Diagnosis and Management of Bipolar Disorder

Diagnosis and Management of Bipolar Disorder

Editor: Francisco Watkins

AMERICAN
MEDICAL PUBLISHERS
www.americanmedicalpublishers.com

AMERICAN
MEDICAL PUBLISHERS
www.americanmedicalpublishers.com

Cataloging-in-Publication Data

Diagnosis and management of bipolar disorder / edited by Francisco Watkins.
p. cm.
Includes bibliographical references and index.
ISBN 979-8-88740-055-6
1. Manic-depressive illness. 2. Manic-depressive illness--Diagnosis.
3. Manic-depressive illness--Treatment. 4. Cognitive neuroscience.
5. Depression, Mental. 6. Mania. I. Watkins, Francisco.
RC516 .D53 2023
616.895--dc23

American Medical Publishers,
41 Flatbush Avenue,
1st Floor, New York,
NY 11217, USA

ISBN 979-8-88740-055-6 (Hardback)

Contents

Preface

This book has been a concerted effort by a group of academicians, researchers and scientists, who have contributed their research works for the realization of the book. This book has materialized in the wake of emerging advancements and innovations in this field. Therefore, the need of the hour was to compile all the required researches and disseminate the knowledge to a broad spectrum of people comprising of students, researchers and specialists of the field.

Bipolar disorder refers to a mental illness characterized by extremely low and high mood swings, as well as changes in thinking, sleep, behavior and mood. The primary symptoms of this disorder are hypomanic and manic episodes. The majority of people suffering from bipolar disorder also experience episodes of depression. Cyclothymic, bipolar I disorder and bipolar II disorder are the different types of bipolar disorders. The diagnosis of bipolar disorder can be done through conducting an interview, assessing lab tests and by performing a physical examination. Body scans and blood tests cannot detect bipolar disorder, but they can help rule out other conditions like hyperthyroidism that can resemble the disorder. Talk therapy, lifestyle changes, medication and other treatments can be helpful in managing this condition. Interpersonal and social rhythm therapy (IPSRT), family-focused therapy, cognitive behavioral therapy (CBT) and psychoeducation are the various therapy options that can be used for treating bipolar disorder. This book contains a detailed explanation of the various diagnostic and therapeutic techniques associated with bipolar disorders. It will serve as a reference to a broad spectrum of readers.

At the end of the preface, I would like to thank the authors for their brilliant chapters and the publisher for guiding us all-through the making of the book till its final stage. Also, I would like to thank my family for providing the support and encouragement throughout my academic career and research projects.

Editor

1

Bipolar disorders in ICD-11: current status and strengths

Jules Angst[1*], Vladeta Ajdacic-Gross[1] and Wulf Rössler[1,2,3]

Abstract

Background: The Clinical descriptions and diagnostic guidelines for the ICD-11 Classification of mental and behavioural disorders should soon be finalized. To measure their potential impact, the new proposed definitions of bipolar disorders in ICD-11 were applied to data from the Zurich cohort study and compared with the definitions of ICD-10 and DSM-5.

Results: We found little difference between ICD-11 and ICD-10 in the identification of subjects with bipolar disorders, but compared to DSM-5 a considerable increase in the diagnosis of hypomanic episodes and therefore of bipolar-II disorders.

Conclusions: Compared to ICD-10 and DSM-5 the definition of hypomanic episodes according to ICD-11 represents important progress. A higher prevalence of BP-II disorder makes sense from a clinical point of view. Further transcultural research is needed into whether out-patient treatment should be included as a criterion for hypomania. Pure mania is unfortunately missing as an independent and codable disorder in the international diagnostic manuals, whether ICD-11 or DSM-5.

Keywords: Bipolar, ICD-10, ICD-11, DSM-5

Introduction

The World Health Organization is central to the continuous development of the diagnostic classification of medical disorders. With the ICD-11 officially approved, the next stage in our field will be the publication of the Clinical Descriptions and Diagnostic Guidelines (CDDG) for the manual's Mental and Behavioural Disorders section. The guidelines are currently out for consultation and comment. From 2022 the ICD-11 should be in worldwide use. The ICD review process has taken over ten years, partly overlapping with the fifth revision of the DSM of the American Psychiatric Association, which was completed in 2013. From the outset the general aim was to harmonise their structure and descriptions in order to avoid arbitrary differences (Reed et al. 2019).

Differences persist nonetheless. In its conception the ICD-11 is guided by the principles of clinical usefulness and global applicability. In particular, its descriptions of the "essential features" of mood episodes are not presented as equivalents of strict diagnostic criteria. Symptom counts or duration cut-offs are generally avoided, which is designed to reflect clinical practice and the exercise of clinical judgment. A full account of the changes in ICD-11 and their rationale is to be found in (Reed et al. 2019).

The purpose of this short paper is to compare the definitions of manic and hypomanic episodes in ICD-11 (as it currently stands) (a) briefly with the previous version ICD-10 (World Health Organization 1992) and (b) with DSM-5 of the American Psychiatric Association (American Psychiatric Association 2013). By applying the criteria to data from the Zurich study, described in detail in an earlier publication (Angst et al. 2016), we can provisionally illustrate some consequences of the revisions.

*Correspondence: jules.angst@uzh.ch
[1] Department of Psychiatry, Psychotherapy and Psychosomatics, Psychiatric Hospital, University of Zurich, Zurich, Switzerland
Full list of author information is available at the end of the article

Zurich study sample and definitions

The Zurich study is an epidemiological study, which followed the probands over a period of 30 years from the ages of 19/20 to 49/50. The interview sample was selected from an initial cohort of 4547 people (f = 2346; m = 2201) representative of the canton of Zurich in Switzerland, who were screened in 1978 by the Symptom Checklist 90 (SCL-90-R) (Derogatis 1977) when they were 19 years old (males) or 20 years old (females).

To increase the probability of the development of psychiatric syndromes, a stratified sub-sample of 591 subjects was selected for the longitudinal study. Two-thirds of the sample consisted of high scorers (defined as scoring above the 85th percentile of the global severity index of the SCL-90-R) (n = 396) and one-third of a random sample of those with scores below the 85th percentile (n = 195). The use of stratified samples is not uncommon in epidemiological research (Dunn et al. 1999). Altogether, seven interview waves were conducted: in 1979, 1981, 1986, 1988, 1993, 1999 and 2008. For the present analysis only data collected from 1986 onwards were used; in 1986 an interview section on mania was added to the interview. The initial allocation to the two strata did not change over the study's time span.

The analysis is presented both with the raw figures (n = 475 in the period 1986–2008) and with figures after reweighting to offset the stratification (n = 2051). For the reweighting, the analysis was conducted with the SAS procedure PROC SURVEYFREQ.

For the definitions of ICD-11 we have used the documents available on the internet. For the ICD-10, diagnostic criteria for research were subsequently published, distinct from of the CDDG for clinicians, (ICD-10 DCR) (World Health Organization 1993). These imposed both symptom numbers and duration cut-offs, narrowing the differences between the ICD and DSM-IV. We applied ICD-10 DCR definitions in our analyses of ICD-10 but this approach was not extended to ICD-11, as there is no indication that diagnostic research criteria will be produced for this latest revision.

Bipolar disorders in ICD-11

The mood disorders section in ICD-11 has been reorganized, opening with the description of mood episodes (depressive, manic, mixed and hypomanic), which are not coded. Codes are ascribed to disorders, which are diagnosed on the basis of the pattern of a patient's mood episodes over time. Moreover, in the bipolar and related disorders grouping newer research led to the subdivision of bipolar disorder into types I and II, based on the distinction between mania and hypomania (Reed et al. 2019). This is in line with DSM-5.

Mania as a diagnosis

Historically bipolar disorders (BP) included mania, BP-I, BP-II, hypomania and cyclothymic disorders. The international diagnostic manuals do not reflect the full affective spectrum. In none of them does mania have the status of a separate disorder. Since ICD-10 a manic episode has been codable only within mood disorders. Those with mania/a manic episode are diagnosed as having bipolar-I disorder. ICD-11 continues this tradition, which is in line with the successive versions of the DSM, including DSM-5. This must nonetheless be considered a loss in both clinical and research terms. There is growing evidence from epidemiological, clinical and genetic studies that unipolar mania exists as a distinct disorder (Merikangas et al. 2014; Baek et al. 2014; Angst and Grobler 2015). A recent analysis of data merged from seven epidemiological studies of adults found BP-I (mania with major depressive disorder) in 323 subjects and pure mania in 109, a relatively rare but separate diagnosis (Angst et al. 2018).

Major change in the definitions of manic and hypomanic syndromes and episodes in ICD-11 and DSM-5

The definitions of manic and hypomanic syndromes and episodes in the two manuals are now almost identical as regards entry criteria, duration, hospitalization, and the presence or absence of psychotic features and impairment in social and occupational functioning, albeit with the dissimilarities referred to above (essential features vs. lettered entry criteria, etc.).

All manic and hypomanic episodes in ICD-11 require as defining features:

1. euphoria, irritability or expansiveness, and, increased activity or subjective experience of increased energy
2. plus "several "(ICD-11), three or more (DSM 5) of the following 7 symptoms:
    1. increased talkativeness or pressured speech,
    2. flight of ideas,
    3. increased self-esteem or grandiosity,
    4. decreased need of sleep,
    5. distractibility,
    6. impulsive reckless behaviour,
    7. increase in sexual drive, sociability or goal-directed activity.

Thus, a diagnosis of bipolar mood disorders in both ICD-11 and DSM-5 now requires as an essential entry feature not only the presence of elated/euphoric, expansive or irritable mood but in addition, in all cases, increased activity/energy; this is in contrast to both

ICD-10 and DSM-IV TR (American Psychiatric Association 2000) which required as criterion A only the presence of mood changes. This development is not without problems. Earlier, we illustrated the consequences of this important conceptual change, as introduced by DSM-5, with data from the Bridge Study. 810 of 3618 (22.5%) patients with Major Depression manifested only one mood criterion for bipolarity (elated or irritable). Following DSM-IV criteria those patients were diagnosed with bipolar disorders, whereas according to DSM-5 they lost their bipolarity and were re-diagnosed as having major depressive disorder (Angst et al. 2014).

Manic and hypomanic episodes in ICD-11 compared to DSM-5

DSM-5 defines manic episodes and hypomanic episodes slightly more restrictively (as had the ICD-10 DCR) in that for cases with mood irritability only (without euphoria) it requires 4 rather than 3 of the 7 symptoms for a diagnosis; ICD-11 does not single out irritability in this way.

Similarly the minimum duration of a hypomanic episode is 4+ days in DSM-5 and "several days" in ICD-11 For the purposes of our analysis several was interpreted as 4+ consecutive days.

One further restriction in the definition of a hypomanic episode in DSM-5 relates to changes in functioning. In DSM-5 criterion C: an unequivocal change in functioning uncharacteristic of the person, and criterion D: the disturbance in mood and the change in functioning are observable by others must be met. In ICD-11 this is less categorically expressed as the significant change in the usual range of moods and behaviour would be apparent to people who know the individual well.

Exclusions

Like DSM-5, ICD-11 excludes syndromes caused by the effects of a substance or medication, another medical condition (tumour etc.), but now allows the diagnosis of a manic or hypomanic episode if the full syndrome persists after antidepressant treatment (e.g. medication, ECT, light therapy) is discontinued and its direct effects have ceased or receded.

Causal attributions and exclusions are, however, known to be problematic and not data based.

Table 1 ICD-11 vs ICD-10: manic spectrum including hospitalization lifetime

	ICD-11 Mania	Hypomania	Manic symptoms	Others	Total
ICD-10 mania	28	1	2	0	31
Hypomania	0	40	0	0	40
Manic symptoms	1	7	144	0	152
Others	0	0	0	252	252
Total	29	48	146	252	475

Comparison of diagnostic systems using data from the Zurich study: ICD-10, ICD-11 and DSM-5

ICD-11 and ICD-10: manic symptoms, hypomania and mania

Comparing ICD-11 with ICD-10 (ICD-10 DCR) our analysis (Table 1) found a minimal reduction in the frequency of ICD-11 manic episodes (N=29) compared to ICD-10 (31). On the other hand ICD-11 diagnosed 48 subjects with a hypomanic episode vs. 40 by ICD-10.

Prevalence rates have to be weighted, because in the Zurich study risk cases (high scorers on the SCL-90 R) were purposely over-represented (Table 2).

ICD-11 and DSM-5: manic symptoms, hypomania and mania

ICD-11 and DSM-5 are in close agreement in the diagnosis of manic episodes (Table 3) but hypomanic episodes are far more frequently identified by ICD-11 (N=48) than DSM-5 (N=15); only 10 subjects are classified by both.

Application of ICD-11 results in prevalence of mania in 5.4%, DSM-5 in 4.7%. But hypomania is diagnosed by ICD-11 far more frequently in 9.9% compared to DSM-5 in 2.2%. The prevalence rates are shown in Table 4.

Validity of the ICD-11 diagnoses

As validators we can provide family history (parents, siblings) and lifetime treatment for manic or depressive symptoms.

As is clear in Table 5, a positive family history (FH+) is strongly correlated with the diagnostic groups of mania and hypomania. Both diagnostic subgroups correlate significantly in their FH+ for mania, suicide/attempts, alcohol abuse/dependence and anxiety/panic. But there is no association with a FH+ for depression or smoking.

Table 6 lists percentage treatment rates for manic and depressive symptoms for ICD-11, ICD-10 and DSM-5. The three diagnostic classifications show very similar

Table 2 ICD-11 vs. ICD-10: prevalence rates, weighted (%) with 95% confidence intervals

	ICD-11 Mania	Hypomania	Manic symptoms	Others	Total
ICD-10 Mania	5.4 (2.4–8.4)	0.05 (0.0–0.1)	0.6 (0.0–1.7)	0	6.0 (2.8–9.2)
Hypomania	0	8.5 (4.7–12.3)	0	0	8.5 (4.7–12.3)
Manic symptoms	0.05 (0.0–0.1)	1.3 (0.0–2.9)	27.1 (21.2–33.1)	0	28.5 (22.5–34.6)
Others	0	0	0	57.0 (50.3–63.7)	57.0 (50.3–63.7)
Total	5.4 (2.4 –8.5)	9.9 (5.8–13.9)	27.7 (21.7–33.7)	57.0 (21.7–33.7)	100

Table 3 ICD-11 vs DSM-5: manic spectrum including hospitalization lifetime

	ICD-11 mania	Hypomania	Manic symptoms	Others	Total
DSM-5 mania	23	0	2	0	25
Hypomania	1	10	4	0	15
Manic symptoms	5	37	140	0	182
Others	0	1	0	252	253
Total	29	48	146	252	475

validity regarding the treatment of manic symptoms but none for the treatment of depressive symptoms.

If ICD currently classifies patients who have been hospitalized for manic syndromes as having manic episodes, individuals with manic symptoms who have been treated could reasonably be diagnosed as hypomanic. In Table 6 we show this to be the case for 4 of 149 subjects (2.7%), who, if added to the subjects with hypomania, would increase their number from 48 to 52. The prevalence rate would correspondingly increase from 9.9 to 10.1%. Of course further research into this approach is needed.

In order to test the hypothesis of a continuum from normal to pathological, one might also look at recurrent brief hypomania among those with manic symptoms (Angst 1997). It is present in 37 subjects, with a prevalence of 7.8%. Cumulatively 23.38% of individuals manifested manic, hypomanic or brief hypomanic episodes.

Conclusions

Compared to ICD-10 and DSM-5, the current ICD-11 definition of hypomanic episodes represents important progress. Hypomanic episodes will be diagnosed twice as frequently as manic episodes. From a clinical point

Table 4 ICD-11 vs. DSM-5: prevalence rates, weighted (%) with 95% confidence intervals

	ICD-11 mania	Hypomania	Manic symptoms	Others	Total
DSM-5 mania	4.1 (1.5–6.8)	0	0.6 (0.0–1.7)	0	4.7 (1.9–7.6)
Hypomania	0.05 (0.0–0.1)	1.5 (3.0–15.1)	0.7 (0.0–1.8)	0	2.2 (0.3–4.1)
Manic symptoms	1.2 (0.0–2.8)	8.3 (4.6–12.1)	26.4 (20.5–32.3)	0	36.0 (29.5–42.7)
Others	0	0.05 (0.0–0.1)	0	57.0 (50.3–63.7)	57.0 (50.4–63.7)
Total	5.4 (2.4–8.5)	9.9 (5.8–13.9)	27.7 (21.7–33.7)	57.0 (50.3–63.7)	100

Table 5 ICD-11 mania: family history (parents and siblings)

ICD-11	Mania (29) %	Hypomania (48) %	Manic symptoms (146) %	Others (252) %	Chi square P
Family history					
Mania	24.1	18.7	8.9	3.2	<.0001
Depression	62.1	58.3	57.5	49.6	<.284
Suicidality	37.9	12.5	18.5	16.3	<.025
Anxiety/panic	58.6	47.9	32.2	24.6	<.0001
Alcohol abuse	17.2	12.5	24.7	11.5	<.0061
Smoking	72.4	72.3	79.3	71.1	<.389

Probands' responses only; consent to interview relatives was not given

Table 6 Lifetime treatment for manic or depressive symptoms

	Mania	Hypomania	Manic symptoms	P
%Treatment manic symptoms				
ICD.11	26.7	12.5	2.7[a]	.0001
ICD-10	25.8	15.0	2.6	.0001
DSM-5	32.0	13.3	4.4	.0001
% Treatment depr. symptoms				
ICD.11	70.0	56.2	53.7	.259
ICD-10	67.7	57.5	53.9	.365
DSM-5	64.0	60.0	54.9	.663

[a] 4 of 149 subjects were treated as out-patients

of view it makes sense that the milder condition should occur more often than the severe one. This also means that bipolar-II disorder will become a more common diagnosis. It should be remembered that hypomanic episodes in terms of their social and subjective consequences are not always undesirable. They can be associated with an increased work capacity and heightened creativity. Transcultural research is needed into whether out-patient treatment should be included as a criterion for a diagnosis of hypomania, in parallel with the hospitalization criterion for a manic episode. Finally, ICD-11 allows greater scope for the exercise of clinical judgment, which is an important strength of this classification system.

Acknowledgements
Not applicable.

Authors' contributions
JA drafted the manuscript and conducted all the statistical analyses. WR participated in the critical revision of the manuscript. VAG revised the statistical results. All authors read and approved the final manuscript.

Author details
[1] Department of Psychiatry, Psychotherapy and Psychosomatics, Psychiatric Hospital, University of Zurich, Zurich, Switzerland. [2] Institute of Psychiatry, Laboratory of Neuroscience (LIM 27), University of São Paulo, São Paulo, Brazil. [3] Department of Psychiatry and Psychotherapy, Charité University Medicine, Berlin, Germany.

References

American Psychiatric Association. Diagnostic and statistical manual of mental disorders: DSM-IV-TR. 4th ed. Washington DC: American Psychiatric Association; 2000.

American Psychiatric Association. Diagnostic and statistical manual of mental disorders: DSM-5™. 5th ed. Arlington: American Psychiatric Association; 2013.

Angst J. Recurrent brief psychiatric syndromes: hypomania, depression, anxiety and neurasthenia. In: Judd LL, Saletu B, Filip V, editors. Basic and clinical science of mental and addictive disorders. Basel Freiburg Paris: Karger; 1997. p. 33–8.

Angst J, Grobler C. Unipolar mania: a necessary diagnostic concept. Eur Arch Psychiatry Clin Neurosci. 2015;265:273–80.

Angst J, Bowden CL, Azorin J, Perugi G, Vieta E, Young AH, editors. From DSM-IV to DSM-5: some changes in major mood disorders in the bridge study (abstract). In: XVI World Congress of Psychiatry. Madrid, Spain, September 14–18, 2014: Abstracts Book Oral & Poster Communications.

Angst J, Paksarian D, Cui L, Merikangas KR, Hengartner MP, Ajdacic-Gross V, Rössler W. The epidemiology of common mental disorders from age 20 to 50: results from the prospective Zurich Cohort Study. Epidemiol Psychiatr Sci. 2016;25:24–32.

Angst J, Rössler W, Ajdacic-Gross V, Angst F, Wittchen HU, Lieb R, Beesdo-Baum K, Asselmann E, Merikangas KR, Cui L, Andrade LH, Viana MC, Lamers F, Penninx BW, de Azevedo-Cardoso T, Jansen K, Dias-de-Mattos Souza L, Azevedo-da-Silva R, Kapczinski F, Grobler C, Gholam-Rezaee M, Preisig M, Vandeleur C. Differences between unipolar mania and bipolar-I disorder: evidence from nine epidemiological studies. Bipolar Disord. 2018. https://doi.org/10.1111/bdi.12732.

Baek JH, Eisner LR, Nierenberg AA. Epidemiology and course of unipolar mania: results from the national epidemiologic survey on alcohol and related conditions (NESARC). Depress Anxiety. 2014;31:746–55. https://doi.org/10.1002/da.22261.

Derogatis LR. SCL-90. Administration, scoring and procedures manual-I for the R (revised) version and other instruments of the Psychopathology Rating Scale Series. Baltimore: Johns Hopkins University School of Medicine; 1977.

Dunn G, Pickles A, Tansella M, Vazquez-Barquero J-L. Two-phase epidemiological surveys in psychiatry. Br J Psychiatry. 1999;174:95–100.

Merikangas KR, Cui L, Heaton L, Nakamura E, Roca C, Ding J, Qin H, Guo W, Yao-Shugart Y, Zarate C, Angst J. Independence of familial transmission of mania and depression: results of the NIMH family study of affective spectrum disorders. Mol Psychiatry. 2014;19:214–9.

Reed GM, First MB, Kogan CS, Hyman SE, Gureje O, Gaebel W, Maj M, Stein DJ, Maercker A, Tyrer P, Claudino A, Garralda E, Salvador-Carulla L, Ray R, Saunders JB, Dua T, Poznyak V, Medina-Mora ME, Pike KM, Ayuso-Mateos JL, Kanba S, Keeley JW, Khoury B, Krasnov VN, Kulygina M, Lovell AM, de Jesus Mari J, Maruta T, Matsumoto C, Rebello TJ, et al. Innovations and changes in the ICD-11 classification of mental, behavioural and neurodevelopmental disorders. World Psychiatry. 2019;18:3–19. https://doi.org/10.1002/wps.20611.

World Health Organization. The ICD-10 classification of mental and behavioural disorders. Clinical descriptions and diagnostic guidelines. Geneva: World Health Organization; 1992.

World Health Organization. The ICD-10 classification of mental and behavioural disorders. Diagnostic criteria for research. Geneva: World Health Organization; 1993.

2

Trajectories of adherence to mood stabilizers in patients with bipolar disorder

M. Bauer[1*], T. Glenn[2], M. Alda[3], R. Bauer[1], P. Grof[4], W. Marsh[5], S. Monteith[6], R. Munoz[7], N. Rasgon[8], K. Sagduyu[9^] and P. C. Whybrow[10]

Abstract

Background: Nonadherence with mood stabilizers is a major problem that negatively impacts the course of bipolar disorder. Medication adherence is a complex individual behavior, and adherence rates often change over time. This study asked if distinct classes of adherence trajectories with mood stabilizers over time could be found, and if so, which patient characteristics were associated with the classes.

Methods: This analysis was based on 12 weeks of daily self-reported data from 273 patients with bipolar 1 or II disorder using ChronoRecord computer software. All patients were taking at least one mood stabilizer. The latent class mixed model was used to detect trajectories of adherence based on 12 weekly calculated adherence datapoints per patient.

Results: Two distinct trajectory classes were found: an adherent class (210 patients; 77%) and a less adherent class (63 patients; 23%). The characteristics associated with the less adherent class were: more time not euthymic ($p < 0.001$) and female gender ($p = 0.016$). No other demographic associations were found.

Conclusion: In a sample of motivated patients who complete daily mood charting, about one quarter were in the less adherent class. Even patients who actively participate in their care, such as by daily mood charting, may be nonadherent. Demographic characteristics may not be useful in assessing individual adherence. Future research on longitudinal adherence patterns in bipolar disorder is needed.

Introduction

Mood stabilizers are a fundamental treatment for both acute episodes of bipolar disorder and the prevention of future episodes. Patient nonadherence is an important contributor to medication nonresponse (Osterberg and Blaschke 2005), and nonadherence with mood stabilizers may negatively impact every aspect of bipolar disorder. Poor medication adherence is associated with an increase in relapses (Gutiérrez-Rojas et al. 2010; Franks et al. 2008), suicide and suicide attempts (Gonzalez-Pinto et al. 2006; Pompili et al. 2009), emergency room visits, hospitalizations, involuntary hospitalizations, healthcare costs (Svarstad et al. 2001; Gianfrancesco et al. 2008; Hong et al. 2011; Eaddy et al. 2005; Hassan and Lage 2009; Schuepbach et al. 2008), homelessness (Copeland et al. 2009), and involvement with the criminal justice system (Robertson et al. 2014). The harm from medication nonadherence in bipolar disorder is considerable to both individual patients and society.

Medication adherence refers to the extent to which patients follow the medication regimen prescribed by their physician, often defined as taking ≥ 80% of the prescribed doses (Osterberg and Blaschke 2005). Medication adherence involves three phases: initiation of treatment, implementation or following the dosing regimen, and persistence with treatment (Vrijens et al. 2012; Gellad et al. 2017). Diverse factors and behaviors influence each phase including patient attitudes towards medication, clinical symptoms, adverse reactions, regimen complexity, health literacy, substance

*Correspondence: michael.bauer@uniklinikum-dresden.de
^ Deceased
[1] Department of Psychiatry and Psychotherapy, Medical Faculty, University Hospital Carl Gustav Carus, Technische Universität Dresden, Fetscherstr. 74, 01307 Dresden, Germany
Full list of author information is available at the end of the article

misuse, medication costs and forgetfulness (Jawad et al. 2018; García et al. 2016; Levin et al. 2016; Fredericksen et al. 2018). An adherence rate is difficult to measure, and will vary with the definition, methodology, adherence phase, study design and study population (Sajatovic et al. 2010; Levin et al. 2016). Less than half of patients with bipolar disorder are estimated to be fully adherent (García et al. 2016; Levin et al. 2016; Scott and Pope 2002). For most patients with bipolar disorder, adherence is partial or intermittent, and changes over time (Scott and Pope 2002; Jawad et al. 2018). Sometimes patients take all the prescribed doses, sometimes a partial dose, and sometimes none for one or all drugs in the medication regimen.

The most frequent way that psychiatrists evaluate medication adherence in bipolar disorder is to ask the patient (Vieta et al. 2012). However, estimates are often incorrect and optimistic (Stephenson et al. 2012; Baldessarini et al. 2008; Lopez et al. 2017; De las Cuevas et al. 2013). Although physicians frequently adjust medications at visits for bipolar disorder (Hodgkin et al. 2018), it is challenging to differentiate non- or inadequate adherence from nonresponse (Velligan et al. 2009). A lack of recognition of patient nonadherence may lead to higher dosages, medication switches and increasingly complex medication regimens, which may further reduce adherence (Baldessarini et al. 2008; Eaddy et al. 2005; Velligan et al. 2009; Colom et al. 2005).

More information to help assess adherence in patients with bipolar disorder is needed. Adherence studies generally use conventional longitudinal modeling approaches that assume the individuals in a sample come from a homogeneous population, the outcome of interest has a single growth trajectory, and any defined covariates influence each individual in the same way (Jung and Wickrama 2008; Proust-Lima et al. 2017). In contrast, trajectory analysis accommodates a heterogeneous population, and allows the detection of subgroups or latent classes within a sample that have different trajectories of change over time for an outcome of interest (Nagin and Odgers 2010; Lennon et al. 2018; Jung and Wickrama 2008). Trajectory analysis was previously used to assess medication adherence for several chronic conditions (Greenley et al. 2015; de Vries McClintock et al. 2016; Hommel et al. 2017; Blalock et al. 2019). Based on 12 weeks of daily self-reported data from patients with bipolar disorder, the purpose of this study was twofold: (1) to determine whether distinct classes of adherence trajectories could be identified for patients taking mood stabilizers, and (2) if trajectory classes were present, to detect associations with patient characteristics.

Methods

All data were from outpatients with a diagnosis of bipolar disorder by DSM-IV or DSM-5 criteria that was made by the prescribing psychiatrist during a clinical interview. All participants volunteered, were age 18 years or older, and provided informed written consent. The participants were recruited from a university mood clinic or private practice and received treatment as usual throughout the study. The participants agreed to record medications, mood and sleep daily using computer software in their native language (ChronoRecord). Demographic variables were obtained from the patient by the clinician at the time of enrollment. The demographic characteristics of patients who use ChronoRecord are similar to that for patients in other studies of bipolar disorder (Bauer et al. 2012). Patients were included in this analysis if they had a diagnosis of bipolar I or bipolar II disorder, returned at least 12 weeks of data (84 days), and were taking at least one mood stabilizer during the 12 weeks. Although arbitrary, 12 weeks of data provides sufficient time for adherence analysis, and includes patients that are comfortable with and willing to use ChronoRecord. Data used in this analysis were collected between 2000 and 2016. The ChronoRecord database was previously used for a variety of published analyses. Active collection of ChronoRecord data is ongoing.

Daily data entry

Patients entered mood, sleep, medications taken and life events daily, and weight weekly into ChronoRecord software (Bauer et al. 2004, 2008). All patients received about a half hour of training in person or by phone before entering data. During training, a medication list was created by selecting from a list of psychotropic medications displayed by brand and generic name. The list includes every medication taken for bipolar disorder. For each selected medication, the pill strength was chosen from a list of available strengths. Every day, for each medication, the patient entered the total number of pills taken. Patients could enter partial pills (1/4, 1/2, or 3/4) for tablets but not capsules. If a medication was not taken, the patient entered zero pills for that drug. The patient could modify the drugs taken throughout the study as needed, and a drug not included in the software list could be added by the patient. Data not entered on one day could be entered later. The software prevents entry for a future date, prevents modification of previously entered data, and requires confirmation for entry of a large number of pills for a drug.

To record mood, patients entered a single daily rating that best described the prior 24 h using a 100-unit visual analog scale. During training, the scale was calibrated to the extremes of mania and depression the patient ever experienced. Based upon the validation studies (Bauer et al. 2004, 2008), a mood entry less than 40 was considered depression, 40–60 euthymia, and greater than 60 hypomania/mania. The range of depression varied between mild symptoms (an entry of 20–39) to moderate to severe symptoms (an entry of 0–19). The range of mania varied from hypomania (an entry of 61–80) to moderate to severe symptoms of mania (an entry of 81–100).

Drugs analyzed

The mood stabilizers considered were lithium, valproate, lamotrigine, carbamazepine, oxcarbazepine and second generation antipsychotics: aripiprazole, olanzapine, risperidone, quetiapine, ziprasidone, paliperidone, asenapine, lurasidone, and clozapine. For the analysis of total psychotropic drugs taken and the daily pill burden, the other drugs considered were antidepressants, benzodiazepines, typical antipsychotics, insomnia medications, and other anticonvulsants (topiramate, gabapentin, pregabalin, tiagabine, levetiracetam, zonisamide).

Adherence

All medication data were self-reported, so the prescribed dosage and medication changes were not known. For each patient, adherence was defined as taking at least one pill per day of each prescribed mood stabilizer. An entry of 0 pills or a missing day of data were treated as no pills taken. The adherence was calculated for each day, and then a weekly adherence rate was created for a total of 12 weekly datapoints per patient. For example to calculate a weekly rate, consider a patient taking 2 mood stabilizers. If the patient took at least one pill for drug A on 7 days, and took at least one pill for drug B on 6 days, adherence for that week would be 86% (adherent on 6 days/7 days = 86%). A mood stabilizer that was discontinued by tapering but remained on the medication list was not included in the calculation. If patients returned more than 84 days of data, only the first 12 weeks of data were included to balance the contribution of each patient.

Latent class trajectory modeling

The latent class mixed model (LCMM), an extension of a standard mixed model, was used to identify the trajectory classes for adherence with mood stabilizers (Proust-Lima et al. 2017; Lennon et al. 2018). Instead of one adherence trajectory for the entire sample, the LCMM allows multiple trajectory classes. LCMM identifies the trajectory classes without predefined assumptions as to the number, size or trajectory pattern of the classes. With LCMM, each patient is included in only one class, and each class has a distinct trajectory based on a supplied trajectory function. The individuals within each trajectory class will be similar to each other, and different from individuals in other classes. The package "lcmm" in R software was used for model estimation (Proust-Lima et al. 2017), and "LCMM toolkit" (Lennon et al. 2018) package was used to verify results.

The analysis models were checked for between 1 and 5 trajectory classes based on a quadratic adherence trajectory function over the 12 weeks. Covariates were not included in the trajectory function, and the variance–covariance matrix was not constrained. The probability that each patient was a member of a class was calculated and all patients were classified according to the highest probability. Several measures were used to help select the optimal number of classes (van de Schoot et al. 2017; Lennon et al. 2018), including the lowest Bayesian Information Criteria (BIC), class size, and probabilities of class membership. The choice of preferred model also included concerns for parsimony and interpretability of results (Jung and Wickrama 2008). To verify the model estimates were not influenced by the initial values, a grid search was performed to confirm the model estimates reflected the best estimates.

For the selected number of classes, the patient characteristics within the classes were compared using Chi-squared tests for categorical variables and ANOVA for continuous variables. Demographic characteristics for the entire sample were also determined. SPSS version 25 was used for all demographic calculations.

Results

There were 560 patients with bipolar disorder in the database of which 528 had a diagnosis of bipolar I or bipolar II disorder. Of the 528 patients, 483 were taking a mood stabilizer, and 273 returned ≥ 84 days of data and were included in the analysis. The 273 patients included in the analysis resided in the US (189, 69%), Germany (38, 14%), Canada (27, 10%), Australia (7, 3%), Chile (4, 1%), Austria (3, 1%), Poland (3, 1%), and the UK (2, 1%). Of the 273 patients, 151 (55%) were recruited at a university mood center, and 122 (45%) from a private practice. Of the 273 patients, 173 (63.4%) had bipolar I disorder and 100 (36.6%) had bipolar II disorder. Of the 273 patients, 192 (70.3%) were female and 81 (29.7%) were male. The demographic characteristics of 273 patients are shown in Table 1. The 273 patients took a total of 2.8 ± 1.4 psychiatric drugs daily, with a mean pill burden of 6.3 ± 4.3 as shown in Table 2.

Latent classes

A comparison of the models identified by LCMM for 1–5 trajectory classes are shown in Table 3. Although the BIC for the 3-class model (−2108) was slightly smaller than

Table 1 Patient demographics (N = 273)

Category	N	Percent
Gender		
Female	192	70.3
Male	81	29.7
Diagnosis		
BP I	173	63.4
BP II	100	36.6
Disabled		
No	175	73.5
Yes	63	26.5
Working full time		
No	131	55.0
Yes	107	45.0
Any college		
No	32	12.5
Yes	224	87.5
College graduate		
No	115	44.9
Yes	141	55.1
Married		
No	133	52.2
Yes	122	47.8
	Mean	**SD**
Hospitalizations (N = 248)	2.8	4.51
Age of onset (N = 253)	22.3	10.34
Age (N = 273)	40.8	11.07
Years of illness (N = 253)	18.8	12.12
Percent days depressed (N = 273)	20.5	22.3
Percent days manic/hypomanic (N = 273)	8.4	11.8
Percent days euthymic (N = 273)	64.3	27.5

Table 2 Patient medications (N = 273)

Medication	N	Percent
Lamotrigine	117	42.9
Lithium	97	35.5
Valproate	58	21.2
Carbamazepine/oxcarbazepine	34	12.5
Any antipsychotic	123	45.1
Any antidepressant	135	49.5
Any benzodiazepine	58	21.2
Any insomnia medication	18	6.6
	Mean	**SD**
Total number of medications[a]	2.8	1.4
Total pill burden[a]	6.3	4.3

[a] Only psychiatric drugs

for the 2-class model (−2091), one of the classes in the 3-class model had only 20 members (7%), the probability of class membership was lower, and trajectories for two of the three classes overlapped, making the interpretation of results more difficult. Therefore the 2-class model was selected as the preferred model.

For the preferred model, the actual and predicted weekly adherence trajectory over the 12 weeks for the two classes is shown in Fig. 1. One class has consistently high adherence over the 12 weeks and is referred to as the adherent class, while the other class has consistently lower adherence and is referred to as the less adherent class. The adherent class includes 210 patients or 77% of the group, while the less adherent class includes 63 patients or 23% of the group. The trajectory of the less adherent class was also relatively stable over the 12 weeks.

Only two patient characteristics differed between the classes. The less adherent class spent a smaller percentage of days euthymic, and included more females, as shown in Table 4. There were no significant differences between the two classes in other demographics including age, age of onset, diagnosis, college graduate, marital status, employed full time, number of hospitalizations for bipolar disorder, years of illness, or if receiving government disability payment due to bipolar disorder. There were no significant differences in the total number of psychiatric medications, daily pill burden, specific mood stabilizer taken, or the use of any antidepressant, benzodiazepine, stimulant or insomnia medication. There were no significant differences between the classes in the percentage of days with depression, severe depression, mania/hypomania or mania. The smaller percentage of days euthymic in the less adherent class was due to a larger percentage of days with depressive symptoms in some patients, and to a larger percentage of days with manic/hypomanic symptoms in others.

The mean percent of days missing medication data for all 273 patients was 7.0% ± 13.5. The mean percent of days missing medication data was 2.2% ± 3.4 for the adherent class and 22.9% ± 20.5 for the less adherent class ($p < 0.001$).

Discussion

This analysis detected two distinct patterns of adherence with taking mood stabilizers over 12 weeks—an adherent class and a less adherent class. About one quarter of the patients were in the less adherent class. Patients in the less adherent class spent significantly more time with symptoms (not euthymic). In prior research in bipolar disorder, affective morbidity including frequent or severe episodes, psychosis, rapid cycling, and longer standing

Table 3 LCMM parameter estimates for 1 to 5 classes (N = 273) using a Quadratic Trajectory Function

N classes	Maximum log likelihood	AIC[a]	BIC[b]	Relative entropy	Class parameter	Class 1	Class 2	Class 3	Class 4	Class 5
1	716.85	−1419.69	−1394.43		N	273				
					%	100%				
					APPA[c]	1.000				
2[d]	1076.39	−2130.79	−2091.09	0.878	N	210	63			
					%	77%	23%			
					APPA	0.971	0.968			
3	1095.99	−2161.98	−2107.84	0.889	N	20	202	51		
					%	7%	74%	19%		
					APPA	0.965	0.968	0.905		
4	1095.99	−2153.98	−2085.40	0.549	N	20	198	0	55	
					%	7%	73%	0%	20%	
					APPA	0.965	0.507	0.000	0.870	
5	1095.99	−2145.98	−2062.97	0.428	N	20	0	0	193	60
					%	7%	0%	0%	71%	22%
					APPA	0.965	0.000	0.000	0.344	0.824

Trajectory function was weekly adherence = $a_0 + a_1 * week + a_2 * week^2$. No covariates were included

[a] Akaike Information Criterion

[b] Bayesian Information Criterion

[c] Average posterior probability of assignment

[d] Preferred model

illness were associated with nonadherence (Leclerc et al. 2013; Greene et al. 2018; Baldessarini et al. 2008; Levin et al. 2016; García et al. 2016). Symptoms that may be most severe during episodes, such as impulsivity (Swann et al. 2008) or lack of insight (Dell'Osso et al. 2002), were also associated with poor adherence (Leclerc et al. 2013, García et al. 2016; Pompili et al. 2009; Belzeaux et al. 2015). Other symptoms such as chaotic lifestyles, loss of daily routine, circadian disruption of sleep–wake cycles, and a preference for nighttime activities may make it harder to adhere with medication regimens (Frank et al. 2000; Melo et al. 2017).

Female gender was also associated with the less adherent class in this study. Although poorer adherence in females with bipolar disorder was reported previously (Kessing et al. 2007; Gianfrancesco et al. 2006; Belzeaux et al. 2013; Murru et al. 2013), review articles show contradictory results for a link between gender and adherence in bipolar disorder: no difference (Colom et al. 2005; Jawad et al. 2018; Greene et al. 2018), inconsistent (Levin et al. 2016), and males more associated with nonadherence (Pompili et al. 2009; Leclerc et al. 2013). In the European Social Survey of 45,700 participants from 24 countries, females were more likely to be nonadherent than males (Stavropoulou 2011). In a study in Japan, females with depression were more likely to hide information related to medication adherence (Sawada et al. 2012). However, the reasons for females being associated with the poor adherence class in this study are unknown.

Other demographic characteristics associated with nonadherence in bipolar disorder in prior research were not significant in this study, including less education, younger age, younger age of onset, and a marital status of single (Leclerc et al. 2013; Levin et al. 2016). Adherence involves a wide range of factors related to the individual, culture, language and communication, disease, drugs, physician, and healthcare system (Leclerc et al. 2013, Pompili et al. 2009; McQuaid and Landier 2018). The routinely collected demographic characteristics may not be associated with adherence, as found in non-psychiatric conditions (Franklin et al. 2016; Steiner et al. 2009) including studies using latent trajectory models (Blalock et al. 2019; de Vries McClintock et al. 2016). Additionally, when significant, the relation between adherence and demographic characteristics is usually weak, providing little practical assistance in discriminating between adherent and nonadherent patients (Steiner et al. 2009; Osterberg and Blaschke 2005). The difficulty in inferring individual adherence based on demographics suggests that self-reported measures may be helpful in clinical settings, and a variety of paper and automated tools are available (Steiner 2012; Stirratt et al. 2015). Review articles report moderate to high correlation between self-reported adherence questionnaires and diaries and electronic monitoring (Monnette et al. 2018; Garber et al. 2004; Shi et al. 2010). While all approaches to measure adherence have strengths and weaknesses (Sajatovic et al. 2010; Lehmann et al. 2014; Levin et al. 2015; Di Matteo 2004), good agreement was found between self-reported

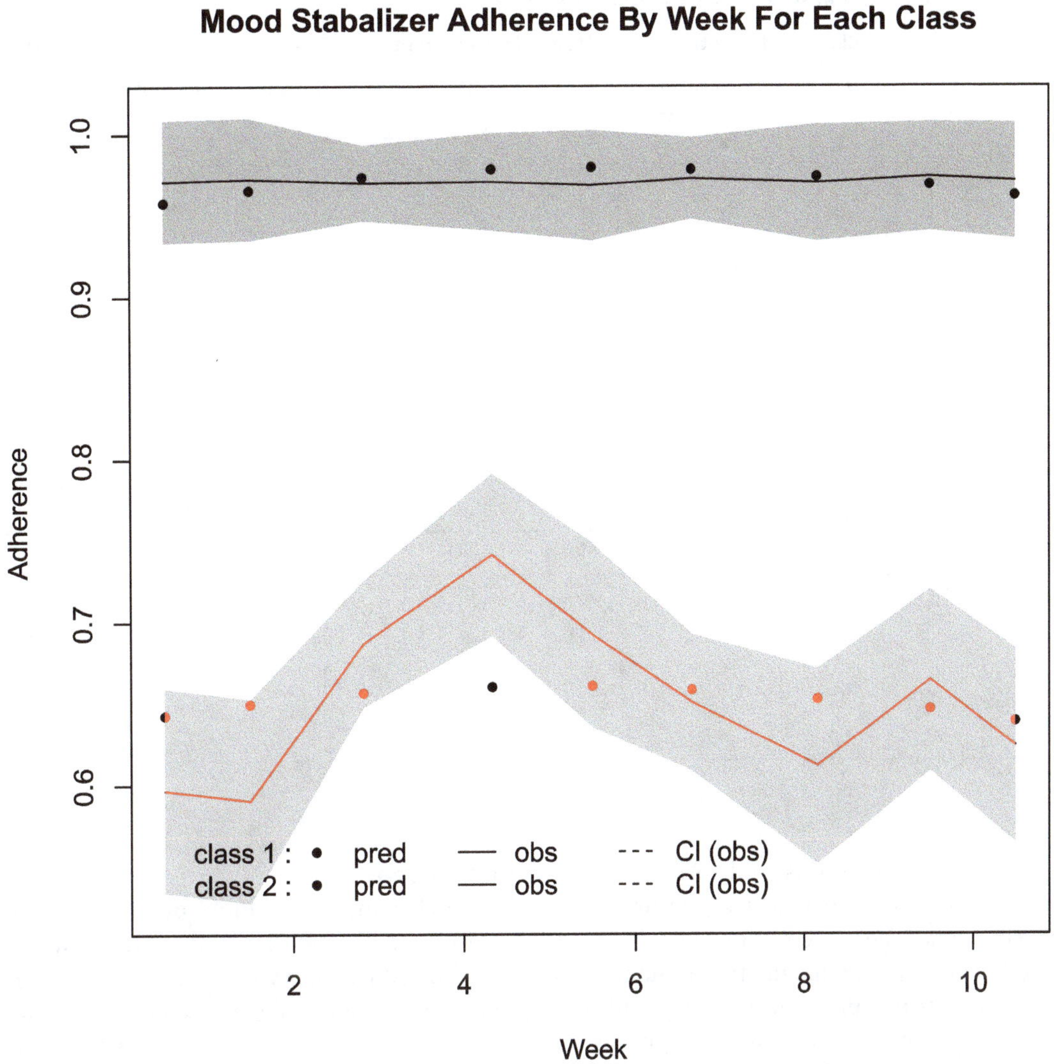

Fig. 1 Mood stabilizer adherence by week for each class. *pred* predicted adherence, *obs* observed adherence, *CI* 91% confidence interval

measures and serum levels of various psychiatric drugs (Jónsdóttir et al. 2010), and with antidepressants (Loayza et al. 2012).

Given the wide range of behaviors that may impact the initiation, implementation and persistence with treatment, understanding the specific reasons for nonadherence is needed to determine the appropriate remedy (Stirratt et al. 2018; Gellad et al. 2017). The detection of two distinct classes in the current study suggests that future research using trajectory analysis, designed to evaluate nonadherence and define membership in trajectory classes, may increase understanding of patterns of adherence in bipolar disorder.

Limitations

This analysis overestimates adherence with mood stabilizers for several reasons. By requiring 12 weeks of data, the sample analyzed was pre-selected for adherence. Since taking one pill of a mood stabilizer was considered adherent, patients taking a lower dose than prescribed were included as adherent. The dosage timing and drug administration instructions were also not considered during the calculation. Drugs taken for general medical conditions and over the counter drugs were not included in the analysis. Complex medication regimens and requirements for dosing more than once daily are associated with decreased adherence in a wide range of chronic illness (Ingersoll and Cohen 2008; Coleman et al. 2012). In our prior research, a larger number of psychiatric medications and greater pill burden were associated with irregularity in daily dosage of mood stabilizers and single day omissions (Pilhatsch et al. 2018; Bauer et al. 2013a), but not with adherence when defined as at least one pill of a mood stabilizer a day (Bauer et al. 2010). The 12 week time period would not provide information about long-term persistence with treatment.

Table 4 Significant differences in the classes by LCMM class (N = 273)

	Class 1 (adherent)		Class 2 (less adherent)		Total		Test	
	N	Percent	N	Percent	N	Percent	X^2 Sig.	DF
Gender								
Male	70	33.3	11	17.5	81	29.7	0.016	1
Female	140	66.7	52	82.5	192	70.3		
Diagnosis								
BP I	135	64.3	38	60.3	173	63.4	0.566	1
BP II	75	35.7	25	39.7	100	36.6		
College graduate								
Yes	108	54.8	33	55.9	141	55.1	0.880	1
No	89	45.2	26	44.1	115	44.9		
Married								
Yes	89	45.9	33	54.1	122	47.8	0.262	1
No	105	54.1	28	45.9	133	52.2		
	Mean	**SD**	**Mean**	**SD**	**Mean**	**SD**	**F Sig.**	**DF**
Percent days euthymic	68.7	26.0	49.7	27.4	64.3	27.5	< 0.001	1271
Age of onset	22.5	10.3	21.6	10.5	22.3	10.3	0.547	1251
Age	40.9	11.0	40.5	11.5	40.8	11.1	0.834	1271
Total number of medications[a]	2.7	1.4	3.1	1.5	2.8	1.4	0.097	1271
Total pill burden[a]	6.1	4.2	6.9	4.3	6.3	4.3	0.145	1271

[a] Only psychiatric drugs

There are other limitations to this study. All data were self-reported and there was no objective confirmation of the medication data. There were more females than males. Only oral drugs were included. The optimal rates to define adherence are not uniform, but vary with the pharmacokinetic and pharmacodynamic properties of the drug (Morrison et al. 2017). Adherence to specific mood stabilizers was not investigated, as drug regimens for bipolar disorder are highly customized in clinical practice (Bauer et al. 2013b). Adherence rates may be larger than one if patients take more than the prescribed dose, as noted in some newly admitted inpatients (Geretsegger et al. 2019). The least adherent patients who would not use mood charting, and those who never fill the initial prescription for a mood stabilizer were not included. In a year-long study of 195,930 new electronic prescriptions, the rate of non-filling for adults was 30.2% overall, with 27.7% for drugs classified as neuropsychiatric, and 29.5% for antidepressants (Fischer et al. 2010). ChronoRecord was not designed to evaluate the reasons for nonadherence. Many important variables were not available for analysis relating to patient attitudes, cultural issues, financial concerns, and the use of adherence tools such as pill boxes. Finally, it was not known if patients were receiving any type of psychosocial interventions for bipolar disorder.

Conclusion

In conclusion, in a sample of motivated patients who complete daily mood charting, there were two trajectories of adherence with taking at least one pill of each prescribed mood stabilizer, adherent and less adherent. About one quarter of the patients were in the less adherent class. Characteristics associated with being in the less adherent class were more time with symptoms (not euthymic), and female gender. Motivated patients may be nonadherent, and demographic characteristics may not be useful to assess individual adherence. Future research to identify longitudinal adherence trajectory patterns is needed in bipolar disorder.

Acknowledgements
None.

Authors' contributions
MB and TG worked on the conception and design of the study, interpreted the results and drafted the manuscript. TG performed the analyses. MA, RB, PG, WM, SM, NR, KS and PW performed data collection, and interpretation of the findings. All authors read and approved the final manuscript.

Author details
[1] Department of Psychiatry and Psychotherapy, Medical Faculty, University Hospital Carl Gustav Carus, Technische Universität Dresden, Fetscherstr. 74, 01307 Dresden, Germany. [2] ChronoRecord Association Inc., Fullerton, CA, USA. [3] Department of Psychiatry, Dalhousie University, Halifax, NS, Canada. [4] Mood Disorders Center of Ottawa, University of Toronto, Toronto, Canada.

[5] Department of Psychiatry, University of Massachusetts, Worcester, MA, USA. [6] Michigan State University College of Human Medicine, Traverse City Campus, Traverse City, MI, USA. [7] Department of Psychiatry, University of California San Diego, San Diego, CA, USA. [8] Department of Psychiatry and Behavioral Sciences, Stanford School of Medicine, Palo Alto, CA, USA. [9] Department of Psychiatry, University of Missouri Kansas City School of Medicine, Kansas City, MO, USA. [10] Department of Psychiatry and Biobehavioral Sciences, Semel Institute for Neuroscience and Human Behavior University of California Los Angeles (UCLA), Los Angeles, CA, USA.

References

Baldessarini RJ, Perry R, Pike J. Factors associated with treatment nonadherence among US bipolar disorder patients. Hum Psychopharmacol. 2008;23:95–105.

Bauer M, Grof P, Gyulai L, Rasgon N, Glenn T, Whybrow PC. Using technology to improve longitudinal studies: self-reporting with ChronoRecord in bipolar disorder. Bipolar Disord. 2004;6:67–74.

Bauer M, Wilson T, Neuhaus K, Sasse J, Pfennig A, Lewitzka U, et al. Self-reporting software for bipolar disorder: validation of ChronoRecord by patients with mania. Psychiatry Res. 2008;159:359–66.

Bauer M, Glenn T, Grof P, Marsh W, Sagduyu K, Alda M, et al. The association between concurrent psychotropic medications and self-reported adherence with taking a mood stabilizer in bipolar disorder. Hum Psychopharmacol. 2010;25:47–54.

Bauer M, Glenn T, Keil M, Bauer R, Marsh W, Grof P, et al. Brief depressive symptoms in patients with bipolar disorder: analysis of long-term self-reported data. Aust N Z J Psychiatry. 2012;46:1068–78.

Bauer M, Glenn T, Alda M, Sagduyu K, Marsh W, Grof P, et al. Regularity in daily mood stabilizer dosage taken by patients with bipolar disorder. Pharmacopsychiatry. 2013a;46:163–8.

Bauer M, Glenn T, Alda M, Sagduyu K, Marsh W, Grof P, et al. Drug treatment patterns in bipolar disorder: analysis of long-term self-reported data. Int J Bipolar Disord. 2013b;1:5.

Belzeaux R, Correard N, Boyer L, Etain B, Loftus J, Bellivier F, et al. Depressive residual symptoms are associated with lower adherence to medication in bipolar patients without substance use disorder: results from the FACE-BD cohort. J Affect Disord. 2013;151:1009–15.

Belzeaux R, Boyer L, Mazzola-Pomietto P, Michel P, Correard N, Aubin V, et al. Adherence to medication is associated with non-planning impulsivity in euthymic bipolar disorder patients. J Affect Disord. 2015;184:60–6.

Blalock DV, Bosworth HB, Reeve BB, Voils CI. Co-occurring reasons for medication nonadherence within subgroups of patients with hyperlipidemia. J Behav Med. 2019;42:291–9.

Coleman CI, Limone B, Sobieraj DM, Lee S, Roberts MS, Kaur R, et al. Dosing frequency and medication adherence in chronic disease. J Manag Care Pharm. 2012;18:527–39.

Colom F, Vieta E, Tacchi MJ, Sánchez-Moreno J, Scott J. Identifying and improving non-adherence in bipolar disorders. Bipolar Disord. 2005;7(Suppl 5):24–31.

Copeland LA, Miller AL, Welsh DE, McCarthy JF, Zeber JE, Kilbourne AM. Clinical and demographic factors associated with homelessness and incarceration among VA patients with bipolar disorder. Am J Public Health. 2009;99:871–7.

De las Cuevas C, Peñate W, Sanz EJ. Psychiatric outpatients' self-reported adherence versus psychiatrists' impressions on adherence in affective disorders. Hum Psychopharmacol. 2013;28:142–50.

de Vries McClintock HF, Morales KH, Small DS, Bogner HR. Patterns of adherence to oral hypoglycemic agents and glucose control among primary care patients with type 2 diabetes. Behav Med. 2016;42:63–71.

Dell'Osso L, Pini S, Cassano GB, Mastrocinque C, Seckinger RA, Saettoni M, et al. Insight into illness in patients with mania, mixed mania, bipolar depression and major depression with psychotic features. Bipolar Disord. 2002;4:315–22.

Di Matteo MR. Variations in patients' adherence to medical recommendations: a quantitative review of 50 years of research. Med Care. 2004;42:200–9.

Eaddy M, Grogg A, Locklear J. Assessment of compliance with antipsychotic treatment and resource utilization in a Medicaid population. Clin Ther. 2005;27:263–72.

Fischer MA, Stedman MR, Lii J, Vogeli C, Shrank WH, Brookhart MA, et al. Primary medication non-adherence: analysis of 195,930 electronic prescriptions. J Gen Intern Med. 2010;25:284–90.

Frank E, Swartz HA, Kupfer DJ. Interpersonal and social rhythm therapy: managing the chaos of bipolar disorder. Biol Psychiatry. 2000;48:593–604.

Franklin JM, Shrank WH, Lii J, Krumme AK, Matlin OS, Brennan TA, et al. Observing versus predicting: initial patterns of filling predict long-term adherence more accurately than high-dimensional modeling techniques. Health Serv Res. 2016;51:220–39.

Franks M, Macritchie KA, Mahmood T, Young AH. Bouncing back: is the bipolar rebound phenomenon peculiar to lithium? A retrospective naturalistic study. J Psychopharmacol. 2008;22:452–6.

Fredericksen RJ, Gibbons L, Brown S, Edwards TC, Yang FM, Fitzsimmons E, et al. Medication understanding among patients living with multiple chronic conditions: implications for patient-reported measures of adherence. Res Soc Adm Pharm. 2018;14:540–4.

Garber MC, Nau DP, Erickson SR, Aikens JE, Lawrence JB. The concordance of self-report with other measures of medication adherence: a summary of the literature. Med Care. 2004;42:649–52.

García S, Martínez-Cengotitabengoa M, López-Zurbano S, Zorrilla I, López P, Vieta E, et al. Adherence to antipsychotic medication in bipolar disorder and schizophrenic patients: a systematic review. J Clin Psychopharmacol. 2016;36:355–71.

Gellad WF, Thorpe CT, Steiner JF, Voils CI. The myths of medication adherence. Pharmacoepidemiol Drug Saf. 2017;26:1437–41.

Geretsegger C, Pichler EM, Gimpl K, Aichhorn W, Stelzig R, Grabher-Stoeffler G, et al. Non-adherence to psychotropic medication assessed by plasma level in newly admitted psychiatric patients: prevalence before acute admission. Psychiatry Clin Neurosci. 2019;73:175–8.

Gianfrancesco FD, Rajagopalan K, Sajatovic M, Wang RH. Treatment adherence among patients with bipolar or manic disorder taking atypical and typical antipsychotics. J Clin Psychiatry. 2006;67:222–32.

Gianfrancesco FD, Sajatovic M, Rajagopalan K, Wang RH. Antipsychotic treatment adherence and associated mental health care use among individuals with bipolar disorder. Clin Ther. 2008;30:1358–74.

Gonzalez-Pinto A, Mosquera F, Alonso M, López P, Ramírez F, Vieta E, et al. Suicidal risk in bipolar I disorder patients and adherence to long-term lithium treatment. Bipolar Disord. 2006;8:618–24.

Greene M, Paladini L, Lemmer T, Piedade A, Touya M, Clark O. Systematic literature review on patterns of pharmacological treatment and adherence among patients with bipolar disorder type I in the USA. Neuropsychiatr Dis Treat. 2018;14:1545–59.

Greenley RN, Karazsia B, Schurman JV, Gumidyala AP, Nguyen EU, Thomason MM, et al. Trajectories of oral medication adherence in youth with inflammatory bowel disease. Health Psychol. 2015;34:514–21.

Gutiérrez-Rojas L, Jurado D, Martínez-Ortega JM, Gurpegui M. Poor adherence to treatment associated with a high recurrence in a bipolar disorder outpatient sample. J Affect Disord. 2010;127:77–83.

Hassan M, Lage MJ. Risk of rehospitalization among bipolar disorder patients who are nonadherent to antipsychotic therapy after hospital discharge. Am J Health Syst Pharm. 2009;66:358–65.

Hodgkin D, Stewart MT, Merrick EL, Pogue YZ, Reilly-Harrington NA, Sylvia LG, et al. Prevalence and predictors of physician recommendations for medication adjustment in bipolar disorder treatment. J Affect Disord. 2018;238:666–73.

Hommel KA, McGrady ME, Peugh J, Zacur G, Loreaux K, Saeed S, et al. Longitudinal patterns of medication nonadherence and associated health care costs. Inflamm Bowel Dis. 2017;23:1577–83.

Hong J, Reed C, Novick D, Haro JM, Aguado J. Clinical and economic consequences of medication non-adherence in the treatment of patients with a manic/mixed episode of bipolar disorder: results from the European Mania in Bipolar Longitudinal Evaluation of Medication (EMBLEM) study. Psychiatry Res. 2011;190:110–4.

Ingersoll KS, Cohen J. The impact of medication regimen factors on adherence to chronic treatment: a review of literature. J Behav Med. 2008;31:213–24.

Jawad I, Watson S, Haddad PM, Talbot PS, McAllister-Williams RH. Medication nonadherence in bipolar disorder: a narrative review. Ther Adv Psychopharmacol. 2018;8:349–63.

Jónsdóttir H, Opjordsmoen S, Birkenaes AB, Engh JA, Ringen PA, Vaskinn A, et al. Medication adherence in outpatients with severe mental disorders: relation between self-reports and serum level. J Clin Psychopharmacol. 2010;30:169–75.

Jung T, Wickrama KAS. An introduction to latent class growth analysis and growth mixture modeling. Soc Personal Psychol Compass. 2008;2:302–17.
Kessing LV, Søndergård L, Kvist K, Andersen PK. Adherence to lithium in naturalistic settings: results from a nationwide pharmacoepidemiological study. Bipolar Disord. 2007;9:730–6.
Leclerc E, Mansur RB, Brietzke E. Determinants of adherence to treatment in bipolar disorder: a comprehensive review. J Affect Disord. 2013;149:247–52.
Lehmann A, Aslani P, Ahmed R, Celio J, Gauchet A, Bedouch P, et al. Assessing medication adherence: options to consider. Int J Clin Pharm. 2014;36:55–69.
Lennon H, Kelly S, Sperrin M, Buchan I, Cross AJ, Leitzmann M, et al. Framework to construct and interpret latent class trajectory modelling. BMJ Open. 2018;8:e020683.
Levin JB, Sams J, Tatsuoka C, Cassidy KA, Sajatovic M. Use of automated medication adherence monitoring in bipolar disorder research: pitfalls, pragmatics, and possibilities. Ther Adv Psychopharmacol. 2015;5:76–87.
Levin JB, Krivenko A, Howland M, Schlachet R, Sajatovic M. Medication adherence in patients with bipolar disorder: a comprehensive review. CNS Drugs. 2016;30:819–35.
Loayza N, Crettol S, Riquier F, Eap CB. Adherence to antidepressant treatment: what the doctor thinks and what the patient says. Pharmacopsychiatry. 2012;45:204–7.
Lopez LV, Shaikh A, Merson J, Greenberg J, Suckow RF, Kane JM. Accuracy of clinician assessments of medication status in the emergency setting: a comparison of clinician assessment of antipsychotic usage and plasma level determination. J Clin Psychopharmacol. 2017;37:310–4.
McQuaid EL, Landier W. Cultural issues in medication adherence: disparities and directions. J Gen Intern Med. 2018;33:200–6.
Melo MCA, Abreu RLC, Linhares Neto VB, de Bruin PFC, de Bruin VMS. Chronotype and circadian rhythm in bipolar disorder: a systematic review. Sleep Med Rev. 2017;34:46–58.
Monnette A, Zhang Y, Shao H, Shi L. Concordance of adherence measurement using self-reported adherence questionnaires and medication monitoring devices: an updated review. Pharmacoeconomics. 2018;36:17–27.
Morrison A, Stauffer ME, Kaufman AS. Relationship between adherence rate threshold and drug 'forgiveness'. Clin Pharmacokinet. 2017;56:1435–40.
Murru A, Pacchiarotti I, Amann BL, Nivoli AM, Vieta E, Colom F. Treatment adherence in bipolar I and schizoaffective disorder, bipolar type. J Affect Disord. 2013;151:1003–8.
Nagin DS, Odgers CL. Group-based trajectory modeling in clinical research. Annu Rev Clin Psychol. 2010;6:109–38.
Osterberg L, Blaschke T. Adherence to medication. N Engl J Med. 2005;353:487–97.
Pilhatsch M, Glenn T, Rasgon N, Alda M, Sagduyu K, Grof P, et al. Regularity of self-reported daily dosage of mood stabilizers and antipsychotics in patients with bipolar disorder. Int J Bipolar Disord. 2018;6:10.
Pompili M, Serafini G, Del Casale A, Rigucci S, Innamorati M, Girardi P, et al. Improving adherence in mood disorders: the struggle against relapse, recurrence and suicide risk. Expert Rev Neurother. 2009;9:985–1004.
Proust-Lima C, Philipps V, Liquet B. Estimation of extended mixed models using latent classes and latent processes: the R Package lcmm. J Stat Softw. 2017;78:1–56.
Robertson AG, Swanson JW, Van Dorn RA, Swartz MS. Treatment participation and medication adherence: effects on criminal justice costs of persons with mental illness. Psychiatr Serv. 2014;65:1189–91.
Sajatovic M, Velligan DI, Weiden PJ, Valenstein MA, Ogedegbe G. Measurement of psychiatric treatment adherence. J Psychosom Res. 2010;69:591–9.
Sawada N, Uchida H, Watanabe K, Kikuchi T, Suzuki T, Kashima H, et al. How successful are physicians in eliciting the truth from their patients? A large-scale Internet survey from patients' perspectives. J Clin Psychiatry. 2012;73:311–7.
Schuepbach D, Novick D, Haro JM, Reed C, Boeker H, Noda S, et al. Determinants of voluntary vs. involuntary admission in bipolar disorder and the impact of adherence. Pharmacopsychiatry. 2008;41:29–36.
Scott J, Pope M. Nonadherence with mood stabilizers: prevalence and predictors. J Clin Psychiatry. 2002;63:384–90.
Shi L, Liu J, Koleva Y, Fonseca V, Kalsekar A, Pawaskar M. Concordance of adherence measurement using self-reported adherence questionnaires and medication monitoring devices. Pharmacoeconomics. 2010;28:1097–107.
Stavropoulou C. Non-adherence to medication and doctor-patient relationship: evidence from a European survey. Patient Educ Couns. 2011;83:7–13.
Steiner JF. Rethinking adherence. Ann Intern Med. 2012;157:580–5.
Steiner JF, Ho PM, Beaty BL, Dickinson LM, Hanratty R, Zeng C, et al. Sociodemographic and clinical characteristics are not clinically useful predictors of refill adherence in patients with hypertension. Circ Cardiovasc Qual Outcomes. 2009;2:451–7.
Stephenson JJ, Tunceli O, Gu T, Eisenberg D, Panish J, Crivera C, et al. Adherence to oral second-generation antipsychotic medications in patients with schizophrenia and bipolar disorder: physicians' perceptions of adherence vs. pharmacy claims. Int J Clin Pract. 2012;66:565–73.
Stirratt MJ, Dunbar-Jacob J, Crane HM, Simoni JM, Czajkowski S, Hilliard ME, et al. Self-report measures of medication adherence behavior: recommendations on optimal use. Transl Behav Med. 2015;5:470–82.
Stirratt MJ, Curtis JR, Danila MI, Hansen R, Miller MJ, Gakumo CA. Advancing the science and practice of medication adherence. J Gen Intern Med. 2018;33:216–22.
Svarstad BL, Shireman TI, Sweeney JK. Using drug claims data to assess the relationship of medication adherence with hospitalization and costs. Psychiatr Serv. 2001;52:805–11.
Swann AC, Steinberg JL, Lijffijt M, Moeller FG. Impulsivity: differential relationship to depression and mania in bipolar disorder. J Affect Disord. 2008;106:241–8.
Van De Schoot R, Sijbrandij M, Winter SD, Depaoli S, Vermunt JK. The GRoLTS-checklist: guidelines for reporting on latent trajectory studies. Struct Equ Model. 2017;24:451–67.
Velligan DI, Weiden PJ, Sajatovic M, Scott J, Carpenter D, Ross R, et al. The expert consensus guideline series: adherence problems in patients with serious and persistent mental illness. J Clin Psychiatry. 2009;70(Suppl 4):1–46.
Vieta E, Azorin JM, Bauer M, Frangou S, Perugi G, Martinez G, et al. Psychiatrists' perceptions of potential reasons for non- and partial adherence to medication: results of a survey in bipolar disorder from eight European countries. J Affect Disord. 2012;143:125–30.
Vrijens B, De Geest S, Hughes DA, Przemyslaw K, Demonceau J, Ruppar T, et al. A new taxonomy for describing and defining adherence to medications. Br J Clin Pharmacol. 2012;73:691–705.

3

Treating winter depressive episodes in bipolar disorder: an open trial of light therapy

Lotte J. E. van Hout[1*], Lisette E. P. Rops[1] and Claudia J. P. Simons[1,2]

Abstract

Background: Light therapy has been used to treat winter depression in bipolar disorder, although the dose, duration, and timing of treatment have differed. The present study is an open trial of light therapy for depressive episodes in autumn/winter using a Dutch protocol specific for patients with a bipolar disorder.

Methods: Data were collected for the seasons September–April 2017–2018 and September–April 2018–2019. In total, 58 patients received light therapy for a minimum of 7 days and a maximum of 21 days; there was a follow-up measurement after two weeks. Outcomes were quick inventory of depressive symptomatology (QIDS) scores and side effects.

Results: QIDS scores were significantly lower at the last day of therapy ($B = -6.00$, $p < 0.001$) and 2 weeks after the end of treatment ($B = -6.55$, $p < 0.001$) compared with pre-intervention. Remission (QIDS ≤ 5) was reached in 55% of the treatments and response (50% symptom reduction) in 57% of the treatments. Side effects were mild; two hypomanic periods occurred.

Conclusions: The Dutch light therapy protocol for patients with a bipolar disorder may be effective in treating a seasonal depression and side effects are mild. Light therapy deserves a prominent place in the treatment because effects may be large and quick.

Keywords: Light therapy, Bipolar disorder, Seasonal affective disorder, Winter depression

Introduction

For decades, light therapy has been an effective method for the treatment of seasonal affective disorder and non-seasonal affective disorder (Rosenthal 1984; Kripke 1998; Ruhrmann et al. 1998; Tuunainen et al. 2002; Golden et al. 2005). Since the first article on this subject in 1984 by Rosenthal (1984), research has focused on the optimization of the treatment for these groups of patients. For a long time, patients with a bipolar disorder were excluded from this research because of fear that the therapy can induce a (hypo)manic state.

In the last decade, however, research has shown that there is a remarkable resemblance between the pathophysiology of seasonal affective disorder and a bipolar disorder (Geoffroy et al. 2014, 2015). It has even been suggested that 11–50% of the patients with a seasonal depression actually can be diagnosed with a bipolar disorder (Sohn and Lam 2004). This, in combination with low response rates for antidepressants and their potential risk of inducing a (hypo)manic state, prompted clinical studies to investigate the effects and risks of light therapy for bipolar depression (Zhang et al. 2013; Goldberg and Truman 2003; Tondo et al. 2009).

However, research on these effects is still limited and results regarding the effectivity are inconclusive. In their meta-analysis, Tseng et al. (2016) found a significant decrease in severity of bipolar depression after light therapy. In 2018, Sit et al. (2018) found that patients with a bipolar depression treated with bright white light had a significantly higher remission rate and lower depression scores compared to a placebo group. Dauphinais

*Correspondence: Lotte.van.hout@ggze.nl
[1] GGzE, Institute for Mental Health Care Eindhoven, Dr. Poletlaan 40, 5626 ND Eindhoven, The Netherlands
Full list of author information is available at the end of the article

et al. (2012), however, found no evidence for a difference between light therapy and placebo. A recent study of Zhou et al. (2018) showed a positive effect of light therapy in comparison to a control group in patients with a bipolar depression. A possible explanation for the mixed findings may be that previous studies differed in the way light therapy was given. There are, for example, differences in length of the treatment, time of day of receiving light therapy, the amount of lux, the type of light, the exposure time, and the combination with other interventions (Sit et al. 2018; Dauphinais et al. 2012; Zhou et al. 2018; Wu et al. 2009; Knapen et al. 2014; Dimitrova et al. 2017; Suzuki et al. 2018; Meesters et al. 2018; Kupeli et al. 2018).

Looking at the risk for developing a (hypo)manic state, a meta-analysis by Benedetti (2018) shows a 0.9% risk for a switch into mania and a 1.4% risk for a switch into hypomania. In comparison, the switch rate during placebo treatment was estimated at 4%. Although these low switch rates are reported, light therapy is not used in common practice.

Because of the potential that light therapy has, and since the risk of developing a (hypo)manic state is considered limited, the Dutch Chronotherapy Comity of the national center for bipolar disorders (Kenbis) wrote a treatment protocol (Eldering et al. 2018). This protocol was optimized for safety, effectiveness and clinical practicality in treating patients with a bipolar depression.

Aim of the study

The aim of this study was to evaluate the safety and effectiveness of light therapy for treating depressive symptoms in patient with a bipolar disorder using the Dutch protocol. This study reflects on the results of light therapy focusing on the effectiveness and the risk of developing a (hypo)manic state in patients with a bipolar depression. The Dutch protocol of light therapy for bipolar disorders was followed for two consecutive years in the autumn/winter at the center for bipolar disorders Eindhoven, the Netherlands.

Methods

Treatment setting

Data were collected at the Center for Bipolar Disorders of GGzE, Eindhoven, the Netherlands. This center is an outpatient clinic specialized in the treatment of bipolar disorders for adults. Patients receive pharmacological, psychological, and/or supportive care.

All data were collected retrospectively, as light therapy was offered as standard care. Written consent was not collected since all data were collected for clinical purposes. Patients had the opportunity to refuse the use of their anonymized data for scientific research. The institutional review board of GGzE gave ethical clearance for the retrospective, anonymized use of the clinical data for research purposes and provided a waiver of informed consent. Identifying information was not provided to the researchers outside of the treatment team.

Indication for light therapy

All patients of the treatment facility who were diagnosed with a bipolar disorder (type I or II) and experienced depressive symptoms in the period September 2017–March 2018 and/or September 2018–March 2019 were offered light therapy at our center. Light therapy was recommended as therapy of first choice but participation was not obligated, no changes in medication were made right before or during the light therapy.

A current (hypo)manic or mixed state was considered a contra-indication for light therapy. Based on theoretical considerations, no contra-indications regarding ocular diseases, medical conditions, or medication use that influence photosensitivity seem to be indicated (Brouwer et al. 2017). If there was any doubt, an ophthalmologist could be consulted to check if light therapy was safe. Photo-sensitive medication also includes lithium. Because clinical studies did not find a negative effect of long-term lithium use on the retina, use of lithium was not seen as a contra-indication for the use of light therapy (Lam et al. 1997).

Screening protocols

If patients experienced depressive symptoms and there were no contra-indications for treatment with light therapy, the severity of depressive symptoms was assessed with the quick inventory of depressive symptomatology (QIDS). The QIDS is a questionnaire containing 16 questions rating the nine symptom domains defining a depressive episode according to the DSM-IV. Symptoms are rated for the prior seven days (Rush et al. 2003; Bernstein et al. 2010). A QIDS score of six or higher indicated a depression and was reason to start light therapy (Rush et al. 2003; Bernstein et al. 2010; Trivedi et al. 2004; Maaren et al. 2013; Meesters et al. 2016).

Treatment protocol

Patients were treated with an intensity of 10,000 lx for at least seven sequential days. On weekdays, light therapy was given with a Davita PhysioLight LD 220 lamp with a strength of 10,000 lx. Distance to the lamp was 50 cm. Screen size of this device is 60 × 40 cm. This lamp generates white light with a light filter that reduces the energy of light emitted in the infrared and UV range to a minimum. Patients were instructed to sit in front of the lamp for 30 min. Patients could also opt to take a lamp (multiple manufacturers, all 10,000 lx) home instead of coming to the treatment center. In the weekends, all patients received these types of lamps to use at home. Patients were instructed about the use of and the distance to these lamps as well (30 cm). Light therapy was conducted between 8:00 a.m. and 11:00 a.m., as several studies suggest that light therapy in the morning has been proven more effective than light therapy in the mid-day (Tuunainen et al. 2002; Golden et al. 2005; Eastman et al. 1998; Terman et al. 1998). At the start, after scoring the QIDS, patients were instructed by a clinical professional on the correct use of the lamp.

After 1 week, patients had an appointment with a clinical professional to evaluate the light therapy, including an assessment of depressive symptoms using the QIDS and an evaluation of the adverse effects of the light therapy. The Young Mania Rating Scale (YMRS) was scored if there was a suspicion of a switch to a (hypo)manic state *or a mixed state* based on the clinical presentation or on the anamnestic complaints of the patient (Young et al. 1978). The score together with the clinical impression of the clinical professional was used to come to the conclusion whether light therapy could be continued or was stopped. If patients had a QIDS ≤ 5, indicating remission, light therapy stopped. If the QIDS score was > 5, patients received seven more days of light therapy with the same treatment conditions as the first week. After this week (i.e. after 14 days of treatment), the QIDS was scored for the third time. Again, if the QIDS score was five or lower, remission was reached and the treatment was stopped. If not, another week of light therapy was offered. After a maximum of 21 days, the treatment stopped even if remission was not yet reached. Fourteen days after light therapy ended, a follow-up assessment with the QIDS was conducted. This was to see if the effects remained after light therapy ceased.

Statistical analysis

As QIDS observations were clustered within light therapy interventions, within patients, we conducted multilevel mixed effects regression analyses with light therapy intervention and patients as random effect (i.e., random intercepts). The QIDS score after the last light therapy session (either at day 7, 14, or 21) was used as the post score. The QIDS score 14 days after the last light therapy session was the follow-up score. The regression models were run with QIDS total scores as dependent variable and session (model 1: 0 = pre or 1 = post; model 2: 0 = pre and 1 = follow-up) as dependent variable. The model was fitted with the State mixed command (Stata version 13; StataCorp) using restricted maximum likelihood estimation (reml). Remission and response were calculated, as they provide information on the clinical relevance of the effects. A QIDS score < 6 was seen as remission of the depressive episode. Response was defined as a reduction of $\geq 50\%$ on the QIDS. In addition, QIDS severity was established using the cut-off scores defined by Rush et al. (2003).

Results

We collected data from 58 patients with 67 treatment periods (some patients had more than one treatment period). In total, we collected 237 QIDS observations. For demographic information, see Table 1. A total of 67 treatment periods (in 58 patients) were analysed. At day 7, 15 treatment periods let to remission (22%), two treatment periods (3%) were stopped before day 7. At day 14 another 15 treatment periods (22%) scored below 6 indicating remission. At the end of the three weeks of treatment another 5 treatment periods let to remission (7%). A total of 14 treatment periods stopped before the three weeks of treatment was completed (21%). Sixteen treatment periods did not lead to remission of symptoms even

Table 1 Patient characteristics (n = 58 patients)

	N	%
Female	36	62.1
Male	22	37.9
Diagnosis		
Bipolar I	36	62.1
Bipolar II	22	37.9
Medication[a]		
Mood stabilizers[b]	47	
Lithium	33	
Valproic acid	9	
Carbamazepine	1	
Lamotrigine	4	
Antipsychotics	33	
Anti-depressant[c]	29	
Sedatives[d]	25	
None	3	
Severity depression[e]		
Mild	19	28.4
Moderate	26	38.8
Severe	19	28.4
Very severe	3	4.5
Age	M: 47.6; SD: 14.05; Range: 20–78	

[a] Note that no percentages were given because patients could use more than one medication

[b] Lithium, valproic acid, carbamazepine, lamotrigine

[c] Selective serotonin reuptake inhibitor (SSRI), serotonin-norepinephrine reuptake inhibitor (SNRI), noradrenergic and specific serotonergic antidepressant (NaSSA), tricyclic antidepressant (TCA)

[d] Sedatives: benzodiazepines, melatonin, Z-drugs, Levomepromazine

[e] According to the QIDS cut off points (Rush et al. 2003)

Table 2 Mean depression score according to the quick inventory of depressive symptomatology (QIDS)

	Number	Mean	Standard deviation	Minimum score	Maximum score
Day 0	67	13.18	4.41	6	24
Day 7	64	9.31	4.87	0	20
Day 14	47	8.55	5.24	1	24
Day 21	22	9.68	5.91	3	23
2 weeks follow-up	37	5.97	4.82	0	20

though the three weeks of treatment were completed (24%).

At follow-up, two weeks after light therapy, patients were asked to participate in another QIDS interview, 37 patients replied. Sixteen patients did not complete the light therapy protocol; the main reason seemed to be remission of the complaints (in between the moments of scoring the QIDS) or a lack of effect.

Table 2 presents the QIDS scores at different assessment moments. Multilevel regression analysis revealed that the total QIDS scores at post-assessment (final light therapy session at day 7, 14, or 21) were significantly lower than the QIDS scores at pre-assessment [$B=-6.00$, 95% CI -7.16; -4.85; $\chi^2(1)=103.68$, $p<0.001$]. Two weeks after the final light therapy session, QIDS scores were still significantly lower compared with pre-light therapy scores [$B=-6.55$ 95% CI -7.97; -5.13, $\chi^2(1)=81.58$, $p<0.001$].

We found that 55% of the completed treatments led to remission (QIDS ≤ 5 at day 7, 14 or 21); 57% led to a response (response defined as a 50% decrease of initial QIDS score at day 0). The distribution of the severity of depressive symptoms per assessment can be found in Fig. 1.

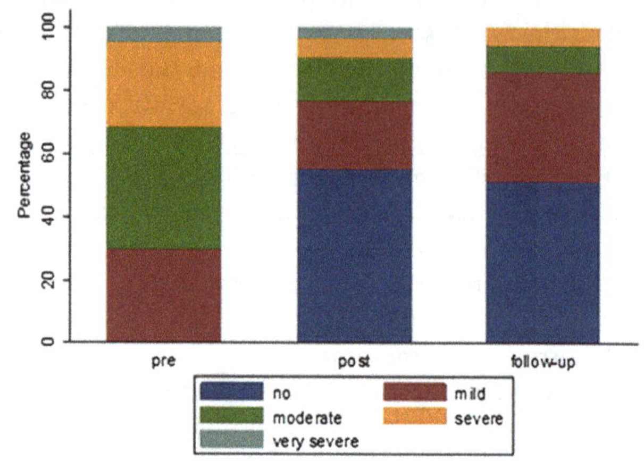

Fig. 1 Severity of depressive symptoms, categorised based on QIDS scores

Adverse effects

Side effects were also monitored during the study. Side effects reported were: nausea (n=1), headache (n=1), and feelings of agitation and restlessness (n=3). These complaints dissolved quickly after the daily dose of light therapy was given and no deviation of the amount of lux or length of the light therapy was needed.

The YMRS interview was conducted once due to suspicion of manic symptoms. Although the patient quitted therapy because of a feeling of restlessness and a decrease in sleep, the YMRS score of 4 indicated that the symptoms did not meet criteria for a (hypo)manic state. Two other patients, however, did switch to a (hypo)manic state, as indicated by notes in the patient file. One patient was admitted because of a hypomanic state seven days after the end of light therapy. After a brief admission with optimisation of the medication, the hypomanic state was in full remission. The other patient was treated with an increase of the dosage of lithium for one week with full recovery after one week. Thus 2.99% of the treatments (i.e., in 3.45% of the patients) led to a hypomanic state.

Discussion

Where light therapy has been a commonly used treatment method for seasonal affective disorder, the use of light therapy for treating patients with a bipolar disorder stayed behind. The current study examined the effectiveness and safety of light therapy for the clinical practice according to the Dutch protocol for light therapy for bipolar disorders.

This study is the first to examine the effect of light therapy in the clinical practice using this treatment protocol and shows positive results with regard to the effectivity of light therapy in treating depressive periods in patients with a bipolar disorder. More than half of the treatments led to remission (55%) and/or response (57%) at the last day of light therapy. There was a significant decrease in QIDS score at the last day of therapy ($B=-6.00$, $p<0.001$) and two weeks after the end of treatment ($B=-6.55$, $p<0.001$). This suggests that light therapy may decrease the severity of depressive symptoms during the treatment and shows that the decrease in depressive symptoms persisted after light therapy was ceased. The quick effect of light therapy is in line with previous studies (Tuunainen et al. 2002; Golden et al. 2005; Terman and Terman 2005). This is an advantage in comparison with anti-depressants or mood-stabilizers, which take more time to show an effect. There is some evidence that light therapy combined with sleep deprivation can be even more effective (Wu et al. 2009), but because of the great impact on daily life of sleep deprivation and the efficacy of light therapy without sleep deprivation, treatment with just light therapy can be a more suitable option for many patients.

An important aim of our study was also to establish the safety of the Dutch light therapy protocol. In the review of Benedetti (2018), the highest reported risk of a (hypo) manic decompensation as a result of light therapy was close to 4%. Similarly, in our study 2.99% of the treatments led to a hypomanic decompensation. No manic decompensation was reported. This supports light therapy is a safe treatment option for this group of patients.

Side effects that were reported in the current study were nausea, headache and a feeling of agitation. This is comparable to previous studies that reported insomnia, headaches, irritability, and dizziness (Dauphinais et al. 2012; Zhou et al. 2018; Kupeli et al. 2018; Levitt et al. 1993; Labbate et al. 1994; Terman and Terman 1999).

The current findings thus suggest that light therapy administered in the morning may be effective in treating winter depression in bipolar disorders. It should be noted however, that the best timing of light therapy has been debated given that light therapy has also been shown to be effective in patients with seasonal depression when administered in midday of evening (Wirz-Justice 1993; Terman et al. 1998). Although several studies suggest that mornings are the optimal timing for light therapy (2002; Golden et al. 2005; Eastman et al. 1998; Terman et al. 1998), the studies by Sit et al. (2007, 2018) advocate light therapy in midday for patients with a bipolar disorder as light therapy may lead to (hypo)mania when administered in morning. The current findings and the review by Benedetti (2018) dispute this, however, and suggest that the risk of switching to mania was not increased after morning light therapy.

This altogether shows that the current light therapy protocol may be effective and safe for treating depressive symptoms in autumn/winter for patients with a bipolar disorder. To strengthen this conclusion, a randomized controlled trial is indicated as the next step. Further research should aim to investigate the predictors for a successful treatment. Also, more research is needed to examine the effectiveness of this treatment in spring and summer.

Limitations

A major limitation of the study is that the data were collected as part of standard care and, hence, there was no control group. We cannot rule out the possibility that, e.g., the depressive symptoms decreased simply as an effect of time or as a placebo effect. Studies in the past showed that the expectations of patients have a significant impact on the antidepressant effect, (Rutherford et al. 2012) thus we cannot rule out that expectations explain a significant part of the effect we found. However, given the short treatment period, the severity of the symptoms, and the population (patients in specialized care with recurrent depressive episodes), we regard it unlikely that the present effects can merely be explained by spontaneous recovery of the depressive symptoms.

Unfortunately, we were not able to see if there was a difference between light therapy at home or at our outpatient clinic. We, therefore, cannot exclude the possibility that effects were (partially) driven by the activation and mobilization that it requires to get out of bed every morning to visit our center. However, previous studies that compared light therapy with a placebo control group also suggest that light therapy is effective in reducing depressive symptoms in patients with a bipolar disorder (Sit et al. 2018; Zhou et al. 2018; Wu et al. 2009; Suzuki et al. 2018; Kupeli et al. 2018; Benedetti et al. 2005).

Other limitations were the relatively small sample size and the fact that the raters were not blinded. Furthermore, the follow-up measurement at two weeks after the end of the light therapy was filled in by 55% of the patients. This means the results of the follow-up measurement must be carefully interpreted, as it is a possibility that the QIDS was predominantly filled in by people with positive results. Compliance with the use of the lamps, especially for the patients who took a lamp home, could not be assessed. This may have led to an underestimation of the treatment effect. This study evaluated the effects of a fixed-dosage protocol in which duration of the light therapy or the amount of lux given was not adjusted based on clinical response or adverse effects. For further research, it may be interesting to see if it is possible to create a more specific treatment protocol for every patient according to the effects and side effects of the treatment.

Finally, to detect potential (hypo)manic decompensation, the clinical observations of the well-trained staff were used. This lead to the discretionary administration of the YMRS, which risks under-detection of (hypo) manic symptoms.

Conclusion

The results of this study show a decline in depressive symptoms after treatment with light therapy for patients with a bipolar disorder with depressive complaints in autumn/winter. The decrease in symptoms may still be observed two weeks after treatment. Risk of developing a (hypo)manic state appears limited and side effects were rare and mild. These findings suggest that the Dutch protocol for light therapy for patients with a bipolar disorder may be effective in ameliorating depressive symptoms and is safe. A randomized, controlled trial would be the next step to make this conclusion more definite.

Acknowledgements
We would like to thank Marijn Groen and the team of Centrum voor Bipolaire Stoornissen GGzE for their help with this research.

Authors' contributions
LEPR and LJEH contributed to the conception and design of the work. LJEH wrote the manuscript. CJPS analysed the data and CJPS and LJEH interpreted the data. All authors read and approved the final manuscript.

Author details
[1] GGzE, Institute for Mental Health Care Eindhoven, Dr. Poletlaan 40, 5626 ND Eindhoven, The Netherlands. [2] Department of Psychiatry and Psychology, School of Mental Health and Neuroscience, Maastricht University Medical Center, Maastricht, The Netherlands.

References
Benedetti F. Rate of switch from bipolar depression into mania after morning light therapy: a historical review. Psychiatry Res. 2018;261:351–6.
Benedetti F, Barbini B, Fulgosi MC, Colombo C, Dallaspezia S, Pontiggia A, et al. Combined total sleep deprivation and light therapy in the treatment of drug-resistant bipolar depression. J Clin Psychiatry. 2005;66(12):1535–40.
Bernstein IH, Rush AJ, Suppes T, Kyotoku Y, Warden D. The quick inventory of depressive symptomatology (clinician and Self-report versions) in patients with bipolar disorder. CNS Spectr. 2010;15(6):367–73.
Brouwer A, Nguyen H-T, Snoek FJ, Raalte DHV, Beekman ATF, Moll AC, et al. Light therapy: is it safe for the eyes? Acta Psychiatrica Scand. 2017;136(6):534–48.
Dauphinais DR, Rosenthal JZ, Terman M, Difebo HM, Tuggle C, Rosenthal NE. Controlled trial of safety and efficacy of bright light therapy vs. negative air ions in patients with bipolar depression. Psychiatry Res. 2012;196(1):57–61.
Dimitrova TD, Reeves GM, Snitker S, Lapidus M, Sleemi AR, Balis TG, et al. Prediction of outcome of bright light treatment in patients with seasonal affective disorder: discarding the early response, confirming a higher atypical balance, and uncovering a higher body mass index at baseline as predictors of endpoint outcome. J Affect Disord. 2017;222:126–32.
Eastman CI, Young MA, Fogg LF, Liu L, Meaden PM. Bright light treatment of winter depression. Arch Gener Psychiatry. 1998;55:883.
Eldering, M, Haarman, B, Kaarsgaren, L, Postma, D, Riemersma, R, Rops, L, Schulte, R. Lichttherapie bij bipolaire stoornissen: protocol. 30 April 2018. In: Kennis Centrum voor Bipolaire Stoornissen. https://www.kenniscentrumbipolairestoornissen.nl/wp-content/uploads/2019/01/Protocol-Lichttherapie-bij-bipolaire-stoornissen.pdf. Accessed 20 July 2019.
Geoffroy PA, Bellivier F, Scott J, Etain B. Seasonality and bipolar disorder: a systematic review, from admission rates to seasonality of symptoms. J Affect Disord. 2014;168:210–23.
Geoffroy PA, Fovet T, Micoulaud-Franchi JA, Boudebesse C, Thomas P, Etain B, et al. Bright light therapy in seasonal bipolar depressions. L'Encéphale. 2015;41(6):527–33.
Goldberg JF, Truman CJ. Antidepressant-induced mania: an overview of current controversies. Bipolar Disord. 2003;5(6):407–20.
Golden RN, Gaynes BN, Ekstrom RD, Hamer RM, Jacobsen FM, Suppes T, et al. The efficacy of light therapy in the treatment of mood disorders: a review and meta-analysis of the evidence. Am J Psychiatry. 2005;162(4):656–62.
Knapen S, Werken MVD, Gordijn M, Meesters Y. The duration of light treatment and therapy outcome in seasonal affective disorder. J Affect Disord. 2014;166:343–6.
Kripke DF. Light treatment for nonseasonal depression: speed, efficacy, and combined 1 Presented at American Psychiatric Association Symposium 54, San Diego, California, May 20, 1997. Supported by AG12364, HL55983, ES08930, and the Sam and Rose Stein Institute for Research on Aging 1. J Affect Disord. 1998;49(2):109–17.
Kupeli NY, Bulut NS, Bulut GC, Kurt E, Kora K. Efficacy of bright light therapy in bipolar depression. Psychiatry Res. 2018;260:432–8.
Labbate LA, Lafer B, Thibault A, Sachs GS. Side effects induced by bright light treatment for seasonal affective disorder. J Clin Psychiatry. 1994 May;55(5):189–91.
Lam RW, Allain S, Sullivan K, Beattie CW, Remick RA, Zis AP. Effects of chronic lithium treatment on retinal electrophysiologic function. Biol Psychiatry. 1997;41(6):737–42.
Levitt AJ, Joffe RT, Moul DE, Lam RW, Teicher MH, Lebegue B, et al. Side effects of light therapy in seasonal affective disorder. American Journal of Psychiatry. 1993;150:650–2.
Maaren YWS-V, Carlier IV, Zitman FG, Hemert AMV, Waal MWD, Does AWVD, et al. Reference values for major depression questionnaires: the Leiden Routine Outcome Monitoring Study. J Affect Disord. 2013;149(1–3):342–9.
Meesters Y, Duijzer WB, Nolen WA, Schoevers RA, Ruhé HG. Inventory of depressive symptomatology en verkorte versie in routine outcome monitoring van Stichting Benchmark GGZ. Tijdschrift voor psychiatrie. 2016;58(1):48–544.
Meesters Y, Duijzer WB, Hommes V. The effects of low-intensity narrow-band blue-light treatment compared to bright white-light treatment in seasonal affective disorder. J Affect Disord. 2018;232:48–51.
Rosenthal NE. Seasonal affective disorder. Arch General Psychiatry. 1984;41(1):72.
Ruhrmann S, Kasper S, Hawellek B, Martinez B, Höflich G, Nickelsen T, et al. Effects of fluoxetine versus bright light in the treatment of seasonal affective disorder. Psychol Med. 1998;28(4):923–33.
Rush A, Trivedi MH, Ibrahim HM, Carmody TJ, Arnow B, Klein DN, et al. The 16-Item quick inventory of depressive symptomatology (QIDS), clinician rating (QIDS-C), and self-report (QIDS-SR): a psychometric evaluation in patients with chronic major depression. Biol Psychiatry. 2003;54(5):573–83.
Rutherford BR, Marcus SM, Wang P, Sneed JR, Pelton G, Devanand D, et al. A randomized, prospective pilot study of patient expectancy and antidepressant outcome. Psychol Med. 2012;43:975–82.
Sit D, Wisner K, Hanusa B, Stull S, Terman M. Light therapy for bipolar disorder: a case series in women. Bipolar Disord. 2007;9(8):918–27.
Sit DK, Mcgowan J, Wiltrout C, Diler RS, Dills J, Luther J, et al. Adjunctive bright light therapy for bipolar depression: a randomized double-blind placebo-controlled Trial. Am J Psychiatry. 2018;175(2):131–9.
Sohn C-H, Lam RW. Treatment of seasonal affective disorder: unipolar versus bipolar differences. Curr Psychiatry Rep. 2004;6(6):478–85.
Suzuki M, Dallaspezia S, Locatelli C, Uchiyama M, Colombo C, Benedetti F. Does early response predict subsequent remission in bipolar depression treated with repeated sleep deprivation combined with light therapy and lithium? J Affect Disord. 2018;229:371–6.
Terman M, Terman JS. Bright Light Therapy. J Clin Psychiatry. 1999;60:798–808.
Terman M, Terman JS. Light therapy for seasonal and nonseasonal depression: efficacy, protocol, safety, and side effects. CNS Spectr. 2005;10:647–63.
Terman M, Terman JS, Ross DC. A controlled trial of timed bright light and negative air ionization for treatment of winter depression. Arch Gener Psychiatry. 1998;55(10):875.
Tondo L, Vázquez G, Baldessarini RJ. Mania associated with antidepressant treatment: comprehensive meta-analytic review. Acta Psychiatrica Scand. 2009;121(6):404–14.
Trivedi MH, Rush AJ, Ibrahim HM, Carmody TJ, Biggs MM, Suppes T, et al. The inventory of depressive symptomatology, clinician rating (IDS-C) and self-report (IDS-SR), and the quick inventory of depressive symptomatology, clinician rating (QIDS-C) and self-report (QIDS-SR) in public sector patients with mood disorders: a psychometric evaluation. Psychol Med. 2004;34(1):73–82.
Tseng P-T, Chen Y-W, Tu K-Y, Chung W, Wang H-Y, Wu C-K, et al. Light therapy in the treatment of patients with bipolar depression: a meta-analytic study. Eur Neuropsychopharmacol. 2016;26(6):1037–47.
Tuunainen A, Kripke DF, Endo T. Light therapy for non-seasonal depression. Cochrane Database Syst Rev. 2004;2004:CD004050.
Wirz-Justice A. Light therapy in seasonal affective disorder is independent of time of day or circadian phase. Arch Gener Psychiatry. 1993;50(12):929.

Wu JC, Kelsoe JR, Schachat C, Bunney BG, Demodena A, Golshan S, et al. Rapid and sustained antidepressant response with sleep deprivation and chronotherapy in bipolar disorder. Biol Psychiatry. 2009;66(3):298–301.
Young RC, Biggs JT, Ziegler VE, Meyer DA. A Rating Scale for Mania: Reliability, Validity and Sensitivity. Br J Psychiatry. 1978;133:429–35.
Zhang Y, Yang H, Yang S, Liang W, Dai P, Wang C, et al. Antidepressants for bipolar disorder: A meta-analysis of randomized, double-blind, controlled trials. Neural Regen Res. 2013;8:2962–74.
Zhou T-H, Dang W-M, Ma Y-T, Hu C-Q, Wang N, Zhang G-Y, et al. Clinical efficacy, onset time and safety of bright light therapy in acute bipolar depression as an adjunctive therapy: a randomized controlled trial. J Affect Disord. 2018;227:90–6.

4

Melanopsin-mediated pupillary responses in bipolar disorder—a cross-sectional pupillometric investigation

Helle Østergaard Madsen[1*], Shakoor Ba-Ali[2], Steffen Heegaard[2], Ida Hageman[3], Ulla Knorr[1], Henrik Lund-Andersen[2], Klaus Martiny[1] and Lars Vedel Kessing[1]

Abstract

Background: Visible light, predominantly in the blue range, affects mood and circadian rhythm partly by activation of the melanopsin-containing intrinsically photosensitive retinal ganglion cells (ipRGCs). The light-induced responses of these ganglion cells can be evaluated by pupillometry. The study aimed to assess the blue light induced pupil constriction in patients with bipolar disorder (BD).

Methods: We investigated the pupillary responses to blue light by chromatic pupillometry in 31 patients with newly diagnosed bipolar disorder, 22 of their unaffected relatives and 35 healthy controls. Mood state was evaluated by interview-based ratings of depressive symptoms (Hamilton Depression Rating Scale) and (hypo-)manic symptoms (Young Mania Rating Scale).

Results: The ipRGC-mediated pupillary responses did not differ across the three groups, but subgroup analyses showed that patients in remission had reduced ipRGC-mediated responses compared with controls (9%, $p=0.04$). Longer illness duration was associated with more pronounced ipRGC-responses (7% increase/10-year illness duration, $p=0.02$).

Conclusions: The ipRGC-mediated pupil response to blue light was reduced in euthymic patients compared with controls and increased with longer disease duration. Longitudinal studies are needed to corroborate these potential associations with illness state and/or progression.

Keywords: Bipolar disorder, Mood disorders, Melanopsin, Pupillary reflex, Pupillometry, Circadian rhythm, Retina

Introduction

In bipolar disorder (BD), a multitude of external factors can interfere with the course of disease and provoke the onset of an affective episode, i.e. depression or mania (Young and Dulcis 2015). Contributing factors include disturbances in biological rhythms caused by e.g. sleep deprivation or change of season. As such, there is evidence for a distinct seasonal pattern in health care utilization in BD with a peak rate of admissions for mania in spring/summer and for depression in winter (Geoffroy et al. 2014) just as patients with BD report increased fluctuations in mood and behavior in relation to change of seasons (Geoffroy et al. 2014). The main driver of this seasonal variation is presumably the change in daylight (Geoffroy et al. 2014; Aguglia et al. 2017). In line with this, chronotherapeutic modalities such as light and dark therapy can be used adjunctively in the treatment of depression and mania, respectively (Gottlieb et al. 2019; van Houl et al. 2020). A hypothesis of so-called retinal super-sensitivity to light has been suggested in BD (Lewy et al. 1985, 1981). Early support for this hypothesis included the findings of increased melatonin suppression

*Correspondence: helle.oestergaard.madsen@regionh.dk
[1] Copenhagen Affective Disorder Research Center (CADIC), Mental Health Center Copenhagen, Rigshospitalet, Edel Sauntes Allé 10, 2100 Copenhagen Ø, Denmark
Full list of author information is available at the end of the article

in response to light in individuals with BD as well as in offspring of patients with BD (Lewy et al. 1985, 1981; Nurnberger et al. 1988). Other studies could not corroborate these findings (Lam et al. 1990; Whalley et al. 1991; Ritter et al. 2019). Aberrant melatonin suppression in patients and offspring could indicate that aberrant light sensitivity constitutes an inherited trait biomarker. Such endophenotypes can potentially inform on underlying biological vulnerability or predict illness emergence in un-affected carriers of the trait. State-dependent biomarkers reflect on the phenotypical presentation of current illness states and can potentially aid in diagnostic and staging processes.

As light reaches the retina, specialized neurons—rods, cones and intrinsically photosensitive retinal ganglion cells (ipRGCs)—perceive the signal (Hattar et al. 2002). The ipRGCs play essential roles in the transmission of light for non-visual purposes such as the pupillary light reflex, suppression of melatonin and regulation of diurnal rhythm, alertness and mood (Lazzerini Ospri et al. 2017; Fernandez et al. 2018). The ipRGCs are predominantly sensitive to high-intensity short wavelength—blue—light (Hattar et al. 2002; Park et al. 2011). IpRGC-activation by blue light elicits the so-called post-illumination pupillary response (PIPR),i.e. a pupillary constriction that persists past the termination of a light stimulus. The PIPR can be swiftly and non-invasively assessed with chromatic pupillometry (Park et al. 2011), i.e. recording and quantification of the pupillary responses to monochromatic light stimuli (Park et al. 2011). Pupillometric evaluation of the ipRGC-mediated responses may provide a potential alternative to the invasive, time consuming, and expensive assessment of circadian system light sensitivity by melatonin suppression experiments. The disadvantages of the method include numerous sources of intra- and inter-individual variation, such as circadian and seasonal timing, iris color, medication, etc. (Kelbsch et al. 2019).

There is some evidence that the PIPR is attenuated in persons with unipolar depression (Roecklein et al. 2013; Berman et al. 2018), but it has not been investigated in persons with BD. In persons without affective disorder, a more pronounced PIPR was associated with higher levels of self-reported lifetime hypomanic/manic-like experiences (Bullock et al. 2019). In this first pupillometric investigation in BD, we assessed trait and state biomarker characteristics of the ipRGC-mediated pupillary response in patients with newly-diagnosed BD and we explored potential associations with illness variables.

Methods

In a cross-sectional design, we investigated the pupillary responses in patients with newly diagnosed BD, their unaffected first-degree relatives and a healthy control group between September 2018 and November 2019. All participants attend the research facility for regular follow-up visits as a part of the Bipolar Illness Onset (BIO)-study (Kessing et al. 2017). BIO-participants who had no prior or current eye disorder, eye trauma, eye surgery or family history of glaucoma were invited to participate in the pupillometric study.

The study was approved by the Committee on Health Research Ethics of the Capital region of Denmark (H-7-2014-007) and complied with the Declaration of Helsinki. Participants all provided written informed consent.

Participants

Patients with bipolar disorder (BD)

BIO-participants with BD have been recruited among outpatients at the Copenhagen Affective Disorder Clinic with a recent ICD-10 diagnosis of BD or single manic episode (WHO 1992). The Copenhagen Affective Disorder Clinic offers a specialized two-year treatment program to all persons with newly diagnosed BD in the greater Copenhagen area. All referred patients undergo a diagnostic assessment by a psychiatrist. The ICD-10 diagnosis of BD is further specified as type I or II as by DSM-V criteria (American Psychiatric Association 2015).

Unaffected first-degree relatives (UR)

Siblings and children to the patients with BD have been included in the BIO-study. These unaffected relatives have had no personal history of substance abuse, psychotic illness or mood disorders according to the ICD-10 at the time of inclusion to the study.

Healthy control participants (HC)

Age-matched control individuals without any personal or family history of psychiatric disorders have been recruited to the BIO-project among blood donors at Rigshospitalet, Copenhagen.

Assessments

Psychiatric evaluation

At inclusion to the BIO-study, all participants underwent a semi-structured diagnostic interview, Schedules in Clinical Assessment in Neuropsychiatry (SCAN), to confirm the clinical diagnosis of BD and to exclude current or prior psychopathology in the UR and HC groups. The interview and clinical evaluation were carried out by trained PhD students (MDs or MSc in psychology). For BD participants, disease duration was recorded as years since their first depressive or (hypo-)manic episode. The severity of current affective symptoms was assessed by interview-based clinical rating scales, i.e. the Hamilton Depression Rating Scale – 17 item version (HDRS) and the Young Mania Rating Scale (YMRS). We used the mood scores to classify the current affective state as follows: remission (both scores ≤ 7), depression (HDRS ≥ 13 and YMRS < 13) and hypomania/mixed state (YMRS ≥ 13) (Kessing et al. 2017; Faurholt-Jepsen et al. 2016). The participants' habitual time of sleep onset and wake-up time within the last 30 days were assessed by the Pittsburgh Sleep Quality Index (PSQI). The time of assessment was defined as the time from habitual wake up time to the recorded time of pupillometry. Current medication and length of day of assessment (http://www.dagenslaengde.dk) was recorded.

Baseline eye examination

We used a Snellen chart to confirm a best corrected visual acuity within normal limits (≥ 0.8). Retinal condition was assessed with optical coherence tomography (OCT), using spectral domain OCT (Heidelberg SD-OCT; Heidelberg Engineering, Heidelberg, Germany). OCT is non-invasive imaging technique that provides high resolution images of the retina through scattering of long-wavelength light. The protocol included macular and peripapillary imaging. Iris color was recorded as dark (brown, black) or light (blue, green, grey).

Pupillometry

We used an automated binocular pupillometer (DP-2000 Human Laboratory Pupillometer, NeurOptics, CA, USA) to elicit monocular monochromatic light stimuli under simultaneous tracking and recording of both pupillary diameters. The light was presented through a diffusing screen (50° × 35° of visual angle) at an illumination level of 100 lux. For the red stimulus with peak wavelength and bandwidth of 633 nm (17 nm), this corresponded to 15.23 log quanta/cm2/second. For the blue stimulus of 463 nm (25 nm), it corresponded to 15.27 log quanta/cm2/second. The study eye was arbitrarily chosen or if there was a difference in visual acuity, we used the better eye. Prior to examination, the study eye was dilated with mydriatic eyedrops (10% phenylephrine hydrochloride and 1% tropicamide) to ensure a pupil diameter > 5 mm before stimulation in order to induce a maximal melanopsin-mediated pupillary response (Ba-Ali et al. 2018). The protocol consisted of 5 min dark adaptation, 10 s baseline recording, 20 s stimulation of the dilated eye with red light and 60 s recording of the pupillary diameters after end of stimulation. After a 5 min break, the protocol was repeated using blue light. Assessments were performed during daytime (8.30 AM – 5 PM) to limit the diurnal variation in the pupillary dynamics.

The raw data on pupillary diameters from the consensual eye—i.e. the non-dilated eye—were imported into the R-statistical software package, version 3.5.1. We inspected a graphic depiction of the pupil diameter (mm) as a function of time (s) to assess the validity of the examination. Blink artefacts were removed with a mathematical algorithm or by manual linear interpolation. Pupillometry outcomes included the pupillary diameter at baseline, the maximal pupil contraction at time 13–15 (3–5 s within the stimulation) and the post-illumination pupil contraction measured at time 40–60 s (10–30 s post-illumination). Mean baseline diameters for the initial 10 s prior to stimulation are reported in millimeter. For the two contraction parameters, the outcomes are reported as the difference between 1 and the mean pupillary diameter for a specified timeframe (see definitions below) divided by the baseline diameter. This normalization to baseline was performed to adjust for the inter-individual differences in pupil size caused by differences in age, sympathetic tone or medication. By the subtraction from 1, the outcomes are interpreted as a degree of contraction, i.e. a higher value reflects a higher contractile response corresponding to a smaller pupil diameter.

The pupillometric outcomes:

Baseline pupil diameter ($PD_{baseline}$): mean pre-stimulus pupil diameter (mm) from time 0–10 s.

Maximal contraction (C_{max}): 1 – (mean pupil diameter (mm) during stimulation from time 13–15 s / $PD_{baseline}$ (mm)).

Post-illumination pupillary response ($PIPR_{late}$): 1 – (mean pupil diameter (mm) from time 40–60 s / $PD_{baseline}$ (mm)).

The C_{max} is a product of joined rod and cone activation. The $PIPR_{late}$ is a product of ipRGC-activation (Ba-Ali et al. 2018).

Statistical analysis

Data were analyzed in the R-statistical software package, version 3.5.1. We report continuous variables as mean and standard deviation (SD) or median and interquartile range (IQR) according to their distribution. Categorical data are presented as numbers and proportions. Comparisons of baseline data were performed in the *tableone* package using Kruskal–Wallis, ANOVA or Fisher's *exact*-test according to the distributions. Spearman correlation tests were performed with the *cor.test* function of the *stats* package.

The a priori analysis plan had the main objective to compare the $PIPR_{late}$ across the 3 groups. Comparisons were performed in a linear mixed effect model (*lme* function in the *nlme* package) to account for the familial relationship between some participants. Estimates of the mean $PIPR_{late}$ and the 95% confidence intervals (CI) for each group were obtained by an initial unadjusted model with the $PIPR_{late}$ as the dependent variable, family relation as a random effect and group as a fixed effect. The model was then adjusted for the covariates of age and sex and lastly a fully adjusted model also included the daylength on time of assessment. To avoid a potential effect of the current affective state in BD, we ran the same models including only patients in remission.

With the secondary objective to evaluate state-dependent variation in the $PIPR_{late}$, we tested the effects of affective scores (HDRS and YMRS) and of current affective state (remission, depression, hypomania/mixed state) on the $PIPR_{late}$ in patients with BD. This was done in separate linear regression models adjusted for sex and age using the *lm* function of the *stats* package. Model fit was assessed by visual inspection of the relevant residual plots.

Thirdly, we investigated associations between the $PIPR_{late}$ and illness variables: psychotropic medication (number of agents (0, 1, ≥ 2) and single agents (lithium, lamotrigine, antidepressants, antipsychotics), BD type (I or II) and illness duration (years since first depressive or (hypo-) manic episode) in separate linear regression models (1:unadjusted, 2: age- and sex-adjusted) within the BD group.

Results

Descriptives

A total of 91 participants underwent pupillometry; 34 patients with BD, 22 UR and 35 HC. We excluded three BD participants due to invalid pupillometric assessments (blinking or deviation of the eye) which left 31 BD participants for analysis (Table 1). There were 4 pairs of relatives in the BD and UR groups, and one pair within the UR group. The median age of the BD and HC samples were 28–29 years and the UR group was slightly younger with a median age of 24 years ($p=0.008$). For all participants, OCT scans and visual acuity assessments were normal. Pupillometry was performed at a similar median time of 12 noon, 11.45 AM and 12 noon in the BD, UR and HC groups, respectively ($p=0.39$) and the groups did not differ in regard to time since habitual wake up time, $p=0.58$ (Table 1). In the BD group, 9 persons were diagnosed with BD type I and 22 persons with BD type II. Median disease duration was 10 years, and 27 persons (77%) had been diagnosed with BD within the last three years. All patients were treated with psychotropic medication and the majority (n=21, 67%) did not meet the criteria for a current affective episode but presented with some residual symptoms (HDRS and YMRS < 13).

Table 1 Characteristics of patients with bipolar disorder (BD), unaffected relatives (UR) and healthy controls (HC)

	BD	UR	HC	$p^{\dagger}$
n	31	22	35	
Age (median [IQR])	29 [25–32.5]	24 [22–28.5]	28 [25–31.5]	0.008
Male sex, n (%)	11 (35.5)	6 (27.3)	12 (34.3)	0.803
Dark eyes, n (%)	7 (22.6)	2 (9.1)	6 (17.1)	0.454
Time of assessment, minutes (mean (SD))	263 (143)	292 (154)	302 (150)	0.578
Daylength, minutes (median [IQR])	778 [685–943]	915 [813–955]	852 [703–972]	0.176
HDRS (median [IQR])	8 [5.5–13]	1 [0–2]	0 [0–1.5]	<0.001
YMRS (median [IQR])	2 [0–7]	0 [0–1]	0 [0–0]	<0.001
Bipolar type 2, n (%)	22 (71)			
Current phase, n (%)				
Remission	9 (29.0)			
Depression	7 (22.6)			
Hypomania/mixed	3 (9.7)			
Lithium, n (%)	12 (38.7)			
Lamotrigine, n (%)	18 (58.1)			
Antipsychotic, n (%)	15 (48.4)			
Antidepressant, n (%)	6 (19.4)			
Number of agents, n (%)				
0	0 (0)			
1	10 (32.3)			
2 or more	21 (67.7)			

Time of assessment: minutes since habitual wakeup time; Daylength: daylight minutes on day of assessment. *HDRS* hamilton depression rating scale, 17 item version. *YMRS* young mania rating scale. Current phase: remission (HDRS and YMRS < 8), depression (HDRS >/= 13 and YMRS < 13), hypomania/mixed (YMRS >/= 13). †Fishers exact test for categorical variables, *t*-test/Kruskal–Wallis for continuous variables

There was no correlation between age and the $PIPR_{late}$ across the total sample ($r=0.15$, $p=0.17$) nor within HC ($r=-0.11$, $p=0.52$) or UR ($r=0.29$, $p=0.19$) subgroups. In the BD group, there was a trend toward increasing PIPR with increasing age ($r=0.34$, $p=0.06$).

The $PIPR_{late}$ as a trait vulnerability marker in BD

The blue induced $PIPR_{late}$ did not differ significantly between the BD, UR and HC groups, nor with adjustment for age-, sex- and photoperiod (Fig. 1a, Table 2). The $PIPR_{late}$ was reduced in the 9 BD participants in current remission ($PIPR_{late}=0.26$ (95% CI: 0.20–0.33)) compared with the HC group ($PIPR_{late}=0.35$ (CI: 0.31–0.38)), $p=0.04$. but not with the UR group, $PIPR_{late}=0.33$ (CI: 0.28–0.38), $p = 0.34$ (Fig. 1, Table 2).

The baseline pupil diameters measured prior to each stimulation did not differ significantly between the groups.

The $PIPR_{late}$ as a state-marker of BD

There were no significant associations between the $PIPR_{late}$ and HDRS-score ($\beta=0.001$, $p=0.77$) or YMRS-score ($\beta=0.004$, $p=0.35$) in patients with BD. This did not change with adjustment for sex and age. There were no significant differences in the $PIPR_{late}$ between BD-participants in different affective states: current remission ($PIPR_{late}=0.25$ (95% CI=0.17–0.32)), depression ($PIPR_{late}=0.30$ (95% CI=0.22–0.39)) or hypomania/mixed state ($PIPR_{late}=0.36$ (95% CI=0.23–0.50)), although the median values displayed a trend towards a more pronounced $PIPR_{late}$ during both depressive and hypomanic/mixed states (Fig. 1c).

Associations between the $PIPR_{late}$ and illness variables in BD

In the BD group, the $PIPR_{late}$ and illness duration was positively associated ($\beta=0.007$, $p=0.02$) corresponding to a 7% increase in the $PIPR_{late}$ for every ten-year increase

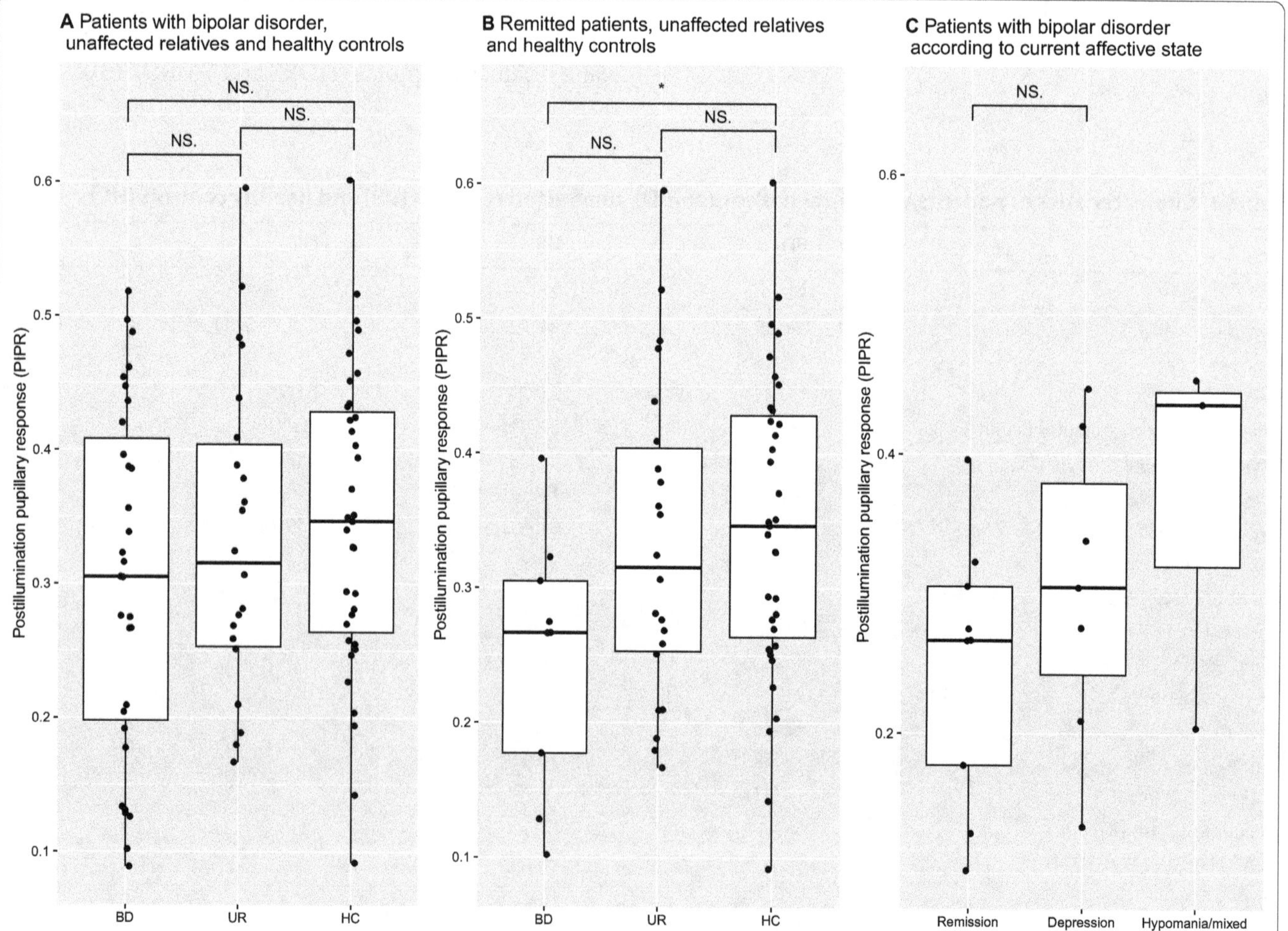

Fig. 1 The post-illumination pupillary response to blue light (PIPR) according to group and affective state. *BD* bipolar disorder, *UR* unaffected relative, *HC* healthy control individual. *NS* nonsignificant comparison. Panel A includes 31 persons with BD, 22 UR and 35 HC. Panel B includes 9 persons with BD in remission, 22 UR and 35 HC. Panel C includes 9 persons with BD in remission, 7 persons in depression and 3 persons in hypomanic/mixed state. *denotes a *p*-value < 0.05

Table 2 Pupillary outcomes in persons with bipolar disorder (BD), unaffected relatives (UR) and healthy controls (HC)

	BD (n = 31)		UR (n = 22)		*p*	HC (n = 35)		*p*	*p*
	Mean	95% CI	Mean	95% CI	BD-UR	Mean	95% CI	BD-HC	UR-HC
Blue light									
$PIPR_{late}$	0.31	0.27–0.35	0.34	0.29–0.39	0.29	0.35	0.31–0.39	0.20	0.87
$PD_{baseline}$ (mm)	7.09	6.81–7.40	7.53	7.17–7.89	0.13	7.32	7.04–7.60	0.28	0.35
C_{max}	0.62	0.60–0.64	0.63	0.61–0.65	0.50	0.62	0.60–0.64	0.80	0.29
Red light									
$PD_{baseline}$ (mm)	7.10	6.81–7.38	7.57	7.23–7.90	0.10	7.31	7.03–7.58	0.28	0.22
C_{max}	0.49	0.46–0.52	0.48	0.45–0.51	0.56	0.51	0.48–0.54	0.33	0.14
	Comparisons of UR and HC with BD in current remission								
	Remission (n = 9)								
Blue light									
$PIPR_{late}$	0.26	0.20–0.33	0.33	0.28–0.38	0.34	0.35	0.31–0.38	0.04	0.67
$PD_{baseline}$ (mm)	7.04	6.49–7.61	7.53	7.17–7.89	0.38	7.32	7.04–7.60	0.38	0.36
C_{max}	0.60	0.56–0.64	0.63	0.61–0.65	0.15	0.62	0.60–0.64	0.36	0.35
Red light									
$PD_{baseline}$ (mm)	7.08	6.55–7.60	7.57	7.23–7.91	0.36	7.31	7.03–7.58	0.44	0.23
C_{max}	0.44	0.39–0.49	0.48	0.44–0.51	0.42	0.51	0.48–0.54	0.02	0.13

$PIPR_{late}$ The mean post-illumination pupillary contraction measured at 10–30 s after stimulation, $PD_{baseline}$ mean pupil diameter during the 10 s before illumination; C_{max} mean pupillary contraction at 3–5 s during illumination. Remission is defined as Hamilton Depression Rating Scale and Young Mania Rating Scale < 8

in illness duration (Fig. 2). This effect was significant with adjustment for sex, but not for sex and age ($\beta = 0.007$, $p = 0.11$).

There were no significant associations between the $PIPR_{late}$ and BD type ($p = 0.88$), number of psychotropic agents ($p = 0.69$) or any single drug type or group (lithium ($p = 0.25$), lamotrigine ($p = 0.93$), antipsychotics ($p = 0.83$), antidepressants, $p = 0.85$)).

Discussion

From this first pupillometric assessment of patients with BD, we report indications that the ipRGC-mediated pupillary responses are altered along with the duration of illness and potentially across different illness states. However, we do not see any indications of aberrant ipRGC-responses being an inherited trait phenomenon in BD.

Although the retinal super-sensitivity hypothesis initially received support from a few studies reporting increased melatonin suppression in patients with BD and in unaffected adolescents with a high-risk profile for BD (Lewy et al. 1985, 1981; Nurnberger et al. 1988; Nathan et al. 1999), later studies challenged the hypothesis (Lam et al. 1990; Whalley et al. 1991; Ritter et al. 2019). Increased melatonin suppression was not found in remitted, drug-free patients (Ritter et al. 2019) nor in a recent well-controlled study using blue light for specific activation of the ipRGC pathway in euthymic patients with BD-I (Ritter et al. 2019). The latter study further reported that the subjective alerting response to blue light was attenuated in patients with BD compared with controls. This is much in line with the group of remitted patients in our study who displayed attenuated ipRGC-responses compared with controls. This finding was, however, based on only 9 remitted patients why it should be interpreted with caution. However, from the larger BIO-cohort, our group has shown, that the BD-group has disordered sleep compared with unaffected relatives and healthy controls even in remitted phases (la Cour Karottki et al. 2020). This inter-episode sleep disturbances may be associated with aberrant ipRGC-transmission. In healthy adolescents and young adults, a more pronounced PIPR is associated with a propensity for delayed sleep timing (Meijden et al. 2016).

We were not able to identify differences in the PIPR across different affective states or associations with symptom severity. This may relate to either sample size (type II error) or the mild-to-moderate symptom load in the present population. The median scores do indicate a trend toward a more pronounced PIPR in depressive and especially in hypomanic/mixed state compared with remission. The prior pupillometric studies in unipolar depression have not assessed the associations between the PIPR and symptom severity (Roecklein et al. 2013; Berman et al. 2018; Laurenzo et al. 2016; Feigl et al. 2018). Moreover, since the studies have used different instruments to assess depression severity, the populations

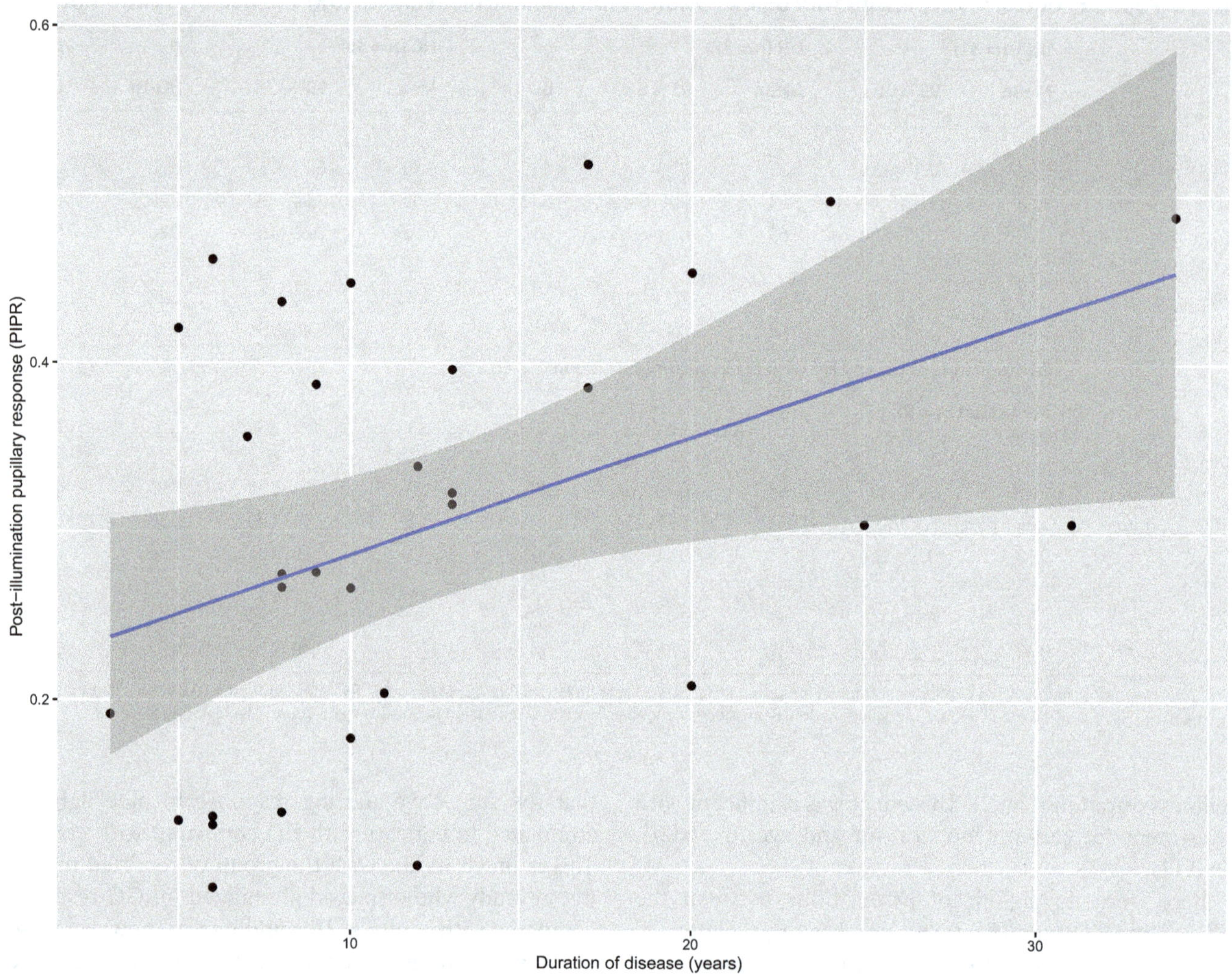

Fig. 2 The post-illumination pupillary response to blue light (PIPR) as a function of illness duration (years since initial depression/mania/hypomania. A higher value indicates a greater post-illumination contraction relative to baseline. The linear regression model predicts a 7% increase in the post-illumination pupillary response to blue light for every 10-year increase in disease duration, $p=0.02$

are not directly comparable. The PIPR was similar in 8 young persons with mild-to-moderate depression and 13 healthy controls (Feigl et al. 2018). In another study of 19 persons with unipolar depression of whom the majority were in remission, there was a trend toward a 7% reduction of the PIPR, $p=0.07$ (Laurenzo et al. 2016). In the largest study to date, 19 in- and outpatients with depression and 20 patients with SAD were assessed with pupillometry during a depressive episode in winter and at follow-up 6 months later (Berman et al. 2018). In both groups with depression, the PIPR was reduced compared with healthy controls. The participants were recruited from a hospital setting which could indicate a more severe illness than in the other studies although their depression scores categorized as mild-to-moderate. In the first pupillometric study in affective disorder performed in persons with SAD, the PIPR was attenuated compared with controls (Roecklein et al. 2013). In SAD, the reduction in ipRGC-responsivity has been suggested as a causal factor, but the association between symptom severity and PIPR remains unresolved in unipolar depression. State marker potential of the PIPR in BD should be evaluated in longitudinal designs of patients across different affective states and preferably with higher symptom severity.

We find a positive association between the $PIPR_{late}$ and illness duration. Due to strong collinearity between age and illness duration, this association was not significant when adjusting for sex and age. As the PIPR is known to be stable across increasing age (Kankipati et al. 2010; Daneault et al. 2016) and since our data do not indicate an association between age and the $PIPR_{late}$ in either the UR or HC groups, we cautiously suggest that the increase in PIPR relates more to illness duration or progression than to higher age. This would be in line with the concept of BD as a progressive disorder presented elsewhere (Kessing and Andersen 2017). A recent OCT study of inpatients with BD did indeed identify a thinning of the retinal nerve fiber layer in BD compared with healthy controls (Khalil et al. 2017). The aforementioned pupillometric studies in unipolar depression have not reported on number of prior episodes or illness duration, hence the association between illness duration and the PIPR constitutes a novel finding. If ipRGC-responsivity is indeed altered in more advanced or severe BD, chronotherapeutic modalities may be more effective in these groups. Blue light-blocking eyewear has been evaluated as an add-on treatment for severe mania in a randomized design in hospitalized patients with a mean illness duration of 20 years (Henriksen et al. 2016). In this population, there was a substantial and rapid reduction in YMRS scores with use of blue-blocking glasses eyewear compared with placebo glasses.

There is a number of limitations to consider in relation to our study. First and foremost, the sample size is modest and do not allow for adjustment for all potential confounding factors. We included only 3 patients with current manic symptoms, why we cannot evaluate any association between hypomania/mania and the PIPR. Importantly, we are also not able to decipher the potential effects of psychotropic medication, since all patients received medication and the majority received combination treatment. By their effects on neurotransmitter systems, psychotropic medications may potentially modify the pupillary motility and/or the sensitivity of the ipRGC-system. A recent study in unmedicated persons found that melatonin suppression was reduced in persons with current but not remitted depression (McGlashan ett al. 2018). No studies have specifically investigated the effects of psychopharmacologic agents on the blue light induced PIPR, but selective serotonin reuptake inhibitors (SSRI) and some antipsychotic agents have been shown to alter the pupil diameter (Koller et al. 2018; Bitsios et al. 1999). An acute dose of the antidepressant citalopram was shown to increase melatonin suppression without affecting the pupillary diameter in a double-blind, placebo-controlled crossover study (McGlashan et al. 2018). No modulatory effects on the PIPR has been reported from post-hoc analyses of antidepressant or anti-manic medications in the referenced pupillometric studies (Roecklein et al. 2013; Berman et al. 2018; Laurenzo et al. 2016; Feigl et al. 2018). Conclusively, medication effects on the pupillary responses or on the circadian system cannot be discarded, although there is no current evidence for drug-related effects on the ipRGC-related pupillary responses, but some evidence for alterations of the resting-state pupillary diameter. We report the $PIPR_{late}$ as percentage pupil constriction relative to baseline in normalized values and not crude numbers, why differences in the resting state pupillary diameters are considered. Another limitation is that we were not able to perform full adjustments for potential effects of photoperiod and time of day due to the sample size. An association between the PIPR and photoperiod has been reported, i.e. a winter-to-summer difference limited to 1–2% (Berman et al. 2018; Laurenzo et al. 2016; Münch et al. 2017) that was primarily related to direct light exposure and not as much to photoperiod (Laurenzo et al. 2016). Our assessments were performed at random dates throughout the year, excluding the winter months, but we made no systematic attempts to match the groups for season or assess light exposure. The main outcome of our study, the comparison of the $PIPR_{late}$ in the 3 groups was adjusted for seasonal but not for diurnal effects. The PIPR undergoes diurnal regulation with an increase in the early morning, a midday plateau and an evening decrease (Münch et al. 2012; Zele et al. 2011). To avoid these morning and evening extremes, we limited the time of assessment to normal office hours, where the PIPR is supposed to display a stable plateau-phase.

Strengths of our study include a thorough diagnostic evaluation to ensure the diagnosis of BD and absence of psychopathology in the two control groups. The inclusion of patients with early BD and their unaffected relatives allows us to specifically assess potential endophenotype features of the ipRGC-responses in BD. We assessed visual acuity and retinal structure to ensure that any pupillometric variation was not related to ocular pathology. Moreover, the implementation of pupillometry in affective disorder research has the potential to add to our understanding of the intertwining of the ipRGC-system and affective regulation. Retinal sensitivity measured during nighttime darkness in melatonin suppression designs may not correspond directly with daytime light sensitivity or ipRGC-function. In glaucoma, where ipRGC degeneration causes attenuations of the PIPR, the correlation between melatonin suppression and the PIPR is rather weak (Munch et al. 2015).

Conclusions

In this first investigation of the ipRGC-related pupillary responses in BD, we find a reduced ipRGC-response in remitted patients compared with controls, but no signs that such aberrant ipRGC-signaling constitutes an inherited trait feature in BD. The positive association between the ipRGC-responses and illness duration could suggest an alteration of the ipRGC-system over the course of disease. This new hypothesis needs corroboration in longitudinal designs. State marker characteristics of the ipRGC-mediated responses in BD should be tested in larger samples in longitudinal designs and include patients with a higher load of affective symptoms.

Acknowledgements
We thank the participants for their contribution and the clinicians at the Department of Ophthalmology, Rigshospitalet for guidance, flexibility and use of equipment. Also, we wish to acknowledge the BIO-team for assisting in recruiting participants.

Authors' contributions
HM, SBA, LVK, UK, HLA and SH conceived and designed the study. SBA and HM obtained the funding. LVK applied for the Data and the Ethical permissions. HM performed participant assessments and data extraction. SBA, HLA and SH assessed OCT scans for pathology. HM performed the statistical analyses under the supervision of LVK. All co-authors made substantial contributions to the interpretation of the data. HM drafted the manuscript. All co-authors contributed with substantial revisions and critical review of the manuscript. All authors read and approved the final manuscript.

Author details
[1] Copenhagen Affective Disorder Research Center (CADIC), Mental Health Center Copenhagen, Rigshospitalet, Edel Sauntes Allé 10, 2100 Copenhagen Ø, Denmark. [2] Department of Ophthalmology, Rigshospitalet, Glostrup, Denmark. [3] Mental Health Services, Capital Region of Denmark, Copenhagen, Denmark.

References

Aguglia A, Borsotti A, Cuniberti F, Serafini G, Amore M, Maina G. The influence of sunlight exposure on hospitalization in emergency psychiatry. Chronobiol Int. 2017;34:1413–22.

Ba-Ali S, Lund-Andersen H, Ahmadi H, Brøndsted AE. Effect of intermittent versus continuous light exposure on pupillary light response, as evaluated by pupillometry. Front Neurol. 2018. https://doi.org/10.3389/fneur.2017.00746.

Berman G, Muttuvelu D, Berman D, Larsen JI, Licht RW, Ledolter J, et al. Decreased retinal sensitivity in depressive disorder: a controlled study. Acta Psychiatr Scand. 2018;137:231–40.

Bitsios P, Szabadi E, Bradshaw CM. Comparison of the effects of venlafaxine, paroxetine and desipramine on the pupillary light reflex in man. Psychopharmacology. 1999;143:286–92.

Bullock B, McGlashan EM, Burns AC, Lu BS, Cain SW. Traits related to bipolar disorder are associated with an increased post-illumination pupil response. Psychiatry Res. 2019;278:35–41.

Daneault V, Dumont M, Massé É, Vandewalle G, Carrier J. Light-sensitive brain pathways and aging. J Physiol Anthropol. 2016. https://doi.org/10.1186/s40101-016-0091-9.

Diagnostic and statistical manual of mental health disorders. Diagnostic and statistical manual of mental health disorders: DSM-5. 5th ed. Arlington: American Psychiatric Association; 2015.

Faurholt-Jepsen M, Brage S, Vinberg M, Kessing LV. State-related differences in the level of psychomotor activity in patients with bipolar disorder - Continuous heart rate and movement monitoring. Psychiatry Res. 2016;237:166–74.

Feigl B, Ojha G, Hides L, Zele AJ. Melanopsin-driven pupil response and light exposure in non-seasonal major depressive disorder. Front Neurol. 2018. https://doi.org/10.3389/fneur.2018.00764.

Fernandez DC, Fogerson PM, Lazzerini Ospri L, Thomsen MB, Layne RM, Severin D, et al. Light affects mood and learning through distinct retina-brain pathways. Cell. 2018;175:71–84.

Geoffroy PA, Bellivier F, Scott J, Etain B. Seasonality and bipolar disorder: A systematic review, from admission rates to seasonality of symptoms. J Affect Disord. 2014;168:210–33.

Gottlieb JF, Benedetti F, Geoffroy PA, Henriksen TEG, Lam RW, Murray G, et al. The chronotherapeutic treatment of bipolar disorders: A systematic review and practice recommendations from the ISBD task force on chronotherapy and chronobiology. Bipolar Disord. 2019;21:741–73.

Hattar S, Liao HW, Takao M, Berson DM, Yau KW. Melanopsin containing retinal ganglion cells: architecture, projections, and intrinsic photosensitivity. Science. 2002;295:1065–70.

Henriksen TE, Skrede S, Fasmer OB, Schoeyen H, Leskauskaite I, Bjørke-Bertheussen J, et al. Blue-blocking glasses as additive treatment for mania: a randomized placebo-controlled trial. Bipolar Disord. 2016;18:221–32.

Kankipati L, Girkin CA, Gamlin PD. Post-illumination pupil response in subjects without ocular disease. Investig Ophthalmol Vis Sci. 2010;51:2764–9.

Kelbsch C, Strasser T, Chen Y, Feigl B, Gamlin PD, Kardon R, et al. Standards in pupillography. Front Neurol. 2019. https://doi.org/10.3389/fneur.2019.00129.

Kessing LV, Andersen PK. Evidence for clinical progression of unipolar and bipolar disorders. Acta Psychiatr Scand. 2017;135:51–64.

Kessing LV, Munkholm K, Faurholt-Jepsen M, Miskowiak KW, Nielsen LB, Frikke-Schmidt R, et al. The Bipolar Illness Onset study: Research protocol for the BIO cohort study. BMJ Open. 2017. https://doi.org/10.1136/bmjopen-2016-015462.

Khalil MA, Saleh AA, Gohar SM, Khalil DH, Said M. Optical coherence tomography findings in patients with bipolar disorder. J Affect Disord. 2017;218:115–22.

Koller D, Belmonte C, Lubomirov R, Saiz-Rodríguez M, Zubiaur P, Román M, et al. Effects of aripiprazole on pupillometric parameters related to pharmacokinetics and pharmacogenetics after single oral administration to healthy subjects. J Psychopharmacol. 2018;32:1212–22.

la Cour Karottki NF, Coello K, Stanislaus S, Melbye S, Kjærstad HL, Sletved KSO, et al. Sleep and physical activity in patients with newly diagnosed bipolar disorder in remission, their first-degree unaffected relatives and healthy controls. Int J Bipolar Disord. 2020. https://doi.org/10.1186/s40345-020-00181-6.

Lam RW, Berkowitz AL, Berga SL, Clark CM, Kripke DF, Gillin JC. Melatonin suppression in bipolar and unipolar mood disorders. Psychiatry Res. 1990;33:129–34.

Laurenzo SA, Kardon R, Ledolter J, Poolman P, Schumacher AM, Potash JB, et al. Pupillary response abnormalities in depressive disorders. Psychiatry Res. 2016;246:492–9.

Lazzerini Ospri L, Prusky G, Hattar S. Mood, the circadian system, and melanopsin retinal ganglion cells. Annu Rev Neurosci. 2017;40:539–56.

Lewy AJ, Wehr TA, Goodwin FK, Newsome DA, Rosenthal NE. Manic-depressive patients may be supersensitive to light. Lancet. 1981;317:383–4.

Lewy AJ, Nurnberger JI, Wehr TA, Pack D, Becker LE, Powell RL, et al. Supersensitivity to light: possible trait marker for manic-depressive illness. Am J Psychiatry. 1985;142:725–7.

McGlashan EM, Nandam LS, Vidafar P, Mansfield DR, Rajaratnam SMW, Cain SW. The SSRI citalopram increases the sensitivity of the human circadian system to light in an acute dose. Psychopharmacology. 2018;235:3201–9.

McGlashan EM, Coleman MY, Vidafar P, Phillips AJK, Cain SW. Decreased sensitivity of the circadian system to light in current, but not remitted depression. J Affect Disord. 2019;256:386–92.

Münch M, Léon L, Crippa SV, Kawasaki A. Circadian and wake-dependent effects on the pupil light reflex in response to narrow-bandwidth light pulses. Investig Ophthalmol Vis Sci. 2012;53:4546–55.

Münch M, Ladaique M, Roemer S, Hashemi K, Kawasaki A. Melanopsin-Mediated acute light responses measured in winter and in summer: seasonal variations in adults with and without cataracts. Front Neurol. 2017. https://doi.org/10.3389/fneur.2017.00464.

Munch M, Leon L, Collomb S, Kawasaki A. Comparison of acute non-visual bright light responses in patients with optic nerve disease, glaucoma and healthy controls. Sci Rep. 2015. https://doi.org/10.1038/srep15185.

Nathan PJ, Burrows GD, Norman TR. Melatonin sensitivity to dim white light in affective disorders. Neuropsychopharmacology. 1999;21:408–13.

Nurnberger JI, Berrettini W, Tamarkin L, Hamovit J, Norton J, Gershon E. Supersensitivity to melatonin suppression by light in young people at high risk for affective disorder. A preliminary report. Neuropsychopharmacology. 1988;1:217–23.

Park JC, Moura AL, Raza AS, Rhee DW, Kardon RH, Hood DC. Toward a clinical protocol for assessing rod, cone, and melanopsin contributions to the human pupil response. Investig Ophthalmol Vis Sci. 2011;52:6624–35.

Ritter P, Wieland F, Skene DJ, Pfennig A, Weiss M, Bauer M, et al. Melatonin suppression by melanopsin-weighted light in patients with bipolar I disorder compared to healthy controls. J Psychiatry Neurosci. 2019;44:1–8.

Roecklein K, Wong P, Ernecoff N, Miller M, Donofry S, Kamarck M, et al. The post illumination pupil response is reduced in seasonal affective disorder. Psychiatry Res. 2013;210:150–8.

Van Der Meijden WP, Van Someren JL, te Lindert BHW, Bruijel J, Van Oosterhout F, Coppens J, et al. Individual differences in sleep timing relate to melanopsin-based phototransduction in healthy adolescents and young adults. Sleep. 2016;39:1305–10.

van Hout LJE, Rops LEP, Simons CJP. Treating winter depressive episodes in bipolar disorder: an open trial of light therapy. Int J Bipolar Disord. 2020. https://doi.org/10.1186/s40345-020-00182-5.

Whalley LJ, Perini T, Shering A, Bennie J. Melatonin response to bright light in recovered, drug-free, bipolar patients. Psychiatry Res. 1991;38:13–9.

World Health Organization. ICD-10: International statistical classification of diseases and related health problems Tenth revision. Geneva: World Health Organization; 1992.

Young JW, Dulcis D. Investigating the mechanism(s) underlying switching between states in bipolar disorder. Eur J Pharmacol. 2015;759:151–62.

Zele AJ, Feigl B, Smith SS, Markwell EL. The circadian response of intrinsically photosensitive retinal ganglion cells. PLoS ONE. 2011. https://doi.org/10.1371/journal.pone.0017860.

5

Associations between the cortisol awakening response and patient-evaluated stress and mood instability in patients with bipolar disorder

Maria Faurholt-Jepsen[1,2*], Vibe Gedsø Frøkjær[1,2,3], Arafat Nasser[3], Niklas Rye Jørgensen[2,4], Lars Vedel Kessing[1,2] and Maj Vinberg[1,2,5]

Abstract

Objective: The Cortisol Awakening Response (CAR) measured as the transient increase in cortisol levels following morning awakening appears to be a distinct feature of the HPA axis. Patients with bipolar disorder (BD) experience daily stress, mood instability (MI) and studies have shown disrupted HPA-axis dynamics. Aims: to evaluate (1) patient-evaluated stress against the CAR, (2) associations between the CAR and mood symptoms, and (3) the effect of smartphone-based treatment on the CAR.

Methods: Patients with BD (n = 67) were randomized to the use of daily smartphone-based monitoring (the intervention group) or to the control group for six months. Clinically rated symptoms according to the Hamilton Depression Rating Scale 17-items (HDRS), the Young Mania Rating Scale (YMRS), patient-evaluated perceived stress using Cohen's Perceived Stress Scale (PSS) and salivary awakening cortisol samples used for measuring the CAR were collected at baseline, after three and six months. In the intervention group, smartphone-based data on stress and MI were rated daily during the entire study period.

Results: Smartphone-based patient-evaluated stress (*B: 134.14, 95% CI: 1.35; 266.92, p = 0.048*) and MI (*B: 430.23, 95% CI: 52.41; 808.04, p = 0.026*) mapped onto increased CAR. No statistically significant associations between the CAR and patient-evaluated PSS or the HDRS and the YMRS, respectively were found. There was no statistically significant effect of smartphone-based treatment on the CAR.

Conclusion: Our data, of preliminary character, found smartphone-based patient-evaluations of stress and mood instability as read outs that reflect CAR dynamics. Smartphone-supported clinical care did not in itself appear to disturb CAR dynamics.

Keywords: Bipolar disorder, Cortisol awakening response, Smartphone

Introduction

The Cortisol Awakening Response (CAR) measured as the transient increase in cortisol levels following morning awakening appears to be a distinct feature of the hypothalamus–pituitary–adrenal (HPA) axis, is associated with a wide range of variables reflecting health status and differs according to age and sex (Fries et al. 2009; Larsson et al. 2009; Stalder et al. 2011; Roelfsema 2017). A meta-analysis including forty-one studies and

*Correspondence: maria@faurholt-jepsen.dk
[1] Copenhagen Affective Disorder Research Center (CADIC), Psychiatric Center Copenhagen, Blegdamsvej 9, Rigshospitalet, 2100 Copenhagen, Denmark
Full list of author information is available at the end of the article

two individual studies showed that bipolar disorder was associated with increased basal levels of cortisol and decreased inhibitory feedback capacity (i.e. increased cortisol post-dexamethasone), and that case–control differences in cortisol levels were positively associated with mania (Jabben 2011; Belvederi Murri et al. 2016; Huang 2017). Familial risk for mood disorders is associated with a compromised inhibitory feedback regulation of the HPA-axis (Modell 1998), which is a significant predictor for relapse of depressive episodes in patients with a history of depression (Zobel 2001; Vrshek-Schallhorn 2013). Overall, previous studies in patients with affective disorders have thus shown changed cortisol patterns during depressive episodes and manic episodes and while in remission. Patients with bipolar disorder further exhibit vulnerability to stress, which in addition to a hyperactive HPA-axis seem to play a key role in the pathophysiology of the disorder (Belvederi Murri et al. 2016; Cervantes et al. 2001; Fries 2014; Coello et al. 2018). Patients with bipolar disorder often report an increased sensitivity to experiencing distress, which is interconnected to mood instability (MI) (Faurholt-Jepsen 2019b; Stanislaus 2020). Further, a substantial proportion of patients with bipolar disorder experience daily subsyndromal mood swings, and MI reflects the amount and degree of mood swings. MI is further associated with poor prognosis including impaired functioning and quality of life, increased perceived stress, increased risk of hospitalization, and a higher risk of relapse (Faurholt-Jepsen 2019b; Bopp 2010; Strejilevich 2013; Patel 2015; Gershon and Eidelman 2015; O'Donnell 2018). Due to the increased focus on the impact of mood instability, mood instability has been suggested as an independent new treatment target and as a more sensitive measure of outcome in randomized controlled trials (RCTs) than for example relapse or recurrence of affective episodes (Bopp 2010; Bonsall et al. 2012; Saunders 2016; Broome et al. 2015). However, previous studies measuring mood instability have included data based on weekly assessments, and data were often collected using paper-based methods thereby increasing the risk of patient recall bias (Strejilevich 2013).

The rapid evolution and ubiquity of mobile networks have resulted in the increasing development tools for remote and real-time self-monitoring (Lal and Adair 2014). Real-time self-monitoring of momentary or very recent experiences have important advantages over retrospective reports, as they contain less bias and allow for unobtrusive monitoring during naturalistic settings (Stone et al. 2003). Studies using daily assessments have found associations between increased CAR and for example chronic stress in daily life and reduced distress responses to daily life stress (Schlotz et al. 2004; Powell and Schlotz 2012; Schlotz 2019). The authors have previously developed and investigated the usability, validity and effect of a smartphone-based self-monitoring system (the previous MONARCA system) in patients with bipolar disorder (Faurholt-Jepsen 2015a, 2015b,2019a). The MONARCA system offers a unique possibility to obtain detailed data on how patients with bipolar disorder experience daily hassles, and in the previous studies patients with bipolar disorders report higher levels of daily stress than healthy control individuals (Faurholt-Jepsen 2019b; Stanislaus 2020). However, it has not previously been investigated whether smartphone-based daily patient-evaluated stress align with aspects of biological stress hormone reactivity, i.e. HPA-axis dynamics in terms of CAR.

Here we report on the tertiary outcome measures collected as part of a randomized controlled trial (RCT) that investigated the effect of a smartphone-based monitoring system on the severity of depressive and manic symptoms in patients with bipolar disorder (the MONARCA I trial) (Faurholt-Jepsen 2014, 2013). In summary, overall the MONARCA I trial found no differences in the severity of depressive and manic symptoms (primary outcome) measured using the Hamilton Depression Rating Scale 17-items (HDRS) (Hamilton 1967) and the Young Mania Rating Scale (YMRS) (Young et al. 1978), respectively, between the intervention group and the control group (Faurholt-Jepsen 2015a). However, sub-group analyses suggested that the smartphone-based monitoring system may sustain the level of depressive symptoms and reduce the level of manic symptoms and thereby affect the level of CAR.

Aims and hypotheses

In patients with bipolar disorder the present study, of preliminary character, aimed to (1) evaluate the association between perceived stress measured using Cohen's perceived stress scale (PSS) (Cohen et al. 1983) and daily smartphone-based measures of stress against the CAR; (2) investigate the association between the CAR and clinically evaluated mood symptoms (measured using the HDRS, the YMRS) and patient-evaluated mood instability (MI) measured using daily smartphone data, respectively, and (3) investigate the effect of smartphone-based treatment on the level of the CAR.

We hypothesized, that there would be a positive association between the CAR and daily patient-evaluated stress and MI, respectively. Further, we hypothesized, that there would be a positive association between the CAR and clinical observed mood symptoms according to the HDRS and the YMRS, respectively, and that smartphone-based treatment could reduce the CAR.

Material and methods

Design, settings and participants

The present study presents data collected as part of a RCT investigating the effect of smartphone-based monitoring in patients with bipolar disorder (the MONARCA I trial) (Faurholt-Jepsen 2015a).

The MONARCA I trial

The patients were recruited from the Copenhagen Clinic for Affective Disorders, Copenhagen, Denmark during a period from September 2011 to March 2013. Patients were invited to participate in the trial following referral to the clinic and were randomized 1:1 to using a smartphone-based monitoring system (the MONARCA system) for daily electronic self-monitoring (the intervention group) (further description below) or to the use of a smartphone without the monitoring system for normal communicative purposes with no daily electronic self-monitoring (the control group). Regardless the allocation group, patients were followed for six months. The inclusion criteria were a bipolar disorder diagnosis according to ICD-10 and DSM-IV using the Schedules for Clinical Assessment in Neuropsychiatry (SCAN) interview (Wing et al. 1990) (conducted by an experienced medical doctor and researcher, MFJ), age between 18 to 60 years, a Hamilton Depression Rating Scale 17-item (HDRS-17) score ≤ 17 (Hamilton 1967) and a Young Mania Rating Scale (YMRS) score ≤ 17 (Young et al. 1978) at the time of inclusion. The exclusion criteria were pregnancy, a lack of Danish language skills, inability to learn the technicalities for using a smartphone, unwilling to use the trial smartphone as the primary cell phone, and severely physical illness or schizophrenia, schizotypal or delusional disorders according to the SCAN interview.

A total of 78 patients with bipolar disorder receiving treatment at the Copenhagen Clinic for Affective Disorder, Denmark at the time of the study were included. Among the 78 patients a total of 67 patients showed up for clinical assessments and were included in the analyses.

Clinical assessments and questionnaires

During the entire trial period of six months, monthly clinical ratings were conducted face-to-face by an MD and trained researcher (MFJ) and questionnaires were collected.

Clinical ratings: The severity of depressive and manic symptoms for the last four days was evaluated using the HDRS (Hamilton 1967) and the YMRS (Young et al. 1978), respectively. Data on functioning were clinically rated using the Functional Assessment Short Test (FAST), which is a 24-item interviewer-administrated interview concerning autonomy, occupational functioning, cognitive functioning, financial issues, interpersonal relationships and leisure time (Rosa 2007); scores above 11 indicate impaired functioning. All clinical ratings were conducted by a clinician (MFJ) who was blinded to the patients' group of allocation during the entire MONARCA I trial, and thus the clinical ratings were blinded.

Patient-based questionnaires: The severity of perceived stress was evaluated by the patients using Cohen's Perceived Stress Scale, which is a 14-item questionnaire measuring the degree to which situations in one's life are appraised as stressful reflecting the last 14 days. Higher scores indicate higher perceived stress (Cohen et al. 1983).

Patient-reported daily monitoring via smartphones

In brief, the MONARCA system consisted of the following: Patients allocated to the intervention group of the MONARCA I trial were provided with an Android smartphone with the MONARCA system installed. At a self-chosen time point on a daily basis during the six months trial period, patients in the intervention group were reminded by an alarm and prompted to use the smartphone-based system for self-assessment of mental distress experienced during that particular day as a whole (Faurholt-Jepsen 2014). The app allowed for anchored daily self-assessment of stress (scored on a scale from 0, 1, 2, 3, 4, 5) and mood (scored on a scale from -3 to $+3$) (and other items such as sleep, medication etc.). The intervention also included a clinical feed-back loop to a study nurse, who went through the smartphone-based data on a daily basis and contacted the patients in case of signs of deterioration. Further details regarding the MONARCA system and the intervention during the MONARCA trial have been described elsewhere (Faurholt-Jepsen 2014, 2013). Patients allocated to the control group did not provide any self-assessed smartphone data during the trial.

Cortisol Awakening Response

Regardless the group of allocation in the MONARCA trial, Cortisol Awakening Response (CAR) samples were collected at baseline, after three months and six months on all patients. The CAR is based on five serial measurements of salivary cortisol over the first hour from awakening (at 0, 15, 30, 45 and 60 min. after awakening) and computed as the area under the curve with respect to increase from baseline level at awakening (AUC_i) controlled for the level of salivary cortisol in sample 1. Patient instructions, home sampling procedures, and cortisol analyses were carried out as described elsewhere (Frokjaer 2013). At each visit, patients returned a paper with handwritten registered timings of collected saliva samples, and it was checked by the researchers that the timings complied with those specified in the home sampling procedures. All samples were collected at the participant's home and were returned at the three assessment days and kept frozen at − 80 °C until assayed in one single batch. Salivary cortisol concentrations were determined by a chemiluminescence immunoassay (CLIA) method on the IDS-iSYS automatic analyzer (IDS PLC, Boldon, UK). The intra- and inter-assay variation was up < 15%, which adhered to the standards of the lab. However, if this variation had been smaller, we might have detected more robust results.

Statistical methods

Descriptive analyses were produced using percentages, medians, interquartile range, means and standard deviations. In one case the 60 min. a salivary cortisol sample was missing, and the CAR was calculated using the available four salivary samples in order to calculate the AUC_i. All statistical analyses including co-variates were defined a priori and computed using linear mixed effect regression models. These regression models allow for both *within*-individual and *between*-individual variations over time with repeated measurements of the variables considered in the analyses. Thus, for each of the analyses we employed a two-leveled linear mixed regression model with the first level representing the repeated measurements per patient of the variables of interest *within*-individuals and the second level representing the *between*-individuals variation of the variables of interest. All models included a fixed effect of visit number (baseline, three-months, six-months) and a participant specific random intercept and a participant specific random effect to account for patient specific correlations between the dependent variables (CAR) and the independent variables (e.g.: PSS, HDRS, YMRS) over time due to repeated measurements. All clinical ratings and questionnaire data from baseline, three-months and six-month) were included corresponding to the CAR at that time point in the analyses. In the linear mixed effect regression models, analyses were conducted assuming that missing data was missing at random. These models will use the full available data set. Thus, we assumed data was missing at random and analyzed data to get an unbiased estimate.

Other covariates were specified as fixed effects in the models. For all analyses, models were adjusted for age and gender, as these covariates may affect the level of the CAR (Larsson et al. 2009; Roelfsema 2017).

Concerning aim 1: to investigate the association between daily smartphone-based measures of patient-evaluated stress collected from patients in the intervention group using the MONARCA system coupling to the CAR, all daily smartphone-based data on stress available from all days during the entire trial period of six months was used in the analyses. There is no consensus on how to report the performance and variance in hierarchical linear models. In the present paper, we reported the Snijders and Bosker's method (Snijders and Bosker 1994), which can be interpreted as the proportion of variance in math achievement explained by the covariates. Values of 0.02 indicate a small proportion of variance explained by the covariates, 0.15 a proportion, and 0.35 a large proportion.

Concerning aim 2: to investigate the association between MI measured using daily smartphone-based data collected from patients in the intervention group using the MONARCA system and the CAR, measures of mood from all days during the entire trial period were used in the analyses. MI was operationalized and calculated as the number of mood changes, on a scale from − 3 to + 3, from day to day divided by the number of weeks followed between baseline to three months and from three months to six months. This method has been used previously by the authors and others (Strejilevich 2013; Faurholt-Jepsen 2015). Thus, the MI measure reflects the number of changes in patient-based mood evaluations, even at a subclinical level, rather than the extent of mood changes.

Concerning aim 3: to investigate the effect of smartphone-based treatment on the CAR, difference in CAR between the two groups (intervention group and control group) during the entire trial period of six months was investigated. The effect of interaction between visit number and randomization group on the CAR was investigated, but not reported ($p = 0.48$).

Model assumptions concerning deviations from normality and heteroscedasticity were checked visually by means of residual plots, and QQ plots for each of the statistical analyses. Since this is the first study to investigate the association between perceived stress measured using smartphones and the CAR, we were not able to conduct statistical power calculations. The variance inflation factor (VIF) identifying the correlation between independent variables and the strength of that correlation was calculated to be < 5, and therefore not severe enough to warrant corrective measures. The statistical significance (two-tailed) limit was set at $p \leq 0.05$. Data were entered using Excel and STATA version 13 (StataCorp, LP, College Station, TX, USA) was used for statistical analyses.

Ethical considerations

The trial was approved by the Regional Ethics Committee of the Capital Region of Denmark (H-2-2011-056) and the Danish Data protection agency (2013-41-1710). The law regarding the handling of personal data was respected. Prior to commencement the trials were registered at

ClinicalTrials.gov (NCT01446406). The electronic data collected from the smartphones were stored at a secure server at Concern IT, Capital Region, Denmark (I-suite number RHP-292 2011-03). The trial complied with the Helsinki Declaration of 1975, as revised in 2008.

Results

Background characteristics

Of the 67 included patient, 33 patients allocated to the intervention group providing daily monitoring of stress and mood via smartphones were included in the present study of analyses concerning only smartphone-based self-monitoring. During the trial period patients randomized to the intervention group provided daily mood monitoring 94.5% of the days and daily stress monitoring 88.6% of the days. The patients had a median stress level of 1 [IQR 0–2] and a median mood level of 0 [IQR 0–1] measured using the smartphone-based system. Further, 34 patients were allocated to the control group and did not provide smartphone-based data, but they were included in the analyses concerning clinical face-to face ratings and PSS data. Two patients, one in the intervention group (due to travelling abroad) and one in the control group (due to non-response), had a discontinued intervention after three months follow-up. Only few patients' visits were missing (3.6% in the intervention group and 3.8% in the control group).

Details on background characteristics and clinical information are presented in Table 1.

A total of 116 samples were excluded due to inadequate saliva volume. Thus, a total of 951 salivary cortisol samples, collected between 6 a.m. and 10 a.m., were available for statistical analyses. None of the samples were excluded due to invalid timing. A total of 79% of the patients provided all three CAR samples during the trial period. Details concerning cortisol levels are presented in Table 2.

The average raw area under the curve with respect to increase of cortisol (AUC_i) at baseline was 91.23 (SD 545.07) nmol/l*min, at visit three months 186.70 (SD 350.20) nmol/l*min, and at six months 297.45 (SD 421.29) nmol/l*min. Raw concentrations of cortisol in the awakening sample are presented in Table 2.

Table 1 Background characteristics and clinical information of study participants, N = 67

	Intervention group (n = 33)	Control group (n = 34)
Age, years	29.1 (7.5)	29.5 (9.4)
Female sex, % (n)	65.7 (22)	68.6 (23)
Clinical history		
BPI diagnosis[a], % (n)	60.0 (20)	74.3 (25)
Previous psychiatric admissions, number	1 [1, 2]	1 [1, 2]
Previous depressive episodes, number	4 [2–10]	4 [2–5]
Previous manic episodes, number	3 [2–6]	2 [1–5]
HDRS-17 score during the study	8 [4–14]	8 [4–14]
YMRS score during the study	2 [0–4]	2 [0–5]
PSS score during the study	18.5 (9.0)	18.9 (9.2)
FAST score during the study	22.1 (16.7)	23.7 (16.5)
Mood measured daily using smartphones[b]	− 0.32 (0.73)	–
Stress measured daily using smartphone[c]	0.93 (1.1)	–

Data are mean (SD), %(n) or median [IQR] unless otherwise stated; [a]Bipolar disorder type I disorder; *HDRS-17* The Hamilton depression rating scale 17 items (median of 7 monthly ratings); *YMRS* The Young mania rating scale (median of 7seven monthly ratings); *PSS* Cohen's Percieved Stress Scale (mean of 7 monthly ratings); *FAST* The Functioning Assessment Short Scale (mean of 7 monthly ratings); [b]Mood measured daily using smartphone was evaluated on a scale from − 3 to + 3; [c]Stress measured daily using smartphone was evaluated on a scale from 0 to 5

Association between the Cortisol Awakening Response and patient-evaluated stress

There was no statistically significant association between patient-evaluated *non-smart-phone-based* stress measured by the PSS and the CAR in the models adjusted for age and gender (*B: − 1.63, 95% CI: − 10.53; 7.26, $p = 0.72$ (N = 67)*) (Snijders and Boskers: 0.17) (Table 3). The estimates were not altered to a large extent when only including patients from the intervention group, and therefore not reported.

There was a statistically significant positive association between daily smartphone-based patient-evaluated stress and the CAR in the models adjusted for age and gender (*B: 134.14, 95% CI: 1.35; 266.92, $p = 0.048$ (n = 33)*) (Snijders and Boskers: 0.05). Thus, for every increase of 1 point on the smartphone-based stress measure there was an increase of 134.14 nmol/l*min of CAR (Table 3 and Fig. 1).

In addition, there was a statistically significant positive association between patient-evaluated stress measured using the PSS and patient-evaluated stress measured using smartphones in the models adjusted for age and gender (*B: 3.33, 95% CI: 2.02; 4.65, $p < 0.0001$* (n = 33)).

Exploratory analyses including bipolar disorder subtype (bipolar disorder type I or II) as a covariate did not alter these estimates.

Association between Cortisol Awakening Response and face-to-face clinician-evaluated depressive symptoms and manic symptoms, repsectively

The results from the adjusted linear mixed effect models regarding the association between the CAR and clinician-evaluated depressive and manic symptoms

Table 2 Salivary cortisol measures in patients with bipolar disorder during a 6 months study period, N=67

Number of salivary samples, total	951
Raw concentration of cortisol (nmol/l) in awakening sample, baseline	11.11 (9.94)
Raw concentration of cortisol (nmol/l) in awakening sample, three months	11.26 (9.55)
Raw concentration of cortisol (nmol/l) in awakening sample, six months	10.08 (5.67)
Area under the curve with respect to increase (nmol/l), baseline	91.23 (545.07)
Area under the curve with respect to increase (nmol/l), three months	186.70 (350.20)
Area under the curve with respect to increase (nmol/l), six months	297.45 (421.29)

Data are mean (SD) unless otherwise stated

Table 3 Associations between cortisol awakening response (CAR) and patient-evaluated perceived stress and mood instability measured daily using smartphones, questionnaire-based perceived stress, clinically evaluated functioning, depressive symptoms and manic symptoms, respectively in patients with bipolar disorder

	Model[a]		
	B	95% CI	*p*
Analyses including all patients, n=67			
CAR			
PSS [c]	− 1.63	− 10.53; 7.26	0.72
FAST	− 1.18	− 6.48; 4.12	0.66
HDRS	− 6.79	− 17.89; 4.30	0.23
YMRS	− 12.88	− 29.92; 4.15	0.14
Analyses including only patients using a smartphone-based monitoring system, n=33			
CAR			
Stress measured using smartphones[b]	134.14	1.35; 266.92	0.048
Mood Instability measured using smartphones[c]	430.23	52.41; 808.04	0.026
PSS	10.73	− 2.78; 24.23	0.12
FAST	3.72	− 5.64; 13.09	0.44
HDRS	4.97	− 12.36; 22.31	0.58
YMRS	− 3.93	− 27.46; 19.61	0.74
Effect of smartphone-based treatment. Control group serve as reference, n=67			
CAR	− 16.57	− 183.11; 216.25	0.87

[a] Model: Adjusted for age and gender

CAR Cortisol Awakening Response; *PSS*: Perceived stress measured using Cohen's Perceived Stress Scale; *FAST* Psychosocial functioning measured using Functional Assessment Short Test; *HDRS* Hamilton Depression Rating Scale; *YMRS* Young Mania Rating Scale; [b]Stress measured using smartphone was evaluated on a scale from 0 to 5; [c]Mood Instability calculated as the number of mood changes from day to day from baseline to three months and from three months to 6 months

measured using the HDRS and the YMRS, respectively are presented in Table 3.

We saw no statistically significant associations between neither clinician-evaluated depressive symptoms according to the HDRS, nor manic symptoms according to the YMRS, and the CAR in the models adjusted for age and gender (HDRS: (*B: − 6.79, 95% CI: − 17.89; 4.30, p=0.23*), YMRS: (*B: − 12.88, 95% CI: − 29.92; 4.15, p=0.14*)).

Association between Cortisol Awakening Response and patients evaluated smartphone-based mood instability

The results from the adjusted linear mixed effect models regarding the association between the CAR and smartphone-based MI, respectively are presented in Table 3.

We saw a statistically significant positive association between smartphone-based MI (based on daily smartphone-based data on mood) and the CAR in the models adjusted for age and gender (*B: 430.23, 95% CI: 52.41; 808.04, p=0.026*). Thus, for every increase of 1 point in MI there was an increase of 430.23 nmol/l*min of the CAR (Table 3).

When restricting the analyses to include data from patients using the smartphone-based monitoring system only (the intervention group) the estimates concerning associations between the CAR and clinician-evaluated depressive and manic symptoms measured using the HDRS and the YMRS, and smartphone-based MI, did not change substantially and were therefore not reported. Likewise, exploratory analyses including bipolar disorder subtype (bipolar disorder type I or II) as a covariate did not alter these estimates in the analyses.

The effect of smartphone-based treatment on the levels of CAR

Difference in the CAR between the intervention group (patients using the smartphone-based MONARCA system) and the control group is presented in Table 3. There was no statistically significant difference in the magnitude of CAR between the intervention group and the control group (*B: − 16.57, 95% CI: − 183.11; 216.25, p=0.87*). Exploratory analyses including bipolar disorder subtype (bipolar disorder type I or II) as a covariate did not alter these estimates in the analyses. The effect of interaction between visit number and randomization

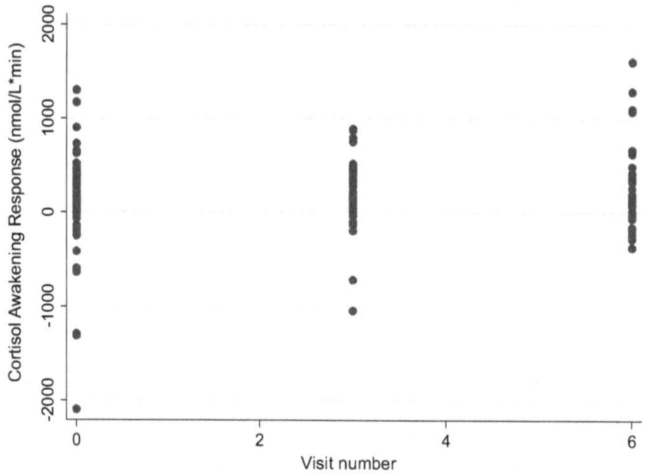

Fig. 1 Scatter plot of CAR and smartphone-based monitoring of stress. Each dot represents multiple smartphone-based patient-reported evaluations of stress level and CAR measures

group on the CAR was investigated but is not reported ($p = 0.48$).

Discussion

For the first time, we here evaluated associations between biological measures of stress-hormone dynamics and high-resolution smartphone-based patient-evaluated daily levels of stress and MI and non-smartphone-based measures of perceived stress, and severity of depressive and manic symptoms in patients with bipolar disorder. Intriguingly, as hypothesized, the CAR was positively associated with daily patient reports of stress and MI measured via smartphones, but not with clinician-rated severity of depressive or manic symptoms or non-smartphone-based patient-reported stress. Also, smartphone-supported clinical care did not in itself reduce the CAR relative to non-smartphone-based care.

Interestingly, we found that increased perceived stress measured daily using smartphones, but not with questionnaire-based perceived stress, was associated with contemporary increased CAR levels. Thus, in contrast to questionnaire-based data and clinical interviews collected at low time-resolution, the fine-grained serial stress and MI measurements capture changes in the CAR. Fine-grained measurements may increase illness insight and improve patients' ability to register symptoms, and thereby facilitate the integrations of psychoeducational elements. Real-time self-monitoring of momentary or very recent experiences have important advantages over retrospective reports, as they contain less bias and allow for unobtrusive monitoring during naturalistic settings (Stone et al. 2003). Other studies in different groups of patients using daily assessments have found associations between increased CAR and for example chronic stress in daily life and reduced distress responses to daily life stress (Schlotz et al. 2004; Powell and Schlotz 2012; Schlotz 2019). However, if the included patients with bipolar disorder had been in a later more progressed stage of their illness it may have translated into more disrupted HPA-axis dynamics expressed as a blunted CAR response (Huang 2017). Nevertheless, the present sample consisted of relatively young patients (mean age 29.4 years), who had relatively low number of previous affective episodes and thus may be in an earlier stage of the disorder that other studies, which seem to be reflected in the present finding of an increased HPA-axis reactivity pattern. So, the HPA axis may express hyper-reactivity in the early stages but could change over the course of illness in line with the kindling hypotheses, in which psychosocial stressors are thought to play a greater role in the initial affective episodes than in subsequent affective episodes (Post 1992). According to this hypothesis, stressors may leave a long-term vulnerability, i.e. a scarring effect. This leads to a lowering of the threshold of the stress exposure required for a new affective episode, so that, over time, relatively minor stressors may trigger new affective episodes (Post 1992). Overall, recent adversities measured as subjective stress seem to impact the patients everyday living as reflected by higher level of MI, which potentially reflects a hypersensitivity to stress. However, in the present study, it is a limitation that we did not measure early adversities e.g. childhood trauma early experiences probably impact vulnerability to developing depressive episodes in response to future stressors (Havermans et al. 2011; Shapero 2017). Finally, whether the kindling hypothesis translates into biological stress measures e.g. the CAR is not possible to reveal from the present study, and there is a lack of longitudinal studies including repeated biological measures of HPA axis dynamics in bipolar disorder.

Strengths of the present study

The included patients were clinically well characterized and were receiving treatment in a specialized mood disorder clinic. Regarding the smartphone-based monitoring system, the MONARCA system has previously been shown to be easy to use and to have a high usability (Bardram et al. 2013). The clinical assessments used for the patients included the HDRS and the YMRS, which, in contrast to the questionnaires, are clinical face to face rating scales administered by an experienced clinical researcher (MFJ) who was blinded to all smartphone and the CAR data during the study. Previous studies on the use of the MONARCA system showed that patients were able to validly evaluate their mood as compared with clinically rated severity of depressive and manic symptoms according to the HDRS and YMRS, respectively (Faurholt-Jepsen 2015b). Finally, all CAR samples were analyzed in one single batch eliminating any measurement variation between batches.

Limitations

Limitations to the present study of preliminary character should be mentioned. First, regarding the scale used for smartphone-based monitoring of stress, the severity of stress was assessed using a scale from 0 to 5, which limited the opportunity to evaluate associations using a scale with higher granularity. Thus, minor symptoms of stress could have been both under- and over-reported by the patients, affecting the associations presented in the present study. Second, the findings were based on the analyses of associations between variables, and thus any potential causality between the measures cannot be evaluated from the present study. Although the included covariates did not alter the estimates to a large extent, other possible confounding factors such as psychopharmacological treatment that were not included in the statistical analyses could have affected the associations, and thus any interpretation should be made with caution. Third, the majority of patients screened for participation in the MONARCA I trial declined to participate for various reasons (Faurholt-Jepsen 2015a). Thus, one might speculate if patients who were favourably oriented towards a technology-based remote monitoring programme may have differed from patients who were not, and our results may not generalize to all segments of a bipolar population. Fourth, we did not have access to adjacent smartphone-based stress measures and CAR in healthy individuals or individuals at high risk for bipolar disorder. Thus, we cannot determine if our findings are specific to patients with bipolar disorder. We collected the CAR samples three times during the present study, and therefore there is a lack of correspondence in time between the CAR samples and the daily smartphone responses. Any potential changes in CAR between the three times where the CAR samples were collected were therefore not available. The association between the CAR and the daily smartphone responses therefore does not reflect this., the use of smartphone-based technology could have been assessed in combination with e.g. actigraphy or a "Fitbit"-like item, which could systematically collect information on energy and activity in more details. Sixth, to date there is no clear consensus on the definition, measurement, use and reporting of MI in patients with bipolar disorder, in the present report we used a combination of measures done in previous studies (Faurholt-Jepsen 2019b, 2015; Strejilevich 2013; O'Donnell 2018; Ebner-Priemer et al. 2009). Using, defining, measuring and reporting MI in a standardized way across studies could improve the quality, reproducibility and comparison of results between studies. Seventh, patients included in the present study were recruited as part of a larger RCT investigating the effect of smartphone-based monitoring. Thus, the sample size and follow up period were defined according to the RCT's design. It is possible that a larger sample with a longer follow up period could have resulted in other findings. Furthermore, the findings that smartphone-based monitoring did not reduce the level of CAR may be due to low power. Studies investigating the effect of smartphone-based monitoring on CAR should include a larger sample and follow patient for longer time to allow for changes in these measures. Since the findings from the present study are hypotheses generating, we did not account for multiple testing in the present study, thus we interpret our results with caution. Finally, as mentioned we did not have access to data on childhood trauma. Information regarding early adverse experiences as childhood trauma would have been of interest to include as a covariate in the analyses, as childhood trauma seems to contribute to alterations of affect regulation, impulse control, and cognitive functioning which might decrease the ability to cope with later stressors (Aas 2016).

Conclusions

Our data, from the present study of preliminary character, found smartphone-based patient-evaluations of stress and mood instability as read outs that reflect the CAR dynamics. Smartphone-supported clinical care did not in itself appear to reduce the CAR dynamics.

Acknowledgements

The authors would like to thank the patients for participating in the study, the nurse Hanne Steenberg Nicolajsen, Psychiatric Center Copenhagen, Rigshospitalet, Denmark for assisting the patients in using the smartphone-based monitoring system and Anne Sophie Jacoby (ASJ) for assisting with the clinical evaluations in the MONARCA I trial.

Authors' contributions

All authors conceived the trial, performed the statistical analyses and wrote the first draft of the manuscript. All authors read and approved the final manuscript.

Author details

[1] Copenhagen Affective Disorder Research Center (CADIC), Psychiatric Center Copenhagen, Blegdamsvej 9, Rigshospitalet, 2100 Copenhagen, Denmark. [2] Faculty of Health and Medical Sciences, University of Copenhagen, Copenhagen, Denmark. [3] Neurobiology Research Unit, Copenhagen University Hospital, Rigshospitalet, Denmark. [4] Department of Clinical Biochemistry, Rigshospitalet, Copenhagen University Hospital, Copenhagen, Denmark. [5] Psychiatric Research Unit, Psychiatric Centre North Zealand, Faculty of Health and Medical Sciences, University of Copenhagen, Hillerød, Denmark.

References

Aas M, et al. The role of childhood trauma in bipolar disorders. Int J Bipolar Disord. 2016;4:1–10.

Bardram, J. E. *et al.* Designing mobile health technology for bipolar disorder: a field trial of the monarca system. In: Proceedings of the SIGCHI Conference on Human Factors in Computing Systems (CHI '13), April 2013, New York, NY, USA: Association for Computing Machinery; 2013.pp. 2627–2636. https://doi.org/10.1145/2470654.2481364.

BelvederiMurri M, et al. The HPA axis in bipolar disorder: systematic review and meta-analysis. Psychoneuroendocrinology. 2016;63:327–42.

Bonsall MB, Wallace-Hadrill SMA, Geddes JR, Goodwin GM, Holmes EA. Nonlinear time-series approaches in characterizing mood stability and mood instability in bipolar disorder. Proc Biol Sci. 2012;279:916–24.

Bopp JM, et al. The longitudinal course of bipolar disorder as revealed through weekly text messaging: a feasibility study. Bipolar Disord. 2010;12:327–34.

Broome MR, Saunders KEA, Harrison PJ, Marwaha S. Mood instability: significance, definition and measurement. Br J Psychiatry. 2015;207:283–5.

Cervantes P, Gelber S, Kin F, Nair VNP, Schwartz G. Circadian secretion of cortisol in bipolar disorder. J Psychiatry Neurosci. 2001;26:411–6.

Coello K, Munkholm K, Nielsen F, Vinberg M, Kessing LV. Hair cortisol in newly diagnosed bipolar disorder and unaffected first-degree relatives. Psychoneuroendocrinology. 2018;99:183–90.

Cohen S, Kamarck T, Mermelstein R. A global measure of perceived stress. J Health Soc Behav. 1983;24:385–96.

Ebner-Priemer UW, Eid M, Kleindienst N, Stabenow S, Trull TJ. Analytic strategies for understanding affective (in)stability and other dynamic processes in psychopathology. J Abnorm Psychol. 2009;118:195–202.

Faurholt-Jepsen M, et al. Daily electronic self-monitoring of subjective and objective symptoms in bipolar disorder-the MONARCA trial protocol (MONitoring, treAtment and pRediCtion of bipolAr disorder episodes): a randomised controlled single-blind trial. BMJ Open. 2013. https://doi.org/10.1136/bmjopen-2013-003353.

Faurholt-Jepsen M, et al. Daily electronic monitoring of subjective and objective measures of illness activity in bipolar disorder using smartphones–the MONARCA II trial protocol: a randomized controlled single-blind parallel-group trial. BMC Psychiatry. 2014;14:309.

Faurholt-Jepsen M, et al. Mood instability in bipolar disorder type I versus type II-continuous daily electronic self-monitoring of illness activity using smartphones. J Affect Disord. 2015;186:342–9.

Faurholt-Jepsen M, et al. Daily electronic self-monitoring in bipolar disorder using smartphones - the MONARCA I trial: a randomized, placebo-controlled, single-blind, parallel group trial. Psychol Med. 2015a;45:2691–704.

Faurholt-Jepsen M, et al. Smartphone data as an electronic biomarker of illness activity in bipolar disorder. Bipolar Disord. 2015b;17:715–28.

Faurholt-Jepsen M, et al. The effect of smartphone-based monitoring on illness activity in bipolar disorder: the MONARCA II randomized controlled single-blinded trial. Psychol Med. 2019a. https://doi.org/10.1017/S0033291719000710.

Faurholt-Jepsen M, et al. Is smartphone-based mood instability associated with stress, quality of life, and functioning in bipolar disorder? Bipolar Disord. 2019b. https://doi.org/10.1111/bdi.12796.

Fries E, Dettenborn L, Kirschbaum C. The cortisol awakening response (CAR): Facts and future directions. Int J Psychophysiol. 2009;72:67–73.

Fries GR, et al. Hypothalamic-pituitary-adrenal axis dysfunction and illness progression in bipolar disorder. Int J Neuropsychopharmacol. 2014. https://doi.org/10.1093/ijnp/pyu043.

Frokjaer VG, et al. Prefrontal serotonin transporter availability is positively associated with the cortisol awakening response. Eur Neuropsychopharmacol. 2013;23:285–94.

Gershon A, Eidelman P. Affective intensity and instability: predictors of depression and functional impairment in bipolar disorder. J Behav Ther Exp Psychiatry. 2015;46:14–8.

Hamilton M. Development of a rating scale for primary depressive illness. Br J Soc Clin Psychol. 1967;6:278–96.

Havermans R, Nicolson NA, Berkhof J, de Vries MW. Patterns of salivary cortisol secretion and responses to daily events in patients with remitted bipolar disorder. Psychoneuroendocrinology. 2011;36:258–65.

Huang M-C, et al. Cortisol awakening response in patients with bipolar disorder during acute episodes and partial remission: a pilot study. Psychiatry Res. 2017;258:594–7.

Jabben N, et al. Co-occurring manic symptomatology influences HPA axis alterations in depression. J Psychiatr Res. 2011;45:1208–13.

Lal S, Adair CE. E-Mental health: a rapid review of the literature. Psychiatr Serv. 2014;65:24–32.

Larsson CA, Gullberg B, Råstam L, Lindblad U. Salivary cortisol differs with age and sex and shows inverse associations with WHR in Swedish women: a cross-sectional study. BMC Endocr Disord. 2009;9:16.

Modell S, et al. Hormonal response pattern in the combined DEX-CRH test is stable over time in subjects at high familial risk for affective disorders. Neuropsychopharmacology. 1998;18:253–62.

O'Donnell LA, et al. Mood instability as a predictor of clinical and functional outcomes in adolescents with bipolar I and bipolar II disorder. J Affect Disord. 2018;236:199–206.

Patel R, et al. Mood instability is a common feature of mental health disorders and is associated with poor clinical outcomes. BMJ Open. 2015;5:e007504.

Post RM. Transduction of psychosocial stress into the neurobiology of recurrent affective disorder. Am J Psychiatry. 1992;149:999–1010.

Powell DJ, Schlotz W. Daily life stress and the cortisol awakening response: testing the anticipation hypothesis. PLoS ONE. 2012;7:e52067.

Roelfsema F, et al. Impact of age, sex and body mass index on cortisol secretion in 143 healthy adults. Endocr Connect. 2017;6:500–9.

Rosa AR, et al. Validity and reliability of the Functioning Assessment Short Test (FAST) in bipolar disorder. Clin Pract Epidemiol Ment Health. 2007;3:5.

Saunders KEA, et al. Oxford Lithium Trial (OxLith) of the early affective, cognitive, neural and biochemical effects of lithium carbonate in bipolar disorder: study protocol for a randomised controlled trial. Trials. 2016. https://doi.org/10.1186/s13063-016-1230-7.

Schlotz W. Investigating associations between momentary stress and cortisol in daily life: What have we learned so far? Psychoneuroendocrinology. 2019;105:105–16.

Schlotz W, Hellhammer J, Schulz P, Stone AA. Perceived work overload and chronic worrying predict weekend-weekday differences in the cortisol awakening response. Psychosom Med. 2004;66:207–14.

Shapero BG, et al. Kindling of life stress in bipolar disorder: effects of early adversity. Behav Ther. 2017;48:322–34.

Snijders T, Bosker R. Modeled variance in two-level models. Sociol Methods Res. 1994;22:342–63.

Stalder T, Evans P, Hucklebridge F, Clow A. Associations between the cortisol awakening response and heart rate variability. Psychoneuroendocrinology. 2011;36:454–62.

Stanislaus S, et al. Mood instability in patients with newly diagnosed bipolar disorder, unaffected relatives, and healthy control individuals measured daily using smartphones. J Affect Disord. 2020;271:336–44.

Stone AA, Shiffman S, Schwartz JE, Broderick JE, Hufford MR. Patient compliance with paper and electronic diaries. Control Clin Trials. 2003;24:182–99.

Strejilevich SA, et al. Mood instability and functional recovery in bipolar disorders. Acta Psychiatr Scand. 2013;128:194–202.
Vrshek-Schallhorn S, et al. The cortisol awakening response predicts major depression: predictive stability over a 4-year follow-up and effect of depression history. Psychol Med. 2013;43:483–93.
Wing JK, et al. SCAN. Schedules for clinical assessment in neuropsychiatry. Arch Gen Psychiatry. 1990;47:589–93.
Young RC, Biggs JT, Ziegler VE, Meyer DA. A rating scale for mania: reliability, validity and sensitivity. Br J Psychiatry. 1978;133:429–35.
Zobel AW, et al. Cortisol response in the combined dexamethasone/CRH test as predictor of relapse in patients with remitted depression: a prospective study. J Psychiatr Res. 2001;35:83–94.

6

A comparison of the 33-item Hypomania Checklist with the 33-item Hypomania Checklist-external assessment for the detection of bipolar disorder in adolescents

Xu Chen[1†], Wei Bai[2,3,4†], Na Zhao[2,5†], Sha Sha[1†], Teris Cheung[6], Gabor S. Ungvari[7,8], Yuan Feng[1*], Yu-Tao Xiang[2,3,4*] and Jules Angst[9]

Abstract

Background: Adolescents with bipolar disorder (BD) are often misdiagnosed as having major depressive disorder (MDD), which delays appropriate treatment and leads to adverse outcomes. The aim of this study was to compare the performance of the 33-item Hypomania Checklist (HCL-33) with the 33-item Hypomania Checklist- external assessment (HCL-33-EA) in adolescents with BD or MDD.

Methods: 147 adolescents with BD and 113 adolescents with MDD were consecutively recruited. The HCL-33 and HCL-33-EA were completed by patients and their carers, respectively. The sensitivity, positive predictive value (PPV), specificity, negative predictive value (NPV), and area under the curve (AUC) were calculated and compared between the two instruments, using cut-off values based on the Youden's index.

Results: The total scores of the HCL-33 and HCL-33-EA were positively and significantly correlated ($rs=0.309$, $P<0.001$). Compared to the HCL-33, the HCL-33-EA had higher sensitivity and NPV (HCL-33: sensitivity = 0.58, NPV = 0.53; HCL-33-EA: sensitivity = 0.81, NPV = 0.60), while the HCL-33 had higher specificity and PPV (HCL-33: specificity = 0.61, PPV = 0.66; HCL-33-EA: specificity = 0.37, PPV = 0.63).

Conclusion: Both the HCL-33 and HCL-33-EA seem to be useful for screening depressed adolescents for BD. The HCL-33-EA would be more appropriate for distinguishing BD from MDD in adolescents due to its high sensitivity in Chinese clinical settings.

Keywords: Adolescents, Bipolar disorder, HCL-33, Self-assessment, External assessment

Introduction

Bipolar Disorder (BD) is a chronic mood disorder characterized by depressive and manic or hypomanic episodes (Phillips and Kupfer 2013). Compared to manic episodes, bipolar depressive episodes usually have higher rates of morbidity and mortality (McIntyre and Calabrese 2019). A major challenge in clinical practice is to diagnose BD accurately, as it is difficult to differentiate from other psychiatric disorders, in particular major depressive disorder (MDD). The difficulty arises because the first episode of mood disturbance in BD is

*Correspondence: 19558051@qq.com; xyutly@gmail.com
†Xu Chen, Wei Bai, Na Zhao and Sha Sha contributed equally to this work
[1] The National Clinical Research Center for Mental Disorders & Beijing Key Laboratory of Mental Disorders, Beijing Anding Hospital & the Advanced Innovation Center for Human Brain Protection, Capital Medical University, School of Mental Health, Xicheng District, Beijing 100088, China
[2] Unit of Psychiatry, Department of Public Health and Medicinal Administration, & Institute of Translational Medicine, Faculty of Health Sciences, University of Macau, Macao SAR, China
Full list of author information is available at the end of the article

frequently depression (McIntyre and Calabrese 2019). In addition, patients are more likely to seek medical treatment for their depressive symptoms than when they are experiencing manic and/hypomanic symptoms (Cuomo et al. 2020; Zimmerman and Galione 2011). The misdiagnosis of BD as MDD may have serious clinical consequences (Patella et al. 2019; Hwang et al. 2010) due to the delay of appropriate treatment and the inappropriate prescription of antidepressants that increase the risk of chronicity and recurrence of BD (McIntyre and Calabrese 2019; Fagiolini et al. 2013).

To improve accuracy in diagnosing BD, standardized and structured or semi-structured diagnostic interviews have been developed, such as the Mini-International Neuropsychiatric Interview (MINI) (Lecrubier et al. 1997), and the Structured Clinical Interview for DSM-5 (SCID-5) (First et al. 2015). These interviews are comprehensive, but time-consuming and their administration is labor-intensive and expensive in clinical or research settings (Nejati et al. 2020). Although comprehensive clinical assessment is essential and irreplaceable, tailor-made screening tools (Hong et al. 2014, Bae et al. 2014) can assist in detecting BD and minimize the risk of misdiagnosis. A study conducted in advanced practice registered nurses reported that screening depressed patients using validated screening tools (e.g., the Mood Disorder Questionnaire (MDQ)) in primary care may reduce the time-lag to the diagnosis and treatment of BD (Kriebel-Gasparro 2016).

The 32-item Hypomania Checklists (HCL-32) is a widely used self-report screening tool for assessing bipolarity in mood disorders. The 33-item Hypomania Checklist (HCL-33) is a modified version of the HCL-32. The Chinese version of the HCL-33 has been validated in both adult (Feng et al. 2016) and adolescent (Zhang et al. 2021) samples to screen for BD in depressed patients. An HCL-33-external assessment version (HCL-33-EA) has been recently developed to rate patients' symptoms by their carers (e.g., family members, friends, etc.) (Łojko et al. 2016). Given that individuals in a manic or hypomanic state are often unaware of changes in their mood and behavior, carers are privileged observers who can provide valuable additional information to the clinician. The Chinese version of the HCL-33-EA has also been validated in adults (Fang et al. 2019).

To the best of our knowledge, no study has directly compared the properties of the HCL-33 and HCL-33-EA in adolescents. Thus, the aim of this study was to compare the sensitivity, specificity, positive predictive value (PPV), negative predictive value (NPV), and area under the curve (AUC) of the HCL-33 and the HCL-33-EA in Chinese adolescents.

Method

Study sample and sites

This study was conducted between August 2020 and November 2020 in the Department of Child Psychiatry at Beijing Anding Hospital of Capital Medical University, a major tertiary psychiatric hospital in China. Participants who met the following inclusion criteria were consecutively recruited during the study period: (1) aged between 13 and 17 years; (2) diagnosed with BD or MDD according to the International Classification of Diseases, Tenth Revision (ICD-10) (WHO 1992) based on a diagnostic interview by two senior psychiatrists; (3) had a current depressive episode defined as a total score of 7 or higher on the 17-item Hamilton Depression Rating Scale (HAMD) (Hamilton 1960; Xie and Shen 1984); (4) were able to understand the aim and contents of the assessment and to provide verbal informed consent, whilst their legal guardians gave written informed consent. Adolescents with cognitive impairment were excluded. The study protocol was approved by the Ethics Committee of the Beijing Anding Hospital, China.

Instruments and evaluation

Patients' and their carers' demographic information was collected by two research psychiatrists in face-to-face interviews and was supplemented by a review of the electronic medical records. The HCL-33—Chinese version (Feng et al. 2016) was used to assess the patients' hypomanic symptoms. The Chinese version of the HCL-33 has been validated with good psychometric properties in both Chinese adults (Fang et al. 2019) and adolescents (Zhang et al. 2021). Patients' carers completed the HCL-33-EA-Chinese version. Each item of the two scales has the dichotomous response format (yes/no). The total scores of the two HCL scales are calculated by adding up items with a "yes" response.

Statistical analysis

All analyses were performed with the Statistical Package for Social Sciences (SPSS), Version 24.0. Patients' and carers' sociodemographic and clinical characteristics were compared between the BD and MDD groups; categorical variables were compared using chi-square tests, while normally distributed continuous variables were compared with two independent sample t tests; otherwise, Mann–Whitney U tests and Wilcoxon tests were used. Normality was examined with the one-sample Kolmogorov–Smirnov test. In order to explore the threshold for discriminating BD from MDD, receiver-operator curves (ROC) were generated and cut-off values were selected based on the Youden's index from the respective curve (Youden 1950). The criterion validity of the HCL-33 and HCL-33-EA was estimated by sensitivity, specificity, PPV, NPV, and AUC. The association between the HCL-33 and the HCL-33-EA assessments was examined with Spearman correlation analysis. The level of statistical significance was set as P < 0.05 (two-tailed).

Results

Of the 274 potential participants consecutively screened for the study, 260 met the inclusion criteria and completed the assessment;113 with MDD and 147 with BD. Table 1 presents the patients' sociodemographic and clinical information; their mean age was 15.42 (standard deviation (SD) = 1.62) years; 22.69% were male. There was no significant difference of the demographic and clinical features between the MDD and BD groups. The vast majority of carers (93.85%) were married, 22.31% were male, and 12.69% were unemployed; their mean age was 43.10 (SD = 5.28) years, and their mean years in education was 13.17 (SD = 3.02) years (Table 2).

The mean scores of the HCL-33 and the HCL-33-EA were 13.38 (SD = 6.06) and 10.37 (SD = 5.52), respectively. The HCL-33 total score was significantly higher than that of the HCL-33-EA (Wilcoxon test; $Z = -6.478$, $P < 0.001$) and the two scales' scores were significantly and positively correlated (Spearman correlation coefficient: $rs = 0.309$, $P < 0.001$). The frequency of the items' positive responses is shown in Table 3. Table 4 compares the sensitivity, specificity, PPV, NPV, and AUC between the HCL-33 and the HCL-33-EA in differentiating BD from MDD using cut-off values calculated according to Youden' s index. The HCL-33 had a higher specificity and PPV, while the HCL-33-EA had a higher sensitivity and NPV (Table 3 and Fig. 1).

Discussion

An insufficient recognition of hypomanic symptoms by clinicians and by patients' families leads to a failure to diagnose BD and subsequently to delayed or inappropriate treatment (Fagiolini et al. 2013). Although structured diagnostic interviews and screening instruments are available for identifying hypomania, to our knowledge, the HCL-33-EA is the only tool allowing patients' carers to rate patients (Fang et al. 2019). The HCL-33-EA is user-friendly because it takes no more than fifteen

Table 1 Basic demographic and clinical characteristics of the study sample

Variables	Whole sample (n = 260)		MDD (n = 113)		BD (n = 147)		BD vs MDD	
	N	%	N	%	N	%	χ^2	P
Male gender	59	22.69	31	27.43	28	19.05	2.561	0.110
	Mean	SD	Mean	SD	Mean	SD	Z^*	P
Age (years)	15.42	1.62	15.30	1.51	15.51	1.70	− 1.015	0.310
Education level (years)	9.76	1.94	9.45	1.93	10.00	1.93	− 1.848	0.065
Age of onset (years)	14.33	4.21	14.21	5.40	14.41	3.01	− 1.170	0.242
Number of episodes	1.20	0.85	1.24	1.18	1.17	0.46	− 0.294	0.768

BD bipolar disorder, *MDD* major depressive disorder, *SD* standard deviation

* Mann–Whitney U test

Table 2 Demographic information of participants' carers

Variables	Whole sample (n = 260)		Carers of MDD patients (n = 113)		Carers of BD patients (n = 147)		Carers for BD vs carers for MDD patients	
	N	%	N	%	N	%	χ^2	P
Male gender	58	22.31	27	23.89	31	21.09	0.290	0.590
Unemployed	33	12.69	11	9.73	22	14.97	1.578	0.209
Married	244	93.85	108	95.58	136	92.52	1.035	0.309
	Mean	SD	Mean	SD	Mean	SD	Z^*	P
Age (years)	43.10	5.28	43.09	6.42	43.10	4.22	–	0.348
Education level (years)	13.71	3.02	14.02	3.14	13.47	2.91	–	0.062

BD Bipolar Disorder, *MDD* Major Depressive Disorder, *SD* standard deviation

* Mann–Whitney U test

Table 3 Percentage of positive responses by adolescents with Major Depressive Disorder and Bipolar Disorder on the HCL-33 and HCL-33-EA

Items	Percentage of positive responses (%)			
	HCL-33		HCL-33-EA*	
	BD	MDD	BD	MDD
1. I need less sleep	51.7	42.5	36.1	23.0
2. I feel more energetic and more active	64.6	57.5	66.7	52.2
3. I am more self-confident	41.5	39.8	52.4	43.4
4. I enjoy my work more	48.3	38.1	36.7	32.7
5. I am more sociable (make more phone calls, go out more)	53.7	41.6	38.8	38.1
6. I want to travel and/or do travel more	44.9	48.7	44.9	41.6
7. I tend to drive faster or take more risks when driving	27.2	17.7	8.8	8.0
8. I spend more money/too much money	56.5	46.9	37.4	23.9
9. I take more risks in my daily life (in my work and/or other activities)	32.7	29.2	11.6	8.0
10. I am physically more active (sport etc.)	39.5	30.1	27.9	15.9
11. I plan more activities or projects	57.1	42.5	47.6	32.7
12. I have more ideas, I am more creative	53.7	46.9	51.7	45.1
13. I am less shy or inhibited	40.8	28.3	38.1	24.8
14. I wear more colourful and more extravagant clothes/make-up	28.6	19.5	22.4	15.9
15. I want to meet or actually do meet more people	40.8	33.6	22.4	18.6
16. I am more interested in sex and/or I am more sexually active	19.7	11.5	9.5	5.3
17. I talk more	66.7	61.1	61.2	53.1
18. I think faster	55.1	54.9	61.2	54.0
19. I make more jokes or puns when I am talking	60.5	67.3	56.5	45.1
20. I am more easily distracted	53.1	54.9	36.7	40.7
21. I engage in lots of new things	51.7	41.6	42.9	35.4
22. My thoughts jump from topic to topic	68.0	65.5	32.0	30.1
23. I do things more quickly and/or more easily	45.6	46.0	49.0	37.2
24. I am more impatient and/or get irritable more easily	66.0	52.2	53.7	51.3
25. I can be exhausting or irritating for others	49.0	38.9	37.4	36.3
26. I get into more quarrels	43.5	35.4	27.2	23.9
27. My mood is higher, more optimistic	46.3	47.8	51.0	41.6
28. I drink more coffee	15.6	8.8	4.8	8.0
29. I smoke more cigarettes	8.2	2.7	2.7	2.7
30. I drink more alcohol	13.6	2.7	5.4	0.9
31. I take more drugs (sedatives, anxiolytics, stimulants...)	15.0	7.1	5.4	4.4
32. I game or gamble more	29.9	20.4	22.4	15.0
33. I eat more or I binge more	42.2	34.5	21.8	15.0

BD Bipolar Disorder, *MDD* Major Depressive Disorder, *HCL-33* 33-item Hypomania Checklist (HCL-33), *HCL-33-EA* 33-item Hypomania Checklist (HCL-33) external assessment

* The subject for each question of the HCL-33-EA is "He/She"

Table 4 Sensitivity, specificity, PPV, NPV, and AUC for the HCL-33 and HCL-33-EA in adolescents with Major Depressive Disorder and Bipolar Disorder

Scales	Cut-off value*	Sensitivity	Specificity	PPV	NPV	AUC	95% CI
HCL-33	14	0.58	0.61	0.66	0.53	0.57	0.48–0.65
HCL-33-EA	7	0.81	0.37	0.63	0.60	0.53	0.45–0.61

95% CI 95% confidence interval for AUC, *AUC* area under the curve, *BD* bipolar disease, *HCL-33* 33-item Hypomania Checklist (HCL-33), *HCL-33-EA* 33-item Hypomania Checklist (HCL-33) external assessment, *MDD* Major Depressive Disorder, *NPV* negative predictive value, *PPV* positive predictive value

* The cut-off values were selected by Youden index from present study

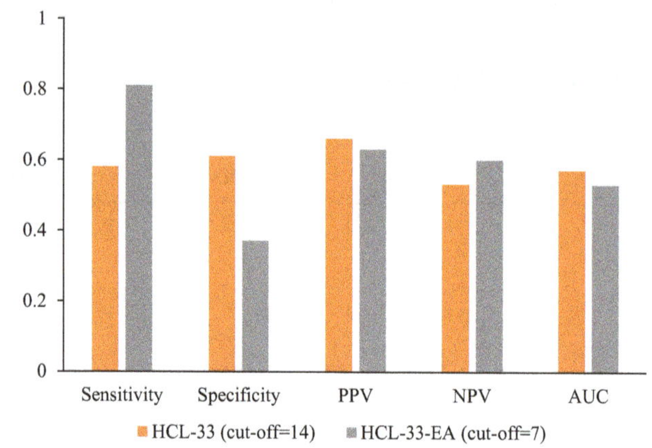

Fig. 1 Sensitivity, specificity, positive predictive value (PPV), negative predictive value (NPV), and area under the curve (AUC) for the Hypomania Checklist-33 (HCL-33) and Hypomania Checklist-33 external assessment (HCL-33-EA) for Bipolar Disorder versus Major Depressive Disorder in adolescents

minutes to administer and through the carers' informed insight into the patient's mood and behavior it can facilitate the early identification of hypomanic symptoms (Fang et al. 2019).

To the best of our knowledge, this was the first study that compared the psychometric properties of the self- and external assessment versions of the HCL-33 in adolescents. A significant and positive association between the total scores of the HCL-33 and the HCL-33-EA was found, similar to findings of the comparison between the HCL-33 and the HCL-33-EA in adult patients (Fang et al. 2019). More specifically, the mean score of the HCL-33-EA in this adolescent sample (10.37) was close to what was found in adults (11.0) (Feng et al. 2016). The total score of the HCL-33-EA was significantly lower than that of the HCL-33 in this study, which is also consistent with previous findings (Fang et al. 2019). In addition, compared to the HCL-33 self-assessment, external assessment with the HCL-33-EA had a higher sensitivity and negative predictive value, and a lower specificity and positive predictive value. This finding was consistent with that of a study comparing the HCL-33 and HCL-33-EA in an adult sample (Wang et al. 2021). Whilst the satisfactory sensitivity indicates that the HCL-33-EA may be an effective tool for differentiating BD from MDD, the lower specificity of HCL-33-EA may be the result of false positives. The discrepancy between the psychometric properties of the HCL-33 and HCL-33-EA in this study may be attributed to their different cut-off values. In a validation study in Russian adults (Mosolov et al. 2021), the HCL-33 cut-off value was 16, which is higher than the corresponding figure in this study. This discrepancy may be due to different target populations, i.e., adolescents vs. adults. A previous validation study on the HCL-33 in Chinese adolescents (Zhang et al. 2021) proposed a cut-off value of 18, which is higher than the cut-off value of 14 in this study. The discrepancy between the two studies is possibly due to different clinical characteristics of the participants. Similarly, the psychometric properties of the HCL-33-EA were less robust (specificity = 0.37), indicating that the HCL-33-EA needs further refinement for adolescent patients.

There were several limitations that need to be addressed. First, the study was conducted in a single center, which limits the generalizability of the findings. Second, due to the relatively small sample size, the two scales' psychometric properties could not be compared separately by basic demographic variables, such as gender and age. Third, the ICD-10 is the official classification manual in clinical practice in China, therefore, we cannot identify bipolar subtypes I and II and compare psychometric properties between the HCL-33 and HCL-33-EA in distinguishing different BD subtypes from MDD. Fourth, information on psychiatric comorbidities is lacking in the electronic medical record system, preventing exploration of potentially confounding effects on the psychometric properties of the two instruments. Fifth, the adolescents included in this study were very young, therefore some of them diagnosed with MDD may be diagnosed with BD in the future, which may bias the findings of this study to an uncertain extent. Finally, although the consecutive sampling method was adopted, the proportion of girls was higher than expected, which may influence the findings of the study. However, the higher proportion of girls reflects the actual distribution of genders in clinical practice.

Conclusion

In adolescents the sensitivity and negative predictive values of the HCL-33-EA were higher, while the specificity and positive predictive value were lower than the corresponding values in the HCL-33. In view of its high sensitivity, the HCL-33-EA would be more appropriate for screening for BD in depressed adolescents in Chinese clinical settings.

Abbreviations

AUC: Area under the curve; BD: Bipolar disorder; HAMD: Hamilton Depression Rating Scale; HCL-33: 33-Item Hypomania Checklist; HCL-33-EA: 33-Item Hypomania Checklist- external assessment; ICD-10: International Classification of Diseases, Tenth Revision; MDD: Major depressive disorder; MDQ: Mood Disorder Questionnaire; MINI: Mini-International Neuropsychiatric Interview; NPV: Negative predictive value; PPV: Positive predictive value; ROC: Receiver-operator curve; SCID-5: Structured Clinical Interview for DSM-5; SD: Standard deviation.

Acknowledgements
Not applicable.

Authors' contributions
Study design: XC, WB, YF, Y-TX. Data collection, analysis and interpretation: WB, NZ, SS. Drafting of the manuscript: WB, Y-TX. Critical revision of the manuscript: TC, GS.U, Y-TX, JA. All authors have read and approved the final manuscript.

Author details
[1]The National Clinical Research Center for Mental Disorders & Beijing Key Laboratory of Mental Disorders, Beijing Anding Hospital & the Advanced Innovation Center for Human Brain Protection, Capital Medical University, School of Mental Health, Xicheng District, Beijing 100088, China. [2]Unit of Psychiatry, Department of Public Health and Medicinal Administration, & Institute of Translational Medicine, Faculty of Health Sciences, University of Macau, Macao SAR, China. [3]Centre for Cognitive and Brain Sciences, University of Macau, Macao SAR, China. [4]Institute of Advanced Studies in Humanities and Social Sciences, University of Macau, Macao SAR, China. [5]Center for Cognition and Brain Disorders, Institutes of Psychological Sciences, Hangzhou Normal University, Hangzhou, China. [6]School of Nursing, Hong Kong Polytechnic University, Hong Kong SAR, China. [7]Division of Psychiatry, School of Medicine, University of Western Australia, Perth, Australia. [8]Section of Psychiatry, University of Notre Dame Australia, Fremantle, Australia. [9]Zurich University Psychiatric Hospital, Lenggstrasse 31, P.O. Box 8032, Zurich, Switzerland.

References

Bae SO, Kim MD, Lee JG, Seo J-S, Won S-H, Woo YS, et al. Is it useful to use the Korean version of the mood disorder questionnaire for assessing bipolar spectrum disorder among Korean college students? Asia Pac Psychiatry. 2014;6(2):170–8.

Cuomo A, Aguglia A, Aguglia E, Bolognesi S, Goracci A, Maina G, et al. Mood spectrum symptoms during a major depressive episode: differences between 145 patients with bipolar disorder and 155 patients with major depressive disorder. Arguments for a dimensional approach. Bipolar Disords. 2020;22(4):385–91.

Fagiolini A, Forgione R, Maccari M, Cuomo A, Morana B, Dell'Osso MC, et al. Prevalence, chronicity, burden and borders of bipolar disorder. J Affect Disord. 2013;148(2):161–9.

Fang M, Wang YY, Feng Y, Ungvari GS, Ng CH, Wang G, et al. Exploration of the psychometric properties of the 33-item Hypomania Checklist - external assessment (HCL-33-EA). J Affect Disord. 2019;245:987–90.

Feng Y, Xiang YT, Huang W, Wang G, Feng L, Tian TF, et al. The 33-item Hypomania Checklist (HCL-33): a new self-completed screening instrument for bipolar disorder. J Affect Disord. 2016;190:214–20.

First M, Williams J, Karg R, Spitzer R. Structured clinical interview for DSM-5—research version (SCID-5 for DSM-5, research version; SCID-5-RV). Arlington: American Psychiatric Association; 2015. p. 1–94.

Hamilton M. A rating scale for depression. J Neurol Neurosurg Psychiatry. 1960;23:56–62.

Hong N, Bahk W-M, Yoon B-H, Shin YC, Min KJ, Jon D-I. Characteristics of bipolar symptoms in psychiatric patients: pattern of responses to the Korean version of the Mood Disorder Questionnaire. Asia Pac Psychiatry. 2014;6(2):120–6.

Hwang SHJ, Childers ME, Wang PW, Nam JY, Keller KL, Hill SJ, et al. Higher prevalence of bipolar I disorder among Asian and Latino compared to Caucasian patients receiving treatment. Asia Pac Psychiatry. 2010;2(3):156–65.

Kriebel-Gasparro AM. Advanced practice registered nurses: gateway to screening for bipolar disorder in primary care. Open Nurs J. 2016;10:59–72.

Lecrubier Y, Sheehan DV, Weiller E, Amorim P, Bonora I, Sheehan KH, et al. The Mini International Neuropsychiatric Interview (MINI) A short diagnostic structured interview reliability and validity according to the CIDI. Eur Psychiatry. 1997;12(5):224–31.

Łojko D, Dudek D, Angst J, Siwek M, Michalak M, Rybakowski J. The 33-item Hypomania Checklist (HCL-33)—a study of the consistency between self- and external assessments in Polish bipolar patients. Psychiatr Pol. 2016;50(6):1085–92.

McIntyre RS, Calabrese JR. Bipolar depression: the clinical characteristics and unmet needs of a complex disorder. Curr Med Res Opin. 2019;35(11):1993–2005.

Mosolov SN, Yaltonskaya PA, Senko OV, Angst J. Validation of the Russian version of the hypomania checklist (HCL-33) for the detection of bipolar disorder in patients with a current diagnosis of recurrent depression. J Affect Disord Rep. 2021;4: 100086.

Nejati S, Ariai N, Björkelund C, Skoglund I, Petersson E-L, Augustsson P, et al. Correspondence between the neuropsychiatric interview M.I.N.I. and the BDI-II and MADRS-S self-rating instruments as diagnostic tools in primary care patients with depression. Int J Gen Med. 2020;13:177–83.

Patella AM, Jansen K, Cardoso TA, Souza LDM, Silva RAD, Coelho F. Clinical features of differential diagnosis between unipolar and bipolar depression in a drug-free sample of young adults. J Affect Disord. 2019;243:103–7.

Phillips ML, Kupfer DJ. Bipolar disorder diagnosis: challenges and future directions. Lancet. 2013;381(9878):1663–71.

Wang Y-Y, Feng Y, Fang M, Guo C, Ungvari GS, Hall BJ, et al. Comparing screening abilities of the 33-item hypomania checklist (HCL-33) and the 33-item hypomania checklist external assessment (HCL-33-EA) for the detection of bipolar disorder. Front Psychiatry. 2021. https://doi.org/10.3389/fpsyt.2021.518722.

World Health Organization. The ICD-10 classification of mental and behavioural disorders: clinical descriptions and diagnostic guidelines. Geneva: World Health Organization; 1992.

Xie G, Shen Q. Use of the Chinese version of the Hamilton rating scale for depression in general population and patients with major depression. Chin J Nerv Ment Dis. 1984;10:346.

Youden WJ. Index for rating diagnostic tests. Cancer. 1950;3(1):32–5.

Zhang Y, Li W, Zhang WY, He F, Pan HP, Cheung T, et al. Validation of the 33-item Hypomania Checklist (HCL-33) in screening adolescents with bipolar disorder. J Affect Disord. 2021;281:786–91.

Zimmerman M, Galione JN. Screening for bipolar disorder with the mood disorders questionnaire: a review. Harv Rev Psychiatry. 2011;19(5):219–28.

7

Mania and bipolar depression: complementing not opposing poles—a post-hoc analysis of mixed features in manic and hypomanic episodes

Christoph Born[1,2], Heinz Grunze[1,2*], Robert M. Post[3,4], Lori L. Altshuler[5,6], Ralph Kupka[7], Susan L. McElroy[8,9], Mark A. Frye[10], Trisha Suppes[11,12], Paul E. Keck[8,9], Willem A. Nolen[13] and Lars Schaerer[14]

Abstract

Background: Depending on the classification system used, 5–40% of manic subjects present with concomitant depressive symptoms. This post-hoc analysis evaluates the hypothesis that (hypo)manic subjects have a higher burden of depression than non-(hypo)manic subjects.

Methods: Data from 806 Bipolar I or II participants of the Stanley Foundation Bipolar Network (SFBN) were analyzed, comprising 17,937 visits. A split data approach was used to separate evaluation and verification in independent samples. For verification of our hypotheses, we compared mean IDS-C scores ratings of non-manic, hypomanic and manic patients. Data were stored on an SQL-server and extracted using standard SQL functions. Linear correlation coefficients and pivotal tables were used to characterize patient groups.

Results: Mean age of participants was 40 ± 12 years (range 18–81). 460 patients (57.1%) were female and 624 were diagnosed as having bipolar I disorder (77.4%) and 182 with bipolar II (22.6%). Data of 17,937 visits were available for analyses, split into odd and even patient numbers and stratified into three groups by YMRS-scores: not manic < 12, hypomanic < 21, manic < 30. Average IDS-C sum scores in manic or hypomanic states were significantly higher ($p < .001$) than for non-manic states. (Hypo)manic female patients were likely to show more depressive symptoms than males ($p < .001$). Similar results were obtained when only the core items of the YMRS or only the number of depressive symptoms were considered. Analyzing the frequency of (hypo)manic mixed states applying a proxy of the DSM-5 mixed features specifier extracted from the IDS-C, we found that almost 50% of the (hypo)manic group visits fulfilled DSM-5 mixed features specifier criteria.

Conclusion: Subjects with a higher manic symptom load are also significantly more likely to experience a higher number of depressive symptoms. Mania and depression are not opposing poles of bipolarity but complement each other.

Keywords: Bipolar disorder, Depression, Hypomania, Mania, Mixed states

*Correspondence: heinz.grunze@icloud.com
[1] Paracelsus Medical University, Nuremberg, Germany
Full list of author information is available at the end of the article

Introduction

Depressive symptomatology during a manic episode (also termed mixed, depressive, or dysphoric mania) is commonly seen in daily practice (Vieta and Valenti 2013) and, compared to pure mania, predicts a course of bipolar disorder (BD) with a younger age at onset, more frequent and longer episodes, more treatment resistance with delayed symptomatic remission, more frequent relapses, suicidality and suicidal acts, irritability, anxiety and substance abuse comorbidity (Grunze et al. 2018). According to the Systematic Treatment Enhancement Program for Bipolar Disorder (STEP-BD) study mixed states are less commonly experienced than euthymic and depressed states, but more temporally unstable, and uniquely associated with rapid cycling, substance use, and psychosis (Prisciandaro et al. 2019). In addition, quality of life, functioning in several domains, e.g., self-esteem, family, love and social life, physical wellbeing, and working capability seem to be severely affected by mixed states (Lee Mortensen et al. 2015).

Older studies applying research-based categorial definitions of mixed mania (Cincinnati criteria, Pisa criteria) indicate that relevant depressive symptoms, i.e. fulfilling the respective mixed features criteria, are present in about 30–40% of acutely manic patients (Akiskal et al. 2000; Hantouche et al. 2006; McElroy et al. 1992) whereas using full Diagnostic and Statistical manual, 4th edition (DSM-IV TR) criteria (American Psychiatric Association 1994) brings the prevalence down to 6.7% (Hantouche et al. 2006). Acknowledging that categorial DSM-IV criteria of mixed mania are too restrictive for deriving meaningful clinical implications, Diagnostic and Statistical manual, 5th edition (DSM-5) (American Psychiatric Association 2013) introduced a more dimensional approach defining depressive symptoms in manic patients and manic symptoms in depression as specifier, requiring ≥ 3 core symptoms of the opposite polarity. First results of studies using proxies for the DSM-5 mixed feature specifier suggest that again about 40% of acutely manic bipolar patients fulfil mixed features specifier criteria (McIntyre et al. 2013; Reinares et al. 2015; Vieta et al. 2014; Young and Eberhard 2015). Mixed mania across definitions appears to be more frequent in adolescents (Birmaher et al. 2006; Geller et al. 2004) and in patients with a high number of previous episodes (Gonzalez-Pinto et al. 2011; Mazzarini et al. 2018), especially in females (Kessing 2008).

The Stanley Foundation Bipolar Treatment Outcome Network (SFBN) recruited 935 bipolar outpatients from 1995 to 2002 from four sites in the United States and three in the Netherlands and Germany. Together with the "Systematic treatment enhancement program for bipolar disorder" (STEP-BD) (Sachs et al. 2003) the SFBN constitutes one of the largest, naturalistic and prospective follow-up studies in bipolar patients. The NFS was funded from 1995 until end of 2002. When funding was discontinued, the database was closed but the international group of investigators continued to analyse the wealth of data together as the Bipolar Collaborative Network (BCN). SFBN participants were rated extensively with several psychometric scales (Leverich et al. 2001), including daily self- and clinician ratings on the National Institute of Mental Health-Life Chart Method (LCM) (Born et al. 2014; Denicoff et al. 1997; Leverich and Post 1996). Having simultaneous ratings at defined time points enables us to examine the temporal relationship between diverse symptom domains, e.g., mania, depression, psychosis, functionality, and quality of life. Examples include previous analyses of depressive symptoms in hypomania (Suppes et al. 2005), manic symptoms while depressed (Miller et al. 2016) or the influence of subsyndromal symptoms on functionality (Altshuler et al. 2006).

Aims of the study

This post-hoc analysis was conducted to clarify the relationship between manic and depressive symptom severity in acutely manic states. The term bipolar suggests that mania and depression do not co-occur. With the awareness of our previous study in hypomanic patients showing a reasonable depressive symptom load (Suppes et al. 2005), and after evaluating our so-called ODD sample (see "Methods" and "Results") we post-hoc formulated and tested the following hypotheses:

1. Primary hypothesis: Patients in a manic state have higher Inventory of Depressive Symptoms—Clinician Version (IDS-C) values than patients in a non-manic state.
2. Secondary hypothesis: Patients in a hypomanic state have higher Inventory of Depressive Symptoms—Clinician Version (IDS-C) values than patients in a non-manic state.

Methods

Data collection

Subjects were drawn from an adult sample with bipolar disorder who participated in the SFBN after signing informed consent. Inclusion criteria for entry into the network and participating in the naturalistic follow-up study (NFS) were the diagnosis of either bipolar I, bipolar II, bipolar not otherwise specified or schizoaffective disorder, bipolar subtype according to the DSM-IV TR (American Psychiatric Association 1994), willingness to attend at least monthly visits and to participate in cross-sectional psychometric self- and clinician ratings and prospective life charting (Leverich et al. 2001). The only exclusion criteria were current active substance abuse or imminent suicidal threat. All diagnoses were based on the DSM-IV-TR criteria set and confirmed by the Structured Clinical Interview for DSM IV (First and Gibbon 2004).

The detailed procedure of the NFS protocol has been reported elsewhere (Born et al. 2014; Leverich et al. 2001). IDS-C (Rush et al. 1986) and Young Mania Rating Scale (YMRS, (Young et al. 1978)) ratings were collected in real-time at each visit as part of the routine assessments. In addition to the NFS participants, this analysis also included subjects who volunteered only for specific intervention trials with YMRS and IDS-C measurements. Thus, this sample slightly differs from those in previous reports from our group on mixed features (Miller et al. 2016; Suppes et al. 2005). Figure 1 illustrates the sequential flow of selection.

Data selection

This post-hoc analysis included only subjects with a diagnosis of bipolar I or II disorder. The final sample consisted of 806 subjects representing 17,937 visits with corresponding YMRS and IDS-C ratings collected at the same occasion. The average number of visits per year was 7.6 (SD ± 4.4), and the average duration of participation was 2.9 years (SD ± 1.8).

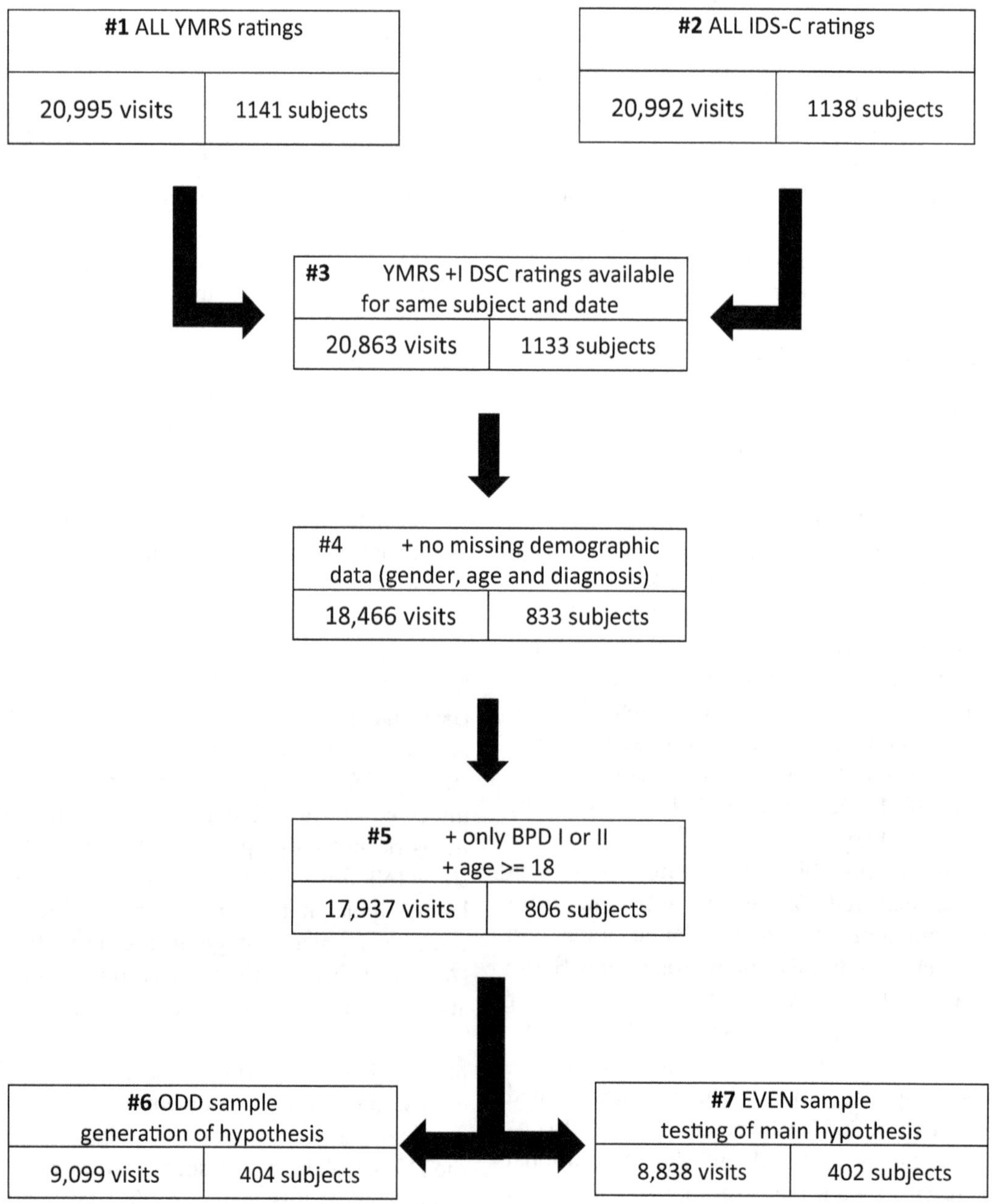

Fig. 1 Flow chart of data selection

In the EVEN sample used for verification (see below) we a priori excluded those with a total YMRS rating of ≥ 30 (0.2%) after observing in the ODD sample a high variance with extreme ratings in this small group distorting regression models and raising considerable doubt how reliable depressive symptoms have been reported while in a highly excited manic state.

Rating scales

The YMRS consists of 11 clinician-rated items measuring severity of distinct manic symptoms over the last 2 weeks. Some of the YMRS items overlap with symptoms observable in depression. To avoid overlap with depression rating scales, the so-called composite "YMRS core-score" consisting of the four items irritability, speech (rate and amount), content and disruptive-aggressive behavior has been created (Ketter et al. 2007) and also been used in subsequent acute mania studies, e.g., (Earley et al. 2018; Vieta et al. 2015). However, the 4 item core score is still not free of distortion as the item "irritability" is also included in the IDS-C. Therefore, we additionally tested a three item YMRS core score consisting of speech (rate and amount), content and disruptive-aggressive behavior only.

In this post-hoc analysis, both the full YMRS and the abbreviated core versions were applied. The four core items are rated with 0 to 8 points, the 7 other items with 0 to 4 points. Thus, the core items account for 32 of the maximum possible score of 60 points in the 4-item YMRS core score, and for 24 of 60 points in the 3-item YMRS core score.

Subjects were divided into three a priori defined groups according to manic severity. A YMRS total score of 12 to 20.5 points was counted as a hypomanic state, a sum score of ≥ 21 points as a manic state and a sum score of less than 12 points was considered as a non-manic state. Using only the YMRS core items for analysis, cut-offs between non-manic, hypomanic and manic were adapted accordingly (Table 1).

The IDS-C consists of 30 items including the DSM-IV criteria for depression, but the scale also covers so called atypical symptoms of depression as weight gain, increased appetite and hypersomnia not rare in bipolar depression (Mitchell et al. 2008). Items are rated taking the last seven days into account. Each item is rated with 0 to 3 points (0, 1, 2 and 3 for no, mild, moderate or severe symptom load, respectively). A sum score of 16 is used as a cut-off value between depression and euthymia (Rush et al. 1996).

Across the four U.S. and the three European sites, interrater reliability was regularly assessed, and rater training was reinforced as needed to maintain consistent performance (kappa values were 0.7 for the YMRS and 0.85 for the IDS-C).

Table 1 Definition of manic, hypomanic and non-manic state by sum scores of all YMRS-items, 4 core YMRS-items and 3 core YMRS-items YMRS-items and core YMRS-items

State	YMRS-Score (total)	YMRS-Score (4 core-items)	YMRS-Score (3 core-items)
Non-manic	0–11.5	0–5.5	0–4
Hypomanic	12–20.5	6–10	4.5–7.5
Manic	21–29.5	10.5–14.5	8–11.5

Data analysis

A split sample approach was applied with subjects divided quasi-randomly into two independent groups using the registration number. Data from subjects with odd registration numbers (ODD-Sample) were used for evaluation/hypothesis building; data from subjects with even registration numbers (EVEN-Sample) constituted the verification/hypothesis testing sample. For preliminary evaluation and hypothesis building, various charting techniques were used to visualize the data from the ODD-Sample, including smoothing and normalization. To test hypotheses derived from ODD-Sample and verification we compared average IDS-C score ratings of non-manic, hypomanic and manic subjects of the EVEN-Sample. After verification of the primary and secondary hypotheses, additional analyses were conducted using the full data set (ODD and EVEN sample).

The database of the SFBN is located on an SQL-server (DB2 Universal Database version 8.2). Data were extracted using standard SQL functions (AVG, STDDEV, COUNT). All graphs were produced with Microsoft Excel 2003. T-tests and ANOVA were calculated with RStudio (Version 1.2.5033, RStudio Inc, Boston, Massachusetts). Considering that there might be a possible overlap of depressive and (hypo) manic symptoms as rated with the scales we tested for both—the total score and only the core items of the YMRS as mentioned above. Categorical variables were reported as frequencies and compared using the chi-square test, while continuous variables were reported as mean ± standard deviation (SD) and compared using the t test. The level of significance was set at $p \leq 0.05$ for the primary and secondary hypotheses, where a compensation for multiple comparisons was not necessary, because of the type of dependency of the subgroups tested. For the additional analyses, following Bonferroni correction the level of significance was set at $p \leq 0.01$ to compensate for multiple comparisons.

Results

Complete data sets were available for 806 subjects. Mean age was 40±12 years (range 18–81 years), and 460 subjects (57.1%) were female. Six hundred twenty-four were diagnosed with bipolar I disorder (77.4%) and 182 with bipolar II (22.6%). 17,937 visits of these subjects were available with corresponding YMRS and IDS-C, both rated at the same occasion. Female subjects contributed 9583 visits (53.4%) for analysis of the total score of the YMRS and 9593 visits (53.5%) for the analysis of the YMRS core items.

There were no significant demographic differences between the ODD and the EVEN sample. The ODD sample included 404 subjects with a mean age of 40±12 years (range 18–81), and 235 subjects (58.2%) were female. In this sample, 320 subjects (79.2%) were diagnosed with bipolar I disorder. The EVEN sample included 402 subjects with a mean age of 40±11 years (range 18–76), and 225 subjects (56.0%) were female. In this sample, 304 subjects (75.6%) were diagnosed with bipolar I disorder. 9099 (50.7%) visits were available from subjects with an odd registration number, 8838 (49.3%) visits were available from subjects with an even registration number.

Table 2 Mean IDS-C scores for the YMRS-groups (total and core items) EVEN SAMPLE

State	Average IDS-Score ± SD grouping by total	Average IDS-Score ± SD grouping by 4 core items	Average IDS-Score ± SD grouping by 3 core items
Non-manic	15.75 ± 12.59	15.46 ± 12.42	15.73 ± 12.52
Hypomanic	19.06 ± 12.43	20.76 ± 13.12	17.94 ± 12.45
Manic	18.29 ± 11.90	21.26 ± 13.23	21.73 ± 13.93

Inspection of the plots "Average IDS-C score by YMRS score "and "Average IDS-C score by core-YMRS score " suggested increasing severity of depressive symptoms with increasing YMRS rating scores in the ODDS sample (see Additional file 1: Fig. S5 and Fig. S6). Subsequently, we tested our primary and secondary hypothesis in the EVEN sample.

For verification of our hypotheses "(1) Subjects in a manic state have higher IDS-C-values than patients in a non-manic state" and "(2) Subjects in a hypomanic state have higher IDS-C values than patients in anon-manic state", data were stratified into three groups defined by YMRS-scores (see Table 1). Average IDS-C Scores of these groups were compared with the t-Test.

Using YMRS total score

When grouping by YMRS total score, 8,102 YMRS ratings (92.3%) felt into the non-manic range between 0 and 11.5 points, 583 YMRS ratings (6.6%) in the hypomanic range between 12 and 20.5 points and 93 YMRS ratings (1.1%) in the manic range between 21 and 29.5 points. 18 YMRS-scores (0.2%) with ≥ 30 points (total) were excluded from final analysis as we were in reasonable doubt how reliable depressive symptoms have been reported while in a highly excited manic state. Forty-two visits (0.5%) had to be excluded because of missing data.

In the non-manic group of the EVEN-Sample the mean IDS-C score was 15.75 ± 12.6 points (range 0–66), in the hypomanic group 19.06 ± 12.4 points (range 0–63) and in the manic group 18.29 ± 11.9 points (range 0–59) (Table 2).

For the YMRS total score, the difference between (hypo)manic groups and the non-manic reached statistical significance ($p < 0.001$ for hypomanic vs non-manic, and $p < 0.05$ for manic vs non-manic) (Table 3).

Table 3 Differences in mean IDS-C scores for the YMRS-groups (total and core items) EVEN SAMPLE

State	Average IDS-Score ± SD Grouping by total YMRS	Average IDS-Score ± SD Grouping by YMRS 4 core items	Average IDS-Score ± SD Grouping by YMRS 3 core items
Hypomanic vs non-manic	19.06–15.75	20.76–15.46	17.94–15.73
Difference [95% CI]	3.3 [2.26; 4.36]	5.3 [4.32; 6.28]	2.21 [0.99; 3.44]
Significance (t-value)	*** (t = 6.2)	*** (t = − 10.6)	*** (t = 3.6)
Manic vs non-manic	18.29–15.75	15.46–12.42	15.73–12.52
Difference [95% CI]	2.54 [0.05–5.01]	*** (t = − 4.7)	*** (t = 6.4)
Significance (t-value)	* (t = 2.0)	21.26 ± 13.23	21.73 ± 13.93

*p < 0.05; ***p < 0.001; 95% CI = 95% confidence interval (two sided)

Using YMRS core-score (4-item and 3-item)

Using the YMRS total score may confound results as there is some overlap with depressive symptom rating scales, including the IDS-C, (e.g., decreased sleep could be due to either depression or (hypo)mania). Using the sum score of the four YMRS core items might minimize this risk. However, as irritability is rated both in the 4-item YMRS core and the IDS-C, we also checked results for a 3-item YMRS core (see "Methods" section).

We identified 7914 4-item YMRS core scores (90.1%) in the non-manic range between 0 and 5.5 points, 748 4-item YMRS core scores (8.5%) in the hypomanic range between 6 and 10 points and 119 4-item YMRS core scores (1.4%) in the manic range between 10.5 and 14.5 points. 39 4-item YMRS core scores (0.4%) with ≥ 15 points (total) were excluded as we were in reasonable doubt how reliable depressive symptoms have been reported while in a highly excited manic state, 18 visits (0.2%) had to be excluded because of missing data.

In the 4-item YMRS core score defined non-manic group of the EVEN-Sample the mean IDS-C score was 15.46 ± 12.42 points (range 0–64), in the hypomanic group 20.76 ± 13.12 points (range 0–66) and in the manic group $21{,}26 \pm 13.23$ points (range 0–59) (Table 2). All differences between all groups reached significance ($p < 0.001$) (Table 3).

Using only the sum score of the other 3 YMRS core items, we identified 8129 3-item YMRS core scores (92.17%) in the non-manic range between 0 and 4 points, 420 3-item YMRS core scores (4.76%) in the hypomanic range between 4.5 and 7.5 points and 230 3-item YMRS core scores (2.6%) in the manic range between 8 and 11.5 points. 39 3-item YMRS core scores (0.46%) with ≥ 12 points (total) were excluded as we were in reasonable doubt how reliable depressive symptoms have been reported while in a highly excited manic state, 18 visits (0.2%) had to be excluded because of missing data.

In the 3-item YMRS core score defined non-manic group of the EVEN-Sample the mean IDS-C score was 15.73 ± 12.52 points (range 0–62), in the hypomanic group $17.94 \pm 12.$ points (range 0–64) and in the manic group 21.73 ± 13.93 points (range 0–64) (Table 2). All differences between all groups reached significance ($p < 0.001$) (Table 3).

Summarizing these results, mean IDS-C scores related to the severity of the manic state as measured with the core items of the YMRS (Table 2). When using the total YMRS score instead of the YMRS core score, we observed significantly higher depressive symptom severity in hypomanic and manic subjects compared to non-manic subjects, too, but no significant difference between hypomanic and manic probands.

Additional analyses in the full sample

After verification of the primary and secondary hypotheses, additional analyses were conducted using the full data set (ODD and EVEN sample).

IDS-C score in relation to mood state (euthymic, hypomanic, manic)

Plotting the average IDS-C sum score for the full data set as a function of the categories non-manic, hypomanic and manic as defined by the 4-item YMRS core score demonstrates significant differences between groups ($p < 0.001$) with the manic group scoring highest, and the non-manic group lowest on the IDS-C (Fig. 2).

Number of depressive symptoms

Plotting only the IDS-C sum score as a function of the YMRS score supplies an estimate of severity of depression, but does not reflect the full symptomatology, e.g., how many mental, social and physical domains are affected. Results for the mean number of depressive symptoms (IDS-C items scoring ≥ 1) in the non-manic, hypomanic and manic group as defined by 4-item YMRS core-scores are shown in Fig. 3. Table 4 illustrates that these results are stable and significant for all three definitions of mood state, by total YMRS score, 4-item and 3-item YMRS core score.

Gender effect on number of depressive symptoms

Previous analyses showed a female preponderance for mixed hypomania (Suppes et al. 2005) and numerically also for mixed mania (Vieta et al. 2014). To test whether this is also true in our study we compared numbers of IDS-C items scoring ≥ 1 as a function of manic severity separately for female and male subjects. Female patients were affected by more depressive symptoms than males,

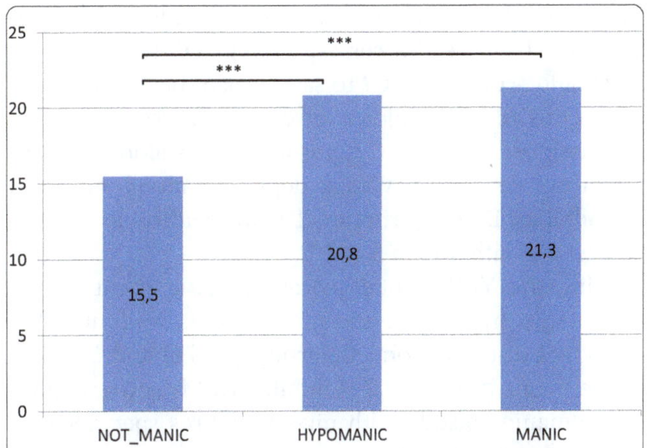

Fig. 2 Average IDS-C scores by state (based on 4-item YMRS core-score), EVEN sample

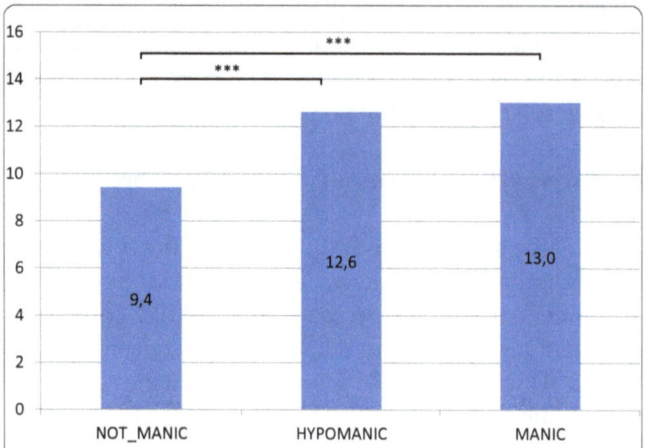

Fig. 3 Average IDS-C-Symptom count by state (based on 4-item YMRS core-score), EVEN sample. ***p < 0.001

especially when manic symptoms were more severe. We observed a linear increase of depressive symptomatology with severity of manic core symptoms (average IDS-C-symptom count vs 4-item YMRS core score, R2 = 0.86), but not in males (R2 = 0.29) (Fig. 4). Thus, the increase of the number of depressive symptoms associated with an increase of YMRS-core scores was mainly carried by women. Factorial analysis of variance testing showed highly significant ($p < 0.001$) effects for all 3 factors, that is (1) YMRS 4 item core score (2) gender as well as (3) the combination of YMRS 4 item core score and gender.

Number of occasions and subjects fulfilling DSM-5 hypomanic or manic with mixed features specifier criteria

Finally, we examined at how many occasions (visits) DSM-5 hypomanic or manic with mixed features specifier criteria were likely to be satisfied, and the corresponding number of subjects. As a proxy we assigned the six depressive A-criteria listed in DSM-5 to corresponding specific IDS-C items (Table 5). Symptom criterion was counted as satisfied with a score of at least 1, except criterion 1 where the corresponding IDS-C items 5 or 10 should score at least 2 to satisfy also the duration criterion of DSM-5 ("majority of days"). To criterion 1, we also assigned two IDS-C items as sadness alone (item 5) might not cover all flavors of depressed mood; however, for fulfilling DSM-5 criterion 1 it was sufficient to score at least 2 in either item 5 or 10.

Using the YMRS total scores for assignment to the non-manic, hypomanic and manic group, we found that 432 visits in the hypomanic group (40,6%) and 58 visits in the manic group (32,2%) fulfilled DSM-5 criteria for a (hypo)manic episode with mixed features specifier (≥3 depressive symptoms).

Applying the 4-item-YMRS core score to group subjects, we found that 652 visits in the hypomanic group (47.7%) and 121 visits in the manic group (48%) fulfilled DSM-5 criteria for a (hypo)manic episode with mixed features specifier (≥3 depressive symptoms). There was no significant difference at $p \leq 0.01$ between the manic and hypomanic group. Examining gender preponderance, we found that in the hypomanic group 55.2% of visits of females and 39.1% of visits of males were likely to satisfy mixed specifier criteria, and in the manic group 53.5% of visits of females and 40.7% of visits of males. Differences between visits of females and males were significant at $p \leq 0.001$ in the hypomanic group, but with the relatively low number of visits only a trend ($p = 0.45$) was observed in the manic group.

Next, we examined how many (hypo)manic subjects fulfilled the mixed feature specifier at least at one visit. As a result, we found that 272 subjects in the hypomanic group (64%) and 77 subjects in the manic group (50%) as defined by 4-item YMRS core score fulfilled DSM-5 criteria for a (hypo)manic episode with mixed features specifier (≥3 depressive symptoms) at some point in time. There was a significant difference at $p \leq 0.01$ between the hypomanic and manic group. Examining gender preponderance, we found that in the hypomanic group 66.7% of females and 60.8% of males were likely to satisfy mixed specifier criteria at some point in time, and in the manic group 51.1% of females and 48.5% of males. There was no significant difference between female and male subjects.

Non-mood symptoms predict more severe depression in (hypo)manic patients

Previous work suggests that the non-mood-symptoms anxiety, agitation and irritability are more prevalent in manic patients suffering from a higher depressive burden and fulfilling DSM-5 mixed feature specifier (Suppes et al. 2017; Vieta et al. 2014). In our sample, we examined the correlation between severity of agitation and irritability vs. average IDS-C score. As a proxy for the degree of agitation, we used the YMRS item 2 and defined a score 0–2 as "no or low degree of agitation", and a score > 2 as "agitated". As a proxy for the degree of irritability, we used the YMRS item 5 and defined a score 0–4 as "no or low degree of irritability", and a score > 4 as "irritable". We could not test for anxiety as there is no appropriate YMRS item as an equivalent. Finally, we compared the average IDS-C value in the group of "High scorer for agitation and irritability", scoring > 2 points for item 2 and > 4 points for YMRS item 5, against the rest of the sample. Confirming previous studies, we found that scoring high on YMRS item 2 (Agitation) or/and 5 (Irritability) significantly predicted more severe depression in (hypo)manic subjects (Table 6).

Table 4 Mean IDS-C SYMPTOMCOUNT for the YMRS-groups (total and core items) in the full sample

State	Average IDS-Symptom Count ± SD Grouping by total	Average IDS-Symptom Count ± SD Grouping by 4 core items	Average IDS-Symptom Count ± SD Grouping by 3 core items
Non-manic vs hypomanic	9.5 ± 6.5 *** (t = 12.1) 11.9 ± 6.1	9.4 ± 6.5 *** (t = 18.4) 12.6 ± 6.2	9.5 ± 6.5 *** (t = 6.8) 11.1 ± 6.3
Non-manic vs manic	9.5 ± 6.5 ** (t = 3.0) 10.9 ± 6.1	9.4 ± 6.5 *** (t = 9.0) 13.0 ± 6.3	9.4 ± 6.5 *** (t = 9.4) 12.5 ± 6.2

***p < 0.001, **p < 0.01

Panic and agitation increase with hypomania

For clinicians it is relevant to know which depressive symptoms have the strongest association with the DSM-5 mixed feature specifier in (hypo-)mania. Therefore, we compared the average values for all IDS-C items between the 3 groups non-manic, hypomanic and manic (see Table 1) for subjects fulfilling criteria for the depressive mixed features specifier.

Compared to the non-manic group, the hypomanic group showed more than 50% increase of the average item score for the IDS-C items interpersonal sensitivity (+ 54%), early morning insomnia (+ 56%), irritable mood (+ 78%), panic/phobic Symptoms (+ 100%), psychomotor agitation (+ 120%).

Compared to the non-manic group, the manic group showed a greater than 50% increase of the average item score for the IDS-C items for anxious mood (+ 50%), sleep onset insomnia (+ 51%), sympathetic arousal (+ 57%), interpersonal sensitivity (+ 66%), suicidal ideation (+ 67%), mid-nocturnal insomnia (+ 67%), weight decrease (+ 67%), panic/phobic symptoms (+ 107%), irritable Mood (+ 114%), early morning insomnia (+ 128%), and psychomotor agitation (+ 206%).

Compared to the hypomanic group, the manic group showed the biggest increase of the average item score for the IDS-C items for mid-nocturnal Insomnia (+ 27%), suicidal ideation (+ 30%), weight decrease (+ 34%), psychomotor agitation (+ 39%) and early morning insomnia (+ 46%),

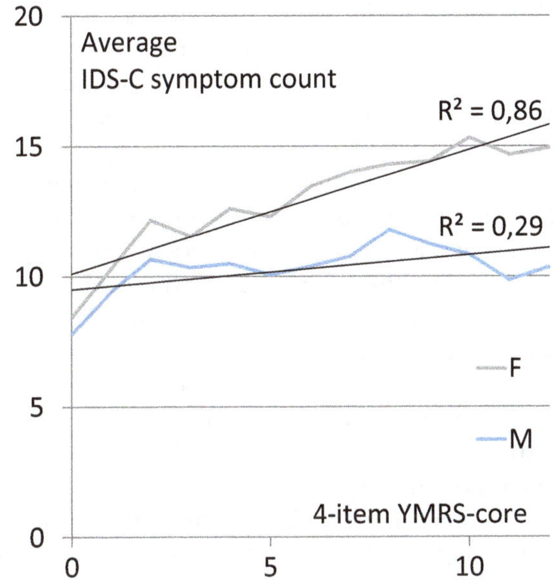

Fig. 4 Average IDS-C-Score by 4 item YMRS CORE SCORE (male vs female)

Discussion

This analysis of a large bipolar I and II cohort participating in the SFBN demonstrates a high depressive burden in subjects fulfilling symptomatic criteria for mania or hypomania as measured with the YMRS total and two different YMRS core sets (with four and with three items). Summarising the different studies looking into gender preference, mixed manic episodes across definitions (mixed mania, dysphoric mania or the manic-depressive dimension) appears more common in females than in males, with the ratio being about 60: 40 (Gonzalez-Pinto et al., 2011), and was also observed in this post-hoc analysis. In the study by Suppes et al. (2005) severity of depressive symptoms was not significantly greater as a function of more severe hypomanic or manic symptoms using only YMRS total scores, but rather resembled a bell-shaped curve. We also observed a flattening of the curve with higher YMRS total scores, with no significant difference in IDS-C scores between hypomanic and manic patients. However, when applying the 4 item YMRS core score we observed a linear increase of depressive severity in females, but not in males, with hypomanic and manic severity. Here we observed not only a significant difference in depressive

Table 5 Assignment of the six DSM-5 depressive symptoms for (hypo)mania with mixed features specifier to selected IDS-C items

DSM-5 depressive symptom (abbreviated)	Corresponding IDS-C item
1. Prominent dysphoria or depressed mood	5 (sad mood) * or 10*
2. Diminished interest or pleasure an all, or almost all, activities	19 (involvement) or 21 (pleasure/enjoyment)
3. Psychomotor retardation nearly every day	23 (psychomotor slowing)
4. Fatigue or loss of energy	20 ((energy/fatiguability)
5. Feelings of worthlessness or excessive or inappropriate guilt	16 (outlook-self)
6. Recurrent thoughts of death	18 (suicidal ideation)

*A minimum score of 2 is needed to satisfy criterion

symptom severity between non-manic and hypomanic or manic patients, but also between hypomanic and manic subjects with a concomitant increase of depressive burden with the severity of mania ratings. The YMRS core score has been frequently used in other studies, however, when used in conjunction with a depression rating such as the IDS-C, the item "irritability" overlaps between scales and has greater weight in the YMRS core set compared to the YMRS due to the smaller number of items. This double counting may, to some degree, skew results, more when using the YMRS core than the full YMRS. However, when applying a 3-item YMRS core leaving out irritability, results remained similar and statistically significant.

Analysing the frequency of manic mixed states applying a proxy of the DSM-5 mixed features specifier extracted from the IDS-C, we found that almost 50% of visits fulfilled criteria and 50–64% of patients at some point in time. The approximate equality of numbers suggests that not a few patients with highly frequent mixed states drive the number of "mixed" visits, but that mixed features do have a wide distribution within our cohort. One of the concerns regarding the validity of the total YMRS score is that depressive symptoms might contribute to and confound the total YMRS score. Different from the total YMRS score, the 4-item YMRS core score excludes all depressive symptoms. If depressive symptoms contribute to the total YMRS score, but do not contribute to the 4-item YMRS score, a lower rate of depressive symptoms associated with manic 4-item YMRS scores appears plausible. On the other hand, if the 4-item YMRS core score separates manic states from non-manic states better than the total YMRS score, and if manic states are associated with more mixed features that non-manic states, it is also plausible to expect a higher rate of mixed features using the 4-item core score opposed to the total YMRS score. Our results, indicating a higher rate of mixed features using the 4-item YMRS core score, would favour the hypothesis that the 4-item YMRS core score is more sensitive than the total YMRS score in separating manic states from non-manic states, and that manic states are associated with more depressive features than non-manic states.

In the IMPACT study (Vieta et al. 2014) non-mood-symptoms as anxiety, agitation and irritability that are known to correlate with inferior outcomes were also more prevalent in the mixed mania group. Thus, the presence of anxiety with irritability or agitation might be an indicator for inferior outcomes in manic patients with mixed features specifier (Vieta et al., 2014), despite the fact that these symptoms are not part of the definition of a mixed feature specifier. Our post-hoc analysis supported that scoring high on YMRS item 2 (Agitation) or/and 5 (Irritability) significantly predicted more severe depression in (hypo)manic subjects. In line with this, a post-hoc analysis of a Phase III medication study also found that the presence of anxiety, irritability and agitation in bipolar mania might enable physicians at the same time to identify patients with more severe depressive symptoms (Suppes et al. 2017). But again, the results for YMRS item 5 (irritability) as a predictor for higher depressive burden needs to interpreted with caution as irritable manic patients also score automatically on IDS-C item 6 (irritable mood).

The abundance of depressive symptoms in hypomanic subjects confirms our previous findings that mixed hypomania is common in patients with symptoms of hypomania and particularly common in women (Suppes et al. 2005), even when only manic core items are considered and overlapping items with depression are omitted. In a previous report on the SFBN cohort we also found that mixed depression, defined as an IDS-C score ≥ 15 and a YMRS score > 2 and < 12 at the same visit, was observed in 43.5% of visits when subjects were depressed (Miller et al. 2016). These three studies together demonstrate again clearly that mania and depression are not opposing poles of bipolarity but complement each other.

Different from simplified neurobiological concepts, psychodynamic and psychoanalytic concepts do not see

Table 6 Scoring high on YMRS item 2 (Agitation) or/and 5 (Irritability) predicted more severe depression in (hypo)manic subjects

YMRS item	IDS-c score for no or low degree of agitation or irritability	IDS-c score for agitated or irritable	p-Value
Agitation (item 2)	20.78	22.38	0.04
Irritability (item 5)	20.47	31.96	<0.001
	IDS-c score for no or low degree of both agitation and irritability	**IDS-c score for agitated or irritable**	**p-Value**
Agitation and irritability	20.07	24.12	<0.001
	IDS-c score for no or low degree of both agitation and irritability	**IDS-c score for both agitated and irritable**	**p-Value**
Agitation and irritability	20.07	30.05	<0.003

a contradiction in a coexistence of depression and mania in what they consider "stable" mixed states (Maggini et al. 2000). They consider depression as the manifestation of losses (e.g., the loss of self-esteem and the sense of worthlessness) and mania serves as a defence against the feelings of depression (Klein 1960). Instability of mixed states, manifesting itself, e.g., as ultradian rapid cycling, might be linked to temperament intruding into an episode of opposite polarity (Akiskal 1992; Marneros 2001).

Limitations of our study include the post-hoc nature of the analysis. Data were collected prospectively without any a priori intention of this analysis for mixed features and we a priori decided for a split sample approach, to make a clear separation between evaluator analysis / hypothesis generation on the one side and hypothesis testing / evidence generation on the other side, but the primary and secondary hypotheses that were tested were generated while aware of a previous, similar evaluation in an overlapping population (Suppes et al. 2005). To minimize overlap between YMRS and IDS-C, we created a 3-item YMRS core set that needs further evaluation of its validity. As far as our results about the proportion of patients and visits fulfilling DSM 5 specifier are concerned, we used a self-developed assignment of specific IDS-C items to mixed feature specifier criteria as a proxy that also has not yet been prospectively evaluated for its validity. Additional analyses suffer from the problems of repeated testing and are reported as findings, in contrast to the evidence generated by testing the primary and secondary hypotheses. A full analysis of the interdependency of manic and depressive symptoms is beyond the scope of this paper. The description of percentual change of average IDS-C values between non-manic, hypomanic and manic state based on this mixed feature specifier is descriptive only, no probabilities have been calculated.

Conclusion

Subjects with a higher manic symptom load were also significantly more likely to experience a higher number of depressive symptoms. In women, we observed a linear increase of depressive burden with increasing YMRS core ratings, and females in general were significantly more likely to experience a larger number of depressive symptoms than males. Approximately half of the patients in the hypomanic and manic group were also likely to fulfill the DSM-5 mixed feature specifier, again with a significant female preponderance. The presence of agitation and irritability, individually and together, was a strong predictor for a higher depressive burden in hypomanic or manic subjects. Future research should consider mania and depression not as opposing poles of bipolarity but as complementing states of manic-depressive disorders.

Abbreviations

BCN: Bipolar Collaborative Network; BD: Bipolar disorder; DSM: Diagnostic and statistical manual; IDS-C: Inventory of Depressive Symptoms—Clinician Version; LCM: Life Chart Method; NFS: Naturalistic follow-up study; SFBN: Stanley Foundation Bipolar Treatment Outcome Network; Step-BD: Systematic Treatment Enhancement Program for Bipolar Disorder; YMRS: Young Mania Rating Scale.

Supplementary Information

Additional file 1: Figure S5. Average IDS-C Score by YMRS score (ODD Sample). **Figure S6.** Average IDS-C Score by 4-item YMRS core score (ODD Sample).

Acknowledgements

The authors wish to recognize the unique contributions of our late colleague Lori Altshuler. Without her energy, inspiration and warmth the SFBN and BCN would not have achieved its success and scientific output.

Authors' contributions

All authors contributed to data acquisition. CB, HG and LS analysed data and completed the initial draft, which was reviewed by all authors. All authors read and approved the final manuscript.

Competing interests
Robert Post has received speaker's honoraria over the past 3 years from AstraZeneca, Validus, Sunovion, Takeda, Pamlabs. Ralph Kupka has received honoraria and royalties over the past 3 years from UpToDate and De Tijdstroom/Boom publishers. Susan McElroy is a consultant to or member of the scientific advisory boards of Bracket, F. Hoffmann-La Roche Ltd., MedAvante, Mitsubishi Tanabe Pharma America, Myriad, Novo Nordisk, Shire, and Sunovion. She is a principal or co-investigator on studies sponsored by the Allergan, Brainsway, Marriott Foundation, Myriad, National Institute of Mental Health, Novo Nordisk, Shire, and Sunovion. She is also an inventor on United States Patent No. 6,323,236 B2, Use of Sulfamate Derivatives for Treating Impulse Control Disorders, and along with the patent's assignee, University of Cincinnati, Cincinnati, Ohio, has received payments from Johnson & Johnson, which has exclusive rights under the patent. Mark A. Frye has received grant support from AssureRx, Mayo Foundation, Myriad, National Institute of Alcohol Abuse and Alcoholism (NIAAA), Nationallnstitute of Mental Health (NIMH), Pfizer. He has served as a consultant (Mayo) to Janssen, Mitsubishi Tanabe Pharma Corporation, Myriad, Neuralstem Inc., Otsuka American Pharmaceutical, Sunovion, Teva Pharmaceuticals. His employer Mayo Clinic has a financial interest in AssureRX and the technology referenced in this publication/presentation. Heinz Grunze received grants/research support, consulting fees and honoraria within the last 3 years from Gedeon Richter, Janssen-Cilag, and Servier. Trisha Suppes, MD, PhD, in the past 36 months, has reported: Grants from Merck, National Institute on Drug Abuse, National Institute of Health, VA Cooperative Studies Program, and VA OR&D PRIME Care, Palo Alto Health Sciences, Stanley Medical Research Institute, Pathways Genomics. Consulting fees from Allergan, Inc., Intracellular Therapies, Sunovion Pharmaceuticals, Inc., and Impel NeuroPharma Inc. Honoraria from CME Institute (Physicians Postgraduate Press, Inc.) and CMEology. Royalties from American Psychiatric Association Publishing, Hogrefe Publishing, Jones and Bartlett, and Wolters Kluwer Health (UpToDate). Travel reimbursement from Sunovion Pharmaceuticals, Inc. Paul Keck Jr has been reimbursed for consulting to Otsuka and Lyndra. He is a co- inventor on United States Patent No. 6387956: Shapira NA, Goldsmith TD, Keck, PE Jr. (University of Cincinnati) Methods of treating obsessive–compulsive spectrum disorder comprises the step of administering an effective amount of tramadol to an individual. Filed March 25, 1999; approved May 14, 2002. Dr. Keck has received no financial gain from this patent. W.A. Nolen has received grants from the Netherlands Organisation for Health Research and Development, the European Union; has received honoraria/speaker's fees over the past 5 years from Lundbeck and Aristo Pharma, and has served over the past 5 years as consultant for Daleco Pharma.

Author details
[1]Paracelsus Medical University, Nuremberg, Germany. [2]Psychiatrie Schwäbisch Hall, Ringstrasse 1, 74523 Schwäbisch Hall, Germany. [3]Bipolar Collaborative Network, Bethesda, MD, USA. [4]Department of Psychiatry and Behavioral Sciences, George Washington University, Washington, DC, USA. [5]Department of Psychiatry and Biobehavioral Sciences, David Geffen School of Medicine, University of California, Los Angeles, CA, USA. [6]Department of Psychiatry, VA Greater Los Angeles Healthcare System, West Los Angeles Healthcare Center, Los Angeles, CA, USA. [7]Department of Psychiatry, Amsterdam UMC, Vrije Universiteit, Amsterdam, The Netherlands. [8]Lindner Center of HOPE, Mason, OH, USA. [9]Biological Psychiatry Program, University of Cincinnati Medical College, Cincinnati, OH, USA. [10]Department of Psychiatry and Psychology, Mayo Clinic, Rochester, MN, USA. [11]Department of Psychiatry and Behavioral Sciences, Stanford University School of Medicine, Palo Alto, CA, USA. [12]V.A. Palo Alto Health Care System, Palo Alto, CA, USA. [13]Department of Psychiatry, University Medical Center Groningen, University of Groningen, Groningen, The Netherlands. [14]Department of Psychiatry and Psychotherapy Medical Center, Faculty of Medicine, University of Freiburg, Freiburg im Breisgau, Germany.

References

Akiskal HS. The distinctive mixed states of bipolar I, II, and III. Clin Neuropharmacol. 1992;15(Suppl 1):632–3.

Akiskal H, Bourgeois ML, Angst J, Post R, Möller HJ, Hirschfeld RM. Re-evaluating the prevalence of and diagnostic composition within the broad clinical spectrum of bipolar disorders. J Affect Disord. 2000;59(Suppl 1):5–30.

Altshuler LL, Post RM, Black DO, Keck PE Jr, Nolen WA, Frye MA, et al. Subsyndromal depressive symptoms are associated with functional impairment in patients with bipolar disorder: results of a large, multisite study. J Clin Psychiatry. 2006;67:1551–60.

American Psychiatric Association Diagnostic and statistical manual of mental disorders. 4th revised edn. Washington, D.C.: APA Press; 1994.

American Psychiatric Association Diagnostic and statistical manual of mental disorders. 5th edn. Washington, D.C.: APA Press; 2013.

Birmaher B, Axelson D, Strober M, Gill MK, Valeri S, Chiappetta L, et al. Clinical course of children and adolescents with bipolar spectrum disorders. Arch Gen Psychiatry. 2006;63:175–83.

Born C, Amann B, Grunze H, Post RM, Schärer L. Saving time and money: a validation of the self ratings on the prospective NIMH Life-Chart Method (NIMH-LCM). BMC Psychiatry. 2014;14:130.

Denicoff KD, Smith-Jackson EE, Disney ER, Suddath RL, Leverich GS, Post RM. Preliminary evidence of the reliability and validity of the prospective life-chart methodology (LCM-p). J Psychiatr Res. 1997;31:593–603.

Earley W, Durgam S, Lu K, Ruth A, Németh G, Laszlovszky I, et al. Clinically relevant response and remission outcomes in cariprazine-treated patients with bipolar I disorder. J Affect Disord. 2018;226:239–44.

First MB, Gibbon M. The structured clinical interview for DSM-IV Axis I disorders (SCID-I) and the structured clinical interview for DSM-IV Axis II disorders (SCID-II. In: Hilsenroth MJ, Segal DL, editors. Comprehensive handbook of psychological assessment, Vol 2: personality assessment. Hoboken, NJ: Wiley; 2004. p. 134–43.

Geller B, Tillman R, Craney JL, Bolhofner K. Four-year prospective outcome and natural history of mania in children with a prepubertal and early adolescent bipolar disorder phenotype. Arch Gen Psychiatry. 2004;61:459–67.

Gonzalez-Pinto A, Barbeito S, Alonso M, Alberich S, Haidar MK, Vieta E, et al. Poor long-term prognosis in mixed bipolar patients: 10-year outcomes in the Vitoria prospective naturalistic study in Spain. J Clin Psychiatry. 2011;72:671–6.

Grunze H, Vieta E, Goodwin G, Bowden C, Licht R, Azorin JM, et al. The World Federation of Societies of Biological Psychiatry (WFSBP) guidelines for the biological treatment of bipolar disorders: acute and long-term treatment of mixed states in bipolar disorder. World J Biol Psychiatry. 2018;19:2–58.

Hantouche EG, Akiskal HS, Azorin JM, Chatenet-Duchene L, Lancrenon S. Clinical and psychometric characterization of depression in mixed mania: a report from the French National Cohort of 1090 manic patients. J Affect Disord. 2006;96:225–32.

Kessing LV. The prevalence of mixed episodes during the course of illness in bipolar disorder. Acta Psychiatr Scand. 2008;117:216–24.

Ketter TA, Jones M, Paulsson B. Rates of remission/euthymia with quetiapine monotherapy compared with placebo in patients with acute mania. J Affect Disord. 2007;100:45–53.

Klein M. Zur Psychogenese der manisch-depressiven Zustände (1937). Psyche. 1960;14:256–83.

Lee Mortensen G, Vinberg M, Lee Mortensen S, Balslev Jørgensen M, Eberhard J. Bipolar patients' quality of life in mixed states: a preliminary qualitative study. Psychopathology. 2015;48:192–201.

Leverich GS, Post RM. Life charting the course of bipolar disorder. Curr Rev Mood Anxiety Disord. 1996;1:48–61.

Leverich GS, Nolen WA, Rush AJ, McElroy SL, Keck PE, Denicoff KD, et al. The Stanley foundation bipolar treatment outcome network. I. Longitudinal methodology. J Affect Disord. 2001;67:33–44.

Maggini C, Salvatore P, Gerhard A, Migone P. Psychopathology of stable and unstable mixed states: a historical view. Compr Psychiatry. 2000;41:77–82.

Marneros A. Origin and development of concepts of bipolar mixed states. J Affect Disord. 2001;67:229–40.

Mazzarini L, Kotzalidis GD, Piacentino D, Rizzato S, Angst J, Azorin JM, et al. Is recurrence in major depressive disorder related to bipolarity and mixed features? Results from the BRIDGE-II-Mix study. J Affect Disord. 2018;229:164–70.

McElroy SL, Keck PE, Pope HG, Hudson JI, Faedda GL, Swann AC. Clinical and research implications of the diagnosis of dysphoric or mixed mania or hypomania. Am J Psychiatry. 1992;149:1633–44.

McIntyre RS, Tohen M, Berk M, Zhao J, Weiller E. DSM-5 mixed specifier for manic episodes: evaluating the effect of depressive features on severity and treatment outcome using asenapine clinical trial data. J Affect Disord. 2013;150:378–83.

Miller S, Suppes T, Mintz J, Hellemann G, Frye MA, McElroy SL, et al. Mixed depression in bipolar disorder: prevalence rate and clinical correlates during naturalistic follow-up in the Stanley bipolar network. Am J Psychiatry. 2016;173:1015–23.

Mitchell PB, Goodwin GM, Johnson GF, Hirschfeld RM. Diagnostic guidelines for bipolar depression: a probabilistic approach. Bipolar Disord. 2008;10:144–52.

Prisciandaro JJ, Tolliver BK, DeSantis SM. Identification and initial validation of empirically derived bipolar symptom states from a large longitudinal dataset: an application of hidden Markov modeling to the Systematic Treatment Enhancement Program for Bipolar Disorder (STEP-BD) study. Psychol Med. 2019;49:1102–8.

Reinares M, Bonnin CM, Hidalgo-Mazzei D, Undurraga J, Mur M, Nieto E, et al. Making sense of DSM-5 mania with depressive features. Aust N Z J Psychiatry. 2015;49:540–9.

Rush AJ, Giles DE, Schlesser MA, Fulton CL, Weissenburger J, Burns C. The inventory for depressive symptomatology (IDS): preliminary findings. Psychiatry Res. 1986;18:65–87.

Rush AJ, Gullion CM, Basco MR, Jarrett RB, Trivedi MH. The inventory of depressive symptomatology (IDS): psychometric properties. Psychol Med. 1996;26:477–86.

Sachs GS, Thase ME, Otto MW, Bauer M, Miklowitz D, Wisniewski SR, et al. Rationale, design, and methods of the systematic treatment enhancement program for bipolar disorder (STEP-BD). Biol Psychiatry. 2003;53:1028–42.

Suppes T, Mintz J, McElroy SL, Altshuler LL, Kupka RW, Frye MA, et al. Mixed hypomania in 908 patients with bipolar disorder evaluated prospectively in the Stanley Foundation Bipolar Treatment Network: a sex-specific phenomenon. Arch Gen Psychiatry. 2005;62:1089–96.

Suppes T, Eberhard J, Lemming O, Young AH, McIntyre RS. Anxiety, irritability, and agitation as indicators of bipolar mania with depressive symptoms: a post hoc analysis of two clinical trials. Int J Bipolar Disord. 2017;5:36.

Vieta E, Valenti M. Mixed states in DSM-5: implications for clinical care, education, and research. J Affect Disord. 2013;148:28–36.

Vieta E, Grunze H, Azorin JM, Fagiolini A. Phenomenology of manic episodes according to the presence or absence of depressive features as defined in DSM-5: results from the IMPACT self-reported online survey. J Affect Disord. 2014;156:206–13.

Vieta E, Durgam S, Lu K, Ruth A, Debelle M, Zukin S. Effect of cariprazine across the symptoms of mania in bipolar I disorder: analyses of pooled data from phase II/III trials. Eur Neuropsychopharmacol. 2015;25:1882–91.

Young AH, Eberhard J. Evaluating depressive symptoms in mania: a naturalistic study of patients with bipolar disorder. Neuropsychiatr Dis Treat. 2015;11:1137–43.

Young RC, Biggs JT, Ziegler VE, Meyer DA. A rating scale for mania: reliability, validity and sensitivity. BrJ Psychiatry. 1978;133:429–35.

8

Electroconvulsive therapy electrode placement for bipolar state-related targeted engagement

Christopher C. Abbott*, Jeremy Miller, Megan Lloyd and Mauricio Tohen

Abstract

Background: Electroconvulsive therapy (ECT) is an effective treatment for all bipolar states. However, ECT remains underutilized, likely stemming from stigma and the risk of neurocognitive impairment. Neuroimaging research has identified state-specific areas of aberrant brain activity that may serve as targets for therapeutic brain stimulation. Electrode placement determines the geometry of the electric field and can be either non-focal (bitemporal) or more focal (right unilateral or bifrontal). Previous research has shown that electrode placement can impact clinical and cognitive outcomes independent of seizure activity. This review critically examines the evidence that focal (unilateral or bifrontal) electrode placements target specific aberrant circuitry in specific bipolar states to optimize clinical outcomes. We hypothesize that optimal target engagement for a bipolar state will be associated with equivalent efficacy relative to bitemporal non-focal stimulation with less neurocognitive impairment.

Methods: We performed a literature search in the PubMed database. Inclusion criteria included prospective, longitudinal investigations during the ECT series with specific electrode placements within a bipolar state from 2000 to 2018.

Results: We identified investigations that met our inclusion criteria with bipolar mania (n = 6), depression (n = 6), mixed (n = 3) and catatonia (n = 1) states. These studies included clinical outcomes and several included cognitive outcomes, which were discussed separately.

Conclusions: While the heterogeneity of the studies makes comparisons difficult, important patterns included the reduced cognitive side effects, faster rate of response, and equivalent efficacy rates of the focal electrode placements (right unilateral and bifrontal) when compared to non-focal (bitemporal) placement. Further avenues for research include more robust cognitive assessments to separate procedure-related and state-related impairment. In addition, future studies could investigate novel electrode configurations with more specific target engagement for different bipolar states.

Keywords: Bipolar disorder, Electroconvulsive therapy, Electrode placement

Introduction

Treatment resistance to pharmacotherapy in bipolar disorder is unfortunately common across all phases of the illness (Thirthalli et al. 2012). Treatment resistance to pharmacotherapy is dependent on the phase of illness and has multiple definitions and thresholds. In the context of bipolar depression, treatment resistance is commonly defined as a failure of two antidepressant trials with concurrent treatment with a mood stabilizer (Gitlin 2006). Despite optimal treatment in the Systematic Treatment Enhancement Program for Bipolar Disorder (STEP-BD), 25% of the bipolar subjects failed to achieve symptom remission in 2 years of follow-up (Perlis et al. 2006). Treatment resistance and acuity are common indications for electroconvulsive therapy (ECT) in bipolar patients. ECT is effective in mania, mixed, and depressed states of bipolar disorder as well as maintenance phases of treatment (Medda et al. 2014). Despite

*Correspondence: cabbott@salud.unm.edu
Department of Psychiatry & Behavioral Sciences, University of New Mexico Health Sciences Center, University of New Mexico School of Medicine, Albuquerque, NM 87131, USA

the overwhelming effectiveness as a true mood stabilizer, patients and clinicians do not consider ECT earlier in the treatment algorithm because of the risk of neurocognitive impairment (Thirthalli et al. 2012; MacQueen et al. 2007; UK ECT Review Group 2003). The risk of ECT-mediated neurocognitive impairment is related to both patient (age, medical comorbidities, cognitive reserve) and treatment related factors (electrode placement, stimulation parameters, treatment number and frequency) (McClintock et al. 2014). The risk and benefit ratio may be optimized by individualizing ECT treatment to maximize mood stabilizing properties while minimizing neurocognitive impairment.

While the exact mechanism of action remains elusive, the therapeutic components of ECT include electric stimulation and generalized seizure activity. Electrode placement dictates the geometry of the electric field and, in conjunction with pulse amplitude, determines the percentage of activated brain volume (Peterchev et al. 2010). The anatomic location and amount of electric field strength may be related to clinical outcomes (Abbott et al. 2016). Bitemporal (BT) electrode placement is the oldest and most effective electrode placement for depressive episodes with respect to clinical efficacy and speed of response (Kellner et al. 2010). BT electrode placement is also the most non-focal method of stimulation and is associated with the greatest risk of neurocognitive impairment (Semkovska et al. 2011). Stimulation of the medial temporal lobes, independent of generalized seizure activity, is associated with increased risk of neurocognitive impairment and prompted efforts to develop more focal methods of stimulation that spare the hippocampus (Nobler et al. 2001; Sackeim et al. 1996; Nahas et al. 2013). For example, bifrontal and right unilateral electrode placement have more targeted engagement to the frontal and non-dominant hemisphere, respectively, relative to the non-focal bitemporal electrode placements.

The more focal electrode placements have unique patterns of brain stimulation that may have differential effectiveness in specific bipolar states. The older lateralization hypothesis of mood control suggests that left hemisphere stimulation may be effective in treating mania (Sackeim et al. 1982). More recent neuroimaging investigations have not confirmed state-related differences in laterality but have identified several candidate circuits for targeted engagement within the corticolimbic model of bipolar disorder (Blumberg et al. 2003; Strakowski et al. 2011; Brooks and Vizueta 2014; Strakowski et al. 2016). Critically, the large-scale networks such as sensorimotor and default mode networks may have unique patterns for depressive and manic phases of bipolar disorder (Martino et al. 2016). Extending state-related neuroimaging biomarkers to different bipolar states suggests that matching the stimulation pattern of the more focal electrode placements (unilateral or bifrontal) with the bipolar state should improve clinical outcomes (match the effectiveness of bitemporal electrode placement with reduced cognitive impairment). Limited evidence suggests that bifrontal electrode placement and prefrontal targeted engagement may have improved efficacy for mania (Blumenfeld et al. 2003). In contrast, right unilateral electrode placement may be ineffective for mania (Small 1985; Small et al. 1985; Milstein et al. 1987) but effective for depressive states with medial temporal lobe engagement (Abbott et al. 2014a). Thus, state-related electrode placements for optimal targeted engagement has the potential to optimize the risk/benefit ratio for ECT in bipolar disorder. However, neuroimaging has yet to confirm targeted engagement with specific electrode placements and bipolar states despite ample evidence with unipolar depression subjects (and combined unipolar and bipolar subjects) (Abbott et al. 2014b). Furthermore, the relative ineffectiveness of right unilateral electrode placement (and medial temporal lobe engagement) for mania is controversial and is based on older studies that did not utilize supra-threshold charge required for improved efficacy with unilateral electrode placements.

Objectives of this review

Efforts to develop more focal stimulation are contingent on identification of state-related anatomic regions for target engagement. Here, we explore the existing evidence of differences in clinical outcomes among three different electrode placements (bitemporal, right unilateral, or bifrontal) for different bipolar states (mania, depressed, mixed, or catatonic episodes). We focused on prospective investigations and highlight the few studies that compared different electrode placements within a specific bipolar state. We hypothesized that the more focal electrode placement (e.g. bifrontal, right unilateral) would target the state-specific neuroanatomic structures implicated in the pathology of a bipolar state (prefrontal cortices for mania, medial temporal lobes for depression), thus maintaining efficacy of bitemporal electrode placement while decreasing the risk of neurocognitive impairment.

Methods

We conducted a PubMed search with the following MeSH terms: "Bipolar Disorder/therapy"[MAJR]) AND "Electroconvulsive Therapy/methods"[MAJR] between January 1, 2000 and December 31, 2018. We selected this date range to acknowledge the development of clinically effective right unilateral supra-threshold (6x's seizure threshold treatments) (Sackeim et al. 2000). Unilateral ECT investigations prior to this date used sub-optimal dosing (seizure threshold or low dose) with right unilateral ECT. Inclusion criterion included prospective investigations that included information on bipolar state (manic, mixed, depressed, subsyndromal, and catatonic) and electrode placement (bitemporal, right unilateral and bifrontal). Exclusion criteria included the following: (1) investigations that did not separate bipolar and unipolar depression subjects, (2) investigations focused exclusively on the maintenance phase of treatment, (3) investigations that did not include a final assessment at the end of the ECT series, and (4) review articles, case reports or case series. The exclusion of maintenance ECT from this search strategy was based on the role of state-specific targeted engagement that may not be applicable to maintenance phases of treatment. *Identification:* Our initial PubMed search identified 106 investigations. *Screening*: We reviewed abstracts and titles to select 24 for detailed review. We excluded two ECT bipolar mania investigation: a retrospective chart review (Thirthalli et al. 2009) and a case series with no summary statistics (Anand 2016). A previous meta-analysis (Dierckx et al. 2012) concluded that ECT was equally effective in bipolar and unipolar depression; however, it did not include electrode placements (Dierckx et al. 2012). We excluded one investigation that did not include information on electrode placement in bipolar and unipolar depression (Prudic et al. 2004). Two investigations were excluded as retrospective chart reviews (Grunhaus et al. 2002; Hallam et al. 2009). Three investigations did not separate bipolar and unipolar depressed subjects (Heikman et al. 2002; Bailine et al. 2000; Ranjkesh et al. 2005). *Eligibility and Identification:* We finalized our review with the selection of 14 ECT bipolar investigations for qualitative synthesis [one investigation reported clinical and cognitive results separately (Kessler et al. 2014; Schoeyen et al. 2015) and another large investigation reported results from all bipolar states (Perugi et al. 2017)]. We organized the results of our review based on bipolar state and highlight the investigations that directly compared electrode placements.

Results: ECT electrode placement and bipolar phase

We have summarized the included investigations and representative electric fields for bitemporal, bifrontal and right unilateral electrode placements (single subject, 800 milliampere pulse amplitude) in Fig. 1.We have also summarized our findings in Tables 1, 2, 3 and 4.

Bipolar Mania

Electrode placement comparisons

Two investigations compared bitemporal with bifrontal electrode placement (Hiremani et al. 2008; Barekatain et al. 2008). Although both investigations included small samples (< 20), the results demonstrated similar effectiveness with both bifrontal and bitemporal electrode placements. Barekatain et al. (2008) compared bifrontal at 1.5 times seizure threshold and bitemporal at seizure threshold. Post-ECT YMRS scores were equivalent for both arms, but attrition was notable in this small study with only 8 of 14 (57%) subjects in the bitemporal arm and 10 of 14 subjects (71%) in the bifrontal arm completing the study. Hiremani et al. (2008) compared bifrontal at 1.5 times seizure threshold and bitemporal at 1.5 times seizure threshold. BF had a faster rate of response evident by the third ECT treatment, but the overall response rates were equivalent (88% response for bifrontal, 72% for bitemporal).

No electrode placement comparisons

Four investigations used one electrode placement (either bitemporal or bifrontal) and focused on stimulus intensities, concurrent psychotropic medications, and anesthetic augmentation strategies. One investigation used bitemporal electrode placement and compared two different stimulation intensities in subjects with bipolar mania with brief pulse ECT (1.5 ms) (Mohan et al. 2009). This investigation had the largest sample size for ECT-mania with 26 subjects in the "seizure threshold" and 24 subjects in the "2.5 times seizure threshold" groups. The primary outcome was the Young Mania Rating Scale (YMRS). The results demonstrated very high and equivalent remission rates (88%) in each arm. The second investigation to use bitemporal electrode placement compared two groups randomized to remifentanil or normal saline to improve clinical outcomes (Rezaei et al. 2012). Overall response rates were not recorded, but both arms demonstrated an equivalent reduction in YMRS. The third bitemporal ECT investigation assessed response rates from a community sample and demonstrated a 75% response rate (Perugi et al. 2017). The only study to focus exclusively on bifrontal electrode placement in mania compared two groups randomized to continue or discontinue sodium valproate (Jahangard et al. 2012). The two groups had an equivalent reduction in YMRS at the "primary" mid-series assessment (after the sixth ECT treatment) but notable attrition (69%) by the end of the ECT series.

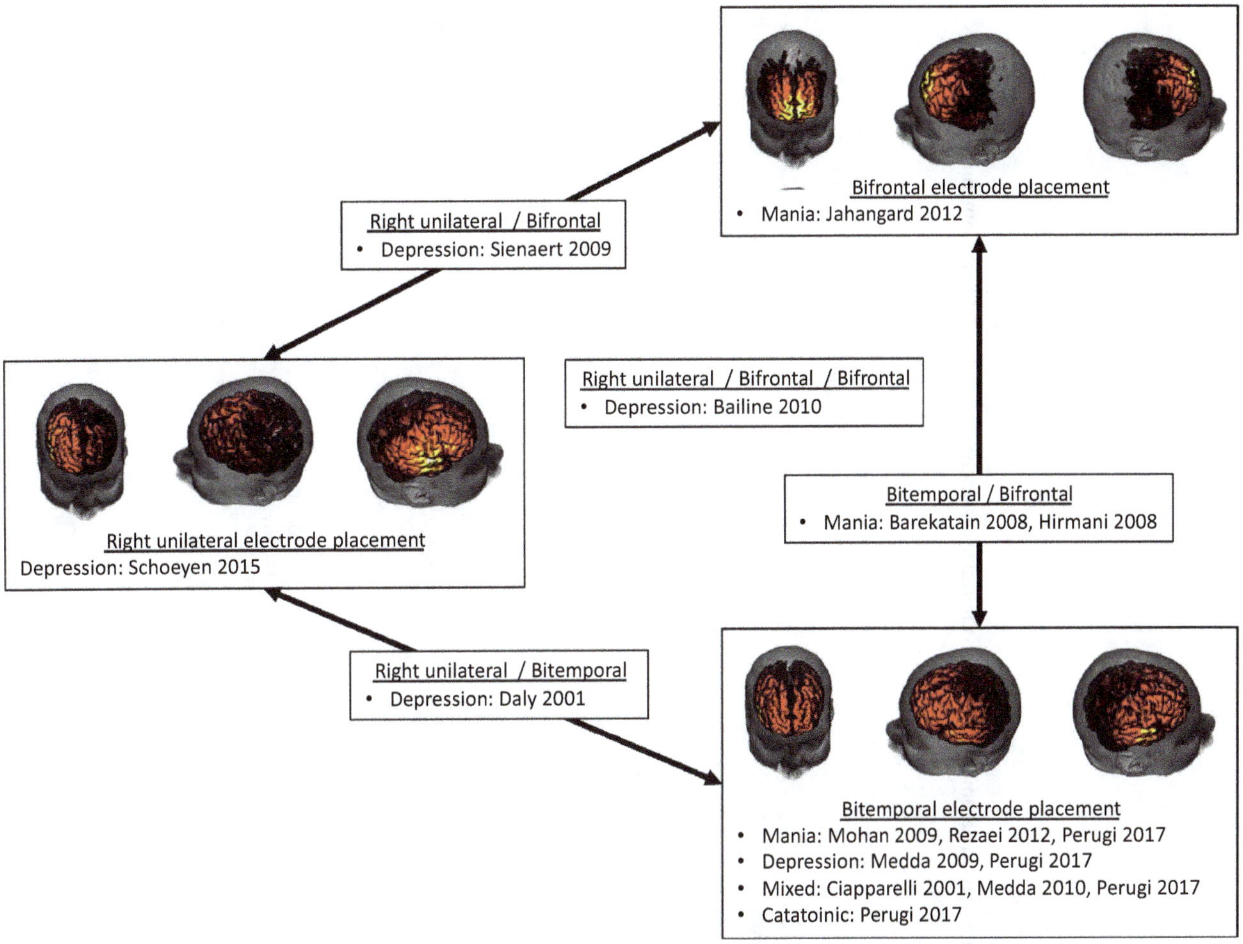

Fig. 1 Electric field modeling for bitemporal, right unilateral and bifrontal electrode placements with the associated studies included in this review. The electric field is modeled for 800 milliamperes with a threshold of 0.35 V/cm (threshold for neuronal firing)

Summary

We are unable to make definitive comparisons between the investigations focused on a single electrode placement due to attrition and inconsistent reporting of clinical ratings. However, both bifrontal and bitemporal electrode placements appear to be effective for mania independent of alternative study aims (comparison of stimulation intensities or pharmacological augmentation strategies). Notably, bifrontal may be associated with a faster rate of response relative to bitemporal electrode placement, but larger studies are needed to prove this relationship.

Bipolar Depression

Electrode placement comparisons

Three investigations compared differences in clinical outcomes among bipolar patients with different electrode placements (Daly et al. 2001; Sienaert et al. 2009; Bailine et al. 2010). Daly et al. (2001) focused on the dose-finding studies with right unilateral and bitemporal electrode placements with different stimulation intensities (right unilateral from seizure threshold to six times threshold, bitemporal from seizure threshold to 2.5 times threshold). For purposes of this review, we focused on the results for the supra-threshold stimulations: right unilateral at six times threshold and bitemporal at 2.5 times threshold. The sub-sample in this analysis was very small ($n=6$ for right unilateral, $n=14$ for bitemporal). The right unilateral supra-threshold treatments included a very small sample ($n=6$) but 100% response and a faster rate of response for the bipolar depressed (7 ± 2 treatments) relative to the unipolar depressed subjects (9 ± 2). The bitemporal supra-threshold treatments also had a robust response (86%). Sienaert et al. (2009) assessed right unilateral and bifrontal electrode placement in a sample of unipolar and bipolar patients. Results did not reveal any diagnostic or electrode placement differences, but bipolar subjects had a faster rate of response. Bailine et al. (2010) assessed the efficacy of right unilateral,

Table 1 Electrode placement and bipolar mania

	Electrode placement, study design	N (age ± SD)	Stimulation parameters	Clinical assessment	Clinical outcome
Electrode placement comparison					
Barekatain et al. (2008)	BT, seizure threshold	14 (27.4 ± 9)	1 ms PW, 900 mA, thrice weekly	Young Mania Rating Scale, response criteria > 50% improvement	No significant difference between groups; all completers met response criteria
	BF, 1.5 times seizure threshold	14 (23.7 ± 4)			
Hiremani et al. (2008)	BT, 1.5 times seizure threshold	19 (28.7 ± 9)	1.5 × ST, 1.5 ms PW, 800 mA, thrice weekly	Young Mania Rating Scale	No significant group differences (88% response for BF, 72% for BT) but BF had a faster response evident by the third ECT treatment
	BF, 1.5 times seizure threshold	17 (25.8 ± 9)			
No electrode placement comparison					
Mohan et al. (2009)	BT, seizure threshold	26 (28.1 ± 7)	1.5 ms pulse width, 800 mA current amplitude, twice weekly	Young Mania Rating Scale, remission < 10	23/26 (88.5%) remitted
	BT, 2.5 times seizure threshold	24 (25.7 ± 7)			21/24 (87.5%) remitted
Jahangard et al. (2012)	BF, 1.5 times seizure threshold with sodium valproate	21 (32.8 ± 10)	Parameters not documented, thrice weekly	Young Mania Rating Scale, Primary assessment completed after 6th ECT treatment	Pre-ECT YMRS = 33 ± 10 to 6th-ECT YMRS = 19 ± 7
	BF, 1.5 times seizure threshold without sodium valproate	21 (31.43 ± 9)			Pre-ECT YMRS = 33 ± 5 to 6th-ECT YMRS = 24 ± 6 (no group differences)
Rezaei et al. (2012)	BT, pre-medicated with remifentanil	15 BT (30.8 ± 9)	1 ms pulse width, other parameters not documented	Young Mania Rating Scale	Pre-ECT YMRS = 29 ± 8 to end-ECT YMRS = 10 ± 9
	BT, pre-medicated with saline	14 BT (29.2 ± 9)			Pre-ECT YMRS = 28 ± 6 to End-ECT YMRS = 13.3 ± 8 (no group differences)
Perugi et al. (2017)	BT, age-based algorithm, community setting	8 BT (41.0 ± 11)	1 ms, pulse width 1.5–4 ms, 800 mA, twice weekly	Clinical Global Impression Improvement Scale, responder ≤ 2	75% response rate

Table 2 Electrode placement and bipolar depression

	Electrode placement, study design	N (age ± SD)	Stimulation parameters	Clinical assessment	Clinical outcome
Electrode placement comparison					
Daly et al. (2001) (studies 2 and 3 with supra-threshold stimulations for RUL and BT)	RUL, six times threshold, bipolar and unipolar depression	14 unipolar depression (overall age: 59 ± 15), 6 bipolar depression (overall age: 56 ± 16)	1.5 ms pulse width, 800 mA pulse amplitude, thrice weekly	Hamilton Depression Rating Scale, initial response rate 60% reduction and maximal score of 16	Initial response rate: 71% for unipolar depression (9 ± 1 treatments), 100% for bipolar depression (7 ± 2 treatments)
	BT, 1.5 times seizure threshold, bipolar and unipolar depression	33 unipolar depression, 14 bipolar depression			Initial response rate: 73% for unipolar depression (9 ± 2 treatments), 86% for bipolar depression (8 ± 2 treatments)
Sienaert et al. (2009)	RUL, 1.5 times seizure threshold BF, six times seizure threshold	51 unipolar depression (55 ± 12), 13 bipolar depression (55 ± 13) randomized to either RUL or BF	0.3 ms pulse width, 800 mA pulse amplitude, twice weekly	Hamilton Depression Rating Scale, moderate remission criteria < 10	Response and remission rates did not differ by diagnosis (unipolar or bipolar diagnosis) or electrode placement; bipolar patients had a faster rate of response, which was independent of electrode placement
Bailine et al. (2010)	RUL, six times threshold; BF, 1.5 times seizure threshold, and BT, 1.5 times seizure threshold	170 unipolar depression (55 ± 16) and 50 bipolar depression (49 ± 13)	900 mA, thrice weekly	Hamilton Depression Rating Scale, moderate remission criteria < 10	EP and diagnosis were not associated with study outcomes (continuous measure with HDRS or remission criteria)
No electrode placement comparison					
Medda et al. (2009)	BT, unipolar depression	17 (54 ± 17)	Age-based settings, 800 mA, pulse width not documented, twice weekly	Hamilton Depression Rating Scale, remission < 8	12/17 (71%) Remission
	BT, bipolar I mre depressed	46 (51 ± 12)			16/46 (35%) Remission (lower remission rates relative to unipolar depression)
	BT, bipolar II mre depressed	67 (53 ± 14)			29/67 (43%) Remission (lower remission rates relative to unipolar depression)

Table 2 (continued)

	Electrode placement, study design	N (age ± SD)	Stimulation parameters	Clinical assessment	Clinical outcome
Schoeyen et al. (2015) (clinical results)	RUL ECT, bipolar I and II	38 (48 ± 10)	Age-based settings, both Thymatron and Mecta ECT devices, 0.5 ms pulse width, thrice weekly	Montgomery-Asberg Depression Rating Scale, remission < 12	Mean MADRS score 15 ± 7 (improved relative to pharmacotherapy), response rate 74% (improved relative to pharmacotherapy), and remission rate 35% (no difference relative to pharmacotherapy)
	Pharmacotherapy, bipolar I and II	35 (48 ± 13)	Algorithm-based pharmacological treatment		Mean MADRS score 20 ± 10, response rate 35%, remission rate 30%
Perugi et al. (2017)	BT, age-based algorithm	295 (49.8 ± 13)	1 ms, pulse width 1.5–4 ms, 800 mA, twice weekly	Clinical Global Impression Improvement Scale, responder ≤ 2	68.1% responders

bifrontal, and bitemporal electrode placements in a large sample of unipolar (n = 170) and bipolar subjects (n = 50). Electrode placement and diagnosis (bipolar or unipolar depression) were not significant. Results from each electrode placement were not reported separately.

No electrode placement comparisons

Three investigations used one electrode placement (bitemporal or right unilateral) to establish outcomes in a large community sample (Perugi et al. 2017), compare differential outcomes across diagnostic categories (Medda et al. 2009), or differences in clinical outcomes relative to pharmacotherapy (Schoeyen et al. 2015). Medda et al. (2009) used bitemporal electrode placement to compare clinical outcomes across three different diagnostic categories: unipolar depression, bipolar I, and bipolar II subjects. The unipolar depressed group was the smallest group but had better rates of remission (12 subjects went to remission out of 17, 71% remission rate) relative to bipolar I (16/46, 35%) and bipolar II (29/67, 43%). Schoeyen et al. (2015) used a randomized controlled trial comparing right unilateral electrode placement (age-based formula) relative to pharmacotherapy for bipolar depression. The right unilateral arm had more clinical improvement and higher response rates relative to the pharmacotherapy arm, but the remission rates (35% in the ECT arm) were similar. Perugi et al. (2017) conducted the largest study to date on bipolar and ECT (total n = 522, bipolar depression n = 295). The study used bitemporal electrode placement and found a high response rates in bipolar depression (68%, response defined as Clinical Global Impression Improvement Subscale (CGI) ≤ 2 or "much improved").

Summary

Perugi et al. (2017) established the rate of response with bipolar depression and bitemporal electrode placement at 68% with a large sample of ~ 300 subjects. The different outcome measures associated with each study (CGI in the Perugi investigation compared to traditional depression ratings with rigorous remission criteria) complicates study and electrode placement comparisons. The low remission rates in the Schoeyen investigation prompted debate regarding right unilateral electrode placement in ECT, but the remission rates are comparable to an earlier bitemporal investigation (Schoeyen et al. 2015; Medda et al. 2009; Kellner and Fink 2015; Kotzalidis et al. 2015). The investigations comparing different types of electrode placements (right unilateral, bifrontal and bitemporal) included both unipolar and bipolar subjects that may have been underpowered to detect differences in response or remission rates within the bipolar group (Daly et al. 2001; Sienaert et al. 2009; Bailine et al. 2010).

Bipolar Mixed and Catatonia

We identified three investigations focused on ECT and bipolar mixed episodes (Perugi et al. 2017; Ciapparelli et al. 2001; Medda et al. 2010). We also identified one investigation that assessed ECT response with bipolar catatonia (Perugi et al. 2017). All investigations (for both bipolar mixed and catatonia) used bitemporal electrode placement and had similar efficacy irrespective of outcome measure. The initial efficacy favoring bipolar mixed relative to bipolar depression (Ciapparelli et al. 2001) was not replicated in a later study, which demonstrated similar, robust response rates for both depressed and mixed episodes (Medda et al. 2010). The bitemporal investigation with catatonia verified the expected high rate of response with this indication (Perugi et al. 2017).

Bipolar state, Electrode Placement and Cogntion

Mania

Two investigations assessed ECT-mediated neurocognitive impairment with bitemporal electrode placement in subjects with mania (Mohan et al. 2009; Rezaei et al. 2012). Both investigations demonstrated decline in cognitive performance with the Mini Mental State Exam (Mohan et al. 2009; Rezaei et al. 2012) and the Weschler Memory Scale (Rezaei et al. 2012). Two investigations measured longitudinal cognitive performance in subjects receiving bifrontal and bitemporal electrode placements (Hiremani et al. 2008; Barekatain et al. 2008). Hiremani et al. (2008) included a thorough cognitive assessment but did not find group differences with bifrontal or bitemporal electrode placements. In contrast, Barekatain et al. (2008) found group differences after the sixth ECT treatment with improved cognitive scores in the bifrontal arm.

Depression

Only one investigation assessed longitudinal cognitive performance during ECT with bipolar depression. Kessler et al. (2014) assessed cognitive performance with the MATRICS Consensus Cognitive Battery, and Autobiographical Memory Interview-Short Form in the right unilateral ECT and pharmacotherapy arms. Both groups demonstrated improvement in every domain of the MATRICS Consensus Cognitive Battery. However, the right unilateral ECT arm had reduced consistency with the Autobiographical Memory Interview-Short Form.

Summary

Although the evidence is sparse, the more focal ECT electrode placements may be associated with less ECT mediated neurocognitive impairment irrespective of

Table 3 Electrode placement and bipolar mixed and bipolar catatonia

	Electrode placement, study design	N (age ± SD)	Stimulation parameters	Clinical assessment	Clinical outcome
Mixed episodes					
Ciapparelli et al. (2001)	BT, bipolar mixed	41 (38 ± 12)	1 to 2 ms pulse width, 550 to 800 mA current amplitude, twice weekly	Montgomery-Asberg Depression Rating Scale (response defined as > 50% reduction), Brief Psychiatric Rating Scale, and Clinical Global Impression (response defined as ≤ "mildly ill")	CGI response criteria = 56%, MADRS response criteria = 78%, higher response rates for mixed episode subjects
	BT, bipolar depressed	23 (41 ± 14)			CGI response criteria = 26%, MADRS response criteria = 52%
Medda et al. (2010)	BT, bipolar mixed	50 (39 ± 13)	Age-based formula, 1.0 ms pulse width, 800 mA current amplitude, twice weekly	Hamilton Depression Rating Scale (response defined as > 50% reduction, remission ≤ 8), Brief Psychiatric Rating Scale, Young Mania Rating Scale, and Clinical Global Improvement Scale (response defined as ≤ "much improved", remission rate as ≤ "very much improved")	CGI response criteria = 76%, similar response and remission rates among both groups irrespective of rating scale
	BT, bipolar depressed	46 (51 ± 12)			CGI response criteria = 67%
Perugi et al. (2017)	BT, age-based algorithm	197 (44 ± 13)	1 ms, pulse width 1.5–4 ms, 800 mA, twice weekly	Clinical Global Impression Improvement Scale, responder ≤ 2	72.9% responders
Catatonic episodes					
Perugi et al. (2017)	BT, age-based algorithm	26 (49.50 ± 13)	1 ms, pulse width 1.5–4 ms, 800 mA, twice weekly	Clinical Global Impression Improvement Scale, responder ≤ 2	80.8% responders

Table 4 Electrode placement and cognition

	Electrode placement	Cognitive assessment	Cognitive outcome
Mania			
Mohan et al. (2009)	BT	Mini Mental State Exam, Wechsler Memory Scale, Scale for autobiographical memory	MMSE and WMS scores declined in both groups, but no group differences between seizure threshold and 2.5 times seizure threshold
Rezaei et al. (2012)	BT	Mini Mental State Exam, Reorientation time	MMSE scores declined in both groups (± remifentanil), but no group differences
Barekatain et al. (2008)	BT and BF	Mini Mental State Exam	BF group had higher MMSE scores after the 6th and final ECT treatment
Hiremani et al. (2008)	BT and BF	Trail Making Test, Verbal Fluency Test (Category), Paired Associate Learning Test, and Complex Figure Test (completed after fifth ECT treatment)	No group differences
Depression			
Kessler et al. (2014)	RUL (and pharmacotherapy)	MATRICS Consensus Cognitive Battery, Autobiographical Memory Interview-Short Form	Both groups demonstrated improvement in every domain of MCCB with no group by time interaction; AMI-SF had a group by time interaction indication reduced autobiographical memory consistency in the ECT arm

bipolar state. The conflicting results in the two bifrontal/bitemporal bipolar mania investigations may be attributed to the different assessment time points. The earlier cognitive assessment (after the fifth ECT treatment) had no differences between bitemporal and bifrontal electrode placements (Hiremani et al. 2008), but traditional end of ECT assessment resulted in group differences despite the use of a less sensitive cognitive measure (Barekatain et al. 2008). The right unilateral electrode placement in bipolar depression was associated with cognitive improvement on most measures and mirrored the cognitive results of pharmacotherapy arm (Kessler et al. 2014). The diminished consistency of the Autobiographical Memory Interview-Short Form must be interpreted in the context of the debatable psychometric properties of this test (Semkovska and McLoughlin 2013, 2014).

Discussion

This review focused on the relationship of electrode placement on clinical outcomes in bipolar states. Bitemporal electrode placement is the most non-focal electrode placement and has higher efficacy rates relative to more focal bifrontal and right unilateral electrode placements. An adequate ECT trial should include bitemporal electrode placement in the context of non-response with focal electrode placements (Kellner and Fink 2015). Bitemporal electrode placement should also be considered the first-line electrode placement when acuity warrants rapid response (e.g., bipolar with catatonia) (Kellner et al. 2010; Perugi et al. 2017). However, the high efficacy rates seen in bitemporal electrode placement comes at a cost of increased risk of ECT-mediated neurocognitive impairment (Semkovska et al. 2011). We hypothesized that efficacy can be maintained, and cognitive risk reduced when more focal electrode placements are matched with state-related targeted engagement. The role of targeted engagement may result in different electrode placements for different bipolar states (e.g., bifrontal for mania, unilateral for depression). The available data is insufficient to support definitive conclusions, but several patterns emerged when reviewing the data. First, focal and non-focal electrode placements are effective for all bipolar states. Second, bifrontal electrode placement appears to have equivalent efficacy relative to bitemporal electrode placement for mania and is associated with less cognitive risk (Hiremani et al. 2008; Barekatain et al. 2008). Third, the more focal electrode placements reduce the cognitive risk across different states of bipolar disorder (Kessler et al. 2014; Barekatain et al. 2008).

Electrode placement is the most important stimulation variable development with respect to geometry of the electric field and electric field current path (Peterchev et al. 2010). To date, the focus on electrode placement development has been reduction of cognitive impairment as opposed to targeting specific state-related neuroanatomic targets (d'Elia 1970; Abrams and Taylor 1973). Novel electrode placements and stimulation methods were not included in this review but represent the next developmental step in improving the risk and benefit ratio for convulsive therapies. Focal Electrically Administered Seizure (FEAST) was recently implemented with a novel electrode placement consisting of a small anode over the right eyebrow and large cathode over the right motor cortex (Nahas et al. 2013; Chahine et al. 2014; Spellman et al. 2009). The intention was to concentrate the current flow to the right subcallosal cingulate and frontal poles and avoid the medial temporal lobes. Magnetic seizure therapy is another form of brain stimulation that uses magnetic pulses to induce seizure activity (Lisanby et al. 2001a, b, 2003). The magnetic stimulation reduces the anatomic variability relevant to electric fields and creates a focal but very superficial stimulation (Lisanby et al. 2003). The cognitive profile of magnetic seizure therapy appears promising, but the clinical efficacy of FEAST and magnetic seizure therapy has yet to be established in bipolar disorder (Cretaz et al. 2015). Other efforts to improve the focality of stimulated brain volume include low amplitude seizure therapy (Radman and Lisanby 2017; Youssef and Sidhom 2017), which has yet to be thoroughly investigated with bipolar disorder. Computer modeling of the ECT induced electric field has promised even more focal methods of stimulation with reduced electrode placement size and diminished distance between stimulation electrodes (Deng et al. 2013).

As the ability to increase the focality with magnetic or electric stimulation improves, the importance of selecting the optimal target region for a diagnosis, state, phenotype or individual becomes increasingly more important. While bitemporal electrode placement may maintain high efficacy rates across different diagnoses (major depressive disorder, bipolar disorder, schizophrenia) with greater risk of cognitive impairment, more focal stimulations may miss the optimal target region for a bipolar state and compromise the efficacy of the procedure (Cretaz et al. 2015). However, the premise of this review is that the efficacy of focal stimulations may be maintained if focused on the optimal anatomic target. This framework is illustrated in a recent investigation with transcranial magnetic stimulation. Sophisticated data-driven analysis methods combined neuroimaging with depression ratings to identify distinct depression "biotypes". These biotypes successfully differentiated response to left dorsolateral or dorsomedial prefrontal cortical transcranial magnetic stimulation (Drysdale et al. 2017). Similar methods could be applied to a large sample of bipolar patients to identify phenotypes and areas of targeted engagement that may represent a more granular classification pattern than manic, depressed or mixed states.

The included investigations had several limitations that limit definitive conclusions from this review. First, the variability of clinical outcomes precluded formal statistical analysis. Second, the included studies were heterogeneous and included alternative outcomes not emphasized in this review (e.g., pharmacotherapy augmentation of ECT). Third, ECT parameters such as pulse width can impact both the efficacy as well as the cognitive risk of ECT but were not included in this review (Semkovska et al. 2011). Fourth, many of the included investigations relied on basic and insensitive cognitive screening measures to capture longitudinal changes in cognitive performance. Only a minority of the included studies included a thorough neuropsychological assessment (Kessler et al. 2014; Hiremani et al. 2008). Finally, seizure metrics (morphology, duration, post-ictal suppression) were not included but are related to the mood stabilizing properties of convulsive therapies.

Conclusions

Recent prospective ECT investigations with different bipolar states (depressed, manic, mixed) have assessed clinical outcomes with different electrode placements. While not definitive, the more focal electrode placements do have the potential to have equivalent efficacy, expedite the rate of response, and reduce cognitive risk. These focal electrode placements may be specific for bipolar states (e.g., bifrontal for mania). However, serious gaps in the literature preclude formal guidelines as suprathreshold right (and left) unilateral electrode placements have not been adequately assessed in bipolar mania and remain controversial in the context of optimizing ECT outcomes for bipolar disorder. If prefrontal networks are specific to bipolar mania, then bifrontal electrode placement should prove to be more efficacious than the suprathreshold unilateral treatments, but this investigation has yet to be completed. In addition, optimal targeted engagement may be more granular than the bipolar state (manic, depressed, or mixed). For example, melancholic or atypical depressive episodes have unique phenomenology and may have different patterns of aberrant circuitry that ultimately require different patterns of stimulation similar to the aforementioned "biotype" research with transcranial magnetic stimulation. Future directions include the development of more focal brain stimulation that will challenge neuroimaging research to optimally define the phenotypically-defined region for targeted engagement. Furthermore, research with more thorough cognitive assessments to disentangle state-related cognitive impairment from procedure-related cognitive impairment is needed. Accurate, focal targeted engagement of the correct anatomic circuit for a given bipolar state will optimize clinical outcomes for bipolar disorder.

Authors' contributions

CCA, JM and ML completed initial draft of manuscript, CA and JM performed literature search, CA, JM, ML, and MT conceptualized manuscript and reviewed final draft. All authors read and approved the final manuscript.

Acknowledgements

Not applicable.

References

Abbott CC, Jones T, Lemke NT, Gallegos P, McClintock SM, Mayer AR, et al. Hippocampal structural and functional changes associated with electroconvulsive therapy response. Transl Psychiatry. 2014a;4:e483.

Abbott CC, Gallegos P, Rediske N, Lemke NT, Quinn DK. A review of longitudinal electroconvulsive therapy: neuroimaging investigations. J Geriatr Psychiatry Neurol. 2014b;27(1):33–46.

Abbott CC, McClintock SM, Jones TR, Deng ZD, editors. Engaging medial temporal lobes with ECT pulse amplitude to improve clinical outcomes. West Hollywood: American College of Neuropsychopharmacology; 2016.

Abrams R, Taylor MA. Anterior bifrontal ECT: a clinical trial. Br J Psychiatry. 1973;122(570):587–90.

Anand S. Ultrabrief electroconvulsive therapy for manic episodes of bipolar disorder. J ECT. 2016;32(4):267–9.

Bailine SH, Rifkin A, Kayne E, Selzer JA, Vital-Herne J, Blieka M, et al. Comparison of bifrontal and bitemporal ECT for major depression. Am J Psychiatry. 2000;157(1):121–3.

Bailine S, Fink M, Knapp R, Petrides G, Husain MM, Rasmussen K, et al. Electroconvulsive therapy is equally effective in unipolar and bipolar depression. Acta Psychiatr Scand. 2010;121(6):431–6.

Barekatain M, Jahangard L, Haghighi M, Ranjkesh F. Bifrontal versus bitemporal electroconvulsive therapy in severe manic patients. J ECT. 2008;24(3):199–202.

Blumberg HP, Leung HC, Skudlarski P, Lacadie CM, Fredericks CA, Harris BC, et al. A functional magnetic resonance imaging study of bipolar disorder: state- and trait-related dysfunction in ventral prefrontal cortices. Arch Gen Psychiatry. 2003;60(6):601–9.

Blumenfeld H, McNally KA, Ostroff RB, Zubal IG. Targeted prefrontal cortical activation with bifrontal ECT. Psychiatry Res. 2003;123(3):165–70.

Brooks JO 3rd, Vizueta N. Diagnostic and clinical implications of functional neuroimaging in bipolar disorder. J Psychiatr Res. 2014;57:12–25.

Chahine G, Short B, Spicer K, Schmidt M, Burns C, Atoui M, et al. Regional cerebral blood flow changes associated with focal electrically administered seizure therapy (FEAST). Brain Stimul. 2014;7(3):483–5.

Ciapparelli A, Dell'Osso L, Tundo A, Pini S, Chiavacci MC, Di Sacco I, et al. Electroconvulsive therapy in medication-nonresponsive patients with mixed mania and bipolar depression. J Clin Psychiatry. 2001;62(7):552–5.

Cretaz E, Brunoni AR, Lafer B. Magnetic seizure therapy for unipolar and bipolar depression: a systematic review. Neural Plast. 2015;2015:521398.

Daly JJ, Prudic J, Devanand DP, Nobler MS, Lisanby SH, Peyser S, et al. ECT in bipolar and unipolar depression: differences in speed of response. Bipolar Disord. 2001;3(2):95–104.

d'Elia G. Unilateral electroconvulsive therapy. Acta Psychiatr Scand Suppl. 1970;215:1–98.

Deng ZD, Lisanby SH, Peterchev AV. Controlling stimulation strength and focality in electroconvulsive therapy via current amplitude and electrode size and spacing: comparison with magnetic seizure therapy. J ECT. 2013;29(4):325–35.

Dierckx B, Heijnen WT, van den Broek WW, Birkenhager TK. Efficacy of electroconvulsive therapy in bipolar versus unipolar major depression: a meta-analysis. Bipolar Disord. 2012;14(2):146–50.

Drysdale AT, Grosenick L, Downar J, Dunlop K, Mansouri F, Meng Y, et al. Resting-state connectivity biomarkers define neurophysiological subtypes of depression. Nat Med. 2017;23(1):28–38.

Gitlin M. Treatment-resistant bipolar disorder. Mol Psychiatry. 2006;11(3):227–40.

Grunhaus L, Schreiber S, Dolberg OT, Hirshman S, Dannon PN. Response to ECT in major depression: are there differences between unipolar and bipolar depression? Bipolar Disord. 2002;4(Suppl 1):91–3.

Hallam KT, Smith DI, Berk M. Differences between subjective and objective assessments of the utility of Electroconvulsive therapy in patients with bipolar and unipolar depression. J Affect Disord. 2009;112(1–3):212–8.

Heikman P, Kalska H, Katila H, Sarna S, Tuunainen A, Kuoppasalmi K. Right unilateral and bifrontal electroconvulsive therapy in the treatment of depression: a preliminary study. J ECT. 2002;18(1):26–30.

Hiremani RM, Thirthalli J, Tharayil BS, Gangadhar BN. Double-blind randomized controlled study comparing short-term efficacy of bifrontal and bitemporal electroconvulsive therapy in acute mania. Bipolar Disord. 2008;10(6):701–7.

Jahangard L, Haghighi M, Bigdelou G, Bajoghli H, Brand S. Comparing efficacy of ECT with and without concurrent sodium valproate therapy in manic patients. J ECT. 2012;28(2):118–23.

Kellner CH, Fink M. Electroconvulsive therapy versus pharmacotherapy for bipolar depression. Am J Psychiatry. 2015;172(3):295.

Kellner CH, Knapp R, Husain MM, Rasmussen K, Sampson S, Cullum M, et al. Bifrontal, bitemporal and right unilateral electrode placement in ECT: randomised trial. Br J Psychiatry. 2010;196(3):226–34.

Kessler U, Schoeyen HK, Andreassen OA, Eide GE, Malt UF, Oedegaard KJ, et al. The effect of electroconvulsive therapy on neurocognitive function in treatment-resistant bipolar disorder depression. J Clin Psychiatry. 2014;75(11):e1306–13.

Kotzalidis GD, Pacchiarotti I, Rapinesi C, Murru A, Colom F, Vieta E. Differential effectiveness of right unilateral versus bilateral electroconvulsive therapy in resistant bipolar depression. Am J Psychiatry. 2015;172(3):294.

Lisanby SH, Luber B, Finck AD, Schroeder C, Sackeim HA. Deliberate seizure induction with repetitive transcranial magnetic stimulation in nonhuman primates. Arch Gen Psychiatry. 2001a;58(2):199–200.

Lisanby SH, Schlaepfer TE, Fisch HU, Sackeim HA. Magnetic seizure therapy of major depression. Arch Gen Psychiatry. 2001b;58(3):303–5.

Lisanby SH, Luber B, Schlaepfer TE, Sackeim HA. Safety and feasibility of magnetic seizure therapy (MST) in major depression: randomized within-subject comparison with electroconvulsive therapy. Neuropsychopharmacology. 2003;28(10):1852–65.

MacQueen G, Parkin C, Marriott M, Begin H, Hasey G. The long-term impact of treatment with electroconvulsive therapy on discrete memory systems in patients with bipolar disorder. J Psychiatry Neurosci. 2007;32(4):241–9.

Martino M, Magioncalda P, Huang Z, Conio B, Piaggio N, Duncan NW, et al. Contrasting variability patterns in the default mode and sensorimotor networks balance in bipolar depression and mania. Proc Natl Acad Sci USA. 2016;113(17):4824–9.

McClintock SM, Choi J, Deng ZD, Appelbaum LG, Krystal AD, Lisanby SH. Multifactorial determinants of the neurocognitive effects of electroconvulsive therapy. J ECT. 2014;30(2):165–76.

Medda P, Perugi G, Zanello S, Ciuffa M, Cassano GB. Response to ECT in bipolar I, bipolar II and unipolar depression. J Affect Disord. 2009;118(1–3):55–9.

Medda P, Perugi G, Zanello S, Ciuffa M, Rizzato S, Cassano GB. Comparative response to electroconvulsive therapy in medication-resistant bipolar I patients with depression and mixed state. J ECT. 2010;26(2):82–6.

Medda P, Toni C, Perugi G. The mood-stabilizing effects of electroconvulsive therapy. J ECT. 2014;30(4):275–82.

Milstein V, Small JG, Klapper MH, Small IF, Miller MJ, Kellams JJ. Uni- versus bilateral ECT in the treatment of mania. Convuls Ther. 1987;3(1):1–9.

Mohan TS, Tharyan P, Alexander J, Raveendran NS. Effects of stimulus intensity on the efficacy and safety of twice-weekly, bilateral electroconvulsive therapy (ECT) combined with antipsychotics in acute mania: a randomised controlled trial. Bipolar Disord. 2009;11(2):126–34.

Nahas Z, Short B, Burns C, Archer M, Schmidt M, Prudic J, et al. A feasibility study of a new method for electrically producing seizures in man: focal electrically administered seizure therapy [FEAST]. Brain Stimul. 2013;6(3):403–8.

Nobler MS, Oquendo MA, Kegeles LS, Malone KM, Campbell CC, Sackeim HA, et al. Decreased regional brain metabolism after ect. Am J Psychiatry. 2001;158(2):305–8.

Perlis RH, Ostacher MJ, Patel JK, Marangell LB, Zhang H, Wisniewski SR, et al. Predictors of recurrence in bipolar disorder: primary outcomes from the Systematic Treatment Enhancement Program for Bipolar Disorder (STEP-BD). Am J Psychiatry. 2006;163(2):217–24.

Perugi G, Medda P, Toni C, Mariani MG, Socci C, Mauri M. The role of electroconvulsive therapy (ECT) in bipolar disorder: effectiveness in 522 patients with bipolar depression, mixed-state. Mania and catatonic features. Curr Neuropharmacol. 2017;15(3):359–71.

Peterchev AV, Rosa MA, Deng ZD, Prudic J, Lisanby SH. Electroconvulsive therapy stimulus parameters: rethinking dosage. J ECT. 2010;26(3):159–74.

Prudic J, Olfson M, Marcus SC, Fuller RB, Sackeim HA. Effectiveness of electroconvulsive therapy in community settings. Biol Psychiatry. 2004;55(3):301–12.

Radman T, Lisanby SH. New directions in the rational design of electrical and magnetic seizure therapies: individualized Low Amplitude Seizure Therapy (iLAST) and Magnetic Seizure Therapy (MST). Int Rev Psychiatry (Abingdon, England). 2017;29(2):63–78.

Ranjkesh F, Barekatain M, Akuchakian S. Bifrontal versus right unilateral and bitemporal electroconvulsive therapy in major depressive disorder. J ECT. 2005;21(4):207–10.

Rezaei F, Nasseri K, Esfandiari GR, Sadeghi SM, Fathie M, Gharibi F. Remifentanil added to propofol for induction of anesthesia can reduce reorientation time after electroconvulsive therapy in patients with severe mania. J ECT. 2012;28(2):124–7.

Sackeim HA, Greenberg MS, Weiman AL, Gur RC, Hungerbuhler JP, Geschwind N. Hemispheric asymmetry in the expression of positive and negative emotions. Neurologic evidence. Arch Neurol. 1982;39(4):210–8.

Sackeim HA, Luber B, Katzman GP, Moeller JR, Prudic J, Devanand DP, et al. The effects of electroconvulsive therapy on quantitative electroencephalograms. Relationship to clinical outcome. Arch Gen Psychiatry. 1996;53(9):814–24.

Sackeim HA, Prudic J, Devanand DP, Nobler MS, Lisanby SH, Peyser S, et al. A prospective, randomized, double-blind comparison of bilateral and right unilateral electroconvulsive therapy at different stimulus intensities. Arch Gen Psychiatry. 2000;57(5):425–34.

Schoeyen HK, Kessler U, Andreassen OA, Auestad BH, Bergsholm P, Malt UF, et al. Treatment-resistant bipolar depression: a randomized controlled trial of electroconvulsive therapy versus algorithm-based pharmacological treatment. Am J Psychiatry. 2015;172(1):41–51.

Semkovska M, McLoughlin DM. Measuring retrograde autobiographical amnesia following electroconvulsive therapy: historical perspective and current issues. J ECT. 2013;29(2):127–33.

Semkovska M, McLoughlin DM. Retrograde autobiographical amnesia after electroconvulsive therapy: on the difficulty of finding the baby and clearing murky bathwater. J ECT. 2014;30(3):187–8 **(discussion 9-90)**.

Semkovska M, Keane D, Babalola O, McLoughlin DM. Unilateral brief-pulse electroconvulsive therapy and cognition: effects of electrode placement, stimulus dosage and time. J Psychiatr Res. 2011;45(6):770–80.

Sienaert P, Vansteelandt K, Demyttenaere K, Peuskens J. Ultra-brief pulse ECT in bipolar and unipolar depressive disorder: differences in speed of response. Bipolar Disord. 2009;11(4):418–24.

Small JG. Efficacy of electroconvulsive therapy in schizophrenia, mania, and other disorders. II. Mania and other disorders. Convuls Ther. 1985;1(4):271–6.

Small JG, Small IF, Milstein V, Kellams JJ, Klapper MH. Manic symptoms: an indication for bilateral ECT. Biol Psychiat. 1985;20(2):125–34.

Spellman T, Peterchev AV, Lisanby SH. Focal electrically administered seizure therapy: a novel form of ECT illustrates the roles of current directionality, polarity, and electrode configuration in seizure induction. Neuropsychopharmacology. 2009;34(8):2002–10.

Strakowski SM, Eliassen JC, Lamy M, Cerullo MA, Allendorfer JB, Madore M, et al. Functional magnetic resonance imaging brain activation in bipolar mania: evidence for disruption of the ventrolateral prefrontal-amygdala emotional pathway. Biol Psychiat. 2011;69(4):381–8.

Strakowski SM, Fleck DE, Welge J, Eliassen JC, Norris M, Durling M, et al. fMRI brain activation changes following treatment of a first bipolar manic episode. Bipolar Disord. 2016;18(6):490–501.

Thirthalli J, Kumar CN, Bangalore RP, Gangadhar BN. Speed of response to threshold and suprathreshold bilateral ECT in depression, mania and schizophrenia. J Affect Disord. 2009;117(1–2):104–7.

Thirthalli J, Prasad MK, Gangadhar BN. Electroconvulsive therapy (ECT) in bipolar disorder: a narrative review of literature. Asian J Psychiatr. 2012;5(1):11–7.

UK ECT Review Group. Efficacy and safety of electroconvulsive therapy in depressive disorder: a systematic review and meta-analysis. Lancet. 2003;361:799–808.

Youssef NA, Sidhom E. Feasibility, safety, and preliminary efficacy of Low Amplitude Seizure Therapy (LAP-ST): a proof of concept clinical trial in man. J Affect Disord. 2017;222:1–6.

9

Variations in seasonal solar insolation are associated with a history of suicide attempts in bipolar I disorder

Michael Bauer[1*], Tasha Glenn[2], Eric D. Achtyes[3], Martin Alda[4], Esen Agaoglu[5], Kürşat Altınbaş[6], Ole A. Andreassen[7], Elias Angelopoulos[8], Raffaella Ardau[9], Edgar Arrua Vares[1], Memduha Aydin[10], Yavuz Ayhan[5], Christopher Baethge[11], Rita Bauer[1], Bernhard T. Baune[12,13,14], Ceylan Balaban[15], Claudia Becerra-Palars[16], Aniruddh P. Behere[17], Prakash B. Behere[18], Habte Belete[19], Tilahun Belete[19], Gabriel Okawa Belizario[20], Frank Bellivier[21], Robert H. Belmaker[22], Francesco Benedetti[23,24], Michael Berk[25,26], Yuly Bersudsky[27], Şule Bicakci[5,28], Harriet Birabwa-Oketcho[29], Thomas D. Bjella[7], Conan Brady[30], Jorge Cabrera[31], Marco Cappucciati[32], Angela Marianne Paredes Castro[25], Wei-Ling Chen[33], Eric Y. Wo Cheung[34], Silvia Chiesa[32], Marie Crowe[35], Alessandro Cuomo[36], Sara Dallaspezia[24], Maria Del Zompo[9], Pratikkumar Desai[37], Seetal Dodd[25,38], Markus Donix[1], Bruno Etain[21], Andrea Fagiolini[36], Frederike T. Fellendorf[39], Ewa Ferensztajn-Rochowiak[40], Jess G. Fiedorowicz[41], Kostas N. Fountoulakis[42], Mark A. Frye[43], Pierre A. Geoffroy[44,45,46], Ana Gonzalez-Pinto[47], John F. Gottlieb[48], Paul Grof[49], Bartholomeus C. M. Haarman[50], Hirohiko Harima[51], Mathias Hasse-Sousa[52], Chantal Henry[53,54], Lone Høffding[55], Josselin Houenou[56,57], Massimiliano Imbesi[32], Erkki T. Isometsä[58,59], Maja Ivkovic[60], Sven Janno[61], Simon Johnsen[62], Flávio Kapczinski[52], Gregory N. Karakatsoulis[42], Mathias Kardell[63], Lars Vedel Kessing[64], Seong Jae Kim[65], Barbara König[66], Timur L. Kot[67], Michael Koval[68], Mauricio Kunz[52], Beny Lafer[20], Mikael Landén[63,69], Erik R. Larsen[70], Melanie Lenger[39], Ute Lewitzka[1], Rasmus W. Licht[71,72], Carlos Lopez-Jaramillo[73], Alan MacKenzie[74], Helle Østergaard Madsen[75], Simone Alberte Kongstad A. Madsen[62], Jayant Mahadevan[76], Agustine Mahardika[77], Mirko Manchia[78,79,80], Wendy Marsh[81], Monica Martinez-Cengotitabengoa[82], Klaus Martiny[75], Yuki Mashima[83], Declan M. McLoughlin[84], Ybe Meesters[50], Ingrid Melle[7], Fátima Meza-Urzúa[16], Mok Yee Ming[85], Scott Monteith[86], Muthukumaran Moorthy[76], Gunnar Morken[87,88], Enrica Mosca[9], Anton A. Mozzhegorov[89], Rodrigo Munoz[90], Starlin V. Mythri[91], Fethi Nacef[92], Ravi K. Nadella[76], Takako Nakanotani[93], René Ernst Nielsen[71,72], Claire O'Donovan[4], Adel Omrani[94], Yamima Osher[27], Uta Ouali[92], Maja Pantovic-Stefanovic[60], Pornjira Pariwatcharakul[95], Joanne Petite[4], Andrea Pfennig[1], Yolanda Pica Ruiz[96], Maximilian Pilhatsch[1,97], Marco Pinna[79,98], Maurizio Pompili[99], Richard Porter[35], Danilo Quiroz[100], Francisco Diego Rabelo-da-Ponte[52], Raj Ramesar[101], Natalie Rasgon[102], Woraphat Ratta-apha[95], Michaela Ratzenhofer[39], Maria Redahan[30], M. S. Reddy[91], Andreas Reif[15], Eva Z. Reininghaus[39], Jenny Gringer Richards[103], Philipp Ritter[1], Janusz K. Rybakowski[40], Leela Sathyaputri[103], Ângela M. Scippa[104], Christian Simhandl[105], Emanuel Severus[1], Daniel Smith[106], José Smith[107], Paul W. Stackhouse Jr.[108],

*Correspondence: Michael.Bauer@uniklinikum-dresden.de
[1] Department of Psychiatry and Psychotherapy, Faculty of Medicine, University Hospital Carl Gustav Carus, Technische Universität Dresden, Dresden, Germany
Full list of author information is available at the end of the article

Dan J. Stein[109], Kellen Stilwell[37], Sergio Strejilevich[107], Kuan-Pin Su[110,111], Mythily Subramaniam[112], Ahmad Hatim Sulaiman[113], Kirsi Suominen[114], Andi J. Tanra[115], Yoshitaka Tatebayashi[93], Wen Lin Teh[112], Leonardo Tondo[116,117], Carla Torrent[118], Daniel Tuinstra[37], Takahito Uchida[83], Arne E. Vaaler[87,88], Julia Veeh[15], Eduard Vieta[118], Biju Viswanath[76], Maria Yoldi-Negrete[119], Oguz Kaan Yalcinkaya[5], Allan H. Young[120], Yosra Zgueb[92] and Peter C. Whybrow[121]

Abstract

Background: Bipolar disorder is associated with circadian disruption and a high risk of suicidal behavior. In a previous exploratory study of patients with bipolar I disorder, we found that a history of suicide attempts was associated with differences between winter and summer levels of solar insolation. The purpose of this study was to confirm this finding using international data from 42% more collection sites and 25% more countries.

Methods: Data analyzed were from 71 prior and new collection sites in 40 countries at a wide range of latitudes. The analysis included 4876 patients with bipolar I disorder, 45% more data than previously analyzed. Of the patients, 1496 (30.7%) had a history of suicide attempt. Solar insolation data, the amount of the sun's electromagnetic energy striking the surface of the earth, was obtained for each onset location (479 locations in 64 countries).

Results: This analysis confirmed the results of the exploratory study with the same best model and slightly better statistical significance. There was a significant inverse association between a history of suicide attempts and the ratio of mean winter insolation to mean summer insolation (mean winter insolation/mean summer insolation). This ratio is largest near the equator which has little change in solar insolation over the year, and smallest near the poles where the winter insolation is very small compared to the summer insolation. Other variables in the model associated with an increased risk of suicide attempts were a history of alcohol or substance abuse, female gender, and younger birth cohort. The winter/summer insolation ratio was also replaced with the ratio of minimum mean monthly insolation to the maximum mean monthly insolation to accommodate insolation patterns in the tropics, and nearly identical results were found. All estimated coefficients were significant at $p < 0.01$.

Conclusion: A large change in solar insolation, both between winter and summer and between the minimum and maximum monthly values, may increase the risk of suicide attempts in bipolar I disorder. With frequent circadian rhythm dysfunction and suicidal behavior in bipolar disorder, greater understanding of the optimal roles of daylight and electric lighting in circadian entrainment is needed.

Keywords: Bipolar disorder, Suicide, Sunlight, Solar insolation, Psychiatry, Circadian, Seasonal variation

Introduction

The risk for suicidal behavior for those with bipolar disorder is estimated to be 20–30 times higher than for the general population (Pompili et al. 2013; Shaffer 2015; Dong et al. 2019; Plans et al. 2019). Risk factors for suicidal behavior in bipolar disorder include depression, agitation, impulsivity, comorbid alcohol or substance abuse, prior suicidal acts, recent discharge from a psychiatric hospital, along with genetic, demographic, socioeconomic and cultural factors, and stressful life events (Pompili et al. 2013; Shaffer 2015; Tondo et al. 2021; Bachmann 2018; Plans et al. 2019; Tidemalm et al. 2014). Additionally, international epidemiology studies of the general population spanning several decades report seasonality in suicide attempts and deaths with a peak in spring or summer (Galvão et al. 2018; Woo et al. 2012; Su et al. 2020; Postolache et al. 2010; Oladunjoye et al. 2020; Christodoulou et al. 2012; Coimbra et al. 2016; Petridou et al. 2002).

There is increasing recognition of the profound and diverse impacts of daylight on human physiology and behavior, and the complexity of the mechanisms underlying the human response to light (Münch et al. 2017; Aranda and Schmidt 2021; Foster 2020). In addition to vision, daylight modulates circadian timing, the sleep–wake cycle, daily neuroendocrine functions, alertness, performance, mood and thermoregulation (Wirz-Justice et al. 2020; Paul and Brown 2019; Prayag et al. 2019; Cajochen 2007; Fisk et al. 2018; LeGates et al. 2014). Alterations in circadian rhythm are a major component of mood disorders (Logan and McClung 2019; Jones and Benca 2015; McClung 2013; Ketchesin et al. 2020), with disruptions in sleep, hormonal secretion, mood regulation and social rhythms occurring frequently in bipolar disorder (Melo et al. 2017; Takaesu 2018; McCarthy 2019; Gonzalez 2014). The effects of circadian disruptions in bipolar disorder are interrelated and can both trigger and exacerbate symptoms (Harvey 2008; Walker et al. 2020; Geoffroy 2018). About 25% of patients exhibit a seasonal pattern in the course of bipolar disorder (Geoffroy et al. 2014; Maruani et al. 2018).

In a prior exploratory study of patients with bipolar I disorder, we found that a history of suicide attempts was associated with living in locations with a large change in solar insolation between winter and summer (Bauer et al. 2019). Solar insolation (incoming solar radiation) is defined as the amount of electromagnetic energy from the sun striking a surface area on earth (Stackhouse et al. 2018). The aim of the current study was to investigate whether a repeat analysis with more data would confirm or contradict the results of the exploratory study. In addition, an analysis using the ratio of the minimum mean monthly insolation to the maximum mean monthly insolation was added to accommodate the insolation patterns in the tropics. The prior analysis included data from 50 collection sites in 32 countries. This analysis used 45% more data both from new and prior collection sites, including data from 71 collection sites in 40 countries with diverse cultures, healthcare systems, and climates.

Methods

Data collection

Data were collected by direct questioning, reviewing records, or both. All patients had a diagnosis of bipolar disorder from a psychiatrist according to DSM-IV or DSM-5 criteria. Study approval was obtained from local institutional review boards, following local requirements. This analysis includes the data used in the exploratory study that were collected between 2010 and 2016, and additional data collected between 2019 and 2020. Details about the project methodology were published previously (Bauer et al. 2012, 2014,2017).

Data collection sites

Researchers from 71 collection sites in 40 countries provided the data, including those at university medical centers, specialty clinics and individual practitioners. Collection sites located in the northern hemisphere were: Aalborg, Denmark; Aarhus, Denmark; Ankara, Turkey; Athens, Greece; Bangkok, Thailand; Barcelona, Spain; Barhir Dar, Ethiopia; Beer Sheva, Israel; Belgrade, Serbia; Bengaluru, India; Cagliari, Sardinia, Italy (2 sites); Calgary, Canada; Dresden, Germany; Dublin, Ireland; Frankfurt, Germany; Halifax, Canada; Helsinki, Finland; Glasgow, UK; Gothenburg, Sweden; Grand Rapids, MI, USA; Hong Kong, China; Hyderabad, India; Iowa City, Iowa, USA; Jincheon, South Korea; Kampala, Uganda; Kansas City, KS, USA; Khanti-Mansiysk, Russia; Konya, Turkey; Kuala Lumpur, Malaysia; Los Angeles, CA, USA; Medellín, Colombia; Mexico City, Mexico; Milan, Italy; Oslo, Norway; Ottawa, Canada; Piacenza, Italy; Palo Alto, CA, USA; Paris, France (2 sites); Poznan, Poland; Rochester, MN, USA; Rome, Italy; San Diego, CA, USA; Siena, Italy; Singapore; Stockholm, Sweden; Tartu, Estonia; Thessaloniki, Greece (2 sites); Tokyo, Japan (3 sites); Taichung, Taiwan; Trondheim, Norway; Tunis, Tunisia; Vitoria, Spain; Wardha, India; Wiener Neustadt, Austria; Worcester, MA, USA, and Würzburg, Germany. Collection sites located in the southern hemisphere were: Adelaide, Australia; Melbourne/Geelong, Australia; Buenos Aires, Argentina; Cape Town, South Africa; Christchurch, New Zealand; Mataram, Indonesia; Porto Alegre, Brazil; Salvador, Brazil; Santiago, Chile (2 sites); and São Paulo, Brazil.

Patient data collected

To facilitate international participation, minimal clinical data were collected for each patient. The patient data collected included gender, age of onset, polarity of first episode, family history of mood disorders, history of psychosis, episode course, history of alcohol and substance abuse, and history of suicide attempts. Three locations were also collected for each patient: birth location, onset location and current location. The same birth cohort groups were used as in the exploratory analysis, and in prior research (Bauer et al. 2014, 2015, 2017; Chengappa et al. 2003).

Country specific data

Country specific socioeconomic data were obtained for all onset locations, including physician density per 1000 population, country median age, unemployment rate, poverty rate, gross domestic product (GDP) per capita (CIA World Factbook 2020), psychiatrists per 100,000 (WHO 2019a), Gini index of income inequality, percent Internet users (World Bank 2020a, b), gender inequality index (UN 2020), and if the country has a state-sponsored or officially favored religion (Pew Research 2017).

Solar insolation

The NASA POWER database provides average monthly solar insolation expressed in kilowatt hours/square meter/day (kWh/m^2/day) based on satellite observations collected between 1983 and the present (Stackhouse et al. 2018; NASA 2020). As in the exploratory study, a 22-year climatology of insolation spanning Jan 1984–December 2013 at spatial resolution of 1° × 1° latitude/longitude was used in this analysis. The actual onset locations were grouped into reference onset locations representing all onset locations within a 1° × 1° grid of latitude and longitude. For example, Dresden, Germany at latitude of 51.1° north and 13.8° east is the reference onset location for all locations between 51° and 52° north, and 13° and 14° east. The latitude and longitude of the reference onset location were used to identify solar insolation values for each patient.

During a year, the pattern of mean monthly solar insolation varies by latitude, with little change near the equator and large changes near the north and south poles. Solar insolation values for locations at the same latitude may vary significantly due to local conditions including cloud cover, aerosols (including dust and pollution), water vapor amounts, and altitude. Locations in the tropics (less than 23.5° north or south of the equator), may have a wet season where clouds reduce solar insolation and a dry season with clear skies rather than a winter/summer insolation pattern. To summarize the changes in solar insolation throughout the year at each reference onset location, two variables were created: (1) the ratio of the mean northern hemisphere winter (December, January, February) to the mean summer (June, July, August) insolation, and (2) the ratio of the minimum mean monthly insolation to the maximum mean monthly insolation. The insolation data from the southern hemisphere were shifted by 6 months for comparison to data from the northern hemisphere to account for the seasonal cycle.

Statistics

The same statistical approach was used as in the exploratory study (Bauer et al. 2019), in which the generalized estimating equations (GEE) statistical technique was used to account for both the correlated data and unbalanced number of patients at reference onset locations. The GEE technique estimates the dependent variable as a function of the entire population, producing a population averaged or marginal estimates of model coefficients (Zeger and Liang 1986). All GEE models in this study were estimated using a binomial distribution, an exchangeable working correlation matrix and a logit link function where a patient history of suicide attempts was the dependent binary variable. The selection process of the best model of a history of suicide attempts first identified individual independent variables with an estimated coefficient significant at the 0.05 level in a univariate GEE model. Significant independent variables from univariate models and variables found in prior suicide research were then combined into multivariate GEE models of a history of suicide attempts. To identify the best model, the multivariate model estimates were compared using the corrected quasi-likelihood independence model criterion (Pan 2001) and confidence intervals at the 0.01 significance level to reduce the chance of type 1 errors. Based on the logit link function, the exponential coefficient can be interpreted as the effect size (Li et al. 2019). Demographic variables were reported using descriptive statistics. SPSS version 26.0 was used for all analyses.

Results

Available data

Data for 10,771 patients were available from the 71 collection sites, including 3379 new patients, 46% more patients than in the exploratory analysis. Of these, 7844 patients had a diagnosis of bipolar I disorder. Of the 7844 patients with bipolar I disorder, a history of suicide attempts was available for 6064 patients. Of the 6064 patients with data on a history of suicide attempts, all 5 variables in the best model were only available for 4876 patients, with 81% of the excluded patients missing data for a history of alcohol or substance abuse. Although 19.6% of the patients with data on a history of suicide attempts were excluded, the other demographics were similar to those included in the best model. The demographics of the 4876 patients included in the best model are shown in Table 1. Of the 4876 patients, 2760 patients (56.6%) were female, and 1496 patients (30.7%) had a history of suicide attempts.

Onset locations

For the 4876 patients analyzed in the best model, there were 479 reference onset locations in 64 countries. The onset location was in the northern hemisphere for 4176 patients (85.6%), and in the southern hemisphere for 700 patients (14.4%), similar to estimates that about 12.5% of the world population lives in the southern hemisphere (Kummu and Varis 2011). Of the 4876 patients, 912 (18.7%) had an onset location in the tropics. For the 4876 patients, 97.6% of the onset locations were in the same country as the current country, and 83.3% of the onset cities were the same as the current city. The average number of patients in each onset location was 10.2, with 256 (5.3%) of the 4876 patients in an onset location with a single patient. As with the exploratory study, the much larger number of onset locations than collection sites reflects worldwide urbanization (WHO 2019b). Figure 1 provides a comparison of the range of latitudes for the onset locations between this analysis and the exploratory study.

Ratio of mean winter solar insolation to mean summer solar insolation

At locations near the equator, there is little change in solar insolation between winter and summer and the ratio of mean winter solar insolation to mean summer solar insolation is large (near 1). At locations near the poles, solar insolation is very small in winter when compared to

Table 1 Demographics of the patients with bipolar I disorder (N = 4876)

Parameter	Value	N	%
Gender			
	Female	2760	56.6
	Male	2116	43.4
Polarity of first episode[a]			
	Manic/hypomanic	2302	48.8
	Depressed	2419	51.2
Family history of mood disorder[a]			
	No	2026	45.3
	Yes	2448	54.7
Alcohol or substance abuse			
	No	3369	69.1
	Yes	1507	30.9
State sponsored religion in country of onset			
	No	2662	54.6
	Yes	2214	45.4
History of suicide attempt			
	No	3380	69.3
	Yes	1496	30.7
Cohort group			
	DOB < 1940	179	3.7
	DOB ≥ 1940 and DOB < 1960	1241	25.5
	DOB ≥ 1960	3456	70.9
Parameter		**Mean**	**SD**
Age at time of data collection		47.8	14.4
Age of onset		25.7	10.6

[a] Missing values excluded

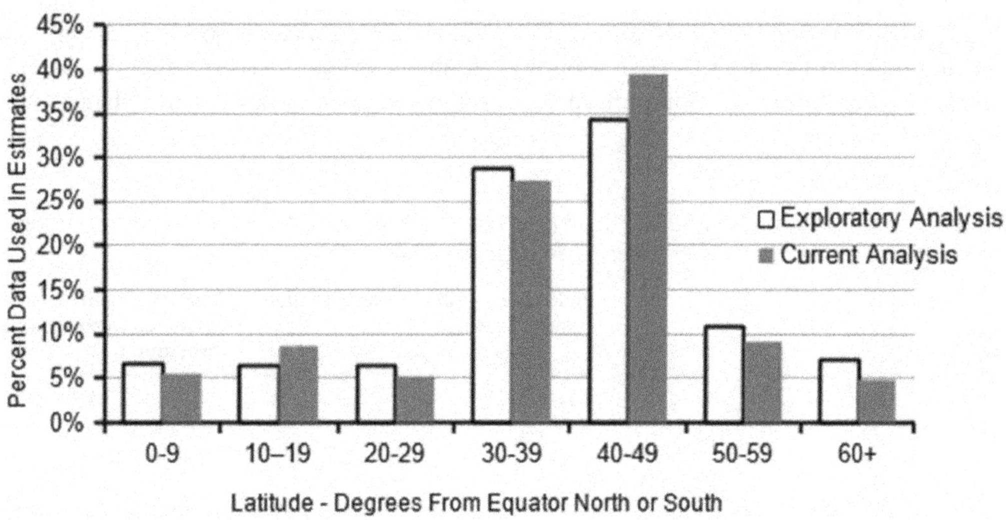

Fig. 1 Comparison of range of onset location latitudes for current and exploratory analyses for patients with bipolar I disorder (N = 4876)

the summer, and the ratio is small (near 0). The ratio of mean winter solar insolation to mean summer solar insolation by latitude groups is shown in Table 2. The ratio of mean winter solar insolation to mean summer solar insolation for example onset locations in the latitude groups is shown in Table 3.

Best model results

The best fitting model for a history of suicide attempts uses the ratio of mean winter solar insolation to the mean summer solar insolation and is shown in Table 4. This is the same model that was selected in the exploratory study as the best model, and the estimated coefficients are similar in value to those in the exploratory analysis. The inclusion of 4876 patients in the best model was a 45% increase over the 3365 patients included in the exploratory analysis.

The estimated coefficients for the model suggest that the odds of a suicide attempt will decrease by 4.8% for every 0.1 increase in the ratio of mean winter to summer insolation. Alternatively stated, comparing a ratio of 1 (near the equator) to a ratio of 0 (near a pole), there was a 48% difference in the odds of a suicide attempt with the lowest odds at the equator. The model estimates that being male will decrease the odds of a suicide attempt by 54%, and living in a country with a state sponsored or favored religion will decrease the odds by 65%. The model also estimates that having a history of alcohol or substance abuse will increase the odds of a suicide attempt by 58%, and being in the youngest cohort will increase the odds of a suicide attempt by 127%.

Ratio of minimum mean monthly insolation to the maximum mean monthly insolation

The ratio of minimum mean monthly insolation to the maximum mean monthly insolation by latitude groups is shown in Table 2. The ratio of minimum mean monthly insolation to the maximum mean monthly insolation for selected onset locations in the latitude groups is shown in Table 3. A second model that substituted the ratio of minimum mean monthly insolation to the maximum mean monthly insolation for the ratio of mean winter solar insolation to mean summer solar insolation was estimated using the same data as with the best model.

The estimated coefficients for the model using the minimum mean monthly insolation to the maximum mean monthly insolation are shown in Table 5, and are very similar to those in the best model. The estimated coefficients for the monthly model suggest that the odds of a suicide attempt will decrease by 4.4% for every 0.1 increase in the ratio of mean winter to summer insolation. Alternatively stated, comparing a ratio of 1 (near the equator) to a ratio of 0 (near a pole), there was a 44% difference in the odds of a suicide attempt with the lowest odds at the equator. The model estimates that being male will decrease the odds of a suicide attempt by 54%, and living in a country with a state sponsored or favored religion will decrease the odds by 69%. The model also estimates that having a history of alcohol or substance will increase the odds of a suicide attempt by 59%, and being in the youngest cohort will increase the odds of a suicide attempt by 124%.

The collection site was thought to be an adequate proxy for the onset location for some or all patients from Barcelona, Cape Town, Christchurch, Frankfurt, Helsinki, Melbourne/Geelong, Porto Alegro, São Paulo, Salvador, Vitoria, and Würzburg, where the patient onset location was not provided. To test the effect of using the current location as a proxy for the onset location, the best model and the minimum mean monthly insolation to the maximum mean monthly insolation model were also estimated excluding these patients. The magnitude of the estimated coefficients did not change substantially and

Table 2 Ratio of mean winter solar insolation/mean summer solar insolation and ratio of minimum mean monthly insolation/maximum mean monthly insolation by latitude for patient onset locations (N = 4876)

Degrees latitude north + south	N	%	Ratio mean winter insolation/mean summer insolation	Ratio minimum mean monthly insolation/maximum mean monthly insolation
0–9	268	5.5	1.0313	0.8076
10–19	420	8.6	1.1074	0.6744
20–29	254	5.2	0.7772	0.6093
30–39	1333	27.3	0.4075	0.3165
40–49	1921	39.4	0.3023	0.2119
50–59	444	9.1	0.1662	0.0903
60+	236	4.8	0.0857	0.0220
Total	4876	100.0	0.4423	0.3135

Table 3 Ratio of mean winter solar insolation/mean summer solar insolation and ratio of minimum mean monthly insolation/maximum mean monthly insolation: example onset locations by latitude group (N = 4876)

Degrees latitude north + south	Onset location	Ratio mean winter insolation/mean summer insolation	Ratio minimum mean monthly insolation/maximum mean monthly insolation
0–9	Kampala, Uganda	1.1400	0.8197
	Kuala Lumpur, Malaysia	0.9702	0.7694
	Mataram, Indonesia	1.0125	0.7831
	Medellín, Columbia	0.9065	0.8370
	Singapore	1.0560	0.7797
10–19	Bahir Dar, Ethiopia	1.1639	0.7713
	Bangkok, Thailand	1.0680	0.7207
	Bengaluru, India	1.1702	0.6814
	Hyderabad, India	1.1762	0.6421
	Mexico City, Mexico	0.9074	0.6855
	Salvador, Brazil	0.6844	0.6246
20–29	Hong Kong, China	0.6603	0.6016
	São Paulo, Brazil	0.7419	0.6050
	Taichung, Taiwan	0.4492	0.3931
	Wardha, India	1.1545	0.5750
30–39	Ankara, Turkey	0.3266	0.2374
	Athens, Greece	0.3148	0.2319
	Beer Sheva, Israel	0.4246	0.3556
	Buenos Aires, Argentina	0.3978	0.3149
	Cagliari, Italy	0.3066	0.2328
	Cape Town, South Africa	0.3873	0.3227
	Los Angeles, CA, USA	0.4235	0.3503
	Melbourne, Australia	0.3628	0.2913
	San Francisco, CA, USA	0.4163	0.3137
	Santiago, Chile	0.3537	0.2879
	Seoul, South Korea	0.6406	0.4404
	Tokyo, Japan	0.7201	0.5574
	Tunis, Tunisia	0.3695	0.2859
40–49	Belgrade, Serbia	0.2832	0.1960
	Barcelona, Spain	0.3622	0.2603
	Boston, MA, USA	0.3626	0.2662
	Christchurch, New Zealand	0.3225	0.2461
	Grand Rapids, MI, USA	0.3281	0.2256
	Halifax, Canada	0.3300	0.2270
	Minneapolis, MN, USA	0.3339	0.2371
	Paris, France	0.2317	0.1540
	Rome, Italy	0.2993	0.2203
	Siena, Italy	0.2988	0.2077
	Vienna, Austria	0.2631	0.1667
	Würzburg, Germany	0.2381	0.1477
50–59	Aarhus, Denmark	0.1432	0.0782
	Calgary, Canada	0.2269	0.1454
	Dresden, Germany	0.2255	0.1379
	Dublin, Ireland	0.1927	0.1149
	Oslo, Norway	0.1126	0.0433
	Poznan, Poland	0.2127	0.1290
	Stockholm, Sweden	0.1087	0.0427
	Tartu, Estonia	0.1353	0.0562
60 +	Helsinki, Finland	0.1095	0.0359
	Khanti-Mansiysk, Russia	0.0951	0.0243
	Trondheim, Norway	0.0673	0.0116

remained significant at the 0.01 level. Estimated models including other patient, country and solar insolation variables were not as significant, or not as meaningful.

Discussion

This analysis confirmed the results of the exploratory study after including 45% more international patient data. Living in locations with a large change in solar

Table 4 Estimated parameters for best model explaining a history of suicide attempts for patients with bipolar I disorder (N = 4876)

Parameters				99% Confidence interval		Coefficient significance	
	Coefficient estimate (β)	Standard error	Exp (β)	Lower	Upper	Wald Chi-squared	P
Intercept	− 0.935	0.2279	0.393	− 1.522	− 0.348	16.815	< 0.001
Ratio mean winter insolation/mean summer insolation	− 0.730	0.1752	0.482	− 1.181	− 0.279	17.357	< 0.001
State sponsored religion in onset country	− 0.438	0.1145	0.645	− 0.733	− 0.143	14.655	< 0.001
Male	− 0.609	0.0792	0.544	− 0.813	− 0.405	59.096	< 0.001
History of alcohol or substance abuse	0.459	0.0726	1.582	0.272	0.646	39.978	< 0.001
DOB ≥ 1960	0.822	0.2289	2.275	0.232	1.414	12.890	< 0.001[a]
DOB ≥ 1940 and DOB < 1960	0.681	0.2064	1.975	0.149	1.212	10.872	0.001[a]

Dependent variable: history of suicide attempts (yes/no). Model: intercept, ratio of mean winter insolation/mean summer insolation at onset location, gender, state sponsored religion in onset country (yes/no), alcohol or substance abuse (yes/no) and birth cohort group (DOB < 1940, DOB ≥ 1940 and DOB < 1960, DOB ≥ 1960)

[a] Individual parameters Wald Chi-square statistics and significance. The model effects Wald Chi-square and significance for the cohort parameter was 12.904 and 0.002, respectively with 2 degrees of freedom

Table 5 Estimated parameters for alternative model explaining a history of suicide attempts for patients with bipolar I disorder (N = 4876)

Parameters				99% Confidence interval		Coefficient significance	
	Coefficient estimate (β)	Standard error	Exp (β)	Lower	Upper	Wald Chi-squared	P
Intercept	− 1.026	0.2302	0.358	− 1.619	− 0.434	19.885	< 0.001
Ratio minimum mean monthly insolation/ maximum mean monthly insolation	− 0.813	0.2552	0.444	− 1.470	− 0.155	10.136	0.001
State sponsored religion in onset country	− 0.378	0.1127	0.685	− 0.668	− 0.088	11.252	0.001
Male	− 0.612	0.0794	0.542	− 0.816	− 0.407	59.438	< 0.001
History of alcohol or substance abuse	0.466	0.0730	1.594	0.278	0.655	40.760	< 0.001
DOB ≥ 1960	0.808	0.2312	2.244	0.213	1.404	12.224	< 0.001[a]
DOB ≥ 1940 and DOB < 1960	0.679	0.2085	1.972	0.142	1.216	10.612	0.001[a]

Dependent variable: history of suicide attempts (yes/no). Model: intercept, ratio minimum mean monthly insolation/maximum mean monthly insolation at onset location, gender, state sponsored religion in onset country (yes/no), alcohol or substance abuse (yes/no) and birth cohort group (DOB < 1940, DOB ≥ 1940 and DOB < 1960, DOB ≥ 1960)

[a] Individual parameters Wald Chi-square statistics and significance. The model effects Wald chi-square and significance for the cohort parameter was 12.224 and 0.002, respectively with 2 degrees of freedom

insolation between winter and summer was associated with increased history of suicide attempts in patients with bipolar I disorder. The onset locations in this analysis were distributed across all latitudes in both hemispheres, and represent a wide range of solar insolation profiles and climatic conditions. The exploratory study results were confirmed in this study in two ways: by identifying the same GEE model as the best model, and by estimating a nearly identical relationship between solar insolation and a history of suicide attempts with slightly better statistical significance. In addition, the estimated coefficients for all other contributing variables in the model, history of alcohol or substance abuse, female gender, birth cohort and state sponsored religion, were similar and slightly more significant. The finding of nearly identical results with an alternative measure of variation in solar insolation, which applies to all locations including the tropics, further confirms the association between a change in solar insolation and a history of suicide attempts.

The largest change in solar insolation between winter and summer occurs at locations near the poles. Suicide is a serious public health problem in the 8 countries with Arctic communities above 60°N (Pollock et al. 2020; Young et al. 2015). For example, in 2017 the suicide rate for the state of Alaska was nearly double the US national suicide rate, and nearly triple for Alaska native people

(AK-IBIS 2019). Additionally, seasonality in suicide is associated with latitude, with little monthly variation or seasonality in suicide rates near the equator, and spring and summer peaks in suicide rates with increasing latitudes north or south (Davis and Lowell 2002; Schwartz 2019).

There is related evidence involving patterns of solar radiation from studies within individual countries. In Finland, an increased suicide risk was associated with the cumulative low solar radiation over the long northern winter (Ruuhela et al. 2009). Several studies reported that an increasing risk of suicidal behavior was associated with increasing solar radiation. In South Korea, increased solar radiation in spring and summer was associated with an increased suicide rate (Jee et al. 2017). In Germany and Greece, increased solar insolation may precede suicidal acts (Müller et al. 2011; Papadopoulos et al. 2005). In Italy, higher solar radiation was associated with an increase in patients admitted to an emergency psychiatric unit with a primary diagnosis of bipolar disorder (Aguglia et al. 2019).

Consistency with prior research

The demographics of the patients are consistent with prior international studies of bipolar disorder, with 30.7% having a history of suicide attempts (Tondo et al. 2016; Dong et al. 2019; Bobo et al. 2018), and 30.9% a history of alcohol or substance abuse (Toftdahl et al. 2016; Hunt et al. 2016; Grant et al. 2004; Nesvåg et al. 2015). Although we previously found a strong, inverse relation between the maximum monthly increase in solar insolation in springtime and the age of onset of bipolar I disorder (Bauer et al. 2017, 2014, 2012), the unadjusted mean age of onset of 25.7 is also similar to international studies (Baldessarini et al. 2012; Morselli et al. 2003; Kalman et al. 2019).

The other variables included in the best model also agree with prior suicide research in bipolar disorder and the general population. Alcohol and substance abuse (Schaffer et al. 2015; Carrà et al. 2014; Østergaard et al. 2017; Bobo 2018; Yuodelis-Flores and Ries 2015; Norström and Rossow 2016), and being female (Schaffer et al. 2015, Dong et al. 2019; Tondo et al. 2016; Bobo 2018) are associated with an increased risk of suicidal behavior. Increased suicide attempts or deaths are reported internationally in younger birth cohorts (Twenge et al. 2019; Odagiri et al. 2011; Page et al. 2013; Yu and Chen 2019; Kwon et al. 2009; Gunnell et al. 2003; Phillips 2014; Chung et al. 2016). Studies involving all major world religions find that religion may be protective against suicidal behavior (Eskin et al. 2020; Wu et al. 2015; VanderWeele et al. 2016; Stack and Kposowa 2011; Dervic et al. 2011; Caribe et al. 2015; Jacob et al. 2019).

Special importance of daylight

The findings of this study highlight the importance of daylight to human wellbeing and behavior. In repeated surveys, people preferred daylight over electric lighting as the source of illumination, although the reasons for the strong daylight preference are not fully established (Knoop et al. 2020; Boyce et al. 2003; Haans 2014). Daylight differs from electric lighting in many fundamental properties, including the spectrum, intensity, temporal characteristics, flicker, and polarization, and the properties of daylight change throughout the day, month and year (Knoop et al. 2020; Aaarts et al. 2017). Many additional factors influence the physiological effects of light. These include individual characteristics such as age, lifestyle, health status, and genetics, environmental issues such as the season, climate, latitude and building design, and the duration of exposure and prior light exposure (Münch et al. 2017; 2020; Turner and Mainster 2008; Prayag et al. 2019).

Researchers emphasize the need to better understand how people respond to daylight and electric lighting in real-life settings (Knoop et al. 2020; Webler et al. 2019; Münch et al. 2020; Foster et al. 2020). Knowledge of non-image forming visual functions including circadian entrainment has grown rapidly. However, many findings are from small studies of healthy young adults exposed to electric lighting in controlled settings, or from animal studies. Even in controlled settings, considerable individual variability in sensitivity to light was detected (Phillips et al. 2019; McGlashan et al. 2018; Chellepa 2020). Understanding of how light intensity and duration of exposure interact for circadian entrainment is limited (Foster et al. 2020). Studies are needed that measure naturally occurring entrainment in large numbers of people of all ages and occupations, including mixed exposure to daylight and electric lighting in the day as well as electric lighting at night (Knoop et al. 2020; Webler et al. 2019; Münch et al. 2020; Foster et al. 2020). It is also not clear how applicable these findings are to patients with bipolar disorder. The optimal mix of daylight and electric lighting for circadian entrainment needs to be clarified to increase understanding of bipolar disorder and suicide risk, and improve the efficacy of chronotherapeutic treatments (Geoffroy and Palagini 2021; Gottlieb et al. 2019; Münch et al. 2020; Wang et al. 2020; Wirz-Justice and Benedetti 2020).

Limitations

Data in this project were collected as a convenience sample. The diagnosis was based on DSM-IV or DSM-5 criteria, but data collection methods and sources were not standardized, including the definition of suicide attempts. Although convenience samples can contain inadvertent biases, this study repeated the results of the exploratory study using substantially more international patient data. This suggests either sample biases in the exploratory study were duplicated in the data collection for this study from 71 international collection sites or, more likely, the relationship found between solar insolation and a history of suicide attempts was confirmed.

Although a large percentage of patients had the same onset city and current city (83.3%), and the same onset and current country (97.6%), there was no confirmation that the suicide attempt occurred at the onset location. There was no data on individual risk factors for suicide attempts, the phase of bipolar disorder when the suicide attempt occurred, or treatments received for bipolar disorder, including those that may lower the risk of suicide such as lithium. There was no data on suicide deaths. The risks for attempted versus completed suicides could not be analyzed, although there are known distinctions (Hansson et al. 2018; Nock et al. 2008). There was no data on individuals who did not seek treatment. There was no individual data on sun exposure, sun-related activities, or lifestyle issues such as shift work. This analysis does not demonstrate causality or predict individual behavior. Characteristics of the forms of electric lighting were not discussed, and other environmental variables were not included. Data from the southern hemisphere were shifted by 6 months, disregarding cultural dimensions of seasonality. Religious and cultural differences may influence data collection related to suicide, and to alcohol and drug abuse. The premature mortality from general medical illness (Roshanaei-Moghaddam and Katon 2009), completed suicides, treatment dropout rates, and the increased rate of diagnosis of bipolar disorder over time (Blader and Carlson 2007) may bias findings related to the birth cohort.

We previously noted two issues related to solar insolation that should be investigated in relation to suicide attempts: the potential impacts of continuous low solar insolation in areas near the poles with winters that last longer than 3 months, and of regional variance in insolation that has occurred over decadal timeframes (Wild 2012). However, we felt it was important to first confirm the results of the exploratory study.

Conclusion

A history of suicide attempts in patients with bipolar I disorder was associated with living in locations with a large change in solar insolation, both between winter and summer and between the minimum and maximum monthly values. Given the frequent presence of circadian rhythm dysfunction and suicidal behavior in bipolar disorder, and the fundamental importance of daylight to human health, greater understanding of the optimal roles of daylight and electric lighting in circadian entrainment in both the normal population and bipolar disorder is needed.

Acknowledgements
None.

Authors' contributions
MB and TG completed the initial draft, which was reviewed by all authors. All authors read and approved the final manuscript.

Competing interests
Rasmus W. Licht has received research Grants from Glaxo Smith Kline, honoraria for lecturing from Pfizer, Glaxo Smith Kline, Eli Lilly, Astra-Zeneca, Bristol-Myers Squibb, Janssen Cilag, Lundbeck, Otsuka, Servier and honoraria from advisory board activity from Glaxo Smith Kline, Eli Lilly, Astra-Zeneca, Bristol-Myers Squibb, Janssen Cilag, Sunovion and Sage. All other authors report no competing interests.

Author details
[1]Department of Psychiatry and Psychotherapy, Faculty of Medicine, University Hospital Carl Gustav Carus, Technische Universität Dresden, Dresden, Germany. [2]ChronoRecord Association, Fullerton, CA, USA. [3]Division of Psychiatry and Behavioral Medicine, Michigan State University College of Human Medicine, Grand Rapids, MI, USA. [4]Department of Psychiatry, Dalhousie University, Halifax, NS, Canada. [5]Department of Psychiatry, Hacettepe University Faculty of Medicine, Ankara, Turkey. [6]Department of Psychiatry, Selcuk University Faculty of Medicine, Mazhar Osman Mood Center, Konya, Turkey. [7]NORMENT Centre, Division of Mental Health and Addiction, Oslo University Hospital and Institute of Clinical Medicine, University of Oslo, Oslo, Norway. [8]Department of Psychiatry, National and Capodistrian University of Athens, Medical School, Eginition Hospital, Athens, Greece. [9]Section of Neurosciences and Clinical Pharmacology, Department of Biomedical Sciences, University of Cagliari, Sardinia, Italy. [10]Department of Psychiatry, Selcuk University Faculty of Medicine, Konya, Turkey. [11]Department of Psychiatry and Psychotherapy, University of Cologne Medical School, Cologne, Germany. [12]Department of Psychiatry, University of Münster, Munster, Germany. [13]Department of Psychiatry, Melbourne Medical School, The University of Melbourne, Melbourne, Australia. [14]The Florey Institute of Neuroscience and Mental Health, The University of Melbourne, Parkville, VIC, Australia. [15]Department of Psychiatry, Psychosomatic Medicine and Psychotherapy, University Hospital Frankfurt, Johann Wolfgang Goethe-Universität Frankfurt am Main, Frankfurt am Main, Germany. [16]National Institute of Psychiatry "Ramón de la Fuente Muñiz", Mexico City, Mexico. [17]Child and Adolescent Psychiatry, Helen DeVos Children's Hospital, Michigan State University-CHM, Grand Rapids, MI, USA. [18]Department of Psychiatry, Jawaharlal Nehru Medical College, Datta Meghe Institute of Medical Sciences (Deemed University), Wardha, India. [19]Department of Psychiatry, College of Medicine and Health Sciences, Bahir Dar University, Bahir Dar, Ethiopia. [20]Bipolar Disorder Research Program, Department of Psychiatry, University of São Paulo Medical School, São Paulo, Brazil. [21]Département de Psychiatrie et de Médecine Addictologique, Assistance Publique-Hôpitaux de Paris, INSERM UMR-S1144, Université de Paris, FondaMental Foundation, Paris, France. [22]Professor Emeritus of Psychiatry, Ben Gurion University of the Negev, Beer Sheva, Israel. [23]University Vita-Salute San Raffaele, Milan, Italy. [24]Psychiatry and Clinical Psychobiology, Division of Neuroscience, San Raffaele Scientific Institute, Milan, Italy. [25]Deakin University, IMPACT-The Institute for Mental and Physical Health and Clinical Translation, School of Medicine, Barwon Health, Geelong, Australia. [26]Orygen, The National Centre of Excellence in Youth Mental Health, Centre for Youth Mental Health, Florey Institute for Neuroscience and Mental Health, Department of Psychiatry, The University of Melbourne, Melbourne, Australia. [27]Department of Psychiatry, Faculty of Health Sciences, Beer Sheva Mental Health Center, Ben Gurion University of the Negev, Beer Sheva, Israel. [28]Department of Psychiatry, Baskent University Faculty of Medicine, Ankara, Turkey. [29]Butabika Hospital, Kampala, Uganda. [30]Department of Psychiatry, Trinity College Dublin, St Patrick's University Hospital, Dublin, Ireland. [31]Mood Disorders Clinic, Dr. Jose Horwitz Psychiatric Institute, Santiago de Chile, Chile. [32]Department of Mental Health

and Substance Abuse, Piacenza, Italy. [33]Department of Psychiatry, Chiayi Branch, Taichung Veterans General Hospital, Chiayi, Taiwan. [34]Private Practice, Central, Hong Kong. [35]Department of Psychological Medicine, University of Otago, Christchurch, New Zealand. [36]Department of Molecular Medicine, University of Siena School of Medicine, Siena, Italy. [37]Pine Rest Christian Mental Health Services, Grand Rapids, MI, USA. [38]Department of Psychiatry, University of Melbourne, Parkville, VIC, Australia. [39]Department of Psychiatry and Psychotherapeutic Medicine, Medical University Graz, Graz, Austria. [40]Department of Adult Psychiatry, Poznan University of Medical Sciences, Poznan, Poland. [41]Department of Psychiatry, School of Epidemiology and Public Health, University of Ottawa, Ottawa, ON, Canada. [42]3rd Department of Psychiatry, School of Medicine, Faculty of Health Sciences, Aristotle University of Thessaloniki, Thessaloniki, Greece. [43]Department of Psychiatry and Psychology, Mayo Clinic Depression Center, Mayo Clinic, Rochester, MN, USA. [44]Département de Psychiatrie et d'addictologie, AP-HP, Hopital Bichat-Claude Bernard, Paris, France. [45]GHU Paris-Psychiatry and Neurosciences, 75014 Paris, France. [46]Université de Paris, NeuroDiderot, Inserm, Paris, France. [47]BIOARABA, Department of Psychiatry, University Hospital of Alava, University of the Basque Country, CIBERSAM, Vitoria, Spain. [48]Department of Psychiatry, Feinberg School of Medicine, Northwestern University, Chicago, IL, USA. [49]Mood Disorders Center of Ottawa and the Department of Psychiatry, University of Toronto, Ottawa, Canada. [50]Department of Psychiatry, University Medical Center Groningen, University of Groningen, Groningen, The Netherlands. [51]Department of Psychiatry, Tokyo Metropolitan Matsuzawa Hospital, Setagaya, Tokyo, Japan. [52]Department of Psychiatry, Universidade Federal do Rio Grande do Sul, Porto Alegre, Brazil. [53]Department of Psychiatry, GHU Paris Psychiatrie & Neurosciences, 75014 Paris, France. [54]Université de Paris, 75006 Paris, France. [55]Department of Clinical Research, University of Southern Denmark, Odense, Denmark. [56]Université Paris Est Créteil, INSERM, IMRB, Translational Neuropsychiatry, Fondation FondaMental, 94010 Créteil, France. [57]Université Paris Saclay, CEA, Neurospin, 91191 Gif-sur-Yvette, France. [58]Department of Psychiatry, University of Helsinki and Helsinki University Hospital, Helsinki, Finland. [59]National Institute for Health and Welfare, Helsinki, Finland. [60]University Clinical Center of Serbia, Clinic for Psychiatry, Belgrade, Serbia. [61]Department of Psychiatry, University of Tartu, Tartu, Estonia. [62]Unit for Psychiatric Research, Aalborg University Hospital, Aalborg, Denmark. [63]Department of Psychiatry and Neurochemistry, Institute of Neuroscience and Physiology, The Sahlgrenska Academy, University of Gothenburg, Gothenburg, Sweden. [64]Copenhagen Affective Disorder Research Center (CADIC), Psychiatric Center Copenhagen, Rigshospitalet, Copenhagen, Denmark. [65]Department of Psychiatry, Cheongju Hospital, Cheongju, South Korea. [66]BIPOLAR Zentrum Wiener Neustadt, Wiener Neustadt, Austria. [67]Khanty-Mansiysk Clinical Psychoneurological Hospital, Khanty-Mansiysk, Russia. [68]Department of Neuroscience, Michigan State University, East Lansing, MI, USA. [69]Department of Medical Epidemiology and Biostatistics, Karolinska Institutet, Stockholm, Sweden. [70]Mental Health Department Odense, University Clinic and Department of Regional Health Research, University of Southern Denmark, Esbjerg, Denmark. [71]Psychiatry, Aalborg University Hospital, Aalborg, Denmark. [72]Department of Clinical Medicine, Aalborg University, Aalborg, Denmark. [73]Mood Disorders Program, Hospital Universitario San Vicente Fundación, Research Group in Psychiatry, Department of Psychiatry, Faculty of Medicine, Universidad de Antioquia, Medellín, Colombia. [74]Forensic Psychiatry, University of Glasgow, NHS Greater Glasgow and Clyde, Glasgow, UK. [75]Copenhagen University Hospitals, Psychiatric Centre Copenhagen, Copenhagen, Denmark. [76]Department of Psychiatry, National Institute of Mental Health and Neuro Sciences (NIMHANS), Bengaluru, India. [77]Department of Psychiatry, Faculty of Medicine, Mataram University, Mataram, Indonesia. [78]Department of Pharmacology, Dalhousie University, Halifax, NS, Canada. [79]Section of Psychiatry, Department of Medical Science and Public Health, University of Cagliari, Cagliari, Italy. [80]Unit of Clinical Psychiatry, University Hospital Agency of Cagliari, Cagliari, Italy. [81]Department of Psychiatry, University of Massachusetts Medical School, Worcester, MA, USA. [82]Osakidetza, Basque Health Service, BioAraba Research Institute, University of the Basque Country, Vitoria, Spain. [83]Department of Neuropsychiatry, Keio University School of Medicine, Tokyo, Japan. [84]Department of Psychiatry, Trinity College Institute of Neuroscience, Trinity College Dublin, St Patrick's University Hospital, Dublin, Ireland. [85]Department of General Psychiatry, Mood Disorders Unit, Institute of Mental Health, Singapore City, Singapore. [86]Michigan State University College of Human Medicine, Traverse City Campus, Traverse City, MI, USA. [87]Department of Mental Health, Norwegian University of Science and Technology-NTNU, Trondheim, Norway. [88]Department of Psychiatry, St Olavs' University Hospital, Trondheim, Norway. [89]Soviet Psychoneurological Hospital, Urai, Russia. [90]Department of Psychiatry, University of California San Diego, San Diego, CA, USA. [91]Asha Bipolar Clinic, Asha Hospital, Hyderabad, Telangana, India. [92]Razi Hospital, Faculty of Medicine, University of Tunis-El Manar, Tunis, Tunisia. [93]Affective Disorders Research Project, Tokyo Metropolitan Institute of Medical Science, Setagaya, Tokyo, Japan. [94]Tunisian Bipolar Forum, Érable Médical Cabinet 324, Lac 2, Tunis, Tunisia. [95]Department of Psychiatry, Faculty of Medicine, Siriraj Hospital, Mahidol University, Bangkok, Thailand. [96]Hospital "Ángeles del Pedregal", Mexico City, Mexico. [97]Department of Psychiatry and Psychotherapy, Elblandklinikum Radebeul, Radebeul, Germany. [98]Lucio Bini Mood Disorder Center, Cagliari, Italy. [99]Department of Neurosciences, Mental Health and Sensory Organs, Sant'Andrea Hospital, Sapienza University of Rome, Rome, Italy. [100]Deparment of Psychiatry, Diego Portales University, Santiago de Chile, Chile. [101]SA MRC Genomic and Precision Medicine Research Unit, Division of Human Genetics, Department of Pathology, Institute of Infectious Diseases and Molecular Medicine, University of Cape Town, Cape Town, South Africa. [102]Department of Psychiatry and Behavioral Sciences, Stanford School of Medicine, Palo Alto, CA, USA. [103]Departments of Psychiatry, Epidemiology, and Internal Medicine, Iowa Neuroscience Institute, The University of Iowa, Iowa City, IA, USA. [104]Department of Neuroscience and Mental Health, Federal University of Bahia, Salvador, Brazil. [105]Bipolar Zentrum Wiener Neustadt, Sigmund Freud Privat Universität, Vienna, Austria. [106]Centre for Clinical Brain Sciences, University of Edinburgh, Edinburgh, Scotland, UK. [107]Bipolar Disorder Program, Neuroscience Institute, Favaloro University, Buenos Aires, Argentina. [108]Science Directorate/Climate Science Branch, NASA Langley Research Center, Hampton, VA, USA. [109]Department of Psychiatry, MRC Unit On Risk and Resilience in Mental Disorders, University of Cape Town, Cape Town, South Africa. [110]College of Medicine, China Medical University (CMU), Taichung, Taiwan. [111]An-Nan Hospital, China Medical University, Tainan, Taiwan. [112]Research Division, Institute of Mental Health, Singapore, Singapore. [113]Department of Psychological Medicine, Faculty of Medicine, University of Malaya, Kuala Lumpur, Malaysia. [114]Department of Social Services and Health Care, Psychiatry, City of Helsinki, Helsinki, Finland. [115]Department of Psychiatry, Faculty of Medicine, Hasanuddin University, Makassar, Indonesia. [116]McLean Hospital-Harvard Medical School, Boston, MA, USA. [117]Mood Disorder Lucio Bini Centers, Cagliari e Roma, Italy. [118]Clinical Institute of Neuroscience, Hospital Clinic, University of Barcelona, IDIBAPS, CIBERSAM, Barcelona, Catalonia, Spain. [119]Subdirección de Investigaciones Clínicas, Instituto Nacional de Psiquiatría Ramón de la Fuente Muñíz, Mexico City, Mexico. [120]Department of Psychological Medicine, Institute of Psychiatry, Psychology and Neuroscience, King's College London, London, UK. [121]Department of Psychiatry and Biobehavioral Sciences, Semel Institute for Neuroscience and Human Behavior, University of California Los Angeles (UCLA), Los Angeles, CA, USA.

References

Aarts MP, Brown S, Bueno B, Gjedde A, Mersch D, Münch M, et al. Reinventing daylight. In: Changing perspectives on daylight: Science, technology and culture. Sponsored supplement to Science/AAS; Science/AAAS Custom Publishing Office: Washington, DC, USA, 2017. p. 33–37.

Aguglia A, Serafini G, Escelsior A, Canepa G, Amore M, Maina G. Maximum temperature and solar radiation as predictors of bipolar patient admission in an emergency psychiatric ward. Int J Environ Res Public Health. 2019;16:1140.

AK-IBIS (Alaska Department of Health and Social Services). Complete health indicator report of suicide mortality rate—all ages. 2019. http://ibis.dhss.alaska.gov/indicator/complete_profile/SuicDth.html. Accessed 3 Feb 2021.

Aranda ML, Schmidt TM. Diversity of intrinsically photosensitive retinal ganglion cells: circuits and functions. Cell Mol Life Sci. 2021;78:889–907.

Bachmann S. Epidemiology of suicide and the psychiatric perspective. Int J Environ Res Public Health. 2018;15:1425.

Baldessarini RJ, Tondo L, Vazquez GH, Undurraga J, Bolzani L, Yildiz A, et al. Age at onset versus family history and clinical outcomes in 1,665 international bipolar-I disorder patients. World Psychiatry. 2012;11:40–6.

Bauer M, Glenn T, Alda M, Andreassen OA, Ardau R, Bellivier F, et al. Impact of sunlight on the age of onset of bipolar disorder. Bipolar Disord. 2012;14:654–63.

Bauer M, Glenn T, Alda M, Andreassen OA, Angelopoulos E, Ardau R, et al. Relationship between sunlight and the age of onset of bipolar disorder: an international multisite study. J Affect Disord. 2014;167:104–11.

Bauer M, Glenn T, Alda M, Andreassen OA, Angelopoulos E, Ardau R, et al. Influence of birth cohort on age of onset cluster analysis in bipolar I disorder. Eur Psychiatry. 2015;30:99–105.

Bauer M, Glenn T, Alda M, Aleksandrovich MA, Andreassen OA, Angelopoulos E, et al. Solar insolation in springtime influences age of onset of bipolar I disorder. Acta Psychiatr Scand. 2017;136:571–82.

Bauer M, Glenn T, Alda M, Andreassen OA, Angelopoulos E, Ardau R, et al. Association between solar insolation and a history of suicide attempts in bipolar I disorder. J Psychiatr Res. 2019;113:1–9.

Blader JC, Carlson GA. Increased rates of bipolar disorder diagnoses among US child, adolescent, and adult inpatients, 1996–2004. Biol Psychiatry. 2007;62:107–14.

Bobo WV, Na PJ, Geske JR, McElroy SL, Frye MA, Biernacka JM. The relative influence of individual risk factors for attempted suicide in patients with bipolar I versus bipolar II disorder. J Affect Disord. 2018;225:489–94.

Boyce P, Hunter C. Howlett O (2003) The benefits of daylight through windows. Troy, New York: Rensselaer Polytechnic Institute; 2003.

Cajochen C. Alerting effects of light. Sleep Med Rev. 2007;11:453–64.

Caribé AC, Studart P, Bezerra-Filho S, Brietzke E, Nunes Noto M, Vianna-Sulzbach M, et al. Is religiosity a protective factor against suicidal behavior in bipolar I outpatients? J Affect Disord. 2015;186:156–61.

Carrà G, Bartoli F, Crocamo C, Brady KT, Clerici M. Attempted suicide in people with co-occurring bipolar and substance use disorders: systematic review and meta-analysis. J Affect Disord. 2014;167:125–35.

Chellappa SL. Individual differences in light sensitivity affect sleep and circadian rhythms. Sleep. 2020;44:zsaa214. https://doi.org/10.1093/sleep/zsaa214.

Chengappa KN, Kupfer DJ, Frank E, Houck PR, Grochocinski VJ, Cluss PA, et al. Relationship of birth cohort and early age at onset of illness in a bipolar disorder case registry. Am J Psychiatry. 2003;160:1636–42.

Christodoulou C, Douzenis A, Papadopoulos FC, Papadopoulou A, Bouras G, Gournellis R, et al. Suicide and seasonality. Acta Psychiatr Scand. 2012;125:127–46.

Chung RY, Yip BH, Chan SS, Wong SY. Cohort effects of suicide mortality are sex specific in the rapidly developed Hong Kong Chinese population, 1976–2010. Depress Anxiety. 2016;33:558–66.

CIA. The World Factbook. 2020. https://www.cia.gov/the-world-factbook/. Accessed 3 Feb 2021.

Coimbra DG, Pereira E, Silva PEAC, de Sousa-Rodrigues CF, Barbosa FT, de Siqueira Figueredo D, et al. Do suicide attempts occur more frequently in the spring too? A systematic review and rhythmic analysis. J Affect Disord. 2016;196:125–37.

Davis GE, Lowell WE. Evidence that latitude is directly related to variation in suicide rates. Can J Psychiatry. 2002;47:572–4.

Dervic K, Carballo JJ, Baca-Garcia E, Galfalvy HC, Mann JJ, Brent DA, et al. Moral or religious objections to suicide may protect against suicidal behavior in bipolar disorder. J Clin Psychiatry. 2011;72:1390–6.

Dong M, Lu L, Zhang L, Zhang Q, Ungvari GS, Ng CH, et al. Prevalence of suicide attempts in bipolar disorder: a systematic review and meta-analysis of observational studies. Epidemiol Psychiatr Sci. 2019;29:e63.

Eskin M, Baydar N, El-Nayal M, Asad N, Noor IM, Rezaeian M, et al. Associations of religiosity, attitudes towards suicide and religious coping with suicidal ideation and suicide attempts in 11 muslim countries. Soc Sci Med. 2020;265:113390.

Fisk AS, Tam SKE, Brown LA, Vyazovskiy VV, Bannerman DM, Peirson SN. Light and cognition: roles for circadian rhythms, sleep, and arousal. Front Neurol. 2018;9:56.

Foster RG, Hughes S, Peirson SN. Circadian photoentrainment in mice and humans. Biology (basel). 2020;9:180.

Galvão PVM, Silva HRSE, Silva CMFPD. Temporal distribution of suicide mortality: a systematic review. J Affect Disord. 2018;228:132–42.

Geoffroy PA. Clock genes and light signaling alterations in bipolar disorder: when the biological clock is off. Biol Psychiatry. 2018;84:775–7.

Geoffroy PA, Palagini L. Biological rhythms and chronotherapeutics in depression. Prog Neuropsychopharmacol Biol Psychiatry. 2021;106:110158.

Geoffroy PA, Bellivier F, Scott J, Etain B. Seasonality and bipolar disorder: a systematic review, from admission rates to seasonality of symptoms. J Affect Disord. 2014;168:210–23.

Gonzalez R. The relationship between bipolar disorder and biological rhythms. J Clin Psychiatry. 2014;75:e323–31.

Gottlieb JF, Benedetti F, Geoffroy PA, Henriksen TEG, Lam RW, Murray G, et al. The chronotherapeutic treatment of bipolar disorders: a systematic review and practice recommendations from the ISBD task force on chronotherapy and chronobiology. Bipolar Disord. 2019;21:741–73.

Grant BF, Stinson FS, Dawson DA, Chou SP, Dufour MC, Compton W, et al. Prevalence and co-occurrence of substance use disorders and independent mood and anxiety disorders: results from the National Epidemiologic Survey on Alcohol and Related Conditions. Arch Gen Psychiatry. 2004;61:807–16.

Gunnell D, Middleton N, Whitley E, Dorling D, Frankel S. Influence of cohort effects on patterns of suicide in England and Wales, 1950–1999. Br J Psychiatry. 2003;182:164–70.

Haans A. The natural preference in people's appraisal of light. J Environ Psychol. 2014;39:51–61.

Hansson C, Joas E, Pålsson E, Hawton K, Runeson B, Landén M. Risk factors for suicide in bipolar disorder: a cohort study of 12 850 patients. Acta Psychiatr Scand. 2018;138:456–63.

Harvey AG. Sleep and circadian rhythms in bipolar disorder: seeking synchrony, harmony, and regulation. Am J Psychiatry. 2008;165:820–9.

Hunt GE, Malhi GS, Cleary M, Lai HM, Sitharthan T. Comorbidity of bipolar and substance use disorders in national surveys of general populations, 1990–2015: systematic review and meta-analysis. J Affect Disord. 2016;206:321–30.

Jacob L, Haro JM, Koyanagi A. The association of religiosity with suicidal ideation and suicide attempts in the United Kingdom. Acta Psychiatr Scand. 2019;139:164–73.

Jee HJ, Cho CH, Lee YJ, Choi N, An H, Lee HJ. Solar radiation increases suicide rate after adjusting for other climate factors in South Korea. Acta Psychiatr Scand. 2017;135:219–27.

Jones SG, Benca RM. Circadian disruption in psychiatric disorders. Sleep Med Clin. 2015;10:481–93.

Kalman JL, Papiol S, Forstner AJ, Heilbronner U, Degenhardt F, Strohmaier J, et al. Investigating polygenic burden in age at disease onset in bipolar disorder: findings from an international multicentric study. Bipolar Disord. 2019;21:68–75.

Ketchesin KD, Becker-Krail D, McClung CA. Mood-related central and peripheral clocks. Eur J Neurosci. 2020;51:326–45.

Knoop M, Stefani O, Bueno B, Matusiak B, Hobday R, Wirz-Justice A, et al. Daylight: what makes the difference? Light Res Technol. 2020;52:423–42.

Kummu M, Varis O. The world by latitudes: a global analysis of human population, development level and environment across the north–south axis over the past half century. Appl Geogr. 2011;31:495–507.

Kwon JW, Chun H, Cho SI. A closer look at the increase in suicide rates in South Korea from 1986–2005. BMC Public Health. 2009;9:72.

LeGates TA, Fernandez DC, Hattar S. Light as a central modulator of circadian rhythms, sleep and affect. Nat Rev Neurosci. 2014;15:443–54.

Li F, Forbes AB, Turner EL, Preisser JS. Power and sample size requirements for GEE analyses of cluster randomized crossover trials. Stat Med. 2019;38:636–49.

Logan RW, McClung CA. Rhythms of life: circadian disruption and brain disorders across the lifespan. Nat Rev Neurosci. 2019;20:49–65.

Maruani J, Anderson G, Etain B, Lejoyeux M, Bellivier F, Geoffroy PA. The neurobiology of adaptation to seasons: relevance and correlations in bipolar disorders. Chronobiol Int. 2018;35:1335–53.

McCarthy MJ. Missing a beat: assessment of circadian rhythm abnormalities in bipolar disorder in the genomic era. Psychiatr Genet. 2019;29:29–36.

McClung CA. How might circadian rhythms control mood? Let me count the ways. Biol Psychiatry. 2013;74:242–9.

McGlashan EM, Poudel GR, Vidafar P, Drummond SPA, Cain SW. Imaging individual differences in the response of the human suprachiasmatic area to light. Front Neurol. 2018;9:1022.

Melo MCA, Abreu RLC, Linhares Neto VB, de Bruin PFC, de Bruin VMS. Chronotype and circadian rhythm in bipolar disorder: a systematic review. Sleep Med Rev. 2017;34:46–58.

Morselli PL, Elgie R. GAMIAN-Europe. GAMIAN-Europe/BEAM survey I-global analysis of a patient questionnaire circulated to 3450 members of 12 European advocacy groups operating in the field of mood disorders. Bipolar Disord. 2003;5:265–78.

Müller H, Biermann T, Renk S, Reulbach U, Ströbel A, Kornhuber J, et al. Higher environmental temperature and global radiation are correlated with increasing suicidality—a localized data analysis. Chronobiol Int. 2011;28:949–57.

Münch M, Brøndsted AE, Brown SA, Gjedde A, Kantermann T, Martiny K, et al. The effect of light on humans. In: Changing perspectives on daylight: Science, technology and culture. Sponsored supplement to Science/AAS; Science/AAAS Custom Publishing Office: Washington, DC, USA, 2017. pp. 16–23.

Münch M, Wirz-Justice A, Brown SA, Kantermann T, Martiny K, Stefani O, et al. The role of daylight for humans: gaps in current knowledge. Clocks Sleep. 2020;2:61–85.

NASA. NASA Power. Solar Data Overview. 2020. https://power.larc.nasa.gov/docs/methodology/solar/ Accessed 3 Feb 2021.

Nesvåg R, Knudsen GP, Bakken IJ, Høye A, Ystrom E, Surén P, et al. Substance use disorders in schizophrenia, bipolar disorder, and depressive illness: a registry-based study. Soc Psychiatry Psychiatr Epidemiol. 2015;50:1267–76.

Nock MK, Borges G, Bromet EJ, Cha CB, Kessler RC, Lee S. Suicide and suicidal behavior. Epidemiol Rev. 2008;30:133–54.

Norström T, Rossow I. Alcohol consumption as a risk factor for suicidal behavior: a systematic review of associations at the individual and at the population level. Arch Suicide Res. 2016;20:489–506.

Odagiri Y, Uchida H, Nakano M. Gender differences in age, period, and birth-cohort effects on the suicide mortality rate in Japan, 1985–2006. Asia Pac J Public Health. 2011;23:581–7.

Oladunjoye AO, Oladunjoye OO, Ayeni OA, Olubiyi O, Fuchs A, Gurski J, et al. Seasonal trends in hospitalization of attempted suicide and self-inflicted injury in United States adults. Cureus. 2020;12:e10830.

Østergaard MLD, Nordentoft M, Hjorthøj C. Associations between substance use disorders and suicide or suicide attempts in people with mental illness: a Danish nation-wide, prospective, register-based study of patients diagnosed with schizophrenia, bipolar disorder, unipolar depression or personality disorder. Addiction. 2017;112:1250–9.

Page A, Milner A, Morrell S, Taylor R. The role of under-employment and unemployment in recent birth cohort effects in Australian suicide. Soc Sci Med. 2013;93:155–62.

Pan W. Akaike's information criterion in generalized estimating equations. Biometrics. 2001;57:120–5.

Papadopoulos FC, Frangakis CE, Skalkidou A, Petridou E, Stevens RG, Trichopoulos D. Exploring lag and duration effect of sunshine in triggering suicide. J Affect Disord. 2005;88:287–97.

Paul S, Brown T. Direct effects of the light environment on daily neuroendocrine control. J Endocrinol. 2019 Aug 1:JOE-19-0302.R1.

Petridou E, Papadopoulos FC, Frangakis CE, Skalkidou A, Trichopoulos D. A role of sunshine in the triggering of suicide. Epidemiology. 2002;13:106–9.

Pew Research Center, Oct. 3, 2017, "Many countries favor specific religions, officially or unofficially". http://www.pewforum.org/2017/10/03/many-countries-favor-specific-religions-officially-or-unofficially/ Accessed 3 Feb 2021.

Phillips JA. A changing epidemiology of suicide? The influence of birth cohorts on suicide rates in the United States. Soc Sci Med. 2014;114:151–60.

Phillips AJK, Vidafar P, Burns AC, McGlashan EM, Anderson C, Rajaratnam SMW, et al. High sensitivity and interindividual variability in the response of the human circadian system to evening light. Proc Natl Acad Sci USA. 2019;116:12019–24.

Plans L, Barrot C, Nieto E, Rios J, Schulze TG, Papiol S, et al. Association between completed suicide and bipolar disorder: a systematic review of the literature. J Affect Disord. 2019;242:111–22.

Pollock NJ, Apok C, Concepcion T, Delgado RA Jr, Rasmus S, Chatwood S, et al. Global goals and suicide prevention in the Circumpolar North. Indian J Psychiatry. 2020;62:7–14.

Pompili M, Gonda X, Serafini G, Innamorati M, Sher L, Amore M, et al. Epidemiology of suicide in bipolar disorders: a systematic review of the literature. Bipolar Disord. 2013;15:457–90.

Postolache TT, Mortensen PB, Tonelli LH, Jiao X, Frangakis C, Soriano JJ, et al. Seasonal spring peaks of suicide in victims with and without prior history of hospitalization for mood disorders. J Affect Disord. 2010;121:88–93.

Prayag AS, Münch M, Aeschbach D, Chellappa SL, Gronfier C. Light modulation of human clocks, wake, and sleep. Clocks Sleep. 2019;1:193–208.

Roshanaei-Moghaddam B, Katon W. Premature mortality from general medical illnesses among persons with bipolar disorder: a review. Psychiatr Serv. 2009;60:147–56.

Ruuhela R, Hiltunen L, Venäläinen A, Pirinen P, Partonen T. Climate impact on suicide rates in Finland from 1971 to 2003. Int J Biometeorol. 2009;53:167–75.

Schaffer A, Isometsä ET, Tondo L, Moreno H, D, Turecki G, Reis C, , et al. International Society for Bipolar Disorders Task Force on Suicide: meta-analyses and meta-regression of correlates of suicide attempts and suicide deaths in bipolar disorder. Bipolar Disord. 2015;17:1–16.

Schwartz PJ. Chris Cornell, the black hole sun, and the seasonality of suicide. Neuropsychobiology. 2019;78:38–47.

Stack S, Kposowa AJ. Religion and suicide acceptability: a cross-national analysis. J Sci Study Relig. 2011;50:289–306.

Stackhouse, PW Jr, Zhang T, Westberg D, Barnett AJ, Bristow T, Macpherson B, Hoell JM. NASA POWER (Prediction of Worldwide Energy Resources). Release 8.01 (with GIS Applications) Methodology (Data Parameters, Sources, & Validation). 2018 https://power.larc.nasa.gov. Accessed 3 Feb 2021.

Su MK, Chan PY, Hoffman RS. The seasonality of suicide attempts: a single poison control center perspective. Clin Toxicol (phila). 2020;58:1034–41.

Takaesu Y. Circadian rhythm in bipolar disorder: a review of the literature. Psychiatry Clin Neurosci. 2018;72:673–82.

Tidemalm D, Haglund A, Karanti A, Landén M, Runeson B. Attempted suicide in bipolar disorder: risk factors in a cohort of 6086 patients. PLoS ONE. 2014;9:e94097.

Toftdahl NG, Nordentoft M, Hjorthøj C. Prevalence of substance use disorders in psychiatric patients: a nationwide Danish population-based study. Soc Psychiatry Psychiatr Epidemiol. 2016;51:129–40.

Tondo L, Pompili M, Forte A, Baldessarini RJ. Suicide attempts in bipolar disorders: comprehensive review of 101 reports. Acta Psychiatr Scand. 2016;133:174–86.

Tondo L, Vázquez GH, Baldessarini RJ. Prevention of suicidal behavior in bipolar disorder. Bipolar Disord. 2021;23:14–23.

Turner PL, Mainster MA. Circadian photoreception: ageing and the eye's important role in systemic health. Br J Ophthalmol. 2008;92:1439–44.

Twenge JM, Cooper AB, Joiner TE, Duffy ME, Binau SG. Age, period, and cohort trends in mood disorder indicators and suicide-related outcomes in a nationally representative dataset, 2005–2017. J Abnorm Psychol. 2019;128:185–99.

UN. Gender Inequality Index (GII). 2020. http://hdr.undp.org/en/content/gender-inequality-index-gii Accessed 3 Feb 2021.

VanderWeele TJ, Li S, Tsai AC, Kawachi I. Association between religious service attendance and lower suicide rates among US women. JAMA Psychiat. 2016;73:845–51.

Walker WH 2nd, Walton JC, DeVries AC, Nelson RJ. Circadian rhythm disruption and mental health. Transl Psychiatry. 2020;10:28.

Wang S, Zhang Z, Yao L, Ding N, Jiang L, Wu Y. Bright light therapy in the treatment of patients with bipolar disorder: a systematic review and meta-analysis. PLoS ONE. 2020;15:e0232798.

Webler FS, Spitschan M, Foster RG, Andersen M, Peirson SN. What is the 'spectral diet' of humans? Curr Opin Behav Sci. 2019;30:80–6.

WHO. Hsuman resources data by country. 2019a. https://apps.who.int/gho/data/node.main.MHHR?lang=en. Accessed 3 Feb 2021.

WHO. WHO Urbanization. 2019b https://ourworldindata.org/urbanization Accessed 3 Feb 2021.

Wild M. Enlightening global dimming and brightening. Bull Am Meteor Soc. 2012;93:27–37.

Wirz-Justice A, Benedetti F. Perspectives in affective disorders: clocks and sleep. Eur J Neurosci. 2020;51:346–65.

Wirz-Justice A, Skene DJ, Münch M. The relevance of daylight for humans. Biochem Pharmacol. 2020;28: 114304. https://doi.org/10.1016/j.bcp.2020.114304.

Woo JM, Okusaga O, Postolache TT. Seasonality of suicidal behavior. Int J Environ Res Public Health. 2012;9:531–47.

World Bank. Gini Index (World Bank estimate). 2020a. https://data.worldbank.org/indicator/SI.POV.GINI. Accessed 3 Feb 2021.

World Bank. Individuals using the Internet (% of population). 2020b. https://data.worldbank.org/indicator/IT.NET.USER.ZS. Accessed 3 Feb 2021.

Wu A, Wang JY, Jia CX. Religion and completed suicide: a meta-analysis. PLoS ONE. 2015;10:e0131715.

Young TK, Revich B, Soininen L. Suicide in circumpolar regions: an introduction and overview. Int J Circumpolar Health. 2015;74:27349.

Yu B, Chen X. Age and birth cohort-adjusted rates of suicide mortality among us male and female youths aged 10 to 19 years from 1999 to 2017. JAMA Netw Open. 2019;2:e1911383.

Yuodelis-Flores C, Ries RK. Addiction and suicide: a review. Am J Addict. 2015;24:98–104.

Zeger SL, Liang KY. Longitudinal data analysis for discrete and continuous outcomes. Biometrics. 1986;42:121–30.

10

Patients' adherence to smartphone apps in the management of bipolar disorder

Marie-Camille Patoz[1], Diego Hidalgo-Mazzei[2], Bruno Pereira[1], Olivier Blanc[1], Ingrid de Chazeron[1], Andrea Murru[2], Norma Verdolini[2], Isabella Pacchiarotti[2], Eduard Vieta[2], Pierre-Michel Llorca[1,3] and Ludovic Samalin[1,3,4*]

Abstract

Background: Despite an increasing number of available mental health apps in the bipolar disorder field, these tools remain scarcely implemented in everyday practice and are quickly discontinued by patients after downloading. The aim of this study is to explore adherence characteristics of bipolar disorder patients to dedicated smartphone interventions in research studies.

Methods: A systematic review following PRISMA guidelines was conducted. Three databases (EMBASE, PsychInfo and MEDLINE) were searched using the following keywords: "bipolar disorder" or "mood disorder" or "bipolar" combined with "digital" or "mobile" or "phone" or "smartphone" or "mHealth" or "ehealth" or "mobile health" or "app" or "mobile-health".

Results: Thirteen articles remained in the review after exclusion criteria were applied. Of the 118 eligible studies, 39 did not provide adherence characteristics. Among the selected papers, study length, sample size and definition of measures of adherence were strongly heterogeneous. Activity rates ranged from 58 to 91.6%.

Conclusion: The adherence of bipolar patients to apps is understudied. Standardised measures of adherence should be defined and systematically evaluated in future studies dedicated to these tools.

Keywords: Smartphone, Mobile application, Bipolar disorder, Systematic review

Introduction

With a lifetime prevalence rate of more than 2% (Merikangas et al. 2007), bipolar disorder (BD) is a common and disabling chronic disease (Pini et al. 2005). BD is characterised by successive mood episodes separated by inter-episodic periods often associated with residual symptoms and poor functioning (Samalin et al. 2014; Murru et al. 2018). The management of BD could be facilitated by the exponential spread of smartphone apps, (Carson et al. 2016) which are easy and useful tools to monitor both subjective and objective mental health status in ecological momentary conditions (Myin-Germeys et al. 2016; Depp et al. 2015; Wenze et al. 2014; Moore et al. 2016) and to provide adjunctive psychosocial interventions (Hollis et al. 2015).

However, despite an increasing number of available mental health apps (Firth et al. 2016) and significant interest from patients (Ben-Zeev et al. 2013) and therapists (Kerst et al. 2019), these tools remain scarcely implemented in everyday practice (Kerst et al. 2019). Furthermore, like any app, mental health apps are quickly discontinued by patients after downloading (Bauer et al.

*Correspondence: lsamalin@chu-clermontferrand.fr
[1] Department of Psychiatry, CHU Clermont-Ferrand, University of Clermont Auvergne, CNRS, Clermont Auvergne INP, Institut Pascal, Clermont-Ferrand, France
Full list of author information is available at the end of the article

2020; Torous et al. 2020). A recent review of digital self-help apps or programmes for depression and anxiety reported that 7–42% of participants continued to actively use the app after 4 weeks but only 0.5–28.6% after 6 weeks (Torous et al. 2020). Despite promising results regarding their interest in the treatment of depression (Kerst et al. 2019) and BD (Depp et al. 2015), the failure of smartphone apps to maintain patient adherence over time could be a major barrier to their implementation in mental healthcare. The low number of scientifically validated apps available on app stores, resulting in a lack of trust from users, and the lack of user-centric designs have often been cited as explanations for this low adherence to apps (Torous et al. 2018; Nicholas et al. 2017). Their integration in therapy has also been described as an important factor in adherence, with higher adherence to adjunctive apps being observed than to unguided ones (Eysenbach 2005; Baumeister et al. 2014). Furthermore, most of the studies reporting positive results do not report adherence, leaving an inaccurate measure of patients receiving or not the intervention, for how long and with which frequency. Thus, a placebo effect cannot be discarded.

An under-studied topic in itself, adherence to smartphone apps have nevertheless been evaluated in several reviews in the field of mental health (Ng et al. 2019; Batra et al. 2017) and depression (Torous et al. 2020; Fleming et al. 2018). To the best of our knowledge, this work has not specifically examined BD, nor has any systematic review been published focused on the adherence characteristics of patients to smartphone apps.

Aims of the study

In this systematic review, we explore the adherence characteristics of bipolar disorder patients to dedicated smartphone interventions in research studies.

Methods

This review was conducted in accordance with the Preferred Reporting Items for Systematic Reviews and Meta-Analyses (PRISMA). It has been registered in PROSPERO (CRD42020218984).

Literature search

A search of the electronic databases MEDLINE, PsycINFO and Embase was conducted to identify peer-reviewed English and French language articles published between January 1st, 2008 and August 1st, 2020. We chose not to include articles published prior to 2008 as this was the year the first app store was released. The existence of articles concerning mental health apps before this date seemed unlikely.

The search terms were designed to capture any smartphone intervention targeting BD patients: ("bipolar disorder" OR "mood disorder" or bipolar) AND (digital OR mobile OR phone OR smartphone OR mHealth OR ehealth OR "mobile health" OR app OR mobile-health).

Study selection process

Articles were included if:

- They included patients with a BD diagnosis
- They involved the delivery of an intervention or collection of data via a smartphone app or a personal digital assistant (PDA), with or without an associated wearable device
- They were randomised or non-randomised trials, with or without a control group, pilot or feasibility studies
- They measured and described the adherence characteristics to the studied app
- They either included or did not include face-to-face therapy in combination with the app intervention

Articles were excluded if:

- They were reviews, commentaries, qualitative studies, conference reports or protocols
- They did not focus on technologies or the disorder of interest (*i.e.* a mobile phone app or PDA and BD)
- They only involved screening or diagnostic tools
- The intervention was only based on SMS
- They discussed data reported in a previous study
- They reported preliminary results only

Data extraction

We utilised a data extraction template developed for this systematic review for the extraction of the following characteristics and data:

- Article reference details and year of publication
- Study characteristics: study design, primary outcomes, study length and main findings.
- Sample characteristics: sample size, mean age, % of female participants, % of participants with BD type 1, clinical state, mean depression and manic scores at baseline.
- Intervention details: name, version and type of app, type of phone used by participants (personal or loaned), existence of notifications, psychoeducation, collection of passive data and feedback, number of sessions (corresponding to one or more items evalu-

ated by the app through questions or tests) a day and number of items actively evaluated in a session.
- Adherence characteristics: activity rate (number of sessions initiated by the patient on the total number of available sessions during the study; when the study protocol included one session a day, the activity rate was then defined as the number of days the patient started a session on the total number of days in the study); completion rate (number of days with a fully completed session on the total number of days in the study); median or mean of use (median or mean time before the patient discontinues the use of the app); retention rate (number of patients still actively using the app at a given time).

Adherence is a generic term that can encompass several aspects. If studies displayed terms as "mean adherence", "compliance rate" or "adherence rate" without providing any definition, we wrote to the corresponding authors for more details. Where the definition of these terms remained unclear, we gathered them under the broad term "undefined adherence characteristics".

Furthermore, to obtain comparable data, we had to discern whether the adherence characteristics were calculated relative to all patients or to active patients only. When this information could not be found in the published paper, we wrote to the corresponding authors for more details. In the event the authors did not reply, we considered that adherence characteristics were calculated relative to all patients, including inactive ones.

When studies included populations with control groups, we selected only data and outcomes regarding BD patients in experimental groups using the studied app.

Statistical analysis

Statistical analysis was performed with Comprehensive Meta-analysis software (Borenstein et al. 2020). To address the non-independence of data due to studies effect, random-effects model using the method of DerSimonian & Laird (with study as random-effect) was performed to estimate mean and standard-deviation (SD) of age of participants in the included studies taking into account the between- and within-study variability (DerSimonian and Laird 2015).

Methodological quality assessment

The quality of each included study was assessed by two independent authors (LS and MCP) using the NIH study Quality Assessment Tools (National Institute of Health 2021). The tool used was adapted to each study design (Quality Assessment of Controlled Intervention Studies, Quality Assessment Tool for Observational Cohort and Cross-Sectional Studies and Quality Assessment Tool for Before-After (Pre-Post) Studies With No Control Group) Discrepancies between the two raters were solved by discussion between them until a consensus was reached.

Results

The search retrieved 1717 records after duplicates were removed. Among them, 228 abstracts were assessed for eligibility and 110 were excluded. A full-text review of the 118 remaining articles was conducted. A total of 13 studies were included in the review (Depp et al. 2015; Wenze et al. 2014, 2016; Faurholt-Jepsen et al. 2014, 2015, 2020; Til et al. 2020; Hidalgo-Mazzei et al. 2016, 2018; Beiwinkel et al. 2016; Tsanas et al. 2016; Stanislaus et al. 2020; Schwartz et al. 2016). The most common reasons for exclusion in the full text article stage were that no adherence characteristics to the studied app were found in the article (n = 39) or that a non-eligible intervention was reported (n = 26). Figure 1 is a flow-chart of the considered and ultimately selected studies, following the PRISMA statements.

Characteristics of included studies and patient populations

The characteristics of the 13 included studies are summarised in Table 1. They were conducted in the United States (Depp et al. 2015; Wenze et al. 2014, 2016; Til et al. 2020; Schwartz et al. 2016), Denmark (Faurholt-Jepsen et al. 2014, 2015, 2020; Stanislaus et al. 2020), England (Tsanas et al. 2016), Spain (Hidalgo-Mazzei et al. 2016), Germany (Beiwinkel et al. 2016) and in spanish language countries (Hidalgo-Mazzei et al. 2018). Among them, three were randomised controlled trials (Depp et al. 2015; Faurholt-Jepsen et al. 2020; Til et al. 2020) and 10 were non randomized studies (Wenze et al. 2014, 2016; Faurholt-Jepsen et al. 2015, 2014; Hidalgo-Mazzei et al. 2016, 2018; Tsanas et al. 2016; Stanislaus et al. 2020; Schwartz et al. 2016). Among the non randomized studies, four were feasibility studies (Wenze et al. 2014, 2016; Hidalgo-Mazzei et al. 2016, 2018) and two were pilot studies (Faurholt-Jepsen et al. 2014; Beiwinkel et al. 2016). Study lengths ranged from 14 to 800 days, with a mean of 213.1 days (SD: 215.3),just over half of the studies (7/13) lasted 6 months or more (Depp et al. 2015; Faurholt-Jepsen et al. 2015, 2020, 2015; Hidalgo-Mazzei et al. 2018; Beiwinkel et al. 2016; Stanislaus et al. 2020).

The quality assessment of the studies included in this systematic review outlines a wide heterogeneity in studies design, populations and outcomes see Additional File 1, 2, 3, Five studies were rated with poor quality because of the small number of participants enrolled (Wenze et al. 2014, 2016; Faurholt-Jepsen et al. 2014; Beiwinkel et al. 2016; Schwartz et al. 2016). Six studies were rated with fair quality (Faurholt-Jepsen et al. 2015; Til et al.

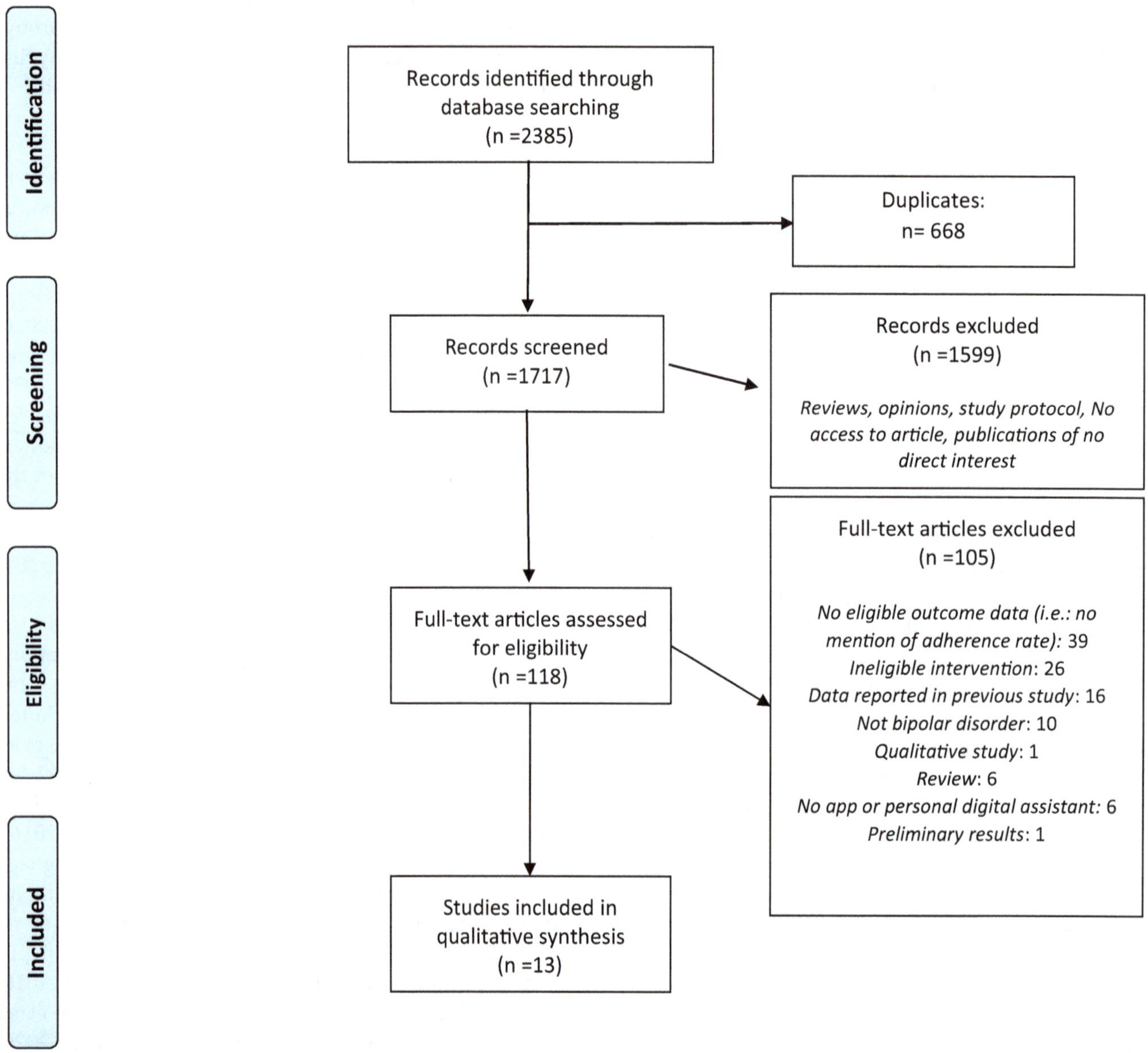

Fig. 1 Prisma flowchart

2020; Hidalgo-Mazzei et al. 2016, 2018; Tsanas et al. 2016; Stanislaus et al. 2020) and 2 were rated with good quality (Depp et al. 2015; Faurholt-Jepsen et al. 2020).

The characteristics of the included patients are summarised in Table 2. They suffered from type 1, 2 or unspecified BD. One study included participants with at least moderate depression and mania (score ≥ 11 on the Quick Inventory of Depressive Symptoms (QIDS-C33) and/or ≥ 16 on the Clinician-Administered Rating Scale for Mania (CARS-M34)) (Wenze et al. 2016), three studies included only euthymic patients, (Depp et al. 2015; Faurholt-Jepsen et al. 2015; Hidalgo-Mazzei et al. 2016) 1 included patients that could be in any mood state at the time of enrolment (Schwartz et al. 2016) and 8 studies did not specify if the participants were euthymic or not (Wenze et al. 2014; Faurholt-Jepsen et al. 2020, 2014; Til et al. 2020; Hidalgo-Mazzei et al. 2018; Beiwinkel et al. 2016; Tsanas et al. 2016; Stanislaus et al. 2020). Participants were predominantly female (n = 481, 62.4%), with a mean age of 39.9 (Inter Quartile Range (IQR): 35.6-44.3,Fig. 2.

Three studies mentioned retribution for participants, among which 1 paid patients for the time they spent on the study (Depp et al. 2015) and two gave compensation for each session completed (Wenze et al. 2014, 2016).

Table 1 Study characteristics

Author, year, location	Study design	Primary outcome	Study length (Weeks)	Main findings	Additional intervention
Van Til et al.; 2020, US (Til et al. 2020)	Randomised Control Trial	To identify how to best engage individuals with BD in monitoring their symptoms using mobile and wearable technology	6	No statistical difference in adherence between the two groups (passive and active monitoring)	
Faurholt-Jepsen et al.; 2020, Denmark (Faurholt-Jepsen et al. 2020)	Randomised Control Trial	To assess the effect of smartphone-based monitoring and mood prediction on depressive and manic symptoms in patients with BD	36	No differences between the intervention group and the control group in levels of depressive and manic symptoms	
Depp et al.; 2015; US (Depp et al. 2015)	Randomised Control Trial	To assess the effect of the PRISM programme on depressive symptoms using an app or paper and pencil in patients with BD	24	Significant effect on depressive symptoms, greater in the app group compared to the paper and pencil group	In-person psycho-educational programme associated with the use of the app
Stanislaus et al.; 2020, Denmark (Stanislaus et al. 2020)	Observational	To compare frequency of mood instability between BD patients and healthy control using a smartphone app	Up to 800 days	Mood instability score was statistically significantly higher for patients with BD compared with HC	
Hidalgo-Mazzei et al.; 2018, Spanish language countries (Hidalgo-Mazzei et al. 2018)	Observational, Feasibility study	To evaluate the long-term retention, usability, perceived helpfulness, and satisfaction among the first 201 users of the SIMPLE programme	24	More than 30% of the participants continued to use the programme after 6 months. Positive outcomes regarding satisfaction, usability, and perceived helpfulness	
Tsanas et al.; 2016, UK (Tsanas et al. 2016)	Observational	To introduce and validate a novel clinical questionnaire used for daily mood monitoring of BD and borderline personality disorder patients as part of a smartphone application	12 to 48	Daily MZ items of negative mood correlated highly with the clinical scores. Correlations were weaker between the daily ratings of positive mood clinical scores	
Schwartz et al., 2016, US (Schwartz et al. 2016)	Observational	To measure completion rates of surveys of mood symptoms on smartphone in BD and healthy control participants	2	Median completion rates did not differ between groups	
Wenze et al.; 2016; US (Wenze et al. 2016)	Observational, Feasibility study	To assess feasibility and acceptability of a 12-week adjunctive, smartphone assisted intervention to improve treatment adherence in bipolar disorder	12	Average Credibility and Expectancy Scale total score was 42.13 (SD = 9.64) out of a possible total of 54. Good adherence to the intervention overall. High satisfaction in qualitative feedbacks	In-person psycho-educational programme associated with the use of the app
Hidalgo-Mazzei et al.; 2016; Spain (Hidalgo-Mazzei et al. 2016)	Observational, Feasibility study	To evaluate acceptability, safety, and satisfaction of the simple app	12	The SIMPLe app represents a satisfactory and acceptable instrument as an add-on to the usual treatment	

Table 1 (continued)

Author, year, location	Study design	Primary outcome	Study length (Weeks)	Main findings	Additional intervention
Beiwinkel et al.; 2016; Germany (Beiwinkel et al. 2016)	Observational, Pilot study	To investigate whether smartphone data predict impending clinical symptoms in bipolar disorder	48	Self-reported mood was found to predict depressive symptom levels above the clinical threshold but not manic symptoms	
Faurholt-Jepsen et al.; 2015; Denmark (Faurholt-Jepsen et al. 2015)	Observational	To determine indicator of illness activity to investigate differences between Bipolar 1 and Bipolar II patients using smartphone self-monitoring	24 or more,	Patients with Bipolar II experienced more severe depressive symptoms and spent almost half of their time with depressive symptoms whereas patients with Bipolar I were euthymic during 75% of their time	
Wenze et al. 2014, US (Wenze et al. 2014)	Observational, Feasibility study	To establish the feasibility and acceptability of using mobile technology to target adherence in BD	2	Participants voiced satisfaction with study procedures. Adherence with EMI sessions was high	
Faurholt -Jepsen et al.; 2014, Denmark (Faurholt-Jepsen et al. 2014)	Observational, Pilot study	To investigate possible correlations between clinically rated depressive and manic symptoms of bipolar disorder and subjective and objective smartphone data	12	Increasing depressive symptoms correlated with decreasing amounts of movement per day. No correlation between smartphone measures and manic symptoms identified	

BD Bipolar disorder, *HC* Healthy control, *SD* Standard deviation, *EMI* Ecological momentary intervention

Table 2 Population characteristics

Reference study	Sample size N	Mean age, Years (SD)	FemaleN (%)	BD type 1 N (%)	Clinical state	Depression score at baseline (SD)	Manic score at baseline (SD)
Til et al. (2020)	47	41.9 (10.8)	25 (53.1)	32 (68.0)	NS	NS	NS
Faurholt-Jepsen et al. (2020)	85	43.0 (12.4)	52 (61.2)	54 (63.5)	NS	NS	NS
Depp et al. (2015)	41	46.9 (11.8)	22 (53.7)	36 (87.8)	Euthymic	MADRS: 11.7 (Moore et al. 2016)	YMRS: 7.4 (Myin-Germeys et al. 2016)
Stanislaus et al. (2020)	203	28.0 [24-35] *	140 (69.0)	68 (33.5)	NS	HAMD17: 9 [5-15] †	YMRS: 2 [0-7][a]
Hidalgo-Mazzei et al. (2018)	201	36.6 (Firth et al. 2016)	127 (63.2)	NS	NS	NS	NS
Tsanas et al. (2016)	48	38.0 (Ng et al. 2019)	32 (66.7)	NS	NS	NS	NS
Schwartz et al. (2016)	10	48.9 (16.8)	7 (70.0)	10 (100)	Any mood state	NS	NS
Wenze et al. (2016)	8	44.0 (11.6)	5 (62.5)	5 (62.5)	At least moderate depression or mania	QIDS-C 15.2 (3.2)	CARS-M 7.2 (4.3)
Hidalgo-Mazzei et al. (2016)	51	43.9 (11.4)	21 (42.9)	33 (67.3)	Euthymic	HAMD-17: 3.2	YMRS: 2.1 (2.6)
Beiwinkel et al. (2016)	13	47.2 (3.8)	5 (38.5)	6 (46.1)	NS	NS	NS
Faurholt-Jepsen et al. (2015)	33	29.1 (7.4)	23 (71.0)	20 (60.6)	Euthymic	HAMD: 9 [4-16][a]	YMRS: 2 [0–7]
Wenze et al. (2014)	14	40.9 (12.1)	10 (71.4)	5 (35.7)	NS	QIDS: 12.5 (4.0)	CARS-M: 9.9 (8.7)
Faurholt-Jepsen et al. (2014)	17	33.4 (9.5)	12 (70.6)	14 (82.4)	NS	NS	NS

BD Bipolar disorder, *SD* Standard deviation, *NS* Not specified, *MADRS* Montgomery and asberg depression scale, *YMRS* Young mania rating scale, *HAMD17* Hamilton depression rating scale with 17 items version, *HAMD* Hamilton depression rating scale, *QIDS-C* Quick inventory of depressive symptomatology-Clinician Rating, *QIDS-C* Quick inventory of depressive symptomatology, *CARS-M* Clinician administered mania rating scale

[a] Median [interquartile range]

Characteristics of interventions

Intervention characteristics are summarised in Table 3. Twelve studies assessed a smartphone app (Depp et al. 2015; Faurholt-Jepsen et al. 2014, 2015, 2020; Wenze et al. 2016; Til et al. 2020; Hidalgo-Mazzei et al. 2016, 2018; Beiwinkel et al. 2016; Tsanas et al. 2016; Stanislaus et al. 2020; Schwartz et al. 2016) and one a PDA (Wenze et al. 2014). All the interventions included self-monitoring sessions. In addition, four apps collected additional passive data (Faurholt-Jepsen et al. 2014, 2020; Til et al. 2020; Beiwinkel et al. 2016), four included the delivery of psychoeducational messages (Wenze et al. 2014, 2016; Hidalgo-Mazzei et al. 2016, 2018) and one included a wearable (Til et al. 2020). Four studies investigated the original or upgraded MONARCA app (Faurholt-Jepsen et al. 2014, 2015, 2020; Stanislaus et al. 2020), two investigated the original or upgraded SIMPLe app (Hidalgo-Mazzei et al. 2016, 2018) and the remaining seven studies investigated an original intervention (Depp et al. 2015; Wenze et al. 2014, 2016; Til et al. 2020; Beiwinkel et al. 2016; Tsanas et al. 2016; Schwartz et al. 2016). Regarding self-monitoring, all the studies offered sessions once- (Faurholt-Jepsen et al. 2014, 2015, 2020; Hidalgo-Mazzei et al. 2016, 2018; Beiwinkel et al. 2016; Tsanas et al. 2016; Stanislaus et al. 2020) or twice-a-day (Depp et al. 2015; Wenze et al. 2014, 2016; Til et al. 2020; Schwartz et al. 2016). The Moodzoom and SIMPLe apps (original or upgraded) added a weekly complementary session (Hidalgo-Mazzei et al. 2016, 2018; Tsanas et al. 2016). The mean number of evaluated items was 7.5 (SD: 4.0). Two interventions evaluated only two items (Beiwinkel et al. 2016; Stanislaus et al. 2020) and five evaluated ten or more items (Wenze et al. 2014, 2016; Faurholt-Jepsen et al. 2014, 2015, 2020). The most frequently evaluated items were mood (12 studies (Depp et al. 2015; Wenze et al. 2014, 2016; Faurholt-Jepsen et al. 2014, 2015, 2020; Til et al. 2020; Hidalgo-Mazzei et al. 2016, 2018; Tsanas et al. 2016; Stanislaus et al. 2020; Schwartz et al. 2016), irritability, anxiety or stress (nine studies (Wenze et al. 2014, 2016; Faurholt-Jepsen et al. 2015, 2020, 2014;

Study name	Mean	Lower limit	Upper limit
Van Til et al. , 2020	41,9	38,8	45,0
Faurholt-Jepsen et al., 2020	43,0	40,4	45,6
Depp et al. , 2015	46,9	43,3	50,5
Stanislaus et al. : 2020	29,0	27,9	30,1
Tsanas et al. , 2016	38,0	32,1	43,9
Schwartz et al. , 2016	48,9	38,5	59,3
Faurholt-Jepsen et al. , 2015	29,1	26,6	31,6
Hidalgo-Mazzei et al. ; 2018	36,6	35,1	38,1
Wenze et al. , 2016	44,0	36,0	52,0
Hidalgo-Mazzei et al. , 2016	43,9	40,8	47,0
Wenze et al., 2014	40,9	34,6	47,2
Beiwinkel et al. , 2016	47,2	45,1	49,3
Faurholt-Jepsen et al., 2014	33,4	28,9	37,9
	39,9	35,6	44,3

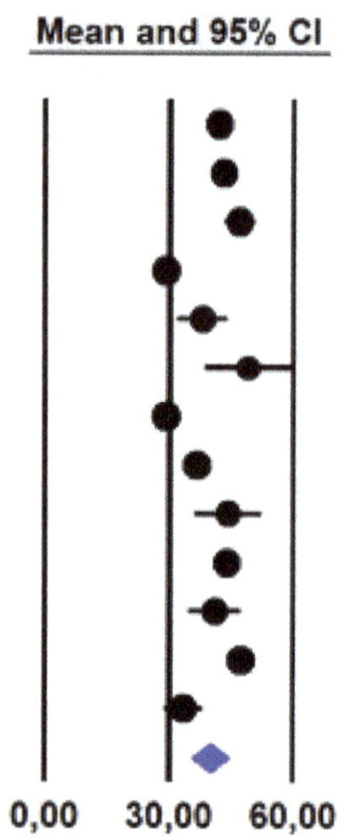

Fig. 2 Mean and standard-deviation of age of participants in the included studies taking into account the between- and within-study variability

Hidalgo-Mazzei et al. 2016, 2018; Tsanas et al. 2016; Schwartz et al. 2016)), sleep [seven studies (Wenze et al. 2014, 2016; Faurholt-Jepsen et al. 2015, 2020, 2014; Hidalgo-Mazzei et al. 2016, 2018)] and medication adherence [seven studies (Wenze et al. 2014, 2016; Faurholt-Jepsen et al. 2014, 2015, 2020; Hidalgo-Mazzei et al. 2016, 2018)]. Nine interventions provided notifications or SMS reminders to complete self-monitoring sessions (Depp et al. 2015; Wenze et al. 2014, 2016; Faurholt-Jepsen et al. 2015; Hidalgo-Mazzei et al. 2016, 2018; Beiwinkel et al. 2016; Stanislaus et al. 2020; Schwartz et al. 2016). Eight interventions provided feedback on self-monitoring through graphics or messages (Depp et al. 2015; Wenze et al. 2014, 2016; Faurholt-Jepsen et al. 2015, 2020; Til et al. 2020; Hidalgo-Mazzei et al. 2016, 2018).

Adherence characteristics

Activity rate

Seven studies calculated an activity rate, ranging from 58.0 to 91.6% (Depp et al. 2015; Wenze et al. 2014, 2016; Faurholt-Jepsen et al. 2020; Hidalgo-Mazzei et al. 2016; Tsanas et al. 2016; Schwartz et al. 2016). Among these seven studies, 6 calculated an activity rate relative to all patients and 1 relative to active patients only (Tsanas et al. 2016).

Schwartz et al. specifically compared the activity rates of the studied app in BD and healthy control groups and did not find a significant difference (79% in the BD group and 71% in the healthy control group, p = 0.22) (Schwartz et al. 2016).

Three studies researched factors influencing the activity rate (Depp et al. 2015; Wenze et al. 2014; Hidalgo-Mazzei et al. 2016). Two studies evaluated the effect of age on the activity rate and failed to find any correlation (Depp et al. 2015; Hidalgo-Mazzei et al. 2016). The third found a trend for a positive association between depressive symptoms and the activity rate (r (Ben-Zeev et al. 2013) = 0.5, p = 0.06) (Wenze et al. 2014).

Completion rate

Only one study focused on the number of study days with a fully completed session and found a completion rate of 81.8% (Til et al. 2020). Its primary objective was to understand how to best engage BD patients in the self-monitoring of their symptoms. The authors compared the monitoring of BD patients with active (self-monitoring) and passive (using an activity tracker) data. As the app offered twice daily sessions, the completion rate was defined as logging at least six of 12 symptoms so the data can be compared to apps offering only one daily session. For the activity tracker, the completion rate was measured as the percent of study days with at least 12 h of activity tracking. There was no statistical difference (p = 0.75) in the completion rate between the two groups (active or passing monitoring). Furthermore, to assess the impact of face-to-face reviewing of monitoring, about 50% of participants in both groups were randomly assigned to review their recorded symptoms weekly with an interviewer. Statistical analysis revealed that reviewing

Table 3 App characteristics

App (study)	Version	Type	Phone	Notifications	Psychoeducation (Type)	Collection of passive data (Type)	Feedback (Type)	Sessions in a day	Number of items evaluated in a session	Adherence Characteristics
No Name (Til et al. 2020)		Self-monitoring + wearable (Fitbit)	Personal	No	No	Yes (Physical activity, sleep and heart rate measured with a wearable device)	Yes (Graphical feedback)	2[a]	6	Completion Rate: 81.8%
MONARCA (Faurholt-Jepsen et al. 2014)	Original	Self-monitoring	Loaned	No	No	Yes (speech duration, social activity, physical activity, and cell tower ID)	No	1	10	88.0%[b]
Faurholt-Jepsen et al. 2015)	Upgraded	Self-monitoring	Loaned	Yes	No	No	Yes (Clinical feed-back loop)	1	11	93.0%[b,c]
Faurholt-Jepsen et al. 2020)	Upgraded	Self-monitoring	Personal or loaned	No	No	Yes (Phone usage, Social activity, Physical activity, Mobility)	Yes (Clinical feed-back loop)	1	10	Activity rate: 72.6%
Stanislaus et al. 2020)	Upgraded	Self-monitoring	Personal or loaned	Yes	No	No	No	1	2	Median of use: 107 days (IQR 157)
PRISM (Depp et al. 2015)		Self-monitoring and evidence-based intervention	Loaned	Yes	No	No	Yes (Graphical Feedback)	2[a]	9	Activity rate: 65.0%
Moodzoom (Tsanas et al. 2016),		Self-monitoring	NS	No	No	No	No	1	6	Activity rate: 81.9%[c]
No Name (Schwartz et al. 2016)		Self-monitoring	Loaned	Yes	No	No	No	2	5	Activity rate: 79.0%
Myexperience (Wenze et al. 2016)		Ecological momentary intervention including self-monitoring	Loaned	Yes	Yes (Messages)	No	Yes (Messages)	2	11	Activity rate 58.0%
SIMPLe (Hidalgo-Mazzei et al. 2016)	Original	Self-monitoring	Personal	Yes	Yes (Messages)	No	Yes (graphical feedback and messages)	1	5	Activity rate: 85.5%
Hidalgo-Mazzei et al. 2018)	Upgraded	Self-Monitoring	Personal	Yes	Yes (Messages)	No	Yes (graphical feedback and messages) °	1	5	Median of use: 60 days. (IQR = 7)

Table 3 (continued)

App (study)	Version	Type	Phone	Notifications	Psychoeducation (Type)	Collection of passive data (Type)	Feedback (Type)	Sessions in a day	Number of items evaluated in a session	Adherence Characteristics
No Name (Wenze et al. 2014)		Self-monitoring	Loaned (PDA)	Yes	Yes (Messages)	No	Yes (messages)	2	16	Activity rate: 91.6%
SIMBA (Beiwinkel et al. 2016)		Self-monitoring	Loaned	Yes	No	Yes (Physical activity and social communication)	No	1	2	55.7%[c]

IQR Inter quartile range, *PDA* Personal digital assistant

[a] Only one session a day taken in account for adherence

[b] Undefined adherence characteristics

[c] Calculated relative to active patients only addition of a weekly complementary session

recorded symptoms did not significantly improve completion rates ($p > 0.80$).

Median of use and retention rate

Hidalgo-Mazzei et al. studied the median of use and retention rate of the SIMPLe app in two studies, the first evaluating the original version (Hidalgo-Mazzei et al. 2016) and the second an upgraded version (Hidalgo-Mazzei et al. 2018).

With the original app, the mean duration of use was 77 days (SD: 26.2). The number of active patients decreased progressively from 46 (94%) after a month to 40 (82%) after 2 months and to 36 after 3 months (end of the study), giving a 74% retention rate. Regarding predictive factors, a high total Functional Assessment Short Test score and more years of smartphone usage were found to be variables weakly related to the retention rate ($p = 0.02$ and $p = 0.04$, respectively).

For the upgraded version, the median of use was 2 months (IQR: 7) and the retention rate was 33.8% at 6 months (end of the study). The mean numbers of users dropping app use each month was 23.3, with almost one-third ($n = 70$, 34.8%) dropping out during the first month. After 6 months, more than 30% of users regularly interacted with the SIMPLe app. Furthermore, increased age was identified as a factor significantly increasing the odds of retention ($OR = 1.0$, $p < 0.001$, CI $95\% = 0.0092–0.033$) (Hidalgo-Mazzei et al. 2018).

Median of use reported for the MONARCA app was 310 days (IQR: 189-437) in a study that investigated differences between BD type 1 and BD type two patients (Faurholt-Jepsen et al. 2015). With an upgraded version, Stanislaus et al. 2020 reported a median of use of 107 days (IQR: 49-206) for BD patients and 84 days (IQR: 42-121) for healthy controls. In both groups, 80% of participants stayed active after a month (Stanislaus et al. 2020).

Undefined adherence characteristics

Three studies did not provide any definition for the adherence characteristics reported (Faurholt-Jepsen et al. 2014, 2015; Beiwinkel et al. 2016). In a pilot study using the SIMBA app, Beiwinkel et al. reported a "compliance rate" of 55.7% (Beiwinkel et al. 2016).

Studying the MONARCA apps, Faurholt-Jepsen et al. reported an "adherence rate" of 88% in a pilot study (Faurholt-Jepsen et al. 2014) and a "mean adherence among time" of 93% in an observational study (Faurholt-Jepsen et al. 2015).

Discussion

Despite a high number of studies selected at the full article level (118), only 13 possessed the requested inclusion criteria. In particular, 39 eligible studies did not provide any information on adherence characteristics to the app. Among the included studies, study length, sample size and definition of measure of adherence were heterogeneous. Seven studies calculated an activity rate, one study calculated a completion rate, three studies provided a median of use or a retention rate and three studies provided undefined adherence characteristics. Activity rates were disparate, ranging from 58 to 91.6%; these were quite high, with five out of seven being over 70%.

Interestingly, the study that paid patients according to the time spent in the study had one of the lowest activity rates (65%) and the two studies paying patients for each completed session displayed the lowest and the highest activity rates of this review (58% and 91.6%, respectively). These results were in accordance with a meta-analysis finding no difference between paid vs. unpaid patients in their adherence to apps (Torous et al. 2020).

Our main findings should be compared to medication adherence in BD which is a pervasive issue in this chronic disease. The study of medication adherence in BD involves the same difficulties that we encountered in this review, especially heterogeneity in adherence descriptions and measures (Tueller et al. 2016; Greene et al. 2018; Averous et al. 2018). As described in several reviews, mean medication adherence in BD ranges from 50 to 80% with good adherence being an exception (Levin et al. 2016; Chakrabarti 2016). Regarding prevalence, 12-month treatment rates are estimated to be between 45 and 51% (Greene et al. 2018). Many predictive factors for poor medication adherence have been reported, the most common being health beliefs and attitudes to medications (Greene et al. 2018; Averous et al. 2018). Additionally, patients' attitudes are influenced by several elements such as their family members' attitude to medication, their knowledge of the illness and their relationship with their clinician (Chakrabarti 2016). This knowledge about medication adherence should be used to guide adherence research in the field of mobile health, both in terms of its predictive factors and ways to improve it.

If the adherence characteristics to the apps found in our review are quite similar to the rates of adherence to treatments found in BD patients, we have to keep in mind that our results are surprisingly high knowing the difficulties encountered by apps to stay attractive over time (Fleming et al. 2018; Baumel et al. 2019). Several aspects could be considered to explain these results.

First, we must recall that a research protocol does not wholly reflect the "real world" conditions; this is particularly true when it comes to mental health and non-drug therapeutic tools. The frame provided by a study, bringing high structuring of participants, is a known adherence-promoting element (Baumel et al. 2019; Ebert and Baumeister 2017). This is confirmed by the studies focusing on the "real world" use of apps that highlighted poor adherence (Bauer et al. 2020; Fleming et al. 2018; Baumel et al. 2019). The included studies in this review are no exception to this bias and it is very likely that the described apps would be less used in real world conditions, without the clinical frame offered by the study protocol. Interestingly, the real-world implementation observational study of the SIMPLe app did not offer clinical interviews to participants but carried out assessments through email only (Hidalgo-Mazzei et al. 2018). This method of evaluation could reduce the bias created by clinical frames in the measure of adherence in studies. However, the lack of face-to-face contact with the patient in fully online study seems to impact negatively the adherence with the app (retention rate of 30% at the end of the study).

Secondly, some of the reviewed studies presented adherence characteristics relative to active patients only. This method of evaluation excludes the notion of retention and so does not allow a reliable assessment of adherence and provides higher rates than if calculated relative to all participants. It provides information about global activity and could help to determine the most suitable rhythm of evaluation for the app (once or twice a day, once a week), but fails to consider participants that discontinued their use of the app in question. Thus, a 93% activity rate calculated on active patients can only hide a 70% drop-out rate.

Another reason for the high adherence characteristics found in our review could be the age of participants. The mean age among studies was 39.9 years (IQR: 35.6-44.3). This mean age and limited dispersion exclude the elderly and could hide the famous "generation gap". Older adults are commonly expected to have difficulties acclimating to new technologies such as smartphone apps (Grossman et al. 2020). This theory tends to be refuted (Bennett et al. 2008) and progressively gives way to the conception of older adults as a heterogeneous population regarding their abilities to use new technologies (Jayasinghe et al. 2019; Mitzner et al. 2010). A review of mobile technology among older adults even suggested that, far from being refractory to mobile intervention, they generally show a desire to engage with these technologies to monitor and improve health conditions (Kuerbis et al. 2017). However, there are still factors that inhibit their use of mobile technologies such as functional capacities, cognitive changes, deterioration of fine motor coordination, visual impairment and previous experience with or exposure to smartphones (Mitzner et al. 2010). In our review, no study found any negative correlation between an older age and adherence; one even identified a positive correlation between increased age and retention (Hidalgo-Mazzei et al. 2016). Further studies should therefore specifically focus on the implication of age in adherence to determine whether there is a generation gap regarding the use of mobile technology in mental health care.

Finally, adherence characteristics can be inflated because of publication bias. In a meta-analysis focusing on clinical trials of smartphone apps for depressive symptoms, Torous et al. reported a drop-out rate of 26.2% (Torous et al. 2020). When they adjusted this estimation to publication bias, it rose to 47.8%. Finding unimportant or negative results is known to be one of the main reasons for non-publication of completed studies (Song 2013). Considering the development of an app, low adherence characteristics could be read as a negative outcome and so lead to the non-publication of results. This element should therefore be taken into account for the interpretation of published adherence characteristics.

Future research

The word "adherence" is a generic term covering many different notions. In articles, it is interchangeably used with the terms "engagement" or "uptake". The most relevant information highlighted by this review was the high number of studies that did not provide any information on adherence characteristics and study heterogeneity regarding method and provided data. This lack of a standardised measure of adherence to smartphone apps has been mentioned in several systematic reviews or meta-analyses focusing on smartphone app interventions for severe mental illness and depression (Kerst et al. 2019; Rathbone and Prescott 2017; Berry et al. 2016). As mentioned in the introduction, adherence is a key factor in the development of apps for BD. Its assessment with standardised methods could allow a meta-analysis to be carried out and statistical determinations of its predictive factors to be made. For further studies involving the use of an app, it could be of interest to systematically assess and report the following items, regardless of the primary study outcomes: activity rate, completion rate, median of use and retention rate. A focus on which features of the apps are more likely used (self-assessment, psychoeducation) could also be of interest. In addition, the collection of patients' feedback regarding the studied app, using Likert scales or a qualitative design, could be potential ways to upgrade apps following a user-centred approach. Beyond these measures, apps adherence should be the object of a broad expert systematic consensus in the scientific community to define all its aspects. In particular, threshold determining a good or acceptable adherence should be defined and its parameters should be standardised. Such a consensus is essential to compare studies with each other and to allow improvement in apps adherence. Furthermore, the access to app usage data is technically simple and should allow these standards to be easily applied to all studies.

Finally, the development of guided apps (i.e., apps used under the supervision of a professional) over self-help apps (i.e., apps freely downloaded and used by patients) should be preferred (Baumel et al. 2019; Ebert and Baumeister 2017). Indeed, several studies focusing on self-help apps found patient reluctance toward these tools (Kerst et al. 2019; Fuller-Tyszkiewicz et al. 2018; Stiles-Shields et al. 2017) and a lower adherence compared to guided one (Torous et al. 2020; Eysenbach 2005; Titzler et al. 2018; Cuijpers et al. 2017; Linardon et al. 2019). Furthermore, the better adherence to apps in research protocols compare to real world highlights the essential role of face-to-face meetings in mental healthcare (Baumel et al. 2019; Ebert and Baumeister 2017). If they are able to facilitate access to psychiatric care to the largest number of individuals (BinDhim et al. 2015; Ramos et al. 2019; Cheng et al. 2016), self-help apps should be restricted to screening tools, and their main purpose should be to guide patients toward medical care. Therapeutic apps should be fully integrated in therapy and be closely monitored by therapists. In addition to increasing adherence, their integration could reinforce the patient-therapist link and offer to the therapist better knowledge of their patient's clinical state, particularly during the in-between visits period.

Limitations

The heterogeneity of apps, study designs, clinical approaches and participant populations analysed limited the generalisation of our results. The lack of standardised reports of adherence forced us to compare similar but not identical data. No study reported on how many features of the apps were used. Furthermore, five studies included were rated with poor quality because of small sample size. They were either pilot study or feasibility studies. Finally, this review included only apps that have been studied in a research protocol. To enlarge the scope of this work, the assessment of adherence to apps available on app stores would be of great interest to future work.

Conclusion

In total, maintaining adherence over time is a key factor to increase apps implementation in daily care and to improve quality of care. This review highlights the overwhelming lack of documentation of adherence to apps in the actual literature, as well as the great disparity of its definition and measures. These results encourage the establishing of a systematic standard evaluation of adherence in study protocols involving smartphone app interventions.

Abbreviations

BD: Bipolar disorder; CARS: Clinician-administered rating scale for mania; IQR: Inter Quartile range; PDA: Personal digital assistant; QIDS: Quick inventory of depressive symptoms; SD: Standard deviation.

Supplementary Information

Additional file1: Table S1. Quality assessment of RCT using the national institutes of health (NIH) quality assessment tool for controlled intervention studies

Additional file2: Table S2. Quality assessment of longitudinal studies using the national institutes of health (NIH) quality assessment tool for observational cohort and cross-sectional studies

Additional file 3: Table S3. Quality assessment of studies with no control group using the national institutes of health (NIH) quality assessment tool for before-after (pre-post) studies with no control group

Acknowledgements

We would like to thank Susan Wenze and Amy Cochran for providing details on their studies included in this report. This study was supported by a grant from the French Ministry of Health (PREPS 17-0121). Dr. Murru thanks the support of the Spanish Ministry of Science and Innovation (PI19/00672).

Authors' contributions

MCP, PML and LS were involved in the study conceptualisation and design. Analyses and interpretation of the data were carried out by all the authors (MCP, DHM, BP, OB, IDC, NV, IP, AM, EV, PML and LS) BP. conducted the statistical analyses. The first draft of the manuscript was written by MCP and LS. All authors (MCP, DHM, BP, OB, IDC, NV, IP, AM, EV, PML and LS) contributed to and approved the final manuscript. All authors read and approved the final manuscript.

Competing interests

Dr. Pacchiarotti has received CME-related honoraria, or consulting fees from ADAMED, Janssen-Cilag and Lundbeck. Dr. Murru has served as a consultant, adviser or speaker for Adamed, AstraZeneca, Bristol-Myers Squibb, Janssen-Cilag, Lundbeck, Otsuka and Sanofi-Aventis and has received a grant (PI19/00672) from the Instituto de Salud Carlos IIISubdirección General de Evaluación y Fomento de la investigación, Plan Nacional 2019–2022. Prof. Vieta has received grants and served as a consultant, advisor or CME speaker for the following entities: AB-Biotics, Abbott, Allergan, Angelini, AstraZeneca, Bristol-Myers Squibb, Dainippon Sumitomo Pharma, Farmindustria, Ferrer, Forest Research Institute, Gedeon Richter, Glaxo-Smith-Kline, Janssen, Lundbeck, Otsuka, Pfizer, Roche, SAGE, Sanofi-Aventis, Servier, Shire, Sunovion, Takeda, the Brain and Behaviour Foundation, the Spanish Ministry of Science and Innovation (CIBERSAM), the EU Horizon 2020 and the Stanley Medical Research Institute. Prof. Llorca has received grants, honoraria or consulting fees from ESAI, Gedeon Richeter, Janssen, Lundbeck, Otsuka and Sanofi. Dr. Samalin has received grants, honoraria or consulting fees from AstraZeneca, Bristol-Myers Squibb, Janssen-Cilag, Lundbeck, Otsuka, Sanofi-Aventis, and Takeda. The other authors declare that they have no conflicts of interest.

Author details

[1]Department of Psychiatry, CHU Clermont-Ferrand, University of Clermont Auvergne, CNRS, Clermont Auvergne INP, Institut Pascal, Clermont-Ferrand, France. [2]Bipolar and Depression Disorders Unit, Institute of Neuroscience, Hospital Clinic, CIBERSAM, University of Barcelona, Barcelona, Catalonia, Spain.

[3]Fondation FondaMental, Créteil, France. [4]Service de Psychiatrie B, Centre Hospitalier Universitaire, 58 rue Montalembert, 63000 Clermont-Ferrand, France.

References

Averous P, Charbonnier E, Lagouanelle-Simeoni MC, Prosperi A, Dany L. Illness perceptions and adherence in bipolar disorder: an exploratory study. Compr Psychiatry. 2018;80:109–15.

Batra S, Baker RA, Wang T, Forma F, DiBiasi F, Peters-Strickland T. Digital health technology for use in patients with serious mental illness: a systematic review of the literature. Med Devices. 2017;10:237–51.

Bauer M, Glenn T, Geddes J, Gitlin M, Grof P, Kessing LV, et al. Smartphones in mental health: a critical review of background issues, current status and future concerns. Int J Bipolar Disord. 2020;8:2.

Baumeister H, Reichler L, Munzinger M, Lin J. The impact of guidance on Internet-based mental health interventions—a systematic review. Internet Interv. 2014;1:205–15.

Baumel A, Muench F, Edan S, Kane JM. Objective user engagement with mental health apps: systematic search and panel-based usage analysis. J Med Internet Res. 2019;21:e14567.

Beiwinkel T, Kindermann S, Maier A, Kerl C, Moock J, Barbian G, et al. Using smartphones to monitor bipolar disorder symptoms: a pilot study. JMIR Ment Health. 2016;3:e2.

Bennett S, Maton K, Kervin L. The 'digital natives' debate: a critical review of the evidence. Br J Educ Technol. 2008;39:775–86.

Ben-Zeev D, Davis K, Kaiser S, Krzsos I, Drake R. Mobile technologies among people with serious mental illness: opportunities for future services. Adm Policy Ment Health. 2013;40:340–3.

Berry N, Lobban F, Emsley R, Bucci S. Acceptability of interventions delivered online and through mobile phones for people who experience severe mental health problems: a systematic review. J Med Internet Res. 2016;18:e121.

BinDhim NF, Shaman AM, Trevena L, Basyouni MH, Pont LG, Alhawassi TM. Depression screening via a smartphone app: Cross-country user characteristics and feasibility. J Am Med Inform Assoc. 2015;22:29–34.

Borenstein M, Hedges L ,Higgins J, Rothstein H. Comprehensive Meta Analysis Version 3.0. https://www.meta-analysis.com/downloads/Meta-Analysis%20Manual%20V3.pdf. Accessed 20 Nov 2020

Carson S, Lundvall A, Möller R, Bävertoft S, Jacobsson A, Sellin G, et al. Ericsson Mobility Report June 2016. https://www.ericsson.com/en/mobility-report/reports. Accessed Aug 23, 2020.

Chakrabarti S. Treatment-adherence in bipolar disorder: a patient-centred approach. World J Psychiatry. 2016;6:399–409.

Cheng PGF, Ramos RM, Bitsch JÁ, Jonas SM, Ix T, See PLQ, et al. Psychologist in a pocket: lexicon development and content validation of a mobile-based app for depression screening. JMIR Mhealth Uhealth. 2016;4:e88.

Cuijpers P, Kleiboer A, Karyotaki E, Riper H. Internet and mobile interventions for depression: opportunities and challenges. Depress Anxiety. 2017;34:596–602.

Depp CA, Ceglowski J, Wang VC, Yaghouti F, Mausbach BT, Thompson WK, et al. Augmenting psychoeducation with a mobile intervention for bipolar disorder: a randomized controlled trial. J Affect Disord. 2015;174:23–30.

DerSimonian R, Laird N. Meta-analysis in clinical trials revisited. Contemp Clin Trials. 2015;45:139–45.

Ebert DD, Baumeister H. Internet-based self-help interventions for depression in routine care. JAMA Psychiat. 2017;74:852–3.

Eysenbach G. The Law of Attrition. J Med Internet Res. 2005;7:e11.

Faurholt-Jepsen M, Frost M, Vinberg M, Christensen EM, Bardram JE, Kessing LV. Smartphone data as objective measures of bipolar disorder symptoms. Psychiatry Res. 2014;217:124–7.

Faurholt-Jepsen M, Ritz C, Frost M, Mikkelsen RL, Margrethe Christensen E, Bardram J, et al. Mood instability in bipolar disorder type I versus type II-continuous daily electronic self-monitoring of illness activity using smartphones. J Affect Disord. 2015;186:342–9.

Faurholt-Jepsen M, Frost M, Christensen EM, Bardram JE, Vinberg M, Kessing LV. The effect of smartphone-based monitoring on illness activity in bipolar disorder: the MONARCA II randomized controlled single-blinded trial. Psychol Med. 2020;50:838–48.

Firth J, Torous J, Yung AR. Ecological momentary assessment and beyond: The rising interest in e-mental health research. J Psychiatr Res. 2016;80:3–4.

Fleming T, Bavin L, Lucassen M, Stasiak K, Hopkins S, Merry S. Beyond the trial: systematic review of real-world uptake and engagement with digital self-help interventions for depression, low mood, or anxiety. J Med Internet Res. 2018;20:e199.

Fuller-Tyszkiewicz M, Richardson B, Klein B, Skouteris H, Christensen H, Austin D, et al. A mobile app-based intervention for depression: end-user and expert usability testing study. JMIR Ment Health. 2018;5:e54.

Greene M, Paladini L, Lemmer T, Piedade A, Touya M, Clark O. Systematic literature review on patterns of pharmacological treatment and adherence among patients with bipolar disorder type I in the USA. Neuropsychiatr Dis Treat. 2018;14:1545–59.

Grossman JT, Frumkin MR, Rodebaugh TL, Lenze EJ. mHealth Assessment and intervention of depression and anxiety in older adults. Harv Rev Psychiatry. 2020;28:203–14.

Hidalgo-Mazzei D, Mateu A, Reinares M, Murru A, Del Mar Bonnín C, Varo C, et al. Psychoeducation in bipolar disorder with a simple smartphone application: feasibility, acceptability and satisfaction. J Affect Disord. 2016;200:58–66.

Hidalgo-Mazzei D, Reinares M, Mateu A, Nikolova VL, Bonnín CDM, Samalin L, et al. OpenSIMPLe: a real-world implementation feasibility study of a smartphone-based psychoeducation programme for bipolar disorder. J Affect Disord. 2018;241:436–45.

Hollis C, Morriss R, Martin J, Amani S, Cotton R, Denis M, et al. Technological innovations in mental healthcare: harnessing the digital revolution. Br J Psychiatry. 2015;206:263–5.

Jayasinghe N, Moallem BI, Kakoullis M, Ojie M-J, Sar-Graycar L, Wyka K, et al. Establishing the feasibility of a tablet-based consent process with older adults: a mixed-methods study. Gerontologist. 2019;59:124–34.

Kerst A, Zielasek J, Gaebel W. Smartphone applications for depression: a systematic literature review and a survey of health care professionals' attitudes towards their use in clinical practice. Eur Arch Psychiatry Clin Neurosci. 2019;270:139–52.

Kuerbis A, Mulliken A, Muench F, A. Moore A, Gardner D. 2017 Older adults and mobile technology: Factors that enhance and inhibit utilization in the context of behavioral health. Ment Health Addict Res 2(2).

Levin JB, Krivenko A, Howland M, Schlachet R, Sajatovic M. Medication Adherence in patients with bipolar disorder: a comprehensive review. CNS Drugs. 2016;30:819–35.

Linardon J, Cuijpers P, Carlbring P, Messer M, Fuller-Tyszkiewicz M. The efficacy of app-supported smartphone interventions for mental health problems: a meta-analysis of randomized controlled trials. World Psychiatry. 2019;18:325–36.

Merikangas KR, Akiskal HS, Angst J, Greenberg PE, Hirschfeld RMA, Petukhova M, et al. Lifetime and 12-Month prevalence of bipolar spectrum disorder in the national comorbidity survey replication. Arch Gen Psychiatry. 2007;64:543–52.

Mitzner TL, Boron JB, Fausset CB, Adams AE, Charness N, Czaja SJ, et al. Older adults talk technology: technology usage and attitudes. Comput Human Behav. 2010;26:1710–21.

Moore RC, Depp CA, Wetherell JL, Lenze EJ. Ecological momentary assessment versus standard assessment instruments for measuring mindfulness, depressed mood, and anxiety among older adults. J Psychiatr Res. 2016;75:116–23.

Murru A, Pacchiarotti I, Verdolini N, Reinares M, Torrent C, Geoffroy P-A, et al. Modifiable and non-modifiable factors associated with functional impairment during the inter-episodic periods of bipolar disorder. Eur Arch Psychiatry Clin Neurosci. 2018;268:749–55.

Myin-Germeys I, Klippel A, Steinhart H, Reininghaus U. Ecological momentary interventions in psychiatry. Curr Opin Psychiatry. 2016;29:258–63.

National institute of health. Study quality assessment tools. https://www.nhlbi.nih.gov/health-topics/study-quality-assessment-tools. Accessed 16 Mar 2021.

Ng MM, Firth J, Minen M, Torous J. User engagement in mental health apps: a review of measurement, reporting, and validity. Psychiatr Serv. 2019;70:538–44.

Nicholas J, Fogarty AS, Boydell K, Christensen H. The reviews are in a qualitative content analysis of consumer perspectives on apps for bipolar disorder. J Med Internet Res. 2017;19:e105.

Pini S, de Queiroz V, Pagnin D, Pezawas L, Angst J, Cassano GB, et al. Prevalence and burden of bipolar disorders in European countries. Eur Neuropsychopharmacol. 2005;15:425–34.

Ramos RM, Cheng PGF, Jonas SM. Validation of an mHealth App for Depression Screening and Monitoring (Psychologist in a Pocket): Correlational Study and Concurrence analysis. JMIR Mhealth Uhealth. 2019;7:e12051.
Rathbone AL, Prescott J. The use of mobile apps and sms messaging as physical and mental health interventions: systematic review. J Med Internet Res. 2017;19:e295.
Samalin L, Llorca PM, Giordana B, Milhiet V, Yon L, El-Hage W, et al. Residual symptoms and functional performance in a large sample of euthymic bipolar patients in France (the OPTHYMUM study). J Affect Disord. 2014;159:94–102.
Schwartz S, Schultz S, Reider A, Saunders EFH. Daily mood monitoring of symptoms using smartphones in bipolar disorder: a pilot study assessing the feasibility of ecological momentary assessment. J Affect Disord. 2016;191:88–93.
Song F, Hooper LY. Publication bias: what is it? how do we measure it? how do we avoid it? Open Access J Clin Trials. 2013;5:51–81.
Stanislaus S, Faurholt-Jepsen M, Vinberg M, Coello K, Kjærstad HL, Melbye S, et al. Mood instability in patients with newly diagnosed bipolar disorder, unaffected relatives, and healthy control individuals measured daily using smartphones. J Affect Disord. 2020;271:336–44.
Stiles-Shields C, Montague E, Lattie EG, Kwasny MJ, Mohr DC. What might get in the way: barriers to the use of apps for depression. Digit Health. 2017;3:205520761771382.
Titzler I, Saruhanjan K, Berking M, Riper H, Ebert DD. Barriers and facilitators for the implementation of blended psychotherapy for depression: a qualitative pilot study of therapists' perspective. Internet Interv. 2018;12:150–64.
Torous J, Nicholas J, Larsen ME, Firth J, Christensen H. Clinical review of user engagement with mental health smartphone apps: evidence, theory and improvements. Evid Based Mental Health. 2018;21:116–9.
Torous J, Lipschitz J, Ng M, Firth J. Dropout rates in clinical trials of smartphone apps for depressive symptoms: a systematic review and meta-analysis. J Affect Disord. 2020;263:413–9.
Tsanas A, Saunders KEA, Bilderbeck AC, Palmius N, Osipov M, Clifford GD, et al. Daily longitudinal self-monitoring of mood variability in bipolar disorder and borderline personality disorder. J Affect Disord. 2016;205:225–33.
Tueller SJ, Deboeck PR, Van Dorn RA. Getting less of what you want: Reductions in statistical power and increased bias when categorizing medication adherence data. J Behav Med. 2016;39:969–80.
Van Til K, McInnis MG, Cochran A. A comparative study of engagement in mobile and wearable health monitoring for bipolar disorder. Bipolar Disord. 2020;22:182–90.
Wenze SJ, Armey MF, Miller IW. Feasibility and acceptability of a mobile intervention to improve treatment adherence in bipolar disorder: a pilot study. Behav Modif. 2014;38:497–515.
Wenze SJ, Armey MF, Weinstock LM, Gaudiano BA, Miller IW. An open trial of a smartphone-assisted, adjunctive intervention to improve treatment adherence in bipolar disorder. J Psychiatr Pract. 2016;22:492–504.

11

Metabolic profile in patients with newly diagnosed bipolar disorder and their unaffected first-degree relatives

Klara Coello[1,2*], Maj Vinberg[1,2], Filip K. Knop[2,3], Bente K. Pedersen[2,4], Roger S. McIntyre[5], Lars V. Kessing[1,2] and Klaus Munkholm[1]

Abstract

Objective: The prevalence of metabolic syndrome and insulin resistance is twice as high in patients with bipolar disorder compared with the general population, and possibly associated with a disabling illness trajectory of bipolar disorder, an increased risk of cardiovascular disease and premature death. Despite these detrimental effects, the prevalence of metabolic syndrome and insulin resistance in patients newly diagnosed with bipolar disorder and their unaffected first-degree relatives is largely unknown.

Methods: In a cross-sectional study of 206 patients with newly diagnosed bipolar disorder, 50 of their unaffected first-degree relatives and 109 healthy age- and sex-matched individuals, we compared the prevalence of metabolic syndrome and insulin resistance (HOMA-IR). In patients with bipolar disorder, we further investigated illness and medication variables associated with the metabolic syndrome and insulin resistance.

Results: Higher rates of metabolic syndrome (odds ratio = 3.529, 95% CI 1.378–9.041, $P = 0.009$) and levels of insulin resistance ($B = 1.203$, 95% CI 1.059–1.367, $P = 0.005$) were found in patients newly diagnosed with bipolar disorder, but not in their unaffected first-degree relatives compared with matched healthy individuals (data adjusted for sex and age). Most patients with bipolar disorder (94.7%) were diagnosed within the preceding 2 years, and the average illness duration, defined as time from first mood episode, was 10 years.

Conclusion: Our findings of elevated prevalence of metabolic syndrome and insulin resistance in patients with newly diagnosed bipolar disorder highlight the importance of screening for these conditions at an early stage to employ adequate and early care reducing the risk of cardiovascular disease and premature death.

Keywords: Bipolar disorder, Insulin resistance, Metabolic syndrome X, Co-morbidity

Introduction

Bipolar disorder (BD) is associated with a decreased life expectancy of 8–12 years (Laursen et al. 2013; Kessing et al. 2015) with cardiovascular disease (CVD) being the leading cause of excess mortality (Osby et al. 2001). Patients with BD have increased risk of developing CVD compared with the general population (Goldstein 2017), and the American Heart Association recognizes BD in youth as a moderate-risk condition for early CVD and accelerated atherosclerosis (Goldstein et al. 2015). Metabolic syndrome (metS) constitutes a cluster of CVD risk factors consisting of abdominal obesity, diabetes and/or raised fasting plasma glucose, dyslipidemia and high blood pressure (Alberti et al. 2006). In general, presence of metS doubles the risk of CVD related mortality (Alberti et al. 2006). In patients with BD the prevalence of metS is doubled compared with the general population, an observation that appears to be a global phenomenon (Vancampfort et al. 2013).

Insulin resistance and central obesity are central components of metS (Alberti et al. 2006). Further, insulin

*Correspondence: klara.coello@regionh.dk
[1] Copenhagen Affective Disorders Research Centre (CADIC), Psychiatric Center Copenhagen, Department O, 6243, Rigshospitalet, Blegdamsvej 9, 2100 Copenhagen, Denmark
Full list of author information is available at the end of the article

resistance, metS and type 2 diabetes may separately be associated with adverse outcomes in patients with BD such as rapid cycling, treatment resistance to BD, and progression into a chronic illness course (Calkin et al. 2015; McIntyre et al. 2010; Cairns et al. 2018). Overweight and obesity have also been associated with increased severity of bipolar depression and a decreased treatment response that diminishes with increasing body mass index (BMI) (Kemp et al. 2010; Calkin et al. 2009). Similarly, the number and frequency of illness episodes seem to be increased in dysglycemic patients with BD compared with euglycemic patients (Calkin et al. 2015) and dysglycemia has been suggested to constitute a moderator of illness progression in BD (Mansur et al. 2016).

Despite robust evidence of the detrimental effects of metabolic comorbidity in BD, it is largely unknown whether risk factors for metS are present in newly diagnosed BD. Three prior case–control studies of metS in a small number of patients newly diagnosed with BD did not find a higher prevalence of metS compared with healthy individuals (Guha et al. 2014; Taylor et al. 2010; Wulsin et al. 2018). However, due to small sample sizes (n = 23–56) a true difference in prevalence may possibly have been overlooked. One of these studies (Guha et al. 2014), additionally, is the only case–control study of insulin resistance in patients newly diagnosed with BD, and they found higher insulin resistance index but not higher rates of metS in medication free, newly diagnosed patients with BD (Guha et al. 2014). However, the age of the participants (43.2 ± 10.6 years) suggested that the patients with BD were in a relatively late illness stage (Guha et al. 2014). Apart from one small study observing decreased high-density lipoprotein (HDL) cholesterol in first-degree unaffected relatives of patients with BD (Sobczak et al. 2004), it is largely unknown whether risk factors for metS, are present in unaffected first-degree relatives of BD.

Aims of the study

The aims of the present study were: (I) to compare the prevalence of metS and levels of insulin resistance, as well as individual risk factors for metS and insulin resistance between patients with newly diagnosed BD and their unaffected first-degree relatives with healthy individuals without personal or first-degree family history of affective disorder; and (II) to determine to what extent illness and medication variables in patients with BD were associated with metS and insulin resistance.

We hypothesized that the prevalence of metS and insulin resistance was higher in patients with newly diagnosed BD and—to a lesser degree—in their unaffected first-degree relatives compared with healthy individuals without a family history of psychiatric disorders.

Materials and methods

Study design

The present report is a cross-sectional investigation of baseline data from the ongoing, longitudinal Bipolar Illness Onset Study (BIO), which aims to identify composite biomarkers for BD (Kessing et al. 2017). Participants were recruited from June 2015 to September 2017. The study protocol was approved by the Committee on Health Research Ethics of the Capital region of Denmark (protocol No. H-7-2014-007) and the Danish Data Protection Agency, Capital Region of Copenhagen (RHP-2015-023). Written informed consent was provided by all participants. The study complied with the Declaration of Helsinki principles (Seoul, October 2008).

Participants

Patients with bipolar disorder

Patients were recruited from the Copenhagen Affective Disorder Clinic that covers the greater Copenhagen area of 1.6 million inhabitants (The Capital Region). All patients having a first episode of (hypo)mania or newly diagnosed with BD were routinely invited to participate in the study by the clinicians in the Copenhagen Affective Disorder Clinic (Kessing et al. 2017). Inclusion criteria were an ICD-10 diagnosis of a single manic episode or BD and age 15–70 years. Exclusion criteria included having an organic BD secondary to brain injury. The patients received treatment as usual without interference from study investigators.

Unaffected first-degree relatives

Siblings and children of the included patients with BD were invited to participate upon consent by the participating patient. Inclusion criteria were being a first-degree relative of an included patient with BD and age 15–40 years. Exclusion criteria included ICD-10 diagnoses of substance abuse, psychotic illnesses and mood disorders. We did not restrict the number of participating unaffected first-degree relatives per patient with BD as we adjusted for familial relationship in our analysis.

Healthy individuals

Age and sex-matched healthy individuals were recruited on random days among blood donors from the Blood Bank at Rigshospitalet, Copenhagen, Denmark. The inclusion criterion was age 15–70 years. Exclusion criteria were a personal or first-degree family history of psychiatric disorders that had required treatment.

Clinical assessments

In the Copenhagen Affective Disorder Clinic, a specialist in psychiatry diagnosed patients with BD according to ICD-10 and classified them as type I or type II according to DSM-5 at the beginning of a two-year treatment program.

All participants were assessed by a medical doctor or a psychologist trained in diagnosing BD. The clinical diagnosis of BD was confirmed using the semi-structured interview: the Schedules for Clinical Assessment in Neuropsychiatry (SCAN) (Wing et al. 1990). Diagnosis of the current affective state was based on ICD-10 criteria. Severity of depressive and manic symptoms was assessed using the Hamilton Depression Rating Scale-17 items (HAMD-17) (Hamilton 1960) and the Young Mania Rating Scale (YMRS) (Young et al. 1978) respectively. Sleep quality was assessed using the Pittsburgh Sleep Quality Index (PSQI) (Buysse et al. 1989) and physical activity was assessed using the International Physical Activity Questionnaire (IPAQ) (Craig et al. 2003), which were both administered at the day of assessment. Medication, alcohol intake and smoking habits were recorded. Alcohol intake was stratified into low intake (0–4 units per week), moderate intake (5–13 units per week) and high intake (> 13 units per week).

Absence of lifetime psychiatric morbidity defined by ICD-10 was confirmed for healthy individuals whereas psychiatric morbidity of F34 and higher (e.g., cyclothymia, anxiety and personality disorders) according to ICD-10 were registered for unaffected relatives.

Anthropometric assessment

After a 10-min rest blood pressure was measured in a sitting position using a calibrated automatic sphygmanometer (Microlife BP A3 plus) at the same day as the clinical assessment. Further, waist circumference was measured at the midpoint between the lowest rib and the iliac crest in an upright position to the nearest millimeter as described in the World Health Organisation's guidelines (Cornier et al. 2011). Lightly dressed and without shoes, height was measured to the nearest millimeter on a rigid stadiometer and weight was measured to the nearest 0.1 kg using a calibrated floor scale (Kern MPE PM®).

Laboratory methods

Fasting blood samples were collected in a resting state between 7.30 AM and 10 AM at the same day as the clinical assessment. Five milliliters of blood was drawn by venipuncture into an EDTA containing vacuum tube (Vacuette®) and within 30 min centrifuged at 1590 g and 4 °C for 15 min. Plasma was aliquoted into Eppendorf® tubes and kept frozen at − 80 °C until P-Insulin was assayed. Plasma/serum concentrations of glucose, triglyceride, HbA1c and HDL cholesterol were measured using standard laboratory routine assays. Blood sampling and all aspects of laboratory processing were done at the Department of Clinical Biochemistry, Rigshospitalet, by laboratory specialists blinded with respect to participant status.

Determination of metabolic syndrome, type 2 diabetes and insulin resistance

Metabolic syndrome was defined according to the International Diabetes Federation 2006 criteria (Alberti et al. 2006). Participants were considered having type 2 diabetes if they met at least one of the following three criteria: a diagnosis of type 2 diabetes, use of antidiabetic treatment (without other indication), and/or having a hemoglobin A1c (HbA1c) level of 48 mmol/mol or above. Insulin resistance was calculated from fasting plasma glucose and insulin using the homeostasis model assessment of insulin resistance (HOMA-IR) (HOMA-IR = (plasma glucose (mmol/L) × plasma insulin (mIU//L)/22.5 (Hermans et al. 1999)). To convert insulin from pmol/L to μIU/ml = mIU/L we divided with six, which has been found to be the most appropriate conversion factor (Larsen et al. 2017).

Statistical analyses

Descriptive data were analyzed by Chi square tests for categorical data and by Student's t test and Mann–Whitney U tests for two independent groups for continuous data, according to whether assumptions of normal distribution were met or not. Continuous data were presented as median and quartiles if assumptions of normal distribution were not met.

For illustrative purposes, we first compared prevalence of metS and levels of insulin resistance in an unadjusted generalized mixed effect model (categorical outcome) and a linear mixed effect model (continuous outcome), respectively, with familial relationship as random effect, to account for the correlation between family-related individuals. In a second model we adjusted for age and sex and as a third fully adjusted model we further added smoking status and alcohol intake as covariates.

In analyses among patients with BD we explored the associations between medication and illness characteristics and metS and insulin resistance, respectively, in separate models to retain sufficient statistical power. In these models, illness duration, BD type (I or II), current medication type in the form of lithium (yes/no), antipsychotics (yes/no), antidepressants (yes/no) and antiepileptics (yes/no) and, finally, receiving psychotropics with metabolic adverse effects were entered as predictors along with the covariates age and sex. All daily psychotropic medication except for lamotrigine and aripiprazole were considered psychotropics with metabolic adverse effects (Abosi et al. 2018). The category 'not receiving psychotropics with metabolic adverse effect' included patients not receiving psychotropic medication as well as patients receiving lamotrigine, aripiprazole or low dose quetiapine (i.e., not exceeding 50 mg daily). Illness duration was defined as time from first episode (depressive, hypomanic, manic or mixed episode). In a separate analysis we explored the association between demographic- and lifestyle variables and metS and insulin resistance among patients with BD, with these as dependent variables, and age, sex, smoking status, alcohol intake, sleep quality and physical activity as independent variables.

For all parametric tests, insulin resistance was transformed by the natural logarithm. Results are presented as back transformed values with a parameter estimate B, expressing the ratio between increments in independent variables. In the generalized linear mixed models, the model estimate, logit, was back transformed and presented as odds ratios. All model assumptions were met. The level of statistical significance was set at $p<0.05$. Statistical analyses were performed using R version 3.3.2 and SPSS version 22.

Results

Demographic and clinical characteristics

We included 206 patients with BD, 50 of their unaffected relatives and 109 healthy individuals. Five patients with BD were Asian, five patients with BD were of mixed Asian and Caucasian ancestry and the remaining participants were Caucasian. Demographic and clinical variables of the study participants are presented in Table 1. Unaffected relatives were from 39 distinct families as 11 patients with BD had two of their unaffected relatives included. The patients with BD and healthy individuals were comparable in age (median [interquartile range] age 29.5 [24–37] vs. 28 [24–36.5] years, $P=0.8$). Sex distribution in the three groups (patients with BD, unaffected relatives, healthy individuals) was similar. The unaffected first-degree relatives were younger than healthy individuals ($P=0.024$). Healthy individuals had higher education level than patients with BD ($P=0.001$), whereas education level did not differ between unaffected relatives and healthy individuals. Levels of activity, measured in metabolic equivalent minutes, were lower in patients with BD compared with healthy individuals ($P=0.013$) and did not differ between unaffected relatives and healthy individuals ($P=0.9$). More patients with BD and unaffected relatives reported sleep disturbances than healthy individuals ($P<0.001$ and $P=0.001$, respectively). Patients with BD had a lower weekly alcohol intake than healthy individuals ($P<0.001$), whereas alcohol units per week were similar in unaffected relatives and healthy individuals ($P=0.1$). Smoking was more common among patients with BD and their unaffected relatives compared to healthy individuals (Chi squared < 0.001). Among the patients with BD, 81.1% (n = 167) were diagnosed within the preceding year; additionally, 13.6% (n = 28) were diagnosed within the last 2 years, whereas the remaining 5.4% (n = 11) were diagnosed within the preceding 7 years.

Metabolic syndrome in patients with bipolar disorder, their unaffected first-degree relatives and healthy individuals

As depicted in Fig. 1, 15.0% of patients with BD, 6.0% of their unaffected first-degree relatives and 5.5% of healthy individuals met criteria for metS. In the unadjusted analysis, the prevalence of metS was higher in patients with BD (B = 3.041, 95% CI 1.227–7.535, $P=0.016$) but not in their unaffected relatives (B = 1.096, 95% CI 0.263–4.570, $p=0.9$) compared with healthy individuals (Table 2, model 1a). Adjusted for age and sex, patients with BD had 3.5 higher risk of having metS than healthy individuals (B = 3.529, 95% CI 1.378–9.041, $P=0.009$), whereas no statistically significant difference was found between unaffected relatives and healthy individuals (B = 1.472, 95% CI 0.334–6.497, $P=0.6$) (Table 2, model 1b). In a fully adjusted model controlling additionally for smoking status and alcohol use, however, the observed difference in metS between the groups was no longer statistically significant (Table 2, model 1c). In a comparable model, there was no statistical difference in the prevalence of metS between unaffected relatives and patients with BD (B = 0.417, 95% CI 0.118–1.467, $P=0.2$). Repeating the main analysis of metS between groups adjusted for age and sex, excluding the two patients with BD with type 2 diabetes, did not change the results (B = 3.250, 95% CI 1.270–8.319, $P=0.009$).

Insulin resistance in patients with bipolar disorder, their unaffected first-degree relatives and healthy individuals

Measurements of insulin were missing in three patients, one unaffected relative and three healthy individuals, consequently these seven participants were only included in analyses of metS but not of insulin resistance. As shown in Fig. 1 the median [interquartile range] of insulin resistance (HOMA-IR) was 2.06 [1.44–3.25] in patients with BD, 2.10 [1.59–2.63] in unaffected relatives and 1.73 [1.35–2.42] in healthy individuals. In the unadjusted model, levels of insulin resistance were 20.3% higher in patients with BD compared with healthy individuals (B = 1.203, 95% CI 1.058–1.367, $P=0.005$) while no difference was found between unaffected relatives and healthy individuals (Table 2, model 2a). After adjusting for age and sex the levels of insulin resistance remained elevated in patients with BD compared with healthy individuals (B = 1.203, 95% CI 1.059–1.367, $P=0.005$) (Table 2, model 2b). In a comparable model, there was no statistical difference in levels of insulin resistance between

Table 1 Demographic and clinical variables in patients with bipolar disorder (BD), their unaffected first-degree relatives (UR) and healthy individuals (HC)

	BD	UR	HC
N	206	50	109
Metabolic syndrome	31 (15)	3 (6)	6 (5.5)
Insulin resistance (HOMA-IR)	2.06 [1.44–3.25]	2.10 [1.59–2.63]	1.73 [1.35–2.42]
Age (years)	29.5 [24–37]	26.5 [22–31.3]	28 [24–36.5]
Sex (% female)	126 (61.2)	25 (50)	66 (60.6)
Education (years total)	15 [12.5–16]	15 [13–17]	15.5 [14.5–17]
Number of smokers (%)	95 (46.1)	13 (27.1)	10 (9.3)
Alcohol, units per week	2 [0–7]	2 [1–8]	5 [2–7]
Exercise (IPAQ, MET-minutes per week)	1680 [698–3051]	2373 [754–5270]	2040 [1160–4320]
Sleep disturbance (PSQI total score)	9 [6–13]	5.5 [3.8–8.3]	4 [2–6]
HDRS-17	9 [5–15]	2 [0–4]	1 [0–2]
YMRS	2 [0–6]	0 [0–2]	1 [0–2]
BD I	75 (34.4)	–	–
BD II	127 (61.7)	–	–
Single manic episode	4 (1.9)	–	–
Age of onset	17 [14–21]	–	–
Illness duration (years)	10 [6–16]	–	–
Untreated bipolar disorder (years)[a]	5 [1–11]	–	–
Manic episodes	0 [0–1]	–	–
Hypomanic episodes	4 [2–15]	–	–
Depressive episodes	6 [3–15]	–	–
Mixed episodes	0 [0–0]	–	–
Total affective episodes	12.5 [6–30]	–	–
Hospitalizations	0 [0–1]	–	–
Current affective episode			
Remission	124 (60.2)	–	–
Mild/moderate depressive episode	42 (20.4)	–	–
Severe depressive episode	6 (2.9)	–	–
Mixed episode	10 (4.9)	–	–
Hypomanic episode	17 (8.3)	–	–
Manic episode	2 (1)	–	–
N.A.	2 (1)	–	–
Medication			
No psychotropic medication	29 (14.1)	–	–
Lithium treatment	74 (35.9)	–	–
Antiepileptic treatment	108 (52.4)	–	–
Antidepressant treatment	55 (26.7)	–	–
Antipsychotic treatment	67 (32.5)	–	–
Psychotropic medication with metabolic adverse effects	127 (61.7)	–	–

Continuous variables are presented as median [interquartile range]. Categorical variables are presented as n (%). *HOMA-IR* the Homeostasis model assessment of insulin resistance, *IPAQ* International Physical Activity Questionnaire, *MET-minutes* metabolic equivalent minutes, *PSQI*: Pittsburgh Sleep Quality Index, *HAMD-17* 17-item Hamilton Depression Rating Scale, *YMRS* Young Mania Rating Scale, *BD I and BD II* Bipolar Disorder type I and II, respectively, *N.A.* not available

[a] Untreated bipolar disorder was defined as time from first manic, hypomanic or mixed episode to time of diagnosing bipolar disorder

patients with BD and unaffected relatives (B = 1.125, 95% CI 0.958–1.321, $P = 0.1$). In a fully adjusted model controlling additionally for smoking status and alcohol use, however, the observed difference in insulin resistance between the groups was no longer statistically significant (Table 2, model 2c). In a post hoc analysis, we added waist circumference as a covariate in the fully adjusted model and it did not alter the findings, however, waist circumference was associated with insulin resistance (B = 1.023, 95% CI 1.018–1.028, $P \leq 0.001$)).

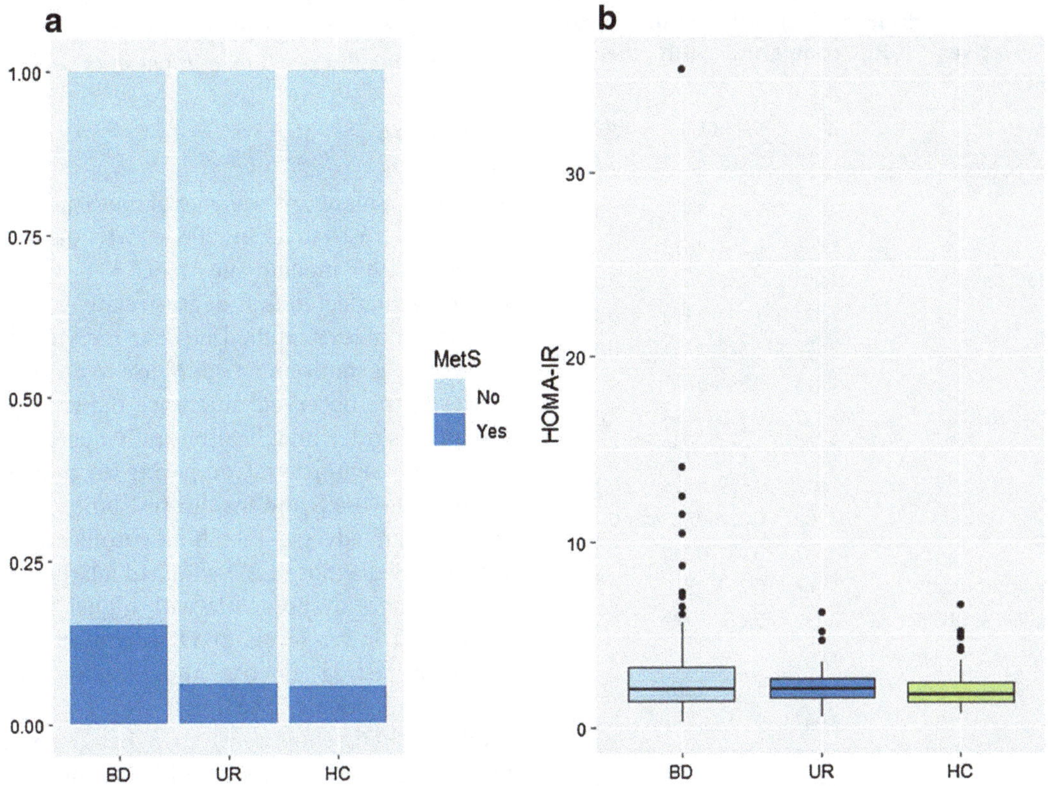

Fig. 1 **a** Clustered bar chart of metabolic syndrome and **b** box plot of insulin resistance in patients with newly diagnosed bipolar disorder (BD), their unaffected first-degree relatives (UR) and healthy individuals (HC). The lower and upper hinges in the box plot correspond to the first and third quartiles and the upper and lower whiskers extend from the hinge to the largest and lower value, respectively, no further than 1.5 times the interquartile range from the hinge. Data beyond the end of the whiskers are plotted individually. MetS: metabolic syndrome; HOMA-IR: homeostasis model assessment of insulin resistance

We repeated our main analysis of insulin resistance adjusted for age and sex, excluding the two patients with BD with type 2 diabetes and this did not change the results (B = 1.199, 95% CI 1.055–1.362, $P = 0.005$).

Individual components of the metabolic syndrome and insulin resistance

Levels of the individual components of the metS and insulin resistance, respectively, are shown in Table 3. Patients with BD had a larger waist circumference ($P = 0.008$) than healthy individuals and in explorative sex-specific analyses female patients with BD had a larger median [interquartile range] waist circumference than healthy female individuals (83 [76–90] cm vs. 78 [74–85] cm $P = 0.014$) whereas male patients with BD did not differ from healthy male individuals (91 [84–104] cm vs. 88 [82–94] cm $P = 0.7$). Compared with healthy individuals, patients with BD had higher levels of triglycerides ($P < 0.001$), fasting glucose ($P = 0.047$) and fasting insulin ($P = 0.009$), and lower levels of HDL cholesterol ($P = 0.001$) and systolic blood pressure ($P = 0.004$). Unaffected relatives had lower levels of HDL cholesterol than healthy individuals ($P = 0.017$), whereas the other components did not differ between these two groups.

Association between illness- and medication variables and metabolic syndrome and insulin resistance among patients with bipolar disorder

Illness duration (B = 0.637, 95% CI 0.409–0.998, $P = 0.047$) was negatively associated with metS (Table 4, model 1). No association between individual psychotropic medication types and metS was observed. Lithium treatment was positively associated with insulin resistance (B = 1.242, 95% CI 1.045–1.478, $P = 0.014$), while no association was observed between illness duration or other individual types of psychotropic medication and insulin resistance (Table 4, model 2). When grouping medication according to their likely metabolic impact, treatment with psychotropic medication with metabolic adverse effects was associated with higher insulin resistance (B = 1.298, 95% CI 1.088–1.550, $P = 0.004$). However, no association was found between treatment with psychotropic medication with metabolic adverse effects and metS (B = 2.325, 95% CI 0.873–6.194, $P = 0.09$). No

Table 2 Metabolic syndrome and insulin resistance in patients with bipolar disorder (BD) and their unaffected first-degree relatives (UR) compared with healthy individuals (HC)

	Model	B	95% CI	*P* value
1	Metabolic syndrome			
a	BD vs. HC	3.041	1.227–7.535	0.016
	UR vs. HC	1.096	0.263–4.570	0.9
b	Male vs. female sex	1.954	1.142–2.168	0.059
	Age	1.574	1.142–2.168	0.056
	BD vs. HC	3.529	1.378–9.041	0.009
	UR vs. HC	1.472	0.334–6.497	0.6
c	Male vs. female sex	2.117	0.998–4.494	0.051
	Age	1.580	1.137–2.197	0.006
	BD vs. HC	1.918	0.669–5.498	0.2
	UR vs. HC	1.108	0.027–0.432	0.9
	No smoking	0.332	0.151–0.730	0.006
	High vs. low alcohol intake	1.107	0.369–3.318	0.9
	Moderate vs. low alcohol intake	0.739	0.317–1.727	0.5
2	Insulin resistance			
a	BD vs. HC	1.203	1.058–1.367	0.005
	UR vs. HC	1.092	0.0910–1.311	0.3
b	Male vs. female sex	1.095	0.977–1.238	0.1
	Age	0.996	0.989–1.002	0.2
	BD vs. HC	1.203	1.059–1.367	0.005
	UR vs. HC	1.069	0.889–1.287	0.5
c	Male vs. female sex	1.129	1.001–1.273	0.048
	Age	0.995	0.982–1.002	0.2
	BD vs. HC	1.129	0.982–1.234	0.1
	UR vs. HC	1.019	0.842–1.234	0.8
	Smoking	1.113	0.974–1.271	0.1
	High vs. low alcohol intake	0.857	0.704–1.044	0.1
	Moderate vs. low alcohol intake	0.905	0.796–1.029	0.1

Model 1: Generalized linear mixed model with metabolic syndrome as the dependent variable. B represents odds ratios

Model 2: Linear mixed model with insulin resistance as the dependent variable. B represents back transformed beta values

association was found between BD subtype and metS or insulin resistance.

Association between demographic- and lifestyle variables and metabolic syndrome and insulin resistance among patients with bipolar disorder

There was no statistically significant association between metS and sex, smoking status, alcohol intake, sleep quality or physical activity among patients with BD. A moderate alcohol intake was associated with lower insulin resistance compared with a low alcohol intake in patients with BD ($B=0.868$, 95% CI 0.763–0.988, $P=0.033$) and male sex was associated with higher insulin resistance ($B=1.174$, 95% CI 1.037–1.328, $P=0.011$). Smoking status, sleep quality and physical activity were not associated with insulin resistance in patients with BD.

Discussion

Main results

We found a higher prevalence of metS and greater degree of insulin resistance in 206 newly diagnosed bipolar patients with a median age of 29.5 [24–37] years, but not in the 50 unaffected first-degree relatives, compared with 109 age and sex-matched healthy individuals. Considering smoking status and alcohol use in an adjusted model, however, the observed difference between patients with bipolar disorder and healthy individuals was no longer statistically significant. Comparing the individual components of the metS and insulin resistance between groups revealed an adverse metabolic profile among patients with newly diagnosed BD who had a larger waist circumference, more dyslipidemia with higher levels of triglycerides and lower levels of HDL cholesterol and higher levels of fasting glucose and insulin compared with healthy individuals. The unaffected relatives had lower levels of HDL cholesterol than healthy individuals. In analyses among patients with BD, treatment with lithium as well as treatment with medication with adverse metabolic effects were associated with higher levels of insulin resistance, whereas illness duration was negatively associated with metS.

Comparison to other case–control studies in patients with newly diagnosed bipolar disorder

Three previous studies investigated metS in patients with newly diagnosed BD compared with healthy individuals (Guha et al. 2014; Taylor et al. 2010; Wulsin et al. 2018) and one of these additionally assessed insulin resistance (Guha et al. 2014). Unlike our study, these prior studies did not include analyses adjusted for alcohol and smoking. Two of these studies found no difference in prevalence of metS in patients newly diagnosed with BD compared with healthy individuals (Guha et al. 2014; Taylor et al. 2010). However, in the study by Guha et al. (2014) including 55 patients with BD and 25 controls, the high mean age 43.2 years (SD: 10.6) of patients with BD indicated that patients were possibly in a later illness stage compared with our population of newly diagnosed patients with BD. Furthermore, their population of patients with BD and healthy individuals had more central obesity than participants in our study sample. The study by Taylor et al. (2010) included only 24 newly diagnosed patients with BD, and may have been underpowered to detect differences between groups. The third case–control study (Wulsin et al. 2018) found comparable rates of metS to our findings and the lack of statistically

Table 3 Individual components of the metabolic syndrome and insulin resistance in patients with bipolar disorder (BD) and their unaffected first-degree relatives (UR) compared with healthy individuals (HC)

	BD[1]	UR[2]	HC[3]	P-value
N	206	50	109	
Waist circumference (cm)	85 [78–94]	79 [74–89]	82 [75–90]	0.008^{1-3} 0.4^{2-3}
Triglycerides (mmol/L)	0.94 [0.70–1.39]	0.77 [0.66–1.03]	0.76 [0.61–0.97]	$<0.001^{1-3}$ 0.4^{2-3}
HDL cholesterol (mmol/L)	1.49 [1.24–1.83]	1.52 [1.29–1.79]	1.68 [1.35–1.94]	0.001^{1-3} 0.017^{2-3}
Systolic blood pressure (mmHg)	120 [111–129]	124 [114–135]	124 [116–136]	0.004^{1-3} 0.9^{2-3}
Diastolic blood pressure (mmHg)	77 [70–83]	78 [70–84]	77 [72–85]	0.1^{1-3} 0.3^{2-3}
Fasting plasma glucose (mmol/L)	5.0 [4.8–5.4]	5.1 [4.8–5.4]	5.0 [4.7–5.2]	0.047^{1-3} 0.1^{2-3}
Type 2 diabetes	2 (0.9)	0	0	
Insulin (pmol/L)	55.8 [39.7–84.8]	56.8 [42.0–69.9]	48.9 [38.5–63.6]	0.009^{1-3} 0.1^{2-3}

HDL high density lipoprotein, *MmHg* millimeters of mercury. Continuous variables are presented as median [interquartile range]

Table 4 Metabolic syndrome and insulin resistance in patients with bipolar disorder

	Model	B	95% CI	P-value
1	Metabolic syndrome			
a	Illness duration[a]	0.637	0.409–0.993	0.047
b	BD type I vs. type II	0.769	0.345–1.705	0.5
c	Lithium	0.993	0.438–2.252	1.0
d	Antipsychotics	0.845	0.361–1.981	0.7
e	Antiepileptics	0.782	0.350–1.748	0.5
f	Antidepressants	2.517	1.717–3.691	0.7
g	Medication with metabolic adverse effects	2.325	0.873–6.194	0.1
2	Insulin resistance			
a	Illness duration[a]	0.987	0.974–1.000	0.056
b	BD type I vs. type II	0.891	0.745–1.065	0.2
c	Lithium	1.242	1.045–1.478	0.014
d	Antipsychotics	1.082	0.903–1.294	0.4
e	Antiepileptics	0.874	0.736–1.040	0.1
f	Antidepressants	1.075	0.882–1.310	0.3
g	Medication with metabolic adverse effects	1.298	1.088–1.550	0.004

Model 1: Separate generalized linear mixed models of metabolic syndrome (a–g) in patients with BD, adjusted for age and sex. B represents odds ratios

Model 2: Separate linear mixed models of insulin resistance (a–g) in patients with BD, adjusted for age and sex. B represents back transformed beta values

BD I and BD II: Bipolar Disorder type I and II, respectively. [a]Illness duration was defined as time from first episode (depressive, hypomanic, manic or mixed episode)

significance may have been due to lack of power owing to a relatively small group of healthy individuals (n = 56). Further, these three studies of metS in patients with newly diagnosed BD all assessed metS using the National Cholesterol Education Program adult treatment panel III (ATPIII) definition, whereas we used the International Diabetes Federation's criteria, which are the most commonly used criteria in Europe with cut-offs for central obesity specific for populations of Europid origin. The ATPIII definition can be met without having central obesity and the cut-off for central obesity for populations of North American origin is more liberal than the International Diabetes Federation's criteria (Kaur 2014). If these studies had used the International Diabetes Federation's criteria it is possible that they had found similar results to ours (e.g. in the study by Guha et al. (2014) only seven out of 55 patients newly diagnosed with BD fulfilled the ATPIII criteria). Similarly to the results by Guha et al. (2014) we found elevated levels of insulin resistance in patients with newly diagnosed BD, although as discussed above, patients with BD in our study were substantially younger than patients with BD in the study by Guha et al. (2014).

Illness- and medication variables

In patients with BD we observed a negative association between illness duration and metS while extant research appears to have indicated a lack of such an association (Vancampfort et al. 2013). However, the confidence interval for the estimate of the association was wide and although we adjusted the analysis for age and sex it cannot be excluded that the finding is due to residual confounding. We did not replicate previous findings of treatment with antipsychotics being associated with increased prevalence of metS (Vancampfort et al. 2013), but found treatment with lithium associated with increased levels of insulin resistance. However, the observed effect was rather small and due to the observational design and the limitations in estimating effects of single treatment categories in patients receiving several types of medications, caution should be observed when interpreting this finding. Given those limitations, it may be more meaningful to consider medication in their capacity to induce metabolic changes, when estimating the association between medication and metS or insulin resistance. Using this approach, we found that patients using medication with metabolic side effects had more insulin resistance, but not a higher risk of metS, compared with patients that did not use such medication. The association between medication with capacity to induce metabolic changes and metS did not reach statistically significance, however, this may be due to the relatively low power of the analysis, and overall, our results point to medication as an important risk factor for metS.

In accordance with Calkin et al.'s (2015) findings we did not find association between the type of BD and insulin resistance. Finally, the type of BD was neither associated with metS.

Individual components of the metabolic syndrome and insulin resistance

Patients with BD had larger waist circumferences than healthy individuals. Robust epidemiological evidence associates central obesity with increased overall mortality as well as excess death caused by CVD (Cornier et al. 2011; Pischon et al. 2008) and, notably, the median waist circumference of 83 cm in our female patients with BD exceeded the cut-off for central obesity defined by the International Diabetes Federation (≥80 cm) (Alberti et al. 2006), while waist circumference medians of male patients with BD and healthy individuals of both sexes were below the threshold for central obesity. We also found an adverse lipid profile in patients with BD with lower levels of HDL cholesterol and higher levels of triglycerides similar to recent findings in patients with BD compared with healthy individuals (Wulsin et al. 2018). The only individual component of metS not differing in patients with BD compared with healthy individuals was the systolic blood pressure which align with findings of a recent meta-analysis of metS and severe mental illness, where the risk of metS and all its individual components except for hypertension were elevated in patients with BD (Vancampfort et al. 2015).

Fasting insulin levels were higher in patients with BD compared with healthy individuals, supporting the findings by Guha et al. (2014). In contrast to that study, we also detected higher levels of fasting glucose in patients with newly diagnosed BD compared with healthy individuals, although the levels were within normal ranges in all three groups. Only mild non medicated type 2 diabetes is allowed among blood donors and we therefore repeated our main analyses of metS and insulin resistance excluding the two patients with BD with comorbid type 2 diabetes. This, however, did not alter the results of our main analyses, which we find to be most correct, as the two patients with BD were not in treatment for type 2 diabetes and were unaware of having type 2 diabetes at time of assessment, thus not treated, which could happen for blood donors as well.

Possible predictors of metabolic syndrome and insulin resistance in patients with bipolar disorder

In the current study, patients with BD differed further from healthy individuals in regard to active smoking (Sun et al. 2012), alcohol intake (Alkerwi et al. 2009), activity level (Zhang et al. 2017) and sleep disturbances (Pulido-Arjona et al. 2018), which are major predictors of metS and insulin resistance. We found that 46% of the patients with BD were smokers, which is more than twice the prevalence of the Danish general population (SST 2017) versus 27% of their unaffected relatives and 9% of their healthy individuals. Smoking cessation increases the levels of HDL cholesterol (März et al. 2017) and has been shown to reduce the risk of metS (Sun et al. 2012). We found smoking to be associated with metS in our overall analyses (Sun et al. 2012), whereas we found no effect of activity level and sleep disturbances in patients with bipolar disorder. Further, in these models, we did not find associations between insulin resistance level and smoking, activity level and sleep disturbances, respectively. However, interpretation of these analyses should be made with caution as we are comparing relatively small subsamples of patients with BD. In the present study, patients with newly diagnosed BD had a lower alcohol intake than healthy individuals, and whereas alcohol in small amounts seems protective of metS high alcohol intake increases the risk of metS (Alkerwi et al. 2009). We did not find an association between metS and alcohol neither in comparison of the three groups or within patients with BD. However, alcohol intake was relatively low in all three groups in the present study suggesting a minor role of alcohol in the current observations. Our finding of higher insulin resistance level among patients with low alcohol intake compared with patients with moderate alcohol intake was unexpected. However, many patients with BD have had an increased alcohol intake the preceding months before initiating treatment in the Copenhagen Affective Disorder Clinic and were encouraged to restrict or completely avoid alcohol for the initial 3 months in the clinic. A preceding large alcohol intake would not be captured in our measure, thus our finding of a negative association between higher alcohol intake and lower prevalence of insulin resistance among patients with BD, should be interpreted with caution. Patients with BD were less physically active than healthy individuals. This may contribute to the present findings and could be due to symptoms related to BD but may also be related to the use of sedative medication. The lower level of activity could likely contribute to the lower levels of HDL cholesterol observed in the present study, such as observed in other studies of patients with BD (Chen et al. 2017). Finally, sleep disturbances in young adults are associated with dysmetabolism such as higher fasting glucose levels and triglyceride levels and lower levels of HDL cholesterol (Pulido-Arjona et al. 2018) and were more prevalent in patients with BD and in their unaffected first-degree relatives in the current study.

Metabolic syndrome and insulin resistance in unaffected first-degree relatives

Studying unaffected relatives may help to clarify if there is a common shared pathophysiology of BD and type 2 diabetes and/or CVD (de Melo et al. 2017; SayuriYamagata et al. 2017). Apart from lower levels of HDL cholesterol in unaffected relatives compared with healthy individuals, our findings did not indicate dysmetabolism before onset of BD as levels of insulin resistance and rates of metS and their individual components did not differ from healthy individuals. Nonetheless, patients with BD and their unaffected first-degree relatives neither differ in prevalence of metS nor in levels of insulin resistance from patients with BD, thus we may possibly have overseen a true difference between our modest sample size of unaffected relatives and healthy individuals. Unaffected first-degree relatives had smoking prevalence at the same level as the Danish general population (SST 2017) and with respect to metS, where smoking is known to be a major predictor (Sun et al. 2012), the unaffected relatives could possibly be representative of the general population. Nonetheless, whereas the healthy individuals possibly were super healthy indicated by higher education- and activity level than the patients with BD and lower smoking prevalence than the Danish general population, the unaffected first-degree relatives may possibly be less healthy than the general population due to their psychiatric dispositions and consequently would not be a valid control group.

Strengths and limitations

Advantages of the study include thoroughly assessment of a relatively large group of well-characterized patients with newly diagnosed BD and a group of their unaffected first-degree relatives. Further, our study profited from a high degree of standardization (e.g., blood sampling time, collection and analyses) at the same day as clinical and psychiatric evaluation. Most of our patients with BD (81.1%) were diagnosed within the preceding year and the maximum time with diagnosis was 7 years. The average delay in diagnosis of 5 years and illness duration (time from first mood episode) of 10 years accords with prior findings (Kessler et al. 2007; Baldessarini et al. 2007) and further illustrates the challenge of recruiting patients early in their course of illness due to the known diagnostic delay (Baldessarini et al. 2007).

Several limitations of our study should be considered. First, the sample size of unaffected relatives was moderate (n = 50) due to three major reasons; (1) missing consent from patients to contact their relatives, (2) unaffected relatives having a major psychiatric illness themselves and (3) lack of unaffected first-degree relatives satisfying the age range criteria (15–40 years). Due to this limited sample of healthy relatives, we were not able to include the measurements of sleep disturbances and physical activity in our fully adjusted analyses comparing metS and insulin resistance between groups. However, since there were no statistically significant differences between groups in the models including smoking status and alcohol intake, we find it unlikely, that the addition of sleep disturbances and physical activity measurements would have changed the results. Second, due to the cross-sectional study design, we cannot draw final conclusions regarding dysmetabolism before BD based on the findings in unaffected relatives of patients with BD, as the majority proportion of these will not develop BD. Currently we are expanding our study cohort in the longitudinal BIO study (Kessing et al. 2017), and following participants prospectively, including through onset of illness, will enhance our knowledge about dysmetabolism before onset of BD. Third, in contrast to well-established evidence we did not find association between antipsychotics and metS and insulin resistance, respectively (Vancampfort et al. 2013; Correll et al. 2008; Burghardt et al. 2018), however, we found an association between receiving psychotropics with metabolic adverse effects and insulin resistance. Further, lithium was also observed associated with insulin resistance. Caution in interpreting these findings should be made due to our categorization of treatment. Thus, our use of dichotomous treatment categories does not account for neither medication dose nor duration of treatment. Further, the concurrent treatment with multiple medication types reduces or may even eliminate the possibility to identify an isolated effect of one treatment category. We may therefore not fully capture the true effect of psychotropic medication on metabolism in the present study. However, using the variable of receiving psychotropics with metabolic adverse effects may possibly yield the most valid analysis of psychotropic medication in the present study. Nonetheless, our findings should be interpreted with caution and we cannot exclude the possibility that receiving psychotropics with metabolic adverse effects is the main driver of the identified higher metS prevalence and insulin resistance level in patients with BD compared with heatlhy individuals. Fourth, we included blood donors recruited in the Blood Bank at Rigshospitalet as healthy individuals. Blood donors may in some respects be regarded as super healthy individuals, and in our sample they had a longer education level, which is known to increase overall health (Golding et al. 2013) and they had a lower prevalence of smoking than the general population (SST 2017). Contrary to our expectations, the healthy individuals had higher systolic blood pressure and a higher alcohol intake than the patients with BD.

Conclusions

Our findings of higher prevalence of metS and elevated insulin resistance levels in patients with newly diagnosed BD compared with healthy individuals highlight the pivotal role of early individualized prevention strategies targeted against smoking, overweight, dyslipidemia and dysglycemia in this population. Notably, smoking was highly prevalent in patients with newly diagnosed BD and—to a lesser degree—in their unaffected first-degree relatives. The well-established connection between smoking and metS indicate that smoking cessation is highly relevant in these populations. Further, our findings suggest that the high prevalence of smoking in our population of patients with BD was an important driver of the identified higher risk of metS. Similarly, central obesity was strongly associated with insulin resistance in patients with BD and found specifically in female patients newly diagnosed with BD. The major CVD risk accompanying central obesity further highlight the importance of maintaining a healthy fat distribution and intervening against central obesity from time of diagnosing BD. Preventing the development of metS, type 2 diabetes and CVD may diminish the risk of premature death and a chronic, disabling illness course in patients with BD. Clinically, it should be considered to include assessment of metS and insulin resistance aiming to prevent or identify metabolic diseases in patients with BD from the time of diagnosis.

Significant outcomes

Patients with newly diagnosed bipolar disorder but not their unaffected first-degree relatives had higher rates of metabolic syndrome and insulin resistance compared with healthy individuals.
A larger waist circumference, more dyslipidemia and higher levels of fasting glucose and insulin were observed in patients with bipolar disorder compared with matched healthy individuals.
Assessment of the individual components of the metabolic syndrome, insulin resistance and smoking from time of diagnosis should be considered to initiate adequate and early care reducing the risk of cardiovascular disease and premature death.

Limitations

The sample size of unaffected first-degree relatives was modest.
Our categorization of psychotropic medication variables may not capture the true effect of psychotropic medication.

Abbreviations

BD: bipolar disorder; metS: metabolic syndrome; BMI: body mass index; HDL: high-density lipoprotein; HOMA-IR: homeostasis model assessment of insulin resistance.

Authors' contributions

KC did the primary draft, statistical analyses and interpretation of data supervised by KM. KC, KM, LVK and MV contributed in the design and overall statistical plan. LVK and MV also contributed with interpretation of data. FKK, BP and RM, experts within the investigated field, participated with intellectual contributions to the manuscript. All authors read and approved the final manuscript.

Author details

[1] Copenhagen Affective Disorders Research Centre (CADIC), Psychiatric Center Copenhagen, Department O, 6243, Rigshospitalet, Blegdamsvej 9, 2100 Copenhagen, Denmark. [2] Department of Clinical Medicine, Faculty of Health and Medical Sciences, University of Copenhagen, Copenhagen, Denmark. [3] Clinical Metabolic Physiology, Steno Diabetes Center Copenhagen,

Gentofte Hospital, Hellerup, Denmark. [4] Centre of Inflammation and Metabolism (CIM) and the Centre for Physical Activity Research (CFAS), Rigshospitalet, Copenhagen, Denmark. [5] Mood Disorders Psychopharmacology Unit, University Health Network, Toronto, Canada.

Acknowledgements
A special thanks to Anne Præstegaard for her logistic and laboratory assistance throughout the study.

Competing interests
KC and KM declare no conflicts of interest. MV discloses within the last three years consultancy fees from Lundbeck. In the last three years, FKK has served on scientific advisory panels and/or been part of speaker's bureaus for, served as a consultant to and/or received research support from Amgen, AstraZeneca, Boehringer Ingelheim, Carmot Therapeutics, Eli Lilly, Gubra, MedImmune, MSD/Merck, Norgine, Novo Nordisk, Sanofi and Zealand Pharma. BKP has a research grant from Novo Nordisk AS, and is a minority shareholder in Antag Therapeutics.. RSV declares having received honoraria from Lundbech, Pfizer, AstraZeneca, Elli-Lilly, JanssenOrtho, Purdue, Johnson & Johnson, Moksha8, Sunovion, Mitsubishi, Takeda, Forest, Otsuka, Bristoy-Myers Squibb, Shire and Allergan in the preceding three years. LVK has within the preceding three years been a consultant for Sunovion.

References

Abosi O, Lopes S, Schmitz S, Fiedorowicz JG. Cardiometabolic effects of psychotropic medications. Horm Mol Biol Clin Investig. 2018;1:1. https://doi.org/10.1515/hmbci-2017-0065.

Alberti G, Zimmet P, Shaw J, M. Grundy SM. IDF Consensus Worldwide Definition of the Metabolic Syndrome. 2006.

Alkerwi A, Boutsen M, Vaillant M, Barre J, Lair ML, Albert A, et al. Alcohol consumption and the prevalence of metabolic syndrome: a meta-analysis of observational studies. Atherosclerosis. 2009;204(2):624–35.

Baldessarini RJ, Tondo L, Baethge CJ, Lepri B, Bratti IM. Effects of treatment latency on response to maintenance treatment in manic-depressive disorders. Bipolar Disord. 2007;9(4):386–93.

Burghardt KJ, Seyoum B, Mallisho A, Burghardt PR, Kowluru RA, Yi Z. Atypical antipsychotics, insulin resistance and weight; a meta-analysis of healthy volunteer studies. Prog Neuropsychopharmacol Biol Psychiatry. 2018;83:55–63.

Buysse DJ, Reynolds CF 3rd, Monk TH, Berman SR, Kupfer DJ. The Pittsburgh Sleep Quality Index: a new instrument for psychiatric practice and research. Psychiatry Res. 1989;28(2):193–213.

Cairns K, McCarvill T, Ruzickova M, Calkin CV. Course of bipolar illness worsens after onset of insulin resistance. J Psychiatr Res. 2018;102:34–7.

Calkin C, van de Velde C, Ruzickova M, Slaney C, Garnham J, Hajek T, et al. Can body mass index help predict outcome in patients with bipolar disorder? Bipolar Disord. 2009;11(6):650–6.

Calkin CV, Ruzickova M, Uher R, Hajek T, Slaney CM, Garnham JS, et al. Insulin resistance and outcome in bipolar disorder. Br J Psychiatry. 2015;206(1):52–7.

Chen YC, Tsai JC, Liou YM, Chan P. Effectiveness of endurance exercise training in patients with coronary artery disease: a meta-analysis of randomised controlled trials. Eur J Cardiovasc Nurs. 2017;16(5):397–408.

Cornier MA, Despres JP, Davis N, Grossniklaus DA, Klein S, Lamarche B, et al. Assessing adiposity: a scientific statement from the American Heart Association. Circulation. 2011;124(18):1996–2019.

Correll CU, Frederickson AM, Kane JM, Manu P. Equally increased risk for metabolic syndrome in patients with bipolar disorder and schizophrenia treated with second-generation antipsychotics. Bipolar Disord. 2008;10(7):788–97.

Craig CL, Marshall AL, Sjostrom M, Bauman AE, Booth ML, Ainsworth BE, et al. International physical activity questionnaire: 12-country reliability and validity. Med Sci Sports Exerc. 2003;35(8):1381–95.

de Melo LGP, Nunes SOV, Anderson G, Vargas HO, Barbosa DS, Galecki P, et al. Shared metabolic and immune-inflammatory, oxidative and nitrosative stress pathways in the metabolic syndrome and mood disorders. Prog Neuropsychopharmacol Biol Psychiatry. 2017;78:34–50.

SST. 2018. https://www.sst.dk/da/udgivelser/2018/~/media/D76CC35372 3F458E9F978B6BE1BF1BBC.ashx. Accessed 31 Jan 2019.

Golding J, Northstone K, Miller LL, Davey Smith G, Pembrey M. Differences between blood donors and a population sample: implications for case-control studies. Int J Epidemiol. 2013;42(4):1145–56.

Goldstein BI. Bipolar disorder and the vascular system: mechanisms and new prevention opportunities. Can J Cardiol. 2017;33(12):1565–76.

Goldstein BI, Carnethon MR, Matthews KA, McIntyre RS, Miller GE, Raghuveer G, et al. Major depressive disorder and bipolar disorder predispose youth to accelerated atherosclerosis and early cardiovascular disease: a scientific statement from the American Heart Association. Circulation. 2015;132(10):965–86.

Guha P, Bhowmick K, Mazumder P, Ghosal M, Chakraborty I, Burman P. Assessment of insulin resistance and metabolic syndrome in drug naive patients of bipolar disorder. Indian J Clin Biochem. 2014;29(1):51–6.

Hamilton M. A rating scale for depression. J Neurol Neurosurg Psychiatry. 1960;23:56–62.

Hermans MP, Levy JC, Morris RJ, Turner RC. Comparison of insulin sensitivity tests across a range of glucose tolerance from normal to diabetes. Diabetologia. 1999;42(6):678–87.

Kaur J. A comprehensive review on metabolic syndrome. Cardiol Res Pract. 2014;2014:943162.

Kemp DE, Gao K, Chan PK, Ganocy SJ, Findling RL, Calabrese JR. Medical comorbidity in bipolar disorder: relationship between illnesses of the endocrine/metabolic system and treatment outcome. Bipolar Disord. 2010;12(4):404–13.

Kessing LV, Vradi E, Andersen PK. Life expectancy in bipolar disorder. Bipolar Disord. 2015;17(5):543–8.

Kessing LV, Munkholm K, Faurholt-Jepsen J, Miskowiak KW, Nielsen LB, Frikke-Schmidt R, Ekstrøm C, Winther O, Pedersen BK, Poulsen HE, McIntyre RS, Kapczinski F, Gattaz WF, Bardram J, Mads F, Mayora O, Knudsen GM, Phillips M, Vinberg M. The Bipolar illness onset study—research protocol for the BIO cohort study. BMJ Open. 2017. https://doi.org/10.1136/bmjopen-2016-015462.

Kessler RC, Angermeyer M, Anthony JC, De Graaf RO, Demyttenaere K, Gasquet I, et al. Lifetime prevalence and age-of-onset distributions of mental disorders in the World Health Organization's World Mental Health Survey Initiative. World Psychiatry. 2007;6(3):168–76.

Larsen PB, Linneberg A, Hansen T, Friis-Hansen L. Reference intervals for C-peptide and insulin derived from a general adult Danish population. Clin Biochem. 2017;50(7–8):408–13.

Laursen TM, Wahlbeck K, Hallgren J, Westman J, Osby U, Alinaghizadeh H, et al. Life expectancy and death by diseases of the circulatory system in patients with bipolar disorder or schizophrenia in the Nordic countries. PLoS ONE. 2013;8(6):e67133.

Mansur RB, Rizzo LB, Santos CM, Asevedo E, Cunha GR, Noto MN, et al. Impaired glucose metabolism moderates the course of illness in bipolar disorder. J Affect Disord. 2016;195:57–62.

März W, Kleber ME, Scharnagl H, Speer T, Zewinger S, Ritsch A, et al. HDL cholesterol: reappraisal of its clinical relevance. Clin Res Cardiol. 2017. https://doi.org/10.1007/s00392-017-1106-1.

McIntyre RS, Danilewitz M, Liauw SS, Kemp DE, Nguyen HT, Kahn LS, et al. Bipolar disorder and metabolic syndrome: an international perspective. J Affect Disord. 2010;126(3):366–87.

Osby U, Brandt L, Correia N, Ekbom A, Sparen P. Excess mortality in bipolar and unipolar disorder in Sweden. Arch Gen Psychiatry. 2001;58(9):844–50.

Pischon T, Boeing H, Hoffmann K, Bergmann M, Schulze MB, Overvad K, et al. General and abdominal adiposity and risk of death in Europe. N Engl J Med. 2008;359(20):2105–20.

Pulido-Arjona L, Correa-Bautista JE, Agostinis-Sobrinho C, Mota J, Santos R, Correa-Rodriguez M, et al. Role of sleep duration and sleep-related problems in the metabolic syndrome among children and adolescents. Ital J Pediatr. 2018;44(1):9.

SayuriYamagata A, Brietzke E, Rosenblat JD, Kakar R, McIntyre RS. Medical comorbidity in bipolar disorder: the link with metabolic-inflammatory systems. J Affect Disord. 2017;211:99–106.

Sobczak S, Honig A, Christophe A, Maes M, Helsdingen RW, De Vriese SA, et al. Lower high-density lipoprotein cholesterol and increased omega-6 polyunsaturated fatty acids in first-degree relatives of bipolar patients. Psychol Med. 2004;34(1):103–12.

Sun K, Liu J, Ning G. Active smoking and risk of metabolic syndrome: a meta-analysis of prospective studies. PLoS ONE. 2012;7(10):e47791.

Taylor V, McKinnon MC, Macdonald K, Jaswal G, Macqueen GM. Adults with mood disorders have an increased risk profile for cardiovascular disease within the first 2 years of treatment. Can J Psychiatry. 2010;55(6):362–8.
Vancampfort D, Vansteelandt K, Correll CU, Mitchell AJ, De Herdt A, Sienaert P, et al. Metabolic syndrome and metabolic abnormalities in bipolar disorder: a meta-analysis of prevalence rates and moderators. Am J Psychiatry. 2013;170(3):265–74.
Vancampfort D, Stubbs B, Mitchell AJ, De Hert M, Wampers M, Ward PB, et al. Risk of metabolic syndrome and its components in people with schizophrenia and related psychotic disorders, bipolar disorder and major depressive disorder: a systematic review and meta-analysis. World Psychiatry. 2015;14(3):339–47.
Wing JK, Babor T, Brugha T, Burke J, Cooper JE, Giel R, et al. SCAN. Schedules for clinical assessment in neuropsychiatry. Arch Gen Psychiatry. 1990;47(6):589–93.
Wulsin LR, Blom TJ, Durling M, Welge JA, DelBello MP, Adler CM, et al. Cardiometabolic risks and omega-3 index in recent-onset bipolar I disorder. Bipolar Disord. 2018. https://doi.org/10.1111/bdi.12633.
Young RC, Biggs JT, Ziegler VE, Meyer DA. A rating scale for mania: reliability, validity and sensitivity. Br J Psychiatry. 1978;133:429–35.
Zhang D, Liu X, Liu Y, Sun X, Wang B, Ren Y, et al. Leisure-time physical activity and incident metabolic syndrome: a systematic review and dose-response meta-analysis of cohort studies. Metabolism. 2017;75:36–44.

12

Has Bipolar Disorder become a predominantly female gender related condition? Analysis of recently published large sample studies

Bernardo Dell'Osso[1,2,3*], Rita Cafaro[1] and Terence A. Ketter[3]

Abstract

Bipolar Disorders (BD) are disabling and severe psychiatric disorders, commonly perceived as equally affecting both men and women. The prevalence of BD in the general population has been growing over the last decade, however, few epidemiological studies are available regarding BD gender distribution, leaving unanswered the question whether the often reported increment of BD diagnosis could be gender specific. In fact, BD in female patients can often be misdiagnosed as MDD, leaving such women non correctly treated for longer times than their male counterparts. From this perspective, we searched literature for large sample (> 1000 subjects) studies published in the last decade (2010 onward) on BD patients. We included ten large sample studies that reported the gender distribution of their samples, and we therefore analysed them. Our results show a higher preponderance of female patients in every sample and sub-sample of BDI and BDII, supporting our hypothesis of an increase in BD diagnosis in females. BD in women presents with higher rates of rapid cycling, depressive polarity and suicide attempts, characteristics of non inferior severity compared to males; prompt recognition and adequate treatment of BD is therefore crucial to reduce risks and improve quality of life of affected women. In this regard, our results could lead the way for national or international epidemiological studies with the aim of more accurately assessing gender-specific prevalence of BD.

Keywords: Bipolar disorders, Gender differences, Prevalence, Female gender

Introduction

Bipolar Disorder (BD) has been traditionally included among psychiatric conditions with no gender difference in terms of lifetime prevalence in the general population, (Weissman et al. 1988; Mitchell et al. 2004; Grant et al. 2005; Merikangas et al. 2007) in contrast to unipolar Major Depressive Disorder (MDD), which has consistently shown a higher prevalence in the female gender. (Bijil et al. 2002; Kessler 2003; Leach et al. 2008) However, some studies showed specific differences in the clinical course as well as across various behavioural and social outcomes of BD in individuals with male versus female gender. For instance, early (pre-teen) age of onset of first mania, (Grant et al. 2005; Kennedy et al. 2005) substance use disorders, (Kessing 2004; Nivoli et al. 2011) and legal problems, (Baldassano et al. 2005) were reported to be more common in men, while rapid cycling, (Slyepchenko et al. 2017; Tondo and Baldessarini 1998) depressive episodes, (Diflorio and Jones 2010) mixed mania, (Diflorio and Jones 2010; Arnold et al. 2000) and attempted or completed suicides, (Nivoli et al. 2011; Clements et al. 2013) have been reported to be more frequent in women. Indeed, hypomania, and consequently BD type II (BDII), has commonly been more frequently associated with female gender, (Hendrick et al. 2000; Suppes et al. 2005;

*Correspondence: bernardo.dellosso@unimi.it
[1] Department of Biomedical and Clinical Sciences Luigi Sacco, Department of Mental Health, University of Milan, ASST Fatebenefratelli-Sacco, Milano, Italy
Full list of author information is available at the end of the article

Altshuler et al. 2010) while no significant gender difference has been reported in lifetime prevalence of BD type I (BDI) (Diflorio and Jones 2010).

The overall limited epidemiological studies about BD conducted in the last decade showed increasing lifetime prevalence of BD in the general population, (Clemente et al. 2015) possibly due to better diagnostic instruments, especially with the implementation of DSM-IV diagnostic criteria (American Psychiatric Publishing 1994).

On the other hand, these studies did not evaluate the gender composition of recruited samples, leaving unanswered the question whether the better understanding of the disease lead to an improvement in its recognition in the female gender, in which misdiagnosis with unipolar MDD occurs frequently (Culpepper 2014; Lish et al. 1994; Hirschfeld et al. 2003). In this regard, the recognition of an epidemiological trend of gender specificity in BD could help physicians to pursue prompter diagnosis and implement more effective treatments, which are extremely important considering that use of antidepressants (i.e., misdiagnosis unipolar MDD) might lead to inefficacy for misdiagnosed (actually bipolar) depression, treatment-emergent (hypo)manic switching, onset of rapid cycling and, thus, negatively influence the course of the disease (Wehr and Goodwin 1987).

In light of these considerations, we aimed to analyse the gender composition of large samples studies on BD patients published in the last decade (from 2010 onward), to evaluate a possible modification in the trend of representation of the disease in the two genders.

Methods

An electronic systematic review within the online databases PubMed, Medline, PsychINFO, and Cochrane Library was conducted up to May 2020. Keywords used were: "bipolar disorder" OR "mania" AND "gender" OR "gender difference(s)" AND "national cohort" OR "multicentric studies". The results were filtered by year of publication (2011–2020) and number of patients included in the study (> 1000). We then proceeded to exclude studies not adherent to criteria and incomplete studies not providing information on sample composition in terms of (sub)diagnosis and gender distribution.

Table 1. Main large samples (> 1000 patients) studies on Bipolar Disorder published in the last ten years

Authors	Site	Sample	N° of BD patients recruited	Female patients (%)
Bareis et al. 2018	U.S.A.	STEP-BD (1999-2005)	3563	57,65%
Bobo et al. 2018	U.S.A.	Mayo Clinic Biobank (started in 2009)	1465 BD-I = 69,42% BD-II = 30,58%	60,75% BD-I = 58,60% BD-II = 66,10%
Buoli et al. 2019	Italy	RENDiBi Study (April 2014-March 2015)	1675 BD-I = 62,21% BD-II = 37,79%	57,40%
Crump et al. 2013	Sweden	National Registry (2001-2002)	6618	59,20%
Hayes et al. 2017	U.K.	Primary care electronics health records (THIN) (2000-2014)	17341	58,83%
Hou et al. 2016	Australia, Canada, Czech Republic, France, Germany, Italy, Japan, Poland, Romania,Spain, Sweden, Switzerland, Taiwan, U.S.A.	ConLiGen	2563	57,63%
Kalman et al. 2019	Austria, Australia, Canada, Czech Republic, France, Germany, Italy, Poland, Romania, Spain, Sweden, U.S.A.	ConLiGen, Bonn-Mannheim and PsyCourse	1995 (BD-I patients only)	55,10%
Karanti et al. 2015	Sweden	Swedish National Quality Assurance Register for Bipolar Disorder (BipoläR) (2004-2011)	7136 BD-I = 47,09% BD-II = 38,15% BD-NOS = 14,76%	61,27% BD-I = 57,30% BD-II = 64,95% BD-NOS = 64,42%
Vieta et al. 2013	Austria, Belgium, Brazil, France, Germany, Portugal, Romania, Turkey, Ukraine, Venezuela	WAVE-BD (April 2010- June 2011)	2896 BD-I = 68,70% BD-II = 31,3%	65,00%
Yoon et al. 2018	Korea	Korean HIRA-NPS (2013 sample only)	2626	58,80%

THIN = The Health Improvement Network; STEP-BD = Systematic Treatment Enhancement Program for Bipolar Disorder; RENDiBi = National Epidemiological Research on Bipolar Disorder; HIRA-NPS = Health Insurance Review and Assessment Service - National Patient Sample; WAVE-BD = Wide Ambispective of Bipolar Disorder; ConLiGen = The International Consortium on Lithium Genetics; BD-I = Bipolar Disorder type I

Results

Ten clinical studies published in the last ten years, analysing data from more than 1000 bipolar patients per sample, met our inclusion criteria and are therefore presented and discussed here (Table 1). In aggregate, 47,878 patients with BD were included in these studies.

Two of these studies were conducted in Sweden, one including bipolar patients enrolled in the national registry of the years 2001–2002 (n = 6618), (Crump et al. 2013) while the other included bipolar patients from the Swedish National Quality Assurance Register for Bipolar Disorder (BipoläR), recruiting patients from 2004 to 2011 (n = 7136) Karanti et al. 2015). Another study was conducted in the United Kingdom (U.K.), analysing data from patients included in "The Health Improvement Network" (THIN), from 2000 to 2014 (n = 17,341); (Hayes et al. 2017) THIN is a database of primary care electronics health records representative of the general U.K. population in terms of age, gender, medical conditions, and death rates, and has been validated for research purposes against experimental and observational evidences. Similarly, one study was conducted in Korea and was based on the Health Insurance Review and Assessment Service – National Patient Sample (HIRA-NPS) records of 2010, 2011 and 2013; importantly, validity and representativeness of HIRA-NPS data have been extensively demonstrated (Kim et al. 2014). However, as there is no continuity between data for different years, in order to avoid duplicates, we included in our review only data from 2013 (n = 2626) (Yoon et al. 2018). Two studies were based in the United States of America (U.S.A.); one of them analysed data from the "Systematic Treatment Enhancement Program for Bipolar Disorder" (STEP-BD), a nationwide database collected from 1999 to 2005 (n = 3563) (Bareis et al. 2018). The other was based on the Mayo Clinic Biobank, started in 2009 and including patients recruited until 2018 (n = 1465) Bobo et al. 2018). Yet another study was an Italian study collecting data in the context of the National Epidemiological Research on Bipolar Disorder (RENDiBi) project, in which patients were recruited from April 2014 to March 2015 (n = 1675) (Buoli et al. 2019). Finally, three studies were based on multinational multicentric databases; one was the Wide AmbispectiVE study of the clinical management and burden of BD (WAVE-BD), recruiting patients from April 2010 to June 2011 (n = 2896) (Vieta et al. 2013). Another study collected data from the ConLiGen database (n = 2563) (Hou et al. 2016), while the last one included data collected from ConLiGen, Bonn-Mannheim and PsyCourse databases (n = 1995, BDI patients only) (Kalman et al. 2019).

Nine out of ten studies analysed samples of both BDI and BDII patients, while one study only analysed a sample of BDI patients. All the evaluated studies described the general distribution of their samples in terms of gender, reporting a higher prevalence of female patients, with female patient proportions ranging from 57·4% (RENDiBi Study) to 65·0% (WAVE-BD) (Fig. 1a). Of these, three studies (Mayo Clinic Biobank, RENDiBi Study, WAVE-BD) described the distribution of their samples in terms of BDI and BDII (Mayo Clinic Biobank 69·4% of BDI, RENDiBi Study 62·2% of BDI, WAVE-BD 68·7% of BDI), while one of them (BipoläR) further categorised patients in BDI (47·1%), BDII (38·1%), and Bipolar Disorder – Not Otherwise Specified (BD NOS) (14·8%). In these four studies, a higher prevalence of BDI diagnosis among women can be found (Fig. 1c). Moreover, the Mayo Clinic Biobank study reported the gender distribution of the sub-samples BD-I (F = 58·6%) and BD-II (F = 66·1%), while the BipoläR study reported the gender distribution in the three sub-samples BDI (F = 57·3%), BDII (F = 64·9%), and BD NOS (F = 64·4%). As shown, both these studies reported a higher prevalence of female versus male patients in every sub-sample (Fig. 1b).

Finally, one study evaluated a sample of BDI patients only, reporting a higher prevalence of female versus male patients (55·1%).

Discussion

As shown in the results, 100% (ten out of ten) of our selected large samples studies (n > 1000) published in the last ten years (2011–2020), showed a predominance of female gender in their samples of bipolar patients. These results could support our hypothesis of a relatively recent increase in BD prevalence among individuals with female gender. Even though data published in the Global Burden of Disease Study of 2013 seem to support the findings of a higher prevalence of BD in the female gender (Ferrari et al. 2016), our results seem to be in contradiction with previously published literature about BD prevalence in the two genders (Weissman et al. 1988; Mitchell et al. 2004; Grant et al. 2005; Merikangas et al. 2007; Diflorio and Jones 2010). Causes for this difference could lay in the size of the samples analysed, being that the majority of the studies presented in literature analyse much smaller samples. Moreover, one could argue that the higher percentage of females diagnosed with BD-II could interfere with the gender distribution of the samples analysed, and therefore be the cause of our findings. However, of note, Bobo et al. (Bobo et al. 2018) Buoli et al. (Buoli et al. 2019) Karanti et al. (Karanti et al. 2015) and Vieta et al. (Vieta et al. 2013) had a higher proportion of BDI patients in their samples, and Kalman et al. (Kalman et al. 2019) only had BDI patients in their sample. Findings of a higher prevalence of female patients in these four studies could further support our hypothesis, being

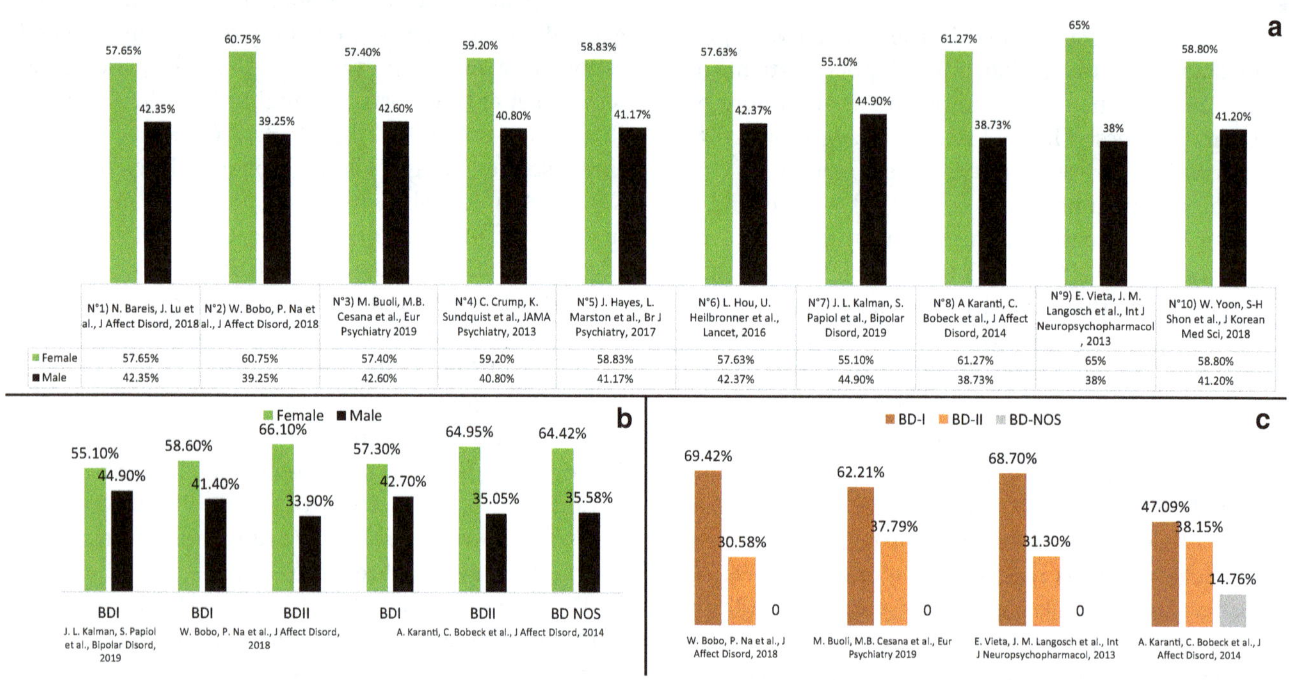

Fig. 1 Gender distribution in Bipolar Disorder as shown in the main large sample studies of the last ten years. **a** Graphic representation of gender distribution in 9 main large sample studies, reported as percentage of female and male participants upon the total number of BD patients; **b** percentages of females and males in BD type-specific samples; **c** gender distribution of three samples, confronted with the BD type-specific composition of the samples. BDI = Bipolar Disorder type I; *BDII* Bipolar Disorder type II.

BDI the type of BD traditionally more commonly associated with equal prevalence in the two genders (Mitchell et al. 2004; Grant et al. 2005).

Even though not all of the studies discussed here are epidemiological, all of them represent the gender distribution of wide national or international coverage studies, with high numbers of patients, and therefore report a fairly realistic picture of the distribution of the disease in the population to which they refer. Buoli et al. (Buoli et al. 2019) analysed the sample of a nationwide epidemiological study, Hayes et al. (Hayes et al. 2017) and Yoon et al. (Yoon et al. 2018) recruited patients from samples representative of the national population, while Crump et al. (Crump et al. 2013) recruited patients from the Swedish National Registry, which included every person at least 20 years of age that lived in Sweden for at least two years as of January 1, 2003.

Overall, the gender distribution of BD reported in these studies, along with the increase of BD diagnosis in the last decade, (Clemente et al. 2015) could be signals of more efficient BD diagnosis, especially in the female gender. Since female gender in BD has already been associated with higher rates of rapid cycling, (Carvalho et al. 2014) dysphoria, and lifetime prevalence of depressive episodes, (Morgan et al. 2005) and suicide attempts, (Nivoli et al. 2011) indicating that BD in women can exhibit characteristics of non-inferior severity of illness and reduced quality of life, compared to their male counterparts, prompt recognition of BD in female patients is crucial in order to provide more adequate treatment. In particular, the frequent observation of a prevalent depressive polarity in female patients (Nivoli et al. 2011), with more frequent first manifestation of BD through a major depressive episode (MDE) and the higher lifetime number of MDEs, represent significant challenges for clinicians who may misdiagnose them as affected by unipolar MDD and consequently treat them with antidepressants rather than with mood stabilizers and atypical antipsychotics, a treatment that, particularly if administered in monotherapy, could concur in the onset of rapid cycling (Valentí et al. 2015). In this regard, although some studies in literature support the use of antidepressants as adjunctive short-term treatment in bipolar depression (Gijsman et al. 2004), data on the topic are inconsistent (Sachs et al. 2007), and antidepressants alone yield a high risk for manic switch and therefore mood stabilizers are still the cornerstone of bipolar disorders treatment (Price and Tyrka 2007).

Moreover, BD in women poses a significant burden on pregnancy, with a higher risk of adverse pregnancy outcomes and a higher frequency of relapses during the postpartum period, (Bodén et al. 2012; Wesseloo et al. 2016; Viguera et al. 2011) making prophylactic medication during pregnancy fundamental in order to maintain mood stability postpartum (Wesseloo et al. 2016). Of note, the correlation between the physiology of pregnancy and BD relapses could underlay hormonal and endocrinological influence on BD symptoms and presentation, as it has already been demonstrated for unipolar MDD (Studd and Panay 2009; Joffe 2011; Graziottin and Serafini 2009). The extensively reported correlations between sex hormones and mood dysregulation in women, could be significant also for BD, not only in terms of prevalence, but also for providing better care for female BD patients, which could benefit from personalized and hormonal treatments, as it already happens for unipolar MDD (Graziottin and Serafini 2009). It has already been suggested, in this regard, that women treated for BD show greater degrees of menstrual-entrained mood fluctuations, which could be mitigated by mood stabilizing treatments (i.e. Lamotrigine) (Robakis et al. 2015).

In conclusion, as BDs represent highly comorbid, disabling, difficult-to-treat and life-threatening conditions, clinicians should be aware of the recently reported increase in the prevalence of such conditions in the female gender and pay additional attention in the differential diagnosis with unipolar MDD, particularly when the first manifestation of BD is represented by a MDE. Prompter diagnosis and appropriate treatment for females with BD, in fact, could reduce acute inefficacy, longer-term relapses, suicide attempts, treatment-emergent affective switching, and onset of rapid-cycling.

Although in the ten large samples studies analysed here it is possible to identify a higher prevalence of female BD patients, the majority of these studies are not epidemiological, and their samples are collected over many years, many in BD Specialty Clinics, which commonly report having more female than male patients. In this regard, female patients, especially in younger generations, are more often willing to seek help for their symptoms, leading to a possible sampling bias. On the other hand, the often reported comorbid substance use disorders in male patients might concur in the fewer men seeking treatment in Bipolar Disorder Specialty Clinics, enhancing this possible sampling bias. Adding to this, female patients often seek help for ruminative thinking associated to life events stressors (Michl et al. 2013), and ruminative thinking is often interpreted as a sign of depression (McLaughlin and Nolen-Hoeksema 2011). To avoid these confounding factors, nationwide or international epidemiological studies are needed in order to confirm our preliminary observation.

Being the samples analysed here only based on longitudinal diagnosis of BD, another limitation of our study is the lack of data on mood presentation at the time of the studies, therefore not addressing one of the greatest differences in BDs presentation between genders.

Moreover, the studies analysed here recruited samples from specific areas or nations. It could be, from this point of view, that our conclusions cannot be extended to the international population but are only true for the specific regions of interest. It is well known, in fact, that the gender distribution of the general population varies across the world, with some countries (especially eastern countries) with a predominant male population. It is therefore possible that, for these countries, further and more specific studies on the subject should be carried out.

Lastly, even though the higher number of reported BD diagnosis in the last years could be connected to better diagnostic criteria implemented in the most recent editions of the DSM, (American Psychiatric Publishing 1994) on the other hand, more comprising diagnostic criteria could misleadingly help diagnose BD when it is not present, and therefore lead to a selection bias. In this regard, a right diagnose and a thorough follow-up are extremely important in order to provide the right treatment to patients presenting with depressive symptoms.

Acknowledgements
Not applicable.

Authors' contributions
All authors contributed equally to this manuscript. All authors read and approved the final manuscript.

Author details
[1] Department of Biomedical and Clinical Sciences Luigi Sacco, Department of Mental Health, University of Milan, ASST Fatebenefratelli-Sacco, Milano, Italy. [2] CRC Aldo Ravelli, Milano, Italy. [3] Department of Psychiatry and Behavioural Sciences, Stanford University, Stanford, CA, USA.

References

Altshuler LL, Kupka RW, Hellemann G, et al. Gender and depressive symptoms in 711 patients with bipolar disorder evaluated prospectively in the Stanley Foundation Bipolar Treatment Outcome Network. Am J Psychiatry. 2010;167(6):708–15. https://doi.org/10.1176/appi.ajp.2009.09010105.

American Psychiatric Association. Diagnostic and statistical manual of mental disorders. 4th ed. Arlington: American Psychiatric Publishing Inc.; 1994.

Arnold LM, McElroy SL, Keck PE. The role of gender in mixed mania. Compr Psychiatry. 2000;41(2):83–7. https://doi.org/10.1016/S0010-440X(00)90137-8.

Baldassano CF, Marangell LB, Gyulai L, et al. Gender differences in bipolar disorder: retrospective data from the first 500 STEP-BD participants. Bipolar Disord. 2005;7(5):465–70. https://doi.org/10.1111/j.1399-5618.2005.00237.x.

Bareis N, Lu J, Kirkwood CK, Kornstein SG, Wu E, Mezuk B. Identifying clinical net benefit of psychotropic medication use with latent variable techniques: Evidence from Systematic Treatment Enhancement Program for Bipolar Disorder (STEP-BD). J Affect Disord. 2018;238:147–55. https://doi.org/10.1016/j.jad.2018.05.063.

Bijl RV, de Graaf R, Ravelli A, Smit F, Vollebergh WAM. Gender and age-specific first incidence of DSM-III-R psychiatric disorders in the general population Results from the Netherlands mental health survey and incidence study (NEMESIS). Soc Psychiatry Psychiatr Epidemiol. 2002;37(8):372–9. https://doi.org/10.1007/s00127-002-0566-3.

Bobo WV, Na PJ, Geske JR, McElroy SL, Frye MA, Biernacka JM. The relative influence of individual risk factors for attempted suicide in patients with bipolar I versus bipolar II disorder. J Affect Disord. 2018;225:489–94. https://doi.org/10.1016/j.jad.2017.08.076.

Bodén R, Lundgren M, Brandt L, Reutfors J, Andersen M, Kieler H. Risks of adverse pregnancy and birth outcomes in women treated or not treated with mood stabilisers for bipolar disorder: Population based cohort study. BMJ. 2012. https://doi.org/10.1136/bmj.e7085.

Buoli M, Cesana BM, Maina G, et al. Correlates of current rapid-cycling bipolar disorder: Results from the Italian multicentric RENDiBi study. Eur Psychiatry. 2019;62:82–9. https://doi.org/10.1016/j.eurpsy.2019.09.001.

Carvalho AF, Dimellis D, Gonda X, Vieta E, McIntyre RS, Fountoulakis KN. Rapid cycling in bipolar disorder: a systematic review. J Clin Psychiatry. 2014. https://doi.org/10.4088/JCP.13r08905.

Clemente AS, Diniz BS, Nicolato R, et al. Bipolar disorder prevalence: A systematic review and meta-analysis of the literature. Rev Bras Psiquiatr. 2015;37(2):155–61. https://doi.org/10.1590/1516-4446-2012-1693.

Clements C, Morriss R, Jones S, Peters S, Roberts C, Kapur N. Suicide in bipolar disorder in a national English sample, 1996–2009: Frequency, trends and characteristics. Psychol Med. 2013;43(12):2593–602. https://doi.org/10.1017/S0033291713000329.

Crump C, Sundquist K, Winkleby MA, Sundquist J. Comorbidities and mortality in bipolar disorder: a Swedish national cohort study. JAMA Psychiatry. 2013;70(9):931–9. https://doi.org/10.1001/jamapsychiatry.2013.1394.

Culpepper L. Misdiagnosis of bipolar depression in primary care practices. J Clin Psychiatry. 2014. https://doi.org/10.4088/JCP.13019tx1c.

Diflorio A, Jones I. Is sex important Gender differences in bipolar disorder. Int Rev Psychiatry. 2010;22(5):437–52. https://doi.org/10.3109/09540261.2010.514601.

Ferrari AJ, Stockings E, Khoo JP, et al. The prevalence and burden of bipolar disorder: findings from the Global Burden of Disease Study 2013. Bipolar Disord. 2016;18(5):440–50. https://doi.org/10.1111/bdi.12423.

Gijsman HJ, Geddes JR, Rendell JM, Nolen WA, Goodwin GM. Antidepressants for bipolar depression: A systematic review of randomized, controlled trials. Am J Psychiatry. 2004;161(9):1537–47. https://doi.org/10.1176/appi.ajp.161.9.1537.

Grant BF, Stinson FS, Hasin DS, et al. Prevalence, correlates, and comorbidity of bipolar I disorder and axis I and II disorders: results from the National Epidemiologic Survey on Alcohol and Related Conditions. J Clin Psychiatry. 2005;66(10):1205–15. https://doi.org/10.4088/JCP.v66n1001.

Graziottin A, Serafini A. Depression and the menopause: Why antidepressants are not enough? Menopause Int. 2009;15(2):76–81. https://doi.org/10.1258/mi.2009.009021.

Hayes JF, Marston L, Walters K, King MB, Osborn DPJ. Mortality gap for people with bipolar disorder and schizophrenia: UK-based cohort study 2000–2014. Br J Psychiatry. 2017;211(3):175–81. https://doi.org/10.1192/bjp.bp.117.202606.

Hendrick V, Altshuler LL, Gitlin MJ, Delrahim S, Hammen C. Gender and bipolar illness. J Clin Psychiatry. 2000;61(5):393–6. https://doi.org/10.4088/JCP.v61n0514.

Hirschfeld RMA, Lewis L, Vornik LA. Perceptions and impact of bipolar disorder: How far have we really come? Results of the National Depressive and Manic-Depressive Association 2000 Survey of individuals with bipolar disorder. J Clin Psychiatry. 2003;64(2):161–74. https://doi.org/10.4088/JCP.v64n0209.

Hou L, Heilbronner U, Degenhardt F, et al. Genetic variants associated with response to lithium treatment in bipolar disorder: a genome-wide association study. Lancet. 2016;387(10023):1085–93. https://doi.org/10.1016/S0140-6736(16)00143-4.

Joffe RT. Hormone treatment of depression. Dialogues Clin Neurosci. 2011;13(1):127–38.

Kalman JL, Papiol S, Forstner AJ, et al. Investigating polygenic burden in age at disease onset in bipolar disorder: findings from an international multicentric study. Bipolar Disord. 2019;21(1):68–75. https://doi.org/10.1111/bdi.12659.

Karanti A, Bobeck C, Osterman M, et al. Gender differences in the treatment of patients with bipolar disorder: a study of 7354 patients. J Affect Disord. 2015;174:303–9. https://doi.org/10.1016/j.jad.2014.11.058.

Kennedy N, Boydell J, Kalidindi S, et al. Gender differences in incidence and age at onset of mania and bipolar disorder over a 35-year period in Camberwell England. Am J Psychiatry. 2005;162(2):257–62. https://doi.org/10.1176/appi.ajp.162.2.257.

Kessing LV. Gender differences in the phenomenology of bipolar disorder. Bipolar Disord. 2004;6(5):421–5. https://doi.org/10.1111/j.1399-5618.2004.00135.x.

Kessler RC. Epidemiology of women and depression. J Affect Disord. 2003;74:5–13. https://doi.org/10.1016/S0165-0327(02)00426-3.

Kim L, Kim J-A, Kim S. A guide for the utilization of Health Insurance Review and Assessment Service National Patient Samples. Epidemiol Health. 2014. https://doi.org/10.4178/EPIH/E2014008.

Leach LS, Christensen H, Mackinnon AJ, Windsor TD, Butterworth P. Gender differences in depression and anxiety across the adult lifespan: The role of psychosocial mediators. Soc Psychiatry Psychiatr Epidemiol. 2008;43(12):983–98. https://doi.org/10.1007/s00127-008-0388-z.

Lish JD, Dime-Meenan S, Whybrow PC, Price RA, Hirschfeld RMA. The National Depressive and Manic-depressive Association (DMDA) survey of bipolar members. J Affect Disord. 1994;31(4):281–94. https://doi.org/10.1016/0165-0327(94)90104-X.

McLaughlin KA, Nolen-Hoeksema S. Rumination as a transdiagnostic factor in depression and anxiety. Behav Res Ther. 2011;49(3):186–93. https://doi.org/10.1016/j.brat.2010.12.006.

Merikangas KR, Akiskal HS, Angst J, et al. Lifetime and 12-month prevalence of bipolar spectrum disorder in the national comorbidity survey replication. Arch Gen Psychiatry. 2007;64(5):543–52. https://doi.org/10.1001/archpsyc.64.5.543.

Michl LC, McLaughlin KA, Shepherd K, Nolen-Hoeksema S. Rumination as a mechanism linking stressful life events to symptoms of depression and anxiety: Longitudinal evidence in early adolescents and adults. J Abnorm Psychol. 2013;122(2):339–52. https://doi.org/10.1037/a0031994.

Mitchell PB, Slade T, Andrews G. Twelve-month prevalence and disability of DSM-IV bipolar disorder in an Australian general population survey. Psychol Med. 2004;34(5):777–85. https://doi.org/10.1017/S0033291703001636.

Morgan VA, Mitchell PB, Jablensky AV. The epidemiology of bipolar disorder: Sociodemographic, disability and service utilization data from the Australian National Study of Low Prevalence (Psychotic) Disorders. Bipolar Disord. 2005;7(4):326–37. https://doi.org/10.1111/j.1399-5618.2005.00229.x.

Nivoli AMA, Pacchiarotti I, Rosa AR, et al. Gender differences in a cohort study of 604 bipolar patients: the role of predominant polarity. J Affect Disord. 2011;133(3):443–9. https://doi.org/10.1016/j.jad.2011.04.055.

Price LH, Tyrka AR. Adjunctive antidepressant treatment for bipolar depression [1]. N Engl J Med. 2007;357(6):614–6. https://doi.org/10.1056/NEJMc071459.

Robakis TK, Holtzman J, Stemmle PG, Reynolds-May MF, Kenna HA, Rasgon NL. Lamotrigine and GABAA receptor modulators interact with menstrual cycle phase and oral contraceptives to regulate mood in women with bipolar disorder. J Affect Disord. 2015;175:108–15. https://doi.org/10.1016/j.jad.2014.12.040.

Sachs GS, Nierenberg AA, Calabrese JR, et al. Effectiveness of adjunctive antidepressant treatment for bipolar depression. N Engl J Med. 2007;356(17):1711–22. https://doi.org/10.1056/NEJMoa064135.

Slyepchenko A, Frey BN, Lafer B, Nierenberg AA, Sachs GS, Dias RS. Increased illness burden in women with comorbid bipolar and premenstrual dysphoric disorder: data from 1 099 women from STEP-BD study. Acta Psychiatr Scand. 2017;136(5):473–82. https://doi.org/10.1111/acps.12797.

Studd J, Panay N. Are oestrogens useful for the treatment of depression in women? Best Pract Res Clin Obstet Gynaecol. 2009;23(1):63–71. https://doi.org/10.1016/j.bpobgyn.2008.11.001.

Suppes T, Mintz J, McElroy SL, et al. Mixed hypomania in 908 patients with bipolar disorder evaluated prospectively in the Stanley Foundation Bipolar Treatment Network: a sex-specific phenomenon. Arch Gen Psychiatry. 2005;62(10):1089–96. https://doi.org/10.1001/archpsyc.62.10.1089.

Tondo L, Baldessarini RJ. Rapid cycling in women and men with bipolar manic-depressive disorders. Am J Psychiatry. 1998;155(10):1434–6. https://doi.org/10.1176/ajp.155.10.1434.

Valentí M, Pacchiarotti I, Undurraga J, et al. Risk factors for rapid cycling in bipolar disorder. Bipolar Disord. 2015;17(5):549–59. https://doi.org/10.1111/bdi.12288.

Vieta E, Langosch JM, Figueira ML, et al. Clinical management and burden of bipolar disorder: results from a multinational longitudinal study

(WAVE-bd). Int J Neuropsychopharmacol. 2013;16(8):1719–32. https://doi.org/10.1017/S1461145713000278.
Viguera AC, Tondo L, Koukopoulos AE, Reginaldi D, Lepri B, Baldessarini RJ. Episdes of mood disorders in 2,252 pregnancies and postpartum periods. Am J Psychiatry. 2011;168(11):1179–85. https://doi.org/10.1176/appi.ajp.2011.11010148.
Wehr TA, Goodwin FK. Can antidepressants cause mania and worsen the course of affective illness? Am J Psychiatry. 1987;144(11):1403–11. https://doi.org/10.1176/ajp.144.11.1403.
Weissman MM, Leaf PJ, Tischler GL, et al. Affective disorders in five United States communities. Psychol Med. 1988;18(1):141–53. https://doi.org/10.1017/S0033291700001975.
Wesseloo R, Kamperman AM, Munk-Olsen T, Pop VJM, Kushner SA, Bergink V. Risk of postpartum relapse in bipolar disorder and postpartum psychosis: a systematic review and meta-analysis. Am J Psychiatry. 2016;173(2):117–27. https://doi.org/10.1176/appi.ajp.2015.15010124.
Yoon W, Shon SH, Hong Y, Joo YH, Lee JS. Antidepressant prescription patterns in bipolar disorder: a nationwide, register-based study in Korea. J Korean Med Sci. 2018. https://doi.org/10.3346/jkms.2018.33.e290.

13

Overview of lithium's use: a nationwide survey

Xabier Pérez de Mendiola[1,2*], Diego Hidalgo-Mazzei[2], Eduard Vieta[2] and Ana González-Pinto[1,2]

Abstract

Background: Lithium is considered the gold standard treatment for bipolar disorder (BD). Current clinical guidelines and scientific evidence support its use as a first-line treatment in BD. However, over the last two decades, there has been a downward tendency in lithium's use in several developed countries. Based on a nationwide survey, this study's objective is to analyze in a large sample of psychiatrists relevant issues of the use of lithium salts in BD.

Methods: Data were collected through an anonymous survey sent by email among 500 psychiatrists who belong to a National Society of Psychiatry (Spanish Society of Biological Psychiatry). The survey is a self-administered questionnaire consisting of 21 items on the most key aspects of lithium's use (indication, dosage, monitoring, and information for patients).

Results: 212 psychiatrists completed the survey. 70% of psychiatrists prescribe lithium to more than 50% of patients diagnosed with BD. Adverse effects are the main reason not to use lithium salts. Over 75% of the participants consider lithium salts the treatment of choice for the maintenance phase of BD, both in women and men. Most of the participants (> 50%) start lithium after the first affective episode, use conservative plasma concentrations (0.6–0.8 mmol/L), and generally prescribe it twice a day. 57% of psychiatrists who treat patients under 18 do not use lithium in this population. About 70% of the survey respondents use official protocols to inform and monitor patients on lithium treatment.

Conclusions: From the results of the present study, it can be concluded that the use of lithium in Spain is in line with the recommendations of the main international clinical guidelines and current scientific literature. The first reason not to prescribe lithium in our country is the perception of its adverse effects and not the aspects related to its practical use or its effectiveness. Considering that BD is a chronic disease with a typical onset in adolescence, the low rate of prescription of lithium salts in patients under 18 must be thoroughly studied.

Keywords: Lithium, Bipolar disorder, Survey, Psychiatrists' attitude, Adverse effects, First episode, Adolescence onset, Dosing schedule

Introduction

Even though more than 70 years have passed since the Australian psychiatrist John Cade reported the antimanic efficacy of lithium carbonate (Cade 1949), the main current clinical guidelines still consider it a first-choice treatment for Bipolar Disorder (BD) (Fountoulakis et al. 2017; Yatham et al. 2018). It has proved useful not only in acute manic episodes (Yildiz et al. 2014) but also in depressive (Baldessarini et al. 2020; Malhi et al. 2017) and mixed episodes (Sani and Fiorillo 2019). Nevertheless, lithium is noted for its outstanding efficacy in the maintenance or prophylactic treatment of BD (Jauhar and Young 2019; Severus et al. 2018). Bearing in mind the frequent chronic, recurrent and disabling nature of BD (a disease that affects more than 1% of the world population) (Vieta et al., 2018), a long-term treatment which

*Correspondence: xabier.perezdemendiolaetxezarraga@osakidetza.eus
[1] Bioaraba, Research Group on Severe Mental Illness; Osakidetza, Araba University Hospital, Psychiatry Service; Faculty of Medicine, Department of Neurosciences, University of the Basque Country UPV / EHU, Vitoria-Gasteiz, Spain
Full list of author information is available at the end of the article

allows preventing relapses or recurrences is vital. In this regard, lithium continues to be the gold standard treatment supported by extensive scientific evidence (Carvalho et al., 2020). Both in controlled clinical trials and observational studies, lithium has shown its efficacy and superiority in the prophylaxis of any type of affective episode (Berk et al. 2017; González-Pinto et al. 2018; Kessing et al. 2018; Lähteenvuo et al. 2018; Miura et al. 2014; Severus et al. 2014).

In addition to its mood-stabilizing properties, lithium has a distinctive, independent, and proven anti-suicide action (Barjasteh-Askari et al. 2020; González-Pinto et al. 2006; Smith and Cipriani 2017; Song et al., 2017). This is a relevant quality in BD since up to 15% of patients diagnosed with BD die by suicide (Gordovez and McMahon 2020). In fact, a systematic review and meta-analysis showed that treatment with lithium among people with mood disorders could reduce the risk of death and suicide up to 60% compared to placebo (Cipriani et al. 2013). Remarkable neuroprotective and antiviral properties have also been attributed to lithium (Post 2018; Rybakowski 2018; Murru et al. 2020; Van Gestel et al. 2019). It slows brain aging (Van Gestel et al. 2019) and reduces the risk of dementia by almost 50% in patients with BD (Velosa et al. 2020). It could also attenuate the cognitive and functional decline in patients (without BD) with mild cognitive impairment (Forlenza et al. 2019). Moreover, the use of lithium has recently been proposed as a potential treatment for CoViD-19 (Murru et al. 2020).

Despite the undeniable evidence in favor of its application in BD, a descendent tendency in the use of lithium has been noticed in the US (Rhee et al. 2020) and in numerous European countries (Bohlken et al. 2020; Karanti et al., 2016; Kessing et al., 2016; Lyall et al., 2019). In several of them, it has changed from being the most prescribed drug to the least one, even behind the controversial antidepressants. (Kessing et al., 2016; Lyall et al., 2019). The emergence of new effective drugs for BD, such as second-generation antipsychotics and certain antiepileptics, has overturned the prescription pattern of BD (Malhi et al., 2020; Anmella et al., 2020). The absence of pharmaceutical marketing, the toxic perception of its adverse effects, the slow onset of action and the need for venipuncture monitoring are some of the possible causes of this declining trend (Gitlin, 2016a; Rybakowski, 2018). Neither the main clinical guidelines nor current scientific literature supports the idea of replacing lithium with other drugs. In fact, over the last two decades, the decrease in lithium's use is not widespread, and in certain countries, lithium's prescription rate has remained high. In some countries, more than 50% of bipolar patients are treated with lithium, while in the US, for example, only 17% (Kessing 2019; Parabiaghi et al. 2015; Renes et al. 2018; Rhee et al. 2020) (Table 1).

Table 1 Changes in the lithium prescription rate in several European countries over the last two decades

Study	Country	Period	Data source	Results
Bohlken et al. 2020	Germany	2009–2018	Neuropsychiatric private practices' records	The percentage of patients with bipolar disorder receiving lithium declined from 31,4% (2009) to 26,2% (2018)
Rhee et al. 2020	United States	1997–2000 vs. 2013–2016	Outpatient physician reports of patient visits	The percentage of patients with bipolar disorder receiving lithium declined from 30,4% (1997–2000) to 17,6% (2013–2016)
Lyall et al. 2019	Scotland	2009–2016	Records of outpatient clinic attendance, general/acute hospital admissions and psychiatric hospital admissions	The percentage of patients with bipolar disorder receiving lithium declined from 26% (2009) to 22% (2016)
Renes et al. 2018	Netherlands	2009–2014	Outpatient psychiatrists' and patients' surveys	Lithium was used by 70% of patients with bipolar disorder or schizoaffective disorder, bipolar type
Karanti et al. 2016	Sweden	2007–2013	Records of private and public psychiatric outpatient health care units	The percentage of patients with bipolar disorder receiving lithium declined from 51% (2007) to 41% (2013)
Kessing et al. 2016	Denmark	2000–2011	Records of all Danish patients with a first-ever contact with mental healthcare	The one-year prescription rate of lithium in bipolar patients decreasedfrom 41% (2000) to 34% (2011)
Parabiaghi et al. 2015	Italy	2000–2010	A population-based database of dispensing records	The prevalence of lithium treatment grew by 38% duringthe observation period
Hayes et al. 2011	England	1995–2009	Records of primary care patients	The prescriptionrate for lithium increased from 22.5% (1995) to 29.3% (2009)
Castells et al. 2006	Spain	1985–2003	Pharmacy sales data of medicinal products	Lithium daily dose per 1000 inhabitants per day (DID) increased from 0.21 (1985) to 0.79 (2003)

In this context, an anonymous survey was carried out among psychiatrists. The primary objective of this study was to evaluate the use and current perception of lithium's treatment on the most relevant aspects of the drug: indication, dosage, monitoring, and information for patients. The results presented below could be used to elaborate new consensus or national protocols, which will promote and optimize the use of lithium in our country.

Methods

Study design and sample

Between 11 May and 11 July 2020, an anonymous online survey was conducted on the use of lithium, thanks to the support of the Spanish Society of Biological Psychiatry (SEPB). All the members of the SEPB (500 psychiatrists) received an email in which they were informed about the purpose of the study. They were invited to participate in it by completing the questionnaire attached to the same message. The collaboration was voluntary, and responses were recorded, eliminating the identity of the participants. Two reminder emails were sent during the mentioned period to maximize the response rate. The survey was created and performed with Google Forms, and Microsoft Office Excel 2019 was used for the analysis and representation of the data. The study was approved by the Clinical Research Ethics Committee of the Araba University Hospital (Spain).

Questionnaire

The survey was designed to obtain a general perspective on lithium's use from a sample of Spanish psychiatrists. In order to encourage participation, a brief self-administered questionnaire (21 items) with multiple-choice questions (Additional file 1: Appendix S1) was elaborated. The first 5 questions are related to demography: age, sex, and origin of the respondents. The following 3 points address the prescription rate of lithium in BD and the main reasons not to prescribe it. The next 5 requests explore its status compared to the rest of the drugs and the stage in the course of the illness when lithium is usually introduced. Subsequently, there are 2 specific questions about two practical and relevant aspects of lithium's use: plasma concentrations and dose distribution. The next 4 refer to the use of lithium in special clinical circumstances (minors, elderly and psychiatric comorbidity). The final issues are about the availability of official documents or protocols to monitor and inform patients undergoing lithium treatment.

Analysis

Data are analyzed using descriptive statistics. The results are represented by graphs based on percentages and absolute numbers using Microsoft Office Excel 2019.

Results

Demographics

A total of 212 responses are obtained from almost all Spain regions (Additional file 1: Appendix S2. Figure S1). The majority of respondents (86%) come from Catalonia (28%), the Community of Madrid (27%), Basque Country (15%), Andalusia (8%), and Valencian Community (8%). The distribution between sexes and age groups is practically homogeneous as it is the percentage of professionals who work at hospitals (psychiatric or general) and outpatient settings (Table 2).

Lithium's prescription and reasons not to use it

Only 3% of respondents never prescribe lithium salts. 70% of participants prescribe lithium to more than 50% of patients diagnosed with BD and 20% to more than 75% of them (Additional file 1: Appendix 2. Figure S2).

Almost 62% of psychiatrists affirm that the main reason not to prescribe lithium is its side effects. A significantly lower percentage of specialists state that the leading cause not to prescribe it is the rejection by the patient (13%) and the need for monitoring by venipuncture (10%) (Fig. 1).

Over 75% of the participants choose lithium as the first option in the maintenance treatment of BD, both in women and men (Additional file 1: Appendix S2. Figure S3). As a second option, antipsychotics (34%) and valproate (31%) stand out in women. For men, valproate (64%) is clearly the second preferred option.

Table 2 Demographic profile of the participants

Profile of psychiatrists	n (%)
Sex	
Man	100 (47%)
Woman	112 (53%)
Age range	
25–35	54 (26%)
36–45	57 (27%)
46–55	42 (20%)
56–65	39 (18%)
> 65	20 (9%)
Work center	
General hospital	88 (41%)
Psychiatric hospital	23 (11%)
Outpatient consultation	101 (48%)
Total	212 (100%)

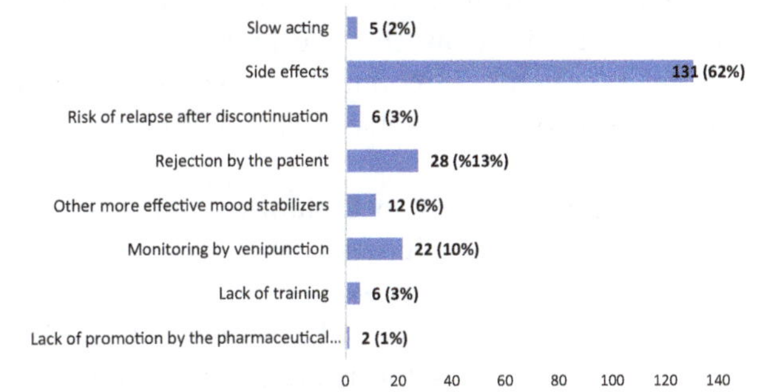

Fig. 1 Main reasons not to prescribe lithium

Finally, more than 80% of respondents usually initiate treatment with lithium salts after the first affective episode. Most of them prescribe it after the first manic episode. More than 25% of psychiatrists, when there is a family history of BD, tend to start lithium treatment after the first depressive episode (Additional file 1: Appendix S2. Table S1).

Serum levels and dose distribution

50% of the participants use serum lithium levels between 0.6 and 0.8 mmol/L for the maintenance phase of BD. 21% consider adequate any concentration within the therapeutic range established between 0.6 and 1.2 mmol/L. Another 20% utilizes higher lithium serum levels between 0.8 and 1 mmol/L to prevent relapse or recurrence in BD (Fig. 2).

Regarding the distribution of the lithium dose, more than 75% of psychiatrists prescribe it in 2 daily doses. 13% in 3 daily doses and only 9% in a single daily dose (Fig. 2).

Specific populations

60% of respondents (128) do not deal with children and adolescents. Among the psychiatrists who care for underage BD patients, most (57%) do not use lithium salts in this population (Additional file 1: Appendix S2. Table S2). By contrast, the majority of survey respondents do use lithium in older age BD (Additional file 1: Appendix S2. Table S2).

Over 80% of specialists do not have any trouble prescribing lithium to patients with a comorbid Substance Use or a Personality Disorder (Additional file 1: Appendix S2. Table S2).

Information for patients and monitoring protocols

One-third of psychiatrists who prescribe lithium do not have documentation for patients at their workplace. Furthermore, a quarter of respondents do not follow a formal protocol for monitoring lithium and its adverse effects (Additional file 1: Appendix S2. Figure S4).

Discussion

This is the first study referring to the use of lithium that analyzes psychiatrists' current general perspective. In 2018, an interesting international survey was published focused exclusively on lithium monitoring (Nederlof et al. 2018). In order to understand the international framework of lithium's underuse, it is essential to know the specialists' point of view (Malhi et al. 2020).

According to the National survey results on the use of lithium, the vast majority of Spanish psychiatrists in this sample, which includes professionals from all the autonomous communities, comply with the recommendations of the latest clinical guidelines and the scientific literature. 70% of the survey respondents prescribed lithium to

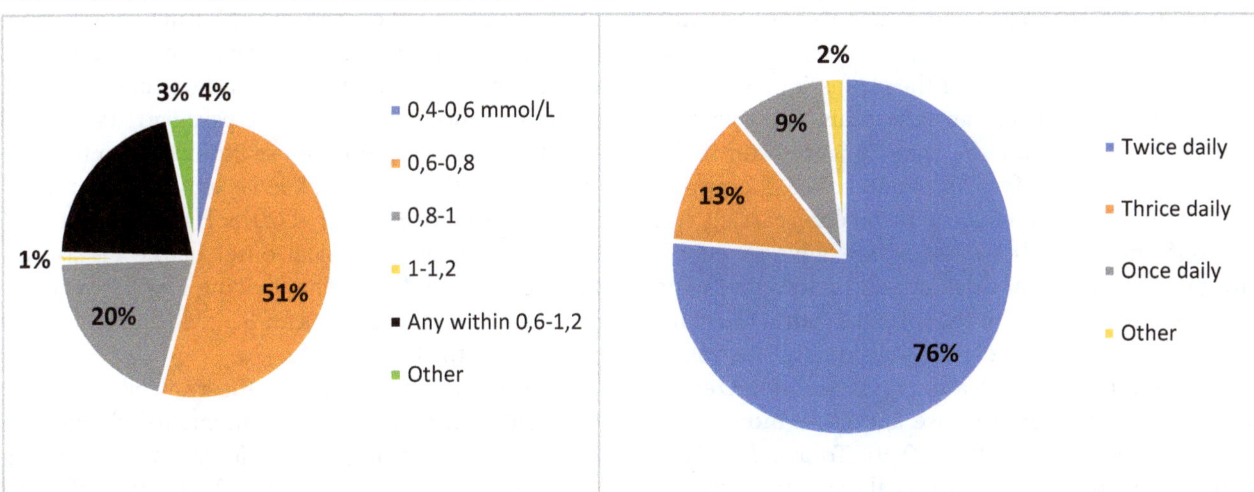

Fig. 2 The preferred serum level and dose distribution of lithium

more than 50% of patients diagnosed with BD and 20% to over 75%. In this line, more than 75% of national psychiatrists who participated in this study chose lithium as their first-choice treatment in the maintenance phase of BD both in men and women.

The apparently high lithium's prescription by Spanish psychiatrists agrees with the recently observed results in the Netherlands, where 70% of patients diagnosed with BD or Schizoaffective Disorder were treated with lithium (Renes et al. 2018). Nevertheless, as it is mentioned above, this percentage is significantly higher than in other neighboring countries (Kessing 2019). In Sweden, the prescription rate for lithium in BD is 55%, in Denmark 41.7%, in Germany 26.2%, and in Scotland 22% (Bohlken et al. 2020; Karanti et al. 2016; Kessing et al. 2016; Lyall et al. 2019) (Table 1).

In the current study, we asked participants about the reasons not to prescribe lithium in the long-term treatment of BD. Most agree that lithium's adverse effects are the main barrier to its use. Only 6% of the participants believe that lithium's non-prescription is due to the availability of other more effective mood stabilizers. This fact shows the conviction that participating psychiatrists have in the efficacy of lithium above other effective drugs. Practical aspects related to lithium's use, such as the need for monitoring or the slow onset of action, are not considered obstacles for the drug's prescription. As suggested for clozapine (Bachmann et al. 2017; Verdoux et al. 2018), the high use of lithium in Spain could be the consequence of a local "culture" that favors the use of the drug. This could be because of the transmission of personal experience from expert therapists to beginners, institutional support that facilitates the adequate infrastructure for patients' follow-up on lithium treatment (lithium clinics and national registries, for example), and the promotion of its use by scientific societies. Knowing exactly why lithium is not prescribed in other countries would help to understand better its international underuse.

Despite the fact that most of the professionals believe that lithium's side effects are the main limiting factor for its prescription, more than 75% consider it the first-choice treatment for the maintenance therapy of BD for both women and men. In recent years, it has been confirmed that the most severe adverse effects of lithium, that is, kidney dysfunction and teratogenic risk, were overestimated in the former reports (Fornaro et al. 2020; Nielsen et al. 2017). Additionally, the risk of suffering from both complications can be minimized by using a minimum effective dose and close monitoring of plasma levels (Tondo et al. 2019). To avoid making the survey extensive and more challenging to answer, we decided not to ask about the short- and long-term adverse effects of lithium in the current study, although we did consider it. Now that we know this result, it would be interesting to conduct a new survey in the future, focusing on the adverse effects of lithium and its management.

Therapeutic alternatives to lithium are not exempted from significant risks. Valproate has a high teratogenic risk, discouraging its use in women of childbearing age (European Medicines Agency 2018; Anmella et al. 2019). That is why it is striking the relatively high percentage of psychiatrists (31%) who choose valproate as a second option for women suffering from BD. On the other hand, antipsychotics are associated with a more significant weight gain and a worse metabolic profile than lithium (Hayes et al. 2016; Jauhar and Young 2019). Besides, they can cause extrapyramidal and sexual symptoms, too (Huhn et al. 2019). Although it is clear that there is a reasonable concern about its negative effects, these data would explain the high percentage of psychiatrists who choose lithium as the first option for the long-term treatment of BD in both sexes. Moreover, lithium has potential long-term benefits related to neurogenesis that are being studied (Berk et al. 2017; Forlenza et al., 2019; Sun et al., 2019; Zanni et al., 2019; Ciftci et al. 2020). Emphasizing the benefits of lithium without forgetting its adverse effects (Gitlin 2016b; Tondo et al. 2017) could help improve the outcome of patients with BD.

The most used serum lithium levels for the maintenance treatment of BD (0.6–0.8 mmol/L) are also in line with current scientific advice (Nolen et al. 2019). This is a crucial issue because the use of conservative plasma levels could prevent lithium intoxication, renal, and central nervous system adverse effects (Nielsen et al. 2018; Schoot et al. 2019). Another practice that could minimize the risk of renal impairment is the schedule of a single lithium daily dose (Schoot et al. 2019). However, this regimen is the least used among the respondents who prefer to distribute lithium dosage in 2 or 3 daily doses.

Another point that differs from the latest scientific publications is the little use of lithium among children and adolescents with BD. Most psychiatrists who take care of minors (57%) do not use lithium when the literature suggests that it is an effective and safe treatment in this population (Amerio et al. 2018; Hafeman et al. 2019). Considering that the typical onset of the disease is in adolescence, and due to the dividing line between child and adult care in Spain, it can be challenging to supply lithium since the first episode.

Finally, it must be stated that the availability of official documentation on lithium for patients (67%) and protocols for its monitoring (72%) is similar to the mentioned international study (Nederlof et al. 2018). The publication of expert consensuses, such as the one which has recently been prepared by the SEPB (González-Pinto et al. 2021), is an initiative that can improve these figures.

This study has several strengths and limitations. As underlined before, this is the first research that evaluates the general perspective on lithium's use among a large group of psychiatrists. The fact that 86% of the responses come from 5 autonomous communities limits the generalization of the results to the whole country. Nonetheless, they are 5 of the most populated autonomous communities, representing 64% of the Spanish population. So, this is a somewhat expected finding. Furthermore, these 5 regions attract specialists trained in other territories because of their greater job offer. The number (212) and the rate (42.5%) of responses are higher or similar to other surveys addressed to professionals (Campos et al. 2020; Daod et al. 2019; Nederlof et al. 2018). The social desirability and selection bias could have overestimated the use of lithium in our country. The survey was distributed only among members of a single national society of Psychiatry, not considering the perspective of psychiatrists who are not members of the SEPB. As part of SEPB, members might be exposed to a more continuous update and training on guidelines due to the continuous education and training opportunities offered within the society. Research participants could have chosen the most socially desirable or acceptable responses rather than responses that reflected their true thoughts or practices. However, the anonymous nature of the survey could have favored obtaining honest and real answers.

Finally, the present study does not analyze national prescription registers. Thus, it would be interesting to complement the current essay with a pharmaco-epidemiological analysis, such as those carried out in other countries that have already been pointed out (Table 1). Nevertheless, it should be noted that the results obtained in this study are congruent with the pharmaco-epidemiological research performed in other countries (Parabiaghi et al. 2015; Renes et al. 2018) and with the only one published in Spain (Castells et al. 2006). In a forthcoming paper, it would also be interesting to explore lithium's use in the acute phases (mania, depression, and mixed states). Its efficacy and role are different from the maintenance phase and vary across the distinct acute phases (Baldessarini et al. 2020; Malhi et al. 2017). Moreover, most recent guidelines state that clinicians should consider the maintenance phase when selecting acute phase treatments (Yatham et al. 2018).

Conclusions

This survey results suggest that, at least in Spain, the use of lithium is consistent with the latest clinical guidelines. Based on these results, except for children and adolescents, one cannot speak of an underuse of lithium in Spain. The use of valproate as one of the main alternatives to lithium in women is one of the few matters that differ from the recommendations of the main scientific societies. The main barrier to prescribe lithium is its side effect profile. Behind this apparent high use of lithium could be a local culture that favors the dissemination of scientific and practical information about the drug.

Supplementary Information

Additional file 1: Appendix S1. The questionnaire. **Appendix S2:** Complementary figures and tables.

Abbreviation

BD: Bipolar disorder.

Acknowledgements

The authors want to acknowledge the Center for Biomedical Research in Mental Health (CIBERSAM), Carlos III Health Research Institute, the Basque Government, and the University of the Basque Country (UPV/EHU).

Authors' contributions

XPM and AG-P performed the survey, analyzing, writing, and editing the data. DH-M and EV provided a critical appraisal of the manuscript. All authors read and approved the final manuscript.

Author details

[1] Bioaraba, Research Group on Severe Mental Illness; Osakidetza, Araba University Hospital, Psychiatry Service; Faculty of Medicine, Department of Neurosciences, University of the Basque Country UPV / EHU, Vitoria-Gasteiz, Spain. [2] Hospital Clinic, Institute of Neuroscience, University of Barcelona, IDIBAPS, Centre for Biomedical Research Network on Mental Health (CIBERSAM), Barcelona, Spain.

References

Amerio A, Ossola P, Scagnelli F, et al. Safety and efficacy of lithium in children and adolescents: a systematic review in bipolar illness. Eur. Psychiatry. 2018;54:85–97.

Anmella G, Pacchiarotti I, Cubała WJ, Dudek D, Maina G, Thomas P, Vieta E. Expert advice on the management of valproate in women with bipolar disorder at childbearing age. Eur Neuropsychopharmacol. 2019;29(11):1199–212.

Anmella G, Vieta E, Hidalgo-Mazzei D. Commentary on: "Make lithium great again!" Bipolar Disord. 2020. https://doi.org/10.1111/bdi.12998.

Bachmann CJ, Aagaard L, Bernardo M, et al. International trends in clozapine use: a study in 17 countries. Acta Psychiatr Scand. 2017;136:37–51.

Baldessarini RJ, Vazquez GH, Tondo L. Bipolar depression: a major unsolved challenge. Int J Bipolar Disord. 2020;8(1):1.

Barjasteh-Askari F, Davoudi M, Amini H, Ghorbani M, Yaseri M, Yunesian M, et al. Relationship between suicide mortality and lithium in drinking water: a systematic review and meta-analysis. J Afect Disord. 2020;264:234–41.

Berk M, Dandash O, Daglas R, Cotton SM, Allott K, Fornito A, Suo C, Klauser P, Liberg B, Henry L, Macneil C, Hasty M, McGorry P, Pantelis C, Yücel M. Neuroprotection after a first episode of mania: a randomized controlled maintenance trial comparing the effects of lithium and quetiapine on grey and white matter volume. Transl Psychiatry. 2017;7(1):e1011.

Bohlken J, Bauer M, Kostev K. Drug treatment for patients with bipolar disorders in psychiatric practices in Germany in 2009 and 2018. Psychiatry Res. 2020;289:112965.

Cade JFK. Lithium salts in the treatment of psychotic excitement. Med J Aust. 1949;36:349–52.

Campos P, Carrió M, Vicedo A, Bioque M. Actitud de los psiquiatras respecto al uso de olanzapina en la práctica clínica: una encuesta nacional. Psiquiatría Biológica. 2020;27:3–8.

Carvalho AF, Firth J, Vieta E. Bipolar disorder. N Engl J Med. 2020;383(1):58–66.

Castells X, Vallano A, Rigau D, et al. Trends in lithium prescription in Spain from1985 to 2003. J Affect Disord. 2006;91:273–6.

Ciftci E, Karacay R, Caglayan A, Altunay S, Ates N, Altintas MO, Doeppner TR, Yulug B, Kilic E. Neuroprotective effect of lithium in cold- induced traumatic brain injury in mice. Behav Brain Res. 2020;17(392):112719.

Cipriani A, Hawton K, Stockton S, Geddes JR. Lithium in the prevention of suicide in mood disorders: updated systematic review and meta-analysis. BMJ. 2013;2013(346):f3646.

Daod E, Krivoy A, Shoval G, Zubedat S, Lally J, Vadas L, et al. Psychiatrists' attitude towards the use of clozapine in the treatment of refractory schizophrenia: a nationwide survey. Psychiatry Res. 2019;275:155–61.

European Medicines Agency (EMA). New measures to avoid valproate exposure in pregnancy endorsed. EMA/375438/2018.

Forlenza OV, Radanovic M, Talib LL, Gattaz WF. Clinical and biological effects of long-term lithium treatment in older adults with amnestic mild cognitive impairment: randomised clinical trial. Br J Psychiatry. 2019;5:1–7.

Fornaro M, Maritan E, Ferranti R, Zaninotto L, Miola A, Anastasia A, et al. Lithium exposure during pregnancy and the postpartum period: a systematic review and meta-analysis of safety and efficacy outcomes. Am J Psychiatry. 2020;177(1):76–92.

Fountoulakis KN, Grunze H, Vieta E, Young A, Yatham L, Blier P, et al. The International College of Neuro-Psychopharmacology (CINP) treatment guidelines for bipolar disorder in adults (CINP-BD-2017), Part 3: the clinical guidelines. Int J Neuropsychopharmacol. 2017;20:180–95.

Gitlin M. Why is lithium not prescribed more often? Here are the reasons. J Psychiatry Neurol Sci. 2016a;29:293–7.

Gitlin MJ. Lithium side effects and toxicity: prevalence and management strategies. Int J Bipolar Disord. 2016b;4:27.

González-Pinto A, Mosquera F, Alonso M, et al. Suicidal risk in bipolar I disorder patients and adherence to long-term lithium treatment. Bipolar Disord. 2006;8:618–24.

González-Pinto A, López-Peña P, Bermúdez-Ampudia C, Vieta E, Martinez-Cengotitabengoa M. Can lithium salts prevent depressive episodes in the real world? Eur Neuropsychopharmacol. 2018;28(12):1351–9.

González-Pinto A, Balanzá-Martínez V, Benabarre Hernández A, et al. Consenso de expertos sobre propuestas de información al paciente en tratamiento con sales de litio. Revista de Psiquiatría y Salud Mental. 2021;14:27–39.

Gordovez FJA, McMahon FJ. The genetics of bipolar disorder. Mol Psychiatry. 2020;25:544–59.

Hafeman DM, Rooks B, Merranko J, Liao F, Gill MK, Goldstein TR, et al. Lithium versus other mood stabilizing medications in a longitudinal study of bipolar youth. J Am Acad Child Adolesc Psychiatry. 2019, S0890–8567(19)31399-1.

Hayes J, Prah P, Nazareth I, et al. Prescribing trends in bipolar disorder: cohort study in the United Kingdom THIN primary care database 1995–2009. PLoS One. 2011;6:e28725.

Hayes JF, Marston L, Walters K, Geddes JR, King M, Osborn DP. Lithium vs. valproate vs. olanzapine vs. quetiapine as maintenance monotherapy for bipolar disorder: a population-based UK cohort study using electronic health records. World Psychiatry. 2016;15:53–8.

Huhn M, Nikolakopoulou A, Schneider-Thoma J, et al. Comparative efficacy and tolerability of 32 oral antipsychotics for the acute treatment of adults with multi-episode schizophrenia: a systematic review and network meta-analysis. Lancet. 2019;394:939–51.

Jauhar S, Young AH. Controversies in bipolar disorder; role of second-generation antipsychotic for maintenance therapy. Int J Bipolar Disord. 2019;7(1):10.

Karanti A, Kardell M, Lundberg U, Landén M. Changes in mood stabilizer prescription patterns in bipolar disorder. J Affect Disord. 2016;195:50–6.

Kessing L. Lithium as the drug of choice for maintenance treatment in bipolar disorder. Acta Psychiatr Scand. 2019;140(2):91–3.

Kessing LV, Vradi E, Andersen PK. Nationwide and population-based prescription patterns in bipolar disorder. Bipolar Disord. 2016;18:174–82.

Kessing LV, Bauer M, Nolen WA, Severus E, Goodwin GM, Geddes J. Effectiveness of maintenance therapy of lithium vs. other mood stabilizers in monotherapy and in combinations: a systematic review of evidence from observational studies. Bipolar Disord. 2018;20:419–31.

Lahteenvuo M, Tanskanen A, Taipale H, et al. Real-world effectiveness of pharmacologic treatments for the prevention of rehospitalization in a finnish nationwide cohort of patients with bipolar disorder. JAMA Psychiatry. 2018;75(4):347–55.

Lyall LM, Penades N, Smith DJ. Changes in prescribing for bipolar disorder between 2009 and 2016: national-level data linkage study in Scotland. Br J Psychiatry. 2019;215(1):415–21.

Malhi GS, Gessler D, Outhred T. Use of lithium for treatment of bipolar disorder: recommendations from clinical practice guidelines. J Affect Disord. 2017;217:266–80.

Malhi GS, Bell E, Boyce P, Hazell P, Murray G, Bassett D, Bryant RA, Hopwood M, Lyndon B, Mulder R, Porter RJ, Singh A, Gershon S. Make lithium great again! Bipolar Disord. 2020;22(4):325–7.

Miura T, Noma H, Furukawa TA, Mitsuyasu H, Tanaka S, Stockton S, Salanti G, Motomura K, Shimano-Katsuki S, Leucht S, et al. Comparative efficacy and tolerability of pharmacological treatments in the maintenance treatment of bipolar disorder: a systematic review and network meta-analysis. Lancet Psychiatry. 2014;1:351–9.

Murru A, Manchia M, Hajek T, Nielsen RE, Rybakowski JK, Sani G, Schulze TG, et al. International group for the study of lithium treated, lithium's antiviral effects: a potential drug for CoViD-19 disease? Int J Bipolar Disord. 2020;8:21.

Nederlof M, Heerdink ER, Egberts ACG, et al. Monitoring of patients treated with lithium for bipolar disorder: an international survey. Int J Bipolar Disord. 2018;6:12.

Nolen WA, Licht RW, Young AH, Malhi GS, Tohen M, Vieta E, et al. What is the optimal serum level for lithium in the maintenance treatment of bipolar disorder? A systematic review and recommendations from the ISBD/IGSLI Task Force on treatment with lithium. Bipolar Disord. 2019;21:394–409.

Parabiaghi A, Barbato A, Risso P, Fortino I, Bortolotti A, Merlino L, et al. Lithium use from 2000 to 2010 in Italy: a population-based study. Pharmacopsychiatry. 2015;48:89–94.

Post RM. The new news about lithium: an underutilized treatment in the United States. Neuropsychopharmacology. 2018;43:1174–9.

Renes JW, Regeer EJ, Hoogendoorn AW, Nolen WA, Kupka RW. A nationwide study on concordance with multimodal treatment guidelines in bipolar disorder. Int J Bipolar Disord. 2018;6:22.

Rhee TG, Olfson M, Nierenberg AA, et al. 20-Year trends in the pharmacologic treatment of bipolar disorder by psychiatrists in outpatient care settings. Am J Psychiatry. 2020;177:706–15.

Rybakowski JK. Challenging the negative perception of lithium and optimizing its long-term administration. Front Mol Neurosci. 2018;11:349.

Sani G, Fiorillo A. The use of lithium in mixed states. CNS Spectr. 2019. https://doi.org/10.1017/S1092852919001184.

Schoot TS, Molmans THJ, Grootens KP, Kerckhoffs APM. Systematic review and practical guideline for the prevention and management of the renal side effects of lithium therapy. Eur Neuropsychopharmacol. 2019;31:16–32.

Severus E, Taylor MJ, Sauer C, et al. Lithium for prevention of mood episodes in bipolar disorders: Systematic review and meta-analysis. Int J Bipolar Disord. 2014;2:15.

Severus E, Bauer M, Geddes J. Efficacy and effectiveness of lithium in the longterm treatment of bipolar disorders: an update 2018. Pharmacopsychiatry. 2018;51(5):173–6.

Smith KA, Cipriani A. Lithium and suicide in mood disorders: updated meta-review of the scientific literature. Bipolar Disord. 2017;19:575–86.

Song J, Sjölander A, Joas E, Bergen SE, Runeson B, Larsson H, et al. Suicidal behavior during lithium and valproate treatment: a within-individual 8-year prospective study of 50,000 patients with bipolar disorder. Am J Psychiatry. 2017;174:795–802.

Sun YR, Herrmann N, Scott CJM, Black SE, Swartz RH, Hopyan J, Lanctôt KL. Lithium carbonate in a poststroke population: exploratory analyses of neuroanatomical and cognitive outcomes. J Clin Psychopharmacol. 2019;39(1):67–71.

Tondo L, Abramowicz M, Alda M, Bauer M, Bocchetta A, Bolzani L, Calkin CV, Chillotti C, Hidalgo-Mazzei D, Manchia M, Müller-Oerlinghausen B, Murru A, Perugi G, Pinna M, Quaranta G, Reginaldi D, Reif A, Ritter P Jr, Rybakowski JK, Saiger D, Sani G, Selle V, Stamm T, Vázquez GH, Veeh J, Vieta E, Baldessarini RJ. Long-term lithium treatment in bipolar disorder: effects on glomerular filtration rate and other metabolic parameters. Int J Bipolar Disord. 2017;5(1):27.

Tondo L, Alda M, Bauer M, Bergink V, Grof P, Hajek T, Lewitka U, Licht RW, Manchia M, Müller-Oerlinghausen B, Nielsen RE, Selo M, Simhandl C, Baldessarini RJ, International Group for Studies of Lithium (IGSLi). Clinical use of lithium salts: guide for users and prescribers. Int J Bipolar Disord. 2019;7(1):16.

Van Gestel H, Franke K, Petite J, Slaney C, Garnham J, Helmick C, Uher R, Alda M, Hajek T. Brain age in bipolar disorders: effects of lithium treatment. Aust N Z J Psychiatry. 2019;53(12):1179–88.

Velosa J, Delgado A, Finger E, Berk M, Kapczinski F, de Azevedo CT. Risk of dementia in bipolar disorder and the interplay of lithium: a systematic review and meta-analyses. Acta Psychiatr Scand. 2020. https://doi.org/10.1111/acps.13153.

Verdoux H, Quiles C, Bachmann CJ, Siskind D. Prescriber and institutional barriers and facilitators of clozapine use: a systematic review. Schizophr Res. 2018;201:10–9.

Vieta E, Berk M, Schulze T, et al. Bipolar disorder. Nat Rev Dis Primers. 2018;4:18008.

Yatham LN, Kennedy SH, Parikh SV, Schaffer A, Bond DJ, Frey BN, et al. Canadian Network for Mood and Anxiety Treatments (CANMAT) and International Society for Bipolar Disorders (ISBD) 2018 guidelines for management of patients with bipolar disorder. Bipolar Disord. 2018;20:97–170.

Yildiz A, Nikodem M, Vieta E, Correll CU, Baldessarini RJ. A network meta-analysis on comparative efficacy and all-cause discontinuation of antimanic treatments in acute bipolar mania. Psychol Med. 2014;45:299–317.

Zanni G, Goto S, Fragopoulou AF, Gaudenzi G, Naidoo V, Di Martino E, Levy G, Dominguez CA, Dethlefsen O, Cedazo-Minguez A, et al. Lithium treatment reverses irradiation-induced changes in rodent neural progenitors and rescues cognition. Mol Psychiatry. 2019. https://doi.org/10.1038/s41380-019-0584-0.

14

Cortisol levels in unmedicated patients with unipolar and bipolar major depression using hair and saliva specimens

Andrés Herane-Vives[1,2*], Danilo Arnone[3], Valeria de Angel[1], Andrew Papadopoulos[1], Toby Wise[2], Luis Alameda[4,5], Kia-Chong Chua[1], Allan H. Young[1] and Anthony J. Cleare[1]

Abstract

Background: Differentiating between unipolar and bipolar depression can be clinically challenging, especially at first presentation. Patterns of cortisol secretion could aid diagnostic discrimination in affective disorders although there has been little comparative research to date. In this study, we investigated acute (saliva) and chronic (hair) cortisol levels concurrently in unmedicated unipolar and bipolar disorders by using conventional diagnostic criteria and self-report measures.

Methods: Patients with unipolar and bipolar major depression and healthy controls were recruited and assessed. Cortisol levels were extracted from saliva and hair specimens. Depressive features were investigated according to diagnostic groups and with a continuous self-report measure of bipolarity using the Hypomania Checklist (HCL-33).

Results: Whilst a trend towards a reduction in the total daily salivary cortisol output—area under the curve with respect to the ground (AUCg)—was detected in depressive disorders across diagnosis, the self-administrated bipolarity index suggested that an increase in bipolarity symptoms predicted lower cortisol levels using AUCg. Chronic cortisol measurement did not discriminate unipolar from bipolar depression.

Conclusion: Results suggested that whilst a low total daily salivary cortisol output (AUCg) might be associated with depressive symptoms, a self-reported measure of bipolarity predicts lower daily cortisol output.

Introduction

Early detection of bipolar depression can be clinically challenging as major depression is the commonest first clinical presentation for both unipolar and bipolar disorders. Especially in the case of bipolar type II disorder, symptoms can be difficult to detect based on their relatively shorter duration and propensity to lesser intensity than bipolar type I. Furthermore, collateral information can be difficult to obtain in many clinical settings in case of sub-threshold symptoms (Angst 2006).

The crude application of diagnostic criteria based on the unipolar vs. bipolar dichotomy can frequently result in underreporting of bipolar disorder, potentially worsening clinical outcome as the treatment for the two conditions differs (Angst et al. 2011). Although it is clearly important to achieve correct syndromic differentiation, not least to optimise treatment and clinical outcome (Sharma et al. 2005), the absence of salient clinical features to guide differentiation of unipolar from bipolar depression is largely part of the current diagnostic limitations (Benazzi et al. 2002). A relatively new concept is to consider bipolarity as a spectrum on a continuum which allows sub-threshold symptoms to be considered as clinically relevant (Akiskal and Pinto 1999). Method of assessment is also important. For example, Jabben et al. (2011) found that among their large depressive sample,

*Correspondence: andres.herane@kcl.ac.uk
[1] Centre for Affective Disorders, Department of Psychological Medicine, Institute of Psychiatry, Psychology & Neuroscience, King's College London, 103 Denmark Hill, London SE5 8AF, UK
Full list of author information is available at the end of the article

only 5.5% of them were bipolar patients when diagnosed through clinical assessment, but when self-reported (hypo)manic symptoms before the depressive episode were also considered, the bipolar group accounted for 10.5% of the depressive sample.

Another aid to help to differentiate affective disorders is the possibility to utilise putative biological markers to increase the specificity of illness detection. A large amount of evidence suggests that differences in cortisol levels might help correctly identify depressive syndromes (Rybakowski and Twardowska 1999). Hypercortisolemia is most commonly associated with unipolar major depression (Pariante and Lightman 2008), often in the context of severe presentations (Maes et al. 1994). Some evidence also points towards relative peripheral hypocortisolism in bipolar depression (Maripuu et al. 2014) in the presence of treatment resistance (Markopoulou 2013). However, although hypothalamic pituitary adrenal axis abnormalities in affective disorders are widely reported (Daban et al. 2005), the direction of the abnormalities in unipolar vs. bipolar major depression is not clearly defined. Jabben and colleagues recently demonstrated that bipolar spectrum patients had a higher diurnal cortisol slope in saliva measures compared to patients with unipolar major depressive disorder (Jabben et al. 2011). Nonetheless, other reports have shown no alterations in cortisol levels in this condition (Strickland and Percival. 2002; Ciufolini et al. 2014). Furthermore, cortisol levels have not differed when large meta-analyses have studied these alterations in unipolar and bipolar depression (Belvederi Murri et al. 2014, 2016).

The heterogeneity of major depressive disorders is a likely contributor to the lack of homogeneity in the findings. One other possible explanation for the inconsistencies in the literature is the wide variance of the methods used to assess cortisol concentrations, some providing acute measures, others chronic.

A study combining acute and chronic measures by using a viable validated approach to test cortisol concentrations in a relatively homogeneous sample of unmedicated unipolar and bipolar major depression might prove helpful to disentangle this uncertainty. Hair can be used to reliably sample chronic cortisol concentrations in humans (Russell et al. 2012), whereas the measurement of cortisol in saliva samples is a well-established approach to evaluate acute concentrations and variations in levels. Using such an approach previously, we found, for instance, that atypical depression may be better described by alterations in cortisol rhythm, rather than total concentration, when short and long-term cortisol levels were concurrently collected in 1 day (Herane-Vives 2018). This suggestion arose from our finding that patients with atypical depression had normal hair cortisol concentrations (HCC) but reduced daily output measured using salivary cortisol. Some authors have also found that atypical depression is the most frequent form of depressive episode in bipolar disorder patients (Benazzi 2001). By contrast, the large percentage of our depressive sample that did not exhibit any acute or chronic cortisol level alterations was mainly characterised by non-atypical cross-sectional and unipolar longitudinal features.

To date, few case–control studies that studied hair cortisol concentration in affective disorders (Dettenborn et al. 2012; Wei et al. 2015; Dowlati et al. 2010; Hinkelmann et al. 2013; Herane Vives et al. 2015). Among those that have specifically studied HCC in bipolar patients, Aas et al. (2019) found that patients in a current mood episode had higher HCC levels compared to euthymic patients, but HCC was not significantly different when euthymic and non-euthymic bipolar patients were compared to controls. HCC was also similar for schizophrenia and bipolar disorder patients. Conversely, Streit et al. (2016) found that HCC was higher in bipolar disorder compared to schizophrenia. Staufenbiel and Koenders (2014) and Manenschijn et al. (2012) both found that HCC was not associated with bipolar disorder. Only Streit et al. (2016) and Coello et al. (2019) found that HCC was higher in bipolar patients compared with healthy individuals. However, when hair cortisol data have meta-analytically been integrated, results have not shown the presence of an association between HCC alterations and mood disorders (Stalder et al. 2017). To date, no affective disorder research study has used a combination of hair and saliva measures, and compared unipolar vs. bipolar major depression in medication-free individuals.

In this study, we measured acute and chronic cortisol concentrations in a sample of medication free unipolar and bipolar depressed individuals vs. healthy controls. Another point of interest is to use a continuous measure of self-reported bipolarity, as a bipolarity index, to better represent subthreshold bipolarity symptoms in unipolar and bipolar depression and to reflect variations in cortisol concentrations irrespective of clinical diagnosis.

Although prior data as summarised above were inconsistent, we tested the hypothesis that whereas unipolar depression would be characterised by hypercortisolemia, hypocortisolemia would be associated with bipolar depression. We also explored whether a continuous index of bipolarity would correlate more closely with cortisol alterations than a categorical approach, such that the higher the bipolarity index the lower the measured cortisol concentration. Finally, we were interested in whether there were differences when acute and chronic cortisol levels were assessed in the same patients, similar to our previous findings in patients with atypical depression.

Methods

Participants

Participants were recruited in London, UK (77) and Santiago, Chile (34) from public advertisements (Wise et al. 2016) and from local psychological therapy and psychiatric services (Table 1). All participants were screened with the Mini International Neuropsychiatric Interview (MINI, Sheehan et al. 1998) and psychometric scales validated in both Spanish and English languages.

Patients were included if they met axis I DSM-IV criteria for unipolar major depression (59) or bipolar (12) disorder. A severity criterion on the 17-item Hamilton Depression rating scale (HAMD-17, Hamilton 1960) was not imposed for two reasons; first, as the HAMD-17 emphasises more typical symptoms of depression over atypical symptoms (e.g. it does not score hypersomnia or increased appetite but does score insomnia and reduced appetite), using a severity inclusion would have risked biasing recruitment because atypical MDE patients would have needed to be more unwell to meet the same HAMD-17 score; and second, so as to reflect the full range of depressive severity seen in out-patients with a MDE. We did, however, require patients to have a score ≥ 11 to ensure they had clinically significant ongoing depressive symptoms. Patients also needed to be medication free for ≥ 2 weeks (≥ 4 weeks for fluoxetine) and not receiving any psychological intervention at the time of the assessment. Depressive symptoms ratings were evaluated on an independent set of patients and showed high inter-rater-reliability among assessors (intraclass correlation coefficient 0.96, $p < 0.01$). Self-reported symptoms of depression were assessed using the Quick Inventory of Depressive Symptoms (QIDS, Rush et al. 2003). The longitudinal categorical diagnoses of unipolar major depression or bipolar depression were made using the MINI, and a current diagnosis of mania/hypomania was also excluded using the MINI. The Young Mania Rating scale (YMRS, Young et al. 1978) was also used to explore a wider range of mood elation symptoms, and only those with scores of < 10 were included to avoid including those with a mixed affective state. Historical self-reported hypomanic symptoms were assessed using the 33-item hypomania checklist (HCL-33) (Feng et al.

Table 1 Clinical and demographic characteristics

	Major depression		Healthy controls	p values
	Unipolar	Bipolar		
Controls, *n*				
Total			40	NA
UK			32	
Chile			8	
Unipolar subtype, *n*				
Total	59			NA
UK	37			
Chile	22			
Bipolar subtype, I/II, *n*				
Total		6/6	NA	NA
UK		5/3		
Chile		1/3		
Atypical/non-atypical depression, *n*	24/35	3/9	NA	0.24^{λ}
Mean age [years] (SD)	34 (10.5)	31.2 (10.6)	33.2 (8.9)	0.66
M/F	17/42	6/6	11/29	0.3
Episodes; mean (SD)	2.3 (4.0)	10.2 (18.7)	0 (0)	<0.01
Admissions; mean (SD)	0.1 (0.4)	0.6 (0.9)	0 (0)	<0.01
Mean duration of illness [weeks], (SD)	91.6 (132.9)	76.6 (151.1)	0 (0)	<0.01
HAMD-17; mean (SD)	18.2 (4.6)	13.0 (6.8)	0.3 (0.9)	<0.01
QIDS; mean (SD)	18.2 (4.2)	15.4 (6.7)	0.5 (1.4)	<0.01
YMRS; mean (SD)	1.1 (1.4)	1.4 (2.7)	0.1 (0.3)	<0.01

NA not applicable, *HAMD–17* 17-item Hamilton Depression Rating Scales, *QIDS* Quick Inventory of Depressive Symptoms, *YMRS* Young Mania Rating Scale, *SD* standard deviation

$^{\lambda}$ p-value was obtained using Fisher's exact test

2016). Atypical depression was defined according to its DSM-5 specifier.

Healthy controls had no current or past psychiatric diagnoses, nor did their first-degree relatives (40). All participants required a minimum of 3 cm hair length for inclusion. Any use of illicit substance in the previous 3 months or any unstable medical condition which could affect data analyses or interpretation were exclusion criteria. Differences in cortisol level covariates for hair and saliva specimens, such as age, gender, menstrual cycle phase, hair washing frequency, different hair treatment, and oral contraceptive use were noted and compared between groups. The relevant local ethics committee approved the research and informed consent was obtained from each participant. All participants received a small compensation for taking part in the research.

Biological specimens

Hair specimens

A trained practitioner collected hair samples of suitable participants. The presence and frequency of any biological confounders and procedures potentially affecting hair cortisol levels were measured, including cosmetic treatments (dyeing, bleaching, permanent straightening or waving), hair washing frequency and oral contraceptive use (Stalder et al. 2017a). Collection procedure and analyses for each participant were standardised according to a strict protocol to produce approximately 3 months of hair growth equivalent to 3-month retrospective assessment of endogenous cortisol production. Cortisol levels were determined using a commercially available competitive ELISA (Salimetrics LLC, USA) and the results expressed in picograms of cortisol per milligram of hair (pg/mg). All hair samples were analysed at Salimetrics Laboratory, Cambridge, UK (http://www.salimetrics.com) (Albermann and Musshoff 2012) (see Additional files 1, 2 for procedural details).

Saliva specimens

Saliva samples collection was taken at the time of the baseline assessment on a weekday Tuesday to Friday following hair sampling. In a typical test day subjects were asked to provide six saliva samples using plain salivettes (Sarstedt, Leicester, UK) as per Roberts' protocol (Roberts et al. 2004) and instructions were given in writing at the time of the assessment. Saliva samples were taken (1) immediately after awakening, (2) 30 min after awakening, (3) 60 min after awakening, (4) at noon, (5) at 4 p.m., and (6) at 8 p.m. They were also instructed to avoid extremes in the time of collections (before 6 a.m and after 10 p.m.). Analyses of saliva cortisol concentrations were carried out in the Bethem Royal Hospital, London UK. The area under the curve with respect to the ground (AUCg) was used for calculating the daily cortisol output using the six samples. Two measures of cortisol reactivity in saliva were analysed in this study including the cortisol awakening response (CAR) and the delta of cortisol (DELTA). The CAR was calculated as the area under the curve with respect to increase (AUCi) using the first three-morning saliva samples collected over a 1-h period and the DELTA was defined as the difference between cortisol measured at waking time and the sample taken at 30-min. All cortisol measures were calculated in nanomoles per litre (nmol/l) (see Additional files 1, 2 for procedural details).

Statistical analyses

Demographics, clinical features and questionnaire measurements were compared with ANOVA or t-test for continuous variables and Chi square or Fisher's exact test for categorical variables. Differences in cortisol levels in unipolar and bipolar depression and healthy controls were tested with analysis of variance (ANOVA) corrected with Bonferroni post-hoc tests for multiple comparisons. Analysis of covariance (ANCOVA) was used to control for any biological confounder potentially affecting cortisol level measurements among the unipolar and bipolar groups. Correlation analysis was used to control for any biological confounder potentially affecting cortisol levels measurements among the whole group of depressed patients. A regression model was used to evaluate the relationship between the bipolarity index, calculated as the total HCL-33 score, and measures of cortisol concentrations in the whole sample.

Results

Subjects

Fifty-nine patients with unipolar major depression (UD) and 12 participants with bipolar depression (BD) (6 type I and 6 type II) were matched with a group of 40 healthy individuals (Table 1). There were no significant differences across groups in terms of confounding biological variables aside from hair washing occurring more frequently in bipolar subjects, and higher use of contraceptives in depressed subjects (Table 2).

Hair cortisol concentrations

Analyses of hair cortisol concentration in the combined group of major depression ($N=71$) (8.3, SD 4.6 pg/mg) vs. healthy individuals (8.3, SD 3.9 pg/mg) did not show significant group differences ($p=0.96$). Similarly, hair cortisol concentration in each comparison of UD group (7.9, SD 4.3 pg/mg) vs. BD (10.2, SD 5.3 pg/mg) vs. HC (8.3, SD 3.9 pg/mg) did not show significant results ($F(2,108)=1.32$, p:0.27). Analysis of covariance controlling for frequency of washing hair and contraceptive use remained non-significant ($F(4,71)=0.42$, $p=0.79$).

Table 2 Distribution of biological variables in the samples

	Major depression		Healthy controls	p-value
	Unipolar depression	Bipolar depression		
Mean BMI (SD)	25.9 (4.5)	25.9 (7.2)	24.3 (3.6)	0.22
Mean waist circumference in cm (SD)	87.1 (12.9)	87.2 (17.3)	82.1 (10.7)	0.15
Follicular phase, *n* (%)	12 (20.3)	1 (8.3)	9 (22.5)	0.44
Medication, *n* (%)	22 (37.3)	3 (25)	13 (32.5)	0.70
Contraceptives, *n* (%)	3 (5.1)	2 (16.6)	10 (25)	0.04
Medical comorbidities, *n* (%)	12 (20.3)	2 (16.7)	2 (5.0)	0.07
Mean hair washes/week (SD)	3.9 (1.7)	5.7 (2.1)	4.5 (1.7)	0.02
Cosmetic treatments[a], *n* (%)	33 (55.9)	9 (75)	27 (67.5)	0.47

BMI body mass index, *NA* not applicable, *SD* standard deviation

[a] Dyeing, bleaching, permanent straightening or waving

Saliva cortisol concentrations

There was a trend towards significant reduction in the total daily salivary cortisol output (AUCg) in the combined group of depressed individuals (105.8, SD 34.8 nmol/l h) vs. the healthy controls (120.8, SD 38.9 nmol/l h), $p = 0.06$ although neither the UD (108.3, SD 34.8 nmol/l h) nor the BD group (87.8; SD 32.0 nmol/l h) significantly differed from the healthy individuals (all $p > 0.05$). Correlation analysis between the use of contraceptives and AUCg or HCC did not show a significant association ($r = 0.11$; $p = 0.35$ and $r = 0.02$; $p = 0.83$, respectively). Neither CAR nor DELTA of cortisol showed a significant difference in any of the comparisons (all $p > 0.05$) (See Fig. 1 for daily salivary cortisol levels over 6 time-points by groups).

Relationship between saliva, hair cortisol concentrations and self-measure of bipolarity in the whole sample

A linear regression carried out to investigate the relationship between cortisol and the bipolarity index as a continuum in the whole sample indicated a significant negative correlation between AUCg and HCL-33 score

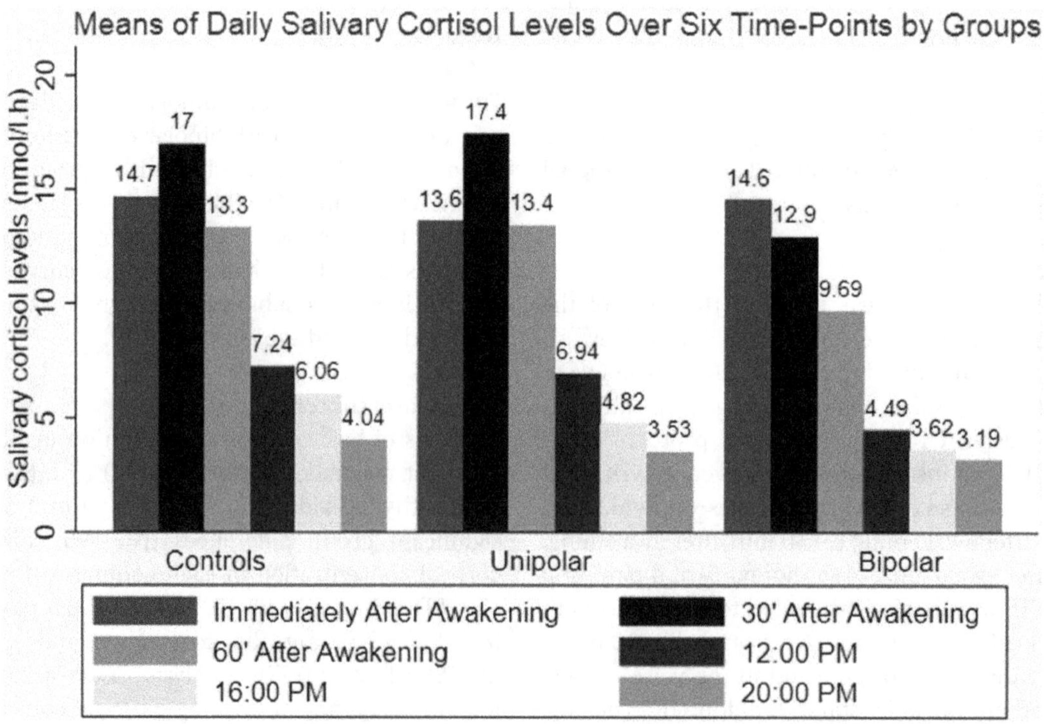

Fig. 1 Daily salivary cortisol levels over 6 time-points by groups

(β −1.32; CI −2.53, −0.12; p=0.03). On average AUCg decreased 1.32 nmol/l h for every point increase in the HCL-33 scale (Fig. 2). Regression analyses between HCL-33 scores and CAR (β −0.05, p=0.58, CI −0.25, −0.14) or DELTA of cortisol (β 0.01, p=0.73,CI −0.09, −0.13) were not significant (Fig. 2). No significant relationship was found with hair cortisol concentrations (β 0.02; CI −0.09, 0.15; p=0.64).

Discussion

In this work, we set out to measure acute and chronic cortisol concentrations in major unipolar and bipolar depression. We also indexed bipolarity in the whole sample, measured using a self-rated scale, to test whether this approach might increase the power to identify predictable changes in cortisol concentrations irrespective of clinical diagnosis. Whereas acute and chronic cortisol concentrations did not significantly differ across clinically defined groups, a linear pattern of cortisol variation emerged so that a higher self-reported bipolarity index was associated with lower AUCg.

We did not find hypercortisolaemia in unipolar major depression as we postulated either using hair or saliva measures. This is different from studies by Dettenborn et al. (2012) and Wei et al. (2015) that showed higher cortisol concentration in this group of patients compared to healthy controls. In the studies by Dettenborn et al. (2012a, b) patients were medicated while Wei et al. (2015) studied unipolar unmedicated patients who were experiencing their first depressive episode. Their findings suggest that that hypercortisolaemia is a frequent finding in more severe patients and suggest that hypothalamic pituitary adrenal axis responses might be increased at first presentation. The patients included in the present study were not purely first presenters which in combination with other factors (e.g. different subtypes of depression such as atypical and non-atypical) add additional heterogeneity and might explain the finding of an absence of hypercortisolaemia.

When major depression was considered irrespective of clinical diagnosis, hair cortisol concentrations did not differ from healthy controls. There was however a trend towards lowered daily cortisol output in this group. Although this was not a significant finding (confirmed after controlling for biological confounders), the direction is different than the hypercortisolaemia suggested in other work (Pariante and Lightman 2008). The present study measured cortisol output over a period of 12 h. Taking into account the results of our hair cortisol measurements which covered 3 months, it is possible that the presence of large spikes of hypercortisolaemia on some days but not others create an average chronic normocortisolaemia as reflected in hair. The contrast between acute and chronic measurements might, therefore, suggest an intermittently hyperactive pattern of cortisol secretion in major depression or perhaps a compensatory increase in cortisol levels during the night, which would be undetected when measuring day time cortisol output, as suggested in some studies (Krieger et al. 1971; Hellman et al. 1970). Other salivary measurements, such as

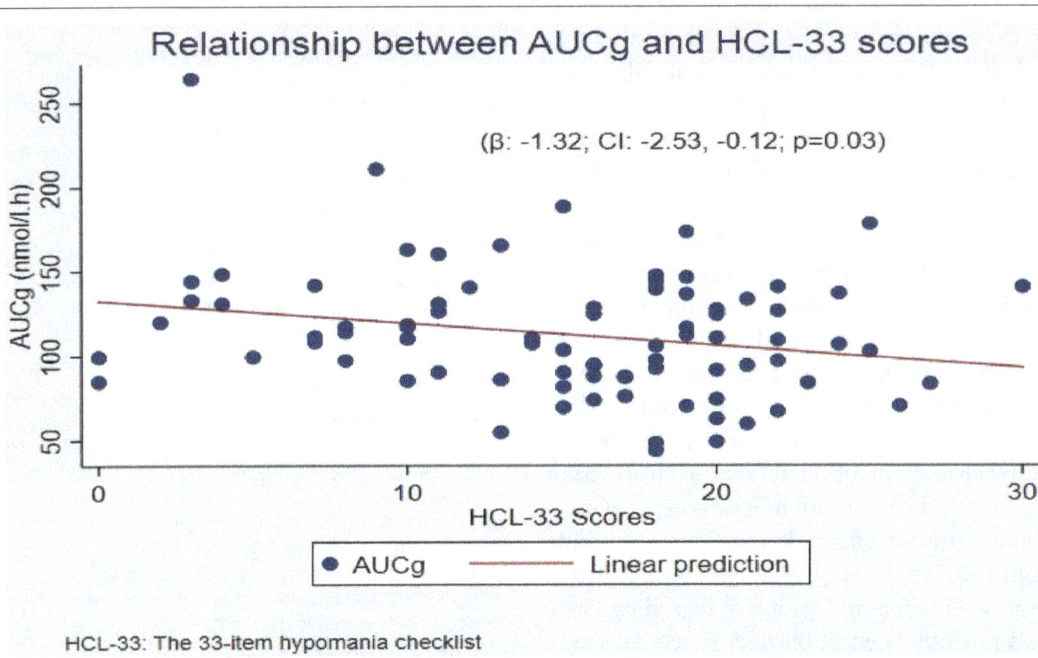

Fig. 2 Relationship between AUCg and HCL-33 scores

those related to cortisol reactivity e.g. CAR and DELTA of cortisol, were not discriminative in this study.

One of the reasons for hypothesising there might be hypocortisolaemia in bipolar depression was the anticipated frequency of atypical depression. Previously, Benazzi (2001) showed that atypical depression was the most frequent type of depressive episode related to bipolar disorder. However, atypical depressive episodes were not the most frequent cross-sectional depressive subtype in our bipolar sample (33%). Furthermore, only half of our sample were diagnosed with Bipolar II disorder (see Table 1), which according to (Benazzi 2001) is the subtype most frequently associated with atypical episodes. Whilst bipolar subtypes may have different chronic cortisol secretion profiles, our sample of bipolar patients was too small to allow meaningful comparison of cortisol concentrations between Bipolar I and Bipolar II.

Overall, our results are then more closely related to Staufenbiel and Koenders (2014) and Manenschijn et al. (2012) who both found normocortisolaemia in hair in a similar studies in samples of bipolar subjects.

However, conversely to results from Girshkin et al. (2014) our linear regression model indicated that a short term measure of daily salivary cortisol output, the AUCg, was the only saliva measure that acted as an explanatory variable when HCL-33 scores were used to define bipolarity dimensionally in the whole sample. The model showed that increases in the HCL-33 scores were significantly associated with a decrease in cortisol levels in the AUCg. This finding suggests a significant inverse relationship between average AUCg and HCL-33 score.

One of the main limitations of this study is that, although the majority of the work to date supports the use of hair to measure cortisol levels (Kalra et al. 2007; Van Uum et al. 2008; D'Anna-Hernandez et al. 2011; van Holland et al. 2012; Grass et al. 2015), there is still some uncertainty on the validity of this method (e.g. Sharpley 2012). In addition, while hair growth differences have been found in white, black and Asian ethnicities (Loussouarn et al. 2005), there is no report to date supporting or discounting differences between English and Chilean people. There is also uncertainty concerning cosmetic treatments, which are known to affect measurement taken from the outside of the hair (Sauvé et al. 2007; Manenschijn et al. 2011) although we measured cortisol from inside of the shaft (see Additional files 1, 2). We also assumed the irrelevance of other factors such as body sweat, shown not to affect cortisol measurements (Grass et al. 2015), and washout effects known to be relevant with hair lengths above 4 cm (Dettenborn et al. 2010). Another limitation is that a new protocol regarding CAR assessment has recently been published. It recommends routinely assessing CAR on two consecutive days, rather than on 1 week day (Stalder et al. 2016), which was not the case in the current study. Finally, we cannot generalize our result to the large percentage of the population that has less than 3 cm of hair length.

In conclusion, we did not find statistically significant differences in patterns of secretion of cortisol measured by using saliva and hair samples between unipolar and bipolar depression. However, self-reported bipolarity measures may be more dimensionally linked to short-term cortisol output variations.

Supplementary information

Additional file 1. Hair collection procedures.

Additional file 2. Saliva specimen collection procedures.

Acknowledgements
The authors would like to thank the staff of the NIHR/Wellcome Trust Clinical Research Facility at King's College Hospital, the Clínica Psiquíatrica Universitaria and OAIC of University of Chile, Dean Broadhurst, and Michael Kelly of the MHRN for their support in the conduct of the study. We are grateful to Mrs Irene Papadopoulos for performing the saliva cortisol Immunoassays. We thank all participants of this study for their support. This study represents independent research part funded by the NIHR/Wellcome Trust, King's Clinical Research Facility and the NIHR Biomedical Research Centre at South London and Maudsley NHS Foundation Trust and King's College London. The views expressed are those of the author(s) and not necessarily those of the NHS.

Authors' contributions
AHV designed the research. He conducted, collected, managed analysed and interpreted the data. He wrote, prepared and reviewed the manuscript. He approved the manuscript; and participated in the decision to submit the manuscript for publication. DA interpreted the data. He reviewed the manuscript. He approved the manuscript; and participated in the decision to submit the manuscript for publication. VA conducted, collected, managed the data. She reviewed the manuscript. She approved the manuscript; and participated in the decision to submit the manuscript for publication. LA interpreted the data. He reviewed the manuscript. He approved the manuscript. AP analysed the data. He reviewed the manuscript. He approved the manuscript. TW conducted, collected and managed the data. He reviewed the manuscript. He approved the manuscript. DA interpreted the data. He reviewed the manuscript. He approved the manuscript. KC provided statistical analysis of the data. He approved the manuscript. AY reviewed the manuscript. He approved the manuscript; and participated in the decision to submit the manuscript for publication. AC designed the research. He prepared and reviewed the manuscript. He approved the manuscript; and participated in the decision to submit the manuscript for publication. All authors read and approved the final manuscript.

Competing interests
AHV has received travel grants from Janssen-Cilag. AJC has in the last three years received honoraria for speaking from Lundbeck; honoraria for consulting from Livanova, Lundbeck and Janssen; sponsorship for conference attendance from Janssen; and research grant support from the Medical Research Council (UK), Wellcome Trust (UK), the National Institute for Health Research (UK) and Protexin Probiotics. AHY has given paid lectures and sits on advisory boards for all major pharmaceutical companies with drugs used in affective and related disorders. DA has received travel grants from Janssen-Cilag and Servier. No other disclosures were reported.

Author details
[1] Centre for Affective Disorders, Department of Psychological Medicine, Institute of Psychiatry, Psychology & Neuroscience, King's College London, 103 Denmark Hill, London SE5 8AF, UK. [2] Neuroscience and Mental Health Group, Institute of Cognitive Neuroscience, University College London, London, UK. [3] Department of Psychiatry, College of Medicine and Health Sciences, United Arab Emirates University, Abu Dhabi, United Arab Emirates. [4] Department of Psychosis Studies, Institute of Psychiatry, Psychology & Neuroscience, King's College London, London, UK. [5] Unit for Research in Schizophrenia, Center for Psychiatric Neuroscience, Department of Psychiatry, Lausanne University Hospital (CHUV), Lausanne, Switzerland.

References

Aas M, et al. Elevated hair cortisol is associated with childhood maltreatment and cognitive impairment in schizophrenia and in bipolar disorders. Schizophr Res. 2019;213:65–71.

Akiskal HS, Pinto O. The evolving bipolar spectrum: prototypes I, II, III, and IV. Psychiatr Clin N Am. 1999;22(3):517–34.

Rush AJ, Trivedi MH, Ibrahim HM, Carmody TJ. The 16-item quick inventory of depressive symptomatology (QIDS), clinician rating (QIDS-C), and self-report (QIDS-SR): a psychometric evaluation in patients with. Biological. 2003;54(5):573–83.

Albermann ME, Musshoff F. Investigations on the influence of different grinding procedures on measured ethyl glucuronide concentrations in hair determined with an optimized and validated LC. Anal Bioanal Chem. 2012. https://doi.org/10.1007/s00216-012-5926-6.

Angst J. Do many patients with depression suffer from bipolar disorder? Can J Psychiatry. 2006. http://search.proquest.com/openview/0eb8b51ac00dd3ea3895e9b45229651e/1?pq-origsite=gscholar. Accessed 24 May 2016.

Angst J, et al. Prevalence and characteristics of undiagnosed bipolar disorders in patients with a major depressive episode: the BRIDGE study. Arch Gen Psychiatry. 2011;68(8):791–8.

Belvederi Murri M, Pariante C, Mondelli V, Masotti M, Atti AR, Mellacqua Z, Antonioli M, Ghio L, Menchetti M, Zanetidou S, Innamorati M, Amore M. HPA axis and aging in depression: systematic review and meta-analysis. Psychoneuroendocrinology. 2014;41:46–62.

Belvederi Murri M, Prestia D, Mondelli V, Pariante C, Patti S, Olivieri B, Arzani C, Masotti M, Respino M, Antonioli M, Vassallo L, Serafini G, Perna G, Pompili M, Amore M. The HPA axis in bipolar disorder: systematic review and meta-analysis. Psychoneuroendocrinology. 2016;63:327–42.

Benazzi F. Atypical depression with hypomanic symptoms. J Affect Disord. 2001;65(2):179–83.

Benazzi F, Helmi S, Bland L. Agitated depression: unipolar? Bipolar? Or both? Ann Clin Psychiatry. 2002;14(2):97–104.

Ciufolini S, et al. HPA axis response to social stress is attenuated in schizophrenia but normal in depression: evidence from a meta-analysis of existing studies. Neurosci Biobehav Rev. 2014;47:359–68.

Coello K, et al. Hair cortisol in newly diagnosed bipolar disorder and unaffected first-degree relatives. Psychoneuroendocrinology. 2019;99:183–90.

D'Anna-Hernandez KL, Ross RG, Natvig CL, Laudenslager ML. Hair cortisol levels as a retrospective marker of hypothalamic-pituitary axis activity throughout pregnancy: comparison to salivary cortisol. Physiol Behav. 2011;104(2):348–53.

Daban C, Vieta E, Mackin P, Young AH. Hypothalamic–pituitary–adrenal axis and bipolar disorder. Psychiatric Clin North. 2005;28(2):469–80.

Dettenborn L, Tietze A, Bruckner F, Kirschbaum C. Higher cortisol content in hair among long-term unemployed individuals compared to controls. Psychoneuroendocrinology. 2010;35(9):1404–9.

Dettenborn L, Tietze A, Kirschbaum C, Stalder T. The assessment of cortisol in human hair: associations with sociodemographic variables and potential confounders. Stress. 2012a. https://doi.org/10.3109/10253890.2012.65447.

Dettenborn L, et al. Introducing a novel method to assess cumulative steroid concentrations: increased hair cortisol concentrations over 6 months in medicated patients with depression. Stress (Amsterdam, Netherlands). 2012b;15(3):348–53.

Dowlati Y, et al. Relationship between hair cortisol concentrations and depressive symptoms in patients with coronary artery disease. Neuropsychiatric Dis Treat. 2010;6:393–400.

Feng Y, Xiang YT, Huang W, Wang G. The 33-item hypomania checklist (HCL-33): a new self-completed screening instrument for bipolar disorder. J Affect Disord. 2016;190:214–20.

Girshkin L, Matheson SL, Shepherd AM, Green MJ. Morning cortisol levels in schizophrenia and bipolar disorder: a meta-analysis. Psychoneuroendocrinology. 2014;49:187–206.

Grass J, et al. Sweat-inducing physiological challenges do not result in acute changes in hair cortisol concentrations. Psychoneuroendocrinology. 2015;53:108–16.

Hamilton M. A rating scale for depression. J Neurol Neurosurg Psychiatry. 1960;23(1):56.

Hellman L, Nakada F, Curti J. Cortisol is secreted episodically by normal man. J Clin Endocrinol Metab. 1970. https://doi.org/10.1210/jcem-30-4-411.

Herane-Vives A, et al. Short-term and long-term measures of cortisol in saliva and hair in atypical and non-atypical depression. Acta Psychiatr Scand. 2018. https://doi.org/10.1111/acps.12852/full.

Herane Vives A, De Angel V, Papadopoulos A, Strawbridge R, Wise T, Young AH, Arnone D, Cleare AJ. The relationship between cortisol, stress and psychiatric illness: new insights using hair analysis. J Psychiatr Res. 2015;70:38–49.

Hinkelmann K, et al. Association between childhood trauma and low hair cortisol in depressed patients and healthy control subjects. Biol Psychiat. 2013;74(9):e15–7.

van Holland BJ, Frings-Dresen MH, Sluiter JK. Measuring short-term and long-term physiological stress effects by cortisol reactivity in saliva and hair. Int Arch Occup Environ Health. 2012;85(8):849–52.

Jabben N, et al. Co-occurring manic symptomatology influences hpa axis alterations in depression. J Psychiatr Res. 2011;45(9):1208–13.

Kalra S, et al. The relationship between stress and hair cortisol in healthy pregnant women. Clin Invest Med. 2007;30(2):E103–7.

Krieger DT, Allen W, Rizzo F. Characterization of the normal temporal pattern of plasma corticosteroid levels. J Clin. 1971. https://doi.org/10.1210/jcem-32-2-266.

Loussouarn G, El Rawadi C, Genain G. Diversity of hair growth profiles. Int J Dermatol. 2005;44(Suppl 1):6–9.

Maes M, Calabrese J, Meltzer HY. The Relevance of the in-versus outpatient status for studies on hpa-axis in depression: spontaneous hypercortisolism is a feature of major depressed inpatients and not of major depression per se. Prog Neuropsychopharmacol Biol Psychiatry. 1994;18(3):503–17.

Manenschijn L, Koper JW, Lamberts SW. Evaluation of a method to measure long term cortisol levels. Steroids. 2011;76(10–11):1032–6.

Manenschijn L, et al. Long-term cortisol in bipolar disorder: associations with age of onset and psychiatric co-morbidity. Psychoneuroendocrinology. 2012;37(12):1960–8.

Markopoulou K. 2013. HPA axis dysfunction in treatment resistant affective disorders. https://kclpure.kcl.ac.uk/portal/files/13067988/Studentthesis-Kalypso_Markopoulou_2013.pdf Accessed 5 Feb 2015.

Maripuu M, Wikgren M, Karling P, Adolfsson R, Norrback KF. Relative hypo- and hypercortisolism are both associated with depression and lower quality of life in bipolar disorder: a cross-sectional study. PLoS One. 2014;9(6):e98682.

Pariante CM, Lightman SL. The HPA axis in major depression: classical theories and new developments. Trends Neurosci. 2008;31(9):464–8.

Roberts AD. Salivary cortisol response to awakening in chronic fatigue syndrome. Br J Psychiatry. 2004;184(2):136–41. https://doi.org/10.1192/bjp.184.2.136.

Russell E, Koren G, Rieder M, Van Uum S. Hair cortisol as a biological marker of chronic stress: current status, future directions and unanswered questions. Psychoneuroendocrinology. 2012;37(5):589–601.

Rybakowski JK, Twardowska K. The dexamethasone/corticotropin-releasing hormone test in depression in bipolar and unipolar affective illness. J Psychiatr Res. 1999;33(5):363–70.

Sauvé B, et al. Measurement of cortisol in human hair as a biomarker of systemic exposure. Clin Invest Med. 2007;30(5):E183–91.

Sharma V, Khan M, Smith A. A closer look at treatment resistant depression: is it due to a bipolar diathesis? J Affect Disord. 2005;84(2–3):251–7.

Sharpley CF. Stress-linked cortisol concentrations in hair: what we know and what we need to know. Rev Neurosci. 2012. http://www.degruyter.com/view/j/revneuro.2012.23.issue 1/rns.2011.058/rns.2011.058.xml

Sheehan DV, et al. The Mini-international neuropsychiatric interview (MINI): the development and validation of a structured diagnostic psychiatric interview for DSM-IV and ICD-10. J Clin Psychiatr. 1998;59(Suppl 2):22–33.
Stalder T, et al. Assessment of the cortisol awakening response: expert consensus guidelines. Psychoneuroendocrinology. 2016;63:414–32.
Stalder T, Steudte-Schmiedgen S, Alexander N, Klucken T, Vater A, Wichmann S, Kirschbaum C, Miller R. Stress-related and basic determinants of hair cortisol in humans: a meta-analysis. Psychoneuroendocrinology. 2017;77:261–74.
Staufenbiel SM, Koenders MA. Recent negative life events increase hair cortisol concentrations in patients with bipolar disorder. Stress. 2014. https://doi.org/10.3109/10253890.2014.968549.
Streit F, et al. Perceived stress and hair cortisol: differences in bipolar disorder and schizophrenia. Psychoneuroendocrinology. 2016;69:26–34.
Strickland PL, DEAKIN JFW, Percival C. Bio-social origins of depression in the community interactions between social adversity, cortisol and serotonin neurotransmission. Br J Psychiatry. 2002. http://bjp.rcpsych.org/content/180/2/168.short.
Van Uum SHM, et al. Elevated content of cortisol in hair of patients with severe chronic pain: a novel biomarker for stress. Stress. 2008;11(6):483–8.
Wei J, et al. Analysis of hair cortisol level in first-episodic and recurrent female patients with depression compared to healthy controls. J Affect Disord. 2015;175:299–302.
Wise T, et al. Recruiting for research studies using online public advertisements: examples from research in affective disorders. Neuropsychiatric Dis Treat. 2016;12:279–85.
Young, RC, Biggs JT, Ziegler VE, Meyer DA. A rating scale for mania: reliability, validity and sensitivity. Br J Psychiatry. 1978. http://bjp.rcpsych.org/content/133/5/429.short. Accessed 24 Nov 2014.

15

Lurasidone in the long-term treatment of Japanese patients with bipolar I disorder: a 52 week open label study

Teruhiko Higuchi[1,2], Tadafumi Kato[3,4], Mari Miyajima[5], Kei Watabe[5], Takahiro Masuda[5], Katsuhiko Hagi[5*] and Jun Ishigooka[6]

Abstract

Background: The current study evaluated the long-term (52 week) safety and impact on symptom measures of lurasidone (with or without lithium or valproate) for the treatment of bipolar I disorder in Japanese patients.

Methods: Bipolar patients for this open-label flexibly dosed lurasidone (20–120 mg/day) study were recruited from those with a recent/current depressive episode who completed an initial 6 week, double-blind, placebo-controlled, lurasidone study (depressed group), and those with a recent/current manic, hypomanic, or mixed episode (non-depressed group) who agreed to enroll directly into the long-term study. Measures of adverse events and safety included treatment-emergent adverse events, vital signs, body weight, ECG, laboratory tests, and measures of suicidality and extrapyramidal symptoms. Symptom measures included Montgomery Åsberg Depression Rating Scale (MADRS) and Young Mania Rating Scale (YMRS).

Results: The most common adverse events associated with lurasidone were akathisia (30.7%), nasopharyngitis (26.6%), nausea (12.1%), and somnolence (12.1%). Minimal changes in lipids and measures of glycemic control occurred. Mean change in body weight was + 1.0 kg in the non-depressed group and − 0.8 kg in the depressed group. MADRS total scores declined by a mean (SD) of 2.0 (14.7) points from long-term baseline to endpoint in the depressed group who had received placebo in the prior 6 week trial. The depressed group that had received lurasidone during the prior 6 week study maintained their depressive symptom improvements. For the non-depressed group, YMRS total scores decreased over time.

Limitations: No control group was included, treatment was open-label, and 49.7% of patients completed the 52 week study.

Conclusions: Long-term treatment with lurasidone 20–120 mg/day for Japanese patients with bipolar disorder maintained improvements in depressive symptoms for depressed patients who were treated in a prior 6 week trial and led to improvements in manic symptoms among a newly recruited subgroup of patients with a recent/current manic, hypomanic, or mixed episode. Few changes in weight or metabolic parameters were evident.

Clinical trial registration: JapicCTI-132319, clinicaltrials.gov—NCT01986114.

Keywords: Lurasidone, Bipolar disorder, Atypical antipsychotic

Introduction

Bipolar disorder is a chronic and disabling disorder that affects both social and occupational functioning to an extensive degree (Dean et al. 2004; Fajutrao et al. 2009; Gardner et al. 2006; Vos et al. 2012). The lifetime

*Correspondence: katsuhiko-hagi@ds-pharma.co.jp
[5] Sumitomo Dainippon Pharma Co., Ltd, 13-1, Kyobashi 1-Chome, Chuo-ku, Tokyo 104-8356, Japan
Full list of author information is available at the end of the article

prevalence of bipolar disorder worldwide is about 1.0% (bipolar I disorder: 0.6%; bipolar II disorder: 0.4%), with an additional 1.4% experiencing a subthreshold version of the disorder (Merikangas et al. 2011). Bipolar disorder is associated with the loss of more disability-adjusted life years than Alzheimer's disease and all forms of cancer (World Health Organization 2002). Though the majority of patients with bipolar disorder experience recurrent depressed episodes more commonly than manic or hypomanic episodes (Calabrese et al. 2004; Judd et al. 2002), about half of those with mania experience severe role impairment (Merkiangas et al. 2011). Those individuals with bipolar I disorder have been found to be symptomatic on average approximately 70% of the time (Forte et al. 2015).

In Japan, clinical guidelines have recommended the use of lithium, sodium valproate (VPA), and several atypical antipsychotic agents in the treatment of mania episodes associated with bipolar disorder (Kanba et al. 2013). In the treatment of bipolar depression, three medications (quetiapine, olanzapine, and lurasidone) have received approval in Japan. Because of the chronic nature of bipolar disorder, long-term safety and effectiveness data is critical for ongoing management of recurring episodes. The long-term management of bipolar disorder takes on further significance given the high rates of metabolic syndrome and cardiovascular disease associated with this disorder (de Jong et al. 2018; Vancampfort et al. 2013) and the association of metabolic syndrome with adverse clinical outcomes in those with bipolar disorder (Bai et al. 2016). Given the fact that medical conditions related to metabolic syndrome and obesity emerge over time, and the episodic nature of bipolar depression, it is important to evaluate safety and symptom changes for medications for bipolar depression over the course of long-term treatment. Only a few studies of one year or more have investigated safety and symptom changes of agents for bipolar disorder in a Japanese population (e.g., Kanba et al. 2019; Katagiri et al. 2014).

The atypical antipsychotic drug lurasidone has high affinity for D2, 5-HT7 and 5-HT2A receptors (antagonist), moderate affinity for 5-HT1A receptor (partial agonist), and no appreciable affinity for H1 and M1 receptors (Ishibashi et al. 2010). The efficacy of lurasidone as a monotherapy and as an adjunctive therapy with lithium or VPA has been established for the acute treatment of bipolar depression (Loebel et al. 2014a, b; Kato et al. 2020). Two longer terms studies of lurasidone for bipolar depression have been conducted. In one extension study, 24 weeks of open-label lurasidone treatment was well tolerated with minimal effects on weight and metabolic parameters and continued improvements in depressive symptoms (Ketter et al. 2016). A second 28 week open-label extension study of lurasidone monotherapy also found minimal changes in body weight and metabolic parameters and further improvements in depressive symptoms (Ishigooka et al. 2021). In the first study (Ketter et al. 2016), 16.6% of the sample had an Asian background. In the second study, 28.3% of patients were Japanese (Ishigooka et al. 2021).

Despite the three short-term positive trials of lurasidone as a monotherapy or adjunctive therapy for bipolar depression (Loebel et al. 2014a, b; Kato et al. 2020), and the two extension trials of 24 and 28 weeks (Ketter et al. 2016; Ishigooka et al. 2021), the generalizability of the results to a Japanese population and to bipolar patients with a most recent manic, hypomanic, or mixed episode is uncertain. In addition, safety and symptom changes over the course of longer term (beyond 28 weeks) lurasidone treatment for bipolar disorder has not been reported. The aims of the current study were to provide data on safety and symptom changes over the course of one year of open-label lurasidone treatment for bipolar disorder, including those with a most recent depressed, manic, hypomanic, or mixed episode, among Japanese patients.

Methods

Patients

The study population consisted of two groups of Japanese patients. In the first group were Japanese patients who had completed an initial 6 week, double-blind, placebo-controlled, evaluation (Kato et al. 2020) of lurasidone in the treatment of bipolar depression and enrolled in a subsequent 52 week open-label extension phase. This group is labeled the "depressed episode" sample here. In the second group were Japanese patients with bipolar I disorder whose current or most recent episode was a mania (ie, meeting criteria for DSM-IV-TR specifier 296.4x), hypomania (DSM-IV-TR specifier 296.40), or mixed (DSM-IV specifier 296.6×) episode. This group is labelled the "non-depressed episode" sample here. This latter group of patients enrolled directly into a 52 week long-term lurasidone study (without a preliminary 6 week double-blind phase).

Patients from both routes of enrollment were male and female outpatients 18–74 years of age. For the non-depressed group, patients who were willing to initiate treatment with lithium or VPA adjunctively were enrolled. The 6 week, double-blind study enrolled patients with a DSM-IV-TR diagnosis of bipolar I disorder (with or without rapid cycling) who were currently experiencing a major depressive episode of at least 4 weeks but less than 12 months in duration. Patients who had completed the 6 week double-blind trial and were considered to be without safety concerns were eligible for the subsequent long-term study. For the second route of enrolment, patients with a DSM-IV-TR diagnosis of bipolar I disorder (with or without rapid cycling) were eligible if their current or most recent episode was a mania, hypomania, or mixed episode. For both the group of patients who had participated in the prior 6 week trial and the newly recruited patients who did not have an initial 6 week double-blind phase, the key exclusion criteria were: (1) presence of another Axis I or Axis II disorder other than bipolar disorder that was the focus of treatment received in the 3 months prior to screening, (2) a score of ≥ 4 on MADRS item 10 (suicidal thoughts) (at week 6 for those who participated in the prior 6 week double-blind study; at screening or baseline for those newly recruited patients who did not have an initial 6 week double-blind phase), (3) had a history of nonresponse to an adequate (6 week) trial of three or more antidepressants, antipsychotics, lithium, or VPA during the current episode, and (4) were judged to be an imminent risk of suicide, injury to self, others, or property. Diagnosis was determined using the Mini-International Neuropsychiatric Interview (Sheehan et al. 1998).

The 6 week double-blind study, the subsequent long-term extension phase, and the study recruiting patients with a manic, hypomanic, or mixed episode directly into a 52 week long-term treatment period, were each reviewed and approved by institutional review boards at each investigational site. The studies were conducted in accordance with the International Conference on Harmonization Good Clinical Practices guidelines and with the ethical principles of the Declaration of Helsinki. All patients reviewed and signed an informed consent document explaining study procedures and potential risks prior to enrollment in the 52 week long-term treatment study.

Study design

This study was a 52 week open-label flexible-dose study of lurasidone with or without a lithium or VPA. The initial 6 week double-blind study recruited patients at 102 centers in 8 countries. Only those recruited at 76 centers in Japan were included in the current report. The study, including the double-blind treatment phase and 52 week open-label phase, was conducted between January 22, 2014 and February 17, 2018.

All patients who had participated in the prior 6 week double-blind study started the 52 week extension study at a lurasidone dose of 60 mg/day for 1 week to maintain the blind of the 6 week trial until the 6 week dataset was ready for analysis. For the newly recruited patients who did not participate in an initial 6 week double-blind study, the starting dose was 20 mg/day followed by a gradual dose escalation. Lurasidone was taken once daily, within 30 min after the evening meal and administered at a flexible dose (20–120 mg/day) for 52 weeks. The dose of lurasidone could be increased or decreased by 20 mg/day at the scheduled visits, and could be increased by 20 mg/day at unscheduled visits at least 7 days after the prior visit. Dose increases were only permitted once a week between scheduled visits. When any safety concerns were raised, the dose could be reduced by 20 mg/day at unscheduled visits without waiting for 7 days.

Concomitant medications

Concomitant use of either lithium or VPA was not mandatory for the completers of the prior 6 week double-blind study because these drugs were prohibited in that prior study. The decision to add a mood stabilizer for patients who had completed the prior 6 week study was a clinical decision by the investigator at each site based on patient symptoms. For patients who had not participated in the prior study (non-depressed episode sample), concomitant use of either lithium or VPA was mandatory in order to evaluate the long-term efficacy and safety of lurasidone adjunctive to a mood stabilizer. The dose of lithium and VPA could be modified based on the patient's condition and serum concentrations that were obtained at each study visit. If necessary, the investigator could use either lithium or VPA at a lower or higher dose than approved with prior consultation with the medical monitor. If any safety concerns were raised, treatment with either lithium or VPA was to be terminated.

Prohibited during the 6 week double-blind and the 52 week long-term study were CYP3A4 inhibitors and inducers, Chinese herbal medications, Ginkgo Biloba extract, Kava Kava, depot antipsychotics, MAO inhibitors, clozapine, fluoxetine, olanzapine/fluoxetine combination, electroconvulsive therapy, and St. John's wort. Lorazepam (≤ 2 mg/day) was permitted as needed (but prohibited within 8 h of an assessment) for the treatment of anxiety, agitation, irritation, and other psychiatric symptoms/signs. Hypnotics were permitted for insomnia. For patients untreated with antiparkinson agents at screening, such medications were prohibited from screening until the initiation of the study treatment. For patients who had completed the prior 6 week study and who had received antiparkinson drugs or other drugs for extrapyramidal symptoms at the initiation of the study treatment, the drugs were to be continued without any dosage modification. For patients who had not participated in the prior study and who had received antiparkinson drugs or other drugs for the treatment of extrapyramidal symptoms at screening, drugs for extrapyramidal symptoms were titrated down and terminated before initiating study treatment. If any extrapyramidal symptoms developed or worsened after the initiation of the study treatment, permitted antiparkinson medications included biperiden (≤16 mg), trihexyphenidyl (≤10 mg), benztropine (≤6 mg), and diphenhydramine (≤300 mg). For akathisia, propranolol (≤120 mg/day), amantadine (≤300 mg/day), or one of the allowable antiparkinson medications was permitted.

Safety and tolerability assessments

Safety and tolerability were assessed throughout the study by the incidence and severity of treatment-emergent adverse events (TEAEs), laboratory measures of prolactin, glucose metabolism, and lipid metabolism, vital signs, body weight, and QTc interval determined from electrocardiography (ECG) measurements. Treatment-emergent mania was defined in depressed group as a YMRS total score of ≥ 16 at any 2 consecutive post-long-term-baseline visits or at the final assessment, or an adverse event of mania or hypomania. The influence of treatment on extrapyramidal symptoms was evaluated by the occurrence of extrapyramidal AEs, the proportion of patients using concomitant antiparkinson drugs, changes on the Drug-Induced Extrapyramidal Symptoms Scale (DIEPSS; Inada et al. 2003) total score (excluding overall severity). The proportion of patients with any instance of suicide attempt or suicidal ideation was measured by the Columbia-Suicide Severity Rating Scale (C-SSRS; Chappell et al. 2012). The DIEPSS, C-SSRS, body weight, and vital signs were obtained at long-term study baseline and post-long-term baseline weeks 1, 2, 4, and every 4 weeks up to week 52. ECGs and laboratory tests were obtained at long-term baseline and week 4 and every 8 weeks up to week 52.

Symptom and functioning assessments

Symptom and functioning measures included the Montgomery-Åsberg Depression Rating Scale (MADRS; Montgomery and Åsberg 1979) total score (range: 0–60), Young Mania Rating Scale (YMRS; Young et al. 1978) (range: 0–60), the Clinical Global Impression: Bipolar Version -Severity of Illness (CGI-BP-S; Spearing et al. 1997) depression score (range: 1–7), the Sheehan Disability Scale (SDS; Sheehan 1983) total score (range: 0–30), and the Hamilton Anxiety Rating Scale (HAM-A; Hamilton 1959) (range: 0–56). Trained raters conducted the assessments at each visit. The MADRS, YMRS, and CGI-BP-S were obtained at long-term baseline and post-long-term baseline weeks 1, 2, 4, and every 4 weeks up to week 52. The SDS and HAM-A were obtained at long-term baseline and week 4 and every 8 weeks up to week 52.

An additional endpoint was the proportion of patients who experienced a recurrence or relapse of a mood event from clinical stability. Recurrence/relapse of a mood event was defined as the occurrence of any of the following: (1) fulfilled DSM-IV-TR criteria for major depressive, manic, hypomanic, or mixed episode; (2) required treatment intervention for depressive, manic, hypomanic, or mixed symptoms with antipsychotics (other than the study drug), antidepressants, mood stabilizers (other than lithium and VPA), anxiolytics, or benzodiazepines (treatment with lorazepam, temazepam, zolpidem, zolpidem CR, eszopiclone, or zaleplon within the permitted dose range was not applied to this criterion), (3) psychiatric hospitalization for any bipolar mood episode, (4) YMRS or MADRS total score ≥ 18 or at least one of the CGI-BP-S (overall, depression, mania) scores ≥ 4 at 2 consecutive visits no more than 10 days apart, or (5) discontinuation from the study because of a mood event (as determined by the investigator). Clinical stability (sustained response) of bipolar disorder was defined as total scores of ≤ 12 on the MADRS and YMRS over at least 12 weeks, with the allowance of 2 exceptions (the YMRS and/or MADRS total scores up to 13 or 14, respectively) as long as these exceptions did not occur during the last 4 weeks before achieving clinical stability. Time to recurrence/relapse following the achievement of clinical stability was also analyzed, as was time until all-cause discontinuation.

Statistical analysis

All analyses were performed on the population of patients who took at least one dose of long-term study drug. Week 6 of the double-blind study was considered to be the baseline of the long-term study for patients who were enrolled in the prior study. Descriptive statistics were used to summarize safety and symptom/functioning data. Number and percent of patients with TEAEs over the course of the 52 weeks were summarized. Mean (SD) change from long-term baseline to week 52 was calculated for laboratory tests, vital signs, body weight, ECG parameters, and the DIEPSS. Symptom and functioning variables were examined in terms of mean changes from long-term baseline to endpoint (LOCF). For time to clinical stability and time to all cause discontinuation, median and its 95% confidence interval using the product-limit method were calculated. The numbers and percentages of subjects who experienced a recurrence/relapse and clinical stability were summarized. Analyses were conducted for all patients, and also separately for patients who received lurasidone and for those who received placebo in the prior 6 week double-blind study, as well as for the patients who had not participated in the prior study as a group and separately by type of current/recent episode.

Results

Patients and disposition

Figure 1 presents the full flow of patients starting with the 6 week double-blind, placebo-controlled trial and the additional recruitment of patients with bipolar I disorder who had a most recent episode of mania, hypomania, or mixed features and did not participate in the prior 6 week trial. Enrolled in the 52 week long-term study were 41 Japanese patients who received placebo and 76 who received lurasidone during the 6 week double-blind study, plus an additional 82 Japanese patients who did not participate in the prior 6 week trial, for a total sample of 199. All of these patients received at least one dose of study drug and were included in the safety population for analyses. Of the Japanese patients who completed the 6 week trial, only 7 did not enroll in the 52 week trial. The demographic and clinical characteristics of these 7 patients were comparable to the characteristics of the patients who did enroll in the 52 week trial. Of the Japanese patients enrolled in the 52 week long-term study who received placebo during the initial 6 week double-blind trial, 51.2% (n = 21) discontinued the long-term study prior to 52 weeks. Of the Japanese patients who received lurasidone during the initial 6 week trial, 57.9% (n = 44) discontinued prior to the end of the 52 week long-term phase. Of the patients who did not participate in the 6 week double-blind trial, 42.7% (n = 35) discontinued prior to the end of the 52 week long-term study. Overall, 20.1% (n = 40) of those enrolled in the 52 week long-term study discontinued because of adverse events; 7.5% (n = 15) discontinued due to lack of efficacy and 17.1% (n = 34) chose to withdraw from the study.

The full group of patients enrolled in the 52 week long-term study were on average 41.6 years of age with approximately an equal percent of men and women (Table 1).

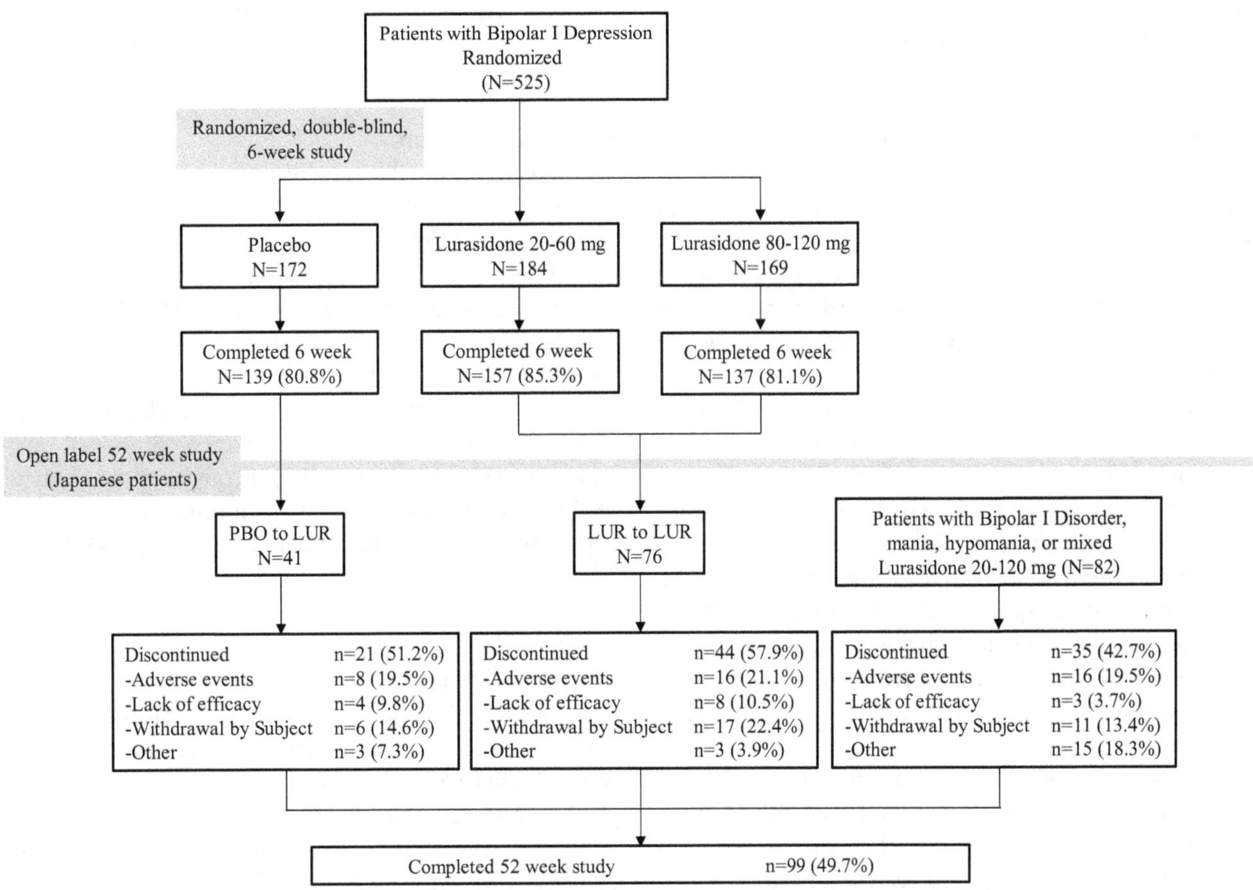

Fig. 1 Study flow diagram and subject disposition during 52 weeks of long-term treatment with lurasidone. Depressed episode group consisted of Japanese patients who had completed an initial 6 week, double-blind, placebo-controlled, evaluation of lurasidone. PBO to LUR = received placebo during prior 6 week trial followed by lurasidone (flexibly dosed 2–120 mg/day) in 52 week long-term trial. LUR to LUR = received lurasidone (flexibly dosed at either 20–60 or 80–120 mg/day) during prior 6 week trial followed by lurasidone (flexibly dosed 20 to 120 mg/day) in 52 week long-term trial. Non-depressed episode group consisted of Japanese patients with bipolar I disorder whose current or most recent episode was a mania, hypomania, or mixed episode. *LUR* lurasidone, *PBO* placebo

Table 1 Baseline characteristics of patients treated in 52 week long-term study

	Most recent or current episode of bipolar I disorder		
	All Patients (n = 199)	**Depressed episode (n = 117)**	**Non-Depressed episode (n = 82)**
Demographics and clinical characteristics			
Male, n (%)	102 (51.3)	63 (53.8)	39 (47.6)
Age years, mean (SD)	41.6 (12.0)	40.0 (10.9)	43.8 (13.1)
Duration of bipolar I disorder, mean years (SD)	13.5 (11.1)	13.8 (10.6)	13.0 (11.7)
With rapid cycling, n (%)	30 (15.1)	15 (12.8)	15 (18.3)
Efficacy measure at long-term study baseline			
MADRS, mean (SD)	12.4 (10.3)	16.0 (10.2)	7.3 (8.0)
CGI-BP-S Overall, mean (SD)	2.98 (1.29)	3.10 (1.25)	2.80 (1.33)
CGI-BP-S Depression, mean (SD)	2.51 (1.39)	3.03 (1.31)	1.77 (1.13)
CGI-BP-S Mania, mean (SD)	1.77 (1.18)	1.23 (0.56)	2.55 (1.39)
SDS, mean (SD)#	11.9 (8.7)	13.7 (9.03)	9.2 (7.6)
YMRS, mean (SD)	4.7 (6.7)	2.0 (2.8)	8.7 (8.6)
HAM-A, mean (SD)	8.3 (7.2)	10.6 (7.5)	5.0 (5.2)
Safety measure at long-term study baseline			
DIEPSS (excluding overall severity), mean (SD)	0.36 (0.78)	0.50 (0.87)	0.16 (0.60)

[#] Number of patients: All = 181, Depressed = 109, Non-Depressed = 72

CGI-BP-S Clinical Global Impression Bipolar Version Severity of illness score, *DIEPSS* Drug-Induced Extrapyramidal Symptoms Scale, *HAM-A* Hamilton Rating Scale for Anxiety total score, *LUR* lurasidone, *MADRS* Montgomery-Åsberg Depression Rating Scale, *PBO* placebo, *SD* Standard Deviation, *SDS* Sheehan Disability Scale, *YMRS* Young Mania Rating Scale

Among the patients in the non-depressed episode group, the most recent episode was manic for 43 patients, hypomanic for 27 patients, and mixed for 12 patients. As expected, the average level of depressive symptoms, as measured by the MADRS and CGI-BP-S depression score was higher for those patients who participated in the prior double-blind study that required a current episode of depression at double-blind baseline, compared to the patients who did not participate in the prior double-blind trial and who had a most recent manic, hypomanic, or mixed bipolar episode (for the MADRS, Cohen's d effect size using the larger SD of the two groups = 0.85; for the CGI-BP-S, d = 0.96). Similarly, the mean YMRS score was higher for non-depressed episode group compared to the depressed episode group (d = 0.78). The long-term baseline demographic and clinical characteristics of patients who had received placebo in the prior 6 week trial were similar to those that had received lurasidone (Additional file 1: Table S1).

At long-term baseline, 53.7% of the non-depressed episode sample had been receiving a mood stabilizer. Of the 44 patients in the non-depressed episode group who were already taking a mood stabilizer at long-term baseline, 23 (52.3%) were receiving lithium, 19 (43.2%) were receiving VPA, and 2 (4.5%) were receiving both lithium and VPA. As per protocol, all of the remaining patients in the non-depressed episode sample received a mood stabilizer going forward from the long-term study baseline.

Study drug exposure

The mean (SD) daily dose of lurasidone for all patients (n = 199) during the 52 week study was 57.0 (26.1) mg and the modal dose was 57.0 mg/day. The number (percent) of patients who received a modal daily dose for each possible lurasidone dosage was: 20 mg: 50 (25.1%), 40 mg: 37 (18.6%), 60 mg: 54 (27.1%), 80 mg: 24 (12.1%), 100 mg: 19 (9.5%), and 120 mg: 15 (7.5%). In the overall safety population, the mean (minimum, maximum) percent compliance (number of tablets taken / number of tablets should have been taken) × 100) throughout the study was 98.9%. The mean (SD, median) number of days of drug exposure for the 199 participants was 233.8 (143.3, 343).

Safety

Overall, 84.9% (n = 169) of patients in the 52 week study experienced at least one treatment-emergent adverse events (Table 2). The most common adverse events were akathisia (30.7%), nasopharyngitis (26.6%), nausea (12.1%), and somnolence (12.1%). Rates of adverse events were generally similar for the depressed episode group compared to the non-depressed episode group. Rates of TEAEs were also generally similar for patients who had received placebo vs lurasidone during the prior 6 week trial and also for type of recent or current episode among patients in the non-depressed patients (Additional file 1: Table S2).

Table 2 Treatment-emergent adverse events (safety population; *N* [%]; incidence ≥ 5%)

Adverse event	Most recent or current episode of bipolar I disorder		
	All patients (n = 199)	Depressed episode (n = 117)	Non-Depressed episode (n = 82)
At least one adverse event	169 (84.9%)	96 (82.1)	73 (89.0%)
Akathisia	61 (30.7%)	40 (34.2%)	21 (25.6%)
Nasopharyngitis	53 (26.6%)	24 (20.5%)	29 (35.4%)
Nausea	24 (12.1%)	12 (10.3%)	12 (14.6%)
Somnolence	24 (12.1%)	10 (8.5%)	14 (17.1%)
Weight increased	17 (8.5%)	8 (6.8%)	9 (11.0%)
Headache	16 (8.0%)	7 (6.0%)	9 (11.0%)
Parkinsonism	15 (7.5%)	10 (8.5%)	5 (6.1%)
Disease progression	13 (6.5%)	9 (7.7%)	4 (4.9%)
Vomiting	13 (6.5%)	8 (6.8%)	5 (6.1%)
Diarrhoea	10 (5.0%)	4 (3.4%)	6 (7.3%)
Dystonia	10 (5.0%)	5 (4.3%)	5 (6.1%)

The incidence of TEAEs did not increase with duration. The most common TEAEs leading to discontinuation were disease progression (n = 10), followed by akathisia (n = 8), and insomnia, mania, suicidal ideation, and suicide attempt (n = 2 each).

For the full sample, TEAEs related to extrapyramidal symptoms were reported for 17.6% (35 of 199) of patients up to week 52. None of these TEAEs were serious and all were mild or moderate in severity. Treatment-emergent metabolic AEs were reported for 13.1% (26 of 199) of patients across the long-term treatment period. Among these, glucose urine present and diabetes mellitus in 1 patient each were recorded as serious. Mood-event related TEAEs were reported for 13.1% (26 of 199) patients up to week 52. Among these, disease progression in 3 patients, mania and suicide attempt in 1 patient each were serious TEAEs. Treatment-emergent mania occurred in 0.9% (1 of 117) patients of the depressed group. Other significant adverse events are presented in Additional file 1: Table S3, separately for placebo vs lurasidone for those enrolled in the prior 6 week trial and separately for type of most recent/current episode for those non-enrolled in the prior 6- week trial. Suicidality-related TEAEs up to week 52 included suicide attempt in 2 patients and suicidal ideation in 4 patients. No patients had a completed suicide and no other deaths occurred in the study. A weight increase of ≥ 7% occurred for 17.7% (n = 35) of patients; a weight decrease of ≥ 7% occurred for 14.5% (n = 29) of patients.

An increase in the mean HOMA-IR (fasting) from long-term study baseline to week 52 was evident (mean change = 0.37) for the full sample, with similar mean changes in both the depressed episode and non-depressed episode groups (Table 3). The mean concentration of triglycerides (fasting) increased from long-term study baseline to week 52 (mean change = 5.4 mg/dl). This change was primarily driven by a mean change of 10.0 mg/dl for the depressed group (enrolled from the prior 6 week trial) compared to a mean change of 0.3 mg/dl in the non-depressed group (who did not participate in the prior trial). Except for the above, no clinically relevant changes from long-term baseline were noted in clinical chemistry, hematology, urinalysis, endocrine parameters, or vital signs. No meaningful differences in laboratory parameters or body weight were evident for those who received placebo vs. lurasidone in the prior 6 week trial, or depending on type of recent/current episode within the non-depressed sample (Additional file 1: Table S4). Overall mean change in body weight to week 52 was 0 kg (-0.8 kg in the depressed group; + 1.0 kg in the non-depressed group). Mean changes from long-term baseline to week 52 in ECG parameters were not clinically meaningful. No subject had a post-long-term baseline QTcF interval of > 500 ms.

No notable changes (LOCF) from long-term baseline were found in the DIEPSS total score at week 52 (mean change = 0.0). Based on the results of C-SSRS, any suicidality after long-term baseline was reported for 26.3% (52 of 198) of patients in the full sample.

The proportion of patients in the full sample who received one or more concomitant medications during the 52 week treatment period was 94.5%. There were 38.2% who received antiparkinson medications, 57.3% mood stabilizers, 41.2% anxiolytics, and 67.3% hypnotics. When the results were summarized by the most recent or current episode of bipolar I disorder (depressed vs.

Table 3 Body weight and laboratory parameters: mean (SD) change from long-term baseline to week 52 (observed case analysis)

Parameter	Most recent or current episode of bipolar I disorder		
	All	**Depressed episode**	**Non-Depressed episode**
Body Weight, kg	n=99	n=52	n=47
Mean change	0.0 (5.6)	− 0.8 (5.6)	(5.5)
Median change	0.1	0.1	0.1
Triglycerides (mmol/L) -fasting	n=99	n=52	n=47
Mean change	0.061 (0.667)	0.113 (0.734)	0.003 (0.587)
Median change	0.068	0.073	0.057
Total cholesterol (mmol/L) -fasting	n=99	n=52	n=47
Mean change	− 0.080 (0.656)	− 0.065 (0.695)	− 0.098 (0.617)
Median change	− 0.026	− 0.091	0.052
LDL cholesterol (mmol/L) -fasting	n=97	n=50	n=47
Mean change	− 0.039 (0.545)	− 0.064 (0.603)	− 0.012 (0.482)
Median change	0.026	0.039	0.026
HDL cholesterol (mmol/L) -fasting	n=99	n=52	n=47
Mean change	− 0.047 (0.276)	− 0.018 (0.255)	− 0.079 (0.297)
Median change	− 0.052	− 0.039	− 0.052
Blood Glucose (mmol/L) -fasting	n=99	n=52	n=47
Mean change	0.044 (0.606)	0.045 (0.690)	0.044 (0.504)
Median change	0.111	0.111	0.056
Insulin (pmol/L) -fasting	n=98	n=51	n=47
	9.68 (63.54)	8.42 (76.05)	11.05 (47.14)
	9.72	9.03	10.42
HOMA-IR -fasting	n=98	n=51	n=47
Mean change	0.37 (2.76)	0.34 (3.46)	0.40 (1.73)
Median change	0.33	0.30	0.35
Hemoglobin A1C (%)	n=99	n=52	n=47
Mean change	0.00 (0.29)	− 0.01 (0.35)	0.01 (0.20)
Median change	0.00	0.00	0.00
Prolactin, (μg/L), Overall	n=98	n=51	n=47
Mean change	− 1.7 (17.6)	− 5.5 (18.7)	2.3 (15.5)
Median change	− 0.5	− 1.3	1.3
Prolactin, (μg/L), Male	n=44	n=24	n=20
Mean change	− 0.3 (9.2)	0.3 (7.5)	− 0.9 (11.1)
Median change	− 0.3	− 0.5	0.3
Prolactin, (μg/L), Female	n=54	n=27	n=27
Mean change	− 3.0 (22.2)	− 10.6 (23.8)	4.7 (17.9)
Median change	− 0.6	− 2.6	3.7

non-depressed), the proportion of patients using concomitant medications was similar in the depressed episode group (90.6%) and the non-depressed episode group (100%). Antiparkinson medications were more commonly used in patients with a depressive episode (47.9% for depressed, 24.4% for non-depressed; the same order applies hereafter), while mood stabilizers (27.4%, 100%) and hypnotics (59.8, 78.0%) were more commonly used in patients with a non-depressed episode. The proportions of patients with anxiolytics were relatively similar in the two groups (37.6, 46.3%).

Changes in symptoms and functioning

Table 4 summarizes the effect of up to 52 weeks of treatment with lurasidone on measures of affective symptoms and functioning based on a conservative LOCF-endpoint analysis. For both subgroups of depressed patients (double-blind placebo and double-blind lurasidone) minimal mean changes were noted during up to 52 weeks of treatment in depressive symptom measures (MADRS or CGI-BP-S depression), in mania symptom measures (YMRS or CGI-BP-S mania), and in the SDS functional measure. Similarly, for the group with a non-depressed episode, minimal mean changes were noted during up to 52 weeks of treatment in both depressive and mania symptom measures, and the SDS functional measure. On an observed case analysis (Additional file 1: Figures S1 and S2), improvement in the mean MADRS was noted during up to 52 weeks of treatment with lurasidone in both subgroups of depressed patients (double-blind placebo and double-blind lurasidone).

Changes in symptom and functioning measures based on type of recent/current episode for the non-depressed episode group are shown in Additional file 1:

Table 4 Mean change (SD) from long-term baseline to LOCF endpoint in efficacy measures

Measure	Most recent or current episode of bipolar I disorder		
	Depressed episode		Non-Depressed episode (n = 81)
	PBO to LUR (n = 41)	LUR to LUR (n = 76)	
	Mean (SD)	Mean (SD)	Mean (SD)
MADRS	− 2.0 (14.7)	1.4 (12.9)	2.5 (10.9)
YMRS	− 0.6 (3.4)	0.2 (3.6)	− 4.8 (9.0)
CGI-BP-S overall	− 0.39 (1.60)	0.12 (1.43)	− 0.14 (1.66)
CGI-BP-S depression	− 0.32 (1.64)	0.13 (1.58)	0.38 (1.53)
CGI-BP-S mania	− 0.07 (0.52)	0.03 (0.73)	− 0.86 (1.43)
HAM-A†	− 1.1 (8.5)	− 0.3 (8.9)	0.9 (6.2)
SDS#	− 0.4 (10.7)	0.8 (9.7)	− 0.9 (9.9)

[†] Number of patients: All = 197, PBO to LUR = 41, LUR to LUR = 75, Non-Depressed = 81

[#] Number of patients: All = 177, PBO to LUR = 38, LUR to LUR = 69, Non-Depressed = 70

PBO to LUR = received placebo during prior 6 week trial followed by lurasidone (flexibly dosed 20 to 120 mg/day) in 52 week long-term trial

LUR to LUR = received lurasidone (flexibly dosed at either 20–60 or 80–120 mg/day) during prior 6 week trial followed by lurasidone (flexibly dosed 20–120 mg/day) in 52 week long-term trial

CGI-BP-S Clinical Global Impression Bipolar Version Severity of illness score, *HAM-A* Hamilton Rating Scale for Anxiety total score, *LUR* lurasidone, *MADRS* Montgomery-Åsberg Depression Rating Scale, *PBO* placebo, *SD* Standard Deviation, *SDS* Sheehan Disability Scale, *YMRS* Young Mania Rating Scale

Table S5. On the YMRS, substantial improvement over the first 12 weeks was seen for the non-depressed episode group, regardless of type or presence of concomitant mood stabilizer (Additional file 1: Figures S3 and S4).

The proportions of patients with all-cause discontinuation were similar across the all treatment groups continuing from the prior study and newly recruited subjects. The median time to all-cause discontinuation was 343 days. Based on the Kaplan–Meier analysis, the probability of all-cause discontinuation at week 52 was 50.3%.

Of the 199 enrolled patients, 103 (51.8%) achieved clinical stability over the course of the 52 week treatment period (Additional file 1: Table S6). The mean duration of treatment until achieving stabilization was 141.3 ± 79.94 days. The proportion of subjects achieving clinical stability was 44.4% (52 of 117) in patients with a depressed episode (51.2% for those who had receive placebo 40.8% for those who had received lurasidone in the prior 6 week trial), and 62.2% (51 of 82) in patients with a most recent non-depressed episode. Within the non-depressed group, clinical stability was achieved those with a most recent manic, hypomanic, and mixed episode by 69.8%, 41.7%, and 59.3%, respectively. The mean duration of treatment until achieving stabilization was 160.6 ± 92.41 days for the depressed episode group and 121.7 ± 59.58 days for the non-depressed episode group. The proportion of subjects with recurrence/relapse of any mood event up to Week 52 was 12.5% (6 of 48) in patients with a depressed episode and 23.5% (12 of 51) in patients with a non-depressed episode. The median time to recurrence/relapse could not calculated.

Discussion

This 52 week long-term study found no new safety concerns over the course of long-term treatment with 20–120 mg/day of flexibly-dosed lurasidone with or without a mood stabilizer within a sample of Japanese patients with bipolar disorder. There were no notable differences in the incidence of TEAEs and common TEAEs between patients with a most recent/current depressed episode and those with a most recent/current non-depressed episode. The incidence of TEAEs did not increase with duration of treatment. No patients in the current study had a post-long-term baseline QTcF interval of > 500 ms and there were no completed suicides. Overall, the results of the current study suggest that 52 weeks of treatment with lurasidone, in doses up to 120 mg/day, has a relatively low potential for causing adverse weight and metabolic effects. As such, the current study extends the safety findings of previous studies of lurasidone (Loebel et al. 2014a; Kato et al. 2020; Ketter et al. 2016) for bipolar depression to a Japanese population and to bipolar patients with a most recent manic, hypomanic, or mixed episode. Importantly, the current safety findings also extend the shorter-term findings of previous studies of lurasidone for bipolar disorder to a full year of safety monitoring.

The most common reported TEAEs were akathisia (30.7%), nasopharyngitis (26.6%), nausea (12.1%), and somnolence (12.1%). The results of the current study found lurasidone to have a low incidence of acute EPS and suggest that long-term treatment with lurasidone is associated with a low risk of tardive extrapyramidal symptoms. However, akathisia was notably higher than reported in two previous short-term studies of lurasidone in bipolar depression. In the Loebel et al. study (2014a) akathisia rates were 7.9% and 10.8% for the 20–60 mg and 80–120 mg dosage groups, respectively. In the Kato et al. study (2020) akathisia rates were 13.0% and 23.7% for the 20–60 mg and 80–120 mg dosage groups, respectively. The higher rate of akathisia observed in the current study appears to be attributable to the fact that the placebo-treated subgroup of depressed patients, that entered the current study after completing the Kato et al. study (2020) was switched to an initial dose of 60 mg of lurasidone with no titration. In contrast, patients in the previous short-term studies (Loebel et al. 2014a; Kato et al. 2020) were treated initially with a 20 mg dose for 7 days prior to gradual titration up to their assigned fixed dosage group.

Over the course of 52 weeks of lurasidone treatment, there were no meaningful mean changes (largely decreases) in total cholesterol, LDL cholesterol, blood glucose, haemoglobin A1C, or prolactin. Small mean increases in triglycerides (mean change = 5.4 mg/dL) and HOMA-IR (mean change = 0.37) were observed. By way of comparison, in the Kanba et al. (2019) study of 52 weeks of quetiapine monotherapy for Japanese patients with bipolar depression, the mean change in triglycerides was 11.8 mg/dL. In the Katagiri et al. (2014) study of 42 or 48 weeks of olanzapine treatment in Japanese patients with bipolar depression, the mean increase in triglycerides was 35.1 mg/dL.

Fifty-two weeks of lurasidone treatment was associated with an average gain of 1.0 kg in body weight in the non-depressed group and a reduction of 0.8 kg in the depressed group. The 6 week study of lurasidone monotherapy for bipolar depression in a non-Japanese sample found a mean change in body weight of 0.6 kg for 20–60 mg/day and 0.0 kg for 80–120 mg/day (Loebel et al. 2014a), and the 6 week study of lurasidone (20–120 mg/day) as an adjunct to a mood stabilizer found a mean change in body weight of 0.2 kg. Mean changes in body weight for long-term treatment with olanzapine and quetiapine in Japanese patients with bipolar depression have been reported to be 3.5 kg and 1.02 kg, respectively (Katagiri et al. 2014; Kanba et al. 2019).

The rates of concomitant medication use in this study was high, with 38.2% of patients receiving antiparkinson medications, 41.2% anxiolytics, and 67.3% hypnotics. It is difficult to compare these concomitant medication rates with other long-term bipolar antipsychotic treatment studies in the literature for multiple reasons, including differences between studies in design (eg., open-label vs. double-blind; adjunctive treatment vs. monotherapy), restrictions on concomitant medications in some studies, failure to report concomitant medication use in certain studies, differences in the patient populations of studies (eg., percent of patients with recent manic/hypomanic vs. depressive episode; Japanese patients vs. other countries), and unique aspects of the current study (eg., mood stabilizers were mandatory for the newly recruited patients but not for those entering the 52 week trial after participating in the 6 week prior trial). It is worth noting that the rate of use of antiparkinson medications was twice as high among the depressed group compared to the non-depressed group in the current study (47.9% vs 24.4%). This may suggest that clinicians should particularly attend to Parkinson symptoms for bipolar patients with a recent depressive episode. However, in a previous 24 week study of lurasidone for bipolar depression, only 9.5% of patients receiving adjunctive lurasidone, and 4.4% of those receiving monotherapy lurasidone, received treatment with anticholinergic medication for acute extrapyramidal symptoms.

About half (50.3%) of the sample did not complete the full 52 week treatment period. This discontinuation rate appears to be comparable to discontinuation rates reported in previous studies of atypical antipsychotics for the long-term treatment of bipolar disorder. For example, 52 weeks of treatment with the extended-release formulation quetiapine (monotherapy) was associated with a 43% discontinuation rate (Kanba et al. 2019); 46 weeks of treatment with aripiprazole (in combination with lithium or valproate) was associated with a 48% discontinuation rate (Vieta et al. 2010); and 48 weeks of olanzapine monotherapy was associated with a 57% discontinuation rate (Katagiri et al. 2014). For olanzapine monotherapy, discontinuation rates of 42% have been reported at 18 weeks (Katagiri et al. 2012), and 34% at 24 weeks (Corya et al. 2006), that are consistent with the 50.3% rate of discontinuation reported in the current study.

Reasons for the 50% discontinuation rate in the current study are uncertain. One possible reason is that the patient group switching from placebo in the initial double-blind study was started on 60 mg of lurasidone, which might be considered to be a high dose associated with an increased likelihood of adverse events. However, the overall discontinuation rate was similar in the placebo group and the group of patients continuing on lurasidone; and the discontinuation rate due to an adverse event, was also similar for both groups.

Effectiveness

Notable in the descriptive analysis of symptom measures for the depressed episode group was the maintenance of improvements that had been achieved during the initial 6 week double-blind study. For the non-depressed episode group who had not participated in an initial 6 week study, substantial improvements in mania symptoms occurred during the first 3 months of lurasidone treatment and these improvements were then maintained out to 52 weeks. Overall, about half of those who began the long-term study met a rigorous definition of clinical stability during the 52 week treatment period. Only 12.5% of those in the depressed episode group and 23.5% in those in the non-depressed episode group experienced a relapse/recurrence of a mood event. Though differences in patient populations and definitions of relapse make comparisons to the literature difficult, these rates compare favourably to estimates of a one-year relapse rate of 75% for bipolar disorder patients receiving placebo and 30–40% for bipolar disorder patients receiving lithium (Fleiss et al. 1978).

Limitations

Study limitations include most notably that no comparison or control group was included and no inferential statistical tests were conducted. Because there was no control group, the changes over time that were found may be due to the passage of time or other factors besides treatment with lurasidone. Another limitation is that treatment was open-label. Any potential differences between patients with a current/recent depressed versus manic/hypomanic would need to be tested in future hypothesis-testing double-blind studies. A further limitation is that about half of the patients who began the study did not complete the full 52 weeks of treatment. A final limitation is that the inclusion/exclusion criteria ruled out patients with psychiatric comorbidities. The generalizability of the current findings to bipolar patients with additional psychiatric disorders is uncertain.

Conclusion

In summary, over the course of 52 weeks of lurasidone (20–120 mg/day) treatment with or without a mood stabilizer in Japanese patients with bipolar disorder there were no new safety concerns and no average changes in metabolic parameters were small. Body weight increased on average 1.0 kg in the non-depressed group and decreased on average 0.8 kg in the depressed group. Overall, 49.7% completed 52 weeks of study treatment. Akathisia occurred for 30.7%, and nausea for 12.1%, of patients. Patients with a current/recent depressed episode showed continued improvement in depressive symptoms over the treatment period; patients with a current/recent manic, hypomanic, or mixed episode showed reduction in manic symptoms. These findings support the use of lurasidone as a long-term treatment of bipolar disorder in Japanese patients.

Supplementary Information

Additional file 1. Additional efficacy and safety tables and figures.

Acknowledgements
Medical writing support was funded by Sumitomo Dainippon Pharma Co., Ltd. Japan and provided by Edward Schweizer, M.D. of Paladin Consulting Group, Princeton, NJ.

Authors' contributions
TH contributed to the conception and design of the study, acquisition and interpretation of data. TK and JI contributed to the acquisition and interpretation of data. KW contributed to the conception and design of the study and analysis and interpretation of data. MM, TM and KH contributed to analysis and interpretation of data. All authors contributed to and approved the final draft prior to submission. All authors read and approved the final manuscript.

Competing interests
Teruhiko Higuchi reports personal fees from Meiji Seika Pharma, MSD, Allergan, Eisai, Pfizer, Janssen, Lundbeck, Shionogi, Yoshitomi, Kyowa Hakko Kirin, Mochida, Otsuka, Sumitomo Dainippon, Mitsubishi Tanabe, Eli Lilly, and Takeda. ***Tadafumi Kato*** reports personal fees from Kyowa Hakko Kirin, Eli Lilly, Otsuka Pharmaceutical, GlaxoSmithKline, Taisho Toyama Pharmaceutical, Sumitomo Dainippon Pharma, Meiji Seika Pharma Pfizer, Mochida Pharmaceutical, Shionogi, Janssen Pharmaceutical, Janssen Asia Pacific, Yoshitomiyakuhin, Astellas Pharma, Wako Pure Chemical Industries, Wiley Publishing Japan, Nippon Boehringer Ingelheim Kanae Foundation for the Promotion of Medical Science, MSD, Kyowa Pharmaceutical, and Takeda Pharmaceutical, and also reports a research grant from Takeda Pharmaceutical. ***Mari Miyajima, Kei Watabe, Takahiro Masuda,*** and ***Katsuhiko Hagi*** are full-time employees of Sumitomo Dainippon Pharma Co., Ltd. ***Jun Ishigooka*** reports grants from Sumitomo Dainippon during the conduct of the study, personal fees from Meiji Seika Pharma, MSD, Astellas, Novartis, Pfizer, Otsuka, Eli Lilly, Takeda, and Eisai.

Author details
[1]Japan Depression Center, Tokyo, Japan. [2]The National Center of Neurology and Psychiatry, Kodaira, Japan. [3]Laboratory for Molecular Dynamics of Mental Disorders, RIKEN Center for Brain Science, Wako, Saitama, Japan. [4]Department of Psychiatry, Juntendo University, Tokyo, Japan. [5]Sumitomo Dainippon Pharma Co., Ltd, 13-1, Kyobashi 1-Chome, Chuo-ku, Tokyo 104-8356, Japan. [6]Institute of CNS Pharmacology, Tokyo, Japan.

References

Bai Y, Li C, Tsai S, Tu PC, Chen MH, Su TP. Metabolic syndrome and adverse clinical outcomes in patients with bipolar disorder. BMC Psychiatry. 2016;16:448.

Calabrese JR, Hirschfeld RM, Frye MA, Reed ML. Impact of depressive symptoms compared with manic symptoms in bipolar disorder: results of a US community based sample. J Clin Psychiatry. 2004;65:1499–504.

Chappell P, Feltner DE, Makumi C, Stewart M. Initial validity and reliability data on the Columbia-Suicide Severity Rating Scale. Am J Psychiatry. 2012;169:662–3.

Corya SA, Perlis RH, Keck PE Jr, Lin DY, Case MG, Williamson DJ, Tohen MF. A 24 week open-label extension study of olanzapine-fluoxetine combination and olanzapine monotherapy in the treatment of bipolar depression. J Clin Psychiatry. 2006;67:798–806.

de Jong M, Belleflamme J, Dale C, Gard T, Gamel C, Mischoulon D, Peeters F. Metabolic syndrome in Dutch patients with bipolar disorder: a cross-sectional study. Prim Care Companion CNS Disord. 2018. https://doi.org/10.4088/PCC.18m02366.

Dean BB, Gerner D, Gerner RH. A systematic review evaluating health-related quality of life, work impairment, and healthcare costs and utilization in bipolar disorder. Curr Med Res Opin. 2004;20:139–54.

Fajutrao L, Locklear J, Priaulx J, Heyes A. A systematic review of the evidence of the burden of bipolar disorder in Europe. Clin Pract Epidemiol Mental Health. 2009;5:3.

Fleiss JL, Prien RF, Dunner DL, Fieve RR. Actuarial studies of the course of manic-depressive illness. Compr Psychiatry. 1978;19:355–62.

Forte A, Baldessarini RJ, Tondo L, Vázquez GH, Pompili M, Girardi P. Long-term morbidity in bipolar-I, bipolar-II, and major depressive disorders. J Affect Disord. 2015;178:71–8.

Gardner HH, Kleinman NL, Brook RA, Rajagopalan K, Brizee TJ, Smeeding JE. The economic impact of bipolar disorder in an employed population from an employer perspective. J Clin Psychiatry. 2006;67:1209–18.

Hamilton M. The assessment of anxiety states by rating. Br J Med Psychol. 1959;32:50–5.

Inada T, Beasley CM Jr, Tanaka Y, Walker DJ. Extrapyramidal symptom profiles assessed with the Drug-Induced Extrapyramidal Symptom Scale: comparison with Western scales in the clinical double-blind studies of schizophrenic patients treated with either olanzapine or haloperidol. Int Clin Psychopharmacol. 2003;18:39–48.

Ishibashi T, Horisawa T, Tokuda K, Ishiyama T, Ogasa M, Tagashira R, Matsumoto K, Nishikawa H, Ueda Y, Toma S, Oki H, Tanno N, Saji I, Ito A, Ohno Y, Nakamura M. Pharmacological profile of lurasidone, a novel antipsychotic agent with potent 5-hydroxytryptamine 7 (5-HT7) and 5-HT1A receptor activity. J Pharmacol Exp Ther. 2010;334:171–81.

Ishigooka J, Kato T, Miyajima M, Watabe K, Masuda T, Hagi K, Higuchi T. Lurasidone in the long-term treatment of bipolar I depression: a 28 week open label extension study. J Affect Disord. 2021;281:160–7.

Judd LL, Akiskal HS, Schettler PJ, Endicott J, Maser J, Solomon DA, Leon AC, Rice JA, Keller MB. The long term natural history of the weekly symptomatic status of bipolar I disorder. Arch Gen Psychiatry. 2002;59:530–7.

Kanba S, Kato T, Terao T, Yamada K. Committee for Treatment Guidelines of Mood Disorders, Japanese Society of Mood Disorders, Guideline for treatment of bipolar disorder by the Japanese Society of Mood Disorders. Psychiatry Clin Neurosci. 2013;2012(67):285–300.

Kanba S, Murasaki M, Koyama T, Takeuchi M, Shimizu Y, Arita E, Kuroishi K, Takeuchi M, Kamei S, et al. Long-term mood/antidepressant effects of quetiapine extended-release formulation: an open-label, non-controlled extension study in Japanese patients with bipolar depression. BMC Psychiatry. 2019;19:198.

Katagiri H, Takita Y, Tohen M, Higuchi T, Kanba S, Takahashi M. Safety and efficacy of olanzapine monotherapy and olanzapine with a mood stabilizer in 18-week treatment of manic/mixed episodes for Japanese patients with bipolar I disorder. Curr Med Res Opin. 2012;28:701–13.

Katagiri H, Tohen M, McDonnell DP, Fujikoshi S, Case M, Kanba S, Takahashi M, Gomez JC. Safety and efficacy of olanzapine in the long-term treatment of Japanese patients with bipolar I disorder, depression: an integrated analysis. Psychiatry Clin Neurosci. 2014;68:498–505.

Kato T, Ishigooka J, Miyajima M, Watabe K, Fujimori T, Masuda T, Higuchi T, Vieta E. Double-blind, placebo-controlled study of lurasidone monotherapy for the treatment of bipolar I depression. Psychiatry Clin Neurosci. 2020;74:635–44.

Ketter TA, Sarma K, Silva R, Kroger H, Cucchiaro J, Loebel A. Lurasidone in the long-term treatment of patients with bipolar disorder: a 24 week open-label extension study. Depress Anxiety. 2016;33:424–34.

Loebel A, Cucchiaro J, Silva R, Kroger H, Hsu J, Sarma K, Sachs G. Lurasidone monotherapy in the treatment of bipolar I depression: a randomized, double-blind, placebo-controlled study. Am J Psychiatry. 2014a;171:160–8.

Loebel A, Cucchiaro J, Silva R, Kroger H, Sarma K, Xu J, Calabrese JR. Lurasidone as adjunctive therapy with lithium or valproate for the treatment of bipolar I depression: a randomized, double-blind, placebo-controlled study. Am J Psychiatry. 2014b;171:169–77.

Merikangas KR, Jin R, He JP, Kessler RC, Lee S, Sampson NA, Viana MC, Andrade LH, Hu C, Karam EG, Ladea M, Medina-Mora ME, Ono Y, Posada-Villa J, Sagar R, Wells JE, Zarkov Z. Prevalence and correlates of bipolar spectrum disorder in the World Mental Health Survey Initiative. Arch Gen Psychiatry. 2011;68:241–51.

Montgomery SA, Åsberg M. A new depression scale designed to be sensitive to change. Br J Psychiatry. 1979;134:382–9.

Sheehan DV. The anxiety disease. New York: Bantam Books; 1983.

Sheehan DV, Lecrubier Y, Sheehan KH, Amorim P, Janavs J, Weiller E, Hergueta T, Baker R, Dunbar GC. The Mini-International Neuropsychiatric Interview (MINI): The development and validation of a structured diagnostic psychiatric interview for DSMIV and ICD-10. J Clin Psychiatry. 1998;59(Suppl 20):22–33.

Spearing MK, Post RM, Leverich GS, Brandt D, Nolen W. Modification of the Clinical Global Impressions (CGI) Scale for use in bipolar illness (BP): The CGI-BP. Psychiatry Res. 1997;73:159–71.

Vancampfort D, Vansteelandt K, Correll CU, Mitchell AJ, De Herdt A, Sienaert P, Probst M, De Hert M. Metabolic syndrome and metabolic abnormalities in bipolar disorder: A meta-analysis of prevalence rates and moderators. Am J Psychiatry. 2013;170:265–74.

Vieta E, Owen R, Baudelet C, McQuade RD, Sanchez R, Marcus RN. Assessment of safety, tolerability and effectiveness of adjunctive aripiprazole to lithium/valproate in bipolar mania: a 46 week, open-label extension following a 6 week double-blind study. Curr Med Res Opin. 2010;26:1485–96.

Vos T, Flaxman AD, Naghavi M, et al. Years lived with disability (YLDs) for 1160 sequelae of 289 diseases and injuries 1990–2010: a systematic analysis for the Global Burden of Disease Study 2010. Lancet. 2012;380:2163–9.

World Health Organization. The world health report 2002: reducing risks, promoting healthy life. Geneva: World Health Organization; 2002.

Young RC, Biggs JT, Ziegler VE, Meyer DA. A rating scale for mania: reliability, validity and sensitivity. Br J Psychiatry. 1978;133:429–35.

The course of bipolar disorder in pregnant versus non-pregnant women

Anja W. M. M. Stevens[1,2*†], Stasja Draisma[2,3†], Peter J. J. Goossens[1,4], Birit F. P. Broekman[2,5], Adriaan Honig[2,5], Elise A. M. Knoppert-van der Klein[6], Willem A. Nolen[7,8], Robert M. Post[8,9] and R. W. Kupka[2,3,8]

Abstract

Background and rationale: Although it has been suggested that pregnancy may influence the course of bipolar disorder (BD), studies show contradictory results. Until now, no studies included a finegrained validated method to report mood symptoms on a daily basis, such as the lifechart method (LCM). The aim of the present study is to investigate the course of BD during pregnancy by comparing LCM scores of pregnant and non-pregnant women.

Methods: Study design: Comparison of LCM scores of two prospective observational BD cohort studies, a cohort of pregnant women (n = 34) and a cohort of non-pregnant women of childbearing age (n = 52). Main study parameters are: (1) proportions of symptomatic and non-symptomatic days; (2) symptom severity, frequency, and duration of episodes; (3) state sequences, longitudinal variation of symptom severity scores.

Results: No differences in clinical course variables (symptomatic days, average severity scores, frequency, and duration of episodes in BD were found between pregnant and non-pregnant women. With a combination of State Sequence Analysis (SSA) and cluster analysis on the sequences of daily mood scores three comparable clusters were found in both samples: euthymic, moderately ill and severely ill. The distribution differences between pregnant and non-pregnant women were significant, with a majority of the pregnant women (68%) belonging to the moderately ill cluster and a majority of the non-pregnant women (46%) to the euthymic cluster. In pregnant women the average daily variation in mood symptoms as assessed with Shannon's entropy was less than in non-pregnant women (respectively 0.43 versus 0.56).

Conclusions: Although the use of daily mood scores revealed no difference in overall course of BD in pregnant versus non-pregnant women, more pregnant than non-pregnant women belonged to the moderately ill cluster, and during pregnancy the variation in mood state was less than in non-pregnant women. Further research is necessary to clarify these findings.

Keywords: Bipolar disorder, Course, Pregnancy, Life chart method

Introduction and rationale

Bipolar disorder (BD) is a recurrent mental illness characterized by depressive, hypomanic, and/or manic episodes separated by euthymic intervals and usually manifests in young adulthood (Goodwin and Jamison 2007). The lifetime prevalence ranges from 1.3% to 2.4% (Merikangas et al. 2011; Graaf et al. 1996).

Patients with BD show considerable illness-related morbidity (Post et al. 2003; Ferrari et al. 2016) and the disorder significantly influences their wellbeing and social, occupational, and general functioning (Altshuler et al. 2006; Bonnin et al. 2012; Parker et al. 2018).

In clinical practice, women with BD often ask their physician about the impact of pregnancy on the course of their illness. However, research into the relation between

*Correspondence: a.stevens@dimence.nl
†Anja W. M. M. Stevens and Stasja Draisma are first author
[1] Center for Bipolar Disorders, Dimence Mental Health, Deventer, The Netherlands
Full list of author information is available at the end of the article

pregnancy and course of BD is scarce. Unlike repeated findings that the postpartum period has a negative influence on the course of BD, with an overall risk of relapse of 35% (66% or medication-free women and 23% for women who used prophylactic medication) (Wesseloo et al. 2016), the impact of pregnancy itself on the course BD is still uncertain, and various studies have reported conflicting results (McNeil et al. 1984; Sharma and Persad 1995).

While some population-based studies suggest that pregnancy could be protective with low rates of new onset and relapse during this period (Munk-Olsen et al. 2006,2009), clinical studies provide conflicting findings. Most of the older studies are retrospective, and most of the prospective studies report high recurrence rates in women who discontinue mood stabilizers (Sharma and Pope 2012).

In a retrospective study (Viguera et al. 2011), clinical data were pooled of 2252 pregnancies of women with BD and unipolar depression. Rates of affective episodes and risk factors were identified during pregnancy and the postpartum period. Among women with BD, 23% had illness episodes during pregnancy, compared to 4.6% of women with unipolar depression. Risk factors were younger age at illness onset, previous postpartum episodes, shorter duration of illness, having fewer children, and not being married.

Freeman et al. (2002) interviewed 30 women with BD after pregnancy with a structured clinical interview, and found that 15 (50%) reported no change or fewer mood symptoms during pregnancy, while the other half reported more symptoms. The experience of worsening of mood symptoms during pregnancy also predicted postpartum recurrence (Freeman et al. 2002). A limitation of this study is that the assessment was retrospective and thus prone to recall bias.

Grof et al. found a protective effect of pregnancy on the frequency and duration of mood episodes in a sample of 28 women with BD (with 56 pregnancies), who had become pregnant prior to receiving successful lithium prophylactic treatment (Grof et al. 2000). Retrospectively, they compared illness severity during the 9 months of pregnancy with the 9 months before pregnancy intra-individually. The recurrence risk during pregnancy was markedly lower and recurrences of mood episodes were significantly shorter during pregnancy in comparison to pre-pregnancy.

In a recent review of the influence of pregnancy on the course of BD we concluded that despite the importance of the topic there is a paucity of evidence on recurrence rates of mood episodes during pregnancy among women with BD (Stevens et al. 2019). Another review also stated that the literature cannot answer the question of how pregnancy affects the course of BD, but merely informs us about the effect of discontinuation of medication in pregnancy (Salim et al. 2018). Retrospective studies are more sensitive to recall bias and results are therefore less reliable, while prospective studies focused mainly on the effect of discontinuation of medication and hardly on the relation between pregnancy and course of illness.

Moreover, none of these studies used a detailed mood monitoring method to assess course of illness during pregnancy. The LifeChart Method (LCM) (Leverich et al. 2001; Denicoff et al. 2000) is a prospective assessment of fluctuations and severity in mood on a daily basis, resulting in more precision, with less risk for recall bias as compared with retrospective self reported data that were collected in most studies (Draisma et al. 2015).

The aim of the present study is to prospectively investigate the relationship between pregnancy and the course of BD.

Methods

LCM-data of two observational, prospective cohort studies were used to compare the course of BD in pregnant versus non-pregnant women.

Study samples

The research samples were (1) pregnant Dutch women with an established DSM-IV diagnosis of BD, who participated in the Sleepreg-BD study between 2012 and 2018 (n = 34), and (2) non-pregnant Dutch women of childbearing age with an established DSM-IV diagnosis of BD, who participated in The Stanley Foundation Bipolar Treatment Outcome Network study between 1995 and 2000 (n = 52).

The Sleepreg-BD study was a multi-site study in the Netherlands investigating the effect of sleep disturbance in pregnancy and the perinatal period on postpartum psychopathology in Dutch women with BD (Stevens et al. 2014). Pregnant women, aged 18–45 year, with a diagnosis of BD were asked to fill in the LCM from week 13 of pregnancy till 12 weeks postpartum. To avoid including women whose pregnancy ended prematurely, we recruted pregnant women at the end of the first trimester of pregnancy. To investigate the illness course during pregnancy, for this study LCM postpartum scores were not included in the analysis. The LCM was completed by 46 women, of these 34 met the inclusion criterion of at least 60 days of LCM reports.

The Stanley Foundation Bipolar Network (SFBN) was a multi-site research program coordinated at the National Institute of Mental Health (NIMH), with four clinical centers in the USA, two in Germany and one in the Netherlands, as described in detail elsewhere (Leverich et al. 2001; Post et al. 2001). Its main aim was to evaluate the long-term illness course and define longitudinal illness patterns, and to investigate the effectiveness of conventional and novel pharmacological treatments in a large group of patients with BD. The SFBN database consisted of over 900 patients, including n = 174 from the Netherlands. For this current study we included data of the 52 non-pregnant women, age 18–45 year, and included in the Netherlands, who had completed at least one full year of LCM. Since the pregnant women delivered a maximum of 272 daily severity scores, we selected the 272 completed last lifechart ratings from the first year of prospective follow-up of the SFBN women for comparison with the Dutch women of the Sleepreg-BD study.

Assessment instruments and outcome variables

Patient and clinician questionnaires:

The Stanley Foundation Bipolar Treatment Outcome Network designed two questionnaires to collect basic demographic and clinical data from both patients and clinicians. These questionnaires (Questionnaire for Bipolar disorder, QBP) generate a comprehensive overview of the characteristics of participants as well as illness and treatment history (Leverich et al. 2001; Suppes et al. 2001), and were translated into Dutch.

QBP reports of medication use were transformed into categories (0: no medication; 1: one mood stabilizer; 2: more than one mood stabilizer; 3: mood stabilizer and other psychotropic medications; 4: only other psychotropic medications).

LCM

The LCM provides a graphic representation of minor mood swings and major mood episodes, and can be used both retrospectively and prospectively (Denicoff et al. 2000,1997). The impact of daily mood symptoms on functioning is rated on a 5-point scale (0 = no dysfunction or euthymia, 1 = mild, 2 = low moderate, 3 = high moderate, 4 = severe dysfunction). Since severity is rated for two poles: mania and depression, this results in nine different ratings. Patients of both cohort studies were asked to complete a prospective LCM on a daily basis during the entire study period. Illness course variables could be calculated, thus allowing longitudinal assessment of illness patterns (Born et al. 2009; Kupka et al. 2007; Nolen et al. 2004). Relevant variables were: number, duration, and severity of mood symptoms and mood episodes, and proportion of time ill during the observation period. A validation study reported high correlations between LCM ratings and ratings on the Young Mania Rating Scale (YMRS) ($r = 0.656$, $p < 0.001$) and the Inventory of Depressive Symptomatology-Clinician (IDS-C) ($r = 0.875$, $p < 0.001$) (Denicoff et al. 2000). Draisma et al. found a Spearman's Rho of 0.61 between LCM depression scores and Clinical Global Impression (CGI-BD) rated depression, and a Rho of 0.63 between LCM mania scores and CGI-C rated mania in a sample of Dutch patients with BD (n = 137), denoting a strong association between LCM ratings and CGI scores (Draisma et al. 2015).

Thus, main study parameters where threefold: (1) demographical variables at baseline: age, marital status, educational level and work status at baseline; (2) clinical variables at baseline consisting of diagnosis, illness duration, age of onset, number of lifetime manic and depressive episodes, number of hospitalizations, use of medication, lifetime alcohol/drugs abuse, number of serious suicide attempts; and (3) LCM derived clinical variables such as proportion of time ill or impaired, number of days with scores not equal to five (i.e. the euthymic state), average illness severity scores, average duration of episodes, and frequency of episodes.

Statistical analysis

Analyses were done in four steps: (1) demographic and clinical characteristics of the pregnant and non-pregnant samples were compared with descriptive statistics; (2) complete series of illness states – the LCM mood scores – were analyzed and typified for the two samples with the use of state sequence analysis (SSA); (3) cluster analysis was performed on the state sequences; and (4) two regression analyses were done, one on clusters with a set of predictors and another on variation in daily states with the same set of predictors.

The set of predictors were illness duration, marital status, work status, educational level, use of medication (Viguera et al. 2011; Akdeniz et al. 2003).

Differences in demographical and clinical variables were analyzed with descriptive statistics, using t-tests for continuous variables with normal distribution, Mann-Whitey tests for non-normal continuous variables and chi square tests for categorical variables. Descriptive analyses were performed in SPSS version 27. Missing lifechart scores of the 34 pregnant women within the observation period (less than 0.3% of the data) were imputed through intrapolation of the surrounding daily scores.

Complete series of illness states as expressed in fluctuations of daily severity scores of the pregnant and non-pregnant women were analysed with SSA (Roux et al. 2019; Gabadinho et al. 2011). The time series of a maximum of 272 daily severity scores resulted in so-called sequences of successive states. The goal of SSA is to describe complete sequences of events as trajectories of subjects though possible states. It is a non-parametric approach with no assumptions regarding underlying processes and aimed at description of sequences as a whole (Courgeau 2018).

Dissimilarities between state sequences were calculated with a dissimilarity measure based on the number of operations necessary to translate a specific sequence into another. The similarities and differences were based on optimal matching techniques. Subsequently, clustering methods were applied to build similar types of sequences (Abbott 1990). By clustering sequences, groups were formed that were as homogenous as possible within the group and as different as possible from other groups. In the analysis, hierarchical clustering was applied using Ward's linkage on the distance matrix. The clustering procedures resulted in a typology of sequence courses. Sequences within a cluster had the lowest dissimilarity scores with each other, and between clusters dissimilarity was optimal. Distributions of women over the clusters found in the sample of pregnant women (n = 34) were subsequently compared to those found in the non-pregnant women (n = 52).

Shannon entropy, an indicator of diversity of states (~ severity scores) within sequences was calculated for all day. Entropy can vary between 0 (all sequences in the same state at time T), to 1 (maximum diversity at time T).

Multinomial regression of clusters on the predictors was performed. In the same vain regression of entropy on this set of covariates was applied.

The package TraMineR (version 2.2–0.1) within R-software was used for sequence analysis.

Results

First, descriptive statistics with respect to the comparisons of sample characteristics are presented in Tables 1, 2, 3. Next the distribution of states over days is presented in an index plot for all women in Fig. 1. Cluster solutions for both samples are also presented graphically as index plots in Fig. 2. Mean time spent in a cluster is given in Fig. 3. Results of multinomial regression of clusters in the combined set of samples on predictors are provided in Table 4. Finally, results of regression of entropy on the same set of predictors are presented.

No age differences were present between the samples. Pregnant women were significantly more often married, attained higher educational levels and were more often unable to work (Table 1). Pregnant women had less previous hospitalisations and used less medication than the non-pregnant group (Table 2). Of the pregnant women three women used antidepressant medication without a mood stabilizer, while in the non-pregnant group none of the women used an antidepressant without a mood stabiliser. No significant differences were found regarding lifetime illness duration, age of onset, lifetime number of experienced manic or depressive episodes, lifetime substance abuse or dependence, and number of attempted suicides.

Comparison of the course of BD in both samples showed no significant differences in LCM variables (Table 3) regarding episodes or number of ill days during the observation episode.

Table 1 Demographic characteristics of non-pregnant and pregnant women with BD recruited from two study cohorts from the Netherlands

	Non-pregnant (n = 52)	Pregnant (n = 34)	Test statistic
Age[a] Mean (SD)			
Years	35.2 (6.3)	34.1 (3.9)	T = -0.95 p = 0.35
Marital status n (%)			
Married/cohabitating	24 (46.2)	33 (97.1)	
Widowed/separated	3 (5.8)	0 (0)	
Single	25 (48.1)	1 (2.9)	$\chi^2 = 23.2$ $p < 0.01$
Educational level n (%)			
Low (some high school or less)	1 (1.9)	1 (3.0)	
Middle(high school-2 year college)	43 (82.7)	8 (24.2)	
High (graduate of professional school)	8 (15.4)	24 (72.7)	$\chi^2 = 29.2$ $p < 0.01$
Work n (%)			
Regular work, school or household	29 (59.2)	26 (78.8)	
Other work	19 (38.8)	2 (6.1)	
Unable to work	1 (2.0)	5 (15.2)	$\chi^2 = 14.0$ $p < 0.01$

[a] Age was normally distributed (Kolmogorov_Smirnov > 0.05, Shapiro–Wilk > 0.05)

Table 2 Lifetime clinical characteristics of non-pregnant and pregnant women with BD recruited from two study cohorts from The Netherlands

Clinical characteristics	Non-pregnant (n-52)	Pregnant (n = 34)	Test statistic
Diagnosis, n (%)			
Bipolar I	38 (76.0)	19 (59.4)	
Bipolar II	12 (24.0)	13 (40.6)	$\chi^2 = 2.541$ $p = 0.11$
Illness duration[a]			
Mean duration in years (SD)	15.4 (7.29)	14.6 (6.18)	T = -5.02 $p = 0.62$
Less than 5 years	3 (5.8)	3 (9.1)	
5–9 years	9(17.3)	3 (9.1)	
10–19 years	21 (40.4)	17 (51.5)	
20–29 years	19 (36.5)	10 (30.3)	$\chi^2 = 2.071$ $p = 0.56$
Age of onset[a] (mean, SD)	19.9 (5.93)	19.5 (5.23)	U = 828.5 $p = 0.790$
No. of depressive episodes, n (%)			
0 episodes	0 (0)	3 (9.1)	
1 episode	6 (11.5)	1 (3.0)	
2–4 episodes	16 (30.8)	16 (48.5)	
5–10 episodes	13 (25.0)	7 (21.2)	
11–20 episodes	5 (9.6)	4 (12.1)	
> 20 episodes	12 (23.1)	2 (6.1)	$\chi^2 = 11.977$ $p = 0.04$
No. of manic episodes, n (%)			
0	0	1 (3.0)	
1 episode	4 (7.7)	6 (18.2)	
2–4 episodes	20 (38.5)	19 (57.6)	
5–10 episodes	16 (30.8)	4 (12.1)	
11–20 episodes	7 (13.5)	1 (3.0)	
> 20 episodes	5 (9.6)	2 (6.1)	$\chi^2 = 10.699$ $p = 0.06$
Hospitalizations[a], mean (SD)	4.1 (5.8)	1.4 (1.7)	
Medication, n (%)			
Without medication	0 (0.0)	8(23.5)	
1 Mood stabilizer	23 (44.2)	8 (23.5)	
> 1 Mood stablizers	20 (38.5)	0 (0.0)	
Moodstabilizer and other medication	9 (17.3)	8 (23.5)	
Other medication only	0 (0.0)	10 (29.4)	$\chi^2 = 43.453$ $p < 0.01$
Substance abuse/dependence, n (%)			
Alcohol	9 (17.3)	3 (9.1)	$\chi^2 = 1.124$ $p = 0.29$
Drugs	7 (13.5)	7 (21.5)	$\chi^2 = 0.881$ $p = 0.35$
Serious suicide attempts			
None	36 (69.2)	28 (84.8)	
One or more	16(30.8)	5 (15.2)	$\chi^2 = 2.547$ $p = 0.10$

[a] Mean illness duration was normally distributed (Kolmogorov_Smirnov > 0.05, Shapiro–Wilk > 0.05), age of onset and number of hospitalizations were not (Kolmogorov_Smirnov < 0.05, Shapiro–Wilk < 0.05)

Sequence analysis results

Distributions of proportions of severity scores per day were plotted for the whole observation periods in an index plot (Fig. 1).

Figure 1 shows that most time of women with BD was spent in the euthymic state. This state covered the largest surface per day during the whole observation period. The percentage of women in this state was the highest, followed by 'mildly depressed' and 'mildly manic'.

Figure 2 gives the graphic results of a cluster analysis with three clusters for the separate samples.

Women in the clusters 'severely ill' of both samples showed sequences with mainly severe and moderate depressive or manic days and few euthymic states. The second set of clusters, 'moderately ill' contained state

Table 3 Clinical lifechart results of non-pregnant and pregnant women with BD recruited from two study cohorts from The Netherlands

Averages (SD)[a]	Non-pregnant (n = 52)	Pregnant (n = 34)	Test statistic T	p
No. depressive episodes[a]	3.43 (11.95)	0.55 (0.94)	1.40	0.16
No. manic episodes[a]	0.35 (0.68)	0.38 (1.35)	−0.14	0.89
No. hypomanic episodes[a]	1.10 (2.95)	1.29 (1.59)	−0.40	0.69
No. manic days[a]	14.06 (36.53)	8.90 (20.81)	0.75	0.46
No. hypomanic days[a]	16.19 (23.12)	18.83 (33.25)	−0.43	0.66
No. depressive days[a]	71.85 (76.07)	56.78 (80.20)	0.88	0.38
No. days ill (depressed, manic, hypomanic)[a]	102.10 (84.53)	84.51 (93.17)	0.91	0.37
Average mania score	0.39 (1.01)	0.23 (0.54)	0.85	0.40
Average depression score	0.45 (0.58)	0.34 (0.55)	0.88	0.38

[a] Corrected for the number of observations

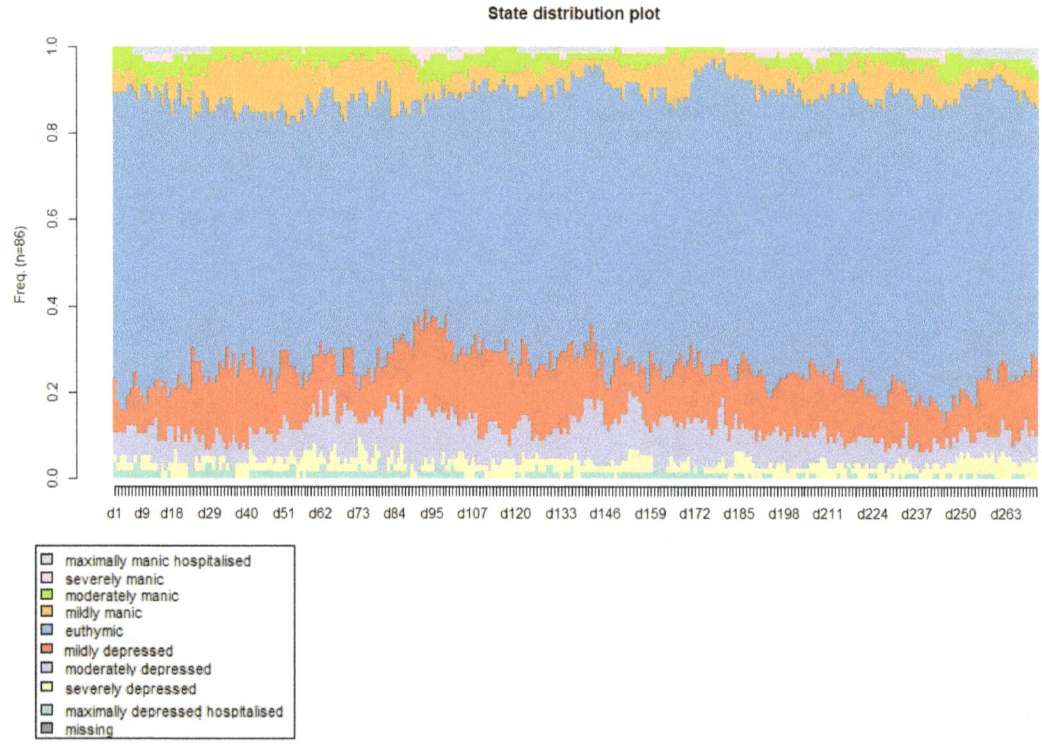

Fig. 1 Index plot: distribution of states (daily self rated severity score) for both samples (pregnant and non-pregnant women, n = 86) over the observation period of 272 days. X-axis: time in days, Y axis: proportions women distributed over states described in the legend

sequences with some illness, days with mild to moderately ill days with respect to both mania as well as depression. Finally, clusters 'euthymic' were typified by sequences with mainly euthymic days, the main area of these clusters were taken up by euthymic states. This three cluster solution shows that the severely ill cluster in the non-pregnant sample consisted of 21% (11/52) of the participants and in the pregnant sample 18% (6/34) of the participants. The euthymic cluster in the pregnant sample consisted of 16% (5/34) the women, whereas this euthymic cluster in the non-pregnant sample was larger, consisting of 46% (24/52) of the women. The majority of the pregnant women were clustered as 'moderately ill': the percentage in this cluster is twice as high as the percentage of non-pregnant women in this cluster (68% and 32%, respectively). These distribution differences between samples were significant: $\chi^2 = 48.02$, df = 2, p-value < 0.001.

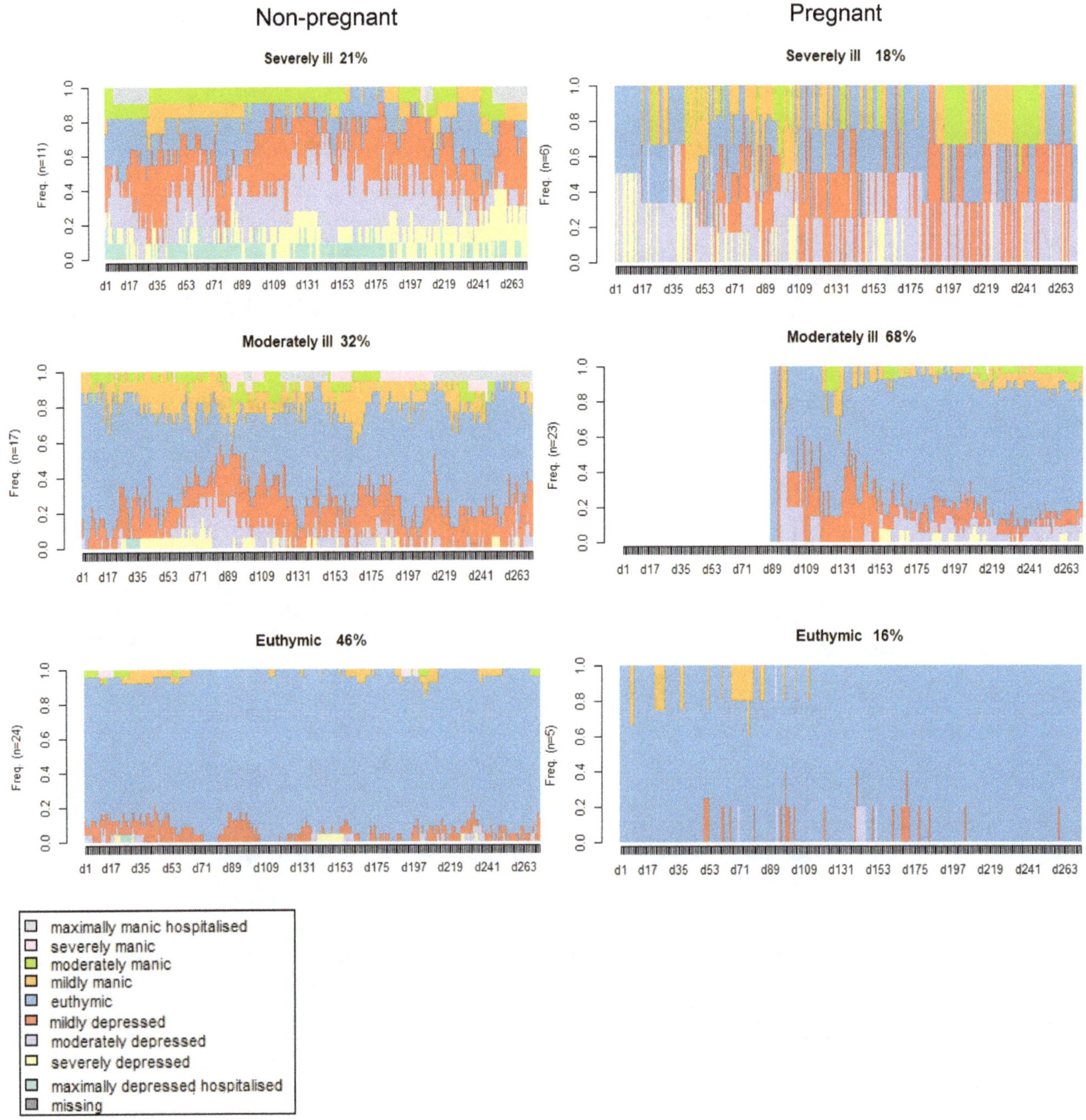

Fig. 2 Index plots of three cluster solution for the pregnant sample and non-pregnant sample; X-axis: time in days (d1 means dey 1), Y axis: proportions women distributed over states in cluster

Number of days spent in each of the nine states obviously differed over the three clusters. Evidently, more days were spent in the euthymic state in the euthymic cluster as compared to the other clusters. Interestingly, daily scores were not normally distributed over mania and depression. There was a tendency that more days were rated as depressed (left side of the cluster figures) than manic (right side of the figures) (Fig. 3).

The level of entropy of scores, i.e., the diversity of states on each day for both samples, for the non-pregnant women were higher (average 0.56) than for the pregnant women (average 0.43).

In multinomial regression the dependent variable (cluster) has three different categorical values. Regression of the three clusters on three demographic variables (educational level, marital status and work) and two clinical

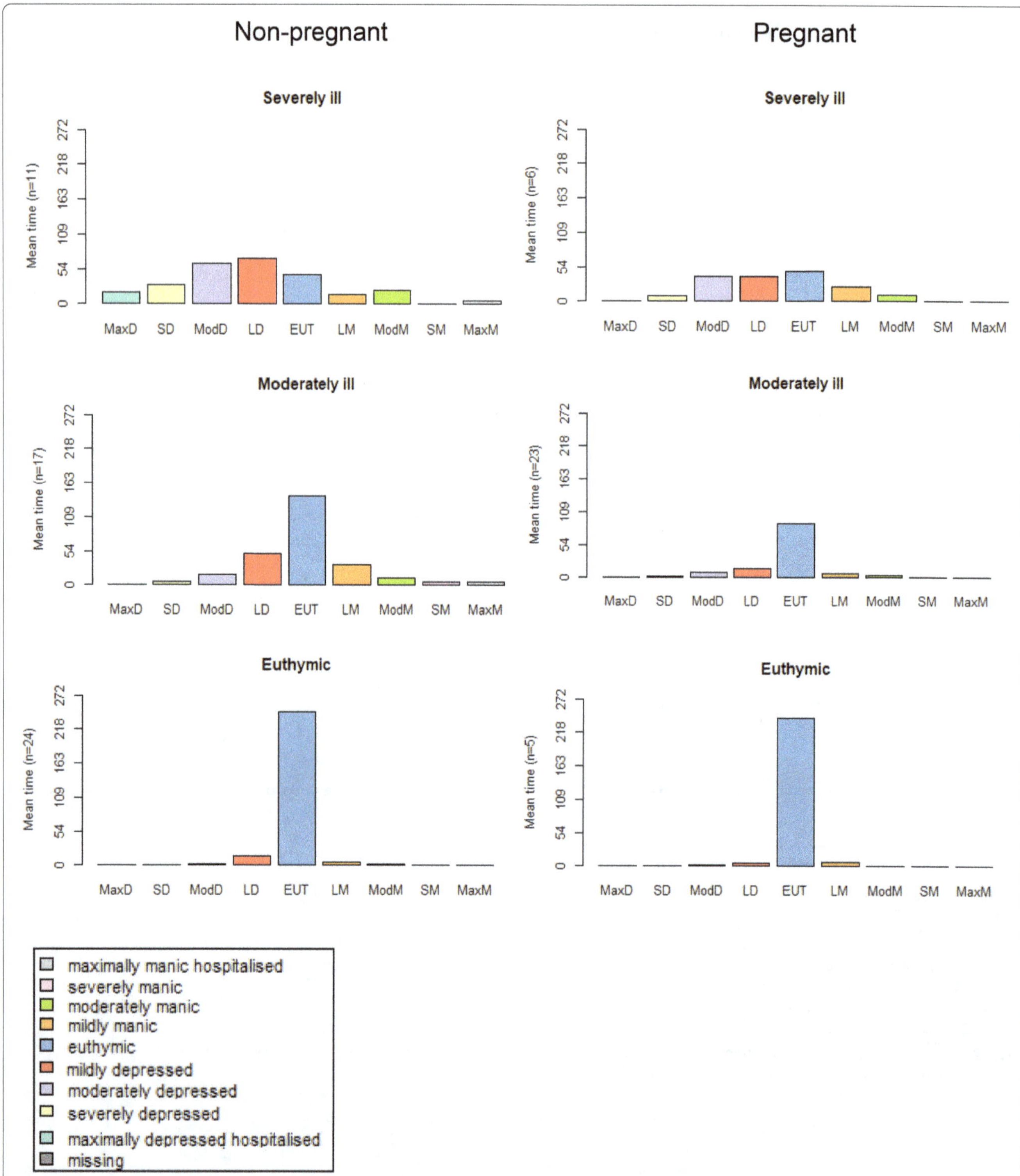

Fig. 3 Mean time (in days) spent in each state for three clusters, pregnant women on the left, non-pregnant women on the right

variables (medication, illness duration) showed only one significant relation, namely between educational level: the odds of going from cluster 1 (severely ill) to cluster 2 (moderately ill). Thus, the higher the level of education, the higher the odds of going from severely ill to moderately ill (Table 4).

Subsequently, the results of regression of entropy (n = 86) on the same set of predictors is shown (Table 5).

Table 4 Multinomial regression of clusters on a selection of predictors (n = 86)

	Odds ratio (Std. Error)	
	Cluster 2 (moderately ill)	Cluster 3 (euthymic)
Educational level	6.71 (0.67)**	1.64 (0.57)
Marital status	1.3e−06 (245.87)	1.2e−00 (0.48)
Work	1.59 (0.57)	1.14 (0.49)
Medication	1.06 (0.25)	0.87 (0.26)
Illness duration	0.75 (0.41)	1.29 (0.32)
Pseudo R^2	0.19	

Odds ratio's and standard errors. Base outcome (reference category) cluster 1: severely ill. **p < 0.01

Table 5 Regressing Entropy on a selection of covariates (n = 86)

Variable	Beta	Std. error	*t* value	Pr. (>|t|)
Intercept	0.594	0.214	2.779	0.007**
Educational level	−0.134	0.054	−2.481	0.016*
Marital status	−0.002	0.053	−0.039	0.969
Work	−0.015	0.046	−0.332	0.741
Medication	0.025	0.023	1.080	0.283
Illness duration	0.011	0.032	0.339	0.736

The only covariate that produced a significant effect in regression of entropy on predictors was educational level. This suggests that the lower the educational level, the more instability occurred in the course of BD.

Discussion

While previous prospective studies have investigated risk of, and/or time to, recurrence of mood episodes during pregnancy in BD (Viguera et al. 2007; Bergink et al. 2012), this is the first study comparing fine-graded prospective illness course with the lifechart method (LCM) in pregnant and non-pregnant women with BD. No differences were found in illness severity variables, such as number of days ill, including days depressed, hypomanic, or manic, or average severity scores. However, with a cluster analysis of LCM data within both samples to reveal longitudinal illness patterns, within the study period, more pregnant women were moderately ill, whereas more non-pregnant women were euthymic.

In addition, pregnant women showed less variation of mood states than non-pregnant women. Women with a higher educational level in both samples were more likely to belong to a cluster moderately ill than to a cluster severely ill. An explanation for the relation between educational level and less mood instability could be that more adequate psycho-education is obtained by higher educated women. The higher educational level in the cluster moderately ill than in the cluster severely ill could be due to the fact that those women had a milder course of BD and therefore were able to get a higher education level.

Constructing typologies/groups, according to temporal data, of patients with BD has been done by other investigators. Post et al. determined the severity of illness in the first 258 outpatients in the SFBN who had 1 year of prospective LCM ratings (Post et al. 2003). Their typologies contain groups of patients who remained severely and almost continuously ill (26.4%), intermittently ill (40.7%), or minimally ill (32.9%) over the course of that year. The patterns of the ratings were visually assigned to the three groups by two independent investigators. Nowadays, with the application of state sequence analysis, clustering methods can be used to build similar types of illness course and so defining groups that are as homogenous as possible on the one hand and as different as possible from other groups on the other. This clustering method does not depend on subjective clinician ratings, but can be applied automatically using algorithms, enhancing reliability.

A possible explanation for the difference between our two samples, especially the higher proportion of euthymic days in non-pregnant women versus pregnant women, could be that more non-pregnant women used psychotropic medication during the observation period. The use of medication prevents recurrences in pregnant and non-pregnant women (Stevens et al. 2019; Larsen and Saric 2017; Kishi et al. 2020; Geddes and Miklowitz 2013). In more detail, in our study 23.5% of pregnant women used no medication at all, compared to none (0%) of the non-pregnant women, whereas 38.5% of the non-pregnant women used more than one mood stabilizer compared to none of the pregnant women. Although the use of antidepressant medication without a mood stabilizer is not recommended in bipolar disorder because of the risk of mood instability and switch to mania (Pacchiarotti et al. 2013), three pregnant women but none of the non-pregnant women used an antidepressant without a mood stabilizer.

All women in both samples received psychiatric treatment and most of the pregnant women had pre-pregnancy consultations. It is possible that women with a more severe BD, who would not stop medication because of fear for recurrence, decided not to attempt to conceive, which could explain why the number of medications used in the pregnant women in our study was relatively low.

In general, women with a childwish are recommended to be stabilized for a period of at least six months before becoming pregnant (Thomson and Sharma 2018). In a study of 70 women with BD, 45% who sought consultation for treatment options and risks during pregnancy had been advised to avoid pregnancy by a health care professional before consultation (Viguera et al. 2002). After the consultation 37% chose to avoid pregnancy with the most commonly reported reason being fears of adverse effect of medication on the development of the fetus (56%) or concerns of genetic transmission of BD to offspring (22%).

There still is a paucity of systematic data on the effects of pregnancy on the course of BD. In our study, with use of daily mood monitoring, no differences were found in the course of BD in pregnant versus non-pregnant women. Comparing trajectories may be a better way to study the effect of pregnancy on the course of BD. A major challenge would be to investigate the role of pregnancy on the 'naturalistic' (i.e. untreated) course of BD, since it is recommended to prescribe some form of preventive medication in patients with BD also during pregnancy (Yatham et al. 2018).

Our study has several strengths. It is the first study comparing prospective daily mood ratings in a sample of pregnant and non-pregnant women with BD. The samples did not differ in demographic characteristics such as nationality and age, nor in clinical variables such as type of diagnosis (BD I or II), illness duration, age of onset, lifetime number of manic and depressive episodes, lifetime substance abuse, and serious suicide attempts. Also, this is the first study using SSA and clustering methods on LCM data to reveal different clusters of illness course.

However, there are also several limitations. Since the design consists of two cohorts from different studies, and cases were not assigned at random or via case control procedures, the comparability of both samples remains uncertain. The pregnant women had a higher educational level and were more often married than the non-pregnant women. The use of medication differed between the two cohorts, with a potential impact on the course of BD. Also, LCM data from pregnant women were reported from week 12 of pregnancy untill giving birth, hence data on the first trimester are not included. An obvious limitation of this study is the relatively small sample sizes of pregnant and non-pregnant women. Selection bias cannot be ruled out completely: the fact that pregnant women more often belonged to the moderately ill cluster and non-pregnant women to the euthymic cluster may be due to the possibility that pregnant moderately ill women were more likely to participate, or that euthymic non-pregnant women were more inclined to enter such a study than moderately ill non-pregnant women. Randomization in a study with regard to a comparison of pregnant and non-pregnant women with BD however is not feasible. Obviously more research with larger sample sizes about the effect of pregnancy on the course of BD is required. However, the fact that these small samples did not differ with respect to descriptive clinical course variables, such as number of manic and number of ill days, yet did show clear differences in illness pattern during the observation period adds further strength to the approach of sequential analysis of daily mood monitoring in BD, even with small sample sizes.

Conclusion

No differences in average values of clinical course variables in BD were found among pregnant women compared to non-pregnant women. The application of SSA to reveal patterns in the overall course in the observational period did show differences in proportions of pregnant versus non-pregnant women distributed over three clusters of sequences. More pregnant women showed a moderately ill pattern of daily mood scores whereas more non-pregnant women showed a euthymic pattern. One explanation is that more non-pregnant women used (more) psychotropic medications than pregnant women, which may have a protective effect. Pregnant women showed less variation in mood than non-pregnant women.

To answer the question whether pregnancy influences the course of BD, ideally, we need large, prospective case–control studies comparing pregnant and non-pregnant women. Another option is to compare within individuals the course of BD during pregnancy and during the year before.

Acknowledgements
Not applicable.

Authors' contributions
All authors contributed to conceptualization, writing, editing and revision of the manuscript, and all approved the final article. AS, SD, BB, PG, EK, AH, RK designed the study and SD and AS interpreted the data. SD en AS performed the analyses. SD prepared the figures and SD and AS performed the tables. All authors read and approved the final manuscript.

Author details
[1]Center for Bipolar Disorders, Dimence Mental Health, Deventer, The Netherlands. [2]Amsterdam UMC, Vrije Universiteit, Psychiatry, Amsterdam Public Health Research Institute, Amsterdam, The Netherlands. [3]GGZinGeest Specialized Mental Health Care, Research and Innovation Amsterdam, Amsterdam, The Netherlands. [4]Department of Public Health, Faculty of Medicine and Health Sciences, University Centre for Nursing and Midwifery, Ghent University, Ghent, Belgium. [5]Department of Psychiatry, OLVG Hospital, Amsterdam, The Netherlands. [6]GGZ Rivierduinen Alphen a/d Rijn, Amsterdam, The Netherlands. [7]Department of Psychiatry, University Medical Center Groningen, University of Groningen, Groningen, The Netherlands. [8]Bipolar Collaborative Network, Bethesda, MD, USA. [9]Department of Psychiatry and Behavioral Sciences, District of Columbia, George Washington University, Washington, USA.

References

Abbott AH. Measuring Resemblance in Sequence Data: An Optimal Matching Analysis of Musicians' Careers. Am J Sociol. 1990;96(1):144–85.
Akdeniz F, Vahip S, Pirildar S, Vahip I, Doganer I, Bulut I. Risk factors associated with childbearing-related episodes in women with bipolar disorder. Psychopathology. 2003;36(5):234–8.
Altshuler LL, Post RM, Black DO, Keck PE Jr, Nolen WA, Frye MA, et al. Subsyndromal depressive symptoms are associated with functional impairment

in patients with bipolar disorder: results of a large, multisite study. J Clin Psychiatry. 2006;67(10):1551–60.

Bergink V, Bouvy PF, Vervoort JS, Koorengevel KM, Steegers EA, Kushner SA. Prevention of postpartum psychosis and mania in women at high risk. Am J Psychiatry. 2012;169(6):609–15.

Bonnin CM, Sanchez-Moreno J, Martinez-Aran A, Sole B, Reinares M, Rosa AR, et al. Subthreshold symptoms in bipolar disorder: impact on neurocognition, quality of life and disability. J Affect Disord. 2012;136(3):650–9.

Born C, Seitz NN, Grunze H, Vieta E, Dittmann S, Seemuller F, et al. Preliminary results of a fine-grain analysis of mood swings and treatment modalities of bipolar I and II patients using the daily prospective life-chart-methodology. Acta Psychiatr Scand. 2009;120(6):474–80.

Courgeau C. Do different approaches in population science lead to divergent or convergent models? In: Studer R, editor. Sequence analysis and related apporaches. Cham: Springer; 2018.

de Graaf R, ten Have M, van Gool C, van Dorsselaer S. Prevalence of mental disorders and trends from 1996 to 2009. Results from the Netherlands Mental Health Survey and Incidence Study-2. Soc Psychiatry Psychiatr Epidemiol. 2012;47(2):203–13.

Denicoff KD, Smith-Jackson EE, Disney ER, Suddath RL, Leverich GS, Post RM. Preliminary evidence of the reliability and validity of the prospective life-chart methodology (LCM-p). J Psychiatr Res. 1997;31(5):593–603.

Denicoff KD, Leverich GS, Nolen WA, Rush AJ, McElroy SL, Keck PE, et al. Validation of the prospective NIMH-Life-Chart Method (NIMH-LCM-p) for longitudinal assessment of bipolar illness. Psychol Med. 2000;30(6):1391–7.

Draisma S, van Zaane J, Smit JH. Data quality indicators for daily life chart methodology: prospective self-ratings of bipolar disorder and alcohol use. BMC Res Notes. 2015;8:473.

Ferrari AJ, Stockings E, Khoo JP, Erskine HE, Degenhardt L, Vos T, et al. The prevalence and burden of bipolar disorder: findings from the Global Burden of Disease Study 2013. Bipolar Disord. 2016;18(5):440–50.

Freeman MP, Smith KW, Freeman SA, McElroy SL, Kmetz GE, Wright R, et al. The impact of reproductive events on the course of bipolar disorder in women. J Clin Psychiatry. 2002;63(4):284–7.

Gabadinho A, Ritschard G, Müller NS, Studer M. Analyzing and visualizing state sequences in R with TraMineR. J Stat Softw. 2011;40(4):1–37.

Geddes JR, Miklowitz DJ. Treatment of bipolar disorder. Lancet. 2013;381(9878):1672–82.

Goodwin FK, Jamison KR. Manic Depressive Illness: Bipolar disorders and Recurrent Depression. 2nd ed. NewYork: Oxford University Press; 2007.

Grof P, Robbins W, Alda M, Berghoefer A, Vojtechovsky M, Nilsson A, et al. Protective effect of pregnancy in women with lithium-responsive bipolar disorder. J Affect Disord. 2000;61(1–2):31–9.

Kishi T, Matsuda Y, Sakuma K, Okuya M, Mishima K, Iwata N. Recurrence rates in stable bipolar disorder patients after drug discontinuation v. drug maintenance: a systematic review and meta-analysis. Psychol Med. 2020;78:1–9.

Kupka RW, Altshuler LL, Nolen WA, Suppes T, Luckenbaugh DA, Leverich GS, et al. Three times more days depressed than manic or hypomanic in both bipolar I and bipolar II disorder. Bipolar Disord. 2007;9(5):531–5.

Larsen ER, Saric K. Pregnancy and bipolar disorder: the risk of recurrence when discontinuing treatment with mood stabilisers: a systematic review. Acta Neuropsychiatr. 2017;29(5):259–66.

Leverich GS, Nolen WA, Rush AJ, McElroy SL, Keck PE, Denicoff KD, et al. The Stanley Foundation Bipolar Treatment Outcome Network. I Longitudinal Methodology J Affect Disord. 2001;67(1–3):33–44.

McNeil TF, Kaij L, Malmquist-Larsson A. Women with nonorganic psychosis: factors associated with pregnancy's effect on mental health. Acta Psychiatr Scand. 1984;70(3):209–19.

Merikangas KR, Jin R, He JP, Kessler RC, Lee S, Sampson NA, et al. Prevalence and correlates of bipolar spectrum disorder in the world mental health survey initiative. Arch Gen Psychiatry. 2011;68(3):241–51.

Munk-Olsen T, Laursen TM, Pedersen CB, Mors O, Mortensen PB. New parents and mental disorders: a population-based register study. JAMA. 2006;296(21):2582–9.

Munk-Olsen T, Laursen TM, Mendelson T, Pedersen CB, Mors O, Mortensen PB. Risks and predictors of readmission for a mental disorder during the postpartum period. Arch Gen Psychiatry. 2009;66(2):189–95.

Nolen WA, Luckenbaugh DA, Altshuler LL, Suppes T, McElroy SL, Frye MA, et al. Correlates of 1-year prospective outcome in bipolar disorder: results from the Stanley Foundation Bipolar Network. Am J Psychiatry. 2004;161(8):1447–54.

Pacchiarotti I, Bond DJ, Baldessarini RJ, Nolen WA, Grunze H, Licht RW, et al. The International Society for Bipolar Disorders (ISBD) task force report on antidepressant use in bipolar disorders. Am J Psychiatry. 2013;170(11):1249–62.

Parker G, McCraw S, Tavella G, Hadzi-Pavlovic D. Measuring the consequences of a bipolar or unipolar mood disorder and the immediate and ongoing impacts. Psychiatry Res. 2018;269:70–4.

Post RM, Nolen WA, Kupka RW, Denicoff KD, Leverich GS, Keck PE Jr, et al. The Stanley Foundation Bipolar Network. I. Rationale and methods. Br J Psychiatry Suppl. 2001;41:169–76.

Post RM, Denicoff KD, Leverich GS, Altshuler LL, Frye MA, Suppes TM, et al. Morbidity in 258 bipolar outpatients followed for 1 year with daily prospective ratings on the NIMH life chart method. J Clin Psychiatry. 2003;64(6):680–90.

Roux J, Grimaud O, Leray E. Use of state sequence analysis for care pathway analysis: The example of multiple sclerosis. Stat Methods Med Res. 2019;28(6):1651–63.

Salim M, Sharma V, Anderson KK. Recurrence of bipolar disorder during pregnancy: a systematic review. Arch Womens Ment Health. 2018;21(4):475–9.

Sharma V, Persad E. Effect of pregnancy on three patients with bipolar disorder. Ann Clin Psychiatry. 1995;7(1):39–42.

Sharma V, Pope CJ. Pregnancy and bipolar disorder: a systematic review. J Clin Psychiatry. 2012;73(11):1447–55.

Stevens AWMM, Goossens PJJ, Hoogendoorn AW, Knoppert-vanderKlein EAM, Honig A, et al. The effect of sleep disturbance during pregnancy and perinatal period on postpartum psychopathology in women with bipolar disorder. J Women's Health Care. 2014;196:78.

Stevens A, Goossens PJJ, Knoppert-vander Klein EAM, Draisma S, Honig A, Kupka RW. Risk of recurrence of mood disorders during pregnancy and the impact of medication: A systematic review. J Affect Disord. 2019;249:96–103.

Suppes T, Leverich GS, Keck PE, Nolen WA, Denicoff KD, Altshuler LL, et al. The Stanley Foundation Bipolar Treatment Outcome Network. II. Demographics and illness characteristics of the first 261 patients. J Affect Disord. 2001;67(1–3):45–59.

Thomson M, Sharma V. Weighing the Risks: the Management of Bipolar Disorder During Pregnancy. Curr Psychiatry Rep. 2018;20(3):20.

Viguera AC, Cohen LS, Bouffard S, Whitfield TH, Baldessarini RJ. Reproductive decisions by women with bipolar disorder after prepregnancy psychiatric consultation. Am J Psychiatry. 2002;159(12):2102–4.

Viguera AC, Whitfield T, Baldessarini RJ, Newport DJ, Stowe Z, Reminick A, et al. Risk of recurrence in women with bipolar disorder during pregnancy: prospective study of mood stabilizer discontinuation. Am J Psychiatry. 2007;164(12):1817–24.

Viguera AC, Tondo L, Koukopoulos AE, Reginaldi D, Lepri B, Baldessarini RJ. Episodes of mood disorders in 2,252 pregnancies and postpartum periods. Am J Psychiatry. 2011;168(11):1179–85.

Wesseloo R, Kamperman AM, Munk-Olsen T, Pop VJ, Kushner SA, Bergink V. Risk of Postpartum Relapse in Bipolar Disorder and Postpartum Psychosis: A Systematic Review and Meta-Analysis. Am J Psychiatry. 2016;173(2):117–27.

Yatham LN, Kennedy SH, Parikh SV, Schaffer A, Bond DJ, Frey BN, et al. Canadian Network for Mood and Anxiety Treatments (CANMAT) and International Society for Bipolar Disorders (ISBD) 2018 guidelines for the management of patients with bipolar disorder. Bipolar Disord. 2018;20(2):97–170.

17

Voice analyses using smartphone-based data in patients with bipolar disorder, unaffected relatives and healthy control individuals, and during different affective states

Maria Faurholt-Jepsen[1*†], Darius Adam Rohani[2†], Jonas Busk[3], Maj Vinberg[1,4], Jakob Eyvind Bardram[2] and Lars Vedel Kessing[1]

Abstract

Background: Voice features have been suggested as objective markers of bipolar disorder (BD).

Aims: To investigate whether voice features from naturalistic phone calls could discriminate between (1) BD, unaffected first-degree relatives (UR) and healthy control individuals (HC); (2) affective states within BD.

Methods: Voice features were collected daily during naturalistic phone calls for up to 972 days. A total of 121 patients with BD, 21 UR and 38 HC were included. A total of 107.033 voice data entries were collected [BD (n =78.733), UR (n =8004), and HC (n = 20.296)]. Daily, patients evaluated symptoms using a smartphone-based system. Affective states were defined according to these evaluations. Data were analyzed using random forest machine learning algorithms.

Results: Compared to HC, BD was classified with a sensitivity of 0.79 (SD 0.11)/AUC =0.76 (SD 0.11) and UR with a sensitivity of 0.53 (SD 0.21)/AUC of 0.72 (SD 0.12). Within BD, compared to euthymia, mania was classified with a specificity of 0.75 (SD 0.16)/AUC = 0.66 (SD 0.11). Compared to euthymia, depression was classified with a specificity of 0.70 (SD 0.16)/AUC = 0.66 (SD 0.12). In all models the user dependent models outperformed the user independent models. Models combining increased mood, increased activity and insomnia compared to periods without performed best with a specificity of 0.78 (SD 0.16)/AUC = 0.67 (SD 0.11).

Conclusions: Voice features from naturalistic phone calls may represent a supplementary objective marker discriminating BD from HC and a state marker within BD.

Keywords: Voice analysis, Classification, Random Forest, Bipolar disorder, openSMILE

Introduction

Bipolar disorder (BD) is characterized by recurrent affective episodes with significant alterations in core features of mood, activity and sleep (Goodwin and Jamison 1996). There is a substantial diagnostic delay and a progression of illness severity during untreated years, stressing the need for earlier diagnosis and intervention (Baldessarini et al. 2007; Kessing et al. 2014). However, due to the lack of objective tests, the diagnostic process as well as the clinical assessment of illness activity relies on patient

*Correspondence: maria@faurholt-jepsen.dk
†Maria Faurholt-Jepsen and Darius Adam Rohani contributed equally to this work and are shared first authors
[1] Copenhagen Affective Disorder Research Center (CADIC), Psychiatric Center Copenhagen, Rigshospitalet, Blegdamsvej 9, 2100 Copenhagen, Denmark
Full list of author information is available at the end of the article

information, clinical evaluation and rating scales (Phillips and Kupfer 2013). This evaluation process involves a risk of individual observer bias and recall distortions at various levels (Silva et al. 2015; Silva et al. 2016). Therefore, objective supplementary methods for assisting clinicians in the diagnosis and the assessment of illness activity in BD would be a tremendous advantage.

It is well established that 20–30% of unaffected first-degree relatives (UR) of patients with BD develop affective illness, compared to 2–5% among healthy control individuals (HC) (Vedel Kessing et al. 2021). Further, functioning is substantially and broadly decreased within education, employment, income, cohabitating and being married in UR compared with HC (Sletved et al. 2021). Therefore, it is likely that UR to patients with BD will show alterations in prodromal symptoms and features related to illness intermediate between patients with BD and HC.

Speech is individual for each person like 'a fingerprint', and speech patterns have shown to provide indicators of mental disorders. In 1921, Emil Kraepelin emphasized that patients with depression tended to have lower pitch, lower speech rate and more monotonous speech (Lord et al. 1921), and studies analyzing the spoken language in affective disorders date back as early as 1938 (Newman and Mather 1938). Differences in language structure between patients with BD and HC have been described, and changes in speech has been suggested as objective, sensitive and valid measures of depressive and (hypo-) manic episodes in BD (Mundt et al. 2012; Raucher-Chéné et al. 2017; Arevian 2020). A recent systematic review concerning automated assessment of psychiatric disorders using speech suggested that speech processing technology could aid mental health assessments (Low et al. 2020). However, this review also addressed obstacles concerning the lack of larger, transdiagnostic and longitudinal studies (Low et al. 2020).

Digital phenotyping refers to approaches in which personal data gathered from mobile devices and sensors is analyzed to provide health information on physiological functions, or behavioral indicators, such as the user's speech (Insel 2017; Ebner-Priemer 2020). These data can be seen as digital footprints/digital markers—or data traces arising as a by-product from interactions with technology. Software for ecologically extracting data on voice features from naturalistic phone calls has been developed (Eyben et al. 2010). Previous studies concerning voice features collected digitally within BD have investigated the use of speech to classify affective states and suggested that (hypo)manic states more accurately were classified than depressive states (Karam et al. 2014; Muaremi et al. 2014; Maxhuni et al. 2016; Gideon et al. 2016; Zhang et al. 2018; Vanello et al. 2012; Guidi et al. 2015). A previous study conducted by the authors found, that voice features collected in naturalistic settings using smartphones may represent objective state markers in patients with BD (Faurholt-Jepsen 2016). However, this previous study included a small number of patients and thus hold less strength. Moreover, it has not been investigated whether voice features collected from naturalistic phone calls can discriminate between BD, UR and HC. Smartphone-based voice technology could potentially aid clinicians in early diagnosing of BD and in identifying and targeting prodromal symptoms and states in UR.

Objectives

The present study aimed to investigate whether voice features collected from naturalistic phone calls (1) could discriminate between patients with BD, UR, and HC; (2) within patients with BD could discriminate between (a) mania and euthymia and (b) depression and euthymia; and (3) within patients with BD could discriminate between (a) periods with increased activity and neutral activity, (b) periods with decreased activity and neutral activity, (c) periods with insomnia and periods without, and (d) periods with combined increased mood, increased activity and insomnia and periods without. We hypothesized that voice features would be able to discriminate between patients with BD and HC, and between UR and HC (with UR intermediate between patients with BD and HC), and further discriminate between states within patients with BD.

Methods and materials

Study design and participants

The present study included data from two studies—the RADMIS trial (Faurholt-Jepsen et al. 2020) and the larger ongoing Bipolar Illness Onset study (BIO study) (Kessing 2017). Data were collected during the period from 2017 to 2020. All participants underwent The Schedules of Clinical Assessment in Neuropsychiatry (SCAN) interview (Wing et al. 1990) to confirm the clinical diagnosis of (or the lack of) BD.

The RADMIS trial

Patients with a diagnosis of BD who were hospitalized due to an affective episode and being discharged from one of five psychiatric centers at the Mental Health Services, Capital Region of Denmark, Denmark in the period from May 2017 to August 2019 were invited to participate in the RADMIS trial. Inclusion criteria: age above 18 years, BD diagnosis (ICD-10), discharge from a psychiatric hospital in The Capital Region of Denmark following an affective episode (depression, mania or mixed episode). Exclusion criteria: pregnancy and a lack of Danish language skills. In addition to standard treatment, patients were randomized with a balanced allocation ratio to either (1) daily use of a smartphone-based monitoring system (the Monsenso system—se description below) (the intervention group) or to (2) normal use of smartphones (the control group) during a 6 months follow-up period. Only patients from the intervention group providing smartphone-based data were included in the present study.

The BIO study

Three groups of participants were included in the BIO study: patients with newly diagnosed BD, UR, and HC.

Patients with BD

Inclusion criteria: a newly diagnosis of a single manic episode or BD (ICD-10) and ages between 15 and 70 years.

UR

UR, siblings or children, to the patients included in the BIO study, were recruited after permission from patients. Exclusion criteria: any previous or current psychiatric diagnosis lower than F34.0 (CD-10) (i.e., organic mental disorders, mental and behavioral disorders due to psychoactive substance use including alcohol, schizophrenia or other psychotic disorders, affective disorders).

HC

HC were recruited among blood donors, aged between 15 and 70 years, from the Blood Bank at Rigshospitalet, Copenhagen. Exclusion criteria: treatment requiring psychiatric disorder in the individual or one of the individuals' first-degree family members. All participants in the BIO study were offered to use a smartphone-based monitoring system on a daily basis (the Monsenso system—see description below) during the study period.

Clinical assessments

Clinical evaluations of the severity of depressive and manic symptoms were conducted by a trained researcher using the Hamilton Depression Rating Scale 17-items (HDRS) (Hamilton 1967) and the Young Mania Rating Scale (YMRS) (Young et al. 1978).

Patient-reported smartphone-based data

A smartphone-based monitoring system (the Monsenso system) was installed on the participants own smartphones (both iPhone and Android smartphones). The smartphone-based monitoring system developed by the authors was used by the patients with BD on a daily basis to collect fine-grained real-time recordings of mood, activity, and sleep duration (Bardram et al. 2013). Mood was evaluated with scores on a 9-point scale ranging from depressed to manic (− 3, − 2, − 1, − 0.5, 0, 0.5, 1, 2, 3). Euthymia mood was defined a priori as a mood score of − 0.5, 0, 0.5. Depression was defined as mood score < -0.5, and mania was defined as mood score > 0.5. Daily activity levels were rated on a 7-point scale (− 3, − 2, − 1, 0, 1, 2, 3) with 0 representing normal activity level. Sleep duration was calculated based on daily reports of bedtime and wake-up time. Insomnia was defined as total sleep duration < 360 min. In addition, a broader definition of mania was made by combining increased mood (> 0.5), increased activity (> 0) and decreased sleep (< 360 min.).

Voice features

Voice features were collected from the participants' phone calls (only Android smartphones) during their everyday life using the open-source Speech and Music Interpretation by Large-space Extraction (openSMILE vs. 2.1.0, Emo-Large) toolkit (Eyben et al. 2010; Schuller et al. 2010). The toolkit is a feature extractor for signal processing and machine learning applications, and it is designed for real-time processing. The toolkit used a built-in voice activity detection to live record voice samples from each incoming and outgoing phone call on the participants' smartphone. The voice activity detection was run solely on the study participants' onboard microphone such that the voice segments represented one recorded audio stream from the participant's voice. The audio stream was used to extract acoustic features 'online', e.g., directly on the study participants' smartphones for each phone call. Voice samples were deleted locally on the smartphone after each phone call, and thus there was not access to any content related material from phone calls. The Emo-Large was a predefined set consisting of 6552 features, e.g., pitch, loudness, and energy, represented through various 1st level descriptive statistics including means, regression coefficients, and percentiles. The set has been found to be particularly relevant for classifying emotions (Pfister and Robinson 2010).

Statistical methods

Data were imported to and processed in Python (version 3.8) with packages sklearn (v. 0.23.2), imblearn (v. 0.7.0), and pandas (v. 1.1.4).

Aim 1 concerned the discrimination between patients with BD, UR, and HC based on the use of collected voice features. Aims 2 and 3 concerned the use of voice data from patients with BD to classify the symptom class labels within mood, energy, and sleep collected daily from smartphones, and a combination of the three.

For all analyses Random Forest (RF) classifiers were built to discriminate between classes (Breiman 2001). The RF classifiers combine several decision tree classifiers into a single classifier. A RF model uses the ensemble technique to yield a prediction from multiple independent decision tree classifiers. RF models were chosen as they generally can handle large number of features while being robust to overfitting. Each tree is generated from a subsample of the data and using a random subset of features to ensure maximal degree of independence among the trees. The classifier uses supervised learning, i.e., information of the group status/affective state, to build nodes that split the dataset into groups. These splits continue until the model either has a group with only a single class, or if further splits are unable to improve the classification. Call entries with missing voice feature values and features with identical values (i.e., zero variance) were removed.

All classifications were binary (e.g., patients with BD versus HC). For aim 2 and 3 patient-reported smartphone-based data for any specific day during the study period were included in the analyses if both voice features and patient-reported smartphone-based on mood, activity or sleep were available for the same day. We evaluated RF models on the resulting data set through a five-fold participant-based cross-validation. Five-fold cross-validation partitions the data in 5 parts of approximately the same size. Five to one partitions of the data were used to train the model, while the last partition was used to test the model, thereby evaluating the performance on unseen data samples. This was repeated 5 times so all samples were used for testing once to yield an average performance across all folds. We used a participant-based cross-validation version, where the test partition included participants that were not part of the training partition and vice versa. The participant-based method is particularly important for aim 1 since all voice data for each participant is identically labeled (i.e., either BD, UR, or HC). If the same participant is represented in the training and test partition the model would falsely learn to discriminate participant-based characteristics instead of clinical diagnose or state. Ad-hoc analyses without the participant-based cross-validation displayed significant better results. Therefore, to avoid learning on participant traits, all analyses included participant-based cross-validation.

In each cross-validation fold, the training set was used to calculate standardization parameters that transform the voice features training set to zero mean, unit variance. The calculated parameters were then applied to the test set. We used this standardization approach to create an unbiased data transformation invariant for factors such as gender, age, or microphone types selected by the phone vendors. As we used a participant-based cross-validation approach, the standardization was done for each voice feature across all participants.

Analyses concerning aims 2 and 3 were separated in two model types. First, a user-independent model that—as for aim 1—combines data from all participants in the same model. The model uses information from known participants to classify symptoms of unknown patients. Second, a user-dependent model personalized model for each patient was built.

We observed significant class imbalance in the data for all aims (e.g., fewer cases of symptoms of 'mania' compared with 'euthymia'). Therefore, we applied a resampling process on the training data to balance the two classes. We did a combination with SMOTE oversampling (Chawla et al. 2002) of the minority class to represent 33% of the cases, followed by random under sampling of the majority class until the sample size was identical to the minority class. The combination of oversampling with SMOTE and under sampling has previously been shown effective to counter class imbalance (García et al. 2016). Without a resampling scheme, the RF classifier would favor overrepresented classes. However, resampling was only performed on the training data, to keep the test set class distribution representative for the collected data. In the cases where class distribution was less than 33% skewed, we only performed random under sampling.

Classifier performance

We applied several standard metrics for binary classification computed on a test set held out data and compared the results to a majority vote baseline model.

The metrics included a) 'accuracy' (defined as the number of correct classifications of the positive and negative cases divided by the total number of cases); (b) 'F1-score' (estimates the model's ability to identify the positive class correctly, and was defined as the true positives divided by the true positives and the average between false positives and false negatives); (c) 'sensitivity' (defined as true positives divided by positives); (d) 'specificity' (defined as true negatives over all negatives); (e) 'area under the characteristic curve' (AUC) which is the area under the entire Receiver Operating Characteristic (ROC) curve. A ROC curve displays the model performance of sensitivity and specificity at all probability thresholds. The sensitivity and specificity reported in the tables are based on a threshold of 50%. An AUC value of 0.5 represents random guessing, while a value of one is a perfect classifier. To further strengthen performance interpretation a Bayesian inference framework with intrinsic priors was added (B10) (Leon-Novelo et al. 2012). The method handles unbalanced data well as proven through various simulated and real work examples (Olivetti et al. 2015). The measure is based on a statistical foundation through a test of statistical independence between, here, our predicted results and the actual symptom registered. Therefore, a direct standardized guideline exists. A value below 0 indicates a negative evidence for a statistically dependency, a value between 1 and 3 suggests a more positive indication, 3–5 a strong indication, while a value above 5 is a decisive indication of statistically dependence.

All classification metrics were computed within each cross-validation fold to yield a mean (M) and standard deviation (SD) value across all five-folds. In the personalized model we further averaged across all patients.

For aim 1, we ran a randomized permutation model (Berry et al. 2002) to test whether voice data from the three populations were statistically significantly different from each other. We randomly shuffled the class label for each participant and re-ran the entire RF classification. This was repeated 200 times to generate a non-parametric null-distribution of AUC scores (Fig. 1). Statistically significance was determined if the RF test AUC statistics with true class labels exceeds the null distribution with a significance level of $p = 0.05$.

For aims 2 and 3, we developed a majority vote model and a random classifier as a baseline. Unlike the RF model, the baseline models did not include voice data. Simply, in the majority vote model, the most frequently observed class label in the training data, was used to classify test data. In cases where there was an equal class distribution, the test data was classified at random. The random classifier used a uniform distribution to randomly choose a class label.

Ethical considerations

The RADMIS trial

The RADMIS trial was approved by the Regional Ethics Committee in The Capital Region of Denmark and the data agency, Capital Region of Copenhagen (H-16046093, RHP-2017-005, I-Suite: 05365) and registered at ClinicalTrials.gov (NCT03033420).

The BIO study

The study protocol was approved by the Committee on Health Research Ethics of the Capital region of Denmark (protocol No. H-7-2014-007) and the Danish Data Protection Agency, Capital Region of Copenhagen (RHP-2015-023).

Both studies complied with the Declaration of Helsinki (Seoul, October 2008). All participants provided written informed consent. Data from smartphones were stored by Monsenso subject to a data management agreement between Monsenso and The Capital Region of Denmark.

Results

Background characteristics

Overall, a total of 254 participants were included in the present study. A total of 27 participants dropped out of the study (mainly due to not having the time to participate), and a total of 47 participants did not provide voice data. Thus, a total 180 participants were available and included in the present report (patients with BD $n = 121$, UR $n = 21$, and HC $n = 38$). The participants provided on average 157 ($SD = 174$) days

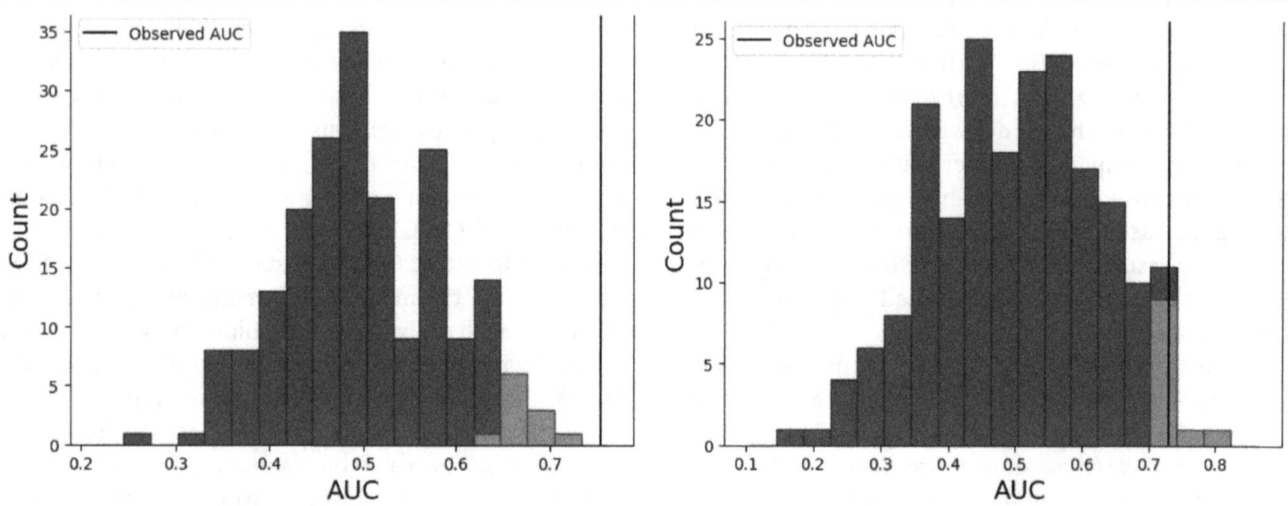

Fig. 1 A generated null distribution of AUC values from a permutation test where the class labels (e.g., patients with bipolar disorder and healthy controls) are randomly shuffled 200 times and an AUC value for each permutation is plotted. The light grey region represents the critical area with the 5% largest values. The vertical lines represent the observed AUC values from the true class labels. **A** Generated null-distribution for the Random Forest classification of patients with bipolar disorder against healthy control individuals. **B** Generated null-distribution for the Random Forest classification of patients with bipolar disorder against unaffected relatives

with at least one voice recording with a range between 1 and 972 days.

A total of 107.033 voice data entries were collected across patients with BD (n =78.733), UR (n =8004), and HC (n =20.296).

Overall, the participants had a mean age of 34.5 (SD 11.5) years with a range from 18 to 67 years. A total of 56% (n =101) were women.

A total of 41% (n =49) of patients with BD had a HDRS score ≥ 13 at inclusion, and a mean score on the YMRS of 3.76 (SD 4.71). Only 5% (n =6) of the patients had an YMRS score ≥13 at inclusion. There were no statistically significant differences in age or sex distribution across the three populations. There was a statistically significant difference in education level (BD: HC, p =0.03) and unemployment (BD: HC, p =0.001; BD: UR, p =0.021) between patients with BD, HC and UR. Further background characteristics are presented in Table 1.

Classification of groups

Table 2 present the results for classification of patients with BD (78.731 observations), HC (20.296 observations) and UR (8004 observations) based on voice features.

The sensitivity and specificity for classifying patients with BD versus HC was 0.79 (SD 0.11) and 0.54 (SD 0.20), respectively and with an AUC of 0.76 (SD 0.11). The sensitivity and specificity for classifying patients with BD versus UR was 0.73 (SD 0.07) and 0.28 (SD 0.11), respectively with an AUC of 0.52 (SD 0.09). The sensitivity and specificity for classifying UR versus HC was 0.53 (SD 0.21) and 0.67 (SD 0.24), respectively and with an AUC of 0.72 (SD 0.12). Figure 1A, B presents the generated null-distribution of AUC scores from permuted class labels as generated from the randomized permutation model. The lighter area shows the critical level for a one-tail test with a significance level of 0.05, e.g., values that are high enough to be considered statistically significant at

Table 1 Background characteristics of participants, n =180

	Patients with bipolar disorder (BD)	Healthy control individuals (HC)	Unaffected relatives (UR)	p
n, % female	121 (60.0)	38 (45.0)	21 (52.0)	p >0.16
Age	35.71 (12.35)	31.66 (10.87)	32.29 (10.57)	p >0.16
Employed, % (n)	17 (20)	50 (19)	57 (12)	BD:HC (p =0.002) UR:HC (p =0.88)
Student, % (n)	31 (37)	39 (15)	33 (7)	p >0.42
Unemployed, % (n)	30 (36)	8 (3)	10 (2)	BD:HC (p =0.001) UR:HC (p =0.76)
Education (years)	13.68 (4.66)	15.58 (1.57)	15.07 (2.62)	BD:HC (p =0.03) UR:HC (p =0.89)
Bipolar subtype I, % (n)	38 (46)	N/A	N/A	N/A
HAMD at inclusion	10.84 (6.93)	0.95 (1.62)	3.10 (3.32)	BD:HC (p <0.001) UR:HC (p =0.38)
YMRS at inclusion	3.76 (4.71)	0.51 (0.98)	1.25 (1.92)	BD:HC (p <0.001) UR:HC (p =0.77)
Previous hospitalizations (number)	4 [1–50]	N/A	N/A	N/A
Previous depressive episodes (number)	10 [1–80]	N/A	N/A	N/A
Previous (hypo)manic episodes (number)	14 [1–182]	N/A	N/A	N/A
Illness duration (years)	14.86 (10.37)	N/A	N/A	N/A
Psychotropic medication				
Anticonvulsant, % (n)	42 (51)	N/A	N/A	N/A
Lithium, % (n)	48 (58)	N/A	N/A	N/A
Antipsychotics, % (n)	49 (59)	N/A	N/A	N/A
Antidepressants, % (n)	18 (22)	N/A	N/A	N/A

Data are mean (SD), median [IQR] or proportions (%, n) unless otherwise stated

HAMD Hamilton Depression Rating Scale 17-items score

YMRS Young Mania Rating Scale score

Table 2 Discrimination between patients with bipolar disorder (BD) (n =121), unaffected relatives (UR) (n =21) and healthy control individuals (HC) (n =38) based on voice features collected from smartphones, n =180

Binary classifier (n = number of observations)	Model type	Accuracy (SD)	F1 score (SD)	Sensitivity (SD)	Specificity (SD)	AUC (SD)
BD (n =78,731) compared with HC (n =20,296)	Random Forest model	0.72 (0.09)	0.81 (0.07)	0.79 (0.11)	0.54 (0.20)	0.76 (0.11)
	Majority vote	0.67 (0.00)	0.88 (0.06)	1.0 (0.00)	0.00 (0.00)	0.50 (0.00)
BD (n =78,731) compared with UR (n =8004)	Random Forest model	0.68 (0.049)	0.81 (0.03)	0.73 (0.07)	0.28 (0.11)	0.52 (0.09)
	Majority vote	0.95 (0.00)	0.95 (0.02)	1.00 (0.00)	0.00 (0.00)	0.50 (0.00)
UR (n =8004) compared with HC (n =20,296)	Random Forest model	0.59 (0.13)	0.38 (0.15)	0.53 (0.21)	0.67 (0.24)	0.72 (0.12)
	Majority vote	0.80 (0.00)	0.00 (0.00)	0.00 (0.00)	1.00 (0.00)	0.50 (0.00)

the 0.05 level. The horizontal line represent the observed AUC value from Table 2 for the correct class labels. In both cases, the observed AUC for patients with BD versus HC (0/200, p <0.001) and UR versus HC (6/200, p =0.03) differed statistically significantly. Thus, there was a statistically significant difference in voice feature between patients with BD versus HC and a statistically significant difference in voice features between UR and HC.

Classifications of states within bipolar disorder

A total of 100 patients with BD provided both voice features and smartphone-based patient-reported data. Table 3 present the results for classification of different states in patients with BD. In all the models presented in Table 3, the personalized user-dependent models outperformed the general user-independent models. Therefore, the results from the user-dependent models are presented below.

Mania (1205 observations) versus euthymia (38.329 observations)

The sensitivity and specificity for classifying mania versus euthymia was 0.42 (SD 0.22) and 0.75 (SD 0.16), respectively and with an AUC of 0.66 (SD 0.11).

Depression (5329 observations) versus euthymia

The sensitivity and specificity for classifying depression versus euthymia was 0.53 (SD 0.22) and 0.70 (SD 0.16), respectively and with an AUC of 0.66 (SD 0.12).

Increased activity (12.890 observations) versus neutral activity (21.661 observations)

The sensitivity and specificity for classifying increased activity versus neutral activity was 0.55 (SD 0.26) and 0.58 (SD 0.24), respectively and with an AUC of 0.61 (SD 0.10).

Decreased activity (10.228 observations) versus neutral activity

The sensitivity and specificity for classifying decreased activity versus neutral activity was 0.53 (SD 0.20) and 0.65 (SD 0.21), respectively and with an AUC of 0.62 (SD 0.10).

Insomnia (8474 observations) versus periods without (36.140)

The sensitivity and specificity for classifying insomnia versus periods without was 0.39 (SD 0.22) and 0.73 (SD 0.17), respectively and with an AUC of 0.59 (SD 0.08).

Combined increased mood, increased activity and insomnia (471 observations) versus periods without (43.243 observations)

The sensitivity and specificity for classifying combined increased mood, increased activity and insomnia versus periods without was 0.41 (SD 0.21) and 0.78 (SD 0.16), respectively and with an AUC of 0.67 (SD 0.11).

Figure 2 presents the association between patient-reported mood and clinical ratings of depressive and manic symptoms according to the HDRS (r =− 0.64, p <0.001) and the YMRS (r =0.39, p <0.001). In both cases the correlation coefficients were statistically significant.

The ROC curves generated by aggregating all model estimates and the corresponding true class labels in each cross-validation fold, as well as each patient in the user-dependent classifiers, are presented in Fig. 3. As can be seen, the ROC curve for the sleep model is the closest to random, while the combined increased mood, increased activity and insomnia versus periods without performed best.

Discussion

The present study investigated the use of voice features collected during naturalistic phone calls for classifications of patients with BD, HC and UR, as well as state classifications within patients with BD. First, and in accordance with our hypotheses, voice features rather sensitively discriminated BD from HC, but in contrast

Table 3 Classification within patients with bipolar disorder (n =100) according to patient-reported smartphone-based data on mood, activity and sleep[a]

Binary classifier n = number of observations	Model type	Accuracy (SD)	F1 score (SD)	Sensitivty (SD)	Specificity (SD)	AUC (SD)	B10 (SD)[b]
Mood							
Mania (n =1205) versus euthymia (n =38,329)	Random Forest model-user independent	0.72 (0.18)	0.05 (0.03)	0.23 (0.12)	0.73 (0.19)	0.51 (0.07)	− 2.65 (0.34)
	Random Forest model-user dependent	0.74 (0.16)	0.25 (0.22)	0.42 (0.22)	0.75 (0.16)	0.66 (0.11)	0.53 (3.69)
	Majority vote-user independent	0.94 (0.00)	0.00 (0.00)	0.00 (0.00)	1.00 (0.00)	0.50 (0.00)	− 3.18 (1.61)
	Majority vote-user dependent	0.97 (0.00)	0.08 (0.25)	0.11 (0.31)	0.89 (0.31)	0.48 (0.02)	− 3.23 (1.35)
	Random model-user independent	0.49 (0.00)	0.06 (0.03)	0.49 (0.05)	0.50 (0.01)	0.50 (0.00)	− 2.82 (0.27)
	Random model-user dependent	0.49 (0.00)	0.15 (0.09)	0.52 (0.03)	0.48 (0.03)	0.50 (0.00)	− 2.21 (0.59)
Depression (n =5329) versus euthymia (n =38,329)	Random Forest model-user independent	0.63 (0.06)	0.21 (0.07)	0.40 (0.07)	0.66 (0.05)	0.55 (0.05)	− 1.82 (0.22)
	Random Forest model-user dependent	0.70 (0.13)	0.40 (0.21)	0.53 (0.22)	0.70 (0.16)	0.66 (0.12)	2.78 (5.49)
	Majority vote-user independent	0.89 (0.00)	0.00 (0.00)	0.00 (0.00)	1.00 (0.00)	0.50 (0.00)	− 3.78 (1.31)
	Majority vote-user dependent	0.71 (0.00)	0.11 (0.28)	0.13 (0.33)	0.88 (0.33)	0.49 (0.02)	− 3.29 (0.00)
	Random model-user independent	0.50 (0.00)	0.24 (0.06)	0.51 (0.01)	0.49 (0.00)	0.50 (0.00)	− 2.07 (0.16)
	Random model-user dependent	0.46 (0.0)	0.31 (0.17)	0.55 (0.07)	0..44 (0.05)	0.50 (0.00)	− 1.80 (0.46)
Activity							
Increased (n =12,890) versus neutral (n =21,661)	Random Forest model-user independent	0.46 (0.08)	0.43 (0.10)	0.55 (0.07)	0.41 (0.09)	0.48 (0.07)	− 1.38 (0.20)
	Random Forest model-user dependent	0.67 (0.13)	0.55 (0.25)	0.55 (0.26)	0.58 (0.24)	0.61 (0.10)	1.85 (5.92)
	Majority vote-user independent	0.48 (0.00)	0.00 (0.00)	0.00 (0.00)	1.00 (0.00)	0.50 (0.00)	− 3.52 (0.00)
	Majority vote-user dependent	0.57 (0.00)	0.45 (0.40)	0.56 (0.49)	0.44 (0.49)	0.49 (0.01)	− 0.02 (0.15)
	Random model-user independent	0.50 (0.00)	0.45 (0.07)	0.50 (0.01)	0.49 (0.01)	0.50 (0.00)	− 1.76 (0.07)
	Random model-user dependent	0.53 (0.00)	0.50 (0.13)	0.56 (0.05)	0.45 (0.05)	0.50 (0.00)	− 1.44 (0.63)
Decreased (n =10,288) versus neutral (n =21,661)	Random Forest model-user independent	0.50 (0.03)	0.42 (0.06)	0.58 (0.04)	0.47 (0.05)	0.54 (0.02)	− 1.43 (0.42)
	Random Forest model-user dependent	0.66 (0.11)	0.53 (0.18)	0.53 (0.20)	0.65 (0.21)	0.62 (0.10)	3.13 (6.40)
	Majority vote-user independent	0.69 (0.00)	0.00 (0.00)	0.00 (0.00)	1.00 (0.00)	0.50 (0.00)	− 3.04 (0.00)
	Majority vote-user dependent	0.71 (0.00)	0.27 (0.37)	0.35 (0.47)	0.65 (0.47)	0.49 (0.02)	− 0.02 (0.15)
	Random model-user independent	0.50 (0.00)	0.41 (0.07)	0.51 (0.01)	0.49 (0.01)	0.50 (0.00)	− 1.77 (0.10)
	Random modeluser dependent	0.55 (0.00)	0.45 (0.12)	0.55 (0.05)	0.44 (0.05)	0.50 (0.00)	− 1.39 (0.66)

Table 3 (continued)

Binary classifier n = number of observations	Model type	Accuracy (SD)	F1 score (SD)	Sensitivty (SD)	Specificity (SD)	AUC (SD)	B10 (SD)[b]
Sleep							
Insomnia (n =8474) versus normal sleep (n =36,140)	Random Forest model-user independent	0.70 (0.05)	0.13 (0.03)	0.16 (0.10)	0.82 (0.09)	0.48 (0.04)	− 1.49 (0.43)
	Random Forest model-user dependent	0.70 (0.16)	0.33 (0.18)	0.39 (0.22)	0.73 (0.17)	0.59 (0.08)	0.28 (2.66)
	Majority vote-user independent	0.85 (0.00)	0.00 (0.00)	0.00 (0.00)	1.00 (0.00)	0.50 (0.00)	− 3.13 (1.17)
	Majority vote-user dependent	0.90 (0.00)	0.05 (0.17)	0.06 (0.24)	0.93 (0.24)	0.49 (0.01)	− 3.36 (1.19)
	Random model-user independent	0.50 (0.00)	0.25 (0.07)	0.50 (0.01)	0.49 (0.00)	0.50 (0.00)	− 2.03 (0.13)
	Random model-user dependent	0.48 (0.00)	0.32 (0.13)	0.55 (0.05)	0.44 (0.04)	0.50 (0.00)	− 1.77 (0.48)
A broader definition of mania							
Combined increased mood, activity and decreased sleep							
Combined increased mood, activity and decreased sleep (n =471) versus rest (n =43,243)	Random Forest model-user independent	0.77 (0.10)	0.03 (0.02)	0.29 (0.17)	0.77 (0.11)	0.58 (0.06)	− 1.68 (0.28)
	Random Forest model-user dependent	0.77 (0.15)	0.17 (0.16)	0.41 (0.21)	0.78 (0.16)	0.67 (0.11)	2.15 (6.02)
	Majority vote-user independent	0.98 (0.00)	0.00 (0.00)	0.00 (0.00)	1.00 (0.00)	0.50 (0.00)	− 3.44 (0.00)
	Majority vote-user dependent	0.99 (0.00)	0.00 (0.00)	0.00 (0.00)	1.00 (0.00)	0.48 (0.02)	− 3.43 (1.30)
	Random model-user independent	0.49 (0.00)	0.13 (0.05)	0.50 (0.00)	0.49 (0.00)	0.50 (0.00)	− 2.39 (0.18)
	Random model-user dependent	0.46 (0.00)	0.46 (0.18)	0.56 (0.02)	0.44 (0.04)	0.50 (0.00)	− 1.78 (0.24)

The number of observations is the recorded samples before any resampling or cross-validation partitioning

[a] Euthymia was defined as a mood score of − 0.5, 0, 0.5. Depression was defined as a mood score < − 0.5, and mania was defined as a mood score > 0.5. Increased activity was defined as a score > 0, and decreased activity was defined as a score < 0. Insomnia was defined as total sleep duration < 360 min. A broader definition of mania was made by combining increased mood, increased activity and decreased sleep

[b] Bayesian inference framework

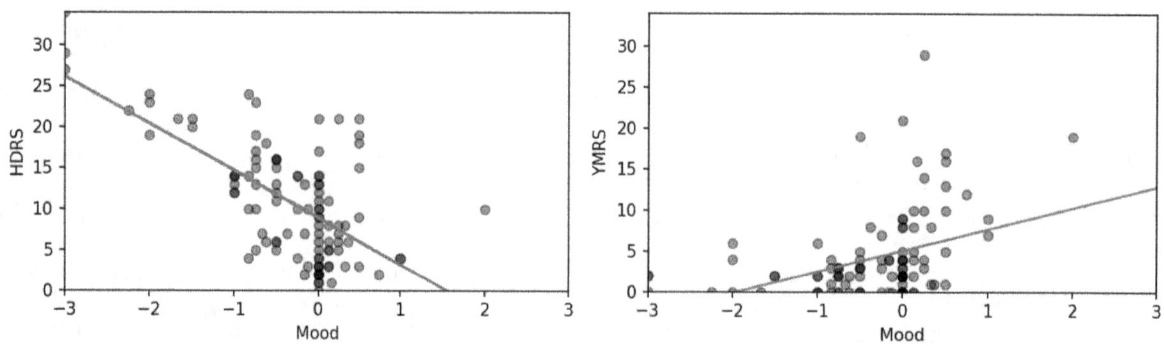

Fig. 2 The association between Hamilton Depression Rating Scale 17-items score (HDRS), Young Mania Rating Scale (YMRS) and patient-reported smartphone-based data on mood. The grey line indicates the linear least square fit for each combination

to our hypotheses with low specificity. Further, voice features statistically significantly differed between UR and HC, but in contrast to our hypotheses discriminated between the two groups with a modest accuracy.

Second, within patients with BD, voice features during mania (and to a lesser degree during depression) rather specifically discriminated from voice features during euthymia, but with low sensitivity. In addition, voice

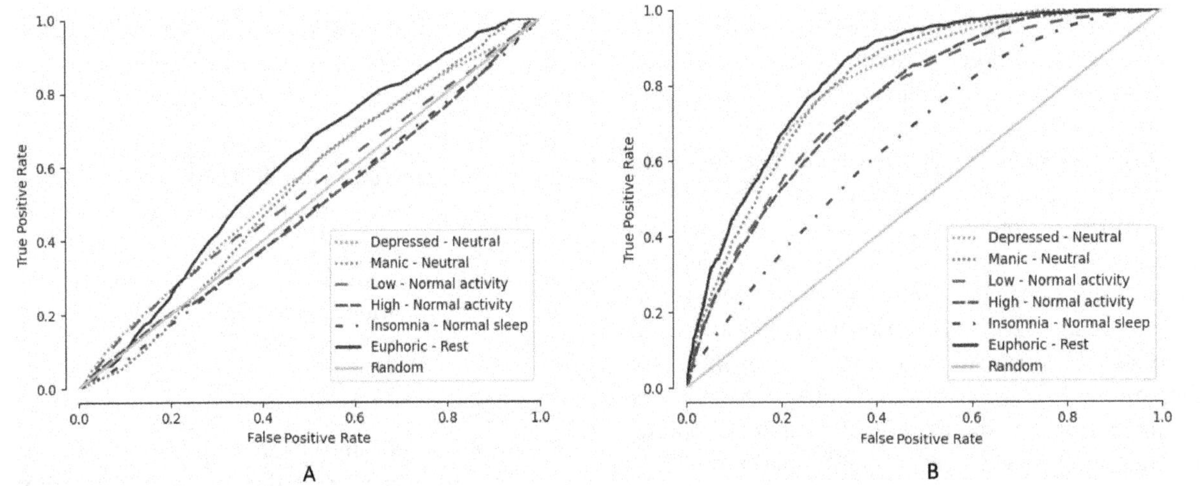

Fig. 3 The ROC curve for the classifications of different states based on voice features in patients with bipolar disorder. **A** The user-independent models; **B** the user-dependent models. Euphoric defined as combined increased mood and increased activity

features during periods with insomnia quite specifically discriminated from periods without insomnia. The model including voice features during periods with combined increased mood, increased activity and insomnia performed best among all the models as reflected by the specificity and the AUC. In line with our previous study (Faurholt-Jepsen 2016), within patients with BD the user dependent models clearly performed the best for classifications of different states, suggesting that changes in voice features is individual, like 'a fingerprint'.

Increased energy or activity has been highlighted in the DSM-5 and must now be present alongside mood changes to diagnose hypomania/mania raising energy/activity to criterion A (Kessing et al. 2021; Fredskild et al. 2021). Nevertheless, in contrast to our hypotheses, the sensitivity and specificity for discriminating between increased activity and neutral activity, and decreased activity and neutral activity was low.

Interestingly, the findings from the present study are in line with findings from previous studies suggesting that voice features may be used as a trait (Zhang et al. 2018) and state (Karam et al. 2014; Gideon et al. 2016; Vanello et al. 2012; Guidi et al. 2015; Faurholt-Jepsen 2016) marker in BD. However, previous studies included rather small samples of patients with BD and did not compare voice features to UR and HC.

A recent systematic review concerning automated assessment of psychiatric disorders using speech suggested that speech processing technology could aid mental health assessments (Low et al. 2020). Many people own and use a smartphone and smartphones comprise a unique platform for unobtrusive and continuous monitoring. Due to the limited access to treatment facilities, during the past 10 years, and especially during the COVID-19 pandemic, there has been an increase in the international interest in the use of mHealth technologies within mental health (Insel 2017; Wang et al. 2018; Anthes 2016; Patoz et al. 2021; Lagan 2020).

Within BD there is a substantial diagnostic delay, a progression of illness severity during untreated years, and a potential delayed intervention on subsyndromal symptoms. Assessments within BD are intermittent and may be limited partly due to the episodic nature of the disorder. The findings from the present study suggest that voice features may be used as an objective supplementary assessment method for diagnosis and identification of deterioration following initial informed consent. Such data has the additional advantage that they may be available when patients suffer from severe mood episodes and even when patients are non-adherent to treatment and don't attend clinical appointments.

Advantages and limitations

The present study was the first to include a large sample of both patients with BD, HC and UR, and is therefore hypothesis generating within the field. Furthermore, the patients with BD were followed for a long time period allowing for collection of both fine-grained voice and daily patient-reported data. The affective states within patients with BD were defined according to daily patient-reported smartphone-based data on mood, activity and sleep. In this way voice features and information on states was available for a larger proportion of days than if states were solely defined according to clinical ratings, which were conducted less frequently. While patient-reported smartphone-based mood was associated with scores on the HDRS and YMRS, a larger error margin was observed in the euthymic state (− 0.5 to 0.5). The ability for the model to discriminate from a euthymic state might be affected by the patient's ability to self-assess when situated in the border between different states. Exploratory analyses investigating the classification of manic episodes using a cut-off on patient-reported smartphone-based mood >1 did not alter the estimates. Further, there may be a risk that the patient-reported smartphone-based data on mood were not missing at random, and thus voice feature during the most severe affective states might not have been included. The three included populations were well-characterized according to clinical as well as research-based assessments using the SCAN interview, and the patients with BD were newly diagnosed increasing the impact of the findings. A potential confounding effect of factors related to the mental health status of the included participants such as psychopharmacological treatment cannot be ruled out (Bock 2019). Future studies could consider investigating this aspect further.

In the present study, the sensitivity of discriminating between different affective states within BD was quite low, as reflected by the relatively modest AUCs. Considerations between the trade-off between the sensitivity and the specificity should be a priority in future studies.

The available voice features were collected unobtrusively during naturalistic settings reducing the Hawthorne effect (Wickström and Bendix 2000). The study included a large amount of fine-grained repeated data for each participant during long-term follow-up. However, in some of the analyses a low number of observations were included. The finding that within patients with BD, the user dependent models outperformed the user independent models, and the user independent models performed close to random, suggest that change in voice features are highly individual, and thus hard to generalize between individuals.

The present study included the Speech and Music Interpretation by Large-space Extraction (openSMILE emolarge) feature set. It is possible that other configurations of the openSMILE toolkit or other feature extraction technologies, and subsequent features selections, to the one used in the present study could be feasible while keeping or improving the classification. This would help to reduce computational costs and save storage space. Further, from the present study, it was not possible to extract which of the included voice features that were most contributing to the classification models. The present study included patients with BD, but not patients with other psychiatric disorders. Future studies investigating the use of voice features for differentiating between psychiatric disorders could provide exciting information within the area. The voice features were extracted during regular phone calls, and thus we did not have access to voice feature from communication using other smartphone-based platforms.

Perspectives and future implications

Using voice features reflects a potential innovative, objective and unobtrusive supplementary method for discriminating patients with BD and UR from HC and as a state marker within patients with BD.

Conclusions

The present study investigated for the first time the use of voice features collected during naturalistic phone calls in a large sample of patients with BD, HC and UR and for state classifications within BD. It was shown that voice features can discriminate BD from HC with high sensitivity, but with low specificity, and that voice features significantly can differentiate between UR and HC. Within patients with BD, mania was rather specifically discriminated from euthymia. However, the trade-off between the sensitivity and the specificity was in all models reflected by the modest AUCs.

Within patients with BD the user dependent models clearly performed the best for classifications of different states, suggesting that changes in voice features is individual, like 'a fingerprint'. These results show that voice features collected during naturalistic phone calls could potentially be used as a supplementary objective marker discriminating patients with BD from HC and as a state marker within patients with BD.

Abbreviations

BD: Bipolar disorder; UR: Unaffected first-degree relatives; HC: Healthy control individuals; SCAN: The Schedules of Clinical Assessment in Neuropsychiatry interview; HDRS: Hamilton Depression Rating Scale 17-items; YMRS: Young Mania Rating Scale; RF: Random Forest classifier; AUC: Area under the characteristic curve; ROC: Receiver operating characteristic; B10: Bayesian inference framework with intrinsic priors; M: Mean; SD: Standard deviation.

Acknowledgements

The authors would like to thank the patients for participating in the studies, the nurses and PhD students involved in the studies.

Authors' contributions

MFJ, LVK and MV designed and conducted the study. MFJ, DR and JoB performed the statistical analyses. JB contributed to the design of the study and the statistical analyses. All authors have contributed to the manuscript. All authors read and approved the final manuscript.

Author details
[1]Copenhagen Affective Disorder Research Center (CADIC), Psychiatric Center Copenhagen, Rigshospitalet, Blegdamsvej 9, 2100 Copenhagen, Denmark. [2]Department of Health Technology, Technical University of Denmark, Lyngby, Denmark. [3]Department of Energy Conversion and Storage, Technical University of Denmark, Lyngby, Denmark. [4]Psychiatric Centre North Zealand, Hilleroed, Denmark.

References

Anthes E. Mental health: there's an app for that. Nature. 2016;532:20–3.
Arevian AC, et al. Clinical state tracking in serious mental illness through computational analysis of speech. PLoS ONE. 2020;15:e0225695.
Baldessarini RJ, Tondo L, Baethge CJ, Lepri B, Bratti IM. Effects of treatment latency on response to maintenance treatment in manic-depressive disorders. Bipolar Disord. 2007;9:386–93.
Bardram JE, et al. Designing mobile health technology for bipolar disorder: a field trial of the monarca system. In: Proceedings of the SIGCHI conference on human factors in computing systems. France: SIGCHI; 2013. p. 2627–36.
Berry KJ, Mielke PW, Mielke HW. The Fisher-Pitman permutation test: an attractive alternative to the F test. Psychol Rep. 2002;90:495–502.
Bock JM. Medications and vocal function. Otolaryngol Clin North Am. 2019;52:693–702.
Breiman L. Random forests. Mach Learn. 2001;45:5–32.
Chawla NV, Bowyer KW, Hall LO, Kegelmeyer WP. SMOTE: synthetic minority over-sampling technique. J Artif Intell Res. 2002;16:321–57.
da Silva RDA, et al. Insight across the different mood states of bipolar disorder. Psychiatr Q. 2015;86:395–405.
da Silva RDA, Mograbi DC, Bifano J, Santana CMT, Cheniaux E. Insight in bipolar mania: evaluation of its heterogeneity and correlation with clinical symptoms. J Affect Disord. 2016;199:95–8.
Ebner-Priemer UW, et al. Digital phenotyping: towards replicable findings with comprehensive assessments and integrative models in bipolar disorders. Int J Bipolar Disord. 2020. https://doi.org/10.1186/s40345-020-00210-4.
Eyben F, Wöllmer M, Schuller B. openSMILe—the Munich versatile and fast open source audio feature extractor. Proc ACM Multimed. 2010. https://doi.org/10.1186/s40345-020-00210-4.
Faurholt-Jepsen M, et al. Voice analysis as an objective state marker in bipolar disorder. Transl Psychiatry. 2016;6:e856.
Faurholt-Jepsen M, et al. Reducing the rate of psychiatric Re-ADMISsions in bipolar disorder using smartphones the RADMIS trial. Acta Psychiatr Scand. 2020. https://doi.org/10.1111/acps.13274.
Fredskild MU, et al. Impact of modification to DSM-5 criterion A for hypomania/mania in newly diagnosed bipolar patients: findings from the prospective BIO study. Int J Bipolar Disord. 2021;9:14.
García S, Ramírez-Gallego S, Luengo J, Benítez JM, Herrera F. Big data preprocessing: methods and prospects. Big Data Anal. 2016;1:9.
Gideon J, Provost EM, McInnis M. Mood state prediction from speech of varying acoustic quality for individuals with bipolar disorder. Proc IEEE Int Conf Acoust Speech Signal Process. 2016;2016:2359–63.
Goodwin FK, Jamison KR. Manic-depressive illness, vol. 1996. Oxford: New Oxford University Press; 1996.
Guidi A, et al. Smartphone application for the analysis of prosodic features in running speech with a focus on bipolar disorders: system performance evaluation and case study. Sensors. 2015;15:28070–87.
Hamilton M. Development of a rating scale for primary depressive illness. Br J Soc Clin Psychol. 1967;6:278–96.
Insel TR. Digital phenotyping: technology for a new science of behavior. JAMA. 2017;318:1215–6.
Karam ZN, et al. Ecologically valid long-term mood monitoring of individuals with bipolar disorder using speech. Proc Int Conf Acoust Speech Signal Process. 2014;2014:4858–62.
Kessing LV, et al. Do young adults with bipolar disorder benefit from early intervention? J Affect Disord. 2014;152–154:403–8.
Kessing LV, et al. The bipolar illness onset study: research protocol for the BIO cohort study. BMJ Open. 2017;7:e015462.
Kessing LV, et al. DSM-5 and ICD-11 criteria for bipolar disorder: Implications for the prevalence of bipolar disorder and validity of the diagnosis—a narrative review from the ECNP bipolar disorders network. Eur Neuropsychopharmacol. 2021. https://doi.org/10.1016/j.euroneuro.2021.01.097.
Lagan S, et al. Digital health developments and drawbacks: a review and analysis of top-returned apps for bipolar disorder. Int J Bipolar Disord. 2020. https://doi.org/10.1186/s40345-020-00202-4.
Leon-Novelo L, Moreno E, Casella G. Objective Bayes model selection in probit models. Stat Med. 2012;31:353–65.
Lord JR. Manic-depressive Insanity and Paranoia. By Prof. Emil Kraepelin; translated by R. Mary Barclay, M. A., M. B.; edited by George M. Robertson, M. D., F. R. C. P. Edin. Edinburgh: E. & S. Livingstone, 1921. Demy 8vo. Pp. 280. Forty-nine illustrations, eighteen in colour. Price 12s. 6d. J Mental Sci. 1921;67:342–6.
Low DM, Bentley KH, Ghosh SS. Automated assessment of psychiatric disorders using speech: a systematic review. Laryngoscope Investig Otolaryngol. 2020;5:96–116.
Maxhuni A, et al. Classification of bipolar disorder episodes based on analysis of voice and motor activity of patients. Pervasive Mob Comput. 2016;31:50–66.
Muaremi A, Gravenhorst F, Grünerbl A, Arnrich B, Tröster G. Assessing bipolar episodes using speech cues derived from phone calls. Pervasive Comput Paradig Ment Health. 2014;2014:103–14.
Mundt JC, Vogel AP, Feltner DE, Lenderking WR. Vocal acoustic biomarkers of depression severity and treatment response. Biol Psychiatry. 2012;72:580–7.
Newman S, Mather VG. Analysis of spoken language of patients with affective disorders. AJP. 1938;94:913–42.
Olivetti E, Greiner S, Avesani P. Statistical independence for the evaluation of classifier-based diagnosis. Brain Inform. 2015;2:13–9.
Patoz M-C, et al. Patients' adherence to smartphone apps in the management of bipolar disorder: a systematic review. Int J Bipolar Disord. 2021;9:19.
Pfister T, Robinson P. Speech emotion classification and public speaking skill assessment. In: Salah AA, Gevers T, Sebe N, Vinciarelli A, editors. Human behavior understanding. Berlin: Springer; 2010. p. 151–62.
Phillips ML, Kupfer DJ. Bipolar disorder diagnosis: challenges and future directions. Lancet. 2013;381:1663–71.
Raucher-Chéné D, Achim AM, Kaladjian A, Besche-Richard C. Verbal fluency in bipolar disorders: a systematic review and meta-analysis. J Affect Disord. 2017;207:359–66.
Schuller B, et al. The INTERSPEECH 2010 paralinguistic challenge. Japan: INTERSPEECH; 2010. p. 2794–7.
Sletved KSO, Ziersen SC, Andersen PK, Vinberg M, Kessing LV. Socio-economic functioning in patients with bipolar disorder and their unaffected siblings—results from a nation-wide population-based longitudinal study. Psychol Med. 2021. https://doi.org/10.1017/S0033291721002026.
Vanello N, et al. Speech analysis for mood state characterization in bipolar patients. Conf Proc IEEE Eng Med Biol Soc. 2012;2012:2104–7.
Vedel Kessing L, Ziersen SC, Andersen PK, Vinberg M. A nationwide population-based longitudinal study mapping psychiatric disorders during lifetime in siblings to patients with bipolar disorder. Acta Psychiatr Scand. 2021;143:284–93.
Wang K, Varma DS, Prosperi M. A systematic review of the effectiveness of mobile apps for monitoring and management of mental health symptoms or disorders. J Psychiatr Res. 2018;107:73–8.
Wickström G, Bendix T. The 'Hawthorne effect'—what did the original Hawthorne studies actually show? Scand J Work Environ Health. 2000;26:363–7.
Wing JK, et al. SCAN. Schedules for clinical assessment in neuropsychiatry. Arch Gen Psychiatry. 1990;47:589–93.
Young RC, Biggs JT, Ziegler VE, Meyer DA. A rating scale for mania: reliability, validity and sensitivity. Br J Psychiatry. 1978;133:429–35.
Zhang J, et al. Analysis on speech signal features of manic patients. J Psychiatr Res. 2018;98:59–63.

18

An evidence map of actigraphy studies exploring longitudinal associations between rest-activity rhythms and course and outcome of bipolar disorders

Jan Scott[1,2,3], Francesc Colom[4,5], Allan Young[2,8], Frank Bellivier[3,6,7] and Bruno Etain[3,6,7]*

Abstract

Background: Evidence mapping is a structured approach used to synthesize the state-of-the-art in an emerging field of research when systematic reviews or meta-analyses are deemed inappropriate. We employed this strategy to summarise knowledge regarding longitudinal ecological monitoring of rest-activity rhythms (RAR) and disease modifiers, course of illness, treatment response or outcome in bipolar disorders (BD).

Structure: We had two key aims: (1) to determine the number and type of actigraphy studies of in BD that explored data regarding: outcome over time (e.g. relapse/recurrence according to polarity, or recovery/remission), treatment response or illness trajectories and (2) to examine the range of actigraphy metrics that can be used to estimate disruptions of RAR and describe which individual circadian rhythm or sleep–wake cycle parameters are most consistently associated with outcome over time in BD. The mapping process incorporated four steps: clarifying the project focus, describing boundaries and 'coordinates' for mapping, searching the literature and producing a brief synopsis with summary charts of the key outputs. Twenty-seven independent studies (reported in 29 publications) were eligible for inclusion in the map. Most were small-scale, with the median sample size being 15 per study and median duration of actigraphy being about 7 days (range 1–210). Interestingly, 17 studies comprised wholly or partly of inpatients (63%). The available evidence indicated that a discrete number of RAR metrics are more consistently associated with transition between different phases of BD and/or may be predictive of longitudinal course of illness or treatment response. The metrics that show the most frequent associations represent markers of the amount, timing, or variability of RAR rather than the sleep quality metrics that are frequently targeted in contemporary studies of BD.

Conclusions: Despite 50 years of research, use of actigraphy to assess RAR in longitudinal studies and examination of these metrics and treatment response, course and outcome of BD is under-investigated. This is in marked contrast to the extensive literature on case–control or cross-sectional studies of actigraphy, especially typical sleep analysis metrics in BD. However, given the encouraging findings on putative RAR markers, we recommend increased study of putative circadian phenotypes of BD.

Keywords: Evidence map, Actigraphy, Longitudinal, Bipolar, Response, Course, Modifiers, Lithium, Phenotype, Domains

Introduction

In the 2017 update on the global burden of disease demonstrates that, the four most burdensome non-communicable conditions (in terms of DALYs: disability adjusted

*Correspondence: bruno.etain@inserm.fr
[3] Université Paris Diderot, Sorbonne Paris Cité, UMR-S 1144, 75013 Paris, France
Full list of author information is available at the end of the article

life years) are: cardiovascular disease (CVD), cancers, musculoskeletal conditions, and mental disorders (GBD 2017; Whiteford et al. 2013). In individuals aged 15–49, mental disorders in general, and mood disorders specifically, are regarded as the most burdensome conditions worldwide. In the last 3 to 4 decades, considerable progress has been made in the management of CVD and cancer through precision medicine. The application of precision medicine is in its infancy in psychiatry, but funding initiatives (such as the European H2020 platform) are supporting studies of personalized diagnostics and therapeutics across a range of mental conditions including bipolar disorders (BD) (Schumann et al. 2014). Like precision approaches to other chronic disorders, these studies have largely focused on more quantifiable metrics (such as 'omics' and brain scanning) as an attempt to increase the biological validity of observed symptoms (Frey et al. 2013; Hellwig and Domschke 2019; MacDonald et al. 2019). This strategy also reflects the proposals described in the RDOC (research domain criteria) paradigm that identifies key domains and analytic units for translational research (Cuthbert and Insel 2013; Insel 2014). Although personalized diagnostics for BD are likely to remain a long-term aspiration, there is emerging evidence that multi-platform, integrated science approaches could offer a pathway for stratifying individuals with BD to improve outcome prediction, namely treatment response, relapse and recurrence, and individual illness trajectories (Scott et al. 2018). However, as these efforts progress, there is a need to extent the search for phenotypes beyond laboratory settings and to test potential biomarkers in real-world settings, such as field and cohort studies, comparative effectiveness research, and large-scale pragmatic trials (Brietzke et al. 2019; Scott et al. 2019).

One of the domains identified by RDOC is the arousal and regulatory system, and RDOC suggests that sleep–wake cycle and circadian rhythms (which we will refer to as rest-activity rhythms or RAR) represent a core construct for investigation (Insel 2014; Smagula 2016). This is of relevance to BD, as converging evidence indicates that RAR disruptions can differentiate BD cases from healthy controls (HC) and/or other comparator groups (Ritter et al. 2011; Geoffroy et al. 2015; Ng et al. 2015; De Crescenzo et al. 2017; Scott et al. 2017). Further, real-time monitoring of most of these phenomena may be possible with wrist-worn devices. Of course, there has been an exponential increase in the development and use of consumer grade wearables (and smart phone apps) in clinical populations (Faurolt-Jepson et al. 2012; Krane-Gartiser et al. 2019). However, many demonstrate low inter-device reliability, none of the apps or programmes are currently validated against 'gold standard' measures and few can accurately estimate key markers of circadian timing (Zee et al. 2014; FDA 2019; Depner et al. 2020). The lack of regulatory approval and absence of basic research on or rigour of testing their performance quality means consumer devices are not currently recommended for use in this research field (Baron 2018; FDA 2019; Moar 2018). Currently, RDOC indicates that actigraphy could be applied as an 'analytic unit' for longitudinal studies of circadian rhythms and sleep–wake cycles (Cuthbert 2014). Such studies are now underway, but there is no consensus regarding the most useful actigraphy-derived RAR parameters to estimate and/or report (Scott et al. 2019; Smagula 2016. Also, a preliminary scoping exercise of this topic suggested that relatively few actigraphy studies have employed a longitudinal or prospective design in BD. Therefore, we decided to collate any existing publications on these issues and synthesise the current state of knowledge.

This paper has three aims:

(a) To determine the number and type of actigraphy studies of samples comprised wholly or partly of individuals with BD that explore data regarding: outcome over time (e.g. relapse/recurrence according to polarity, or recovery/remission), treatment response or illness trajectories.
(b) To examine the range of actigraphy metrics that can be used to estimate disruptions of RAR and describe which individual circadian rhythm or sleep–wake cycle parameters are most consistently associated with outcome over time in BD.
(c) To demonstrate the use of evidence mapping as a process for synthesising the state-of-the-art in the field of ecological monitoring of RAR and disease modifiers, course of illness, treatment response or outcome in BD.

Methods

As the use of evidence-mapping dictates the structure of the paper, we provide a brief overview of this approach in Table 1. Below, we outline the application to the project described in this article.

Rationale for use of mapping

As noted in the introduction, the goal of this evidence map is to present an overview of the extent, range, nature, and findings of clinical research on RAR metrics measured by actigraphy and a range of potential outcomes of BD. Like many evidence maps, the rationale for using this process was determined by prior knowledge of the field. Many research groups, including our own, have synthesized research findings or undertaken meta-analyses of

Table 1 Brief overview of evidence mapping

Evidence Mapping

Evidence mapping is defined as-

"a form of knowledge synthesis that addresses an exploratory research question aimed at mapping key concepts, types of evidence, and gaps in research related to a defined area or field by systematically searching, selecting, and synthesizing existing understanding"

The gold standard methods used in evidence-based research are systematic review and meta-analysis. These classic approaches are both rigorous and provide readers with detailed information about narrow questions (e.g. the efficacy of drug X for disorder Y). However, developments from this archetypal model are now being developed to meet more diverse needs regarding evidence synthesis (Arksey 2003; Miake-Lye et al. 2016). The obvious example is the use of rapid reviews (which address urgent topics and do not always fully adhere to systematic methodologies) or scoping reviews (that identify extensive bodies of literature but do not usually provide detailed synthesis) (Colquhoun et al. 2014). In this context, evidence mapping has emerged as another process that allows researchers and their audience to develop an understanding of the extent and distribution of evidence in on a broad topic, highlighting what is known and also where gaps exist (Katz et al. 2003; Hetrick et al. 2010). Although it applies systematic and replicable methodology, the process is iterative, as expert consensus and preliminary literature searches inform the next steps in the review, so the final product is broader and less detailed than the traditional approaches (Vallarino et al. 2015). Furthermore, the goal is not to provide detailed statistical comparisons, but rather to offer an essential snapshot of what is or is not known at this moment in time. It is presumed that an evidence map for any given field will be followed up in the future when research develops to a point where it becomes justifiable to apply more formal reviews and pooled analyses

The depth of evidence synthesized will differ depending on its purpose of an evidence map e.g. an overview of the extent, range and nature of research activity might entirely exclude any details of study findings (Miake-Lye et al. 2016). However, if the latter are considered, they can be represented by graphs and figures, instead of or as well as a detailed table such as the summary tables provided in systematic reviews (Hetrick et al. 2010)

Given the proposed scope of this map, we determined that a simple written summary with basic tables and figures would be offered in the results section of the paper. A detailed Table summarizing sample characteristics and research findings (in an Appendix) and citations in the reference list only would ensure readers focused on key findings we summarize. Individual readers could then choose to examine supporting evidence and relevant references for themes that they wished to investigate further

pooled data regarding BD cases compared with HC or other (comparator) groups (Ritter et al. 2011; Geoffroy et al. 2015). Some of those projects identified small-scale studies that used real-time monitoring of BD cases and/or that examined associations between baseline actigraphy recordings and longitudinal course and outcome of BD (Scott et al. 2017). Nearly all of those projects were undertaken several decades ago and differences in sampling, diagnosis or research methods meant the publications failed to meet eligibility criteria for systematic reviews focused on a specific research question (De Crescenzo et al. 2017). Further, it was known that most of the reported data were insufficient (in terms of amount or quality) to merit inclusion in meta-analyses (Ng et al. 2015). As such, an evidence map offered a realistic option to gain an understanding of existing research in this area, especially capturing insights from multiple small-scale studies and mapping provides a means of summarizing the range of publications and findings in a transparent way (Vallarino et al. 2015). The potential advantage over a basic narrative or selective review is that the search process is reproducible, and the map specifically addresses gaps in the knowledgebase (Hetrick et al. 2010). However, findings are described in brief, so a map does not aim to offer the detailed lists of citations and extensive tables included in systematic reviews or meta-analyses.

Mapping process

The process usually incorporates four steps (clarifying focus; describing boundaries and 'coordinates' for mapping; literature search; charting the output maps). After consultation among the co-authors, the questions and scope of the mapping project were defined as follows-

Step 1: Clarification of the focus of the map.

It was agreed that the focus would be:

(a) What evidence exists on this topic and based on a review of study characteristics and methodologies: what conclusions can be drawn about the quality of evidence?
(b) What areas are, or are not, well-researched?
(c) Based on the available evidence, what advice can be offered to clinicians and investigators in the field?

Step 2: Description of the eligibility criteria (boundaries for inclusion and exclusion), specification of co-ordinates to be mapped (study characteristics associated with outcome/response, etc.) and definition of key variables (RAR metrics):

(a) Studies were eligible if:

Inclusion criteria-

i) The sample or cohort was wholly or partly comprised of BD cases that met clinical or research diagnostic criteria
ii) It reported associations between any RAR actigraphy metric recorded at baseline and a clinical or research-defined outcome assessed at follow-up in BD cases (or vice versa). Note: For the purposes of the map, the focus was on BD cases, so we extracted informa-

tion on inter-individual or intra-individual changes in actigraphy or outcomes in the clinical cases (i.e. we aimed to avoid focusing on findings of case–control studies or cross-sectional comparisons of RAR metrics between BD and HC, which have been reviewed many times before).

iii) The publication reported any association between RAR metrics recorded by actigraphy and the outcome or response of BD in the short or long term (this could include e.g. naturalistic observational studies of treatment interventions and/or randomized controlled trials).

iv) Presence of comorbidities was not an exclusion criterion, but details were noted.

v) Findings from self-report questionnaires, consumer grade wearables or smartphone apps were eligible if the study also reported data for actigraphy recordings and/or the RAR findings extracted from questionnaires or wearables were reported alongside the equivalent metric derived from actigraphy.

Exclusion criteria-

The map aimed to capture the extent of the existing literature, so there were minimal exclusion criteria. The most significant criterion was that studies that failed to report any measures (quantity and/or or timing) of daytime activity were ineligible. Also excluded were single case reports or studies where the recruitment of participants was not based on a current diagnosis of BD or depression (UP and BD) e.g. studies of individuals at risk of BD or of individuals attending medical clinics (actigraphy has been used to assess treatment outcome in CVD and cancer).

(b) Study Coordinates.

It was agreed that the following would be mapped: year and geographic location of study (we also noted if the study specified seasonality, etc.); sample characteristics (demographics; diagnoses e.g. BD subtypes, inclusion of UP and BD; phase of illness at recruitment); community or clinical setting (e.g. in- or outpatient); duration of study; duration of actigraphy recording; and outcomes reported. The latter could include: outcome prediction; response to introduction of treatment or treatment withdrawal; acute or long-term treatment effects; longitudinal course of BD (continuous or repeated cross-sectional assessment) in terms of illness progression (naturalist follow-up or associated with treatment introduction or withdrawal), symptom exacerbation, relapse/recurrence/recovery/remission and/or putative disease course modifiers (as defined in a study). Also eligible were: naturalistic observational studies in clinician settings (unspecified/uncontrolled treatment), naturalistic monitoring of illness with unspecified/uncontrolled treatment and/or randomized controlled trials that incorporated actigraphy (if not identified via previous criteria).

(c) Definitions of Rest-Activity Rhythms.

It is clear from actigraphy studies in BD that the metrics reported have differed by location (i.e. geography) and decade of study. However, researchers have repeatedly acknowledged the close connection between sleep and circadian structure and that actigraphy data can be used for 'rhythmometric analysis' of RAR (Calogiuri et al. 2013; Smagula, 2016; Wirz-Justice, 2007). As such, all the metrics listed in Table 2 are considered as potentially relevant RAR markers in this project.

Table 2 gives an overview of the key RAR metrics that have been derived from actigraphy recordings in psychiatry (definitions and descriptions of each metric are provided in Table 3 in Appendix) (Calogiuri et al. 2013; Ancoli-Israel et al. 2003). As shown, investigators have focused on different rhythmometric procedures, which need to be considered when interpreting the map. For instance, early studies were likely to report parametric statistics (especially in the USA) (Nelson et al. 1979). Three variables (mesor, acrophase and amplitude) were estimated using cosinor methods (with the p value

Table 2 Potential measures of rest-activity rhythms (further details are given in Appendix)

Parametric (Cosinor) Model	Non-parametric Model	Sleep Quantity Analysis Model (Mean or Variability)	Sleep Analysis- Circadian Phase Model
Midline estimating statistic of rhythm (MESOR)	Inter-daily Stability (IS)	Mean Activity (MA)	Sleep Onset
Amplitude	Intra-daily Variability (IV)	Time in Bed (TIB) (± Lights Off)	Sleep Offset
Acrophase	Least active period: L5/ L5 Onset	Total Sleep Time (TST)	Sleep Midpoint
	Most active period:M10/M10 Onset	Sleep Onset Latency (SOL)	Sleep Regularity Index (SRI)
	Amplitude	Sleep Efficiency (SE %)	
	Relative Amplitude	Fragmentation Index (FI %)	
		Wake after sleep onset (WASO) (± N awakenings > 5 min)	

signifying the probability that the data really show circadian periodicity), whilst more recently these metrics have been derived using regression techniques (which report similar variables but assume more complex patterns and rhythms and are more robust for larger study populations) (Fernandez and Hermida 1998). Non-parametric methods report a wider range of variables to describe the quantity and timing of activity and rest, and especially provide insights into variability/stability of rhythms and any RAR disruptions (Calogiuri et al. 2013; Natale et al. 2009). They are often preferred to parametric models and it is argued that non-parametric models better represent the complexity of RAR than cosinor models (van Someren et al. 1997). Variables derived from basic sleep analysis (such as total sleep time: TST) are probably the most widely reported measures in research in BD. One reason for this is that these sleep quantity are much easier to estimate from raw data (and do not rely on more complex algorithms). Sleep variables are useful for estimating duration and fragmentation of sleep patterns but are less reflective of circadian rhythmicity. Estimation of variability in values for each sleep parameter is encouraged in contemporary literature on RAR and greater reporting of sleep onset/offset/midpoint or sleep regularity index has been employed to give a greater insight into rhythmometrics (Bei et al. 2016).

Step 3: Literature Search

The search approach was the same as utilized in systematic reviews. Search terms were applied to PubMed, MEDLINE, PsycINFO, EMBASE, CINAHL and Web of Science databases No limits were set for language, type of study or date of publication (the original telemetric motion sensors and actometers were used in BD in the early 1970s). The search terms included the full range of RAR metrics and potential outcomes listed in Step 2, supplemented by searches using names of medications (e.g. lithium, carbamazepine) or for research groups known to have contributed publications when this topic initially emerged in the literature. This approach was used to ensure the broadest possible range of publications were identified. Furthermore, hand-searches were undertaken of all reference lists of studies noted in narrative reviews, systematic reviews, and meta- analyses on this or similar topics. The final list of eligible studies was generated based on broad relevance to the scope of this map. Key drivers of selection of publications were that:

a) The study reported the use of an actigraphy device to undertake daytime or 24-h monitoring of RAR in BD
b) The study endpoint was described in terms of a recognizable clinical outcome or measure of response or change in RAR (if combined with baseline or follow-up clinical measures).

Step 4. Charting: screening and positioning the relevant evidence within the map

Based on the specified aims of the study, we agreed three core outputs:

a) Nature & quality of research: a Table of study coordinates was planned. Co-authors would review the Table independently and produce a brief written synopsis of the key characteristics of the available research. This information was used to formulate a consensus on the nature and quality of the extant literature.
b) Extent of research: two maps would be generated. The first would describe year and country of study to provide a snapshot of research in this field by geography and over time. The second map would give an overview of the most common methodologies and research themes. These would be identified by extracting information regarding study coordinates and coding each of these separately, e.g. setting (e.g. inpatient); type (e.g. naturalistic observational; treatment outcome; response criteria; etc.); reported interventions (e.g. proportion of individuals taking lithium; numbers allocated to psychological intervention); whether interventions were compared (e.g. lithium versus quetiapine). These data could be combined to show the overall pattern of research.
c) A map would be generated to identify the range of RAR parameters reported across all studies and which individual metrics appeared to be consistently found to be associated with course and outcome of BD. Such a map can offer a heuristic framework and be the starting point for a systematic review or meta-analysis at a future date.

Results

Twenty-seven independent studies (reported in 29 publications) were included in the map. Table 4 in Appendix gives an overview of the studies and the core characteristics. To maintain the simplicity expounded in evidence mapping we have not included all the citations after every statement (the citations are in the reference list and the key studies can be easily identified from Table 3).

In the studies in the evidence map, the median age of all participants was 45 years and 60% were female. The median sample size was 15 per study (range: 2–75); 484 individuals with BD (out of a total of 560) participated in actigraphy and the median duration of recordings was

7 days (range 1–210). Studies before 1990 tended to be smaller, but sample size did not appear to be determined by decade of publication, with several small-scale projects or BD subsamples (included in larger samples or cohorts) being followed-up longitudinally in recent studies. Overall, 17 studies comprised wholly or partly of inpatients (63%). Two studies reported daytime activity monitoring only, one study used actigraphy primarily to confirm reported patterns of hypersomnia whilst a RCT examined changes in objective levels of morning activity following a psychological intervention targeted at sleep inertia.

There was evidence that statistical analyses of RAR have become more sophisticated over time, but earlier studies were more likely to address directly the association between RAR and phase of BD (e.g. transitions between mania, and depression), and change in RAR following initiation or withdrawal of treatment (especially lithium) (e.g. Kripke et al. 1979; Wolff et al. 1985). The sampling, design, and analytic strategies of most studies demonstrate several methodological flaws (e.g. repeated testing of small samples with correction, absence of reporting of non-significant outcomes). Overall, the consensus judged the quality of the studies to be modest.

Figure 1 shows that > 50% studies (14 of 27) were undertaken in the USA and it is only in the last decade that the number of studies undertaken across Europe has matched the USA. The earliest studies reported the seminal work undertaken by Kupfer and associates and pursued by researchers at NIMH; more recent studies represent projects exploring RAR as disease course modifiers or examining RAR as potential predictors of treatment response and/or to monitor treatment outcomes. Table 3 also demonstrates that there were no studies (meeting our eligibility criteria) that reported RAR in BD for more than a decade (1994–2006). This is most likely a consequence of the fact that psychiatry research shifted towards the reporting of metrics favoured by experts in sleep/sleep disorders, rather than focusing on metrics most relevant to specific psychiatric disorders. Reviewing publications after 2006 suggests this this trend started to reverse when BD researchers increased their focus on sleep–wake cycles and also with the rise in interest in precision diagnostics and therapeutics.

As shown in Fig. 2, only 22% studies reported follow-up assessments at > 6 months (N = 6). Naturalistic observational studies and treatment outcome studies are equally common (N = 10; 37%). In nine studies, > 50% of the sample were taking lithium or the study specifically explored RAR and lithium treatment.

Although our preliminary work for the evidence-map identified > 30 possible RAR parameters (parametric and non-parametric measures; mean or variable measures of sleep analysis; putative circadian phase markers extracted from sleep quantity analysis), the eligible studies only consistently reported estimates for seven metrics (see Fig. 3). Early studies mainly reported cosinor metrics (amplitude, acrophase and mesor), whilst the more recent studies increasingly report all raw data (either in the main text of the study or Appendices). However, in the middle decades, there was a tendency to only report statistically significant findings, without any indication as to whether other parameters were measured and/or which were found to be non-significant. Interestingly, when number of studies measuring a parameter is compared with the likelihood that a statistically significant association would be found, five variables were associated with outcome in > 50% of the studies. Namely: Variability/Rigidity of RAR (4 out of 4), 24 h rest activity cycle (22 out of 25), amplitude (5 out of 6), acrophase/phase advance (5 out of 7), and sleep efficiency (SE: 5 out of 8). In contrast, most measures of sleep quantity show weaker links: wake after

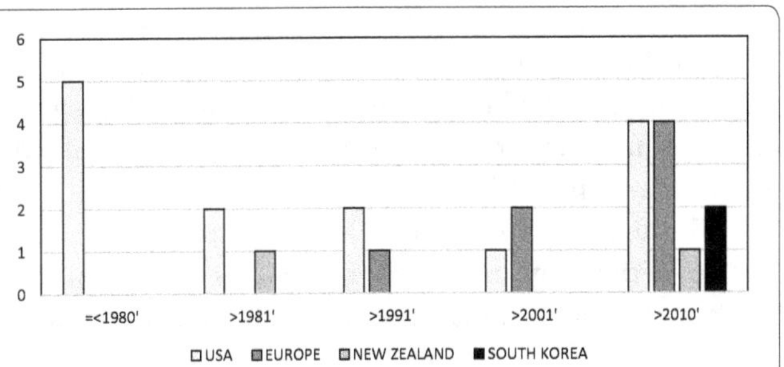

Fig. 1 Location of study & decade of publication (Total = 27). (Note: if > 1 publication was identified relating to a dataset from a particular location, we included the date of the first publication only)

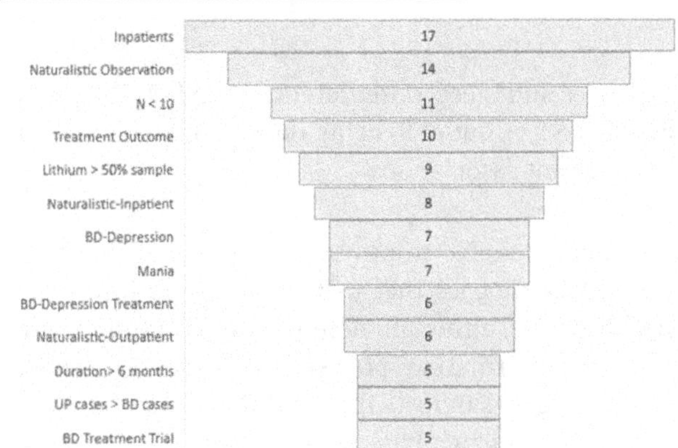

Fig. 2 Key coordinates of actigraphy studies – the graph shows the main characteristics or reported purpose of the publications. Note: Only descriptors reported in > = 5 studies are included in the chart. However, the Total N reported in the graph exceeds the number of citations (n = 28) as most studies are counted in > 1 descriptor category

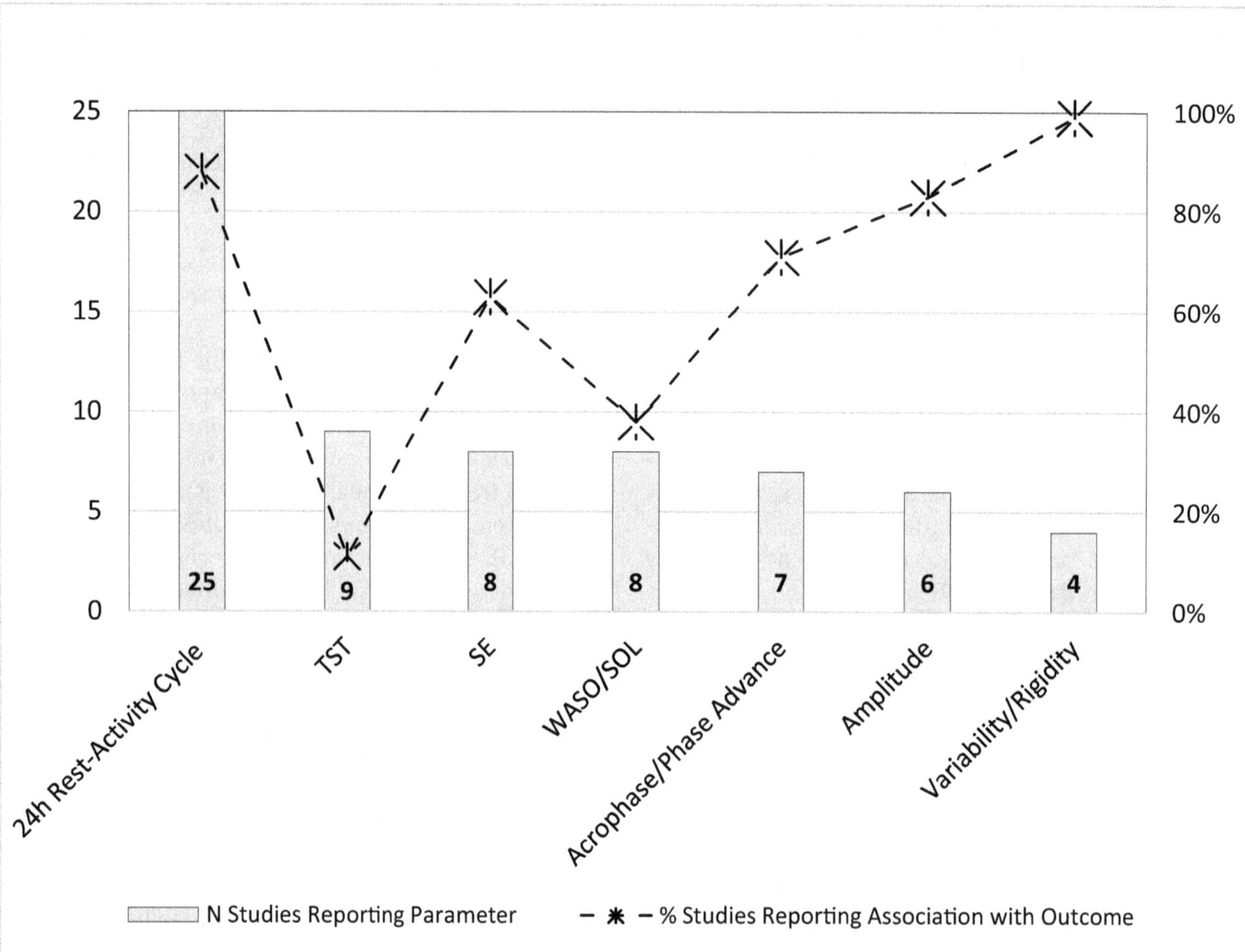

Key - SE: Sleep efficiency; SOL: Sleep onset latency; TST: Total sleep time; WASO: Wake after sleep onset

Fig. 3 Comparison of number of studies reporting each actigraphy metric & proportion of those studies (%) in which the parameter shows a significant association with an outcome of interest

sleep onset and sleep onset latency (WASO/SOL: 3 out of 8) and TST (1 out of 9) being the only metrics showing any significant associations.

It was not possible to provide specific evidence of the nature of the metrics that were most useful in different types of studies, although there was some trend of interest. Using information précised in Table 3, available evidence largely supports the view that mania is associated with circadian phase advance and BD-depression with phase delay. The latter was not obvious in studies of mixed samples of UP and BD depression. Interestingly, treatment may be associated with phase change, and treatments may have different effects on phase in BD-II, and phase shifts may can be associated with outcome at follow-up. The variable 24 h rest-activity cycle represents a global estimate of RAR and its primary value to the map is that it confirms that RAR can be used to assess a range of clinical outcomes in BD. Amplitude appeared to be a useful marker of illness course and treatment response or outcome. It was noted that variability/rigidity of RAR was only estimated in four small samples (Ns = 3, 8, 10, 12). These studies reported extended continuous durations of actigraphy and found the metrics to be significant markers of longitudinal course (including admissions).

However, the studies did not report sufficient raw data or basic analyses to allow further investigation or interpretation of the findings.

Discussion

This article explores associations between RAR metrics measured via actigraphy and course, outcome and/or treatment response in BD. The project arose from three converging strands of work. First, a background scoping exercise undertaken for the H2020-funded consortium exploring a range of putative markers of lithium response phenotypes (including actigraphy) (Scott et al. 2019); second, scrutiny of RDOC publications that suggest undertaking longitudinal actigraphy to explore RAR phenotypes in BD (Insel 2014); and third, a study of circadian and sleep–wake cycles in lithium responders and non-responders (Scott et al. 2020). These projects provided us with sufficient insights into this research field and, alongside our prior knowledge, led us to conclude that the existing literature on RAR and course/outcome/response was unlikely to be suitable for systematic review or meta-analysis. Furthermore, it appeared it would be counter-productive to use these classic evidence-based techniques as they would prematurely restrict the focus of our investigation to a specific or narrow question of what presently seems to be an imprecise research area. As such, it was agreed that utilizing evidence mapping might enable some synthesis of the diverse range of (predominantly small-scale) studies currently available.

Regarding our first question (what evidence exists and what conclusions can be drawn about the quality of evidence?). We conclude that limited evidence exists, but what is available indicates that a discrete number of RAR metrics are more consistently associated with transition between different phases of BD and/or may be predictive of longitudinal course of illness or treatment response. The metrics that show the most frequent associations represent markers of the amount, timing, or variability of RAR rather than the sleep quality metrics that are frequently targeted in contemporary studies of BD. However, these putative 'circadian' signals should be viewed in context, as there is evidence of selective reporting of both metrics and outcomes, thus increasing the likelihood of publication bias. Notably, the statistical associations reported derive from multiple small-scale studies that together included < 500 individuals with BD. In sum, the findings are of interest, encourage pursuit of research in this field, but clearly expose that the quality of evidence and available published studies is modest.

Next, the second question addressed what areas are, or are not, well-researched? Our findings about the extent, nature and quality of the research, indicate that the available publications demonstrate the diverse ways in which RAR can be studied in the context of BD, but that no single area has been targeted for a prolonged period of research. Notably, the early studies showed a keen interest in treatment response (or change in illness with treatment withdrawal), but these themes were not pursued to a definitive conclusion. However, this theme is now drawing interest again and two recent studies used actigraphy to explore RAR and acute treatment outcome, namely ketamine infusions for depression (albeit in sample with many more UP than BD cases) and inpatient treatment of mania (such as Blue Blocking Glasses) (Duncan et al. 2017; Henriksen et al. 2020). The map also highlights evidence that clinical depressive symptoms are associated with robustness of circadian rhythm (e.g. Hwang et al. 2017), whilst current RAR patterns may predict future mental state (Salvatore et al. 2008). Also, in a small inpatient sample, it was shown that RAR recorded by actigraphy were associated with clinical progress, whilst estimates made with a consumer wearable were not (Averill et al. 2019). This is a useful reminder that research grade devices are still more accurate than consumer grade device and apps (and so actigraphy is likely to continue to have a role in the immediate future). Importantly, individuals with BD are prepared to wear actiwatches and/or consumer devices for extended periods (> 6 months) and this, allied with new conceptualizations of and analytic approaches to of RAR (such as fractal activity as an indicator system adaptability and lagged data analyses, etc.), may lead to a greater understanding of the chronological sequence of change of RAR, mood, cognition and other cardinal features of BD (Knapen et al. 2020; Walker et al. 2020).

The final question asked, based on the available evidence, what are the potential ways forward for the field? We suggest that one important option would be to develop a consensus within research consortia or wider groups of clinicians and investigators regarding the most appropriate RAR metrics to include in future actigraphy studies of BD (Scott et al. 2017). It is particularly important that this dialogue focuses on metrics that offer insights into RAR in BD that will have the optimal clinical as well as research utility for this field. This should be prioritized over simply generating a list of RAR measures recommended for estimation or reporting of sleep or sleep–wake research in general (Sack et al. 2007). These discussions will necessarily consider any RAR metrics that may represent trait or state variables (e.g. there is emerging evidence that relative amplitude, amplitude, interdaily stability and intradaily variability may be markers of disease onset as well as disease progression) (Merikangas et al. 2019; Scott et al. 2020). Developing a consensus is perhaps the most important recommendation that arises from this mapping exercise, as without such a course of action there is a clear possibility that we will continue to lack the means to make detailed cross-study comparisons of the metrics that would offer most promise as diagnostic or response biomarkers.

An obvious gap in the available literature is the lack of youth studies of actigraphy that take a longitudinal perspective. Given the interest in staging models and temperament, research on the transition between sub-threshold conditions or at-risk mental states and the onset of full-threshold illness episodes would be welcome. In individuals with established BD, consideration should be given to RAR metrics that might be combined in multi-platform research of precision diagnostics and therapeutics (Scott et al. 2019). For instance, precision studies that focus on prediction of response to mood stabilizers such as lithium, and the identification of biosignatures (rather than single biomarkers) might consider giving priority to reporting RAR markers such as amplitude and variablility (given our mapping findings regarding emerging evidence for their importance). The mapping exercise demonstrated that actigraphy studies are viable in inpatient as well as outpatient settings, as such, wider consideration should be given to monitoring inpatient progress using objective measures such as actigraphy, with the option of continuation to post-discharge settings. Of course, longitudinal monitoring that allows early warning signs of relapse or recurrent is also feasible with this ecological measure (Bellivier et al. 2015; Ritter et al. 2011). The above steps would address some of the explicit aims outlined by RDOC publications but could be valuable for clinicians e.g. they might consider using electronic monitoring or including sleep diaries as part of the clinical assessment of BD. The latter could be scrutinized not only to identify mean sleep duration and timing but also variability between weekdays and weekends or large differences in duration of sleep onset/offset/duration over 2–3 weeks.

Whilst consumer grade wearables and smart phone apps are attractive to many, it is important to remember that they all await regulatory approval for use as clinical devices (and commercial developments of longer battery life to avoid repeated need for charging). However, their use alongside actigraphy could be helpful, both to validate different measures of RAR that might be derived from consumer devices but also to facilitate ecological momentary assessment (EMA) research (Merikangas et al. 2019; Depner et al. 2020). Research in this area is ongoing and has the advantage of combining self-report ratings of events, cognition, energy, and mood states with objective RAR data (de Wild-Hartmann et al. 2013; Merikangas et al. 2019). However, these advances necessarily require researchers to work more closely alongside statisticians and computational data scientists as the optimal methods for analyzing and understanding links between RAR, symptoms and behaviours are more sophisticated (including non-linear dynamics, entropy) than the basic approaches that are most commonly used and/or the algorithms that are currently available. Assuming this dialogue can occur, combining these approaches would allow to comprehensive exploration of the course of illness, prediction of treatment response and a range of patient reported outcomes (Moskowitz and Young, 2006; Marino et al. 2013). For clinicians, actigraphy offers access to objective ecological monitoring that provides a far more reliable and valid measure of RAR than can be obtained by self-rating scales (Depner et al. 2020; Mulligan 2016). However, not all clinicians feel confident in extracting data and metrics from the devices and this is likely to mitigate against wider dissemination beyond specialist settings. Another advantage of actigraphy is that it is a more feasible option for routine clinical practice than putative 'omic' and brain scanning markers of treatment response or illness outcome as these are less available, more expensive and often concentrated in research settings (Gooley and Chua 2014). Also, if the focus is on RAR, then actigraphic monitoring would be easier to integrate into a clinical management and monitoring package than evaluation of other objective circadian markers e.g. measurement of dim light melatonin onset (DLMO) (Depner et al. 2020).

Conclusions

Despite 50 years of research, and several papers identified by this evidence map being highly cited, use of actigraphy to assess RAR in longitudinal research and examination of these metrics and treatment response, course and outcome of BD is under-investigated. This is in marked contrast to the extensive literature on case–control or cross-sectional studies of actigraphy, especially typical sleep analysis metrics in BD, which are reported in independent studies, systematic reviews, meta-analyses and meta-regressions. The most obvious reason for this marked disparity in the amount of research undertaken using these different methodologies, is that case–control and cross-sectional studies are easier to undertake, usually involve much briefer time frames, and have lower resource requirements than longitudinal research. Also, it was notable that prospective studies identified in this evidence map were still predominantly shorter-term projects, often reporting outcomes over weeks rather than months.

This evidence map suggests that the existence of several often-quoted publications has probably led to an overestimation of the extent and robustness of existing evidence of longitudinal associations between RAR and treatment response, course, and outcome in BD. However, we are aware of promising emerging findings in this area (McCarthy et al. 2019; Scott et al. 2020) and there is tremendous potential for expanding this field of research to inform precision medicine projects in psychiatry. Further, there is a strong argument that, rather than actigraphy being replaced by consumer grade devices and apps, it may be more fruitful to establish frameworks for clinical and research projects that combine these approaches.

Abbreviations

BD: Bipolar disorders; CVD: Cardiovascular disease; d: Days; DALYs: Disability adjusted life years; DLMO: Dim light melatonin onset; EMA: Ecological momentary assessment; HC: Healthy controls; IS: Inter-daily stability; IV: Intra-daily variability; Li: Lithium; N: Number; NIMH: National Institute of Mental Health; RDOC: Research domain criteria; RAR: Rest activity rhythms; SD: Standard deviation; SE: Sleep efficiency; SOL: Sleep onset latency; TST: Total sleep time; UP: Unipolar; WASO: Wake after sleep onset; wks: Weeks; yrs: Years.

Authors' contributions

All authors identified the key questions and coordinates for the map. Scott collated papers for the evidence map, Etain and Scott created summary tables and charts. Scott, Etain and Colom created the first full draft of the manuscript. All authors read and approved the final manuscript.

Competing interests

The authors report no financial affiliation or other relationship relevant to the subject matter of this article. JS is a Visiting Professor at Diderot University, Paris and an Honorary Professor at Kings College, London. AY declares paid lectures and advisory boards for the following companies with drugs used in affective and related disorders: AstraZeneca, Eli Lilly, Lundbeck, Sunovion, Servier, Livanova, and Janssen. He is a paid consultant to Johnson & Johnson, is lead Investigator for Embolden Study (AstraZeneca), BCI Neuroplasticity study and a pharma sponsored Aripiprazole in Mania study. His institution has received funding for investigator-initiated studies from AstraZeneca, Eli Lilly, Linova, Lundbeck, Wyeth, and Janssen.

Author details

[1] Institute of Neuroscience, Newcastle University, Newcastle upon Tyne, UK. [2] Centre for Affective Disorders, Department of Psychological Medicine, Institute of Psychiatry, Psychology & Neuroscience, King's College London, London, UK. [3] Université Paris Diderot, Sorbonne Paris Cité, UMR-S 1144, 75013 Paris, France. [4] IMIM-Hospital del Mar-CIBERSAM, Barcelona, Catalonia, Spain. [5] Universitat Autònoma de Barcelona Barcelona-Catalonia, Barcelona, Spain. [6] Département de Psychiatrie Et de Médecine Addictologique, AP-HP, GH Saint-Louis – Lariboisière – F. Widal, 75475 Paris, France. [7] Inserm U114475006, Paris, France. [8] South London and Maudsley NHS Foundation Trust, Bethlem Royal Hospital, Kent, UK.

Appendix

See Tables 3 and 4.

Table 3 Parameters reported in studies of Rest–Activity Rhythms: additional details

Cosinor model (parametric)	
Midline estimating statistic of rhythm (MESOR)	Estimates the arithmetic mean of the values throughout the 24-h period
Amplitude	Distance from the rhythmic mean to the peak or trough of a mathematical model
Acrophase	Time interval during which the highest values are expected
Nonparametric approach	
Interdaily stability	Quantifies the degree of resemblance between the activity patterns on individual days; ranges from 0 to 1 and may typically be about 0.6 for healthy adults
Intradaily Variability	Quantifies the fragmentation of periods of rest and activity; ranges from 0 to 2 and typically is < 1 for healthy adults, with higher values indicating a more fragmented rhythm
L5	Average of the activity values for the 5 least active consecutive hours in the 24-h cycle
L5 Onset	Onset time of the five most restful consecutive hours
M10	Average of the activity values for the 10 most active consecutive hours in the 24-h cycle
M10 Onset	Onset time of the 10 most active consecutive hours
Amplitude	Difference between M10 and L5
Relative Amplitude	Calculated by dividing AMP by the sum of L5 and M10; ranges from 0 to 1, with higher values indicating higher amplitude of the rhythm
Sleep quantity analysis (reported as Individual Mean values or Intra-Individual Variability e.g. SD, RMSSD)	
Time in bed (TIB) (Lights Off (LO))	Difference between the get-up time and bedtime (Lights Off: time bedroom lights are turned off is reported in some therapy studies)
Total sleep time (TST)	Duration of the sleep episode, calculated on the actual time of sleep start and sleep end
Sleep latency (SOL)	Difference between time in bed and the actual time the monitored subject starts sleeping
Mean activity (MA)	Number of movements within specified epoch (usually 1 min)
Number of awakenings longer than 5 min (NA > 5)	Number of awakenings longer than 5 min
Wake after sleep onset (WASO)	Wake time (min) after sleep onset
Sleep efficiency (SE %)	Percentage of effective sleep during time in bed
Fragmentation Index (FI %)	% of sleep continuity/discontinuity. It is calculated as the amount of time associated with movement (restlessness) during the sleep period expressed as a percentage
Putative Circadian Phase Measures (derived from Sleep quantity analysis data)	
Sleep Onset	Time is the clock time (HH:MM) of the first epoch scored as sleep in each main rest interval
Sleep Offset	Mean sleep offset time is the clock time (HH:MM) of the last epoch scored as sleep in each main rest interval
Sleep midpoint	Calculated as the midpoint between sleep onset and sleep offset
Sleep Regularity Index (SRI)	This is defined as the percentage probability of a person being asleep (or awake) at any two time points 24 h apart

Cosinor model descriptions from Nelson et al (1979); nonparametric approach descriptions from Van Someren et al (1997). Sleep quantity analysis variables and descriptions as from Natale et al (2009), Krane-Gartiser et al. (2019) and Bei et al (2016)

IS quantifies regularity in activity (overall variability in a time-signal after averaging across days) & IV quantifies fragmentation; some argue that SRI best quantifies how rapidly sleep patterns change between consecutive days

Table 4 Studies of actigraphic recordings of treatment outcome or course of illness in samples that include individuals diagnosed with bipolar disorders (BD)

Study: 1st author, location, year	Sample characteristics			Actigraphy: number of days (d)[a]	Findings and comments
	N (BD)	Total N*, Diagnoses	Mean Age (SD) yrs; % Female		
Kupfer, USA (1974)	4	N = 11; Bipolar Depression (N = 4) & Unipolar Depression (n = 7)	~52 [b]; 80%	3d at baseline & 3d at wk 3	Baseline (pre-treatment) mean levels of day-time motor activity in un-medicated unipolar depression > BD depression, with significant differences between 19:00 & mid-day (but not mid-day until 19:00) BD cases treated with lithium; UP cases treated with amitriptyline Post-treatment activity differences were no longer evident; (response in Unipolar Depression showed the greatest improvement in activity)
Weiss, USA (1974)	6	Mania (N = 3) & Bipolar Agitated Depression (N = 3)	~38 [b]; 66%	7-9d; additional recording at 20 wks	3 manic inpatients were assessed pre-treatment; then all 6 inpatients were assessed before & after initiation of Lithium. Some individuals repeated actigraphy recordings at 5 months Baseline (pre-treatment) levels of motor activity (counts per minute) in un-medicated mania > agitated depressed, with the most significant differences reported between 22:00 and 02:00 h
Heninger, USA (1977)	13	N = 15; BD-I = 11; BD-II = 2; Unipolar Disorder = 2	55[b] 84%	2d pre-lithium & 2d at 2 wks	All participants were inpatients who initiated lithium treatment Duration of sleep increased by > 60 min after starting lithium (~6.3 h to 7.5 h). When data were reviewed for mania and depression separately, individuals with mania showed reduction in motor activity in parallel with symptom reduction, whilst individuals with depression showed increased motor activity with reduction in symptoms
Kripke, USA (1978)	7	BD: across episodes	28% [b]	3d (repeated)	Adults assessed through complete cycles of mania and depression. In 5 individuals there was evidence that a circadian rhythm 'free-ran' fast & in 5 individuals, evidence suggested that lithium slowed a circadian rhythm. The authors concluded that the prophylactic benefit of lithium may derive from slowing or delaying an overfast circadian clock to prevent desynchronization

Table 4 (continued)

Study: 1st author, location, year	Sample characteristics			Actigraphy: number of days (d)[a]	Findings and comments
	N (BD)	Total N*, Diagnoses	Mean Age (SD) yrs; % Female		
Wehr, USA (1980)#	10	Mania & Bipolar Depression	~40[b]	2d	Motor activity levels were significantly different across 24 h and indicated 'phase advance' of 1–3 h in mania or depression (compared with 14 HC) Acrophase for motor activity was significantly earlier in Mania (13:37 h) & Depression (14:10 h) compared to HC (15:57 h) Acrophase did not differ in 8 BD cases that were assessed in both the Manic & Depressive phases of illness
Godfrey, New Zealand (1984)	4	N=9; Unipolar Disorder=5; BD-II, Hypomania=4	77%[b]	Median ~12d	Inpatients wore an actiwatch during the daytime only for 7-27d of the admission. Data were also collected on 9 HC. Daytime activity level was lowest in Depression and highest in HC. During actigraphy, mean daytime activity level increased in Depression & reduced in Hypomania. Change in activity was not correlated with change in depressed mood (no measures reported for hypomania). However, patients continued to show much lower levels of activity compared with HC. (The study abandoned some speech recordings due to low cooperation by some hypomanic patients)
Wolff, USA (1984)#	30	Mania, Bipolar Depression or Euthymia	42±13; 66%	3d	Intra-individual recordings demonstrated that: Mean amount of motor activity in Mania > Depression with the most significant differences being early & later in the daytime Activity levels did not differ significantly in Mania versus Euthymia Total activity (count/24 h) in 18 HC > Euthymic BD

Table 4 (continued)

Study: 1st author, location, year	Sample characteristics			Actigraphy: number of days (d)[a]	Findings and comments
	N (BD)	Total N*, Diagnoses	Mean Age (SD) yrs; % Female		
Joffe, USA (1987)	15	N = 19, BD Depression = 15; Unipolar Disorder = 2; Schizoaffective = 1	43 ± 3; 58%	3d pre- & 3d post-initiation of -carbamazepine	Inpatients were included who began carbamazepine treatment after a placebo washout of > 2 wks; actigraphy was undertaken during washout and ~ 35 days later. 7 individuals (37%) met response criteria. Baseline patterns of motor activity were not significantly different in Responders vs. Non-responders Mean 24 h activity increased over time (& mean depression score decreased), with a trend toward greater change in Responder. When time of day was considered, Responders showed higher activity from 13:00 h onwards, with significantly greater activity during evening & night-time
Klein, USA (1991)	4	BD, in remission	Not reported[b]	3d with lithium; 3d at ~ 3 wks post-lithium withdrawal	Long-term lithium was discontinued, and outpatients were followed for 3 months of placebo treatment and up to 12 months. Two individuals experienced manic relapse with symptoms commencing within 2 wks of discontinuation, 2 remained well. Relapse was characterized by fragmentation of sleep–wake patterns, disorganization of 24 h rest-activity cycles & increased motor activity, especially at night. The latter was accompanied by a marked reduction in SE
Klein, USA (1992)	10	BD, in remission	49 ± 12[b]	3d with lithium; 3d at ~ 3 wks post- lithium withdrawal	As with the previous publication, long-term lithium was discontinued, and outpatients were followed for 3 months of placebo treatment. Seven experienced manic relapse: 4 within 3 weeks and all 7 within 3 months of lithium discontinuation. These individuals had higher baseline levels of motor activity (daytime) even though asymptomatic and showed higher daytime & night-time activity (during follow-up) than individuals who remained well (N = 3)

Table 4 (continued)

Study: 1st author, location, year	Sample characteristics: N (BD)	Sample characteristics: Total N*, Diagnoses	Sample characteristics: Mean Age (SD) yrs; % Female	Actigraphy: number of days (d)[a]	Findings and comments
Raoux, France, (1994)	5	N = 26; Unipolar Depression = 21; BD Depression = 5	44 ± 21; 77%	3d treatment-onset & 3d pre-discharge	Inpatients were assessed at beginning & end of admission for melancholic depression (median stay = 26d). All patients had current or past exposure to benzodiazepines. Diurnal hypoactivity, reduced amplitude & longer TST were found at admission. Overall activity level and amplitude increased by discharge. There was an inverse correlation between baseline activity level & clinical improvement (daytime hypoactivity), with a trend for Responders (N = 21) to a lower baseline activity levels than Non-responders (N = 5). Amplitude was a robust marker of response, but acrophase was difficult to interpret because of large intragroup phase variability (~ 25% showed a phase shift of ~ 1 hr)
Todder (2006) & Baune, Germany (2007)	6	N = 26; Treatment-resistant depression: Unipolar = 21; BD-II = 6	49 ± 13; 58%	2 × 11d with 6d gap	Todder reported 4-week follow-up of patients & 27 HC. Sleep parameters in patients showed significant change in the 1st week of follow-up (increased TST & reduced SOL). Even with depression improvement, many sleep parameters differed from HC Baune reported the 4-week study of antidepressant & quetiapine. At final follow-up, 16 individuals were classified as Responders. Amount of activity had increased significantly at follow-up (& depression score had decreased)
Benedetti, Italy (2007)	39	BD-I Depression	44 ± 10; 54%	7d	Study examined antidepressant effects of sleep deprivation & light therapy; 14 individuals were receiving lithium (36%) Responders (N = 26) & Non-responders (N = 13) did not differ on actigraphy parameters at baseline (although mesor was higher in Responders). Responders showed increase in daytime activity especially in the morning compared with Non-responders. Total sleep was shorter in Responders. Acrophase was advanced in Responders (of ~ 57 min) but delayed by 5 min in Non-responders

Table 4 (continued)

Study: 1st author, location, year	Sample characteristics			Actigraphy: number of days (d)[a]	Findings and comments
	N (BD)	Total N*, Diagnoses	Mean Age (SD) yrs; % Female		
Salvatore, USA (2008)#	36	BD-I: Mania/ Mixed States & Remission	44 ± 10; 81%	3d in episode & 3d in remission	BD-I cases were in and outpatients; 72% were prescribed lithium 36 acutely ill BD-I cases were compared with 32 HC at baseline. Then recordings from the BD-I cases when ill & in remission were compared Manic cases showed phase advance (~ 2 h) compared with HC & lower amplitude (mesor & TST did not differ from HC) Mean daytime activity (counts/minute were higher in HC (67 ± 10) than Mania/Mixed States (59 ± 32; but Mania ~ Remission (60 ± 11) Total sleep was significantly longer in remission (Remission > HC; HC = Mania/Mixed States) Acrophase was significantly earlier in Mania/ Mixed States (14:01 hrs) < Remission (14:26 h) < HC (16:05 h)
Scott, UK (2011)$	10	N = 18 Unipolar Disorder = 8; BD-I = 10	43 ± 12; 60%	30-200d	Naturalistic longitudinal follow-up of individuals attending a lithium clinic who were invited to wear actiwatch for > 1 month (many continued for > 6 months) Lower mean daytime activity (counts/minute) and variability in sleep pattern/duration (alongside psychological measures such as self-esteem) was associated with shorter time to hospital admission during ~ 15-month follow-up (but admissions according to polarity were not reported)

Table 4 (continued)

Study: 1st author, location, year	Sample characteristics			Actigraphy: number of days (d)[a]	Findings and comments
	N (BD)	Total N*, Diagnoses	Mean Age (SD) yrs; % Female		
Kim, (2014) & Hwang (2017) South Korea	29	BD-II = 26; BD Depression	36 ± 10; 55%	56d	Open label trial of lithium v. quetiapine (actual N for each group included in analyses varied slightly between the two publications). Individuals were drug free at baseline Quetiapine group (N = 10–12): SE increased (~6%) & WASO decreased at 6 weeks follow-up & SE improvement maintained at final follow-up (8 weeks) Lithium group (N = 15–17): Modest improvement in SE (~1.5%), other parameters showed some fluctuation without obvious improvement Both quetiapine & lithium affected several circadian parameters, including peak activity time and robustness of circadian rhythm, but exerted different effects on acrophase; clinical depressive symptoms were associated with robustness of circadian rhythm during the 8-week treatment phase
Novak, Czech Republic (2014)	6	BD-I	~37 [b]; 66%	Median ~210d	8 individuals were recruited, 7 agreed to participate and 6 of them provided long-term recordings (5–80 months, but about 30% loss of data). 4 individuals reported no relapses, one reported 3 episodes (over 37 months) & one reported 14 (over 80 months). No manic relapses occurred The best signal for identifying relapse was for IS (inter-daily stability)- a marker of regularity of rest-activity patterns (overall classification ~66%)

Table 4 (continued)

Study: 1st author, location, year	Sample characteristics: N (BD)	Total N*, Diagnoses	Mean Age (SD) yrs; % Female	Actigraphy: number of days (d)[a]	Findings and comments
Kaplan, USA (2015)	75	N = 159, BD-I = 143, BD-II = 13; BD NOS = 3	36 ± 11; 66%	7d	159 individuals with BD spectrum disorders were assessed for hypersomnia & followed-up at 7 months later (222 ± 73d). Baseline actigraphy recordings in 75 individuals identified 2 forms of hypersomnia: 'long sleepers' (although actigraphy showed these individuals spent longer in bed but did not have longer TST) and those with excessive sleepiness (lower daytime activity) During follow-up, 21 individuals (17.5%) had a hypomanic/manic & 37 (30.1%) a major depressive episode. Self-reported 'Excessive daytime sleepiness' predicted relapse into hypomania/mania ($p < 0.01$); actigraphy was not used to directly assess objective markers of relapse
Gershon, USA (2016)	37	BD-I	35 ± 10; 62%	42d	Lower amount of daytime activity & later daily onset of activity were both associated with greater likelihood of onset of a depressive episode &/or increase in depressive symptom severity. Weaker evidence suggested a slightly elevated mid-day peak & less evening activity were also noted
Moon, South Korea (2016)	26	BD-I = 23 Manic = 21; Depressed = 4. (Manic & Depressive Episodes = 1)	30 ± 11; 62%	At admission; 2 wks, 4 wks & recovery	All BD cases were recruited during a hospital admission. Analyses included 26 manic and 5 depressive episodes. Final wake time was delayed by ~ 1 h and SE improved by ~ 4% during admission Advanced phase was recorded in mania but returned to normal after treatment; likewise, delayed phase in depression returned to normal after treatment. These shifts led to BD cases more closely resembling HC (N = 18) Phase advance or delay observed in biochemical rhythms (such as cortisol) were much greater than sleep–wake cycle changes identified by actigraphy

Table 4 (continued)

Study: 1st author, location, year	Sample characteristics			Actigraphy: number of days (d)[a]	Findings and comments
	N (BD)	Total N*, Diagnoses	Mean Age (SD) yrs; % Female		
Bewernick, Germany (2017)	2	N = 16; Unipolar Depression = 14; BD Depression = 2	49 ± 9; 66%	7d	12 individuals (10 inpatients) completed the study. Actigraphy was not undertaken during sleep. Individuals with higher activity levels at baseline showed a larger reduction in symptoms of depression after one week. Change in severity of depression correlated with increased in amount of daytime activity (with significance for some but not all ratings). Activity also showed a lagged correlation with mood rating in the following hours (but not vice versa)
Duncan, USA (2017)	21	N = 51; Bipolar Depression = 21; Unipolar Depression = 30	~42; 59%	9d: (4-days pre- & 5 days post-ketamine	Data from 51 trial participants receiving ketamine (21 responders; 30 non-responders) were compared with data from 38 who received placebo Pre-ketamine infusion: evidence of phase advanced activity pattern (acrophase) & lower mesor (144 vs. 167) was associated with good response. Persistent response (day 1 & 3 post-infusion) was characterized by higher amplitude & increased mesor
Krane-Gartiser, Norway (2018)	3	Series of BD-I cases with > = 2 admissions (over 1–6 months)	~50[b]	1d per admission	Intra-individual 24-h activity patterns for recurrences of the same polarity show similar patterns; but episodes with different polarity show intra-individual differences in activity patterns. Acute phases were characterized by greater variation between rest-activity and periods with distinct irregularity in activity (measured by sample entropy) in all cases
Averill, New Zealand (2018)	2	N = 24; 22 Unipolar Depression; 2 BD Depression	38 ± 14; 37%	17d	Inpatients were recruited to a study of activity, psychomotor speed & treatment response; usable actigraphy data available from 16 individuals (2 receiving lithium) Change in 24-h activity count was correlated with treatment response Data from consumer grade activity monitor did not correlate with outcomes

Table 4 (continued)

Study: 1st author, location, year	Sample characteristics			Actigraphy: number of days (d)[a]	Findings and comments
	N (BD)	Total N*, Diagnoses	Mean Age (SD) yrs; % Female		
Kaplan, USA (2018)	40	Inter-episode BD I (with insomnia)	39 ± 14; 70%	14d (7d pre- & 7d post-intervention)	58 patients were randomized to a two-arm trial; 40 participated in a one session intervention experiment actigraphy data were available on 29 A behavioural intervention (Rise-Up: aimed at overcoming sleep inertia) was compared with a control condition (education: PE) Individuals in the Rise-Up group were significantly more active in the 1st hour upon waking compared to PE
Henriksen, Norway (2020)	20	BD-I, Mania	45 ± 13; 70%	2d (baseline & day 5)	The trail recruited 32 individuals: this study reports data for 20; 10 inpatients were allocated to the blue blocking glasses (BBG) & 10 to placebo glasses 60% of all cases were receiving lithium At day 5: SE improved more in the BBG compared with the control group (4% v 0%). The BBG group showed lower activity count during the sleep period (L5) & lower WASO & a trend for lower FI
Knapen, Netherlands (2020)	14	BD-I	45 ± 12; 79%	~ 180d	Continuous monitoring of temporal relationship between sleep, daily rhythm (measured by actigraphy) and mood changes. Time-lagged association showed significant negative correlation between depression and fractal patterns of motor activity (a measure of rigidity or adaptability of physiological systems) with higher level of depression associated with greater rigidity (with 5–7-day delay)

%, Mean and SD: percentages, means and standard deviations are reported to the nearest whole number; *BD* Bipolar Disorder, *BD-I/II/NOS* Bipolar I/II Disorder, *BD* Not Otherwise Specified, *d* day, *h* hours, *HC* Healthy Controls, *N* number, *NA* not available, *SD* Standard Deviation, *SE* Sleep Efficiency, *SOL* Sleep Onset Latency, *TST* Total Sleep Time, *yrs* years. *Total N is reported only if sample contains cases with other diagnoses (as well as BD); [a] Estimated for some studies that did not specify exact time frames; [b]This either indicates that data were reported as medians and/or data were missing for some variables; [#]The same sample of BD cases was studied in different mental states; [$]

Analysis reported by Scott (2011) is described in Scott et al. (2017)

References

Ancoli-Israel S, Cole R, Alessi C, Chambers M, Moorcroft W, Pollak CP. The role of actigraphy in the study of sleep and circadian rhythms. Sleep. 2003;26(3):342–92.

Arksey H. Scoping the field: services for carers of people with mental health problems. Health Soc Care Community. 2003;11(4):335–44.

Averill I, Beaglehole B, Douglas K, Crowe M, Inder M, Lacey L, et al. Activation therapy for the treatment of inpatients with depression - protocol for a randomised control trial compared to treatment as usual. BMC Psychiatry. 2019;19(1):52.

Baron K. Feeling validated yet? A scoping review of the use of consumer-targeted wearable and mobile technology to measure and improve sleep. Sleep Med Rev. 2018;40:151–9.

Baune BT, Caliskan S, Todder D. Effects of adjunctive antidepressant therapy with quetiapine on clinical outcome, quality of sleep and daytime motor activity in patients with treatment-resistant depression. Hum Psychopharmacol. 2007;22(1):1–9.

Bei B, Wiley JF, Trinder J, Manber R. Beyond the mean: a systematic review on the correlates of daily intraindividual variability of sleep/wake patterns. Sleep Med Rev. 2016;2(8):108–24.

Bellivier F, Geoffroy P, Etain B, Scott J. Sleep-and circadian rhythm–associated pathways as therapeutic targets in bipolar disorder. Expert Opin Ther Targets. 2015;19:747–63.

Benedetti F, Dallaspezia S, Fulgosi MC, Barbini B, Colombo C, Smeraldi E. Phase advance is an actimetric correlate of antidepressant response to sleep deprivation and light therapy in bipolar depression. Chronobiol Int. 2007;24(5):921–37.

Bewernick BH, Urbach AS, Bröder A, Kayser S, Schlaepfer TE. Walking away from depression-motor activity increases ratings of mood and incentive drive in patients with major depression. Psychiatry Res. 2017;247:68–72.

Brietzke E, Hawken ER, Idzikowski M, Pong J, Kennedy SH, Soares CN. Integrating digital phenotyping in clinical characterization of individuals with mood disorders. Neurosci Biobehav Rev. 2019;104:223–30.

Calogiuri G, Weydahl A, Carandente F. Methodological issues for studying the rest-activity cycle and sleep disturbances: a chronobiological approach using actigraphy data. Biol Res Nurs. 2013;15(1):5–12.

Colquhoun H, Levac D, O'Brien K, Straus S, Tricco A, Perrier L, et al. Scoping reviews: time for clarity in definition, methods, and reporting. J Clin Epidemiol. 2014;67(12):1291–4.

Cuthbert BN. Translating intermediate phenotypes to psychopathology: the NIMH Research Domain Criteria. Psychophysiology. 2014;51(12):1205–6.

Cuthbert B, Insel T. Toward the future of psychiatric diagnosis: the seven pillars of RDoC. BMC Medicine. 2013;11:126.

De Crescenzo F, Economou A, Sharpley A, Gormez A, Quested D. Actigraphic features of bipolar disorder: a systematic review and meta-analysis. Sleep Med Rev. 2017;33:58–69.

Depner C, Cheng P, Devine J, Khosla S, de Zambotti M, Robillard R, Vakulin A, Drummond S. Wearable technologies for developing sleep and circadian biomarkers: a summary of workshop discussions. Sleep. 2020;43(2):254.

de Wild-Hartmann J, Wichers M, van Bemmel A, Derom C, Thiery E, Jacobs N, van Os J, Simons C. Day-to-day associations between subjective sleep and affect in regard to future depression in a female population-based sample. Br J Psychiatry. 2013;202:407–12.

Duncan W, Slonena E, Hejazi N, Brutsche N, Yu K, Park L, et al. Motor-activity markers of circadian timekeeping are related to ketamine's rapid antidepressant properties. Biol Psychiat. 2017;82(5):361–9.

Faurholt-Jepsen M, Brage S, Vinberg M, Christensen EM, Knorr U, Jensen HM, Kessing LV. Differences in psychomotor activity in patients suffering from unipolar and bipolar affective disorder in the remitted or mild/moderate depressive state. J Affect Disord. 2012;141(2–3):457–63.

Fernandez J, Hermida R. Inferential statistical method for analysis of non-sinusoidal hybrid time series with unequidistant observations. Chronobiol Int. 1998;15:191–204.

Food and Drug Administration (FDA). 2019. Digital Health Software Precertification (Pre-Cert) Program. https://www.fda.gov/medical-devices/digital-health/digital-health-software-precertification-pre-cert-program). Accessed 20 May 2020.

Frey B, Andreazza AC, Houenou J, Jamain S, Goldstein B, Frye M, et al. Biomarkers in bipolar disorder: a positional paper from the International Society for Bipolar Disorders Biomarkers Task Force. Aust N Z J Psychiatry. Apr ;47(4):321–32.

GBD 2017 Disease and Injury Incidence and Prevalence Collaborators.Global, regional, and national incidence, prevalence, and years lived with disability for 354 diseases and injuries for 195 countries and territories, 1990–2017: a systematic analysis for the Global Burden of Disease Study 2017. The Lancet. 8 Nov 2018; 392:1789–858.

Geoffroy P, Scott J, Boudebesse C, Lajnef M, Henry C, Leboyer M, Bellivier F, Etain B. Sleep in patients with remitted bipolar disorders: a meta-analysis of actigraphy studies. Acta Psychiatr Scand. 2015;131(2):89–99.

Gershon A, Ram N, Johnson SL, Harvey AG, Zeitzer JM. Daily actigraphy profiles distinguish depressive and inter-episode states in bipolar disorder. Clin Psychol Sci. 2016;4(4):641–50.

Godfrey H, Knight R. The validity of actometer and speech activity measures in the assessment of depressed patients. Br J Psychiatry. 1984;145(2):159–63.

Gooley J, Chua E. Diurnal regulation of lipid metabolism and applications of circadian lipidomics. J Genet Genomics. 2014;41:231–50.

Hellwig S, Domschke K. Update on PET imaging biomarkers in the diagnosis of neuropsychiatric disorders. Curr Opin Neurol. 2019;32(4):539–47.

Heninger GR, Kirstein L. Effects of lithium carbonate on motor activity in mania and depression. J Nerv Ment Dis. 1977;164(3):168–75.

Henriksen T, Gronli J, Assmus J, Fasmer O, Schoeyen H, Leskauskaite I, et al. Blue-blocking glasses as additive treatment for mania: effects on actigraphy-derived sleep parameters. J Sleep Res. 2020;2020:e12984.

Hetrick S, Parker A, Callahan P, Purcell R. Evidence mapping: illustrating an emerging methodology to improve evidence-based practice in youth mental health. J Eval Clin Pract. 2010;16:1025–30.

Hwang JY, Choi JW, Kang SG, Hwang SH, Kim SJ, Lee YJ. Comparison of the effects of Quetiapine XR and lithium monotherapy on actigraphy-measured circadian parameters in patients with bipolar ii depression. J Clin Psychopharmacol. 2017;37(3):351–4.

Insel T. The NIMH Research Domain Criteria (RDoC) Project: precision medicine for psychiatry. Am J Psychiatry. 2014;171:395–7.

Joffe RT, Uhde TW, Post RM, Minichiello MD. Motor activity in depressed patients treated with carbamazepine. Biol Psychiatry. 1987;22(8):941–6.

Kaplan KA, McGlinchey EL, Soehner A, Gershon A, Talbot LS, Eidelman P, Gruber J, Harvey AG. Hypersomnia subtypes, sleep, and relapse in bipolar disorder. Psychol Med. 2015;45(8):1751–63.

Kaplan KA, Talavera DC, Harvey AG. Rise and shine: A treatment experiment testing a morning routine to decrease subjective sleep inertia in insomnia and bipolar disorder. Behav Res Ther. 2018;111:106–12.

Katz DL, Williams A, Girard C, Goodman J, Comerford B, Behrman A, Bracken M. The evidence base for complementary and alternative medicine: methods of evidence mapping with application to CAM. Altern Ther Health Med. 2003;9(4):22–30.

Kim SJ, Lee YJ, Lee YJ, Cho SJ. Effect of quetiapine XR on depressive symptoms and sleep quality compared with lithium in patients with bipolar depression. J Affect Disord. 2014;157:33–40.

Klein E, Lavie P, Meiraz R, Sadeh A, Lenox RH. Increased motor activity and recurrent manic episodes: predictors of rapid relapse in remitted bipolar disorder patients after lithium discontinuation. Biol Psychiatry. 1992;31(3):279–84.

Klein E, Mairaz R, Pascal M, Hefez A, Lavie P. Discontinuation of lithium treatment in remitted bipolar patients: relationship between clinical outcome and changes in sleep-wake cycles. J Nerv Ment Dis. 1991;179(8):499–501.

Knapen S, Li P, Riemersma-van der Lek R, Verkooijen S, Boks M, Schoevers R, Scheer F, Hu K. Fractal biomarker of activity in patients with bipolar disorder. Psychol Med. 2020: 1, 1–8.

Krane-Gartiser K, Scott J, Nevoret C, Benard V, Benizri C, Brochard H, et al. Which actigraphic variables optimally characterize the sleep-wake cycle of individuals with bipolar disorders? Acta Psychiatr Scand. 2019;139(3):269–79.

Kripke DF, Mullaney DJ, Atkinson M, Wolf S. Circadian rhythm disorders in manic-depressives. Biol Psychiat. 1978;13(3):335–51.

Kripke DF, Judd LL, Hubbard B, Janowsky DS, Huey LY. The effect of lithium carbonate on the circadian rhythm of sleep in normal human subjects. Biol Psychiatry. 1979;14(3):545–8.

Kupfer D, Weiss B, Foster G, Detre T, McPartland R. Psychomotor activity in affective states. Arch Gen Psychiatry. 1974;30(6):765–8.
MacDonald K, Krishnan A, Cervenka E, Hu G, Guadagno E, Trakadis Y. Biomarkers for major depressive and bipolar disorders using metabolomics: a systematic review. Am J Med Genet B Neuropsychiatr Genet. 2019;180(2):122–37.
Marino M, Li Y, Rueschman M. Measuring sleep: accuracy, sensitivity, and specificity of wrist actigraphy compared to polysomnography. Sleep. 2013;36:1747–55.
McCarthy M, Wei H, Nievergelt C, Stautland A, Maihofer A, Welsh DK. Chronotype and cellular circadian rhythms predict the clinical response to lithium maintenance treatment in patients with bipolar disorder. Neuropsychopharmacology. 2019;44:620–8.
Merikangas KR, Swendsen J, Hickie IB, Cui L, Shou H, Merikangas A, et al. Real-time mobile monitoring of the dynamic associations among motor activity, energy, mood, and sleep in adults with bipolar disorder. JAMA Psychiatry. 2019;76(2):190–8.
Miake-Lye I, Hempel S, Shanman R. What is an evidence map? A systematic review of published evidence maps and their definitions, methods, and products. Syst Rev. 2016;5:28.
Moar J. Where Now for Wearables. 2018; https://www.juniperresearch.com/document-library/white-papers/where-now-for-wearables. Accessed 20 May 2020.
Moon J, Cho C, Son G, Geum D, Chung S, Kim H, et al. Advanced circadian phase in mania and delayed circadian phase in mixed mania and depression returned to normal after treatment of bipolar disorder. EBioMedicine. 2016;11:285–95.
Moskowitz D, Young S. Ecological momentary assessment: what it is and why it is a method of the future in clinical psychopharmacology. J Psychiatry Neurosci. 2006;31(1):13–20.
Mullington J. Developing biomarker arrays predicting sleep and circadian-coupled risks to health. Sleep. 2016;39(4):727–36.
Natale V, Plazzi G, Martoni M. Actigraphy in the assessment of insomnia: a quantitative approach. Sleep. 2009;32:767–71.
Nelson W, Tong Y, Lee J, Halberg F. Methods for cosinor rhythmometry. Chronobiologia. 1979;6:305–23.
Novak D, Albert F, Spaniel F. Analysis of actigraph parameters for relapse prediction in bipolar disorder: a feasibility study. Conf Proc IEEE Eng Med Biol Soc. 2014;2014:4972–5.
Ng T, Chung K, Ho F, Yeung W, Yung K, Lam T. Sleep-wake disturbance in interepisode bipolar disorder and high-risk individuals: a systematic review and meta-analysis. Sleep Med Rev. 2015;20:46–58.
Raoux N, Benoit O, Dantchev N. Circadian pattern of motor activity in major depressed patients undergoing antidepressant therapy: Relationship between actigraphic measures and clinical course. Psychiatry Res. 1994;52:85–98.
Ritter PS, Marx C, Bauer M, Leopold K, Pfennig A. The role of disturbed sleep in the early recognition of bipolar disorder: a systematic review. Bipolar Disord. 2011;13(4):437.
Sack R, Auckley D, Auger R, Carskadon M, Wright K, Vitiello M, Zhdanov I. Circadian rhythm sleep disorders: Part II, advanced sleep phase disorder, delayed sleep phase disorder, free-running disorder, and irregular sleep-wake rhythm. An American Academy of Sleep Medicine review. Sleep. 2007;30:1484–501.
Salvatore P, Ghidini S, Zita G, De Panfilis C, Lambertino S, Maggini C, Baldessarini R. Circadian activity rhythm abnormalities in ill and recovered bipolar I disorder patients. Bipolar Disord. 2008;10:256–65.
Schumann G, Binder E, Holte A, de Kloet E, Oedegaard K, Robbins T, et al. Stratified medicine for mental disorders. Eur Neuropsychopharmacol. 2014;24(1):5–50.
Scott J. Clinical parameters of circadian rhythms in affective disorders. Eur Neuropsychopharmacol. 2011;21(suppl 4):S671–5.
Scott J, Etain B, Bellivier F. Can an integrated science approach to precision medicine research improve lithium treatment in bipolar disorders? Front Psychiatry. 2018;9:360.
Scott J, Hidalgo-Mazzei D, Strawbridge R, Young A, Resche-Rigon M, Etain B, et al. Prospective cohort study of early biosignatures of response to lithium in bipolar-I-disorders: overview of the H2020-funded R-LiNK initiative. Int J Bipolar Disord. 2019;7(1):20.
Scott J, Murray G, Henry C, Morken G, Scott E, Angst J, Merikangas KR, Hickie IB. Activation in bipolar disorders: a systematic review. JAMA Psychiatry. 2017;74(2):189–96.
Scott J, Hennion V, Meyrel M, Bellivier F, Etain B. (2020) An ecological study of objective rest-activity markers of lithium response in bipolar I disorder. Paper submitted.
Smagula SF. Opportunities for clinical applications of rest-activity rhythms in detecting and preventing mood disorders. Curr Opin Psychiatry. 2016;29(6):389–96.
Todder D, Caliskan S, Baune B. Night locomotor activity and quality of sleep in quetiapine-treated patients with depression. J Clin Psychopharmacol. 2006;26(6):638–42.
Vallarino M, Henry C, Etain B, Gehue L, MacNeill C, Scott E, et al. An evidence map of psychosocial interventions for the earliest stages of bipolar disorder. Lancet Psychiatry. 2015;2(6):548–63.
van Someren E, Kessler A, Mirmiran M, Swaab D. Indirect bright light improves circadian rest-activity rhythm disturbances in demented patients. Biol Psychiat. 1997;41:955–63.
Walker W, Walton J, DeVries A, Nelson R. Circadian rhythm disruption and mental health. Transl Psychiatry. 2020;10(1):28.
Wirz-Justice A. How to measure circadian rhythms in humans. Medicographia. 2007;29:84–90.
Wehr T, Muscettola G, Goodwin F. Urinary 3-methoxy-4-hydroxyphenylglycol circadian rhythm. Early timing (phase-advance) in manic-depressives compared with normal subjects. Arch Gen Psychiatry. 1980 Mar;37(3):257–63.
Weiss B, Foster F, Reynolds C, Kupfer D. Psychomotor activity in mania. Arch Gen Psychiatry. 1974;31(3):379–83.
Whiteford HA, Degenhardt L, Rehm J, Baxter AJ, Ferrari AJ, Erskine HE, et al. Global burden of disease attributable to mental and substance use disorders: findings from the Global Burden of Disease Study 2010. Lancet. 2013;382:1575–86.
Wolff E, Putnam F, Post R. Motor activity and affective illness. The relationship of amplitude and temporal distribution to changes in affective state. Arch Gen Psychiatry. 1985;42(3):288–94.
Zee P, Badr M, Kushida C, Mullington J, Pack A, Parthasarathy S, et al. Strategic opportunities in sleep and circadian research: report of the Joint Task Force of the Sleep Research Society and American Academy of Sleep Medicine. Sleep. 2014;37(2):219–27.

19

Respiratory infections during lithium and valproate medication: a within-individual prospective study of 50,000 patients with bipolar disorder

Mikael Landén[1,2*], Henrik Larsson[2,3], Paul Lichtenstein[2], Johan Westin[4] and Jie Song[2]

Abstract

Background: In vitro studies have demonstrated that lithium has antiviral properties, but evidence from human studies is scarce. Lithium is used as a mood stabilizer to treat patients with bipolar disorder. Here, the aim was to investigate the association between lithium use and the risk of respiratory infections in patients with bipolar disorder. To rule out the possibility that a potential association could be due to lithium's effect on psychiatric symptoms, we also studied the effect of valproate, which is an alternative to lithium used to prevent mood episodes in bipolar disorder.

Method: We followed 51,509 individuals diagnosed with bipolar disorder in the Swedish Patient register 2005–2013. We applied a within-individual design using stratified Cox regression to estimate the hazard ratios (HRs) of respiratory infections during treated periods compared with untreated periods.

Results: During follow-up, 5,760 respiratory infections were documented in the Swedish Patient Register. The incidence rate was 28% lower during lithium treatment (HR 0.73, 95% CI 0.61–0.86) and 35% higher during valproate treatment (HR 1.35, 95% CI 1.06–1.73) compared with periods off treatment.

Conclusions: This study provides real-world evidence that lithium is associated with decreased risk for respiratory infections and suggests that the repurposing potential of lithium for potential antiviral or antibacterial effects is worthy of investigation.

Keywords: Respiratory tract infections, Lithium, Drug repositioning, Viruses, Therapeutic use, Coronavirus

Introduction

The outbreak of the coronavirus SARS-CoV-2, the cause of COVID-19 (Corona virus Disease-2019) respiratory disease, has prompted a search for approved drugs with antiviral properties that might be repurposed to treat covid-19, or shed light on biological mechanisms that might be targeted for antiviral purposes.

Lithium has been suggested to have antiviral properties since the 1970-1980s (Rybakowski 2000; van den Ameele et al. 2016; Murru et al. 2020). In vitro studies have shown that lithium inhibit replication of several viruses (Skinner et al. 1980; Ren et al. 2011; Chen et al. 2016; Zhao et al. 2017; Qian et al. 2018). Interestingly, in vitro studies have also shown lithium to effectively suppress infection with Porcine deltacoronavirus (Zhai et al. 2019) and other viruses that belong to the Coronaviridae family (Murru et al. 2020), albeit usually in concentrations that would be toxic in humans (Nowak and Walkowiak 2020).

As pointed out in a recent review (Murru et al. 2020), however, there is scarce evidence to support that lithium therapy affects the risk of infections or infection severity

*Correspondence: mikael.landen@gu.se
[1] Section of Psychiatry, Institute of Neuroscience and Physiology, The Sahlgrenska Academy at University of Gothenburg, Blå Stråket 15, 413 45 Gothenburg, Sweden
Full list of author information is available at the end of the article

in humans. Small studies in the 1990s suggested reduced rates of herpes virus infections with lithium (Amsterdam et al. 1990a, b; Amsterdam et al. 1990a, b; Amsterdam et al. 1996). A retrospective review of 236 patients with affective disorders found that lithium treated patients showed a small reduction of flu-like illness during lithium therapy (Amsterdam et al. 1998).

Lithium is the mainstay prophylactic treatment of bipolar disorder (Joas et al. 2017). Here, we leveraged a Swedish cohort of more than 50,000 patients with bipolar disorder followed over eight years to investigate if lithium treatment is associated with risk of respiratory infections. We employed a within-individual design to circumvent the problem of confounding by indication. With each person serving as his or her own matched control, the within-individual design controls for fixed confounders (e.g., baseline severity of the illness, genetic predisposition, childhood environment) (Lichtenstein et al. 2012). To rule out the possibility that a potential association between lithium and respiratory infection rate is secondary to the effect on psychiatric symptoms, we also calculated the association between valproate medication and respiratory infections. Valproate is a commonly used alternative to lithium to prevent mood episodes in bipolar disorder (Cipriani et al. 2013), recommended by the National Institute for Health and Care Excellence (NICE) when lithium is not suitable (Kendall et al. 2014).

Methods

Subjects

We linked several longitudinal Swedish population-based registers through unique personal identification numbers (Ludvigsson et al. 2009): the Total Population Register, the Migration Register, the Cause of Death Register, the Patient Register (captures information on inpatient care since 1973 and outpatient visits to specialists care since 2001), and the Prescribed Drug Register (Wettermark et al. 2007). We identified 51,509 individuals with bipolar disorder followed from 1 October 2005, or age 15, or date of bipolar disorder diagnosis (if later than 1 October 2005) until emigration, death, or 31 December 2013, whichever occurred first. This date was chosen because the register linkage was conducted during 2015 with access to data up to December 2013. This study was approved by the Ethics Committee at Karolinska Institutet.

Bipolar disorder cases

To identify cases with bipolar disorder in the Patient Register, we applied a validated algorithm (Sellgren et al. 2011) that has been used in several previous Swedish register-based studies on bipolar disorder (Viktorin et al. 2014, 2017; Song et al. 2017). This algorithm includes bipolar I disorder, bipolar II disorder, bipolar disorder not otherwise specified, or schizoaffective disorder bipolar type.

Medications

The main exposure was defined as dispensed prescriptions of lithium sulphate (Anatomical Therapeutic Chemical classification code: N05AN01) or sodium valproate/valproic acid (N03AG01) as documented in the prescribed drug register. In Sweden, long-term prescribed medications are dispensed for three-month periods. Similar to previous studies (Song et al. 2017), we therefore defined a medication period as a sequence of at least two prescriptions, with no more than three months (92 days) between any two consecutive prescriptions. Thus, for both lithium and valproate, individuals were defined as on medication during the time interval between two dispensed prescriptions, unless the dispensed prescriptions occurred more than three months apart. To determine whether an individual was on/off medication initially, the start of follow-up was set to 1 October 2005 because the prescribed drug register started 1 July 2005.

Outcomes

In Sweden, uncomplicated respiratory infections are commonly treated in primary health care and therefore not recorded in the Patient register. Viral infections complicated by bacterial superinfection may, however, warrant specialist care or warrant hospital in-patient treatment. Hence, patients with a viral respiratory infection are likely to be diagnosed with bacterial pneumonia. A systematic review and meta-analysis of 27 studies, including a total of 3,215 patients, found that bacterial coinfection was very common (up to 65%) among patients hospitalized for influenza (Klein et al. 2016). The authors conclude that bacterial coinfection should always be suspected in all patients with influenza. We therefore defined outcome as being diagnosed with either viral or bacterial respiratory infections. Specifically, the outcomes were defined as influenza or other viral pneumonia (ICD-10 codes: J09, J10, J11.0, J11.1, J12), bacterial pneumonia (ICD-10 codes: J13, J14, J15, J16), pneumonia in other diseases (ICD-10 code: J17.1), pneumonia due to unspecified organisms (ICD-10 code: J18), acute bronchitis (ICD-10 code: J20), acute bronchiolitis (ICD-10 code: J21), and unspecified acute lower respiratory infection (ICD-10 code: J22). In an additional posthoc analysis, we limited outcomes to respiratory infection diagnoses specifically caused by viruses (ICD-10 codes: J09, J10, J11.0, J11.1, J12, J17.1, J20.3-7, and J21.0-1). Dates and diagnoses were retrieved from the National Patient Register that covers in-patient care and doctor visits from private and public caregivers, with the exception of primary care which is not covered.

Statistical analyses

We performed within-individual analyses using stratified Cox regression. By comparing treated and untreated periods within the same individual, this approach automatically controls for all time-stationary confounders and thus reduces the likelihood of confounding by indication. More details about this method are given in a review (Allison 2009).

We split the follow-up time into consecutive periods. A new period started after a medication switch (i.e., from off medication to on medication or vice versa, for either lithium or valproate) or a respiratory infection diagnosis. For the latter, we restarted the following period at baseline (i.e., to set the underlying time scale as the time since last diagnosis). Lithium and valproate treatment status were defined as time-varying dichotomous exposures. Age band (15–51, 51–64, 64–75, 75–100 years, grouped by the quartiles of the baseline age distribution among those who had an event during the follow-up) was adjusted for as a time-varying categorical covariate. We estimated the hazard ratios (HRs) and 95% confidence intervals (CIs) for respiratory infections during periods with treatment as compared with periods off treatment. This method have previously been described in detail (Lichtenstein et al. 2012; Chang et al. 2014; Chen et al. 2014; Molero et al. 2015).

All analyses were performed with Stata 16.0 (StataCorp. 2013).

Results

Among the 51,509 patients with bipolar disorder, a total of 5760 respiratory infections were diagnosed in 3,389 individuals (6.6%) during 217,214 person-years of follow-up (Table 1). Lithium treatment was more prevalent (41.0%) than valproate treatment (15.9%). About 50% patients were not exposed to lithium or valproate during the study period. Additional file 1: Table S1 outlines the characteristics of patients treated with lithium, valproate, or both during the study period.

After excluding individuals without respiratory infections and varying covariates (i.e., treatment status and age band) during follow-up, 3285 individuals were eligible for the within-individual analysis. These patients experienced a total of 5656 respiratory infections.

The rate of respiratory infection diagnoses was 27% lower during periods on lithium treatment compared with periods off lithium (HR 0.73, 95% CI 0.61–0.86). By contrast, the rate of respiratory infections was higher during periods with valproate treatment (HR 1.35, 95% CI 1.06–1.73).

When we in a post hoc analysis limited the diagnoses to viral respiratory infections, the number of events dropped by 97% to 199. In this analysis, neither lithium (HR 1.07, 95% CI 0.35–3.22) nor valproate (HR 0.96, 95%

Table 1 Characteristics at baseline and during follow-up for patients with bipolar disorder with different medication status in Sweden 2005–2013

	Lithium[a]	Valproate[a]	Never treated with lithium/valproate	Total	Eligible for within-individual analysis[c]
Number of individuals (%)	21,126 (41.0)	8410 (15.9)	25,758 (49.7)	51,509	3285 (6.4)
Sex (% male)	8469 (40.1)	3609 (42.9)	9001 (34.9)	19,475 (37.8)	1307 (39.8)
Characteristics at baseline					
Age distribution (N of individuals, %)[b]					
15–51	11,355 (53.7)	5115 (60.8)	16,263 (63.1)	30,808 (59.8)	864 (26.3)
51–64	5513 (26.1)	1998 (23.8)	4986 (19.4)	11,494 (22.3)	899 (27.4)
64–75	2652 (12.6)	887 (10.5)	2498 (9.7)	5496 (10.7)	798 (24.3)
75–100	1606 (7.6)	410 (4.9)	2011 (7.8)	3711 (7.2)	724 (22.0)
Respiratory infection (N of individuals, %)					
At least one respiratory infection event during follow-up	1532 (7.3)	722 (8.6)	1463 (5.7)	3389 (6.6)	3285 (100)
Proportion of time exposed to lithium or valproate medications	41.3	42.3	–	22.4	28.6

[a] 3785 individuals were ever treated with both lithium and valproate (defined as at least 3 months treatment)

[b] Age band was categorized according to the quartiles of age distribution of individuals who ever have any respiratory infection at any time during follow-up

[c] Includes individuals who ever had a respiratory infection during the follow-up; individuals without any of the outcome diagnoses during follow-up do not provide information

CI 0.24–4.37) was significantly associated with the risk of viral respiratory infections.

Discussion

In a large sample of patients with bipolar disorder, we found that rates of respiratory infection diagnosed at hospitals or specialist outpatient care were significantly lower while on lithium medication than during periods off lithium. By contrast, the rate of respiratory infections was increased during medication with the alternative mood stabilizer valproate. Given that we used a within-individual design—and that lithium and valproate both effectively prevent mood episodes in bipolar disorder—the difference is likely to be caused by effects of the medication used.

Overall, the proportion of respiratory infections was higher in patients treated with lithium (7.3%) and valproate (8.6%) than in patients who were treated with any of these drugs (5.7%). However, this difference is likely to be confounded by indication, which is why a between group comparison does not provide information on whether lithium or valproate influence the risk of respiratory infections. For example, cases treated with lithium or valproate are more likely to have a more severe psychiatric disorder, to smoke, or have other unknown risk factors than cases never treated with any of these drugs. Moreover, cases that had used lithium or valproate were older and were more likely to be male than those who had never used lithium or valproate. The within-individual model that we used compares the risk of respiratory infections during periods with lithium (or valproate) medication with the risk during periods without lithium (or valproate) medication *within each individual.* The model thereby corrects for potential group differences such as sex, genetical make up, severity of the psychiatric disorder et cetera.

Bacterial coinfections or superinfections is a common complication of viral respiratory infections, especially in hospitalized patients (Klein et al. 2016). In the present study, it was not possible to distinguish between viral and bacterial respiratory infections because the results are compatible with effects on both viral and bacterial infections. The observed association of lithium treatment and low risk of respiratory infections therefore needs to be addressed in further investigations using broad diagnostic panels for viral as well as bacterial pathogens. The previously reported antiviral properties of lithium might, however, explain our results since an antiviral mechanism may also protect against bacterial complications.

Limited testing for viral pathogens in clinical routine care may explain the dramatic decrease of number of events (97%) when we limited the analysis to viral respiratory only infections in a post hoc analysis. This drop in sample size radically impaired statistical power and the post hoc analysis did not yield any significant results.

Although the antiviral effect of lithium remains speculative in vivo, our findings are in line with a small previous study (N = 236) that found a reduction of flu-like illness during lithium therapy.(Amsterdam et al. 1998) Although lithium is believed to act across several biological pathways and the exact mechanism of actions remains obscure (Alda 2015), it is known to inhibit glycogen synthase kinase 3β (GSK3β) (Malhi and Outhred 2016). GSK3β has been suggested to be involved in inducing apoptosis and release of viral particles in dengue virus-2 infection (Cuartas-Lopez and Gallego-Gomez 2020), and GSK3β suppression is hence one potential mechanism underlying the antiviral effect of lithium (Sarhan et al. 2017). Lithium has also been found to induce leucocytosis (Carmen et al. 1993; Petrini and Azzara 2012), and attenuate anti-inflammatory effects during chronic use (reviewed by (van den Ameele et al. 2016)). Further, lithium may stimulate immunoglobulin production in B-lymphocytes, increase T-lymphocyte proliferation, and affect proinflammatory cytokine production (reviewed by (Maddu and Raghavendra 2015) and (van den Ameele et al. 2016)).

Valproate treatment, by contrast, *increased* the risk of respiratory infections. It is well known that valproate can cause reversible bone marrow suppression leading to leukopenia and neutropenia (Acharya and Bussel 2000). However, a meta-analysis of infectious diseases reported as adverse events during the double-blind phase of placebo-controlled randomized clinical studies failed to show a significant effect of valproate (Zaccara et al. 2017). It should be noted, however, that groups treated with lithium or valproate are likely to differ in several respects (Additional file 1: Table S1). Lithium is the recommended first treatment option in Sweden, why the group treated with valproate is likely to be less responsive to treatment and might also be a more severely ill group.

This is by far the largest study testing the hypothesis that lithium protects against respiratory infections. The within-individual design controls for time-invariant covariates that might confound the results, but the method is susceptible to confounding by factors associated with the exposure that change during the observation period. For example, periods on a mood stabilizer might be associated with better access to healthcare than periods off a mood stabilizer. Although we controlled for this by including valproate in our analyses, it cannot be excluded that time-varying confounding might differ between lithium and valproate. The main limitation is that we cannot discern if lithium protects against viral, bacterial, or other aetiologies. Another limitation is that we lack information on tobacco use and comorbidity, but this should not confound the results in a within-individual model. Limitations finally include the lack of information regarding adherence, but this would if anything be a conservative bias.

In conclusion, we provide real-world evidence that lithium treatment reduces the rate of respiratory infections. Taken together with ample previous literature on antiviral effects of lithium (Murru et al. 2020), the repurposing potential of lithium for antiviral effects is worth pursuing.

Supplementary Information

Additional file 1: Table S1. Characteristics of individuals with bipolar disorder by different treatment.

Acknowledgements
Not applicable.

Authors' contributions
ML conception of the study, study design, analysis and interpretation of data, drafting of the manuscript; HL and PL data acquisition, interpretation of data, revision of the manuscript for important intellectual content; JW interpretation of data, revision of the manuscript for important intellectual content; JS study design, analysis and interpretation of data, revision of the manuscript for important intellectual content. All authors read and approved the final manuscript.

Author details
[1]Section of Psychiatry, Institute of Neuroscience and Physiology, The Sahlgrenska Academy at University of Gothenburg, Blå Stråket 15, 413 45 Gothenburg, Sweden. [2]Department of Medical Epidemiology and Biostatistics, Karolinska Institutet, Stockholm, Sweden. [3]Department of Medical Sciences, Örebro University, Örebro, Sweden. [4]Department of Infectious Diseases, The Sahlgrenska Academy at University of Gothenburg, Gothenburg, Sweden.

References
Acharya S, Bussel JB. Hematologic toxicity of sodium valproate. J Pediatr Hematol Oncol. 2000;22:62–5.
Alda M. Lithium in the treatment of bipolar disorder: pharmacology and pharmacogenetics. Mol Psychiatry. 2015;20:661–70.
Allison PD. Fixed effects regression models. CA: SAGE publications; 2009. p. 160.
Amsterdam JD, Maislin G, Potter L, Giuntoli R. Reduced rate of recurrent genital herpes infections with lithium carbonate. Psychopharmacol Bull. 1990a;26:343–7.
Amsterdam JD, Maislin G, Rybakowski J. A possible antiviral action of lithium carbonate in herpes simplex virus infections. Biol Psychiatry. 1990b;27:447–53.
Amsterdam JD, Maislin G, Hooper MB. Suppression of herpes simplex virus infections with oral lithium carbonate–a possible antiviral activity. Pharmacotherapy. 1996;16:1070–5.
Amsterdam JD, Garcia-Espana F, Rybakowski J. Rates of flu-like infection in patients with affective illness. J Affect Disord. 1998;47:177–82.
Carmen J, Okafor K, Ike E. The effects of lithium therapy on leukocytes: a 1-year follow-up study. J Natl Med Assoc. 1993;85:301–3.
Chang Z, Lichtenstein P, D'Onofrio BM, Sjolander A, Larsson H. Serious transport accidents in adults with attention-deficit/hyperactivity disorder and the effect of medication: a population-based study. JAMA Psychiatry. 2014;71:319–25.
Chen Q, Sjolander A, Runeson B, D'Onofrio BM, Lichtenstein P, Larsson H. Drug treatment for attention-deficit/hyperactivity disorder and suicidal behaviour: register based study. BMJ. 2014;348:g3769.
Chen Y, Kong D, Cai G, Jiang Z, Jiao Y, Shi Y, et al. Novel antiviral effect of lithium chloride on mammalian orthoreoviruses in vitro. Microb Pathog. 2016;93:152–7.
Cipriani A, Reid K, Young AH, Macritchie K, Geddes J. Valproic acid, valproate and divalproex in the maintenance treatment of bipolar disorder. Cochrane Database Syst Rev. 2013;10:CD003196.
Cuartas-Lopez AM, Gallego-Gomez JC. Glycogen synthase kinase 3ss participates in late stages of Dengue virus-2 infection. Mem Inst Oswaldo Cruz. 2020;115:e190357.
Joas E, Karanti A, Song J, Goodwin GM, Lichtenstein P, Landen M. Pharmacological treatment and risk of psychiatric hospital admission in bipolar disorder. Br J Psychiatry. 2017;210:197–202.
Kendall T, Morriss R, Mayo-Wilson E, Marcus E, Guideline Development Group of the National Institute for H, Care E. Assessment and management of bipolar disorder: summary of updated NICE guidance. BMJ. 2014;349:g5673.
Klein EY, Monteforte B, Gupta A, Jiang W, May L, Hsieh YH, et al. The frequency of influenza and bacterial coinfection: a systematic review and meta-analysis. Influenza Other Respir Viruses. 2016;10:394–403.
Lichtenstein P, Halldner L, Zetterqvist J, Sjolander A, Serlachius E, Fazel S, et al. Medication for attention deficit-hyperactivity disorder and criminality. N Engl J Med. 2012;367:2006–14.
Ludvigsson JF, Otterblad-Olausson P, Pettersson BU, Ekbom A. The Swedish personal identity number: possibilities and pitfalls in healthcare and medical research. Eur J Epidemiol. 2009;24:659–67.
Maddu N, Raghavendra PB. Review of lithium effects on immune cells. Immunopharmacol Immunotoxicol. 2015;37:111–25.
Malhi GS, Outhred T. Therapeutic Mechanisms of Lithium in Bipolar Disorder: Recent Advances and Current Understanding. CNS Drugs. 2016;30:931–49.
Molero Y, Lichtenstein P, Zetterqvist J, Gumpert CH, Fazel S. Selective serotonin reuptake inhibitors and violent crime: a cohort study. PLoS Med. 2015;12:e1001875.
Murru A, Manchia M, Hajek T, Nielsen RE, Rybakowski JK, Sani G, et al. Lithium's antiviral effects: a potential drug for CoViD-19 disease? Int J Bipolar Disord. 2020;8:21.
Nowak JK, Walkowiak J. Lithium and coronaviral infections. A scoping review. F1000Research. 2020;9:93.
Petrini M, Azzara A. Lithium in the treatment of neutropenia. Curr Opin Hematol. 2012;19:52–7.
Qian K, Cheng X, Zhang D, Shao H, Yao Y, Nair V, et al. Antiviral effect of lithium chloride on replication of avian leukosis virus subgroup J in cell culture. Arch Virol. 2018;163:987–95.
Ren X, Meng F, Yin J, Li G, Li X, Wang C, et al. Action mechanisms of lithium chloride on cell infection by transmissible gastroenteritis coronavirus. PLoS ONE. 2011;6:e18669.
Rybakowski JK. Antiviral and immunomodulatory effect of lithium. Pharmacopsychiatry. 2000;33:159–64.
Sarhan MA, Abdel-Hakeem MS, Mason AL, Tyrrell DL, Houghton M. Glycogen synthase kinase 3beta inhibitors prevent hepatitis C virus release/assembly through perturbation of lipid metabolism. Sci Rep. 2017;7:2495.
Sellgren C, Landén M, Lichtenstein P, Hultman CM, Långström N. Validity of bipolar disorder hospital discharge diagnoses: file review and multiple register linkage in Sweden. Acta Psychiatr Scand. 2011;124:447–53.
Skinner GR, Hartley C, Buchan A, Harper L, Gallimore P. The effect of lithium chloride on the replication of herpes simplex virus. Med Microbiol Immunol. 1980;168:139–48.
Song J, Sjolander A, Joas E, Bergen SE, Runeson B, Larsson H, et al. Suicidal behavior during lithium and valproate treatment: a within-individual 8-year prospective study of 50,000 patients with bipolar disorder. Am J Psychiatry. 2017;174:795–802.
StataCorp. Stata: release 13. Statistical software. College Station: StataCorp LP; 2013.
van den Ameele S, van Diermen L, Staels W, Coppens V, Dumont G, Sabbe B, et al. The effect of mood-stabilizing drugs on cytokine levels in bipolar disorder: a systematic review. J Affect Disord. 2016;203:364–73.

Viktorin A, Lichtenstein P, Thase ME, Larsson H, Lundholm C, Magnusson PK, et al. The risk of switch to mania in patients with bipolar disorder during treatment with an antidepressant alone and in combination with a mood stabilizer. Am J Psychiatry. 2014;171:1067–73.

Viktorin A, Ryden E, Thase ME, Chang Z, Lundholm C, D'Onofrio BM, et al. The risk of treatment-emergent mania with methylphenidate in bipolar disorder. Am J Psychiatry. 2017;174:341–8.

Wettermark B, Hammar N, Fored CM, Leimanis A, Otterblad Olausson P, Bergman U, et al. The new Swedish Prescribed Drug Register—opportunities for pharmacoepidemiological research and experience from the first six months. Pharmacoepidemiol Drug Saf. 2007;16:726–35.

Zaccara G, Giovannelli F, Giorgi FS, Franco V, Gasparini S, Tacconi FM. Do antiepileptic drugs increase the risk of infectious diseases? A meta-analysis of placebo-controlled studies. Br J Clin Pharmacol. 2017;83:1873–9.

Zhai X, Wang S, Zhu M, He W, Pan Z, Su S. Antiviral effect of lithium chloride and diammonium glycyrrhizinate on porcine deltacoronavirus in vitro. Pathogens. 2019;8:144.

Zhao FR, Xie YL, Liu ZZ, Shao JJ, Li SF, Zhang YG, et al. Lithium chloride inhibits early stages of foot-and-mouth disease virus (FMDV) replication in vitro. J Med Virol. 2017;89:2041–6.

20

Valproic acid autoinduction: a case-based review

Sean Bennett[1] and Mujeeb U. Shad[2,3,4*]

Abstract

Although valproic acid (VPA) induces the metabolism of multiple other drugs, the clinical reports of VPA autoinduction are rare. A comprehensive literature search yielded only one published case series, which provided the rationale to conduct a review of the published cases along with a new case of VPA autoinduction. Although there may be myriad of reasons for lack of published cases of VPA autoinduction, potential underreporting may be one of the core reasons. Lack of understanding into the highly complex metabolism of VPA may also make it difficult to recognize and report VPA autoinduction. However, it is important to mention that in addition to autoinduction increased elimination of VPA may be mediated by several pharmacokinetic (PK) factors, such as drug interactions, genetic polymorphisms of metabolic enzymes, and protein displacement reactions. As VPA is metabolized by multiple metabolic pathways, the risk for drug interactions is relatively high. There is also a growing evidence for high genetic inducibility of some enzymes involved in VPA metabolism. Protein displacement reactions with VPA increase the biologically active and readily metabolizable free fraction and pose a diagnostic challenge as they are usually not requested by most clinicians. Thus, monitoring of free fraction with total VPA levels may prevent clinically serious outcomes and optimize VPA treatment in clinically challenging patients. This case-based review compares the clinical data from three published cases and a new case of VPA autoinduction to enhance clinicians' awareness of this relatively rare but clinically relevant phenomenon along with a discussion of potential underlying mechanisms.

Keywords: Valproic, Acid, Autoinduction, Case-based, Review

Introduction

Valproic acid (VPA) is one of the oldest and most frequently prescribed drugs for epilepsy, bipolar disorder, and migraine prophylaxis (Peterson and Naunton 2005). This is one of the few psychotropic drugs that have fairly well-defined therapeutic levels that range from 50 to 100 μg/mL for epilepsy and 80 to 125 μg/mL for bipolar disorder (Patsalos et al. 2008). These therapeutic levels are usually achieved at VPA doses well under 4000 mg/day. However, VPA doses required to achieve recommended therapeutic levels vary significantly across patients, which could be due to its highly complex metabolism. Valproic acid is metabolized by both phase-I and phase-II enzyme systems as well as fatty acid β-oxidation. Although rarely reported, VPA autoinduction is a clinically-significant phenomenon in a high-risk patient population with bipolar disorder and epilepsy as sub-therapeutic VPA levels may result in clinically serious outcomes, such as suicide and seizures, respectively. A comprehensive literature search yielded only one published case series reporting three cases of VPA autoinduction (Jackson et al. 2015), which could be due to potential under-reporting, lack of understanding into the complex nature of VPA metabolism as well as lesser recognition of drugs as inducers than inhibitors (de Leon 2015a, b). Finding the current case of VPA autoinduction provided us the rationale to conduct a review of the published cases along with the new case in order to analyze and compare clinical data and increase clinicians' awareness into VPA autoinduction. This case-based review also

*Correspondence: mujeebushad@gmail.com
[2] University of Nevada Las Vegas, Las Vegas, NV, USA
Full list of author information is available at the end of the article

provided an opportunity to discuss various pharmacokinetic mechanisms underlying VPA autoinduction to minimize seriously adverse outcomes and optimize clinical outcomes in challenging patients.

Methods

The current case of the bipolar patient hospitalized for inpatient treatment was identified after he required unusually high dose of VPA to achieve therapeutic levels. A comprehensive literature search yielded only one case series comprised of three patients who required unusually high VA doses to be effective. The current case was added to the three cases of VPA autoinduction in the published case series to conduct a case-based review. The literature search was conducted in MEDLINE/PubMed, EMBASE, CINAHL, PsychINFO without any restrictions. The following search terms were employed for this search: ((‘valproic acid’ OR ‘valproate’ OR ‘VPA’) AND (‘autoinduction’ OR ‘auto-induction’ OR ‘induction’ OR ‘inducibility’)). A total of 13 records were found of which four records included both search terms and one record documenting VPA autoinduction in three patients in a case series. All VPA levels were trough levels obtained at the steady state, including the current case. The concentration/dose (C/D) ratio for the current case was calculated using the same methods and rationale as described in the published case series (Jackson et al. 2015). Briefly, the VPA level was divided by the VPA dose and multiplied by 1000 to make the ratio numerically clear.

Results

As can be seen from the Table 1, all reviewed cases were Caucasian males, with a mean age (SD) of 55.25 ± 14.17, receiving a formulation of VPA for various diagnoses, including bipolar disorder, schizophrenia, tuberous sclerosis, and traumatic brain injury. However, the clinical data for three published cases were collected over several years of inpatient treatment as compared to clinical data for the current subject over a much shorter hospital stay of 22 days. The current patient was admitted for severe traumatic brain injury, methamphetamine use, and bipolar symptoms, such as racing thoughts, lack of sleep, increased energy, and pressured speech, but without any other psychiatric or neurological disorders. VPA levels for all cases were trough levels obtained at a steady state using the same clinical laboratory. However, in contrast to several years of data collection for the three published cases, the VPA levels in the current case were obtained only over 22 days. The normal therapeutic ratio of VPA C/D ratio $\times$ 1000 ranged between 112 and 132 μg/mL.

Brief case histories of previously published cases

Case 1

A 34-year old Caucasian male with treatment-refractory schizophrenia developed a seizure disorder before he was hospitalized with four antiepileptic medications: carbamazepine, phenytoin, diazepam, and VPA, but all with subtherapeutic levels. It took several months to titrate off these medications, except VPA. The seizures were not adequately controlled until the VPA dose was increased to 5250 mg/day to achieve therapeutic concentrations. However, VPA had to be switched to divalproex sodium (DVPS) after the patient began to complain about the bad taste of the VPA concentrate. This switch led to an unexpected valproate intoxication despite the absence of any other medication changes.

Case 2

This patient was a 66-year-old Caucasian male with a long history of bipolar disorder and substance use disorder. He was admitted to a psychiatric hospital for bipolar symptoms and psychosis, which was managed by starting 1000 mg/day DVPS. However, he continued to display rapid, pressured speech and flight of ideas, in addition to increased levels of energy, which required a gradual increase in DVPS dose to 4000 mg/day to have an antimanic response with a therapeutic level of around 70 μg/mL.

Case 3

This patient was a middle-aged Caucasian male with tuberous sclerosis manifested as a seizure disorder and mental retardation. He had been in inpatient treatment at a state psychiatric hospital for about 22 years before he started to have complications from tuberous sclerosis, including a right renal tumor, worsening episodes of ataxia and confusion, and a giant cell astrocytoma. Thus, the patient required a progressive increase in the DVPS dose from a baseline dose of 3375 mg/day to a therapeutic dose of 10,500 mg/day. This dose was maintained until it was found that the patient's physical deterioration was due to astrocytoma, resulting in discontinuation of all medications except phenytoin and a reduction in DVPS from a dose of 10,500 to 7000 mg/day.

Current case

A 51-year old Caucasian male with past psychiatric history of bipolar disorder and methamphetamine use disorder, who was consulted by Consult-Liaison (C-L) psychiatry following a three-week inpatient surgical hospitalization after the wreckage of his recreational vehicle while under the influence of methamphetamine.

Table 1 Relationship between age, weight, valproic acid (VPA) formulation, daily VPA dose, average VPA levels, and concentration/dose (C/D) ratio × 1000 mean ± SD and range across cases

Cases	Age	Wt. (kg)	Diagnosis	Hospital Duration	Formulation	VPA dose (mg/day)	VPA level (µg/mL)	C/D ratio × 1000[a]	No. of VPA Levels	Mean C/D ratio × 1000: mean ± SD, range[#]	Comments
Case 1*	34	85	Schizophrenia Seizure disorder	> 3 years	VPA	5250	87	17	44	15 ± 2.6, range = 10–21	Significantly lower C/D ratio than the normal range between 112 and 132 µg/mL, suggesting faster VPA metabolism
				< 1 year	DVPS	2000	78	39	7	39 ± 6.3, range = 28–48	Higher C/D ratio with DVPS than VPA in case 1, suggesting significantly slower DVPS metabolism than VPA
Case 2*	66	90	Bipolar Disorder Substance Use disorder	8 weeks	DVPS	4000	67	17	10	25 ± 5.6, range = 17–33	Significantly lower C/D ratio than the normal range between 112 and 132 µg/mL, suggesting faster VPA metabolism
Case 3*	70	71	Tuberous Sclerosis	> 4 years	DVPS	10,500	10	12	137	8 ± 3.5, range = 3–20	Lowest C/D ratio of all cases, suggesting robust autoinduction with DVPS
New Case	51	71	Bipolar disorder Methamphetamine use disorder Recent Traumatic Brain Injury	22 days	VPA	5000	98.8	19.8	7	18.6 ± 2.9, range = 13–20	Similar C/D ratio to case 1 & 2, suggesting similar rate of auto-induction with VPA

*Reference = Jackson et al. (2015) VPA: valproic acid; DVPS: divalproex sodium; C/D = Mean concentration/dose ratio (therapeutic range between 112 to 132 µg/mL); Number of VPA levels drawn over total hospitalization

[#] Mean C/D ratio × 1000: mean ± SD, range; Calculated from the total number of VPA levels during hospital duration

[a] C/D ratio × 1000; Calculated from the last final VPA dose and the level at that dose

Injuries sustained resulted in a skull fracture and intracranial hemorrhage, requiring neurosurgery. Recovery was then complicated by ongoing aggression and agitated delirium, for which CL psychiatry was consulted. The initial efforts were to reduce the use of as-needed medications, discontinue deliriogenic medications, and transition the patient to high dose IV haloperidol to manage aggression. A dose of 156 mg IV haloperidol over 24 h was administered but had to be discontinued due to prolonged QTc interval, with the highest QTc value reaching 560 ms and a return to 420 ms following haloperidol's discontinuation. Three different second-generation antipsychotic medications, benzodiazepines, and opiate pain medications failed to adequately manage patient's aggression, At this time, a collaborative, multi-team decision was made to intubate the patient and perform a medication washout due to refractory, severe, and persistent agitated delirium. Eventually, valproic acid (Depakene®), quetiapine and risperidone were introduced to manage aggressive and impulsive behavior in a setting of traumatic brain injury (TBI) with a history of possible underlying bipolar mania. Following extubation and washout, the delirium resolved. The patient was alert and able to fully orient and converse; however, he remained agitated and aggressive with staff, demanding to leave against medical advice (AMA). In the meanwhile, repeated VPA dose titrations were required to achieve therapeutic trough levels of 98.8 µg/mL at the steady state at an unusually high total dose of 5000 mg/day. Eventually, the patient stabilized and was discharged on day 22 of hospitalization. Of note, risperidone was discontinued after the 18th day of VPA initiation to reduce polypharmacy.

Discussion

As can be seen from the Table 1, similar to the prior cases, the new case (case 4) required aggressive titration of VPA dose to achieve therapeutic VPA levels required for bipolar disorder (80–125 µg/mL) (Peterson and Naunton 2005). Although it took several years for the published cases to attribute the need for unusually high VPA doses to autoinduction (Jackson et al. 2015), it took only a few days to do so for the current case due to the valuable clinical information provided by the published case series. Since VPA has a highly complex metabolism, an initial discussion of different PK factors involved in VPA autoinduction may be relevant here. About 40% of VPA is metabolized by multiple isoforms of a phase-II enzyme, uridine diphosphate glucuronyl transferase (UGT1A6, UGT1A9, and UGT2B7), (Li et al. 2004; Patsalos and Perucca 2003); while 30% is metabolized via β-oxidation, and the rest by multiple phase-I cytochrome P450 (CYP) enzymes (i.e., CYP2A6, CYP2C9, and CYP2C19) (Ghodke-Puranik et al. 2013; Perucca et al. 2006). It is interesting to note that two of the three UGT isoforms (i.e., UGT2B7, UGT1A9) and one of the CYP enzymes (CYP2C9) that metabolize VPA are actually inhibited by VPA (Morris et al. 2000). In this context, inhibition of UGT2B7 is well-documented to elevate lamotrigine levels when co-administered with VPA (Wang et al. 2016) by 2–3 folds (Morris et al. 2000) increasing the risk for dose-dependent life threatening skin rashes associated with lamotrigine. This is despite some animal studies reporting increased VPA glucuronidation (Fisher et al. 1991) and β-oxidation (Fisher et al. 1991; McLaughlin et al. 2000) but with long-term use of VPA. Another study (McLaughlin et al. 2000) found at least 3 weeks delay in mild VPA autoinduction with a low-dose VPA mediated by the β-oxidation but not UGT. The delayed enzyme induction probably does not explain the relatively fast autoinduction observed in reviewed cases. However, there are many other PK factors that can also alter VPA plasma levels, including drug interactions, protein displacement reactions, genetic polymorphisms, and activation of nuclear receptors.

In terms of drug interactions, VPA is known to elevate plasma levels of only a few drugs, most notably lamotrigine (Wang et al. 2016; Morris et al. 2000). However, VPA is more frequently reported to increase the metabolism of multiple co-administered drugs, such as aripiprazole (Citrome et al. 2005), clozapine (Cerveny et al. 2007; Finley and Warner 1994; Longo and Salzman 1995; Diaz et al. 2014), norclozapine, felbamate (Hooper et al. 1996), irinotecan (Jong et al. 2007), and olanzapine (Bergemann et al. 2006; Haslemo et al. 2012). The relatively rare reports of VPA autoinduction suggest that the VPA-induced induced enzymes may not be relevant in VPA metabolism. Regardless, the high level of long-term polypharmacy in the published cases was not observed in the current subject, who was only treated with two concomitantly administered medications (i.e., 4 mg/day of risperidone & 950 mg/day of quetiapine). Both these medications were co-administered at the same dose for 18 out of 22 days of hospitalization, and none has been reported to significantly interact with VPA. Most of the other concomitant drugs in the published cases are not known to significantly alter VPA metabolism with the only exception of phenytoin in case 3. Phenytoin is a robust inducer for enzymes, including UGT and may have contributed to the VPA autoinduction (Zaccara et al. 2014).

The protein displacement reactions may also enhance VPA metabolism, which may sometimes be confused with autoinduction. Valproic acid is highly protein-bound drug, which can saturate protein binding sites at levels ≥ 50 μg/mL (Jackson et al. 2015), thereby increasing the biologically active and readily metabolizable free fraction (Dutta et al. 2007; Kodama et al. 2001). A similar increase in free fraction may occur if VPA is displaced by more potent protein-bound drugs, such as ibuprofen (Lana et al. 2016a, 2016b). Thus, dose-dependent protein saturation is one of the many non-inducing factors that can magnify VPA autoinduction. Valproic acid, in turn, may displace phenytoin, which is a lesser protein bound drug (Lai and Huang 1993; Perucca et al. 1980), thereby decreasing its plasma levels (Wen et al. 2001). This decrease is often counterbalanced by an increase in phenytoin levels via VPA-induced inhibition of CYP2C9 that metabolizes phenytoin (Franco and Perucca 2015). This observation is consistent with unchanged phenytoin levels in case 3. Since albumin is the plasma protein that binds VPA (Hermida and Tutor 2005; VandenBerg et al. 2017), any change in albumin levels may also alter VPA levels. Thus, an increase in VPA free fraction has been reported in patients with hypoalbuminemia due to acute medical stress and renal or liver dysfunction (Hermida and Tutor 2005; VandenBerg et al. 2017). However, increased free fraction from protein saturation is clinically different from that reported with hypoalbuminemia. Unlike protein saturation, any increase in VPA dose in patients with hypoalbuminemia may overwhelm the metabolic pathways to effectively eliminate significantly elevated levels of biologically active free fraction, thus increasing the risk for VPA toxicity in the absence of a notable increase in total VPA levels (Hermida and Tutor 2005). This underscores the need to obtain free fraction levels in addition to the total VPA levels to guide critical VPA dose adjustments in clinically challenging cases (Maat et al. 2011). A simple subtraction of free fraction from the total VPA levels may help determine protein-bound VPA levels to distinguish between protein saturation and hypoalbuminemia.

Genetic polymorphisms in enzymes that metabolize VPA may explain the high inter-individual variability in VPA levels (Methaneethorn 2018; Ding et al. 2015). The most significant inducible variants for UGT1A6 are 541A > G and 552A > C), which have been associated with increased metabolism of VPA in children (Guo et al. 2012; Hung et al. 2011; Wang and Zhou 2016). A relatively recent metanalysis supported the inducibility of the two UGT1A6 variants in other age groups as well (Kim and Kim 2019). Another study reported a third inducible UGT1A6 variant (i.e., 19T > G) as well as a CYP2C9 variant in VPA-treated patients with severe traumatic brain injury (Sun et al. 2017). Tanner and Tyndale (2017) found a second inducible CYP enzyme, 2A6 to further contribute to the significant inter-individual variation in VPA levels (Tanner and Tyndale 2017). Inducible variants of UGT2B7 (i.e., G211T and C161T) were also reported to require VPA dose adjustments for therapeutic effects in a metanalysis (Wang et al. 2018). Since UGT variance was not assessed in the reviewed cases, the effects of UGT polymorphism(s) on VPA autoinduction cannot be assessed. Nevertheless, genetic testing for CYP2C9 and CYP2C19 that metabolize VPA (Jiang et al. 2009) ruled out any dysfunctional alleles for these enzymes in the published case series (Jackson et al. 2015).

Another potential mechanism for VPA autoinduction could be the activation of a nuclear receptor, peroxisome proliferator-activated (Kallen 2004; Lampen et al. 1999; Werling et al. 2001), which has been associated with induction of UGT enzymes (Fisher et al. 1991; Luci et al. 2006). However, it is unlikely that activation of other nuclear receptors associated with increased expression of CYP3A4 and P-glycoprotein (P-gp) (Cerveny et al. 2007) could have contributed to the VPA autoinduction as VPA is not a substrate for either of the two. This is in contrast to another antiepileptic drug, carbamazepine, which is associated with robust autoinduction as it increases the expression of CYP3A4 and P-gp, for which it is a substrate (Lutz et al. 2018).

This review has several limitations including the retrospective nature of the clinical data, the lack of VPA free fraction level monitoring, the significant difference in hospital duration between the current and published cases, the lack of post-discharge follow-up and VPA level monitoring for the current case. Nevertheless, this review underscores the clinical significance of not only monitoring total VPA levels, but also the free fraction, to facilitate diagnosis and management of VPA autoinduction.

Conclusion

The findings from this review are based on a retrospective analysis of only four cases and should be interpreted with caution. However, the clinicians should consider VPA autoinduction in patients with unusually low plasma levels despite conventional VPA doses. It appears that VPA autoinduction is a relatively rare phenomenon probably because of multiple PK factors that may result in or contribute to VPA autoinduction, most notably drug interactions, protein displacement reactions, and genetic polymorphisms in enzymes metabolizing VPA. Until future research addresses the complexities of VPA metabolism, the most logical way to deal with clinically challenging cases is to obtain both total and free fraction VPA levels for safe and effective VPA dose adjustments.

Acknowledgements
N/A.

Authors' contributions
Both authors contributed equally to this review. MUS conceptualized the presentation of a new case along with the only published case series on this topic. SB prepared the first draft and organized the review. Both authors read and approved the final manuscript.

Author details
[1]Samaritan Health Services, Corvallis, OR, USA. [2]University of Nevada Las Vegas, Las Vegas, NV, USA. [3]Touro University Nevada, Las Vegas, NV, USA. [4]Valley Health System, Las Vegas, NV, USA.

References

Bergemann N, Kress KR, Abu-Tair F, Frick A, Kopitz J. Valproate lowers plasma concentration of olanzapine. J Clin Psychopharmacol. 2006;26(4):432–4.

Cerveny L, Svecova L, Anzenbacherova E, Vrzal R, Staud F, Dvorak Z, et al. Valproic acid induces CYP3A4 and MDR1 gene expression by activation of constitutive androstane receptor and pregnane X receptor pathways. Drug Metab Dispos. 2007;35(7):1032–41.

Citrome L, Josiassen R, Bark N, Salazar DE, Mallikaarjun S. Pharmacokinetics of aripiprazole and concomitant lithium and valproate. J Clin Pharmacol. 2005;45(1):89–93.

de Leon J. The effects of antiepileptic inducers in neuropsychopharmacology, a neglected issue. Part II: pharmacological issues and further understanding. Rev Psiquiatr Salud Ment. 2015;8(3):167–88.

de Leon J. The effects of antiepileptic inducers in neuropsychopharmacology, a neglected issue. Part I: a summary of the current state for clinicians. Rev Psiquiatr Salud Ment. 2015b;8(2):97–115.

de Jong FA, Scott-Horton TJ, Kroetz DL, McLeod HL, Friberg LE, Mathijssen RH, et al. Irinotecan-induced diarrhea: functional significance of the polymorphic ABCC2 transporter protein. Clin Pharmacol Ther. 2007;81(1):42–9.

de Maat MM, van Leeuwen HJ, Edelbroek PM. High unbound fraction of valproic acid in a hypoalbuminemic critically ill patient on renal replacement therapy. Ann Pharmacother. 2011;45(3):e18.

Diaz FJ, Eap CB, Ansermot N, Crettol S, Spina E, de Leon J. Can valproic acid be an inducer of clozapine metabolism? Pharmacopsychiatry. 2014;47(3):89–96.

Ding J, Wang Y, Lin W, Wang C, Zhao L, Li X, et al. A population pharmacokinetic model of valproic acid in pediatric patients with epilepsy: a non-linear pharmacokinetic model based on protein-binding saturation. Clin Pharmacokinet. 2015;54(3):305–17.

Dutta S, Faught E, Limdi NA. Valproate protein binding following rapid intravenous administration of high doses of valproic acid in patients with epilepsy. J Clin Pharm Ther. 2007;32(4):365–71.

Finley P, Warner D. Potential impact of valproic acid therapy on clozapine disposition. Biol Psychiat. 1994;36(7):487–8.

Fisher JE, Nau H, Loscher W. Alterations in the renal excretion of valproate and its metabolites after chronic treatment. Epilepsia. 1991;32(1):146–50.

Franco V, Perucca E. CYP2C9 polymorphisms and phenytoin metabolism: implications for adverse effects. Expert Opin Drug Metab Toxicol. 2015;11(8):1269–79.

Ghodke-Puranik Y, Thorn CF, Lamba JK, Leeder JS, Song W, Birnbaum AK, et al. Valproic acid pathway: pharmacokinetics and pharmacodynamics. Pharmacogenet Genomics. 2013;23(4):236–41.

Guo Y, Hu C, He X, Qiu F, Zhao L. Effects of UGT1A6, UGT2B7, and CYP2C9 genotypes on plasma concentrations of valproic acid in Chinese children with epilepsy. Drug Metab Pharmacokinet. 2012;27(5):536–42.

Haslemo T, Olsen K, Lunde H, Molden E. Valproic acid significantly lowers serum concentrations of olanzapine-an interaction effect comparable with smoking. Ther Drug Monit. 2012;34(5):512–7.

Hermida J, Tutor JC. A theoretical method for normalizing total serum valproic acid concentration in hypoalbuminemic patients. J Pharmacol Sci. 2005;97(4):489–93.

Hooper WD, Franklin ME, Glue P, Banfield CR, Radwanski E, McLaughlin DB, et al. Effect of felbamate on valproic acid disposition in healthy volunteers: inhibition of beta-oxidation. Epilepsia. 1996;37(1):91–7.

Hung CC, Ho JL, Chang WL, Tai JJ, Hsieh TJ, Hsieh YW, et al. Association of genetic variants in six candidate genes with valproic acid therapy optimization. Pharmacogenomics. 2011;12(8):1107–17.

Jackson J, McCollum B, Ognibene J, Diaz FJ, de Leon J. Three patients needing high doses of valproic acid to get therapeutic concentrations. Case Rep Psychiatry. 2015;2015:542862.

Jiang D, Bai X, Zhang Q, Lu W, Wang Y, Li L, et al. Effects of CYP2C19 and CYP2C9 genotypes on pharmacokinetic variability of valproic acid in Chinese epileptic patients: nonlinear mixed-effect modeling. Eur J Clin Pharmacol. 2009;65(12):1187–93.

Kallen B. Valproic acid is known to cause hypospadias in man but does not reduce anogenital distance or causes hypospadias in rats. Basic Clin Pharmacol Toxicol. 2004;94(1):51–4.

Kim SC, Kim MG. A meta-analysis of the influence of UGT1A6 genetic polymorphisms on valproic acid pharmacokinetics. Int J Clin Pharmacol Ther. 2019;57:144–51.

Kodama Y, Kodama H, Kuranari M, Tsutsumi K, Ono S, Yukawa E, et al. Gender- or age-related binding characteristics of valproic acid to serum proteins in adult patients with epilepsy. Eur J Pharm Biopharm. 2001;52(1):57–63.

Lai ML, Huang JD. Dual effect of valproic acid on the pharmacokinetics of phenytoin. Biopharm Drug Dispos. 1993;14(4):365–70.

Lampen A, Siehler S, Ellerbeck U, Gottlicher M, Nau H. New molecular bioassays for the estimation of the teratogenic potency of valproic acid derivatives in vitro: activation of the peroxisomal proliferator-activated receptor (PPARdelta). Toxicol Appl Pharmacol. 1999;160(3):238–49.

Lana F, Marti-Bonany J, Fuster J, de Leon J. Reduction in serum concentration of valproic acid secondary to the intake of ibuprofen as an example of valproic acid auto-induction metabolism. Actas Esp Psiquiatr. 2016a;44(4):136–44.

Lana F, Marti-Bonany J, de Leon J. Ibuprofen may increase pharmacological action of valproate by displacing it from plasma proteins: a case report. Am J Psychiatry. 2016b;173(9):941–2.

Li Q, Lugt CB, Looareesuwan S, Krudsood S, Wilairatana P, Vannaphan S, et al. Pharmacokinetic investigation on the therapeutic potential of artemotil (beta-arteether) in Thai patients with severe *Plasmodium falciparum* malaria. Am J Trop Med Hyg. 2004;71(6):723–31.

Longo LP, Salzman C. Valproic acid effects on serum concentrations of clozapine and norclozapine. Am J Psychiatry. 1995;152(4):650.

Luci S, Geissler S, Konig B, Koch A, Stangl GI, Hirche F, et al. PPARalpha agonists up-regulate organic cation transporters in rat liver cells. Biochem Biophys Res Commun. 2006;350(3):704–8.

Lutz JD, Kirby BJ, Wang L, Song Q, Ling J, Massetto B, et al. Cytochrome P450 3A Induction Predicts P-glycoprotein Induction; Part 2: prediction of decreased substrate exposure after rifabutin or carbamazepine. Clin Pharmacol Ther. 2018;104(6):1191–8.

McLaughlin DB, Eadie MJ, Parker-Scott SL, Addison RS, Henderson RD, Hooper WD, et al. Valproate metabolism during valproate-associated hepatotoxicity in a surviving adult patient. Epilepsy Res. 2000;41(3):259–68.

Methaneethorn J. A systematic review of population pharmacokinetics of valproic acid. Br J Clin Pharmacol. 2018;84(5):816–34.

Morris RG, Black AB, Lam E, Westley IS. Clinical study of lamotrigine and valproic acid in patients with epilepsy: using a drug interaction to advantage? Ther Drug Monit. 2000;22:656–60.

Patsalos PN, Perucca E. Clinically important drug interactions in epilepsy: interactions between antiepileptic drugs and other drugs. Lancet Neurol. 2003;2(8):473–81.

Patsalos PN, Berry DJ, Bourgeois BF, Cloyd JC, Glauser TA, Johannessen SI, et al. Antiepileptic drugs–best practice guidelines for therapeutic drug monitoring: a position paper by the subcommission on therapeutic drug monitoring, ILAE Commission on Therapeutic Strategies. Epilepsia. 2008;49(7):1239–76.

Perucca E, Hebdige S, Frigo GM, Gatti G, Lecchini S, Crema A. Interaction between phenytoin and valproic acid: plasma protein binding and metabolic effects. Clin Pharmacol Ther. 1980;28(6):779–89.

Perucca E, Berlowitz D, Birnbaum A, Cloyd JC, Garrard J, Hanlon JT, et al. Pharmacological and clinical aspects of antiepileptic drug use in the elderly. Epilepsy Res. 2006;68(Suppl 1):S49-63.

Peterson GM, Naunton M. Valproate: a simple chemical with so much to offer. J Clin Pharm Ther. 2005;30(5):417–21.

Sun Y, Yu J, Yuan Q, Wu X, Wu X, Hu J. Early post-traumatic seizures are associated with valproic acid plasma concentrations and UGT1A6/CYP2C9 genetic polymorphisms in patients with severe traumatic brain injury. Scand J Trauma Resusc Emerg Med. 2017;25:85.

Tanner JA, Tyndale RF. Variation in CYP2A6 activity and personalized medicine. J Pers Med. 2017;7:18.

VandenBerg A, Broadway J, Lalich C, Kennedy R, Williams K. Valproate serum concentrations in patients with hypoalbuminemia and medical complications. Ment Health Clin. 2017;7:13–5.

Wang S, Zhou N. Removal of carbamazepine from aqueous solution using sono-activated persulfate process. Ultrason Sonochem. 2016;29:156–62.

Wang P, Lin XQ, Cai WK, Xu GL, Zhou MD, Yang M, He GH. Effect of UGT2B7 genotypes on plasma concentration of valproic acid: a meta-analysis. Eur J Clin Pharmacol. 2018;74:433–42.

Wen X, Wang JS, Kivisto KT, Neuvonen PJ, Backman JT. In vitro evaluation of valproic acid as an inhibitor of human cytochrome P450 isoforms: preferential inhibition of cytochrome P450 2C9 (CYP2C9). Br J Clin Pharmacol. 2001;52(5):547–53.

Werling U, Siehler S, Litfin M, Nau H, Gottlicher M. Induction of differentiation in F9 cells and activation of peroxisome proliferator-activated receptor delta by valproic acid and its teratogenic derivatives. Mol Pharmacol. 2001;59(5):1269–76.

Zaccara G, Giovannelli F, Bell GS, Sander JW. Network meta-analyses of antiepileptic drug efficacy and tolerability in drug-resistant focal epilepsies: a clinical perspective. Eur J Clin Pharmacol. 2014;70(6):647–54.

21

Psychological symptoms during and after Austrian first lockdown in individuals with bipolar disorder? A follow-up control-group investigation

Nina Dalkner[1], Jolana Wagner-Skacel[2*], Michaela Ratzenhofer[1], Frederike Fellendorf[1], Melanie Lenger[1], Alexander Maget[1], Adelina Tmava-Berisha[1], René Pilz[1], Robert Queissner[1], Carlo Hamm[1], Susanne Bengesser[1], Martina Platzer[1], Armin Birner[1] and Eva Reininghaus[1]

Abstract

Background: The coronavirus disease (COVID-19) pandemic, a global health crisis, has resulted in widespread socioeconomic restrictions including lockdown, social distancing, and self-isolation. To date, little is known about the psychological impact of the COVID-19 pandemic and lockdown on patients with bipolar disorder as a particularly vulnerable group.

Methods: An online survey was conducted in Austria at two points of measurement (T1 April 2020 during the first lockdown vs. T2 May 2020 at post-lockdown). The sample comprises 20 patients with bipolar disorder (mean age $= 49.4 \pm 15.6$ years) and 20 healthy controls (mean age $= 32.7 \pm 9.6$ years). A 2×2 factorial design to compare two time points (T1 vs. T2) and two groups (patients vs. healthy controls) was used. Main outcome measures included the Brief Symptom Inventory-18 (BSI-18) and a (non-validated and non-standardized) assessment to determine COVID-19 fears and emotional distress due to social distancing. Multiple linear regression analyses were used to assess the longitudinal association of COVID-19 fears/emotional distress due to social distancing during lockdown (T1) and psychological symptoms after lockdown (T2).

Results: At T1, results demonstrated higher scores in BSI-18 subscales depression, anxiety and global severity index as well as emotional distress due to social distancing in bipolar patients compared to controls. There was a significant time x group interaction in the BSI-18 subscale somatization showing a decreasing trend in patients with BD compared to controls. No time effects in BSI-18 subscales or COVID-19 fears/emotional distress due to social distancing were observed. Regression analyses showed that COVID-19 fears during lockdown predicted somatization, only in patients.

Conclusions: There was a connection between the lockdown measures and somatization symptoms observed in patients. When the first steps of easing the social restrictions in May 2020 took place, somatization decreased only in the bipolar compared to the control group. Higher COVID-19 fears during lockdown predicted later symptoms at post-lockdown. Long-term impacts of the COVID-19 pandemic need further investigations to improve current

*Correspondence: jolana.wagner-skacel@medunigraz.at
[2] Department of Medical Psychology and Psychotherapy, Medical University of Graz, Auenbruggerplatz 3, 8036 Graz, Austria
Full list of author information is available at the end of the article

therapeutic approaches and prevent fears and distress during lockdown in individuals with bipolar disorder in times of crisis.

Keywords: Bipolar disorder, COVID-19, Lockdown, Global symptom load, Somatization, Depression, Anxiety

Introduction

The severe acute respiratory syndrome coronavirus-2 (SARS-CoV-2), which can cause the novel coronavirus disease (COVID-19) and its consequences (e.g., quarantine, lockdown, and social distancing), represent a global health crisis, and the whole world has experienced a state of emergency (Guan et al. 2020. To date, in October 2020, the ongoing COVID-19 pandemic has infected more than 33 million people and led to more than one million deaths globally (Johns Hopkins University 2020). The COVID-19 pandemic is leading directly or indirectly to extraordinary challenges for mental health services (Fatke et al. 2020; Rajkumar 2020). Insecurity, confusion, emotional isolation, and stigma may affect mental health and well-being (Pfefferbaum and North 2020). Psychological stress symptoms (including depression, somatization, insomnia, and anxiety) can be consequences of such an extraordinary situation, including feelings of threat and uncertainty (Lieberman et al. 2020; Pérez-Fuentes et al. 2020). The effects may lead to severe emotional reactions, unhealthy behaviours, or noncompliance with public health directives (Pfefferbaum and North 2020). Furthermore, emotional responses to the COVID-19 pandemic can result in relapse or worsening of an already existing psychiatric disorder because of high susceptibility to stress compared with the general population (Pérez-Fuentes et al. 2020).

BD is a recurrent chronic psychiatric disorder characterized by fluctuations in mood state and energy (Vieta et al. 2016), and can cause people to have a more reactive response to stress when compared to healthy controls. Studies show that individuals with BD exhibit a high risk of developing severe affective episodes during periods with high chronic stress (Bender and Alloy 2011; Malkoff-Schwartz et al. 2000; Weiss et al. 2015). The vulnerability-stress model postulates a neurobiological, polygenic genetic predisposition in concatenation with chronic stress and acute triggers (e.g., critical life events, disruption of the sleep–wake rhythm), which determine the course of psychiatric disorders by gene-environment interactions (e.g., infections and inflammation) mediated by epigenetic modifications, gene expression changes, and other cellular mechanisms (Bengesser and Reininghaus 2018; Brietzke et al. 2012; Esterwood and Saeed 2020). The COVID-19 crisis may be a life event in itself. In this paper, we are especially interested whether patients with BD are more susceptible to psychological symptoms in an extreme environmental situation, as it was the case during lockdown.

Since the outbreak of the COVID-19 pandemic, numerous studies evaluating psychiatric symptoms in individuals with severe mental illness including samples with BD have been published (Chang et al. 2020; Costa et al. 2020; Frank et al. 2020; Hao et al. 2020; Iasevoli et al. 2020; Pan et al. 2020; Riblet et al. 2020; Solé et al. 2021; Zou et al. 2020). Rates of high perceived stress severity, anxiety, and severe depressive symptoms were significantly higher in psychiatric patients compared with controls (Frank et al. 2020; Iasevoli et al. 2020, Solé et al. 2021). In addition, patients reported on sleeping problems (Frank et al. 2020) and fatigue (Zou et al. 2020). A very recent study from Australia, focusing on psychosocial distress in patients with mood disorders, highlighted the maladaptive situational and lifestyle changes during the COVID-19 pandemic of this patient group. In particular, patients with BD reported high stress levels and men with BD had even higher levels of depression than women with BD in this study. Respondents with BD were more concerned about financial issues associated with COVID-19 compared to those with depressive disorder and those with no mental disorder. However, mood disorders in this study were self-reported (Van Rheenen et al. 2020). A further reason for psychological stress symptoms caused by the COVID-19 pandemic might be social distancing rules that were promulgated and enforced by many governments to prevent an uncontrolled spread of SARS-CoV-2.

Lockdown and social distancing (also known as physical distancing) included in infection control actions is intended to slow the spread of disease by minimizing close contact between individuals. However, lockdown, quarantine, and social distancing procedures may lead to loss of personal freedom, uncertainty, fear of the future, and financial well-being, and they also may contribute strongly to widespread emotional distress and mental health problems (Pfefferbaum and North 2020; Semo and Frissa 2020; Zandifar and Badrfam 2020). An Italian study by Rossi et al. (2020) identified associations of lockdown measures with high rates of depression, anxiety, insomnia, perceived stress symptoms and adjustment disorder symptoms in the general population. Brooks et al. (2020) reviewed the psychological impact of quarantine and found negative psychological effects, including post-traumatic stress symptoms, confusion, and anger. Stressors included longer quarantine duration, infection fears, frustration, boredom, inadequate supplies, inadequate information, financial loss, and stigma. Accordingly, Tull et al. (2020) found that being under a stay-at-home order was associated with greater health anxiety, financial worry, and loneliness in healthy adults.

In psychiatric samples, lockdown measures including temporary shutdown of medical and mental health treatment and the disrupted rhythm of a healthy life, such as reduced opportunities to exercise, experience sunlight exposure, and participate in meaningful activities, could pose a special risk or relapse during the pandemic (Muruganandam et al. 2020; Youngstrom et al. 2020). Hao et al. (2020) confirmed that patients with psychiatric disorders experienced more psychiatric symptoms during the COVID-19 pandemic. They highlighted the severity of negative psychological impact on psychiatric patients during strict lockdown measures. An Italian study by Carmassi et al. (2020), surveying 100 patients with BD in April 2020, found more post-traumatic stress symptoms, more anxiety, and depressive symptoms during the period of national lockdown and ongoing social distancing measures. Post-traumatic stress symptoms were related to work and financial difficulties. Interestingly, acute manic symptoms seemed to be protective in this study. A Spanish study by González-Blanco et al. (2020) evaluated depression, anxiety, and stress symptoms as early responses to the pandemic and found that patients with severe mental disorders (bipolar and psychotic disorders) reacted to the lockdown restrictions with higher anxiety levels compared to healthy controls. Solé et al. (2021) stated that lockdown had a higher psychological impact in psychiatric patients vs. controls and that psychiatric patients used less adaptive copings strategies to face the lockdown. Moreover, suicidality case reports as well as increased suicidality rates related to the COVID-19 pandemic because of fear and xenophobia have already been reported (Dsouza et al. 2020; Mamun and Griffiths 2020; Sher 2020). Consequently, several adjustment strategies to prevent psychological stress and suicide attempts during the COVID-19 pandemic have already been published (Ho et al. 2020; Klomek 2020; Wu et al. 2020). Interestingly, there are also few studies showing decreased psychiatric symptoms due to the pandemic. A longitudinal study by Orhan et al. (2020) observed less psychiatric symptoms in older patients with BD (age > 50 years) during the course of the COVID-19 pandemic than at baseline. Psychiatric symptoms were associated with loneliness, not having children, more feelings of loneliness, lower mastery, passive coping style and neuroticism.

Yao et al. (2020) pointed out that individuals with psychiatric disorders are generally more susceptible to infections for multiple reasons including cognitive impairment and little awareness of risk, more comorbidities and more barriers in accessing timely health services. Accordingly, it is suggested that patients with BD exhibit more serious COVID-19-related symptoms (Stefana et al. 2020) and that they are at increased infection risks due higher prevalence of obesity, cardiovascular disease, diabetes mellitus, and obstructive pulmonary disease (Staudt et al. 2019; McIntyre et al. 2007; Vancampfort et al. 2013; Vancampfort et al. 2016; Zareifopoulos et al. 2018). There are already recommendations for patients with BD for the time of the COVID-19 pandemic to decrease the vulnerability, such as proactively improving social connections, prioritizing self-care, and learning to use mobile and telehealth effectively (Stefana et al. 2020; Youngstrom et al. 2020). However, more multidisciplinary research on COVID-19 effects on severe symptoms of BD is needed to accomplish a consequent establishment of prevention strategies for psychiatric COVID-19 consequences (Courtet et al 2020; Holmes et al. 2020).

This study aimed at investigating the psychosocial strain of Austrian patients with BD during the COVID-19 pandemic at two time points (April 2020 vs. May 2020) via an online survey. Austria was in the first lockdown from March 15 to the end of April 2020, and the survey was conducted twice: April 9–April 28, 2020 (T1) and the second time from May 5–June 4, 2020 (T2). Individual differences in the emotional response to the pandemic and effects of governmental restrictions including social distancing and lockdown might be critical for the comprehension of psychological pandemic effects and the construction of new management and treatment models. Thus, we conducted a single-institution prospective analysis to address the following research questions:

1. Do patients with BD and healthy controls differ in a) global severity index, anxiety, depression, and somatization in the course of the pandemic (during and post-lockdown) and in b) COVID-19 fears and emotional distress due to social distancing?
2. Do COVID-19 fears and emotional distress due to social distancing during lockdown (T1) can predict psychological symptoms post-lockdown (T2) in patients vs. healthy controls?

We hypothesized that psychological symptoms in individuals with BD depend on lockdown measures and that patients with BD may report more psychological stress symptoms (anxiety, depression, somatization) during the first Austrian lockdown (vs. post-lockdown) in comparison to a healthy control group. In addition, we assumed that COVID-19 fears and emotional response to social distancing will be related to psychological symptoms, resulting in higher effects in patients.

Materials and methods

Study design

Data collection (T1) via online survey began on April 9 and ended on April 28, 2020. Between May 5 and June 4, 2020, the survey was open for answering for a second time (T2) for the same participants. The first survey in April was during the first total lockdown, starting at March 16, 2020 with governmental measures to limit the spread of COVID-19 in Austria. At this time all nonessential shops, schools, nurseries, and leisure premises were closed, all events were cancelled, and home-office rather than in-office work was recommended (except for key workers) or workers were put on furlough. Essential venues were only accessible when wearing face masks and keeping a distance of at least one meter. Furthermore, the public was advised to stay at home and to limit all real-life contacts except for people sharing the same household. Travel to and from Austria was heavily restricted by the government. Up to April 9, 13,120 cases were confirmed in Austria, of which 7585 people were actively infected and 295 people had died in connection with COVID-19; by April 28, 15,357 cases were confirmed, of which 2208 were actively infected and 569 had died (Nussmayr 2020).

The follow-up survey at T2 was conducted when restrictions where loosened, including permission for events with up to 10 people, and all shops, leisure venues, and hairdressers were allowed to open again. In the middle of May, number-restricted reopening of schools, restaurants, and places of worship took place. Wearing a face mask inside and keeping distance was still mandatory, and travel restrictions remained. At the end of May, events up to 100 people were allowed again. Up to May 5, 15,650 cases were confirmed in Austria, of which 1,582 people were actively infected and 606 people had died in connection with COVID-19; by June 4, 16,805 cases were confirmed, of which 418 were actively infected and 670 had died in Austria (Nussmayr 2020). An overview of the governmental measures in Austria at both time points of this study is given in Fig. 1.

Participants

This study surveyed former participants of the BIPLONG study, and all patients were diagnosed earlier with the Structured Clinical Interview for DSM-IV (SCID-I) and treated at the outpatient center for BD at the Medical University of Graz, Department of Psychiatry and Psychotherapeutic Medicine. Participants answered the questionnaires pseudo-anonymously using a participant code of former studies (see our recent report on the BIPLONG study by Dalkner et al. 2020). Inclusion criteria included voluntary participation (informed consent), German native speakers, age above 18 years, and e-mail access. We surveyed 38 patients with BD and 39 healthy controls at T1 and 23 patients with BD and 22 healthy controls at T2. Total data sets at both time points including all relevant variables were available from 20 participants with BD vs. 20 healthy controls. The healthy controls included were also former study participants and had no psychiatric disease or positive family history of a psychiatric disease. This was screened in the BIPLONG study and again in the COVID-19 survey. This study was conducted in accordance with the Declaration

Covid-19 governmental measures in Austria

	Survey Start	Exit regulations	Behaviour guidelines	Travel regulations	Event regulations	Educational institutions	Service sector	Survey End
T1	April 9th Actively infected: 7585 Deaths: 295 [1]	People are required to stay at home and only leave the house for essential reasons: 1) professional work 2) essential errands 3) to help others 4) physical activity	Keeping distance and wearing face masks in shops, offices, public transport is mandatory.	Only essential travel (e.g. for business that cannot be delayed) is permitted. Entry regulations are in effect.	All events such as concerts, plays, exhibitions etc. are prohibited	Nurseries, kindergartens, schools, universities are closed.	Restaurants/bars, health and rehabilitation resorts, sports areas, culture and leisure facilities are closed. Only essential shops are open.	April 28th Actively infected: 2208 Deaths: 569 [1]
T2	May 5th Actively infected: 1582 Deaths: 606 [1]	Restrictions to leave the house are lifted.	Order to keep 1.5 metre distance and wearing face masks in shops, offices, public transport.	Travel regulations remain.	May 1st: Events with participants up to 10 people and funerals up to 30 people are allowed. May 15th: Weddings and funerals of up to 100 people are allowed.	May 15th: Reopening of Nurseries, kindergartens, schools, universities.	May 15th: Number restricted reopening of restaurants/bars, health and rehabilitation resorts, sports areas, culture and leisure facilities, shops, theatres, etc.	June 4th Actively infected: 418 Deaths: 670 [1]

[1] Nussmayr, 2020

Fig.1 Overview of the COVID-19 protective measures in Austria in April 2020 (T1) and May 2020 (T2)

of Helsinki and was approved by the Ethics Committee of the Medical University Graz (EK-number: 25-335 ex 12/13). Participants could withdraw from the survey at any moment without providing any justification.

Psychological inventories

The web-based survey, in German, was accessible online using the survey tool LimeSurvey; it solicited answers to the following question topics:

Global symptom load was assessed using the German version of the Brief Symptom Inventory-18 (BSI-18; Franke et al. 2017) by Derogatis and Fitzpatrick (2004), a short version of the Symptom-Checklist-90 Revised (Derogatis and Unger 2010). The BSI-18 comprises 18 items assessing psychological distress in the last 7 days on three subscales (depression, anxiety, and somatization). The global severity index (GSI) is a global measure of psychological distress. The BSI-18 employs a 5-point rating form ranging from 1 ("absolutely not") to 5 ("very strong"). The subscales (total value of each scale is 24) show an internal consistency with a Cronbach's alpha of $\alpha = 0.82$ for Somatization, $\alpha = 0.87$ for Depression, $\alpha = 0.84$ for Anxiety and $\alpha = 0.93$ for GSI. (Derogatis and Fitzpatrick 2004).

The Beck Depression Inventory (BDI-2) was used as a self-evaluation report to assess the severity of depressive symptoms, with 21 items and a 4-point Likert scoring system. The total score ranges from 0 to 63 points. According to the manual, a score below 18 indicates a lack of clinical depression. The scale has been shown to demonstrate an internal consistency with a Cronbach's alpha of $\alpha \geq 0.84$ and a reliability of $r \geq 0.75$ (Kühner et al. 2007).

The Altman Self-Rating Mania Scale (ASRM) by Altman et al. (1997) is a five-item scale for assessing mood, self-confidence, sleep disturbances, speech, and activity level during 1 week. Each question can be rated with 0 to 4 points, and a total score above five indicates mania.

Demographic information included personal data (sex, age, education, relationship status), information about the living situation (inhabitants in home town, people in household, children), engagement in activities and hobbies, the presence of a daily structure, adherence to medication (changes in current medication) and governmental measures, and contact with a mental health professional (psychiatrist, psychologist, psychotherapist).

A COVID-19 assessment was developed by the Department of Psychiatry and Psychotherapeutic Medicine at the Medical University of Graz assessing COVID-19 fears, as follows (0 = no fears, 10 = extremely high fear):

- On a scale from 0 to 10, how strongly do you rate your concerns and fears about the coronavirus?
- On a scale from 0 to 10, how strongly do you rate your fear of contracting the coronavirus?
- On a scale from 0 to 10, how strongly do you rate your fear of infecting others with the coronavirus?

The three items showed a highly significant intercorrelation (all $p < 0.01$), and a mean index for COVID-19 fears was created, showing a Cronbach's alpha of $\alpha = 0.81$ at T1 and $\alpha = 0.82$ at T2.

Emotional distress due to social distancing was assessed by the following five items on a 6-point rating scale (0 = not at all, 4 = full commitment):

- On a scale from 0 to 4, social distancing makes me feel lonely/bored/frustrated/hopeless/anxious.

Out of these significantly intercorrelated items (all $p <$ .01), a mean index for "Emotional distress due to social distancing" was created, showing a Cronbach's alpha of α = .90 at T1 and α = .86 at T2.

Statistical analyses

A 2 × 2 factorial design to compare two time points (T1 vs. T2) × 2 groups (patients with BD vs. healthy controls) was used. Consequently, repeated measures ANCOVAs (controlling for age, sex, education, and employment) for analyzing global symptom load and subscales of the BSI-18 from same subjects at both time points (combining data from April vs. May) were calculated. For analyses of variance, effect sizes are presented as Cohen's partial eta-squared (η^2). Paired *t*-tests were post-hoc computed to demonstrate changes in psychological scales from T1 to T2 within one group. Multiple linear regression analyses controlling for age, sex, education, and employment were applied to assess whether COVID-19 fears as well as emotional distress due to social distancing during lockdown (T1) as independent variables can predict psychological symptoms (somatization, depression, anxiety, GSI) after lockdown (T2); multiple regression models were compared between groups. Basic statistical requirements to run multiple regression analyses were met and preliminary analyses were conducted to check relevant assumptions of regression analysis including linearity, normality, absence of multicollinearity, and homoscedasticity. Cohen's *f2* were calculated as a measure of effect size interpreted according to Cohen (1988) as small (*f2* = 0.02), medium (*f2* = 0.15), and big effects (*f2* = 0.35). Differences in clinical data between patients with BD and healthy controls at one time point were calculated with chi-square tests (for nominal) and the Freeman–Halton Fisher's exact test, when the expected cell size was < 5, and *t*-tests (for metric data) and Mann–Whitney *U* tests (for nonparametric data). The overall significance was set at 0.05 and all analyses were performed using the Statistical Package for Social Sciences (SPSS version 25.0, IBM).

Results

Sample description

The sociodemographic characteristics of participants are shown in Table 1. Fifty percent of the 20 patients and 75.0% of the 20 controls were females. The mean age of the participants was 49.35 ± 15.55 years in the patient group and 32.65 ± 9.58 years in the control group. Patients were more frequently retired ($\chi^2(6) = 22.01$, $p < 0.001$) and had a lower educational level ($\chi^2(5) = 10.28$, $p = 0.050$; see Table 1). Of all participants, no one had tested positive for COVID-19, no one lived together with someone who tested positive for COVID-19, and no one was put under quarantine (because of contact with positive COVID-19 cases) at the time of testing or before. Patients suffered significantly more from cardiovascular

Table 1 Demographic data

	BD ($n = 20$)	Controls ($n = 20$)	Statistics
Sex			
Male (*N*)	10	5	
Female (*N*)	10	15	$\chi^2(1) = 2.67, p = 0.102$
Age			
Years (*M, SD*)	49.35 (15.55)	32.65 (9.58)	$t(38) = 4.09, p < 0.001$
Highest education			
Compulsory education (*N*)	2	0	$\chi^2(5) = 10.28, p = 0.050$[a]
Apprenticeship (*N*)	7	1	
A-Levels (*N*)	5	4	
University Bachelor's Degree (*N*)	1	4	
University Master's Degree (*N*)	4	7	
University Doctorate (*N*)	1	4	
Marital status			
Married, in relationship (*N*)	12	12	$\chi^2(3) = 5.33, p = 0.149$[a]
Single (*N*)	4	8	
Divorced/Widowed (*N*)	3	0	
Employment			
Unemployed, before the pandemic	1	0	$\chi^2(6) = 22.01, p < 0.001$[a]
Unemployed, due to the pandemic	1	0	
Short-time work	2	1	
Retired/rehabilitation	10	0	
Student	1	3	
Home office	5	10	
Employed	0	6	
Living situation			
Alone (*N*)	5	3	$\chi^2(6) = 4.99, p = 0.605$[a]
With partner (*N*)	5	7	
With partner and children (*N*)	5	3	
With child/children (*N*)	0	1	
In a shared residence (*N*)	1	2	
With parents (*N*)	2	4	
In a multi-generation household (*N*)	2	0	
Inhabitants town of residence			
< 1000 Inhabitants (*N*)	3	1	$\chi^2(3) = 6.27, p = 0.108$
1000–4999 Inhabitants (*N*)	6	1	
5000–9999 Inhabitants (*N*)	2	3	
≥ 10.000 Inhabitants (*N*)	9	15	

BD bipolar disorder

[a] Fisher's exact test

disease than controls ($\chi^2(1)=5.71$, $p=0.017$). No differences between patients and controls were found in history of diabetes ($\chi^2(1)=3.24$, $p=0.231$), obstructive pulmonary disease ($\chi^2(1)=2.11$, $p=0.487$), and hypertension ($\chi^2(1)=2.11$, $p=0.487$; see Table 2). Of the patients, 25% reported using online counseling or online therapy during the pandemic; however, 30% stated not having any contact with their treating psychiatrist or psychologist during the lockdown. In this study, no sex differences in COVID-19 fears, emotional distress due to social distancing, or psychological symptoms were observed (all $p<0.05$). The clinical data (somatic comorbidities, medication, and clinical self-ratings with BDI-2 and ASRM) are presented in Table 2.

In April, 90% (vs. 95% in May) of the patients reported taking their medication regularly, and as prescribed without arbitrary change of dosage. In addition, 45% (n=9) of patients reported subjective negative effects of the COVID-19 pandemic on their mental well-being (vs. 40% of controls; $\chi^2(1)=1.63$, $p=0.202$), and 25% (n=5) (vs. 20% of controls; $\chi^2(1)=0.224$, $p=0.638$) reported positive effects; the rest reported no effect. For a negative valuation of lockdown, patients listed amongst others little social contacts, loss of daily structure, and suspension of psychotherapy. Positive ratings of lockdown comprised amongst others more time for oneself.

Psychological symptoms at the peak of the lockdown in April 2020 vs. post-lockdown in may 2020

Patients with BD differed from healthy controls in the median GSI decrease from T1 to T2 ($\chi^2(2)=6.63$, $p=0.036$). Fourteen patients (vs. six healthy controls) showed a decrease and five patients (vs. eight controls) showed an increase in GSI from T1 to T2, with a minimum of − 16 and a maximum of +9 points in the BD group and −4 to+10 points in healthy controls. The other participants showed no difference in GSI from T1 to T2. Figure 2 displays the median change from T1 to T2 in GSI.

Somatization

For the subscale somatization, a two-tailed repeated measures ANCOVA (controlled for age, sex, education, and employment) showed no main effect time point ($F_{(1, 34)}=1.20$, $p=0.280$, $\eta^2=0.034$) and no main effect group (at T1) ($F_{(1, 34)}=2.82$, $p=0.102$, $\eta^2=0.077$). As shown in Fig. 3, there was a significant interaction between time point (April vs. May) and group (patients vs. controls) in somatization ($F_{(1, 34)}=5.22$, $p=0.029$, $\eta^2=0.133$). Post-hoc paired *t*-tests showed a decreasing trend in BD patients ($T_{(19)}=1.98$, $p=0.062$), but no change in somatization in healthy controls ($T_{(19)}=-0.72$, $p=0.481$). The covariables age ($\eta^2=0.045$), sex ($\eta^2=0.006$), education ($\eta^2=0.002$), and employment ($\eta^2=0.006$) showed no significant effects on somatization (all $p>0.05$). The statistical results, means and standard deviations are presented in Table 3.

Depression

For the subscale depression, there was no main effect time point ($F_{(1, 34)}=0.21$, $p=0.651$, $\eta^2=0.006$), but a main effect group ($F_{(1, 34)}=11.73$, $p=0.002$, $\eta^2=0.256$)

Table 2 Clinical data

	BD ($n=20$)	Controls ($n=20$)	Statistics
Mood stabilizers			
Lithium	30%	–	
Atypical antipsychotics	35%	–	
Anticonvulsants	10%	–	
Others	25%	–	
Somatic comorbidities			
Cardiovascular disease	5	0	$\chi^2(1)=5.71, p=0.017$[a]
Diabetes mellitus	3	0	$\chi^2(1)=3.24, p=0.231$[a]
Obstructive pulmonary disease	2	0	$\chi^2(1)=2.11, p=0.487$[a]
Hypertension	6	2	$\chi^2(1)=2.50, p=0.114$
Symptom self-ratings			
BDI-2 (*M, SD*), April	15.45 (10.74)	3.10 (2.53)	$t(38)=5.00, p<0.001$
BDI-2 (*M, SD*), May	12.20 (11.69)	2.40 (2.21)	$t(38)=3.69, p<0.01$
ASRM (*M, SD*), April	0.95 (2.28)	0.55 (1.19)	$t(38)=0.70, p=0.491$
ASRM (*M, SD*), May	1.5 (2.19)	0.25 (0.55)	$t(38)=2.48, p=0.022$

BD bipolar disorder, *BDI-2* beck depression inventory-2, *ASRM* Altman self-rating mania scale, *M* mean, SD standard deviation

[a] Fisher's exact test

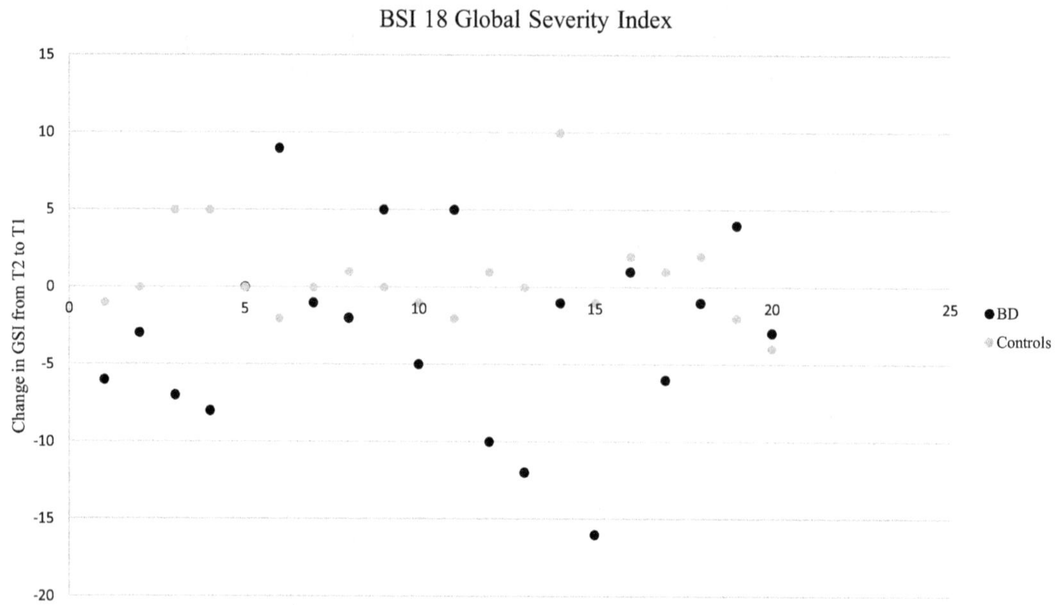

Fig. 2 Median change from T1 to T2 in BSI-18 global severity index(GSI) *BD* bipolar disorder, *GSI* global severity index

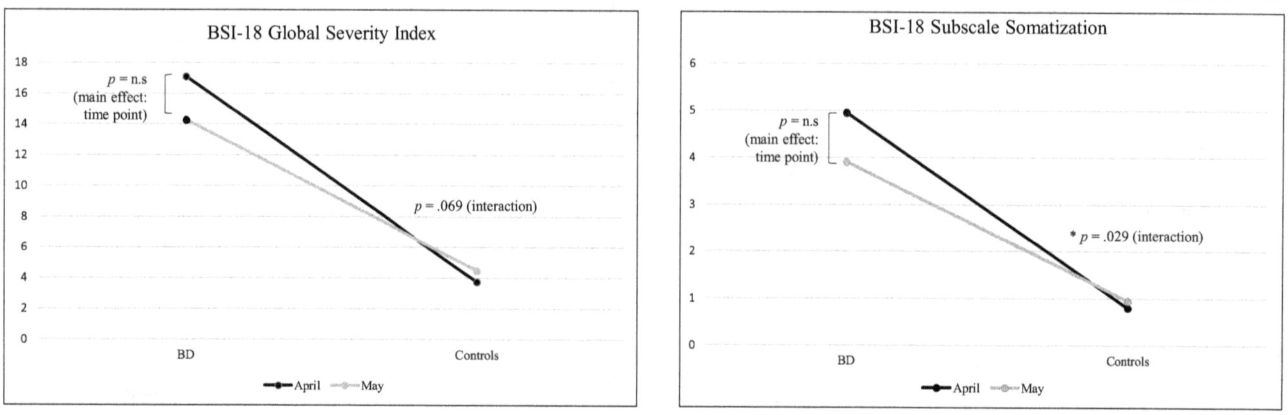

Fig. 3 Main result of the two-tailed repeated measure ANCOVAs for BSI-18 somatization and BSI-18 global severity index (GSI)

Table 3 Results from repeated measures ANCOVAs: Psychological symptoms (BSI-18) in patients with BD vs. healthy controls in April (T1) and May 2020 (T2)

	BD ($n=20$)		Controls ($n=20$)		Statistics					
	T1	T2	T1	T2	Group effect		Time effect		Time x group interaction	
	M (SD)	*M (SD)*	*M (SD)*	*M (SD)*	*F*	*p*	*F*	*p*	*F*	*p*
Somatization	4.95 (5.56)	3.90 (5.43)	0.80 (1.58)	0.95 (1.57)	2.82	0.102	1.2	0.28	5.22	0.029
Depression	7.15 (6.42)	5.50 (6.00)	1.55 (1.90)	1.80 (2.12)	11.73	0.002	0.21	0.651	0.38	0.544
Anxiety	5.00 (4.46)	4.85 (5.37)	1.40 (1.19)	1.70 (2.13)	9.48	0.004	1.3	0.263	1.4	0.245
GSI	17.10 (13.83)	14.25 (14.15)	3.75 (3.42)	4.45 (4.55)	10.08	0.003	0.8	0.378	3.53	0.069

Results from repeated measures ANCOVAs controlling for age, sex, education, and employment

BD bipolar disorder, *BSI-18* brief symptom inventory-18, *GSI* global severity index, *M* mean, *SD* standard deviation

showing higher scores in the patients group compared to controls. No interaction time x group for the BSI-18 subscale depression ($F_{(1, 34)}=0.376$, $p=0.544$, $\eta^2=0.011$) was found (see Table 3). The covariables age ($\eta^2=0.022$), sex ($\eta^2=0.017$), and education ($\eta^2=0.073$) showed no significant effects on depression (all $p>0.05$). There was a significant time x employment effect ($F_{(1, 34)}=5.08$, $p=0.031$, $\eta^2=0.130$).

Anxiety

For the BSI-18 subscale anxiety, there was no main effect time ($F_{(1, 34)}=1.30$, $p=0.263$, $\eta^2=0.037$). A significant group effect indicating higher anxiety scores ($F_{(1, 34)}=9.48$, $p=0.004$, $\eta^2=0.218$) at T1 in the patient compared to the control group was found. No interaction effect time x group in anxiety was found (($F_{(1, 34)}=1.40$, $p=0.245$, $\eta^2=0.040$; see Table 3). The covariables age ($\eta^2=0.001$), sex ($\eta^2=0.108$), education ($\eta^2=0.003$), and employment ($\eta^2=0.003$) showed no significant effects on anxiety (all $p>0.05$).

Global severity index

In GSI, we observed a decreasing trend from April to May in patients (see Fig. 3), however, the time x group interaction was not significant ($F_{(1, 34)}=3.53$, $p=0.069$, $\eta^2=0.094$). At T1, there was a significant group effect indicating higher GSI scores in patients compared with healthy controls ($F_{(1, 34)}=10.08$, $p=0.003$, $\eta^2=0.229$). Time ($\eta^2=0.023$), age ($\eta^2=0.047$), sex ($\eta^2=0.001$), education ($\eta^2=0.021$), and employment ($\eta^2=0.034$) showed no significant effects on GSI (all $p>0.05$). Table 3 shows the means and standard deviations as well as ANCOVA statistics of BSI-18 scales.

COVID-19 fears and emotional distress due to social distancing

Two-tailed repeated measures ANCOVAs for COVID-19 fears and emotional distress due to social distancing showed no significant time effects in COVID-19 fears ($F_{(1, 34)}=2.73$, $p=0.108$, $\eta^2=0.074$) or emotional distress due to social distancing ($F_{(1, 34)}=0.44$, $p=0.511$, $\eta^2=0.013$). At T1, there was a significant group difference in emotional distress due to social distancing indicating more distress in patients compared with controls ($F_{(1, 34)}=6.62$, $p=0.015$, $\eta^2=0.163$), no group difference was found in COVID-19 fears ($F_{(1, 34)}=0.84$, $p=0.366$, $\eta^2=0.024$). There were no significant time x group interactions in COVID-19 fears ($F_{(1, 34)}=0.21$, $p=0.651$, $\eta^2=0.006$) or emotional distress due to social distancing ($F_{(1, 34)}=0.003$, $p=0.958$, $\eta^2=0.000$; see Table 4. Age ($\eta^2=0.027$), sex ($\eta^2=0.004$), education ($\eta^2=0.019$), and employment ($\eta^2=0.054$) showed no significant effects on COVID-19 fears (all $p>0.05$) and on emotional distress due to social distancing (age: $\eta^2=0.007$; sex: $\eta^2=0.015$; education: $\eta^2=0.050$, employment: $\eta^2=0.028$). The means and standard deviations of the COVID-19 fear index and emotional distress due to social distancing index are shown in Table 4.

Effects of COVID-19 fears/emotional distress to social distancing during the lockdown on psychological symptoms post-lockdown

The regression analyses were ran with selected predictor variables (COVID-19 fears and emotional distress due to social distancing at T1) and control variables (age, sex, education, and employment) using the ENTER method, and the BSI-18 subscales as dependent variables. Results of regression analyses confirmed the hypothesis that COVID-19 fears during the lockdown were associated with psychological symptoms post-lockdown, this was bipolar-specific. In detail, in the BD group, the regression models adjusted for age, sex, education, and employment, which accounted for 59% of the variance (see Table 5), demonstrated that COVID-19 fears predicted somatization ($r=0.54$, $p=0.007$; $F_{(6, 19)}=3.15$, $p=0.039$, $R^2=0.59$). Age was identified as significant confounder in the regression model ($r=0.40$, $p=0.041$). No associations between COVID-19 fears and somatization

Table 4 Results from repeated measures ANCOVAs: COVID-19 fears and emotional distress due to social distancing in patients with BD vs. healthy controls in April (T1) and May 2020 (T2)

	BD ($n=20$)		Controls ($n=20$)		Statistics					
	T1	T2	T1	T2	Group effect		Time effect		Time x group interaction	
	M (SD)	*M (SD)*	*M (SD)*	*M (SD)*	*F*	*p*	*F*	*p*	*F*	*p*
COVID-19 fears	4.43 (2.69)	3.98 (2.39)	3.79 (2.15)	3.42 (2.14)	0.83	0.366	2.73	0.108	0.21	0.651
ED-SD	1.56 (1.16)	1.13 (1.04)	0.78 (0.51)	0.79 (0.96)	6.62	0.015	0.442	0.511	0	0.958

Results from repeated measures ANCOVAs controlling for age, sex, education, and employment

BD bipolar disorder, *ED-SD* emotional distress due to social distancing, *M* mean, *SD* standard deviation

Table 5 Multiple linear regression of COVID-19 fears/emotional distress due to social distancing during lockdown (T1) associated with somatization at post-lockdown (T2)

	Unstandardized coefficients		Standardized coefficients	*t*	*p*	*F* (*p*)	*R*	*R2*	*ΔR2*	*Cohens f2*
	B	*SE*	*β*							
Somatization										
BD										
(Constant)						**3.15 (0.039*)**	0.77	0.59	0.40	1.44
COVID-19 fears	1.36	0.45	0.67	3.00	**0.010***					
ED-SD	−0.38	1.04	− 0.08	− 0.37	0.718					
Age	0.18	.06	0.50	2.75	**0.017***					
Sex	− 0.60	2.13	− 0.06	− 0.28	0.783					
Education	0.31	0.73	0.08	0.42	0.680					
Employment	−0.74	0.79	− 0.18	− 0.94	0.363					
Controls										
(Constant)						0.38 (0.878)	0.38	0.15	− 0.24	0.18
COVID-19 fears	− 0.13	0.25	− 0.18	− 0.53	0.605					
ED-SD	0.82	1.25	0.27	.66	0.520					
Age	0.05	0.07	0.30	.74	0.475					
Sex	− 0.08	1.01	− 0.02	−.08	0.941					
Education	0.46	0.39	0.35	1.17	0.263					
Employment	− 0.00	0.28	− 0.00	−.01	0.994					

BD bipolar disorder, *ED-SD* emotional distress due to social distancing

$^{*}p<0.05$ in bold; multiple linear regression results on somatization with COVID-19 fears and ED-SD as predictors corrected for age, sex, education, and employment

was observed in the control group ($r=0.08$, $p=369$; $F_{(6,19)}=0.38$, $p=0.878$, $R^2=0.15$). Table 5 lists the regression coefficients and regression results on somatization in both groups. The other regression models to predict anxiety (BD: $F_{(6,19)}=1.35$, $p=0.305$, $R^2=0.62$; Controls: $F_{(6,19)}=1.01$, $p=0.462$, $R^2=0.56$), depression (BD: $F_{(6,19)}=1.96$, $p=0.146$, $R^2=0.69$; Controls: $F_{(6,19)}=2.02$, $p=0.135$, $R^2=0.70$), and GSI (BD: $F_{(6,19)}=1.92$, $p=0.152$, $R^2=0.69$; Controls: $F_{(6,19)}=1.09$, $p=0.418$, $R^2=0.58$) were not significant. Table 6 shows partial correlations (corrected for sex, age, education, and employment) between the regression variables. In BD, associations between emotional distress due to social distancing at T1 and depression at T2 were observed ($r=0.63$, $p=0.009$). COVID-19 fears at T1 were related to post-lockdown somatization ($r=0.68$, $p=0.004$), anxiety ($r=0.53$, $p=0.035$), and GSI ($r=0.63$, $p=0.009$). No associations between COVID-19 fears/emotional distress due to social distancing and psychological symptoms within the control group were found.

Discussion

This was the first study to survey individuals diagnosed with BD during the COVID-19 pandemic at two points of measurement—at the peak of the first Austrian lockdown in April 2020 and post-lockdown in May 2020—using a follow-up control-group design. Due to very little empirical data on the impact of the pandemic and lockdown

Table 6 Partial correlations between COVID-19 fears/emotional distress due to social distancing at T1 and BSI-18 scales at T2 in BD patients and healthy controls

	Somatization		Depression		Anxiety		GSI	
	BD	Controls	BD	Controls	BD	Controls	BD	Controls
COVID-19 fears	**0.68****	− 0.06	0.43	0.27	**0.53***	− 0.03	**0.63****	0.08
ED-SD	0.32	0.12	**0.63****	0.14	0.13	0.45	0.43	0.31

BD bipolar disorder, *ED-SD* emotional distress due to social distancing, *GSI* global symptom index

$^{**}p<0.01$, $^{*}p<0.05$ in bold letters; partial correlations were corrected for age, sex, education, and employment

on patients with BD, the aim of this study was to explore psychological consequences of the lockdown during the COVID-19 pandemic in this vulnerable group in order to develop possible strategies for patients to cope with the crisis.

Patients experienced social distancing during the first Austrian lockdown in April 2020 as much more burdensome than controls. They reported more emotional distress due to social distancing (including feelings of loneliness, boredom, frustration, hopelessness, and anxiety). Although the regression model revealed no effect, partial correlations in BD showed a relationship between emotional distress due to social distancing and depression scores at post-lockdown. In addition, patients with BD reported high values in depression, anxiety, and psychological distress (measured with GSI) during lockdown. This was in line with previous studies in samples with severe mental disorders during the COVID-19 pandemic in 2020 (Carmassi et al. 2020; González-Blanco et al. 2020; Solé et al. 2021). In comparison to healthy controls, individuals with severe mental illness reported less use of coping strategies, such as having a routine, social interactions, and a healthy lifestyle (Solé et al. 2021).

We suppose that this first lockdown in Austria may have led to high insecurity and anxiety with affective dynamics in patients with BD compared to controls. According to the literature, the ongoing COVID-19 pandemic is suggested to promote worries about health, personal and financial loss, uncertainties, anger, confusion, frustration, boredom, decrease in social contacts, isolation, loss in daily routine, stigma, emotional distress, and exacerbation of psychological symptoms in otherwise healthy individuals (Barzilay et al. 2020; Brooks et al. 2020; Fatke et al. 2020; Lieberman et al. 2020; Pérez-Fuentes et al. 2020; Pfefferbaum and North 2020; Tull et al. 2020). Certain aspects of the pandemic could affect patients with BD, especially concerning the risk of relapse or disruption in biological and social rhythm (Rajkumar 2020). Studies have shown that traits related to emotional instability and anxiety are generally elevated in bipolar spectrum disorder (Evans et al. 2005; Greenwood et al. 2012; Wagner-Skacel et al. 2020). It is suggested that individuals with BD are less securer and more anxious than healthy people in normal situation and that this it getting more severe under extreme situation. Individuals with BD are prone to react to stress more extensively (Stefana et al. 2020), and this is in line with results of past epidemics and natural disasters (Esterwood and Saeed 2020) as well as recent longitudinal studies during the COVID-19 pandemic in individuals with affective disorders (Frank et al. 2020; Pan et al. 2020). The real development of COVID-19 pandemic effects on psychological conditions in patients with BD as a response to the crisis will be objects of further investigations.

There is a link between personality structure and affective dynamics, including depressive, anxiety, and somatization symptoms in BD. An impairment of personality functioning including difficulties in interpersonal relations as well as self-regulation in individuals with BD leads to more psychological distress (Wagner-Skacel et al. 2020). Additionally, we know that patients with BD usually engage in ineffective coping strategies to address stressful situations (Bender and Alloy 2011). These patients may need more stabilization in the affective regulation during the COVID-19 pandemic.

Using a 2 × 2 design, it was evident that patients with BD got closer to healthy controls from April to May in somatization, whereas healthy controls showed no significant change, rather decline, in somatization. This divided reaction of patients and controls may be caused by a rising frustration and strain over time in the control population. For people without a history of mental illness, this period of chronic emotional stress und uncertainty may have been a first-time experience. Possibly, their natural resilience may have hit its limit in May, resulting in a deterioration of their psychological condition. We suggest that patients with BD might be more familiar with such episodes of high stress. In general, we assume that healthy individuals maintain a more active social life than psychiatric individuals, wherefore changes in the social structure could strain them highly.

The decreasing trends in somatization observed in May 2020 in patients might be interpreted as depending on easing of strict lockdown. The second point of measurement was after the lockdown, along with reopening of schools, nurseries, kindergartens, restaurants/bars, hotels, recreational centers, shops, theaters, etc., when social life started to rise. We suppose that the easing of lockdown measures and thus the revival of social contact, reconstitution of psychiatric treatment, and return to "normal life" correlated with the decrease in psychological symptoms, especially somatization symptoms. Somatization is suggested as an indicator for psychological distress in the form of somatic symptoms. A recent meta-analysis revealed that medically unexplained somatic symptoms are highly prevalent among persons with BD at a rate nearly double that of the general population (Edgcomb et al. 2016). The same study group investigated predictors and outcomes of somatization in patients with BD. Somatic symptoms were independently associated with disease severity, defined as earlier age of first seeking psychiatric help and first psychiatric hospitalization, greater probability of attempting suicide, and rapid cycling course of disease (Edgcomb and Kerner 2018). Studies on somatization in patients with BD have been limited to anxiety subscale scores of somatization, establishing that anxiety disorders occur more frequently in persons with BD than in the general population (Pavlova et al. 2015). Research on the psychological reactions to previous epidemics suggest various vulnerability factors for anxiety and fears associated with an infectious virus, such as individual differences in intolerance of uncertainty and perceived vulnerability to disease (Esterwood and Saeed 2020; Taylor et al. 2004). In this study, COVID-19 fears could predict later somatization in the BD group. Somatization refers to psychological stress caused by the perception of physical dysfunctions. The somatization items of the BSI-18 focus on body symptoms with strong autonomous mediation (Franke et al. 2017). Subjective perception, thoughts, emotions, and behaviours associated with the individual somatic status are sometimes clinically more important than a medical diagnosis. In this context, it is very important to identify anxiety and COVID-19 fears in the BD group, but also in the general population, and to find evidence-based ways of addressing these issues for future outbreaks of infection.

Although we suggest that the change in symptoms is related to the easing of restrictions, some patients with BD might adapt and perhaps benefit from the complete stop of social obligations, resulting in decreased somatization scores. Other studies found a decrease of symptoms during the course of the COVID-19 pandemic too (Orhan et al. 2020). According to our results, we see a chance for patients individually, as some might realize that others (normally nonimpaired fellow human beings) are also afraid of the consequences of the COVID-19 pandemic, e.g., fear to contract the coronavirus or to infecting others with the coronavirus.

BD has high comorbidity with obesity; metabolic disorders including diabetes mellitus, coronary heart disease, and obstructive pulmonary disease; and smoking and substance abuse (Staudt Hansen et al. 2018; McInytre et al. 2007; Vancampfort et al. 2013; Vancampfort et al. 2016; Zareifopoulos et al. 2018). These related somatic illnesses compromise immune functioning and heighten the risk for SARS-CoV-2 infection per se as well as a severe course if one is infected (Stefana et al. 2020; Yao et al. 2020). Based on this, it is surprising that our results show that patients with BD are not more afraid to contract the coronavirus than healthy controls. At both time points, patients and controls did not differ in COVID-19 fears, including general concerns and fears about the coronavirus, fear of contracting the coronavirus, and fear of infecting others with the coronavirus. We suppose that patients with BD are not always aware of the high somatic risk factors accompanying their psychiatric disease. Thus, integrating more psychoeducational intervention programs, possibly smartphone based, related to increased somatic risk factors and SARS-CoV-2 infection would be beneficial in the treatment of BD. Otherwise, in this context it must be mentioned that lithium has shown direct antiviral effects, which might possibly protect individuals with BD against SARS-CoV-2 infection (Murru et al. 2020; Nowak and Walkowiak 2020). Stefana et al. (2020) indicated that social stigma flares when societies are under stress. Particularly at risk for stigmatization are vulnerable groups or those considered as "different". They suggested that, as BD is already prone to stigmatization, people with BD will undoubtedly take a second hit when they contract COVID-19 (Stefana et al. 2020).

Limitations

Several limitations should be considered when interpreting the current results. First, we only assessed patients with BD who were former study participants and who were motivated to participate in an online survey. Therefore, results may not be transferable to patients with BD who have not yet received therapy. We have not assessed euthymia by external rating criteria and do not know the affective status of the patients. However, affective state was monitored using self-ratings (BDI-2, ASRM). Additionally, the gender distribution in the control sample was unequal, there were more male patients than healthy controls. In addition, compared to controls, more patients were retired or in rehabilitation or had completed apprenticeship or A-Levels, which could have influenced the results. Since adverse course of COVID-19 is strongly associated with age, it cannot be ruled out, that differences in symptoms may be at least partially due to the differences in age (which has been controlled in all analyses).

Second, all data were self-reported and, thus, may potentially be biased. Although we assessed COVID-19 fears and emotional responses in addition to psychological scales, it cannot be excluded that at least some symptom worsening was not directly attributable to the COVID-19 pandemic. In addition, we do not know whether the participants were being negative tested for COVID-19 or have not being tested, as this discrimination was not assessed at the beginning of the pandemic. Third, COVID-19 fears and emotional distress due to social distancing were self-conducted variables and not measured by validated, standardized questionnaires. Fourth, we only included patients with complete data at both time points, and therefore the sample was relatively small and may be too small to be of much importance. Fifth, the observation period was at the beginning of the crisis and relatively short in order to display the social effects of the pandemic such as job loss or isolation. In this respect, follow-up investigations of this study are of special interest. Sixth, we have no information on BSI-18 scores in our sample before the outbreak of the COVID-19 pandemic or prior to lockdown.

Clinical implications

There is a need for adequate and necessary attention to people with BD in the COVID-19 pandemic and to develop specific health care interventions and treatment approaches for this particular vulnerable group during the crisis. Given the high scores in scales of depression, anxiety, and somatization during the lockdown and the finding that COVID-19 fears during the lockdown predict later symptoms in individuals with BD, interventions aimed at helping patients cope with fears and symptoms might help manage their condition. In this context, telemedicine, which obviates the risk of virus transmission inherent in face-to-face therapy, offers a great potential for delivering treatment during the COVID-19 pandemic (Torous and Wykes 2020; Wind et al. 2020; Zhou et al. 2020). Our findings show that videoconference therapy was used by a small part, only 22% of patients. However, we do not know if there was too little offer or demand. In any case, we believe that online treatment (especially during lockdown) has to be expanded significantly in the future, and it would be worthwhile to provide online or smartphone-based psychological interventions (e.g., cognitive behavioral therapy and mindfulness-based therapy) (Szentagotai and David 2009; Williams et al. 2008). In addition, patients with BD need more information about risk factors (disruption of daily rhythms, social isolation, somatic comorbidities) and their vulnerability to stress in order to protect themselves better during any time of great social disruption, whether caused by pandemic, environmental disaster, or whatnot. Specific psychosocial and psychological interventions during a pandemic could be relaxation methods and maintenance of daily rhythms. The self-awareness of patients with high somatization symptoms could be improved using strategies and skills for emotion regulation, engagement in stress-reducing activities, the regulation of relationships, and healthy lifestyle.

Much like Stefana et al. (2020) and Youngstrom et al. (2020), we are convinced that every crisis could be an opportunity by learning and rethinking and therefore gaining a more in-depth understanding of BD patients' special needs during the pandemic.

Conclusion

Our findings summarize that the COVID-19 pandemic and especially the lockdown measures greatly challenged patients with BD. At the peak of the Austrian lockdown in April 2020, psychological symptoms were observed in patients with BD; somatization decreased in patients from April to May 2020 along with easing of restrictions, in contrast to controls, and we conclude that this was dependent on lockdown measures. Accordingly, we want to emphasize that fears of contracting the coronavirus or fears of infecting others (so called COVID-19 fears) during the lockdown could predict later symptoms of somatization and that these results were bipolar specific. We therefore propose that patients with BD need more information about potential lockdown effects on their psychological well-being and about strategies for stress reduction and dealing with fears during periods of reduced psychosocial care. Patients with a higher vulnerability, including less resilience, maladaptive coping strategies, higher psychological distress, more severe course of disease, and more somatic comorbidities, have to be identified earlier and need frequent clinical contacts with a more active role of the therapist or doctor during times of crisis. Follow-up studies to estimate the long-term effects of the COVID-19 pandemic in individuals with BD are highly needed.

Abbreviations

SARS-CoV-2: Severe acute respiratory syndrome coronavirus-2; COVID-19: Coronavirus disease; BD: Bipolar disorder; SCID-I: Structured Clinical Interview for DSM-IV; BSI-18: Brief Symptom Inventory-18; GSI: Global severity index; BDI-2: Beck depression inventory; ASRM: Altman self rating mania scale; MANCOVA: Multivariate covariance analyses; SPSS: Statistical Package for Social Sciences; ANCOVA: Analysis of covariance.

Acknowledgements

We especially thank all study participants for their kind participation.

Authors' contributions

ND: designed the study, wrote the first and last draft, and was responsible for the study conception, coordination, and publication of data. JW: was involved in the conception of the study and writing. In addition, she supervised and guided us through the whole process of publication. MR: was involved in the conception of the study, creation of graphics, administered the online application tool LimeSurvey, and was responsible for data collection. FF: managed patient schedules and appointments and supervised the testing. ML: was involved in the conception of the study, writing, creation of graphics, and statistical data analysis. AT-B: was responsible for proofreading and revising the manuscript. AB: was responsible for proofreading and revising the manuscript. RQ: was responsible for proofreading and revising the manuscript. SB: was responsible for proofreading and revising the manuscript. CH: was responsible for proofreading and revising the manuscript. AM: was responsible for proofreading and revising the manuscript. RP: supported the implementation of the survey in the online application tool LimeSurvey and was responsible for proofreading and revising the manuscript. MP: was responsible for proofreading and revising the manuscript. ER: supervised the whole study procedure and made revisions for important intellectual content. All authors read and approved the final manuscript.

Author details

[1]Department of Psychiatry and Psychotherapeutic Medicine, Medical University Graz, Auenbruggerplatz 31, Graz 8036, Austria. [2]Department of Medical Psychology and Psychotherapy, Medical University of Graz, Auenbruggerplatz 3, 8036 Graz, Austria.

References

Altman EG, Hedeker D, Peterson JL, Davis JM. The Altman self-rating mania scale. Biol Psychiat. 1997;42(10):948–55. https://doi.org/10.1016/s0006-3223(96)00548-3.

Barzilay R, Moore TM, Greenberg DM, DiDomenico GE, Brown LA, White LK, Gur RE. Resilience, COVID-19-related stress, anxiety and depression during the pandemic in a large population enriched for healthcare providers. Transl Psychiatry. 2020;10(1):1–8.

Bender RE, Alloy LB. Life stress and kindling in bipolar disorder: review of the evidence and integration with emerging biopsychosocial theories. Clin Psychol Rev. 2011;31(3):383–98.

Bengesser S, Reininghaus E. Polygenic risk scores and bipolar disorder. J Psychiatry Brain Sci. 2018;3(6):1–11.

Brietzke E, Mansur RB, Soczynska J, Powell AM, McIntyre RS. A theoretical framework informing research about the role of stress in the pathophysiology of bipolar disorder. Prog Neuropsychopharmacol Biol Psychiatry. 2012;39(1):1–8.

Brooks SK, Webster RK, Smith LE, Woodland L, Wessely S, Greenberg N, Rubin GJ. The psychological impact of quarantine and how to reduce it: rapid review of the evidence. Lancet. 2020;395:912–20. https://doi.org/10.1016/s0140-6736(20)30460-8.

Carmassi C, Bertelloni CA, Dell'Oste V, Barberi FM, Maglio A, Buccianelli B, Cordone A, Dell'Osso L. Tele-psychiatry assessment of post-traumatic stress symptoms in 100 patients with bipolar disorder during the COVID-19 Pandemic social-distancing measures in Italy. Front Psychiatry. 2020. https://doi.org/10.3389/fpsyt.2020.580736.

Chang KC, Hou WL, Pakpour AH, Lin CY, Griffiths MD. Psychometric testing of three COVID-19-related scales among people with mental illness. Int J Ment Heal Addict. 2020. https://doi.org/10.1007/s11469-020-00361-6.

Cohen JE. Statistical power analysis for the behavioral sciences. Hillsdale: Lawrence Erlbaum Associates Inc; 1988.

Costa M, Pavlo A, Reis G, Ponte K, Davidson L. COVID-19 concerns among persons with mental illness. Psychiatr Serv. 2020;71(11):1188–90. https://doi.org/10.1176/APPI.PS.202000245.

Courtet P, Olié E, Debien C, Vaiva G. Keep socially (but not physically) connected and carry on: preventing suicide in the age of COVID-19. J Clin Psychiatr. 2020;81(3):1–3.

Dalkner N, Bengesser S, Birner A, Rieger A, Seebauer J, Platzer M, Hamm C, Maget A, Queissner R, Pilz R, Fellendorf F, Reininghaus B, Strassnig M, Kapfhammer HP, Reininghaus EZ. Body mass index predicts decline in executive function in bipolar disorder: preliminary data of a 12-month follow-up study. Neuropsychobiology. 2020;80:1–11.

Derogatis LR, Fitzpatrick M. The SCL-90-R, the brief symptom inventory (BSI), and the BSI-18. In: Maruish ME, editor. The use of psychological testing for treatment planning and outcomes assessment: instruments for adults. Hillsdale: Lawrence Erlbaum Associates Publishers; 2004. p. 1–41.

Derogatis LR, Unger R. Symptom checklist-90-revised. In: Weiner IB, Craighead WE, editors. The Corsini encyclopedia of psychology. Hoboken: Wiley; 2010. p. 1–2. https://doi.org/10.1002/9780470479216.corpsy0970.

Dsouza DD, Quadros S, Hyderabadwala ZJ, Mamun MA. Aggregated COVID-19 suicide incidences in India: fear of COVID-19 infection is the prominent causative factor. Psychiatr Res. 2020;290:e113145.

Edgcomb JB, Kerner B. Predictors and outcomes of somatization in bipolar I disorder: a latent class mixture modeling approach. J Affect Disord. 2018;227:681–7. https://doi.org/10.1016/j.jad.2017.11.083.

Edgcomb JB, Tseng CH, Kerner B. Medically unexplained somatic symptoms and bipolar spectrum disorders: a systematic review and meta-analysis. J Affect Disord. 2016;204:205–13.

Esterwood E, Saeed SA. Past epidemics, natural disasters, COVID19, and mental health: learning from history as we deal with the present and prepare for the future. Psychiatr Q. 2020. https://doi.org/10.1007/s11126-020-09808-4.

Evans L, Akiskal HS, Keck PE Jr, McElroy SL, Sadovnick AD, Remick RA, Kelsoe JR. Familiality of temperament in bipolar disorder: support for a genetic spectrum. J Affect Disord. 2005;85(1–2):153–68. https://doi.org/10.1016/j.jad.2003.10.015.

Fatke B, Hölzle P, Frank A, Förstl H. Psychische probleme in der pandemie–beobachtungen während der COVID-19-krise. DMW. 2020;145(10):675–81. https://doi.org/10.1055/a-1147-2889

Frank A, Fatke B, Frank W, Förstl H, Hölzle P. Depression, dependence and prices of the COVID-19-Crisis. Brain Behav Immun. 2020. https://doi.org/10.1016/j.bbi.2020.04.068.

Franke GH, Jaeger S, Glaesmer H, Barkmann C, Petrowski K, Braehler E. Psychometric analysis of the brief symptom inventory 18 (BSI-18) in a representative German sample. BMC Med Res Methodol. 2017;17(1):14.

González-Blanco L, Dal Santo F, García-Álvarez L, de la Fuente-Tomás L, Lacasa CM, Paniagua G, et al. COVID-19 lockdown in people with severe mental disorders in Spain: do they have a specific psychological reaction compared with other mental disorders and healthy controls? Schizophr Res. 2020;223:192–8. https://doi.org/10.1016/j.schres.2020.07.01.

Greenwood TA, Akiskal HS, Akiskal KK, Study BG, Kelsoe JR. Genome-wide association study of temperament in bipolar disorder reveals significant associations with three novel Loci. Biol Psychiat. 2012;72(4):303–10. https://doi.org/10.1016/j.biopsych.2012.01.018.

Guan WJ, Ni ZY, Hu Y, Liang WH, Ou CQ, He JXB, et al. Clinical characteristics of coronavirus disease 2019 in China. N Engl J Med. 2020;382(18):1708–20. https://doi.org/10.1056/nejmoa2002032.

Hansen PS, Laursen MF, Grøntved S, StraszekLicht SPVRW, Nielsen RE. Increasing mortality gap for patients diagnosed with bipolar disorder—a nationwide study with 20 years of follow-up. Bipolar Disord. 2019;21(3):270–5. https://doi.org/10.1111/bdi.12684.

Hao F, Tan W, Jiang L, Zhang L, Zhao X. Do psychiatric patients experience more psychiatric symptoms during COVID-19 pandemic and lockdown? A case-control study with service and research implications for immunopsychiatry. Brain Behav Immun. 2020. https://doi.org/10.1016/j.bbi.2020.04.069.

Ho CS, Chee CY, Ho RC. Mental health strategies to combat the psychological impact of COVID-19 beyond paranoia and panic. Ann Acad Med Singap. 2020;49(1):1–3.

Holmes EA, O'Connor RC, Perry VH, Tracey I, Wessely S, Arseneault L, Ford T. Multidisciplinary research priorities for the COVID-19 pandemic: a call for action for mental health science. The Lancet Psychiatry. 2020;7:547–60. https://doi.org/10.1016/s2215-0366(20)30168-1.

Iasevoli F, Fornaro M, D'Urso G, Galletta D, Casella C, Paternoster M, et al. Psychological distress in patients with serious mental illness during the COVID-19 outbreak and one-month mass quarantine in Italy. Psychol Med. 2020. https://doi.org/10.1017/S0033291720001841.

Johns Hopkins University. (2020). COVID-19 dashboard by the Center for Systems Science and Engineering (CSSE) at Johns Hopkins University (JHU). https://coronavirus.jhu.edu/map.html. Accessed 28 Sept 2020.

Klomek AB. Suicide prevention during the COVID-19 outbreak. The Lancet Psychiatry. 2020;7(5):390.

Kühner C, Bürger C, Keller F, Hautzinger M. Reliability and validity of the revised beck depression inventory (BDI-II). Results from German samples. Der Nervenarzt. 2007;78(6):651–6.

Lieberman L, Petrey K, Shankman SA, Phan KL, Gorka SM. Heightened reactivity to uncertain threat as a neurobehavioral marker of suicidal ideation in individuals with depression and anxiety. Int J Psychophysiol. 2020;155:99–104. https://doi.org/10.1016/j.ijpsycho.2020.06.003.

Malkoff-Schwartz S, Frank E, Anderson BP, Hlastala SA, Luther JF, Sherrill JT, et al. Social rhythm disruption and stressful life events in the onset of bipolar and unipolar episodes. Psychol Med. 2000;30(5):1005–16.

Mamun MA, Griffiths MD. First COVID-19 suicide case in Bangladesh due to fear of COVID-19 and xenophobia: possible suicide prevention strategies. Asian J Psychiatr. 2020;51:102073.

McIntyre RS, Soczynska JK, Beyer JL, Woldeyohannes HO, Law CW, Miranda A, et al. Medical comorbidity in bipolar disorder: reprioritizing unmet needs. Curr Opin Psychiatry. 2007;20(4):406–16.

Murru A, Manchia M, Hajek T, Nielsen RE, Rybakowski JK, Sani G, et al. Lithium's antiviral effects: a potential drug for CoViD-19 disease. Int J Bipolar Disord. 2020;8:1–9.

Muruganandam P, Neelamegam S, Menon V, Alexander J, Chaturvedi SK. COVID-19 and severe mental illness: impact on patients and its relation with their awareness about COVID-19. Psychiatry Res. 2020;291:113265. https://doi.org/10.1016/j.psychres.2020.113265.

Nowak JK, Walkowiak J. Lithium and coronaviral infections. A scoping review. F1000Research. 2020. https://doi.org/10.12688/f1000research.22299.2.

Nussmayr K. 15 Grafiken, die die Verbreitung des Coronavirus in Österreich und der Welt erklären. Die Presse. 2020. https://www.diepresse.com/5785804/

15-grafiken-die-die-verbreitung-des-coronavirus-in-osterreich-und-der-welt-erklaren. Accessed 29 Sept 2020.

Orhan M, Korten N, Paans N, de Walle B, Kupka R, van Oppen P, Kok A, Sonnenberg C, Schouws S, Dols A. Psychiatric symptoms during the COVID-19 outbreak in older adults with bipolar disorder. Int J Geriatr Psychiatry. 2020. https://doi.org/10.1002/gps.548910.1002/gps.5489.

Pan KY, Kok AA, Eikelenboom M, Horsfall M, Jörg F, Luteijn RA, et al. The mental health impact of the COVID-19 pandemic on people with and without depressive, anxiety, or obsessive-compulsive disorders: a longitudinal study of three Dutch case-control cohorts. The Lancet Psychiatry. 2020;0366:1–9. https://doi.org/10.1016/S2215-0366(20)30491-0.

Pavlova B, Perlis RH, Alda M, Uher R. Lifetime prevalence of anxiety disorders in people with bipolar disorder: a systematic review and meta-analysis. The Lancet Psychiatry. 2015;2(8):710–7. https://doi.org/10.1016/s2215-0366(15)00112-1.

Pérez-Fuentes MDC, Jurado MDMM, Martínez ÁM, Linares JJG. Threat of COVID-19 and emotional state during quarantine: positive and negative affect as mediators in a cross-sectional study of the Spanish population. PLoS ONE. 2020;15(6):e0235305. https://doi.org/10.1371/journal.pone.0235305.

Pfefferbaum B, North CS. Mental health and the Covid-19 pandemic. N Engl J Med. 2020;383:510–2. https://doi.org/10.1056/nejmp2008017.

Rajkumar RP. COVID-19 and mental health: a review of the existing literature. Asian J Psychiatr. 2020;52:102066. https://doi.org/10.1016/j.ajp.2020.102066.

Riblet NB, Stevens SP, Shiner B, Cornelius S, Forehand J, Scott RC, Watts BV. Longitudinal examination of COVID-19 public health measures on mental health for rural patients with serious mental illness. Mil Med. 2020. https://doi.org/10.1093/milmed/usaa559.

Rossi R, Socci V, Talevi D, Mensi S, Niolu C, Pacitti F, et al. COVID-19 pandemic and lockdown measures impact on mental health among the general population in Italy. Front Psychiatry. 2020;11:790. https://doi.org/10.3389/fpsyt.2020.00790.

Semo BW, Frissa SM. The mental health impact of the COVID-19 pandemic: implications for sub-Saharan Africa. Psychol Res Behav Manag. 2020;13:713.

Sher L. The impact of the COVID-19 pandemic on suicide rates. QJM. 2020;10:707–12.

Solé B, Verdolini N, Amoretti S, Montejo L, Rosa AR, Hogg B, et al. Effects of the COVID-19 pandemic and lockdown in Spain: comparison between community controls and patients with a psychiatric disorder. Preliminary results from the BRIS-MHC STUDY. J Affect Disord. 2021;281:13–23. https://doi.org/10.1016/j.jad.2020.11.099.

Stefana A, Youngstrom EA, Jun C, Hinshaw S, Maxwell V, Michalak E, Vieta E. The COVID-19 pandemic is a crisis and opportunity for bipolar disorder. Bipolar Disord. 2020;22:641–3. https://doi.org/10.1111/bdi.12949.

Szentagotai A, David D. The efficacy of cognitive-behavioral therapy in bipolar disorder: a quantitative meta-analysis. J Clin Psychiatry. 2009;71(1):66–72.

Taylor SE, Lerner JS, Sage RM, Lehman BJ, Seeman TE. Early environment, emotions, responses to stress, and health. J Pers. 2004;72(6):1365–94. https://doi.org/10.1111/j.1467-6494.2004.00300.x.

Torous J, Wykes T. Opportunities from the coronavirus disease 2019 pandemic for transforming psychiatric care with telehealth. JAMA Psychiat. 2020;11:e1-2. https://doi.org/10.1001/jamapsychiatry.2020.1640.

Tull MT, Edmonds KA, Scamaldo K, Richmond JR, Rose JP, Gratz KL. Psychological outcomes associated with stay-at-home orders and the perceived impact of COVID-19 on daily life. Psychiatry Res. 2020;289:1–6.

Van Rheenen TE, Meyer D, Neill E, Phillipou A, Tan EJ, Toh WL, Rossell SL. Mental health status of individuals with a mood-disorder during the COVID-19 pandemic in Australia: initial results from the COLLATE project. J Affect Disord. 2020;275:69–77. https://doi.org/10.1016/j.jad.2020.06.037.

Vancampfort D, Vansteelandt K, Correll CU, Mitchell AJ, De Herdt A, Sienaert P, et al. Metabolic syndrome and metabolic abnormalities in bipolar disorder: a meta-analysis of prevalence rates and moderators. Am J Psychiatry. 2013;170(3):265–74. https://doi.org/10.1176/appi.ajp.2012.12050620.

Vancampfort D, Correll CU, Galling B, Probst M, De Hert M, Ward PB, et al. Diabetes mellitus in people with schizophrenia, bipolar disorder and major depressive disorder: a systematic review and large scale meta-analysis. World Psychiatry. 2016;15(2):166–74. https://doi.org/10.1002/wps.20309.

Vieta E, Berk M, Birmaher B, Grande I. Bipolar disorder: defining symptoms and comorbidities–authors' reply. The Lancet. 2016;388(10047):869–70. https://doi.org/10.1016/S0140 6736(16)30966 7

Wagner-Skacel J, Bengesser S, Dalkner N, Mörkl S, Painold A, Hamm C, et al. Personality structure and attachment in bipolar disorder. Front Psych. 2020;11:410. https://doi.org/10.3389/fpsyt.2020.00410.

Weiss RB, Stange JP, Boland EM, Black SK, LaBelle DR, Abramson LY, Alloy LB. Kindling of life stress in bipolar disorder: comparison of sensitization and autonomy models. J Abnorm Psychol. 2015;124(1):4.

Williams JMG, Alatiq Y, Crane C, Barnhofer T, Fennell MJ, Duggan DS, et al. Mindfulness-based cognitive therapy (MBCT) in bipolar disorder: preliminary evaluation of immediate effects on between-episode functioning. J Affect Disord. 2008;107(1–3):275–9.

Wind TR, Rijkeboer M, Andersson G, Riper H. The COVID-19 pandemic: the 'black swan' for mental health care and a turning point for e-health. Internet Interv. 2020;100317:1–2. https://doi.org/10.1016/j.invent.2020.100317.

Wu W, Zhang Y, Wang P, Zhang L, Wang G, Lei G, et al. Psychological stress of medical staffs during outbreak of COVID-19 and adjustment strategy. J Med Virol. 2020;92:1962–70.

Yao H, Chen JH, Xu YF. Patients with mental health disorders in the COVID-19 epidemic. The Lancet Psychiatry. 2020;7(4):e21. https://doi.org/10.1016/s2215-0366(20)30090-0.

Youngstrom EA, Hinshaw SP, Stefana A, Chen J, Michael K, Van Meter A, et al. Working with bipolar disorder during the COVID-19 pandemic: both crisis and opportunity. Wiki J Med. 2020;7(1):4. https://doi.org/10.31234/osf.io/wg4bj.

Zandifar A, Badrfam R. Iranian mental health during the COVID-19 epidemic. Asian J Psychiatr. 2020;51:101990. https://doi.org/10.1016/j.ajp.2020.101990.

Zareifopoulos N, Bellou A, Spiropoulou A, Spiropoulos K. Prevalence of comorbid chronic obstructive pulmonary disease in individuals suffering from schizophrenia and bipolar disorder: a systematic review. COPD. 2018;15(6):612–20. https://doi.org/10.1080/15412555.2019.1572730.

Zhou X, Snoswell CL, Harding LE, Bambling M, Edirippulige S, Bai X, et al. The role of telehealth in reducing the mental health burden from COVID-19. Telemed e-Health. 2020;26(4):377–9. https://doi.org/10.1089/tmj.2020.0068.

Zou S, Liu ZH, Yan X, Wang H, Li Y, Xu X, et al. Prevalence and correlates of fatigue and its association with quality of life among clinically stable older psychiatric patients during the COVID-19 outbreak: a cross-sectional study. Glob Health. 2020;16(1):1–7.

Permissions

All chapters in this book were first published by Springer; hereby published with permission under the Creative Commons Attribution License or equivalent. Every chapter published in this book has been scrutinized by our experts. Their significance has been extensively debated. The topics covered herein carry significant findings which will fuel the growth of the discipline. They may even be implemented as practical applications or may be referred to as a beginning point for another development.

The contributors of this book come from diverse backgrounds, making this book a truly international effort. This book will bring forth new frontiers with its revolutionizing research information and detailed analysis of the nascent developments around the world.

We would like to thank all the contributing authors for lending their expertise to make the book truly unique. They have played a crucial role in the development of this book. Without their invaluable contributions this book wouldn't have been possible. They have made vital efforts to compile up to date information on the varied aspects of this subject to make this book a valuable addition to the collection of many professionals and students.

This book was conceptualized with the vision of imparting up-to-date information and advanced data in this field. To ensure the same, a matchless editorial board was set up. Every individual on the board went through rigorous rounds of assessment to prove their worth. After which they invested a large part of their time researching and compiling the most relevant data for our readers.

The editorial board has been involved in producing this book since its inception. They have spent rigorous hours researching and exploring the diverse topics which have resulted in the successful publishing of this book. They have passed on their knowledge of decades through this book. To expedite this challenging task, the publisher supported the team at every step. A small team of assistant editors was also appointed to further simplify the editing procedure and attain best results for the readers.

Apart from the editorial board, the designing team has also invested a significant amount of their time in understanding the subject and creating the most relevant covers. They scrutinized every image to scout for the most suitable representation of the subject and create an appropriate cover for the book.

The publishing team has been an ardent support to the editorial, designing and production team. Their endless efforts to recruit the best for this project, has resulted in the accomplishment of this book. They are a veteran in the field of academics and their pool of knowledge is as vast as their experience in printing. Their expertise and guidance has proved useful at every step. Their uncompromising quality standards have made this book an exceptional effort. Their encouragement from time to time has been an inspiration for everyone.

The publisher and the editorial board hope that this book will prove to be a valuable piece of knowledge for researchers, students, practitioners and scholars across the globe.

List of Contributors

Jules Angst and Vladeta Ajdacic-Gross
Department of Psychiatry, Psychotherapy and Psychosomatics, Psychiatric Hospital, University of Zurich, Zurich, Switzerland

Wulf Rössler
Department of Psychiatry, Psychotherapy and Psychosomatics, Psychiatric Hospital, University of Zurich, Zurich, Switzerland
Institute of Psychiatry, Laboratory of Neuroscience (LIM 27), University of São Paulo, São Paulo, Brazil
Department of Psychiatry and Psychotherapy, Charité University Medicine, Berlin, Germany

M. Bauer and R. Bauer
Department of Psychiatry and Psychotherapy, Medical Faculty, University Hospital Carl Gustav Carus, Technische Universität Dresden, Fetscherstr. 74, 01307 Dresden, Germany

T. Glenn
ChronoRecord Association Inc, Fullerton, CA, USA

M. Alda
Department of Psychiatry, Dalhousie University, Halifax, NS, Canada

P. Grof
Mood Disorders Center of Ottawa, University of Toronto, Toronto, Canada

W. Marsh
Department of Psychiatry, University of Massachusetts, Worcester, MA, USA

S. Monteith
Michigan State University College of Human Medicine, Traverse City Campus, Traverse City, MI, USA

R. Munoz
Department of Psychiatry, University of California San Diego, San Diego, CA, USA

N. Rasgon
Department of Psychiatry and Behavioral Sciences, Stanford School of Medicine, Palo Alto, CA, USA

K. Sagduyu
Department of Psychiatry, University of Missouri Kansas City School of Medicine, Kansas City, MO, USA

P. C. Whybrow
Department of Psychiatry and Biobehavioral Sciences, Semel Institute for Neuroscience and Human Behavior University of California Los Angeles (UCLA), Los Angeles, CA, USA

Lotte J. E. van Hout and Lisette E. P. Rops
GGzE, Institute for Mental Health Care Eindhoven, Dr. Poletlaan 40, 5626 ND Eindhoven, The Netherlands

Claudia J. P. Simons
GGzE, Institute for Mental Health Care Eindhoven, Dr. Poletlaan 40, 5626 ND Eindhoven, The Netherlands
Department of Psychiatry and Psychology, School of Mental Health and Neuroscience, Maastricht University Medical Center, Maastricht, The Netherlands

Helle Østergaard Madsen, Ulla Knorr, Klaus Martiny and Lars Vedel Kessing
Copenhagen Affective Disorder Research Center (CADIC), Mental Health Center Copenhagen, Rigshospitalet, Edel Sauntes Allé 10, 2100 Copenhagen Ø, Denmark

Shakoor Ba-Ali, Steffen Heegaard and Henrik Lund-Andersen
Department of Ophthalmology, Rigshospitalet, Glostrup, Denmark

Ida Hageman
Mental Health Services, Capital Region of Denmark, Copenhagen, Denmark
Faculty of Health and Medical Sciences, University of Copenhagen, Copenhagen, Denmark

Vibe Gedsø Frøkjær
Copenhagen Affective Disorder Research Center (CADIC), Psychiatric Center Copenhagen, Blegdamsvej 9, Rigshospitalet, 2100 Copenhagen, Denmark
Faculty of Health and Medical Sciences, University of Copenhagen, Copenhagen, Denmark
Neurobiology Research Unit, Copenhagen University Hospital, Rigshospitalet, Denmark

Arafat Nasser
Neurobiology Research Unit, Copenhagen University Hospital, Rigshospitalet, Denmark

Niklas Rye Jørgensen
Faculty of Health and Medical Sciences, University of Copenhagen, Copenhagen, Denmark
Department of Clinical Biochemistry, Rigshospitalet, Copenhagen University Hospital, Copenhagen, Denmark

Maj Vinberg
Copenhagen Affective Disorder Research Center (CADIC), Psychiatric Center Copenhagen, Blegdamsvej 9, Rigshospitalet, 2100 Copenhagen, Denmark
Department of Clinical Medicine, Faculty of Health and Medical Sciences, University of Copenhagen, Copenhagen, Denmark
Psychiatric Research Unit, Psychiatric Centre North Zealand, Faculty of Health and Medical Sciences, University of Copenhagen, Hillerød, Denmark

Xu Chen, Sha Sha and Yuan Feng
The National Clinical Research Center for Mental Disorders & Beijing Key Laboratory of Mental Disorders, Beijing Anding Hospital & the Advanced Innovation Center for Human Brain Protection, Capital Medical University, School of Mental Health, Xicheng District, Beijing 100088, China

Wei Bai and Yu-Tao Xiang
Unit of Psychiatry, Department of Public Health and Medicinal Administration, & Institute of Translational Medicine, Faculty of Health Sciences, University of Macau, Macao SAR, China
Centre for Cognitive and Brain Sciences, University of Macau, Macao SAR, China
Institute of Advanced Studies in Humanities and Social Sciences, University of Macau, Macao SAR, China

Na Zhao
Unit of Psychiatry, Department of Public Health and Medicinal Administration, & Institute of Translational Medicine, Faculty of Health Sciences, University of Macau, Macao SAR, China
Center for Cognition and Brain Disorders, Institutes of Psychological Sciences, Hangzhou Normal University, Hangzhou, China

Teris Cheung
School of Nursing, Hong Kong Polytechnic University, Hong Kong SAR, China

Gabor S. Ungvari
Division of Psychiatry, School of Medicine, University of Western Australia, Perth, Australia
Section of Psychiatry, University of Notre Dame Australia, Fremantle, Australia

Christoph Born and Heinz Grunze
Paracelsus Medical University, Nuremberg, Germany
Psychiatrie Schwäbisch Hall, Ringstrasse 1, 74523 Schwäbisch Hall, Germany

Lori L. Altshuler
Department of Psychiatry and Biobehavioral Sciences, David Geffen School of Medicine, University of California, Los Angeles, CA, USA
Department of Psychiatry, VA Greater Los Angeles Healthcare System, West Los Angeles Healthcare Center, Los Angeles, CA, USA

Ralph Kupka
Department of Psychiatry, Amsterdam UMC, Vrije Universiteit, Amsterdam, The Netherlands

Susan L. McElroy and Paul E. Keck
Lindner Center of HOPE, Mason, OH, USA
Biological Psychiatry Program, University of Cincinnati Medical College, Cincinnati, OH, USA

Mark A. Frye
Department of Psychiatry and Psychology, Mayo Clinic, Rochester, MN, USA

Trisha Suppes
Department of Psychiatry and Behavioral Sciences, Stanford University School of Medicine, Palo Alto, CA, USA
V.A. Palo Alto Health Care System, Palo Alto, CA, USA

Lars Schaerer
Department of Psychiatry and Psychotherapy Medical Center, Faculty of Medicine, University of Freiburg, Freiburg im Breisgau, Germany

Christopher C. Abbott, Jeremy Miller, Megan Lloyd and Mauricio Tohen
Department of Psychiatry & Behavioral Sciences, University of New Mexico Health Sciences Center, University of New Mexico School of Medicine, Albuquerque, NM 87131, USA

Michael Bauer
Department of Psychiatry and Psychotherapy, Faculty of Medicine, University Hospital Carl Gustav Carus, Technische Universitat Dresden, Dresden, Germany

Tasha Glenn
ChronoRecord Association, Fullerton, CA, USA

Eric D. Achtyes
Division of Psychiatry and Behavioral Medicine, Michigan State University College of Human Medicine, Grand Rapids, MI, USA

Martin Alda
Department of Psychiatry, Dalhousie University, Halifax, NS, Canada

Esen Agaoglu
Department of Psychiatry, Hacettepe University Faculty of Medicine, Ankara, Turkey

Carlos Lopez-Jaramillo
Mood Disorders Program, Hospital Universitario San Vicente Fundacion, Research Group in Psychiatry, Department of Psychiatry, Faculty of Medicine, Universidad de Antioquia, Medellin, Colombia

Alan MacKenzie
Forensic Psychiatry, University of Glasgow, NHS Greater Glasgow and Clyde, Glasgow, UK

Helle Ostergaard Madsen
Copenhagen University Hospitals, Psychiatric Centre Copenhagen, Copenhagen, Denmark

Simone Alberte Kongstad A. Madsen
Unit for Psychiatric Research, Aalborg University Hospital, Aalborg, Denmark

Jayant Mahadevan
Department of Psychiatry, National Institute of Mental Health and Neuro Sciences (NIMHANS), Bengaluru, India

Maria Yoldi-Negrete
Subdireccion de Investigaciones Clinicas, Instituto Nacional de Psiquiatria Ramon de la Fuente Muniz, Mexico City, Mexico

Oguz Kaan Yalcinkaya
Department of Psychiatry, Hacettepe University Faculty of Medicine, Ankara, Turkey

Yosra Zgueb
Razi Hospital, Faculty of Medicine, University of Tunis-El Manar, Tunis, Tunisia

Peter C. Whybrow
Department of Psychiatry and Biobehavioral Sciences, Semel Institute for Neuroscience and Human Behavior, University of California Los Angeles (UCLA), Los Angeles, CA, USA

Marie-Camille Patoz, Bruno Pereira, Olivier Blanc and Ingrid de Chazeron
Department of Psychiatry, CHU Clermont-Ferrand, University of Clermont Auvergne, CNRS, Clermont Auvergne INP, Institut Pascal, Clermont-Ferrand, France

Diego Hidalgo-Mazzei, Andrea Murru, Norma Verdolini, Isabella Pacchiarotti and Eduard Vieta
Hospital Clinic, Institute of Neuroscience, University of Barcelona, IDIBAPS, Centre for Biomedical Research Network on Mental Health (CIBERSAM), Barcelona, Spain

Pierre-Michel Llorca
Department of Psychiatry, CHU Clermont-Ferrand, University of Clermont Auvergne, CNRS, Clermont Auvergne INP, Institut Pascal, Clermont-Ferrand, France
Fondation FondaMental, Créteil, France

Ludovic Samalin
Department of Psychiatry, CHU Clermont-Ferrand, University of Clermont Auvergne, CNRS, Clermont Auvergne INP, Institut Pascal, Clermont-Ferrand, France
Fondation FondaMental, Créteil, France
Service de Psychiatrie B, Centre Hospitalier Universitaire, 58 rue Montalembert, 63000 Clermont-Ferrand, France

Klaus Munkholm
Copenhagen Affective Disorders Research Centre (CADIC), Psychiatric Center Copenhagen, Department O, 6243, Rigshospitalet, Blegdamsvej 9, 2100 Copenhagen, Denmark

Klara Coello and Lars V. Kessing
Copenhagen Affective Disorders Research Centre (CADIC), Psychiatric Center Copenhagen, Department O, 6243, Rigshospitalet, Blegdamsvej 9, 2100 Copenhagen, Denmark
Department of Clinical Medicine, Faculty of Health and Medical Sciences, University of Copenhagen, Copenhagen, Denmark

Filip K. Knop
Department of Clinical Medicine, Faculty of Health and Medical Sciences, University of Copenhagen, Copenhagen, Denmark
Clinical Metabolic Physiology, Steno Diabetes Center Copenhagen, Gentofte Hospital, Hellerup, Denmark

Bente K. Pedersen
Department of Clinical Medicine, Faculty of Health and Medical Sciences, University of Copenhagen, Copenhagen, Denmark
Centre of Inflammation and Metabolism (CIM) and the Centre for Physical Activity Research (CFAS), Rigshospitalet, Copenhagen, Denmark

Roger S. McIntyre
Mood Disorders Psychopharmacology Unit, University Health Network, Toronto, Canada

Rita Cafaro
Department of Biomedical and Clinical Sciences Luigi Sacco, Department of Mental Health, University of Milan, ASST Fatebenefratelli-Sacco, Milano, Italy

Bernardo Dell'Osso
Department of Biomedical and Clinical Sciences Luigi Sacco, Department of Mental Health, University of Milan, ASST Fatebenefratelli-Sacco, Milano, Italy
CRC Aldo Ravelli, Milano, Italy
Department of Psychiatry and Behavioural Sciences, Stanford University, Stanford, CA, USA

Terence A. Ketter
Department of Psychiatry and Behavioural Sciences, Stanford University, Stanford, CA, USA

Xabier Pérez de Mendiola and Ana Gonzalez-Pinto
Bioaraba, Research Group on Severe Mental Illness; Osakidetza, Araba University Hospital, Psychiatry Service; Faculty of Medicine, Department of Neurosciences, University of the Basque Country UPV / EHU, Vitoria-Gasteiz, Spain
Hospital Clinic, Institute of Neuroscience, University of Barcelona, IDIBAPS, Centre for Biomedical Research Network on Mental Health (CIBERSAM), Barcelona, Spain

Valeria de Angel, Andrew Papadopoulos, Kia-Chong Chua, Allan H. Young and Anthony J. Cleare
Centre for Affective Disorders, Department of Psychological Medicine, Institute of Psychiatry, Psychology & Neuroscience, King's College London, 103 Denmark Hill, London SE5 8AF, UK

Andrés Herane-Vives
Centre for Affective Disorders, Department of Psychological Medicine, Institute of Psychiatry, Psychology & Neuroscience, King's College London, 103 Denmark Hill, London SE5 8AF, UK
Neuroscience and Mental Health Group, Institute of Cognitive Neuroscience, University College London, London, UK

Toby Wise
Neuroscience and Mental Health Group, Institute of Cognitive Neuroscience, University College London, London, UK

Danilo Arnone
Department of Psychiatry, College of Medicine and Health Sciences, United Arab Emirates University, Abu Dhabi, United Arab Emirates

Luis Alameda
Department of Psychosis Studies, Institute of Psychiatry, Psychology & Neuroscience, King's College London, London, UK
Unit for Research in Schizophrenia, Center for Psychiatric Neuroscience, Department of Psychiatry, Lausanne University Hospital (CHUV), Lausanne, Switzerland

Teruhiko Higuchi
Japan Depression Center, Tokyo, Japan
The National Center of Neurology and Psychiatry, Kodaira, Japan

Tadafumi Kato
Laboratory for Molecular Dynamics of Mental Disorders, RIKEN Center for Brain Science, Wako, Saitama, Japan
Department of Psychiatry, Juntendo University, Tokyo, Japan

Mari Miyajima, Kei Watabe, Takahiro Masuda and Katsuhiko Hagi
Sumitomo Dainippon Pharma Co, Ltd, 13-1, Kyobashi 1-Chome, Chuo-ku, Tokyo 104-8356, Japan

Jun Ishigooka
Institute of CNS Pharmacology, Tokyo, Japan

Anja W. M. M. Stevens
Center for Bipolar Disorders, Dimence Mental Health, Deventer, The Netherlands
Amsterdam UMC, Vrije Universiteit, Psychiatry, Amsterdam Public Health Research Institute, Amsterdam, The Netherlands

Stasja Draisma
Amsterdam UMC, Vrije Universiteit, Psychiatry, Amsterdam Public Health Research Institute, Amsterdam, The Netherlands
GGZinGeest Specialized Mental Health Care, Research and Innovation Amsterdam, Amsterdam, The Netherlands

Peter J. J. Goossens
Center for Bipolar Disorders, Dimence Mental Health, Deventer, The Netherlands
Department of Public Health, Faculty of Medicine and Health Sciences, University Centre for Nursing and Midwifery, Ghent University, Ghent, Belgium

Birit F. P. Broekman and Adriaan Honig
Amsterdam UMC, Vrije Universiteit, Psychiatry, Amsterdam Public Health Research Institute, Amsterdam, The Netherlands
Department of Psychiatry, OLVG Hospital, Amsterdam, The Netherlands

Elise A. M. Knoppert-van der Klein
GGZ Rivierduinen Alphen a/d Rijn, Amsterdam, The Netherlands

Willem A. Nolen
Department of Psychiatry, University Medical Center Groningen, University of Groningen, Groningen, The Netherlands
Bipolar Collaborative Network, Bethesda, MD, USA

R. W. Kupka
Amsterdam UMC, Vrije Universiteit, Psychiatry, Amsterdam Public Health Research Institute, Amsterdam, The Netherlands
GGZinGeest Specialized Mental Health Care, Research and Innovation Amsterdam, Amsterdam, The Netherlands
Bipolar Collaborative Network, Bethesda, MD, USA

Robert M. Post
Bipolar Collaborative Network, Bethesda, MD, USA
Department of Psychiatry and Behavioral Sciences, District of Columbia, George Washington University, Washington, USA

Maria Faurholt-Jepsen
Copenhagen Affective Disorder Research Center (CADIC), Psychiatric Center Copenhagen, Rigshospitalet, Blegdamsvej 9, 2100 Copenhagen, Denmark

Darius Adam Rohani and Jakob Eyvind Bardram
Department of Health Technology, Technical University of Denmark, Lyngby, Denmark

Jonas Busk
Department of Energy Conversion and Storage, Technical University of Denmark, Lyngby, Denmark

Jan Scott
Institute of Neuroscience, Newcastle University, Newcastle upon Tyne, UK
Centre for Affective Disorders, Department of Psychological Medicine, Institute of Psychiatry, Psychology & Neuroscience, King's College London, London, UK
Université Paris Diderot, Sorbonne Paris Cité, UMR-S 1144, 75013 Paris, France

Francesc Colom
IMIM-Hospital del Mar-CIBERSAM, Barcelona, Catalonia, Spain
Universitat Autònoma de Barcelona Barcelona-Catalonia, Barcelona, Spain

Frank Bellivier and Bruno Etain
Université Paris Diderot, Sorbonne Paris Cité, UMR-S 1144, 75013 Paris, France
Département de Psychiatrie Et de Médecine Addictologique, AP-HP, GH Saint-Louis - Lariboisière - F. Widal, 75475 Paris, France
Inserm U114475006, Paris, France

Allan Young
Centre for Affective Disorders, Department of Psychological Medicine, Institute of Psychiatry, Psychology & Neuroscience, King's College London, London, UK
South London and Maudsley NHS Foundation Trust, Bethlem Royal Hospital, Kent, UK

Mikael Landén
Section of Psychiatry, Institute of Neuroscience and Physiology, The Sahlgrenska Academy at University of Gothenburg, Blå Stråket 15, 413 45 Gothenburg, Sweden
Department of Medical Epidemiology and Biostatistics, Karolinska Institutet, Stockholm, Sweden

Paul Lichtenstein and Jie Song
Department of Medical Epidemiology and Biostatistics, Karolinska Institutet, Stockholm, Sweden

Henrik Larsson
Department of Medical Epidemiology and Biostatistics, Karolinska Institutet, Stockholm, Sweden
Department of Medical Sciences, Örebro University, Örebro, Sweden

Johan Westin
Department of Infectious Diseases, The Sahlgrenska Academy at University of Gothenburg, Gothenburg, Sweden

Sean Bennett
Samaritan Health Services, Corvallis, OR, USA

Mujeeb U. Shad
Samaritan Health Services, Corvallis, OR, USA
University of Nevada Las Vegas, Las Vegas, NV, USA
Touro University Nevada, Las Vegas, NV, USA. 4 Valley Health System, Las Vegas, NV, USA

Nina Dalkner, Michaela Ratzenhofer, Frederike Fellendorf, Melanie Lenger, Alexander Maget, Adelina Tmava-Berisha, Rene Pilz, Robert Queissner, Carlo Hamm, Susanne Bengesser, Martina Platzer, Armin Birner and Eva Reininghaus
Department of Psychiatry and Psychotherapeutic Medicine, Medical University Graz, Auenbruggerplatz 31, Graz 8036, Austria

Jolana Wagner-Skacel
Department of Medical Psychology and Psychotherapy, Medical University of Graz, Auenbruggerplatz 3, 8036 Graz, Austria

Index

www.ingramcontent.com/pod-product-compliance
Lightning Source LLC
LaVergne TN
LVHW082202200926
848484LV00008B/2201